NATURAL HISTORY – AN ILLUSTRATED SELECTION

PLINY THE ELDER

Natural History
An Illustrated Selection

Pliny the Elder

NATURAL HISTORY – AN ILLUSTRATED SELECTION
© 2022 by Daniel Bernardo

ANTIQUA SAPIENTIA

Based upon the translation of:

J. Bostock and *H.T. Riley*
London – 1855-57

All rights reserved under International and
Pan-American Copyright Conventions.

ISBN: 978-1-989586-69-3

Contents

The Life and Writings of Pliny 1

Book I
Dedication 11
Plinius Secundus to his Friend Titus Vespasian. 11

Book II
An Account of the World and the Elements 15
Form and Nature of the World; whence its name is Derived 16
Of the Elements and the Planets 16
Of God 17
Of the Nature of the Stars; of the Motion of the Planets 19
Of the Eclipses of the Moon and the Sun 22
Of the Magnitude of the Stars 23
On the Recurrence of the Eclipses of the Sun and the Moon 23
On the Motion of the Moon 24
Of the Motions of the Planets and the General Laws of these Aspects ... 24
Why the Same Stars Appear at Some Times More Lofty
    and at Other Times More Near 25
Why the Same Stars Have Different Motions 27
General Laws of the Planets 28
The Reason why the Starts are of Different Colours 28

Of the Motion of the Sun and the Cause of the Irregularity
of the Days... 29
Why Thunder is Ascribed to Jupiter 29
Of the Distances of the Stars... 29
Of the Harmony of the Stars... 30
On the Dimensions of the World.................................... 30
Of the Stars Which Appear Suddenly or of Comets........ 31
Their Nature, Situation and Species............................... 31
Of the Air and on the Cause of the Showers of Stones.... 32
Of the Stated Seasons... 33
Of the Regular Influence of the Different Seasons......... 33
Of Thunder and Lightning 34
The Origin of Winds... 34
Invocation of Thunder.. 35
The Rainbow 35
Nature of the Earth... 35
Of the Form of the Earth.. 36
Whether the Ocean Surrounds the Earth 36
What Part of the Earth is Inhabited............................... 37
That the Earth is in the Middle of World 38
Of Earthquakes... 38
Wonderful Circumstances Attending Earthquakes....... 38
In What Places the Sea Has Receded............................. 39
The Mode in Which Islands Rise Up 39
Lands Which have been Totally Changed Into Seas...... 39
Of Certain Lands Which are Always Shaking, and of Floating Islands........ 39
The Wonders of Various Countries Collected Together .. 40
The Power of the Moon Over the Land and the Sea...... 40
The Dimensions of the Earth 40
The Harmonical Proportion of the Universe................. 42

Book III
Europe (I).. 43

Introduction 43
The Boundaries and Gulfs of Europe............................. 44
Of Spain Generally... 44
Of Italy.. 44
The First Region of Italy; the Tiber; Rome.................... 45
Sixty-Four Islands, Among Which are the Baleares...... 46

Book IV
Europe (II)... 47

The Peloponnese (Greece).. 47

Attica	48
The Hellespont — The Lake Mæotis	49
Germany	50
Britannia	51
Gaul	51

Book V

Africa and Asia 53

The Two Mauritanias	53
Mount Atlas	54
Numidia	54
Africa	55
The Syrtes	55
Cyrenaica	55
Countries on the Interior of Africa	55
Egypt and Thebais	56
The River Nile	57
The Cities of Egypt	58
The Coasts of Arabia, Situate on the Egyptian Sea	59
Syria	59
Judæa	59
The Euphrates	60
The Islands Which Lie in Front of Asia	60
Rhodes	60

Book VI

The Black Sea, India and the Far East 61

The Euxine Sea and the Maryandini	61
The Cimmerian Bosporus	62
The Rivers Cyrus and Araxes	62
Albania, Iberia, and the Adjoining Nations	63
The Passes of the Caucasus	63
Nations on the Vicinity of the Scythian Ocean	63
The Caspian and Hyrcanian Sea	63
Media and the Caspian Gates	64
The Seres	64
The Nations of India	65
The Ganges	66
The Indus	66
Taprobane	66
Voyages To India	67
The Persian and the Arabian Gulfs	68
Mesopotamia	68

The Tigris.	69
Arabia...	69
The Gulfs of the Red Sea	70
Troglodytice	70
Æthiopia..	70

Book VII
Man, his Birth, his Organization, and the Invention of the Arts 73

The Wonderful Forms of Different Nations	74
Marvellous Births	76
The Generation of Man.	76
Striking Instances of Resemblance	77
Remarkable Circumstances Connected with the Menstrual Discharge.	78
Some Account of the Teeth, and Some Facts Concerning Infants	78
Examples of Unusual Size..	79
Instances of Extraordinary Strength, Agility, Sight and Memory	79
Vigour of Mind	80
Heroic Exploits	80
Instances of Extreme Courage..	81
Men Of Remarkable Genius and Wisdom..	82
Men Who have been Remarkable for Wisdom	82
Instances of the Highest Degree of Affection.	83
Ten Very Fortunate Circumstances Which Have Happened to the Same Person.	83
The Greatest Length of Life	84
The Variety of Destinies at the Birth of Man ..	85
Death	85
Persons Who Have Come to Life Again After Being Laid Out for Burial..	86
Burial	86
The Manes, or Departed Spirits of the Soul	86
The Inventors of Various Things ..	87
When the First Timepieces Were Made..	89

Book VIII
The Nature of the Terrestrial Animals 91

Elephants.	91
The Instinct of Wild Animals in Perceiving Danger..	92
The Combats of Elephants	93
The Way in Which Elephants are Caught	93
In What Countries the Elephant is Found; the Antipathy of the Elephant and the Dragon	94
Dragons/Serpents	95

Lions. …	95
Combats of Lions at Rome … … … … … … … … … … … … …	96
Wonderful Feats Performed by Lions.. … … … … … … … … …	96
Tigers … … … … … … … … … … … … … … … … … … …	97
Wild Beasts that Kill with its Eyes … … … … … … … … … …	97
Camels.. … … … … … … … … … … … … … … … … … …	98
The Rhinoceros… … … … … … … … … … … … … … … …	98
Werewolf.. … … … … … … … … … … … … … … … … …	98
The Lynx, the Sphinx, the Crocotta, and the Monkey… … … … …	99
About Serpents … … … … … … … … … … … … … … … …	100
The Hippopotamus. … … … … … … … … … … … … … … …	100
Prognostics of Danger Derived from Animals… … … … … … … …	101
Amphibious Animals. … … … … … … … … … … … … … …	101
Stags.. … … … … … … … … … … … … … … … … … …	101
The Chameleon… … … … … … … … … … … … … … … …	102
Bears. … … … … … … … … … … … … … … … … … …	102
Hedgehogs… … … … … … … … … … … … … … … … …	103
The Dog … … … … … … … … … … … … … … … … … …	103
The Nature of the Horse … … … … … … … … … … … … …	104
The Generation of the Horse. … … … … … … … … … … … …	105
The Oxen; their Generation .. … … … … … … … … … … … …	105
The Egyptian Apis .. … … … … … … … … … … … … … …	106
Sheep, and their Propagation … … … … … … … … … … … …	107
The Different Kinds of Wool. … … … … … … … … … … … …	107
Goats and their Propagation. … … … … … … … … … … … …	107
The Wild Boar. … … … … … … … … … … … … … … … …	108
Apes.. … … … … … … … … … … … … … … … … … …	108
Animals Which Are Tamed in Part Only … … … … … … … … …	108

Book IX
The Natural History of Fishes. … … … … … … … … … … … … … 109

The Sea Monsters of the Oceans… … … … … … … … … … … …	110
Tritons and Nereids … … … … … … … … … … … … … … …	110
Whether Fishes Breathe and Sleep… … … … … … … … … … …	111
Dolphins .. … … … … … … … … … … … … … … … … …	111
Turtles and How They are Caught … … … … … … … … … … …	112
Distribution of Aquatic Animals into Various Species . … … … … …	113
Fishes of the Largest Size… … … … … … … … … … … … …	113
Why Fishes Leap Above the Surface of the Water.. … … … … … …	113
Auguries Derived from Fishes.. … … … … … … … … … … …	114
Gills and Scales … … … … … … … … … … … … … … …	114
The Fins of Fish, and their Mode of Swimming. … … … … … … …	114

Eels	114
The Echeneis, and its Uses in Enchantments	115
Fishes Which Emerge and Fly Above the Water	115
The Octopus	115
The Sailing Nauplius	116
Pearls	116
The Murex and the Purple	117
The Sensitiveness of Water animals	118
Sponges	119
The Dog-fish	119
The Generation Of Fishes	120
Land Fishes	121
The Mice of the Nile	121

Book X
The Natural History of Birds ... 123

The Ostrich	123
The Pœnix	123
The Eagle	124
Hawks	125
Crows – Birds of Ill Omen	125
The Wood-Pecker	126
Birds Which Have Hooked Talons	126
The Dunghill Cock	126
The Goose	127
The Cranes	127
The Nightingale	128
The Times of Incubation of Birds	128
The Halcyones	128
Pigeons	129
Different Modes of Flight in Birds	129
A Sedition that Arose Among the Roman People, in Consequence of a Raven Speaking	130
Fabulous Birds	131
The Bat	131

Book XI
The Various Kinds of Insects and Organs of Animals ... 133

Bees	134
How Bees Work	135
Wasps and Hornets	136

Contents

The Silk-worm ... 136
Spiders ... 136
Scorpions ... 137
Locusts ... 137
Insects that are Parasites of Man ... 138
The Pyrallis or Pyrausta ... 138
Different Kinds of Horns ... 138
The Brain ... 139
The Eyes ... 139
The Teeth ... 140
The Heart; the Blood; the Vital Spirit ... 141
The Gall ... 141
Resemblance of the Ape to Man ... 142
Parts of the Human Body to Which Religious Ideas are Attached ... 142
The Sexual Parts — Hermaphrodites ... 142
Signs of Vitality and Moral Disposition of Man, from the Limbs ... 143

Book XII
The Natural History of Trees ... 145

Exotic Trees ... 146
The Trees of India ... 146
Trees of Persia ... 147
Frankincense ... 148
Myrrh 149
Cinnamomum and Cassia ... 149
Balsamum, Opobalsamum and Xylobal-Samum ... 150

Book XIII
The Natural History of Exotic Trees, and an Account of Perfumes ... 153

The Palm-Tree ... 154
Nine Kinds of Gum ... 155
Papyrus – The Use of Paper ... 155
The Lotus ... 157

Book XIV
The Natural History of Vines and Viticulture ... 159

The Nature of the Grape, and the Cultivation of the Vine ... 160
Varieties of the Vine ... 160
The Nature of Wines ... 161
Wines Drunk by the Ancient Romans ... 161
Wine with Miraculous Properties ... 161
Wine-vessels — Wine-cellars ... 162

Book XV
The Olive and Other Fruit-trees 163

The Nature of Olive Oil 164
The Culture of the Olive According to Cato 164
Other Kinds of Fruit-trees 165
The Peach 166
Various Methods of Grafting Trees 166
How to Keep Various Fruits and Grapes 167
Figs 167
Historical Anecdotes Connected with the Fig 168
The Sorb 169
The Walnut 169
The Myrtle 169
The Laurel 171

Book XVI
The Natural History of the Forest Trees 173

The Acorn 175
Uses for the Bark and Wood of the Trees 175
The Pitch-tree 176
Methods of Making Tar and Pitch 177
Germination and Blossom of Trees 178
Trees Which Bear no Fruit, Looked Upon as Ill-omened 179
The Trunks and Branches of Trees 179
The Cypress 180
The Ivy 180
Water Plants 180
The Juices of Trees 181
The Veins and Fibres of Trees 182
The Felling of Trees 182
The Age of Trees 183
Mistletoe 183

Book XVII
The Natural History of the Cultivated Trees 185

The Influence of Weather Upon the Trees 185
What Soils are to be Considered the Best 186
Methods to Enrich the Earth 187
Ashes and Manure 187
Propagation of Trees 188

Contents	xiii

Seed-plots	190
The Holes for Transplanting	190
Trees Propagated From Layers	191
Grafting	191
The Diseases of Trees	191
Prodigies Connected With Trees	193

Book XVIII
The Natural History of Agriculture … 195

The Jugerum of Land	196
The Proper Arrangements for a Farm-house	197
Maxims of the Ancients on Agriculture	197
The Different Kinds of Grain	198
Spelt	199
Wheat	199
Barley – Rice	199
Polenta	199
Ptisan	200
The Nature of Barley	200
Wheat	200
The Mode of Grinding Corn	201
Millet – Leaven	201
When Bakers Were First Introduced at Rome	201
Alica	202
The Leguminous Plants – The Bean	202
The Lupine	203
The Diseases of Grain – The Oat	204
Different Systems of Cultivation Employed by Various Nations	205
Arrangement of the Stars According to the Terrestrial Days and Nights	205
The Epochs of the Seasons	206
Causes of Sterility	207
Remedies Against These Noxious Influences	209
The Harvest	210
The Methods of Storing Corn	210
The Revolutions of the Moon	211
The Theory of the Winds	211
Weather Prognostics	212
Prognostics Derived from the Moon	213
Prognostics Derived from the Stars	214
Prognostics Derived from Thunder	214
Prognostics Derived from Clouds	214
Prognostics Derived from Aquatic Animals and Birds	215

Book XIX
The Nature and Cultivation of Flax, and an Account of Various Garden Plants... 217

How Flax is Sown; Its Varieties. ... 217
The Mode of Preparing Flax. ... 218
Esparto. ... 219
Truffles. ... 219
The Pleasures of the Garden. ... 220
Different Kinds of Plants Which Grow in Gardens ... 220
Vegetables of a Cartilaginous Nature – Cucumbers ... 221
Gourds ... 221
Radishes ... 221
Parsnips ... 222
Onion ... 222
Garlic ... 223
The Nature of the Various Seeds ... 224
The Lettuce ... 224
Beet ... 225
Cabbages ... 225
Wild and Cultivated Asparagus ... 225
Thistles ... 226
Rue ... 226
Parsley ... 226
Mint ... 226
Poppy ... 227
The Maladies of Garden Plants. ... 227
Remedies for Plant Maladies and Insects that Attack Them ... 227

Book XX
Remedies Derived from the Garden Plants. ... 229

The Wild Cucumber ... 230
The Gourd ... 230
Rape ... 231
The Cultivated Radish ... 231
Onions ... 232
Garlic ... 233
Cabbage ... 233
Asparagus ... 234
Parsley ... 235
Rue ... 235
Mint ... 236
Pennyroyal ... 236

Poppy	236
Wild Thyme	237
The Composition of Theriaca	238

Book XXI
Flowers – Garlands – Bees – Wild plants ... 239

Garlands and Chaplets	239
The Rose	241
The Lily	241
The Violet	241
The Iris	241
Shrubs	242
Trefoil	242
Thyme	242
The Duration of Life of Various Flowers	243
Bees and Beehives	243
Poisoned Honey	244
Maddening Honey	244
Beehives	244
The Method of Preparing Wax	245
Wild Plants	245
The Colocasia	246
Prickly Plants	246
The Cactos	246
The Cyperus	247
Medicinal Uses of the Lily and the Narcissus	247
The Violet	248
Medicinal Uses of the Iris	248
Thyme	249

Book XXII
The Properties of Plants and Fruits ... 251

Vegetable Dyes	251
The Grass Crown	252
The Tribulus	252
The Nettle	253
The Anchusa	253
The Heliotropium	254
The Asphodel	254
Mushrooms	255
Fungi	256
Laser	256
Propolis	257

Hidromel	257
Wax	258
Alica	258
Ptisan	259
Bread	259

Book XXIII
Medicinal Uses and Properties of the Cultivated Trees ... 261

The Vine	261
The Leaves and Shoots of the Vine	262
Grapes	263
The White Vine	263
Observations Relative to Wine	264
Vinegar	265
The Leaves of the Olive	265
Omphacium	266
Castor Oil	266
Cyprus and Its Oil	266
Oil of Balsamum	267
The Palm	267
Pears	267
Figs	268
Mulberries	268
Stomatice	269
Pine Cones	270
The Laurel	270
Myrtle	271

Book XXIV
Medicaments Derived from the Forest Trees ... 273

The Antipathies and Sympathies Which Exist Among Trees and Plants	273
The Lotus of Italy	274
Gall-nuts	274
The Cypress	275
The Pitch-tree and the Larch	275
Resins	276
The Lentisk	276
The Poplar	277
The Juniper	277

The Broom	277
The Ivy	278
The Reed	278
The Papyrus	279
Rosemary	279
Gum	279
The Bramble	279
The Trixago	280
The Chamæsyce	280
The Clematis Echites	281
The Millefollium	281
The Aproxis	281
A Plant Growing on the Head of a Statue	282
A Plant Growing on the Banks of a River	282
Plants That Take Root in a Sieve	282
Plants Growing Upon Dunghills	282
Plants That Have Been Moistened with the Urine of a Dog	282
Gramen	282

Book XXV
Medicinal Use of Plants (I) ... 285

Mithridates	285
Greek Writers	286
Medicinal Herbs in Modern Times	287
Moly	289
Pæonia	289
Panaces Asclepion	289
Hyoscyamos	290
Linozostis, Parthenion, Hermupoa, or Mercurialis	290
Achilleos	291
Melampodium, Hellebore or Veratrum	291
Centaurion or Chironion	292
Artemisia	293
Nymphæa or Heracleon	293
The Iberis	293
Plants Discovered by Animals	294
The Aristolochia	294
Hierabotane or Verbenaca	295
The Thelyphonon or Scorpio	296
The Xiphion or Phasganion	296
Medicaments for Diseases of the Eyes	296
Hemlock	297
Preparations for Treating Offensive Breath	298

Book XXVI
Medicinal Use of Plants (II) 299

New Skin Diseases.. 299
The Nature of Lichen 299
Elephantiasis 300
The Old System of Medicine. 301
The New System of Medicine – Asclepiades............................. 301
Remarks Against Superstitions. 302
Cough... 303
Chalcetum 303
Medicaments for Diseases of the Belly 303
Scammony.. 304
Tithymalos Characias 304
Remedies for Griping Pains in the Bowels.. 305
Silaus 306
Scordion... 306
Aphrodisiacs and Anti-Aphrodisiacs.. 306
The Orchids or Serapias. 307
Satyrion 307
Maladies Which Attack the Whole of the Body. 308
Onotheras or Onear.. 308
Medicaments for Jaundice. 308
Remedies for Abscesses and Inflammations............................ 309
Medicaments for Haemorrhage 309
Medicaments for Ruptures and Sprains 309
Medicaments for Warts and Applications for the Removal of Scars 310
Remedies for Female Diseases.. 310

Book XXVII
Medicinal Use of Plants (III) 313

Aconite. 314
Aloe 314
Alsine 315
Aparine 316
Alcibium.. 316
Absinthium or Wormwood.. 316
Two Varieties of Fern. 317
The Lithospermum. 318
Lapidis Muscus or Stone Moss 319
The Natrix 319
The Peplis. 319

Poterion	320
Rhacoma	320
The Ages of Plants	320
How the Greatest Efficacy in Plants May be Ensured	321
Maladies Peculiar to Various Nations	321

Book XXVIII
Medicaments Derived From Living Creatures (I) – Magic and Charms ... 323

Medicaments Derived From Man	324
Whether Words are Possessed of any Healing Efficacy	324
Prodigies and Portents	325
People With Magic Powers	326
Properties of the Human Spittle	327
Medicaments Derived From the Human Blood	327
Medicaments Derived from the Dead	328
Miscellaneous Medicaments	328
Medicaments Derived From the Urine	329
Medicaments Derived from the Female Sex	329
Medicaments Derived from Woman's Milk	330
Facts Connected With the Menstrual Discharge	330
Medicaments Derived from Foreign Animals: Elephant, Lion, Camel, Hyæna	331
Remedies Derived from the Crocodile	332
Medicaments Derived from the Hippopotamus	333
Medicinal Uses of Milk	333
The Various Uses of Fat	334
Gall	334
Blood	335
Peculiar Remedies Derived from Various Animals	335
Remedies Against Enchantments	336
Medicaments for Affections of the Eyes	336
Medicaments for Tooth-ache	336
Medicaments for Cough and for Spitting of Blood	337
Medicaments for Bowel Complaints	337
Medicaments for Gout and for Diseases of the Feet	337
Medicaments for Fevers	338
Medicaments for Sprains, Indurations and Boils	338
Medicaments for the Itch	339
Medicaments for Female Diseases	339
Stimulants for the Sexual Passions	339

Book XXIX
History of Medicine and Medicaments Derived From Living Creatures (II) 341

The Origin of the Medical Art 341
The Opinions Entertained by the Romans on the Ancient Physicians 343
Remedies Derived from Wool and Eggs 343
Remedies Derived from Eggs 344
Remedies Derived from the Dog 344
Remedies Derived from Bugs 345
Remedies Derived from the Salamander 345
Remedies for the Bite of the Mad Dog 346
Remedies for Head-ache and for Wounds on the Head 347
Remedies for Diseases of the Eyes 347
Remedies for Pains and Diseases of the Ears 348

Book XXX
The Magic Art. Medicaments Derived From Living Creatures (III). 349

The Various Branches of Magic 351
Medicaments Derived from Living Creatures – Tooth-ache 351
Remedies for Quinsy and Scrofula 352
Remedies for Pains in the Stomach 352
Remedies for Dysentery 353
Remedies for Urinary Calculi and Affections of the Bladder 353
Remedies for Cold Shiverings 354
Remedies for Jaundice 354
Remedies for Fevers 354
Remedies for Carbuncles 355
Remedies for Burns 355
Methods for Arresting Haemorrhage 355
Remedies for Broken Bones 355
Remedies for Female Complaints 355
Various Kinds of Depilatories 356
Aphrodisiacs and Anti-aphrodisiacs 356
Other Marvellous Facts Connected with Animals 357

Book XXXI
Water and Medicaments Derived from Aquatic Animals (I) 359

The Different Properties of Water 360
Remedies Derived from Water 360
Deadly Waters – Poisonous Fishes 361
The Wholesomeness of Waters 361
The Impurities of Water 362

Prospecting for Water	362
The Qualities of Water at the Different Seasons of the Year	363
Waters Which Have Suddenly Made Their Appearance or Ceased.	364
The Method of Conveying Water.	364
How Mineral Waters Should be Used..	365
The Uses of Sea-water – The Advantages of a Sea-voyage	365
The Various Kinds of Salt..	366
Flower of Salt...	366
The Nature of Salt...	367
The Various Kinds of Nitrum	368
Sponges	369

Book XXXII
Medicaments Derived from Aquatic Animals (II) — 371

The Echeneïs	371
The Torpedo	372
The Instincts of Fishes	373
Coral.	374
Amphibious Animals. The Beaver	374
The Tortoise.	375
Various Frogs ..	376
Oysters .	377
Sea-weed..	378
Remedies for Diseases of the Eyes	378
Remedies for Tooth-ache	378
Remedies for Scrofula	379
Remedies for Pains in the Liver and Side	379
Remedies for Intestinal Hernia, and for Diseases of the Rectum	379
Remedies for Gout, and for Pains in the Feet.	380
Remedies for Fevers	380
Remedies for Ulcers, Carcinomas, and Carbuncles	380
Remedies for Female Diseases..	381
Other Water Creatures...	382

Book XXXIII
The Natural History of Metals (I). — 383

Gold..	383
How Much Gold Possessed the Ancients	384
The Right of Wearing Gold Rings	384
The Decuries of the Judges	385
The Equestrian Order	386
Coins of Gold and Other Metals ..	386
Considerations on Man's Cupidity for Gold	387

Silver Upon the Arena and the Stage ... 387
For What Reasons the Highest Value is Set Upon Gold ... 388
How Gold is Found ... 388
Electrum ... 389
Eight Remedies Derived from Gold ... 390
Silver ... 390
Quicksilver ... 390
Minium ... 391
The Different Kinds of Silver, and the Modes of Testing It ... 391
Mirrors ... 391
Cæruleum ... 392

Book XXXIV
The Natural History of Metals (II) ... 393

The Ores of Brass ... 393
The Different Kinds of Copper ... 393
Corinthian Brass ... 394
Brass Candelabra and the Story of Gegania ... 394
The First Statue of a God Made of Brass at Rome ... 394
Different Kinds and Forms of Statues ... 394
The Most Celebrated Colossal Statues ... 395
The Different Kinds of Copper ... 396
Cadmia ... 396
Verdigris ... 397
Iron Ores ... 397
Seven Remedies Derived from Iron ... 398
The Ores of Lead ... 398
Black Lead ... 399
Remedies Derived from Lead ... 399

Book XXXV
An Account of Paintings, Colours, Plastic Art and Earths ... 401

Portraits ... 401
The History of Painting ... 402
Roman Painters ... 402
When Painting was First Held in High Esteem at Rome ... 403
The Art of Painting – Colours ... 403
Colours Used by the Ancients ... 403
Encaustic Painting ... 404
The Colouring of Tissues ... 404
Plastic Art ... 404
Works in Pottery ... 405
Various Kinds of Earth ... 405

| Contents | xxiii |

Framed Walls	406
Bricks	406
Sulphur	407
Bitumen	407
Alumen	408

Book XXXVI
The Natural History of Stones 409

Marble and Its Sculptors	410
Phidias	410
Praxiteles	411
Scopas	412
When Marble was First Used in Buildings	413
The Method of Cutting Marble into Slabs	413
Varieties of Marbles	413
Onyx and Alabastrites	414
Various Stones	414
Obelisks	415
The Pyramids	416
The Sphinx	416
Labyrinths	417
Hanging Gardens – A Hanging City	418
Temple of Diana at Ephesus	418
Remarkable Stones – The Magnet	418
The Sarcophagus Stone	419
Chernites	419
Pumice	420
Specular Stones	420
Quick-lime	421
Various Kinds of Sand	421
Stucco	421
Maltha	422
Gypsum	422
Paved Floors	422
Terrace-roof Pavements	422
Glass	423
Marvellous Facts Connected with Fire	424

Book XXXVII
The Natural History of Precious Stones 427

Famous Rings and Jewels of Legend	427
Pearls and Precious Stones	428
Rock Crystal	428

Marvellous Histories about Amber.. 429
Several Kinds of Amber. 430
Precious Stones 430
Adamas 431
Emeralds.. 432
Beryls 432
Opals 433
Onyx. 433
Topazos 433
Iaspis. 434
Amethysts 434
Ceraunia 435
Galaxias 436
Heliotrope 436
The Methods of Testing Precious Stones. 436

Index 439

Measurement Units. 447

The Life and Writings of Pliny

Caius Plinius Secundus was born either at Verona or Novum Comum,[1] now Como, in Cisalpine Gaul, in the year A.U.C. 776,[2] A.D. 23. It is supposed that his earlier years were spent in his native province; and that he was still a youth when he removed to Rome, and attended the lectures of the grammarian Apion.

In his twenty-second Pliny visited Africa, Egypt, and Greece and the next year served in Germany under the legatus[3] Pomponius Secundus, whose friendship he soon acquired, and was in consequence promoted to the command of an *ala*, or troop of cavalry. During his military career he wrote a treatise (now lost) "On the Use of the Javelin by Cavalry," and travelled over that country as far as the shores of the German Ocean, besides visiting Belgic Gaul. In his twenty-ninth year he returned to Rome, and applied himself for a time to forensic pursuits, which however he appears soon to have abandoned. About this time he wrote the life of his friend Pomponius, and an account of the "Wars in Germany," in twenty books, neither of which are extant. Though employed in writing a continuation of the "Roman History" of Aufidius Bassus, from the time of Tiberius, he judiciously suspended its publication during the reign of Nero, who appointed him his procurator in Nearer Spain, and not improbably honoured him with equestrian rank. It was during his sojourn in Spain that the death of his brother-in-law, C. Cæcilius, left his nephew

---

1   The weight of testimony inclines to the latter. The mere titles of the works which have been written on the subject would fill a volume.

2   *Ab urbe condita*, 'from the founding of the City' abbreviated as AUC, express a date in years since 753 BC, the traditional founding of Rome.

3   Officer or commander of a legion (TN).

C. Plinius Cæcilius Secundus (the author of the *Letters*) an orphan; whom immediately upon his return to Rome, A.D. 70, he adopted, receiving him and his widowed mother under his roof.

Having been previously known to Vespasian in the German wars, he was admitted into the number of his most intimate friends, and obtained an appointment at court, the nature of which is not known, but Rezzonico conjectures that it was in connexion with the imperial treasury. Though Pliny was on intimate terms also with Titus, to whom he dedicated his *Natural History*, there is little ground for the assertion, sometimes made, that he served under him in the Jewish wars. His account of Palestine clearly shows that he had never visited that country. It was at this period that he published his Continuation of the *History* of Aufidius Bassus.

Prom the titles which he gives to Titus in the dedicatory preface, it is pretty clear that his *Natural History* was published A.D. 77, two years before his death.

In A.D. 73 or 74, he had been appointed by Vespasian præfect of the Roman fleet at Misenum, on the western coast of Italy. It was to this elevation that he owed his romantic death, somewhat similar, it has been remarked, to that of Empedocles, who perished in the crater of Mount Ætna. The closing scene of his active life, simultaneously with the destruction of Herculaneum and Pompeii, cannot be better described than in the language employed by his nephew in an Epistle to his friend Tacitus the historian: "My uncle was at Misenum, where he was in personal command of the fleet. On the ninth day before the calends[4] of September, at about the seventh hour, 1 P.M., my mother, observing the appearance of a cloud of unusual size and shape, mentioned it to him. After reclining in the sun he had taken his cold bath; he had then again lain downn and, after a slight repast, applied himself to his studies. Immediately upon hearing this, he called for his shoes, and ascended a spot from which he could more easily observe this remarkable phenomena. The cloud was to he seen gradually rising upwards; though, from the great distance, it was uncertain from which of the mountains it arose; it was afterwards, however, ascertained to be Vesuvius. In appearance and shape it strongly resembled a tree; perhaps it was more like a pine than anything else, with a stem of enormous length reaching upwards to the heavens, and then spreading out in a number of branches in every direction. I have little doubt that either it had been carried upwards by a violent gust of wind, and that the wind dying away, it had lost its compactness, or else, that being overcome by its own weight, it had decreased in density and become extended over a large surface; at one moment it was white, at another dingy and spotted, just as it was more or less charged with earth or with ashes.

---

4   In the Roman calendar, the first day of the month. From this the days of the preceding month were counted backward to the ides, which in March, May, July, and October corresponded to the 15th, and in all the other months to the 13th day of the month. Thus the 16th day of March by our reckoning was in the Roman calendar the 17th day before the calends of April (the first of April being included), or more briefly 17th calends; the 14th day of January was the 19th day before the calends of February; the 14th day of any month with thirty days being the 18th before the calends of the succeeding month.

"To a man so eager as he was in the pursuit of knowledge, this appeared to be a most singular phenomena, and one that deserved to be viewed more closely; accordingly he gave orders for a light Liburnian vessel to be got ready, and left it at my option to accompany him. To this however I made answer, that I should prefer continuing my studies; and as it so happened, he himself had just given me something to write. Taking his tablets with him, he left the house. The sailors stationed at Retina, alarmed at the imminence of the danger –for the village lay at the foot of the mountain, and the sole escape was by sea– sent to entreat his assistance in rescuing them from this frightful peril. Upon this he instantly changed his plans, and what he had already begun from a desire for knowledge, he determined to carry out as a matter of duty. He had the galleys put to sea at once, and went on board himself, with the intention of rendering assistance, not only to Retina, but to many other places as well; for the whole of this charming coast was thickly populated. Accordingly he made all possible haste towards the spot, from which others were flying, and steered straight onwards into the very midst of the danger; so far indeed was he from every sensation of fear, that he remarked and had noted down every movement and every change that was to be observed in the appearance of this ominous eruption. The ashes were now falling fast upon the vessels, hotter and more and more thickly the nearer they approached the shore; showers of pumice too, intermingled with black stones, calcined and broken by the action of the flames; the sea suddenly retreated from the shore, where the debris of the mountain rendered landing quite impossible. After hesitating for a moment whether or not to turn back, upon the pilot strongly advising him to do so: 'Fortune favours the bold', said he, 'conduct me to Pomponianus.' Pomponianus was then at Stabiæ, a place that lay on the other side of the bay, for in those parts the shores are winding, and as they gradually trend away, the sea forms a number of little creeks. At this spot the danger at present was not imminent, but still it could be seen, and as it appeared to be approaching nearer and nearer, Pomponianus had ordered his baggage on board the ships, determined to take to flight, if the wind, which happened to be blowing the other way, should chance to lull. The wind, being in this quarter, was extremely favourable to his passage, and my uncle soon arriving at Stabise, embraced his anxious friend, and did his best to restore his courage; and the better to reassure him by evidence of his own sense of their safety, he requested the servants to conduct him to the bath. After bathing he took his place at table, and dined, and that too in high spirits, or at all events, what equally shows his strength of mind, with every outward appearance of being so. In the mean time vast sheets of flame and large bodies of fire were to be seen arising from Mount Vesuvius; the glare and brilliancy of which were beheld in bolder relief as the shades of night came on apace. My uncle however, in order to calm their fears, persisted in saying that this was only the light given by some villages which had been abandoned by the rustics in their alarm to the flames; after which he retired to rest, and soon fell fast asleep; for his respiration, which with him was heavy and loud, in consequence of his corpulence, was distinctly heard by the servants who were keeping watch at the door of the apartment. The courtyard which led to his apartment had now become filled with cinders and pumice-stones, to such a degree, that if he had remained any longer in the room, it would have been quite impossible for him to leave it. On being awoke he immediately arose, and rejoined Pomponianus and the others who had in the meanwhile been sitting up. They then consulted together whether it would be better to remain in the house or take their chance in the open air; as the building was now rocking to and fro from the violent and repeated shocks, while the walls, as though rooted up from their very foundations, seemed to be at one moment carried in this direction, at another in that. Having adopted the latter alternative, they were now alarmed at the showers of light calcined pumice-stones that were falling thick about them, a risk however to which as a choice of evils they had to submit. In taking this step I must remark that, while with my uncle it was reason triumphing over reason, with the rest it was only one fear getting the better of the other. Taking the precaution of placing pillows on their heads, they tied them on with towels, by way of protection against the falling stones and ashes. It was now day in other places, though there it was still night, more dark and more profound than any ordinary night; torches however and various lights in some measure served to dispel the gloom. It was then determined to make for the shore, and to ascertain whether the sea would now admit of their embarking; it was found however to be still too stormy and too boisterous to allow of their making the attempt. Upon this my uncle lay down on a sail which had been spread for him, and more than once asked for some cold water, which he drank; very soon however, they were alarmed by the flames and the sulphurous smell which announced their approach, upon which the others at once took to flight, while my uncle arose leaning upon two of the servants for support. Upon making this effort, he instantly fell to the ground; the dense vapour having, I imagine, stopped his respiration and suffocated him; for his chest was naturally weak and contracted, and often troubled with violent palpitations. When day was at last restored, the third after the closing one of his existence, his body was found untouched and without a wound; there was no change to be perceived in the clothes, and its appearance was rather that of a person asleep than of a corpse. In the meantime my mother and myself were at Misenum —that however has nothing to do with the story, as it was only your wish to know the details connected with his death. I shall therefore draw to a conclusion. The only thing that I shall add is the assurance that I have truthfully related all these facts, of which I was either an eye-witness myself, or heard them at the time of their occurrence, a period when they were most likely to be correctly related. You of course will select such points as you may think the most important. For it is one thing to write a letter, another to write history; one thing to write for a friend, another to write for the public. Farewell."

Of the mode of life pursued by Pliny, and of the rest of his works, an equally interesting account has been preserved by his nephew, in an Epistle addressed to Macer. We cannot more appropriately conclude than by presenting this Epistle to the reader: "I am highly gratified to find that you read the works of my uncle with such a degree of attention as to feel a desire to possess them all, and that with this view you inquire. What are their names? I will perform the duties of an index then;

and not content with that, will state in what order they were written; for even that is a kind of information which is by no means undesirable to those who are devoted to literary pursuits. His first composition was a treatise 'on the use of the Javelin by Cavalry,' in one Book. This he composed, with equal diligence and ingenuity, while he was in command of a troop of horse. His second work was the 'Life of Q. Pomponius Secundus,' in two Books, a person by whom he had been particularly beloved. These books he composed as a tribute which was justly due to the memory of his deceased friend. His next work was twenty Books on 'the Wars in Germany,' in which he has compiled an account of all the wars in which we have been engaged with the people of that country This he had begun while serving in Germany, having been recommended to do so in a dream. For in his sleep he thought that the figure of Drusus Nero,[5] stood by him —the same Drusus, who after the most extensive conquests in that country, there met his death. Commending his memory to Pliny's attentive care, Drusus conjured him to rescue it from the decaying effect of oblivion. Next to these came his three books entitled 'The Student', divided, on account of their great size, into six volumes. In these he has given instructions for the training of the orator, from the cradle to his entrance on public life. In the latter years of Nero's reign, he wrote eight books, 'On Difficulties in the Latin Language'; that being a period at which every kind of study, in any way free-spoken or even of elevated style, would have been rendered dangerous by the tyranny that was exercised. His next work was his 'Continuation of the History of Aufidius Bassus,' in thirty-one books; after which came his 'Natural History,' in thirty-seven books, a work remarkable for its comprehensiveness and erudition, and not less varied than Nature herself. You will wonder how a man so occupied with business could possibly find time to write such a number of volumes, many of them on subjects of a nature so difficult to be treated of. You will be even more astonished when you learn, that for some time he pleaded at the bar as an advocate, that he was only in his fifty-sixth year at the time of his death, and that the time that intervened was equally trenched upon and frittered away by the most weighty duties of business, and the marks of favour shewn him by princes. His genius, however, was truly quite incredible, his zeal indefatigable, and his power of application wonderful in the extreme. At the festival of the Vulcanalia,[6] he began to sit up to a late hour by candle-light, not for the purpose of consulting the stars, but with the object of pursuing his studies; while, in the winter, he would set to work at the seventh hour of the night, or the eighth at the very latest, often indeed at the sixth.[7] By nature he had the faculty of being able to fall asleep in a moment; indeed, slumber would sometimes overtake him in his studies, and then leave him just as suddenly. Before daybreak, he was in the habit of attending the Emperor Vespasian —for he, too, was one who made an excellent use of his nights—, and then betook himself to the duties with which he was charged. On his return home, he devoted

---

5   Nero Claudius Drusus, the son of Livia, afterwards the wife of Augustus. He was the father of the Emperor Claudius, and died in Germany of the effects of an accident.
6   23rd of August.
7   At midwinter, this hour would answer at Rome to our midnight.

all the time which was still remaining to study. Taking an early repast, after the old fashion, light, and easy of digestion, in the summer time, if he had any leisure to spare, he would lie down in the sunshine, while some book was read to him, he himself making notes and extracts in the meanwhile; for it was his habit never to read anything without making extracts, it being a maxim of his, that there is no book so bad but that some good may be got out of it. After thus enjoying the sunshine, he generally took a cold bath; after which he would sit down to a slight repast, and then take a short nap. On awaking, as though another day had now commenced, he would study till the hour for the evening meal, during which some book was generally read to him, he making comments on it in a cursory manner. I remember, on one occasion, a friend of his interrupting the reader, who had given the wrong pronunciation to some words, and making him go over them again. 'You understood him, didn't you?' said my uncle. 'Yes,' said the other. 'Why, then, did you make him go over it again? Through this interruption of yours, we have lost more than ten lines.' So thrifty a manager was he of time! In summer he rose from the evening meal by daylight; and, in winter, during the first hour of the night,[8] just as though there had been some law which made it compulsory on him to do so. This is how he lived in the midst of his employments, and the bustle of the city. When in retirement in the country, the time spent in the bath was the only portion that was not allotted by him to study. When I say in the bath, I mean while he was in the water; for while his body was being scraped with the strigil[9] and rubbed, he either had some book read to him, or else would dictate himself. While upon a journey, as though relieved from every other care, he devoted himself to study, and nothing else. By his side was his secretary, with a book and tablets; and, in the winter time, the secretary's hands were protected by gloves, that the severity of the weather might not deprive his master for a single moment of his services. It was for this reason also that, when at Rome, he would never move about except in a litter. I remember that on one occasion he found fault with me for walking: 'You might have avoided losing all those hours,' said he; for he looked upon every moment as lost which was not devoted to study. It was by means of such unremitting industry as this that he completed so many works, and left me 160 volumes of notes, written extremely small on both sides, which in fact renders the collection doubly voluminous. He himself used to relate, that when he was procurator in Spain, he might have parted with his common-place book to Largius Licinius for 400,000 sesterces; and at that time the collection was not so extensive as afterwards. When you come to think of how much he must have read, of how much he has written, would you not really suppose that he had never been engaged in business, and had never enjoyed the favour of princes? And yet, on the other hand, when you hear what labour he expended upon his studies, does it not almost seem that he has neither written nor read enough? For, in fact, what pursuits are those that would not have been interrupted by occupations such as his? While, again,

---

    8   At midwinter, this would be between six and seven in the evening.
    9   An instrument of metal, ivory, or horn, used by the ancients for scraping the skin at the bath and in the gymnasium; a flesh-scraper.

what is there that such unremitting perseverance as his could not have effected? I am in the habit, therefore, of laughing at it when people call me a studious man —me who, in comparison with him, am a downright idler; and yet I devote to study as much time as my public engagements on the one hand, and my duties to my friends on the other, will admit of. Who is there, then, out of all those who have devoted their whole life to literature, that ought not, when put in comparison with him, to quite blush at a life that would almost appear to have been devoted to slothfulness and inactivity? But my letter has already exceeded its proper limits, for I had originally intended to write only upon the subject as to which you made inquiry, the books of his composition that he left. I trust, however, that these particulars will prove no less pleasing to you than the writings themselves; and that they will not only induce you to peruse them, but excite you, by a feeling of generous emulation, to produce some work of a similar nature. — Farewell."

Of all the works written by Pliny, one only, the 'Historia Naturalis' has survived to our times. This work, however, is not a 'Natural History' in the modern acceptation of the term, but rather a vast Encyclopædia of ancient knowledge and belief upon almost every known subject "not less varied than Nature herself," as his nephew says. It comprises, within the compass of thirty-seven books, 20,000 matters of importance, collected from about 2000 volumes (nearly all of which have now perished), the works, as Pliny himself states, of 100 writers of authority; together with a vast number of additional matters unknown to those authorities, and many of them the results of his own experience and observation. Hardouin has drawn up a catalogue of the authors quoted by Pliny; they amount in number to between 400 and 500.

The following is a brief sketch of the plan of this wonderful monument of human industry. After a dedicatory Epistle to Titus, followed by a table of contents of the other Books, which together form the First Book, the author proceeds to give an account of the prevailing notions as to the universe, the earth, the sun, the moon, the stars, and the more remarkable properties of the elements (*partes naturæ*). He then passes on to a geographical description of the face of the earth as known to the ancients. After the Geography comes what may in strict propriety be termed "Natural History," including a history of man, replete indeed with marvels, hut interesting in the highest degree. Having mentioned at considerable length the land, animals, fishes, birds, and insects, he passes on to Botany, which in its various aspects occupies the larger portion of the work. At the same time, in accordance with his comprehensive plan, this part includes a vast amount of information on numerous subjects, the culture of the cereals and the manufacture of oil, wine, paper (*papyrus*), and numerous other articles of daily use. After treating at considerable length of Medical Botany, he proceeds to speak of medicaments derived from the human body, from which he branches off into discussions on the history of medicine, and magic, which last he looks upon as an offshoot from the medical art; and he takes this opportunity of touching upon many of the then current superstitions and notions on astrology. He concludes this portion of his work with an account of the medicinal properties of various waters, and of those of fishes and other aquatic animals. He then presents us with a treatise on Mineralogy, in which he has accumulated every possible kind of information relative to the use of gold, silver, bronze, and other metals; a subject which not unnaturally leads him into repeated digressions relative to money, jewels, plate, statues, and statuaries. Mineral pigments next occupy his attention, with many interesting notices of the great painters of Greece; from which he passes on to the various kinds of stone and materials employed in building, and the use of marble for the purposes of sculpture, including a notice of that art and of the most eminent sculptors. The last Book is devoted to an account of gems and precious stones, and concludes with an eulogium on his native country, as alike distinguished for its fertility, its picturesque beauties, and the natural endowments and high destinies of its people.

From the writings of Pliny we gather of course a large amount of information as to his opinions and the constitution of his mind. His credulity, it must be admitted, is great in the extreme; though, singularly enough, he severely taxes the Greeks with the same failing. Were we not assured from other sources that he was eminently successful in life, was in the enjoyment of opulence, and honoured with the favour and confidence of princes, the remarks which he frequently makes on human life, in the Seventh Book more especially, would have led us to the conclusion that he was a disappointed man, embittered against his fellow-creatures, and dissatisfied with the terms on which the tenure of life is granted to us. He opens that Book with a preface replete with querulous dissatisfaction and repinings at the lot of man —the only 'tearful' animal— he says.[10] He repines at the helpless and wretched condition of the infant at the moment it is ushered into life, and the numerous pains and vices to which it is doomed to be subject. Man's liability to disease is with him a blemish in the economy of nature; "life," he says, "this gift of nature, however long it may be, is but too uncertain and too frail; to those even to whom it is most largely granted, it is dealt out with a sparing and niggardly hand, if we only think of eternity." As we cannot have life on our own terms, he does not think it worthy of our acceptance, and more than once expresses his opinion that the sooner we are rid of it the better. Sudden death he looks upon as a remarkable phenomena, but, at the same time, as the greatest blessing that can be granted to us; and when he mentions cases of resuscitation, it is only to indulge in the querulous complaint, that, "exposed as he is by his birth to the caprices of fortune, man can be certain of nothing; no, not even his own death." Though anything but an Epicurean, in the modern acceptation of the word, he seems to have held some, at least, of the tenets of Epicurus, in reference to the immortality of the soul. Whether he supposed that the soul, at the moment of death, is resolved into its previous atoms or constituent elements, he does not inform us; but he states it as his belief, that after death the soul has no more existence than it had before birth; that all notions of immortality are a mere delusion; and that the very idea of a future existence is ridiculous, and spoils that greatest blessing of nature —death. He certainly speaks

---

10   Even on that point he contradicts himself in the next Book, in reference to the lion and the horse.

of ghosts or apparitions, seen after death; but these he probably looked upon as exceptional cases, if indeed he believed in the stories which he quotes, of which we have no proofs, or rather, indeed, presumptive proofs to the contrary; for some of them he calls *magna fabulosetas*, "most fabulous tales."

In relation to human inventions, it is worthy of remark, that he states that the first thing in which mankind agreed, was the use of the Ionian alphabet; the second, the practice of shaving the beard, and the employment of barbers; and the third, the division of time into hours,

We cannot more appropriately conclude this review of the Life and Works of Pliny, than by quoting the opinions of two of the most eminent philosophers of modern times, Buffon and Cuvier; though the former, it must be admitted, has spoken of him in somewhat too high terms of commendation, and in instituting a comparison between Pliny's work and those of Aristotle, has placed in juxtaposition the names of two men who, beyond an ardent thirst for knowledge, had no characteristics in common.

"Pliny," says Buffon, "has worked upon a plan which is much more extensive than that of Aristotle, and not improbably too extensive. He has made it his object to embrace every subject; indeed he would appear to have taken the measure of Nature, and to have found her too contracted for his expansive genius. His 'Natural History,' independently of that of animals, plants, and minerals, includes an account of the heavens and the earth, of medicine, commerce, navigation, the liberal and mechanical arts, the origin of usages and customs, in a word, the history of all the natural sciences and all the arts of human invention. That, too, is still more astonishing, in each of these departments Pliny shows himself equally great. The grandeur of his ideas and the dignity of his style confer an additional lustre on the profoundness of his erudition; not only did he know all that was known in his time, but he was also gifted with that comprehensiveness of view which in some measure multiplies knowledge. He had all that delicacy of perception upon which depend so materially both elegance and taste, and he communicates to his readers that freedom of thought and that boldness of sentiment, which constitute the true germ of philosophy. His work, as varied as Nature herself, always paints her in her most attractive colours. It is, so to say, a compilation from all that had been written before his time; a record of all that was excellent or useful; hut this record has in it features so grand, this compilation contains matter grouped in a manner so novel, that it is preferable to most of the original works that treat upon similar subjects."

The judgment pronounced by Cuvier on Pliny's work, though somewhat less highly coloured, awards to it a high rank among the most valuable productions of antiquity. "The work of Pliny," says he, "is one of the most precious monuments that have come down to us from ancient times, and affords proof of an astonishing amount of erudition in one who was a warrior and a statesman. To appreciate with justice this vast and celebrated composition, it is necessary to regard it in several points of view; with reference to the plan proposed, the facts stated, and the style employed. The plan proposed by the writer is of immense extent; it is his object to write not merely a Natural History in our restricted sense of the term, not an account merely, more or less detailed, of animals, plants, and minerals, but a work which embraces astronomy, physics, geography, agriculture, commerce, medicine, and the fine arts; and all these in addition to natural history properly so called; while at the same time he continually interweaves with his narrative information upon the arts which bear relation to man considered metaphysically, and the history of nations; so much so indeed, that in many respects this work was the Encyclopaedia of its age. It was impossible in running over, however cursorily, such a prodigious number of subjects, that the writer should not have made us acquainted with a multitude of facts, which, while remarkable in themselves, are the more precious from the circumstance that at the present day he is the only author extant who relates them. It is to be regretted however that the manner in which he has collected and grouped this mass of matter, has caused it to lose some portion of its value, from his mixture of fable with truth, and more especially from the difficulty, and in some cases, the impossibility, of discovering exactly of what object he is speaking. But if Pliny possesses little merit as a critic, it is far otherwise with his talent as a writer, and the immense treasury which he opens to us of Latin terms and forms of expression; these, from the very abundance of the subjects upon which he treats, render his work one of the richest repositories of the Roman language. Wherever he finds it possible to give expression to general ideas or to philosophical views, his language assumes considerable energy and vivacity, and his thoughts present to us a certain novelty and boldness which tend in a very great degree to relieve the dryness of his enumerations, and, with the majority of his readers, excuse the insufficiency of his scientific indications. He is always noble and serious, full of the love of justice and virtue, detestation of cruelty and baseness, of which he had such frightful instances before his eyes, and contempt for that unbridled luxury which in his time had so deeply corrupted the Roman people. For these great merits Pliny cannot be too highly praised, and despite the faults which we are obliged to admit in him when viewed as a naturalist, we are bound to regard him as one of the most meritorious of the Roman writers, and among those most worthy to be reckoned in the number of the classics who wrote after the reign of Augustus."

Book I
Dedication

Plinius Secundus to his Friend Titus Vespasian

This treatise on Natural History, a novel work in Roman literature, which I have just completed, I have taken the liberty to dedicate to you, most gracious Emperor.

I have included in thirty-six books 20,000 topics, all worthy of attention, (for, as Domitius Piso says, we ought to make not merely books, but valuable collections), gained by the perusal of about 2000 volumes, of which a few only are in the hands of the studious, on account of the obscurity of the subjects, procured by the careful perusal of 100 select authors; and to these I have made considerable additions of things, which were either not known to my predecessors, or which have been lately discovered. Nor can I doubt but that there still remain many things which I have omitted; for I am a mere mortal, and one that has many occupations. I have, therefore, been obliged to compose this work at interrupted intervals, indeed during the night, so that you will find that I have not been idle even during this period. The day I devote to you, exactly portioning out my sleep to the necessity of my health, and contenting myself with this reward, that while we are musing on these subjects (according to the remark of Varro), we are adding to the length of our lives; for life properly consists in being awake.

In consideration of these circumstances and these difficulties, I dare promise nothing; but you have done me the most essential service in permitting me to dedicate my work to you. Nor does this merely give a sanction to it, but it determines its value; for things are often conceived to be of great value, solely because they are consecrated in temples.

And because the public good requires that you should be spared as much as possible from all trouble, I have subjoined to this epistle the contents of each of the following books and have used my best endeavours to prevent your being obliged to read them all through. And this, which was done for your benefit, will also serve the same purpose for others, so that any one may search for what he wishes, and may know where to find it. This has been already done among us by Valerius Soranus, in his work which he entitled "On Mysteries."

The 1st book is the Preface of the Work, dedicated to Titus Vespasian Cæesar.
The 2nd is on the World, the Elements, and the Heavenly Bodies.
The 3rd, 4th, 5th and 6th books are on Geography, in which is contained an account of the situation of the different countries, the inhabitants, the seas, towns, harbours, mountains, rivers, and dimensions, and the various tribes, some of which still exist and others have disappeared.
The 7th is on Man, and the Inventions of Man.
The 8th on the various kinds of Land Animals.
The 9th on Aquatic Animals.
The 10th on the various kinds of Birds.
The 11th on Insects,
The 12th on Odoriferous Plants.
The 13th on Exotic Trees.
The 14th on Vines.
The 15th on Fruit Trees.
The 16th on Forest Trees.
The 17th on Plants raised in nurseries or gardens.
The 18th on the nature of Fruits and the Cerealia, and the pursuits of the Husbandman.
The 19th on Flax, Broom,[1] and Gardening.
The 20th on the Cultivated Plants that are proper for food and for medicine.
The 21st on Flowers and Plants that are used for making Garlands.
The 22nd on Garlands, and Medicines made from Plants.
The 23rd on Medicines made from Wine and from cultivated Trees.
The 24th on Medicines made from Forest Trees.
The 25th on Medicines made from Wild Plants.
The 26th on New Diseases, and Medicines made, for certain Diseases, from Plants.
The 27th on some other Plants and Medicines.
The 28th on Medicines procured from Man and from large Animals.

---

1 *Spartum*; this plant was used to make bands for the vines and cables for ships.

Book I - Dedication

The 29th on Medical Authors, and on Medicines from other Animals.
The 30th on Magic, and Medicines for certain parts of the Body.
The 31st on Medicines from Aquatic Animals.
The 32nd on the other properties of Aquatic Animals.
The 33rd on Gold and Silver.
The 34th on Copper and Lead, and the workers of Copper.
The 35th on Painting, Colours, and Painters,
The 36th on Marbles and Stones,
The 37th on Gems.

Book II
An Account of the World and the Elements

Whether the World[1] be Finite, and Whether there be More than One World
The world and whatever other name used to call the heavens, by the vault of which all things are enclosed, we must conceive to be a Deity, to be eternal, without bounds, neither created, nor subject, at any time, to destruction. To inquire what is beyond it is no concern of man, nor can the human mind form any conjecture respecting it. It is sacred, eternal, and without bounds, all in all; indeed including everything in itself; finite, yet like what is infinite; the most certain of all things, yet like what is uncertain, externally and internally embracing all things in itself; it is the work of nature, and itself constitutes nature.

It is madness to harass the mind, as some have done, with attempts to measure the world, and to publish these attempts; or, like others, to argue from what they have made out, that there are innumerable other worlds, and that we must believe there to be so many other natures, or that, if only one nature produced the whole, there will be so many suns and so many moons, and that each of them will have immense trains of other heavenly bodies. As if the same question would not recur

---

1 "Mundus." In translating from one language into another, it is proper, as a general principle, always to render the same word in the original by the same word in the translation. But to this rule there are two exceptions; where the languages do not possess words which precisely correspond, and where the original author does not always use the same word in the same sense. Both these circumstances, I apprehend, apply to the case in question. The term Mundus is used by Pliny, sometimes to mean the earth and its immediate appendages, the visible solar system; and at other times the universe; while I think we may venture to assert, that in some instances it is used in rather a vague manner, without any distinct reference to either one or other of the above designations. I have, in almost all cases, translated it by the term world as approaching nearest to the sense of the original.

at every step of our inquiry, anxious as we must be to arrive at some conclusion; or, as if this infinity, which we ascribe to nature, the former of all things, cannot be more easily comprehended by one single formation, especially when that is so extensive. It is madness, perfect madness, to go out of this world and to search for what is beyond it, as if one who is ignorant of his own dimensions could ascertain the measure of anything else, or as it the human mind could see what the world itself cannot contain.

FORM AND NATURE OF THE WORLD; WHENCE ITS NAME IS DERIVED

That it has the form of a perfect globe we learn from the name which has been uniformly given to it, as well as from numerous natural arguments. For not only does a figure of this kind return everywhere into itself and sustains itself, also including itself, requiring no adjustments, not sensible of either end or beginning in any of its parts, and is best fitted for that motion, with which, as will appear hereafter, it is continually turning round; but still more, because we perceive it, by the evidence of the sight, to be, in every part, convex and central, which could not be the case were it of any other figure.

The rising and the setting of the sun clearly prove, that this globe is carried round in the space of twenty-four hours, in an eternal and never-ceasing circuit, and with incredible swiftness. I am not able to say, whether the sound caused by the whirling about of so great a mass be excessive, and, therefore, far beyond what our ears can perceive, nor, indeed, whether the resounding of so many stars, all carried along at the same time and revolving in their orbits, may not produce a kind of delightful harmony of incredible sweetness. To us, who are in the interior, the world appears to glide silently along, both by day and by night.

Various circumstances in nature prove to us, that there are impressed on the heavens innumerable figures of animals and of all kinds of objects, and that its surface is not perfectly polished like the eggs of birds, as some celebrated authors assert. For we find that the seeds of all bodies fall down from it, principally into the ocean, and, being mixed together, that a variety of monstrous forms are in this way frequently produced. And, indeed, this is evident to the eye; for, in one part, we have the figure of a wain, in another of a bear, of a bull, and of a letter; while, in the middle of them, over our heads, there is a white circle.

With respect to the name, I am influenced by the unanimous opinions of all nations. For what the Greeks, from its being ornamented, have termed κόσμος, we, from its perfect and complete elegance, have termed *mundus*. The name *cœlum*,[2] no doubt, refers to its being engraved, as it were, with the stars, as Varro suggests. In confirmation of this idea we may adduce the Zodiac, in which are twelve figures of animals; through them it is that the sun has continued its course for so many ages.

OF THE ELEMENTS AND THE PLANETS

I do not find that any one has doubted that there are four elements. The highest of these is supposed to be fire, and hence proceed the eyes of so many glittering

---

2   Pliny confuses the word *cœlum* with *cælum*: engraved.

stars. The next is that spirit, which both the Greeks and ourselves call by the same name, air. It is by the force of this vital principle, pervading all things and mingling with all, that the earth, together with the fourth element, water, is balanced in the middle of space. These are mutually bound together, the lighter being restrained by the heavier, so that they cannot fly off; while, on the contrary, from the lighter tending upwards, the heavier are so suspended, that they cannot fall down. Thus, by an equal tendency in an opposite direction, each of them remains in its appropriate place, bound together by the never-ceasing revolution of the world, which always turning on itself, the earth falls to the lowest part and is in the middle of the whole, while it remains suspended in the centre, and, as it were, balancing this centre, in which it is suspended. So that it alone remains immoveable, whilst all things revolve round it, being connected with every other part, whilst they all rest upon it.

Between this body and the heavens there are suspended, in this aerial spirit, seven stars, separated by determinate spaces, which, on account of their motion, we call wandering, although, in reality, none are less so. The sun is carried along in the midst of these, a body of great size and power, the ruler, not only of the seasons and of the different climates, but also of the stars themselves and of the heavens. When we consider his operations, we must regard him as the life, or rather the mind of the universe, the chief regulator and the God of nature; he also lends his light to the other stars. He is most illustrious and excellent, beholding all things and hearing all things, which, I perceive, is ascribed to him exclusively by the prince of poets, Homer.

OF GOD

I consider it, therefore, an indication of human weakness to inquire into the figure and form of God. For whatever God be, if there be any other God, and wherever he exists, he is all sense, all sight, all hearing, all life, all mind, and all within himself. To believe that there are a number of Gods, derived from the virtues and vices of man, as Chastity, Concord, Understanding, Hope, Honour, Clemency, and Fidelity; or, according to the opinion of Democritus, that there are only two. Punishment and Reward, indicates still greater folly. Human nature, weak and frail as it is, mindful of its own infirmity, has made these divisions, so that every one might have recourse to that which he supposed himself to stand more particularly in need of. Hence we find different names employed by different nations; the inferior deities are arranged in classes, and diseases and plagues are deified, in consequence of our anxious wish to propitiate them. It was from this cause that a temple was dedicated to Fever, at the public expense, on the Palatine Hill, and to Orbona, near the Temple of the Lares, and that an altar was elected to Good Fortune on the Esquiline. Hence we may understand how it comes to pass that there is a greater population of the Celestials than of human beings, since each individual makes a separate God for himself, adopting his own Juno and his own Genius. And there are nations who make Gods of certain animals, and even certain obscene things, which are not to be spoken of, swearing by stinking meats and such like. To suppose that marriages are contracted between the Gods, and that, during so long a period, there should have been no issue from them, that some of them should be old and always grey-headed and others young and like children, some of a dark complexion, winged, lame, produced from eggs, living and dying on alternate days, is sufficiently puerile and foolish. But it is the height of impudence to imagine, that adultery takes place between them, that they have contests and quarrels, and that there are Gods of theft and of various crimes. To assist man is to be a God; this is the path to eternal glory. This is the path which the Roman nobles formerly pursued, and this is the path which is now pursued by the greatest ruler of our age, Vespasian Augustus, he who has come to the relief of an exhausted empire, as well as by his sons. This was the ancient mode of remunerating those who deserved it, to regard them as Gods. For the names of all the Gods, as well as of the stars that I have mentioned above have been derived from their services to mankind. And with respect to Jupiter and Mercury, and the rest of the celestial nomenclature, who does not admit that they have reference to certain natural phenomena?

But it is ridiculous to suppose, that the great head of all things, whatever it be, pays any regard to human affairs. Can we believe, or rather can there be any doubt, that it is not polluted by such a disagreeable and complicated office? It is not easy to determine which opinion would be most for the advantage of mankind, since we observe some who have no respect for the Gods, and others who carry it to a scandalous excess. They are slaves to foreign ceremonies; they carry on their fingers the Gods and the monsters whom they worship; they condemn and they lay great stress on certain kinds of food; they impose on themselves dreadful ordinances, not even sleeping quietly. They do not marry or adopt children, or indeed do anything else, without the sanction of their sacred rites. There are others, on the contrary, who will cheat in the very Capitol, and will forswear themselves even by Jupiter Tonans,[3] and while these thrive in their crimes, the others torment themselves with their superstitions to no purpose.

Among these discordant opinions mankind have discovered for themselves a kind of intermediate deity, by which our scepticism concerning God is still increased. For all over the world, in all places, and at all times. Fortune is the only god whom every one invokes; she alone is spoken of, she alone is accused and is supposed to be guilty; she alone is in our thoughts, is praised and blamed, and is loaded with reproaches; wavering as she is, conceived by the generality of mankind to be blind, wandering, inconstant, uncertain, variable, and often favouring the unworthy. To her are referred all our losses and all our gains, and in casting up the accounts of mortals she alone balances the two pages of our sheet. We are so much in the power of chance, that change itself is considered as a God, and the existence of God becomes doubtful.

But there are others who reject this principle and assign events to the influence of the stars and to the laws of our nativity; they suppose that God, once for all, issues his decrees and never afterwards interferes. This opinion begins to gain ground, and both the learned and the unlearned vulgar are falling into it. Hence

---

3   His specific office was to execute vengeance on the impious.

we have the admonitions of thunder, the warnings of oracles, the predictions of soothsayers, and things too trifling to he mentioned, as sneezing and stumbling with the feet reckoned among omens. The late Emperor Augustus relates, that he put the left shoe on the wrong foot, the day when he was near being assaulted by his soldiers. And such things as these so embarrass improvident mortals, that among all of them this alone is certain, that there is nothing certain, and that there is nothing more proud or more wretched than man. For other animals have no care but to provide for their subsistence, for which the spontaneous kindness of nature is all-sufficient; and this one circumstance renders their lot more especially preferable, that they never think about glory, or money, or ambition, and, above all, that they never reflect on death.

The belief, however, that on these points the Gods superintend human affairs is useful to us, as well as that the punishment of crimes, although sometimes tardy, from the Deity being occupied with such a mass of business, is never entirely remitted, and that the human race was not made the next in rank to himself, in order that they might be degraded like brutes. And indeed this constitutes the great comfort in this imperfect state of man, that even the Deity cannot do everything. For he cannot procure death for himself, even if he wished it, which, so numerous are the evils of life, has been granted to man as our chief good. Nor can he make mortals immortal, or recall to life those who are dead; nor can he effect, that he who has once lived shall not have lived, or that he who has enjoyed honours shall not have enjoyed them; nor has he any influence over past events but to cause them to be forgotten. And, if we illustrate the nature of our connexion with God by a less serious argument, he cannot make twice ten not to be twenty, and many other things of this kind. By these considerations the power of Nature is clearly proved, and is shown to be what we call God. It is not foreign to the subject to have digressed into these matters, familiar as they are to every one, from the continual discussions that take place respecting God.

OF THE NATURE OF THE STARS; OF THE MOTION OF THE PLANETS

Let us return from this digression to the other parts of nature. The stars which are described as fixed in the heavens, are not, as the vulgar suppose, attached each of them to different individuals, the brighter to the rich, those that are less so to the poor, and the dim to the aged, shining according to the lot of the individual, and separately assigned to mortals; for they have neither come into existence, nor do they perish in connexion with particular persons, nor does a falling star indicate that any one is dead. We are not so closely connected with the heavens as that the shining of the stars is affected by our death. When they are supposed to shoot or fall, they throw out, by the force of their fire, as if from an excess of nutriment, the superabundance of the humour which they have absorbed, as we observe to take place from the oil in our lamps, when they are burning. The nature of the celestial bodies is eternal, being interwoven, as it were, with the world, and, by this union, rendering it solid; but they exert their most powerful influence on the earth. This, notwithstanding its subtilty, may be known by the clearness and the magnitude of the effect, as we shall point out in the proper place. The account of the circles of the heavens will be better understood when we come to speak of the earth, since they have all a reference to it; except what has been discovered respecting the Zodiac, which I shall now detail.

Anaximander the Milesian, in the 58th olympiad, is said to have been the first who understood its obliquity, and thus opened the road to a correct knowledge of the subject. Afterwards Cleostratus made the signs in it, first marking those of Aries and Sagittarius; Atlas had formed the sphere long before this time. But now, leaving the further consideration of this subject, we must treat of the bodies that are situated between the earth and the heavens.

It is certain that the star called Saturn is the highest, and therefore appears the smallest, that he passes through the largest circuit, and that he is at least thirty years in completing it. The course of all the planets, and among others of the Sun, and the Moon, is in the contrary direction to that of the heavens, that is towards the left, while the heavens are rapidly carried about to the right. And although, by the stars constantly revolving with immense velocity, they are raised up, and hurried on to the part where they set, yet they are all forced, by a motion of their own, in an opposite direction; and this is so ordered, lest the air, being always moved in the same direction, by the constant whirling of the heavens, should accumulate into one mass, whereas now it is divided and separated and beaten into small pieces, by the opposite motion of the different stars. Saturn is a star of a cold and rigid nature, while the orbit of Jupiter is much lower, and is carried round in twelve years. The next star, Mars, which some persons call Hercules, is of a fiery and burning nature, and from its nearness to the sun is carried round in little less than two years. In consequence of the excessive heat of this star and the rigidity of Saturn, Jupiter, which is interposed between the two, is tempered by both of them, and is thus rendered salutary. The path of the Sun consists of 360 degrees; but, in order that the shadow may return to the same point of the dial, we are obliged to add, in each year, five days and the fourth part of a day. On this account an intercalary day is given to every fifth year, that the period of the seasons may agree with that of the Sun.

Below the Sun revolves the great star called Venus, wandering with an alternate motion, and, even in its surnames, rivalling the Sun and the Moon. For when it precedes the day and rises in the morning, it receives the name of Lucifer, as if it were another sun, hastening on the day. On the contrary, when it shines in the west, it is named Vesper, as prolonging the light, and performing the office of the

Book II - An Account of the World and the Elements

moon. Pythagoras, the Samian, was the first who discovered its nature, about the 62nd olympiad, in the 222nd year of the City. It excels all the other stars in size, and its brilliancy is so considerable, that it is the only star which produces a shadow by its rays. There has, consequently, been great interest made for its name; some have called it the star of Juno, others of Isis, and others of the Mother of the Gods, By its influence everything in the earth is generated. For, as it rises in either direction, it sprinkles everything with its genial dew, and not only matures the productions of the earth, but stimulates all living things. It completes the circuit of the zodiac in 348 days, never receding from the Sun more than 46 degrees, according to Timæus.

Similarly circumstanced, but by no means equal in size and in power, next to it, is the star Mercury, by some called Apollo; it is carried in a lower orbit, and moves in a course which is quicker by nine days, shining sometimes before the rising of the sun, and at other times after its setting, but never going farther from it than 23 degrees, as we learn from Timæeus and Sosigenes. The nature of these two stars is peculiar, and is not the same with those mentioned above, for those are seen to recede from the sun through one-third or one-fourth part of the heavens, and are often seen opposite to it. They have also other larger circuits, in which they make their complete revolutions, as will be described in the account of the great year.

But the Moon, which is the last of the stars, and the one the most connected with the earth, the remedy provided by nature for darkness, excels all the others in its admirable qualities. By the variety of appearances which it assumes, it puzzles the observers, mortified that they should be the most ignorant concerning that star which is the nearest to them. She is always either waxing or waning; sometimes her disc is curved into horns, sometimes it is divided into two equal portions, and at other times it is swelled out into a full orb; sometimes she appears spotted and suddenly becomes very bright; she appears very large with her full orb and suddenly becomes invisible; now continuing during all the night, now rising late, and now aiding the light of the sun during a part of the day; becoming eclipsed and yet being visible while she is eclipsed; concealing herself at the end of the month and yet not supposed to be eclipsed. Sometimes she is low down, sometimes she is high up, and that not according to one uniform course, being at one time raised up to the heavens, at other times almost contiguous to the mountains; now elevated in the north, now depressed in the south; all which circumstances having been noticed by Endymion, a report was spread about, that he was in love with the moon. We are not indeed sufficiently fateful to those, who, with so much labour and care, have enlightened us with this light; while, so diseased is the human mind, that we take pleasure in writing the annals of blood and slaughter, in order that the crimes of men may be made known to those who are ignorant of the constitution of the world itself.

Being nearest to the axis, and therefore having the smallest orbit, the Moon passes in twenty-seven days and the one-third part of a day through the same space for which Saturn, the highest of the planets, as was stated above, requires thirty years. After remaining for two days in conjunction with the sun, on the thirtieth day she again very slowly emerges to pursue her accustomed course. I know not whether she ought not to be considered as our instructress in everything that can be known respecting the heavens; as that the year is divided into the twelve divisions of the months, since she follows the sun for the same number of times, until he returns to the commencement of his course; and that her brightness, as well as that of the other stars, is regulated by that of the sun, if indeed they all of them shine by light borrowed from him, such as we see floating about, when it is reflected from the surface of water. On this account it is that she dissolves so much moisture, by a gentle and less perfect force, and adds to the quantity of that which the rays of the sun consume.[4] On this account she appears with an unequal light, because being full only when she is in opposition, on all the remaining days she shows only so much of herself to the earth as she receives light from the sun. She is not seen in conjunction, because, at that time, she sends back the whole stream of light to the source whence she has derived it. That the stars generally are nourished by the terrestrial moisture is evident, because, when the moon is only half visible she is sometimes seen spotted, her power of absorbing moisture not having been powerful enough; for the spots are nothing else than the dregs of the earth drawn up along with the moisture. But her eclipses and those of the sun, the most wonderful of all the phenomena of nature, and which are like prodigies, serve to indicate the magnitude of these bodies and the shadow which they cast.

OF THE ECLIPSES OF THE MOON AND THE SUN

For it is evident that the sun is hid by the intervention of the moon, and the moon by the opposition of the earth, and that these changes are mutual, the moon, by her interposition, taking the rays of the sun from the earth, and the earth from the moon. As she advances darkness is suddenly produced, and again the sun is obscured by her shade; for night is nothing more than the shade of the earth. The figure of this shade is like that of a pyramid or an inverted top; and the moon enters it only near its point, and it does not exceed the height of the moon, for there is no other star which is obscured in the same manner, while a figure of this kind always terminates in a point. The flight of birds, when very lofty, shows that shadows do not extend beyond a certain distance; their limit appears to be the termination of the air and the commencement of the aether. Above the moon everything is pure and full of an eternal light. The stars are visible to us in the night, in the same way that other luminous bodies are seen in the dark. It is from these causes that the moon is eclipsed during the night. The two kinds of eclipses are not, however, at the stated monthly periods, on account of the obliquity of the zodiac, and the irregularly wandering course of the moon, as stated above; besides that the motions of these stars do not always occur exactly at the same points.

---

4   It was a general opinion among the ancients, and one which was entertained until lately by many of the moderns, that the moon possessed the power of evaporating the water of the ocean. This opinion appears to have been derived, at least in part, from the effect which the moon produces on the tides.

BOOK II - AN ACCOUNT OF THE WORLD AND THE ELEMENTS

OF THE MAGNITUDE OF THE STARS

This kind of reasoning carries the human mind to the heavens, and by contemplating the world as it were from thence, it discloses to us the magnitude of the three greatest bodies in nature. For the sun could not be entirely concealed from the earth, by the intervention of the moon, if the earth were greater than the moon. And the vast size of the third body, the sun, is manifest from that of the other two, so that it is not necessary to scrutinize its size, by arguing from its visible appearance, or from any conjectures of the mind; it must be immense, because the shadows of rows of trees, extending for any number of miles, are disposed in right lines, as if the sun were in the middle of space. Also, because, at the equinox, he is vertical to all the inhabitants of the southern districts at the same time; also, because the shadows of all the people who live on this side of the tropic fall, at noon, towards the north, and, at sunrise, point to the west. But this could not be the case unless the sun were much greater than the earth; nor, unless it much exceeded Mount Ida in breadth, could he be seen when he rises, passing considerably beyond it to the right and to the left, especially, considering that it is separated by so great an interval.

The eclipse of the moon affords an undoubted argument of the sun's magnitude, as it also does of the small size of the earth. For there are shadows of three figures, and it is evident, that if the body which produces the shadow be equal to the light, then it will be thrown off in the form of a pillar, and have no termination. If the body be greater than the light, the shadow will be in the form of an inverted cone, the bottom being the narrowest part, and being, at the same time, of an infinite length. If the body be less than the light, then we shall have the figure of a pyramid, terminating in a point. Now of this last kind is the shadow which produces the eclipse of the moon, and this is so manifest that there can be no doubt remaining, that the earth is exceeded in magnitude by the sun, a circumstance which is indeed indicated by the silent declaration of nature herself. For why does he recede from us at the winter half of the year? That by the darkness of the nights the earth may be refreshed, which otherwise would be burned up, as indeed it is in certain parts; so great is his size.

ON THE RECURRENCE OF THE ECLIPSES OF THE SUN AND THE MOON

It is ascertained that the eclipses complete their whole revolution in the space of 223 months, that the eclipse of the sun takes place only at the conclusion or the commencement of a lunation, which is termed conjunction, while an eclipse of the moon takes place only when she is at the full, and is always a little farther advanced than the preceding eclipse. Now there are eclipses of both these stars in every year, which take place below the earth, at stated days and hours; and when they are above it they are not always visible, sometimes on account of the clouds, but more frequently, from the globe of the earth being opposed to the vault of the heavens. It was discovered two hundred years ago, by the sagacity of Hipparchus, that the moon is sometimes eclipsed after an interval of five months, and the sun after an interval of seven; also, that he becomes invisible, while above the horizon, twice in every thirty days, but that this is seen in different places at different times. But the most wonderful circumstance is, that while it is admitted that the moon is darkened by the shadow of the earth, this occurs at one time on its western, and at another time on its eastern side. And farther, that although, after the rising of the sun, that darkening shadow ought to be below the earth, yet it has once happened, that the moon has been eclipsed in the west, while both the luminaries have been above the horizon. And as to their both being invisible in the space of fifteen days, this very thing happened while the Vespasians were emperors, the father being consul for the third time, and the son for the second.

ON THE MOTION OF THE MOON

It is certain that the moon, having her horns always turned from the sun, when she is waxing, looks towards the east; when she is waning, towards the west. Also, that, from the second day after the change, she adds 47½ minutes each day, until she is full, and again decreases at the same rate, and that she always becomes invisible when she is within 14 degrees of the sun. This is an argument of the greater size of the planets than of the moon, since these emerge when they are at the distance of 7 degrees only. But their altitude causes them to appear much smaller, as we observe that, during the day, the brightness of the sun prevents those bodies from being seen which are fixed in the firmament, although they shine then as well as in the night: that this is the case is proved by eclipses, and by descending into very deep wells.

OF THE MOTIONS OF THE PLANETS AND THE GENERAL LAWS OF THESE ASPECTS

The three planets, which, as we have said, are situated above the sun are visible when they come into conjunction with him. They rise visibly in the morning, when they are not more than 11 degrees from the sun; they are afterwards directed by the contact of his rays and when they attain the trine aspect, at the distance of 120 degrees, they take their morning stationary positions, which are termed primary; afterwards, when they are in opposition to the sun, they rise at the distance of 180 degrees from him. And again advancing on the other side to the 120th degree, they attain their evening stations, which are termed secondary, until the sun having arrived within 12 degrees of them, what is called their evening setting becomes no longer visible. Mars, as being nearer to the sun, feels the influence of his rays in the quadrature, at the distance of 90 degrees, whence that motion receives its name, being termed, from the two risings, respectively the first and the second nonagenarian. This planet passes from one station to another in six months, or is two months in each sign; the two other planets do not spend more than four months in passing from station to station.

The two inferior planets are, in like manner, concealed in their evening conjunction, and, when they have left the sun, they rise in the morning the same number of degrees distant from him. After having arrived at their point of greatest elongation, they then follow the sun, and having overtaken him at their morning setting, they become invisible and pass beyond him. They then rise in the evening, at the distances which were mentioned above. After this they return back to the sun and are concealed in their evening setting. The star Venus becomes stationary when at its two points of greatest elongation, that of the morning and of the evening, according to their respective risings. The stationary points of Mercury are so very brief, that they cannot be correctly observed.

WHY THE SAME STARS APPEAR AT SOME TIMES MORE LOFTY AND AT OTHER TIMES MORE NEAR

The above is an account of the aspects and the occultations of the planets, a subject which is rendered very complicated by their motions, and is involved in much that is wonderful; especially, when we observe that they change their size and colour, and that the same stars at one time approach the north, and then go to the south, and are now seen near the earth, and then suddenly approach the heavens. If on this subject I deliver opinions different from my predecessors, I acknowledge that I am indebted for them to those individuals who first pointed out to us the proper mode of inquiry; let no one then ever despair of benefiting future ages.

But these things depend upon many different causes. The first cause is the nature of the circles described by the stars, which the Greeks term *apsides*, for we are obliged to use Greek terms. Now each of the planets has its own circle, and this a different one from that of the world; because the earth is placed in the centre of the heavens, with respect to the two extremities, which are called the poles, and also in that of the zodiac, which is situated obliquely between them. And all these things are made evident by the infallible results which we obtain by the use of the compasses. Hence the apsides of the planets have each of them different centres, and consequently they have different orbits and motions, since it necessarily follows, that the interior apsides are the shortest.

The apsides which are the highest from the centre of the earth are, for Saturn, when he is in Scorpio, for Jupiter in Virgo, for Mars in Leo, for the Sun in Gemini, for Venus in Sagittarius, and for Mercury in Capricorn, each of them in the middle of these signs; while in the opposite signs, they are the lowest and nearest to the centre of the earth. Hence it is that they appear to move more slowly when they are carried along the highest circuit; not that their actual motions are accelerated or retarded, these being fixed and determinate for each of them; but because it necessarily follows, that lines drawn from the highest apsis must approach nearer to each other at the centre, like the spokes of a wheel; and that the same motion seems to be at one time greater, and at another time less, according to the distance from the centre.

Another cause of the altitudes of the planets is, that their highest apsides, with relation to their own centres, are in different signs from those mentioned above. Saturn is in the 20th degree of Libra, Jupiter in the 15th of Cancer, Mars in the 28th of Capricorn, the Sun in the 19th of Aries, Venus in the 27th of Pisces, Mercury in the 15th of Virgo, and the Moon in the 3rd of Taurus.

The third cause of the altitude depends on the form of the heavens, not on that of the orbits; the stars appearing to the eye to mount up and to descend through the depth of the air. With this cause is connected that which depends on the latitude of the planets and the obliquity of the zodiac. It is through this belt that the stars which I have spoken of are carried, nor is there any part of the world habitable, except what lies under it;[5] the remainder, which is at the poles, being in a wild desert state. The planet Venus alone exceeds it by 2 degrees, which we may suppose to be the cause why some animals are produced even in these desert regions of the earth. The moon also wanders the whole breadth of the zodiac, but never exceeds it. Next to these the planet Mercury moves through the greatest space; yet out of the 12 degrees (for there are so many degrees of latitude in the zodiac), it does not pass through more than 8, nor does it go equally through these, 2 of them being in the middle of the zodiac, 4 in the upper part, and 2 in the lower part. Next to these the Sun is carried through the middle of the zodiac, winding unequally through the two parts of his tortuous circuit. The star Mars occupies the four middle degrees; Jupiter the middle degree and the two above it; Saturn, like the sun, occupies two.[6] The above is an account of the latitudes as they descend to the south or ascend to the north. Hence it is plain that the generality of persons are mistaken in supposing the third cause of the apparent altitude to depend on the stars rising from the earth and climbing up the heavens. But to refute this opinion it is necessary to consider the subject with very great minuteness, and to embrace all the causes.

It is generally admitted, that the stars, at the time of their evening setting, are nearest to the earth, both with respect to latitude and altitude that they are at the commencement of both at their morning risings, and that they become stationary at the middle points of their latitudes, what are called the ecliptics. It is, moreover, acknowledged, that their motion is increased when they are in the vicinity of the earth, and diminished when they are removed to a greater altitude; a point which is most clearly proved by the different altitudes of the moon. There is no doubt that it is also increased at the morning risings, and that the three superior planets are retarded, as they advance from the first station to the second. And since this is the case, it is evident, that the latitudes are increased from the time of their morning risings, since the motions afterwards appear to receive less addition; but they gain their altitude in the first station, since the rate of their motion then begins to diminish, and the stars to recede.

And the reason of this must be particularly set forth. When the planets are struck by the rays of the sun, in the situation which I have described, that is, in their quadrature, they are prevented from holding on their straight forward course, and are raised on high by the force of the fire. This cannot be immediately perceived by the eye, and therefore they seem to be stationary, and hence the term

---

5   *Quam quod illi subjace*; under this designation the author obviously meant to include the temperate zones, although it technically applies only to the part between the tropics. It is scarcely necessary to remark, that modem discoveries have shown that this opinion respecting the Arctic zone is not strictly correct.

6   As this remark appears to contradict what was said in the last sentence respecting the sun, we may suspect some error in the text.

Book II - An Account of the World and the Elements

station is derived. Afterwards the violence of the rays increases, and the vapour being beaten back forces them to recede.

This exists in a greater degree in their evening risings, the sun being then turned entirely from them, when they are drawn into the highest apsides; and they are then the least visible, since they are at their greatest altitude and are carried along with the least motion, as much less indeed as this takes place in the highest signs of the apsides. At the time of the evening rising the latitude decreases and becomes less as the motion is diminished, and it does not increase again until they arrive at the second station, when the altitude is also diminished; the sun's rays then coming from the other side, the same force now therefore propels them towards the earth which before raised them into the heavens, from their former triangular aspect. So different is the effect whether the rays strike the planets from below or come to them from above. And all these circumstances produce much more effect when they occur in the evening setting. This is the doctrine of the superior planets; that of the others is more difficult, and has never been laid down by any one before me.

WHY THE SAME STARS HAVE DIFFERENT MOTIONS

I must first state the cause, why the star Venus never recedes from the sun more than 46 degrees, nor Mercury more than 23, while they frequently return to the sun within this distance. As they are situated below the sun, they have both of them their apsides turned in the contrary direction; their orbits are as much below the earth as those of the stars above mentioned are above it, and therefore they cannot recede any farther, since the curve of their apsides has no greater longitude. The extreme parts of their apsides therefore assign the limits to each of them in the same manner, and compensate, as it were, for the small extent of their longitudes, by the great divergence of their latitudes. It may be asked, why do they not always proceed as far as the 46th and the 23rd degrees respectively? They in reality do so, but the theory fails us here. For it would appear that the apsides are themselves moved, as they never pass over the sun. When therefore they have arrived at the extremities of their orbits on either side, the stars are then supposed to have proceeded to their greatest distance; when they have been a certain number of degrees within their orbits, they are then supposed to return more rapidly, since the extreme point in each is the same. And on this account it is that the direction of their motion appears to be changed. For the superior planets are carried along the most quickly in their evening setting, while these move the most slowly; the former are at their greatest distance from the earth when they move the most slowly, the latter when they move the most quickly. The former are accelerated when nearest to the earth, the latter when at the extremity of the circle; in the former the rapidity of the motion begins to diminish at their morning risings, in the latter it begins to increase; the former are retrograde from their morning to their evening station, while Venus is retrograde from the evening to the morning station. She begins to increase her latitude from her morning rising, her altitude follows the sun from her morning station, her motion being the quickest and her altitude the greatest in her morning setting. Her latitude decreases and her altitude diminishes from her evening rising, she becomes retrograde, and at the same time decreases in her altitude from her evening station.

Again, the star Mercury, in the same way, mounts up in both directions from his morning rising, and having followed the sun through a space of 15 degrees, he becomes almost stationary for four days. Presently he diminishes his altitude, and recedes from his evening setting to his morning rising. Mercury and the Moon are the only planets which descend for the same number of days that they ascend. Venus ascends for fifteen days and somewhat more; Saturn and Jupiter descend in twice that number of days, and Mars in four times. So great is the variety of nature! The reason of it is, however, evident; for those planets which are forced up by the vapour of the sun likewise descend with difficulty.

GENERAL LAWS OF THE PLANETS

There are many other secrets of nature in these points, as well as the laws to which they are subject, which might be mentioned. For example, the planet Mars, whose course is the most difficult to observe, never becomes stationary when Jupiter is in the trine aspect, very rarely when he is 60 degrees from the sun, which number is one-sixth of the circuit of the heavens; nor does he ever rise in the same sign with Jupiter, except in Cancer and Leo. The star Mercury seldom has his evening risings in Pisces, but very frequently in Virgo, and his morning risings in Libra; he has also his morning rising in Aquarius, very rarely in Leo. He never becomes retrograde either in Taurus or in Gemini, nor until the 25th degree of Cancer. The Moon makes her double conjunction with the sun in no other sign except Gemini, while Sagittarius is the only sign in which she has sometimes no conjunction at all. The old and the new moon are visible on the same day or night in no other sign except Aries, and indeed it has happened very seldom to any one to have witnessed it. From this circumstance it was that the tale of Lynceus's quick-sightedness originated, Saturn and Mars are invisible at most for 170 days; Jupiter for 36, or, at the least, for 10 days less than this; Venus for 69, or, at the least, for 52; Mercury for 13, or, at the most, for 18.

THE REASON WHY THE STARTS ARE OF DIFFERENT COLOURS

The difference of their colour depends on the difference in their altitudes; for they acquire a resemblance to those planets into the vapour of which they are carried, the orbit of each tinging those that approach it in each direction. A colder planet renders one that approaches it paler, one more hot renders it redder, a windy planet gives it a lowering aspect, while the sun, at the union of their apsides, or the extremity of their orbits, completely obscures them. Each of the planets has its peculiar colour; Saturn is white, Jupiter brilliant, Mars fiery, Lucifer is glowing, Vesper refulgent, Mercury sparkling, the Moon mild; the Sun, when he rises, is blazing, afterwards he becomes radiating. The appearance of the stars, which are fixed in the firmament, is also affected by these causes. At one time we see a dense cluster of stars around the moon, when she is only half-enlightened, and when they are viewed in a serene evening; while, at another time, when the moon is full, there are so few to be seen, that we wonder whither they are fled; and this is also the case when the rays of the sun, or of any of the above-mentioned bodies, have dazzled our sight. And, indeed, the moon herself is, without doubt, differently affected at different times by the rays of the sun; when she is entering them, the convexity of the heavens rendering them more feeble than when they fall upon her more directly. Hence, when she is at a right angle to the sun, she is half-enlightened; when in the trine aspect, she presents an imperfect orb, while, in opposition, she is full. Again, when she is waning, she goes through the same gradations, and in the same order, as the three stars that are superior to the sun.

OF THE MOTION OF THE SUN AND THE CAUSE OF THE IRREGULARITY OF THE DAYS

The Sun himself is in four different states; twice the night is equal to the day, in the Spring and in the Autumn, when he is opposed to the centre of the earth in the 8th degree of Aries and Libra. The length of the day and the night is then twice changed, when the day increases in length, from the winter solstice in the 8th degree of Capricorn, and afterwards, when the night increases in length from the summer solstice in the 8th degree of Cancer. The cause of this inequality is the obliquity of the zodiac, since there is, at every moment of time, an equal portion of the firmament above and below the horizon. But the signs which mount directly upwards, when they rise, retain the light for a longer space, while those that are more oblique pass along more quickly.

WHY THUNDER IS ASCRIBED TO JUPITER

It is not generally known, what has been discovered by men who are the most eminent for their learning, in consequence of their assiduous observations of the heavens, that the fires which fall upon the earth, and receive the name of thunder-bolts, proceed from the three superior stars, but principally from the one which is situated in the middle. It may perhaps depend on the superabundance of moisture from the superior orbit communicating with the heat from the inferior, which are expelled in this manner; and hence it is commonly said, the thunder-bolts are darted by Jupiter. And as, in burning wood, the burnt part is cast off with a crackling noise, so does the star throw off this celestial fire, bearing the omens of future events, even the part which is thrown off not losing its divine operation. And this takes place more particularly when the air is in an unsettled state, either because the moisture which is then collected excites the greatest quantity of fire, or because the air is disturbed, as if by the parturition of the pregnant star.

OF THE DISTANCES OF THE STARS

Many persons have attempted to discover the distance of the stars from the earth, and they have published as the result, that the sun is nineteen times as far from the moon, as the moon herself is from the earth. Pythagoras, who was a man of a very sagacious mind, computed the distance from the earth to the moon to be 126,000 furlongs,[7] that from her to the sun is double this distance, and that it is

---

7   A measure of length equal to the eighth part of a mile, 40 rods, poles, or perches, 220 yards, or 201.17 meters.

three times this distance to the twelve signs; and this was also the opinion of our countryman, Gallus Sulpicius.

OF THE HARMONY OF THE STARS

Pythagoras, employing the terms that are used in music, sometimes names the distance between the Earth and the Moon a tone; from her to Mercury he supposes to he half this space, and about the same from him to Venus. From her to the Sun is a tone and a half; from the Sun to Mars is a tone, the same as from the Earth to the Moon; from him there is half a tone to Jupiter, from Jupiter to Saturn also half a tone, and thence a tone and a half to the zodiac. Hence there are seven tones, which he terms the diapason harmony, meaning the whole compass of the notes. In this, Saturn is said to move in the Doric time, Jupiter in the Phrygian, so forth of the rest; but this is a refinement rather amusing than useful.

ON THE DIMENSIONS OF THE WORLD

The stadium is equal to 125 of our Roman paces, or 625 feet. Posidonius supposes that there is a space of not less than 40 stadia around the earth, whence mists, winds and clouds proceed; beyond this he supposes that the air is pure and liquid, consisting of uninterrupted light; from the clouded region to the moon there is a space of 2,000,000 of stadia, and thence to the sun of 500,000,000. It is in consequence of this space that the sun, notwithstanding his immense magnitude, does not burn the earth. Many persons have imagined that the clouds rise to the height of 900 stadia. These points are not completely made out, and are difficult to explain; but we have given the best account of them that has been published, and if we may be allowed, in any degree, to pursue these investigations, there is one infallible geometrical principle, which we cannot reject. Not that we can ascertain the exact dimensions (for to profess to do this would be almost the act of a madman), but that the mind may have some estimate to direct its conjectures. Now it is evident that the orbit through which the sun passes consists of nearly 366 degrees, and that the diameter is always the third part and a little less than the seventh of the circumference. Then taking the half of this (for the earth is placed in the centre) it will follow, that nearly one-sixth part of the immense space, which the mind conceives as constituting the orbit of the sun round the earth, will compose his altitude. That of the moon will be one-twelfth part, since her course is so much shorter than that of the sun; she is therefore carried along midway between the sun and the earth. It is astonishing to what an extent the weakness of the mind will proceed, urged on by a little success, as in the above-mentioned instance, to give full scope to its impudence! Thus, having ventured to guess at the space between the sun and the earth, we do the same with respect to the heavens, because he is situated midway between them; so that we may come to know the measure of the whole world in inches. For if the diameter consist of seven parts, there will be twenty-two of the same parts in the circumference; as if we could measure the heavens by a plumb-line!

The Egyptian calculation, which was made out by Petosiris and Necepsos, supposes that each, degree of the lunar orbit (which, as I have said, is the least) consists of little more than 33 stadia; in the very large orbit of Saturn the number is double;

Book II - An Account of the World and the Elements

in that of the sun, which, as we have said, is in the middle, we have the half of the sum of these numbers. And this is indeed a very modest calculation, since if we add to the orbit of Saturn the distance from him to the zodiac, we shall have an infinite number of degrees.

OF THE STARS WHICH APPEAR SUDDENLY OR OF COMETS

A few things still remain to he said concerning the world; for stars are suddenly formed in the heavens themselves; of these there are various kinds.

The Greeks name these stars *comets*; we name them *Crinitæ*, as if shaggy with bloody locks, and surrounded with bristles like hair. Those stars, which have a mane hanging down from their lower part, like a long beard, are named *Pogoniæ*. Those that are named *Acontiæ* vibrate like a dart with a very quick motion. It was one of this kind which the Emperor Titus described in his very excellent poem, as having been seen in his fifth consulship; and this was the last of these bodies which has been observed. When they are short and pointed they are named *Xiphiæ*; these are the pale kind; they shine like a sword and are without any rays; while we name those *Discei*, which, being of an amber colour, in conformity with their name, emit a few rays from their margin only. A kind named *Pitheus* exhibits the figure of a cask, appearing convex and emitting a smoky light. The kind named *Cerastias* has the appearance of a horn; it is like the one which was visible when the Greeks fought at Salamis. *Lampadias* is like a burning torch; *Hippias* is like a horse's mane; it has a very rapid motion, like a circle revolving on itself. There is also a white comet, with silver hair, so brilliant that it can scarcely be looked at, exhibiting, as it were, the aspect of the Deity in a human form. There are some also that are shaggy, having the appearance of a fleece, surrounded by a kind of crown. There was one, where the appearance of a mane was changed into that of a spear; it happened in the 109th olympiad, in the 398th year of the City. The shortest time during which any one of them has been observed to be visible is 7 days, the longest 180 days.

THEIR NATURE, SITUATION AND SPECIES

Some of them move about in the manner of planets, others remain stationary. They are almost all of them seen towards the north, not indeed in any particular portion of it, but generally in that white part of it which has obtained the name of the Milky Way. Aristotle informs us that several of them are to be seen at the same time, but this, as far as I know, has not been observed by any one else; also that they prognosticate high winds and great heat. They are also visible in the winter months, and about the south pole, but they have no rays proceeding from them. There was a dreadful one observed by the Æthiopians and the Egyptians, to which Typhon, a king of that period, gave his own name; it had a fiery appearance, and was twisted like a spiral; its aspect was hideous, nor was it like a star, but rather like a knot of fire. Sometimes, there are hairs attached to the planets and the other stars. Comets are never seen in the western part of the heavens. It is generally regarded as a terrific star, and one not easily expiated; as was the case with the civil commotions in the consulship of Octavius, and also in the war of Pompey and Cæsar. And in our own age, about the time when Claudius Cæsar was poisoned and left the

Empire to Domitius Nero, and afterwards, while the latter was Emperor, there was one which was almost constantly seen and was very frightful. It is thought important to notice towards what part it darts its beams, or from what star it receives its influence, what it resembles, and in what places it shines. If it resembles a flute, it portends something unfavourable respecting music; if it appears in the parts of the signs referred to the secret members, something respecting lewdness of manners; something respecting wit and learning, if they form a triangular or quadrangular figure with the position of some of the fixed stars; and that some one will be poisoned, if they appear in the head of either the northern or the southern serpent.

Some persons suppose that these stars are permanent, and that they move through their proper orbits, but that they are only visible when they recede from the sun. Others suppose that they are produced by an accidental vapour together with the force of fire, and that, from this circumstance, they are liable to be dissipated.

OF THE AIR AND ON THE CAUSE OF THE SHOWERS OF STONES

So far I have spoken of the world itself and of the stars. I must now give an account of the other remarkable phenomena of the heavens. For our ancestors have given the name of heavens, or, sometimes, another name, air, to all the seemingly void space, which diffuses around us this vital spirit. It is situated beneath the moon, indeed much lower, as is admitted by every one who has made observations on it, and is composed of a great quantity of air from the upper regions, mixed with a great quantity of terrestrial vapour, the two forming a compound. Hence proceed clouds, thunder and lightning of all kinds; hence also hail, frost, showers, storms and whirlwinds; hence proceed many of the evils incident to mortals, and the mutual contests of the various parts of nature. The force of the stars keeps down all terrestrial things which tend towards the heavens, and the same force attracts to itself those things which do not go there spontaneously. The showers fall, mists rise up, rivers are dried up, bad-storms rush down, the rays of the sun parch the earth, and impel it from all quarters towards the centre. The same rays, still unbroken, dart back again, and carry with them whatever they can take up. Vapour falls from on high and returns again to the same place. Winds arise which contain nothing, but which return loaded with spoils. The breathing of so many animals draws down the spirit from the higher regions; but this tends to go in a contrary direction, and the earth pours out its spirit into the void space of the heavens. Thus nature moving to and fro, as if impeded by some machine, discord is kindled by the rapid motion of the world. Nor is the contest allowed to cease, for she is continually whirled round and lays open the causes of all things, forming an immense globe about the earth, while she again, from time to time, covers this other firmament with clouds. This is the region of the winds. Here their nature principally originates, as well as the causes of almost all other things; since most persons ascribe the darting of thunder and lightning to their violence. And to the same cause are assigned the showers of stones, these having been previously taken up by the wind, as well as many other bodies in the same way. On this account we must enter more at large on this subject.

OF THE STATED SEASONS

It is obvious that there are causes of the seasons and of other things which have been stated, while there are some things which are casual, or of which the reason has not yet been discovered. For who can doubt that summer and winter, and the annual revolution of the seasons are caused by the motion of the stars? As therefore the nature of the sun is understood to influence the temperature of the year, so each of the other stars has its specific power, which produces its appropriate effects. Some abound in a fluid retaining its liquid state, others, in the same fluid concreted into hoar frost, compressed into snow, or frozen into hail; some are prolific in winds, some in heat, some in vapours, some in dew, some in cold. But these bodies must not be supposed to be actually of the size which they appear, since the consideration of their immense height clearly proves, that none of them are less than the moon. Each of them exercises its influence over us by its own motions; this is particularly observable with respect to Saturn, which produces a great quantity of rain in its transits. Nor is this power confined to the stars which change their situations, but is found to exist in many of the fixed stars, whenever they are impelled by the force of any of the planets, or excited by the impulse of their rays; as we find to be the case with respect to the Suculæ which the Greeks, in reference to their rainy nature, have termed the Hyades. There are also certain events which occur spontaneously, and at stated periods, as the rising of the Kids. The star Arcturus scarcely ever rises without storms of hail occurring.

OF THE REGULAR INFLUENCE OF THE DIFFERENT SEASONS

There is moreover a peculiar influence in the different degrees of certain signs, as in the autumnal equinox, and also in the winter solstice, when we find that a particular star is connected with the state of the weather. It is not so much the recurrence of showers and storms, as of various circumstances, which act both upon animals and vegetables. Some are planet-struck, and others, at stated times, are affected in the bowels, the sinews, the head, or the intellect.

The olive, the white poplar, and the willow turn their leaves round at the summer solstice. The herb *pulegium*, when dried and hanging up in a house, blossoms on the very day of the winter solstice, and bladders burst in consequence of their being distended with air. One might wonder at this, did we not observe every day, that the plant named heliotrope always looks towards the setting sun, and is, at all hours, turned towards him, even when he is obscured by clouds. It is certain that the bodies of oysters and of whelks, and of shell-fish generally, are increased in size and again diminished by the influence of the moon. Certain accurate observers have found out, that the entrails of the field-mouse correspond in number to the moon's age, and that the very small animal, the ant, feels the power of this luminary, always resting from her labours at the change of the moon. And so much the more disgraceful is our ignorance, as every one acknowledges that the diseases in the eyes of certain beasts of burden increase and diminish according to the age of the moon. But the immensity of the heavens, divided as they are into seventy-two constellations, may serve as an excuse. These are the resemblances of certain things, animate and inanimate, into which the learned have divided the heavens. In these they have announced 1600 stars, as being remarkable either for their effects or their appearance; for example, in the tail of the Bull there are seven stars, which are named *Vergiliæ*; in his forehead are the *Suculæ*; there is also *Bootes*, which follows the seven northern stars.

OF THUNDER AND LIGHTNING

It cannot therefore be denied, that fire proceeding from the stars which are above the clouds, may fall on them, as we frequently observe on serene evenings, and that the air is agitated by the impulse, as darts when they are hurled whiz through the air. And when it arrives at the cloud, a discordant kind of vapour is produced, as when hot iron is plunged into water, and a wreath of smoke is evolved. Hence arise squalls. And if wind or vapour be struggling in the cloud, thunder is discharged; if it bursts out with a flame, there is a thunderbolt; if it be long in forcing out its way, it is simply a flash of lightning. By the latter the cloud is simply rent, by the former it is shattered. Thunder is produced by the stroke given to the condensed air, and hence it is that the fire darts from the chinks of the clouds. It is possible also that the vapour, which has risen from the earth, being repelled by the stars, may produce thunder, when it is pent up in a cloud; nature restraining the sound whilst the vapour is struggling to escape, but when it does escape, the sound bursting forth, as is the case with bladders that are distended with air. It is possible also that the spirit, whatever it be, may be kindled by friction, when it is so violently projected. It is possible that, by the dashing of the two clouds, the lightning may flash out, as is the case when two stones are struck against each other. But all these things appear to be casual. Hence there are thunderbolts which produce no effect, and proceed from no immediate actual cause; by these mountains and seas are struck, and no injury is done. Those which prognosticate future events proceed from on high and from stated causes, and they come from their peculiar stars.

THE ORIGIN OF WINDS

In like manner I would not deny that winds, or rather sudden gusts, are produced by the arid and dry vapours of the earth; that air may also be exhaled from water, which can neither be condensed into a mist, nor compressed into a cloud; that it may be also driven forward by the impulse of the sun, since by the term 'wind' we mean nothing more than a current of air, by whatever means it may be produced. For we observe winds to proceed from rivers and bays, and from the sea, even when it is tranquil; while others, which are named Altani, rise up from the earth; when they come back from the sea they are named Tropœi, but if they go straight on, Apogœi.

The windings and the numerous peaks of mountains, their ridges, bent into angles or broken into defiles, with the hollow valleys, by their irregular forms, cleaving the air which rebounds from them (which is also the cause why voices are, in many cases, repeated several times in succession), give rise to winds.

There are certain caves, such as that on the coast of Dalmatia, with a vast perpendicular chasm, into which, if a light weight only be let down, and although the day be calm, a squall issues from it like a whirlwind. The name of the place is Senta. And also, in the province of Cyrenaica, there is a certain rock, said to be sacred to the south wind, which it is profane for a human hand to touch, as the south wind immediately rolls forwards clouds of sand. There are also, in many houses, artificial cavities, formed in the walls, which produce currents of air; none of these are without their appropriate cause.

INVOCATION OF THUNDER

It is related in our Annals, that by certain sacred rites and imprecations, thunder-storms may be compelled or invoked. There is an old report in Etruria, that thunder was invoked when the city of Volsinium had its territory laid waste by a monster named Volta. Thunder was also invoked by King Porsenna. And L. Piso, a very respectable author, states in the first book of his Annals, that this had been frequently done before his time by Numa, and that Tullus Hostilius, imitating him, but not having properly performed the ceremonies, was struck with the lightning. We have also groves, and altars, and sacred places, and, among the titles of Jupiter, as Stator, Tonans, and Feretrius, we have a Jupiter Elicius. The opinions entertained on this point are very various, and depend much on the dispositions of different individuals.

THE RAINBOW

What we name Rainbows frequently occur, and are not considered either wonderful or ominous; for they do not predict, with certainty, either rain or fair weather. It is obvious, that the rays of the sun, being projected upon a hollow cloud, the light is thrown back to the sun and is refracted and that the variety of colours is produced by a mixture of clouds, air, and fire. The rainbow is certainly never produced except in the part opposite to the sun, nor even in any other form except that of a semicircle. Nor are they ever formed at night, although Aristotle asserts that they are sometimes seen at that time; he acknowledges, however, that it can only be on the 14th day of the moon. They are seen in the winter the most frequently, when the days are shortening, after the autumnal equinox. They are not seen when the days increase again, after the vernal equinox, nor on the longest days, about the summer solstice, but frequently at the winter solstice, when the days are the shortest. When the sun is low they are high, and when the sun is high they are low; they are smaller when in the east or west, but are spread out wider; in the south they are small, but of a greater span. In the summer they are not seen at noon, but after the autumnal equinox at any hour; there are never more than two seen at once.

NATURE OF THE EARTH

Next comes the earth, on which alone of all parts of nature we have bestowed the name that implies maternal veneration. It is appropriated to man as the heavens are to God. She receives us at our birth, nourishes us when born, and ever afterwards supports us; lastly, embracing us in her bosom when we are rejected by the rest of nature, she then covers us with especial tenderness; rendered sacred to us, inasmuch as she renders us sacred, bearing our monuments and titles, continuing our names, and extending our memory, in opposition to the shortness of life. In our anger we imprecate her on those who are now no more, as if we were ignorant that she is the only being who can never be angry with man. The water passes into showers, is concreted into hail, swells into rivers, is precipitated in torrents; the air is condensed into clouds, rages in squalls; but the earth, kind, mild, and indulgent as she is, and always ministering to the wants of mortals, how many things do we compel her to produce spontaneously! What odours and flowers, nutritive juices, forms and colours! With what good faith does she render hack all that has been entrusted to her!

OF THE FORM OF THE EARTH

Every one agrees that it has the most perfect figure. We always speak of the ball of the earth, and we admit it to be a globe bounded by the poles. It has not indeed the form of an absolute sphere, from the number of lofty mountains and flat plains; but if the termination of the lines be bounded by a curve, this would compose a perfect sphere. And this we learn from arguments drawn from the nature of things, although not from the same considerations which we made use of with respect to the heavens. For in these the hollow convexity everywhere bends on itself, and leans upon the earth as its centre. Whereas the earth rises up solid and dense, like something that swells up and is protruded outwards. The heavens bend towards the centre, while the earth goes from the centre, the continual rolling of the heavens about it forcing its immense globe into the form of a sphere.

WHETHER THE OCEAN SURROUNDS THE EARTH

The whole of the western ocean is now navigated, from Gades and the Pillars of Hercules, round Spain and Gaul. The greater part of the northern ocean has also been navigated, under the auspices of the Emperor Augustus, his fleet having been carried round Germany to the promontory of the Cimbri; from which spot they descried an immense sea, or became acquainted with it by report, which extends to the country of the Scythians, and the districts that are chilled by excessive moisture. On this account it is not at all probable, that the ocean should be deficient in a region where moisture so much abounds. In like manner, towards the east, from the Indian sea, all that part which lies in the same latitude, and which bends round towards the Caspian, has been explored by the Macedonian arms, in the reigns of Seleucus and Antiochus, who wished it to be named after themselves, the Seleucian or Antiochian Sea. About the Caspian, too, many parts of the shores of the ocean have been explored, so that nearly the whole of the north has been sailed over in one direction or another. Nor can our argument be much affected by the point that has been so much discussed, respecting the Palus Mæotis,[8] whether it be a bay of the same ocean, as is, I understand, the opinion of some persons, or whether it be the overflowing of a narrow channel connected with a different ocean. On the

---

8   Sea of Azof (TN).

other side of Gades, proceeding from the same western point, a great part of the southern ocean, along Mauritania, has now been navigated. Indeed the greater part of this region, as well as of the east, as far as the Arabian Gulf, was surveyed in consequence of Alexander's victories. When Caius Cæsar, the son of Augustus had the conduct of affairs in that country, it is said that they found the remains of Spanish vessels which had been wrecked there. While the power of Carthage was at its height, Hanno published an account of a voyage which he made from Gades to the extremity of Arabia; Himilco was also sent, about the same time, to explore the remote parts of Europe. Besides, we learn from Cornelius Nepos, that one Eudoxus, a contemporary of his, when he was flying from king Lathyrus, set out from the Arabian Gulf, and was carried as far as Gades. And long before him, Cælius Antipater informs us, that he had seen a person who had sailed from Spain to Ethiopia for the purposes of trade. The same Cornelius Nepos, when speaking of the northern circumnavigation, tells us that Q. Metellus Celer, the colleague of L. Afranius in the consulship, but then a proconsul in Gaul, had a present made to him by the king of the Suevi, of certain Indians, who sailing from India for the purpose of commerce, had been driven by tempests into Germany. Thus it appears, that the seas which flow completely round the globe, and divide it, as it were, into two parts, exclude us from one part of it, as there is no way open to it on either side. And as the contemplation of these things is adapted to detect the vanity of mortals, it seems incumbent on me to display, and lay open to our eyes, the whole of it, whatever it be, in which there is nothing which can satisfy the desires of certain individuals.

WHAT PART OF THE EARTH IS INHABITED

In the first place, then, it appears, that this should be estimated at half the globe, as if no portion of this half was encroached upon by the ocean. But surrounding as it does the whole of the land, pouring out and receiving all the other waters, furnishing whatever goes to the clouds, and feeding the stars themselves, so numerous and of such great size as they are, what a great space must we not suppose it to occupy! This vast mass must fill up and occupy an infinite extent. To this we must add that portion of the remainder which the heavens take from us. For the globe is divided into five parts, termed zones, and all that portion is subject to severe cold and perpetual frost which is under the two extremities, about each of the poles, the nearer of which is called the north, and the opposite the south pole. In all these regions there is perpetual darkness, and, in consequence of the aspect of the milder stars being turned from them, the light is malignant, and only like the whiteness which is produced by hoar frost. The middle of the earth, over which is the orbit of the sun, is parched and burned by the flame, and is consumed by being so near the heat. There are only two of the zones which are temperate, those which lie between the torrid and the frigid zones, and these are separated from each other, in consequence of the scorching heat of the heavenly bodies. It appears, therefore, that the heavens take from us three parts of the earth; how much the ocean steals is uncertain.

THAT THE EARTH IS IN THE MIDDLE OF WORLD

It is evident from undoubted arguments, that the earth is in the middle of the universe, but it is the most clearly proved by the equality of the days and the nights at the equinox. It is demonstrated by the quadrant, which affords the most decisive confirmation of the fact, that unless the earth was in the middle, the days and nights could not be equal; for, at the time of the equinox, the rising and setting of the sun are seen on the same line, and the rising of the sun, at the summer solstice, is on the same line with its setting at the winter solstice; but this could not happen if the earth was not situated in the centre

OF EARTHQUAKES

According to the doctrine of the Babylonians, earthquakes and clefts of the earth, and occurrences of this kind, are supposed to be produced by the influence of the stars, especially of the three to which they ascribe thunder; and to be caused by the stars moving with the sun, or being in conjunction with it, and, more particularly, when they are in the quartile aspect. If we are to credit the report, a most admirable and immortal spirit, as it were of a divine nature, should be ascribed to Anaximander the Milesian, who, they say, warned the Lacedæmonians to beware of their city and their houses. For he predicted that an earthquake was at hand, when both the whole of their city was destroyed and a large portion of Mount Taygetus, which projected in the form of a ship, was broken off, and added farther ruin to the previous destruction. Another prediction is ascribed to Phcrecydes, the master of Pythagoras, and this was divine; by a draught of water from a well, he foresaw and predicted that there would be an earthquake in that place. And if these things be true, how nearly do these individuals approach to the Deity, even during their lifetime! But I leave every one to judge of these matters as he pleases. I certainly conceive the winds to be the cause of earthquakes; for the earth never trembles except when the sea is quite calm, and when the heavens are so tranquil that the birds cannot maintain their flight, all the air which should support them being withdrawn; nor does it ever happen until after great winds, the gust being pent up, as it were, in the fissures and concealed hollows. For the trembling of the earth resembles thunder in the clouds; nor does the yawning off the earth differ from the bursting of the lightning; the enclosed air struggling and striving to escape.

WONDERFUL CIRCUMSTANCES ATTENDING EARTHQUAKES

Inundations of the sea take place at the same time with earthquakes; the water being impregnated with the same spirit, and received into the bosom of the earth which subsides. The greatest earthquake which has occurred in our memory was in the reign of Tiberius, by which twelve cities of Asia were laid prostrate in one night. They occurred the most frequently during the Punic war, when we had accounts brought to Rome of fifty-seven earthquakes in the space of a single year. It was during this year that the Carthaginians and the Romans, who were fighting at the lake Thrasimenus, were neither of them sensible of a very great shock during the battle. Nor is it an evil merely consisting in the danger which is produced by the motion; it is an equal or a greater evil when it is considered as a prodigy. The city of Rome never experienced a shock, which was not the forerunner of some great calamity.

IN WHAT PLACES THE SEA HAS RECEDED

The same cause produces an increase of the land; the vapour, when it cannot burst out forcibly lifting up the surface. For the land is not merely produced by what is brought down the rivers, as the islands called Echinades are formed by the river Achelous, and the greater part of Egypt by the Nile, where, according to Homer, it was a day and a night's journey from the main land to the island of Pharos; but, in some cases, by the receding of the sea, as, according to the same author, was the case with the Circæan isles. The same thing also happened in the harbour of Ambracia, for a space of 10,000 paces, and was also said to have taken place for 5000 at the Piræus of Athens, and likewise at Ephesus, where formerly the sea washed the walls of the temple of Diana. Indeed, if we may believe Herodotus, the sea came beyond Memphis, as far as the mountains of Ethiopia, and also from the plains of Arabia. The sea also surrounded Ilium and the whole of Teuthrania, and covered the plain through which the Mæander flows.

THE MODE IN WHICH ISLANDS RISE UP

Land is sometimes formed in a different manner, rising suddenly out of the sea, as if nature was compensating the earth for its losses, restoring in one place what she had swallowed up in another.

LANDS WHICH HAVE BEEN TOTALLY CHANGED INTO SEAS

The sea has totally carried off certain lands, and first of all, if we are to believe Plato, for an immense space where the Atlantic ocean is now extended. More lately we see what has been produced by our inland sea; Acarnania has been overwhelmed by the Ambracian gulf, Achaia by the Corinthian, Europe and Asia by the Propontis and Pontus. And besides these, the sea has rent asunder Leucas, Antirrhium, the Hellespont, and the two Bosphori.

OF CERTAIN LANDS WHICH ARE ALWAYS SHAKING, AND OF FLOATING ISLANDS

There are certain lands which shake when any one passes over them; as in the territory of the Gabii, not far from the city of Rome, there are about 200 acres which shake when cavalry passes over it; the same thing takes place at Reate.

There are certain islands which are always floating as in the territory of the Cæcubum, and of the above-mentioned Reate, of Mutina, and of Statonia. In the lake of Vadimonis and the waters of Cutiliæ there is a dark wood, which is never seen in the same place for a day and a night together. In Lydia, the islands named Calaminæ are not only driven about by the wind, but may be even pushed at pleasure from place to place, by poles; many citizens saved themselves by this means in the Mithridatic war. There are some small islands in the Nymphæus, called the Dancers, because, when choruses are sung, they are moved by the motions of those who beat time. In the great Italian lake of Tarquinii, there are two islands with groves on them, which are driven about by the wind, so as at one time to exhibit the figure of a triangle and at another of a circle; but they never form a square.

THE WONDERS OF VARIOUS COUNTRIES COLLECTED TOGETHER

Near Harpasa, a town of Asia, there stands a terrific rock, which may be moved by a single finger; but if it be pushed by the force of the whole body, it resists. In the Tauric peninsula, in the state of the Parasini, there is a kind of earth which cures all wouuds. About Assos, in Troas, a stone is found, by which all bodies are consumed; it is called Sareophagus. There are two mountains near the river Indus; the nature of one is to attract iron, of the other to repel it; hence, if there be nails in the shoes, the feet cannot be drawn off the one, or set down on the other. It has been noticed, that at Loeris and Crotona, there has never been a pestilence, nor have they ever suffered from an earthquake; in Lycia there are always forty calm days before an earthquake. In the territory of Argyripa the corn which is sown never springs up. At the altars of Mucius, in the country of the Veii, and about Tusculum, and in the Cimmerian Forest, there are places in which things that are pushed into the ground cannot be pulled out again. The hay which is grown in Crustuminium is noxious on the spot, but elsewhere it is wholesome.

THE POWER OF THE MOON OVER THE LAND AND THE SEA

Hence we may certainly conjecture, that the moon is not unjustly regarded as the star of our life. This it is that replenishes the earth; when she approaches it, she fills all bodies, while, when she recedes, she empties them. From this cause it is that shell-fish grow with her increase, and that those animals which are without blood more particularly experience her influence; also, that the blood of man is increased or diminished in proportion to the quantity of her light; also that the leaves and vegetables generally, as I shall describe in the proper place, feel her influence, her power penetrating all things.

THE DIMENSIONS OF THE EARTH

Our part of the earth, of which I propose to give an account, floating as it were in the ocean which surrounds it (as I have mentioned above), stretches out to the greatest extent from east to west, viz. from India to the Pillars consecrated to Hercules at Gades, being a distance of 8568 miles, according to the statement of Artemidorus, or according to that of Isidorus, 9818 miles. Artemidorus adds to this 491 miles, from Gades, going round by the Sacred Promontory, to the promontory of Artabrum, which is the most projecting part of Spain.

This measurement may be taken in two directions. From the Ganges, at its mouth, where it discharges itself into the Eastern ocean, passing through India and Parthyene, to Myriandrus, a city of Syria, in the bay of Issus, is a distance of 5215 miles. Thence, going directly by sea, by the island of Cyprus, Patara in Lycia, Rhodes, and Astypalæa, islands in the Carpathian sea, by Tænarum in Laconia, Lilybæum in Sicily and Calaris in Sardinia, is 2103 miles. Thence to Gades is 1250 miles, making the whole distance from the Eastern ocean 8568 miles.

The other way, which is more certain, is chiefly by land. From the Ganges to the Euphrates is 5169 miles; thence to Mazaca, a town in Cappadocia, is 319 miles; thence, through Phrygia and Caria, to Ephesus is 415 miles; from Ephesus, across the Ægean sea to Delos, is 200 miles; to the Isthmus is 212 miles; thence, first by land and afterwards by the sea of Lechseum and the gulf of Corinth, to Patræe in Peloponnese, 90 miles; to the promontory of Leucate 87½ miles; as much more to Corcyra; to the Acroceraunian mountains 132½, to Brundisium 87½, and to Rome 360 miles. To the Alps, at the village of Scingomagum, is 519 miles; through Gaul to Illiberis at the Pyrenees, 927; to the ocean and the coast of Spain, 331 miles; across the passage of Gades 7½ miles; which distances, according to the estimate of Artemidorus, make altogether 8945 miles.

The breadth of the earth, from south to north, is commonly supposed to be about one-half only of its length, viz. 4490 miles; hence it is evident how much the heat has stolen from it on one side and the cold on the other; for I do not suppose that the land is actually wanting, or that the earth has not the form of a globe; but that, on each side, the uninhabitable parts have not been discovered. This measure then extends from the coast of the Æthiopian ocean, the most distant part which is habitable, to Meroë, 1000 miles; thence to Alexandria 1250; to Rhodes 562; to Cnidos 87½; to Cos 25; to Samos 100; to Chios 94; to Mitylene 65; to Tenedos 44; to the promontory of Sigæeum 12½; to the entrance of the Euxine 312½; to the promontory of Carambis 350; to the entrance of the Palus Mæeotis 312½; and to the mouth of the Tanais 275 miles, which distance, if we went by sea, might be shortened 89 miles. Beyond the Tanais the most diligent authors have not been able to obtain any accurate measurement. Artemidorus supposes that everything beyond is undiscovered, since he confesses that, about the Tanais, the tribes of the Sarmatæe dwell, who extend towards the north pole. Isidorus adds 1250 miles, as the distance to Thule; but this is mere conjecture. For my part, I believe that the boundaries of Sarmatia really extend to as great a distance as that mentioned above; for if it were not very extensive, how could it contain the innumerable tribes that are always changing their residence? And indeed I consider the uninhabitable portion of the world to be still greater; for it is well known that there are innumerable islands lying off the coast of Germany, which have been only lately discovered.

The above is all that I consider worth relating about the length and the breadth of the earth. But Eratosthenes, a man who was peculiarly well skilled in all the more subtle parts of learning, and in this above everything else, and a person whom I perceive to be approved by every one, has stated the whole of this circuit to be 252,000 stadia, which, according to the Roman estimate, makes 31,500 miles. The attempt is presumptuous, but it is supported by such subtle arguments that we cannot refuse our assent. Hipparchus, whom we must admire, both for the ability with which he controverts Eratosthenes, as well as for his diligence in everything else, has added to the above number not much less than 25,000 stadia.

Dionysodorus is certainly less worthy of confidence; but I cannot omit this most remarkable instance of Grecian vanity. He was a native of Melos, and was celebrated for his knowledge of geometry; he died of old age in his native country. His female relations, who inherited his property, attended his funeral, and when they had for several successive days performed the usual rites, they are said to have found in his tomb an epistle written in his own name to those left above; it stated that he had descended from his tomb to the lowest part of the earth, and that it was a distance of 42,000 stadia. There were not wanting certain geometricians, who interpreted this epistle as if it had been sent from the middle of the globe, the point which is at the greatest distance from the surface, and which must necessarily be the centre of the sphere. Hence the estimate has been made that it is 252,000 stadia in circumference.

THE HARMONICAL PROPORTION OF THE UNIVERSE

That harmonical proportion, which compels nature to be always consistent with itself, obliges us to add to the above measure, 12,000 stadia; and this makes the earth one ninety-sixth part of the whole universe.

Book III
Europe (I)

INTRODUCTION

Thus far have I treated of the position and the wonders of the earth, of the waters, the stars, and the proportion of the universe and its dimensions. I shall now proceed to describe its individual parts; although indeed we may with reason look upon the task as of an infinite nature, and one not to be rashly commenced upon without incurring censure. And yet, on the other hand, there is nothing which ought less to require an apology, if it is only considered how far from surprising it is that a mere mortal cannot be acquainted with everything. I shall therefore not follow any single author, but shall employ, in relation to each subject, such writers as I shall look upon as most worthy of credit. For, indeed, it is the characteristic of nearly all of them, that they display the greatest care and accuracy in the description of the countries in which they respectively flourished; so that by doing this, I shall neither have to blame nor contradict any one.

The whole globe is divided into three parts, Europe, Asia, and Africa. Our description commences where the sun sets and at the Straits of Gades,[1] where the Atlantic ocean, bursting in, is poured forth into the inland seas. As it makes its entrance from that side, Africa is on the right hand and Europe on the left; Asia lies between them; the boundaries being the rivers Tanais[2] and Nile.

---

1 Now the Straits of Gibraltar.
2 This river today is know as *Don*. In antiquity, this river was viewed as the border between Europe and Asia.

THE BOUNDARIES AND GULFS OF EUROPE

I shall first then speak of Europe, the foster-mother of that people which has conquered all other nations, and itself by far the most beauteous portion of the earth. Indeed, many persons have, not without reason considered it, not as a third part only of the earth, but as equal to all the rest, looking upon the whole of our globe as divided into two parts only, by a line drawn from the river Tanais to the Straits of Gades.

OF SPAIN GENERALLY

The first land situate upon this Gulf is that which is called the Farther Spain or Bætica. Bætica, so called from the river which divides it in the middle, excels all the other provinces in the richness of its cultivation and the peculiar fertility and beauty of its vegetation.

M. Agrippa has also stated the whole length of this province to be 475 miles, and its breadth 257; but this was at a time when its boundaries extended to Carthage, a circumstance which has often caused great errors in calculations.

The ancient form of the Nearer Spain, like that of many other provinces, is somewhat changed, since the time when Pompey the Great, upon the trophies which he erected in the Pyrenees, testified that 877 towns, from the Alps to the borders of the Farther Spain, had been reduced to subjection by him.

The length of the Nearer Spain, from the Pyrenees to the frontier of Castulo, is 607 miles, and a little more if we follow the line of the coast; while its breadth, from Tarraco to the shore of Olarson, is 307 miles. Prom the foot of the Pyrenees, where it is wedged in by the near approach of the two seas, it gradually expands until it touches the Farther Spain, and thereby acquires a width more than double.

Nearly the whole of Spain abounds in mines of lead, iron, copper, silver, and gold; in the Nearer Spain there is also found *lapis specularis*; in Bætica there is cinnabar. There are also quarries of marble.

OF ITALY

Next comes Italy, and we begin with the Ligures, after whom we have Etruria, Umbria, Latium, where are the mouths of the Tiber, and Rome, the Capital of the world, sixteen miles distant from the sea. We then come to the coasts of the Volsci and of Campania, and the districts of Ricenum, of Lucania, and of Bruttium, where Italy extends the farthest in a southerly direction, and projects into the (two) seas with the chain of the Alps, which there forms pretty nearly the shape of a crescent. Leaving Bruttium we come to the coast of (Magna) Græcia, then the Salentini, the Pediculi, the Apuli, the Peligni, the Frentani, the Marrucini, the Vestini, the Sabini, the Picentes, the Galli, the Umbri, the Tusci, the Veneti, the Carni, the Iapydes, the Ilistri, and the Liburni.

I may premise by observing that this land very much resembles in shape an oak leaf, being much longer than it is broad; towards the top it inclines to the left, while it terminates in the form of an Amazonian buckler, in which the spot at the central projection is the place called Cocinthos, while it sends forth two horns at the end of its crescent-shaped bays.

THE FIRST REGION OF ITALY; THE TIBER; ROME

The Tiber flows down from nearly the central part of the chain of the Apennines, in the territory of the Arretini. It is at first small, and only navigable by means of sluices, in which the water is dammed up and then discharged, for which purpose it is found necessary to collect the water for nine days, unless there should happen to be a fall of rain. And even then, the Tiber, by reason of its rugged and uneven channel, is really more suitable for navigation by rafts than by vessels, for any great distance. It winds along for a course of 150 miles, passing not far from Tifernum, Perusia, and Ocriculum, and dividing Etruria from the Umbri and the Sabini.

Below its union with the Glanis from Arretinum the Tiber is swollen by two and forty streams; it is also increased by the numerous aqueducts and springs which are conveyed to the City. Here it becomes navigable by vessels of any burden which may come up from the Italian sea; a most tranquil dispenser of the produce of all parts of the earth, and peopled and embellished along its banks with more villas than nearly all the other rivers of the world taken together. And yet there is no river more circumscribed than it, so close are its banks shut in on either side; but still, no resistance does it offer, although its waters frequently rise with great suddenness, and no part is more liable to be swollen than that which runs through the City itself. In such case, however, the Tiber is rather to be looked upon as pregnant with prophetic warnings to us, and in its increase to be considered more as a promoter of religion than a source of devastation.

It will not perhaps be altogether foreign to the purpose, if I here make mention of one peculiar institution of our forefathers which bears especial reference to the inculcation of silence on religious matters. The goddess Angerona, to whom sacrifice is offered on the twelfth day before the calends of January,[3] is represented in her statue as having her mouth bound with a sealed fillet.

Romulus left the city of Rome, if we are to believe those who state the very greatest number, having three gates and no more. When the Vespasians were emperors and censors, in the year from its building 826, the circumference of the walls which surrounded it was thirteen miles and two-fifths. Surrounding as it does the Seven Hills, the city is divided into fourteen districts, with 265 cross-roads under the guardianship of the Lares. If a straight line is drawn from the mile-column[4] placed at the entrance of the Forum, to each of the gates, which are at present thirty-seven

---

3   21st December.
4   This was a gilded column erected by Augustus in the Forum, and called *milliarium aureum*; on it were inscribed the distances of the principal points to which the "viæ" or high-roads conducted.

in number (taking care to count only once the twelve double gates, and to omit the seven old ones, which no longer exist), the result will be (taking them altogether), a straight line of twenty miles and 765 paces. But if we draw a straight line from the same mile-column to the very last of the houses, including therein the Praetorian encampment, and follow throughout the line of all the streets, the result will then be something more than seventy miles. Add to these calculations the height of the houses, and then a person may form a fair idea of this city, and will certainly be obliged to admit that there is not a place throughout the whole world that for size can be compared to it.

SIXTY-FOUR ISLANDS, AMONG WHICH ARE THE BALEARES

The first islands that we meet with in all these seas are the two to which the Greeks have given the name of Pityussæe[5] from the pine-tree, which they produce. They are separated by a narrow strait of the sea, and are forty-six miles in extent. They are distant from Dianium[6] 700 stadia, Dianium being by land the same distance from New Carthage. At the same distance from the Pityussæe, lie, in the open sea, the two Baleares, and, over against the river Sucre, Colubraria.

The larger island is 100 miles in length, and 475 in circumference.

In the Ligurian Sea, but close to the Tuscan, is Corsica, by the Greeks called Cyrnos, extending, from north to south 150 miles, and for the most part 50 miles in breadth, its circumference being 325.

Leucothea comes next, and after it, but out of sight, as it lies upon the verge of the African Sea, Sardinia. It is situate somewhat less than eight miles from the nearest point of Corsica, and the Straits between them are even still more reduced by the small islands there situate, called the Cuniculariæ. Sardinia extends, upon the east side, a distance of 188 miles, on the west 175, on the south 77, and on the north 125, being 565 miles in circumference.

But more celebrated than all is Sicily, called Sicania by Thucydides, and by many writers Trinaeria or Trinacia, from its triangular appearance. According to Agrippa it is 618 miles in circumference. In former times it was a continuation of the territory of Bruttium, but, in consequence of the overflowing of the sea, became severed from it; thus forming a strait of 15 miles in length, and a mile and a half in width in the vicinity of the Pillar of Rhegium.

In these Straits is the rock of Scylla, as also Charybdis, a whirlpool of the sea, both of them noted for their perils.

---

5 The modern Ibiza and Formentera.
6 Now Denia.

Book IV
Europe (II)

THE PELOPONNESE (GREECE)

The Peloponnese, which was formerly called Apia and Pelasgia, is a peninsula, inferior in fame to no land upon the face of the earth. Situate between the two seas, the Ægaean and the Ionian, it is in shape like the leaf of a plane-tree, in consequence of the angular indentations made in its shores. According to Isidorus, it is 563 miles in circumference; and nearly as much again, allowing for the sea-line on the margin of its gulfs. The narrow pass at which it commences is know by the name of the Isthmus. At this spot the two seas, which we have previously mentioned, running from the north and the east, invade the land from opposite sides, and swallow up its entire breadth, the result being that through these inroads in opposite directions of such vast bodies of water, the sides of the land are eaten away to such an extent, that Hellas (Greece) only holds on to the Peloponnese by the narrow neck, five miles in width, which intervenes. The Gulfs thus formed, the one on this side, the other on that, are known as the Corinthian and the Saronic Gulfs. The

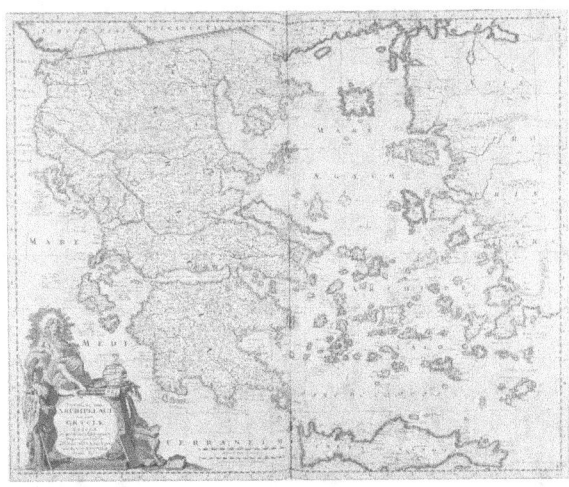

47

ports of Lecheæ, on the one side, and of Cenchreæ on the other, form the frontiers of this narrow passage, which thus compels to a tedious and perilous circumnavigation such vessels as from their magnitude cannot be carried across by land on vehicles. For this reason it is that both King Demetrius, Cæsar the Dictator, the prince Caius, and Domitius Nero, have at different times made the attempt to cut through this neck by forming a navigable canal; a profane design, as may be clearly seen by the result in every one of these instances.

Upon the middle of this intervening neck which we have called the Isthmus, stands the colony of Corinth, formerly known by the name of Ephyre, situate upon the brow of a hill, at a distance of sixty stadia from the shore of either sea. From the heights of its citadel, which is called Acrocorinthos, or the "Heights of Corinth," and in which is the Fountain of Pirene, it looks down upon the two seas which lie in the opposite directions. From Leucas to Patræ upon the Corinthian gulf is a distance of eighty-eight miles. The colony of Patrae is founded upon the most extensive promontory of the Peloponnese, facing Ætolia and the river Evenus, the Corinthian Gulf being, as we have previously stated, less than a mile in width at the entrance there, though extending in length as far as the isthmus, a distance of eighty-five miles.

ATTICA

At the narrow neck of the Isthmus, Hellas begins, by our people known as Græcia (Greece). The first state that presents itself is Attica, anciently called Acte. It touches the Isthmus in that part of it which is called Megaris, from the colony of Megara, lying on the opposite side to Pagæ.

These two towns are situate at the spot where the Peloponnese projects to the greatest distance; being placed, one on each side, upon the very shoulders of Hellas as it were. The Pagæans, as well as the people of Ægosthena, belong to the jurisdiction of Megara.

The other islands are, Myconos, with the mountain of Dimastus, distant from Delos fifteen miles; Siphnus, formerly called Meropia and Acis, twenty-eight miles in circumference; Seriphus, twelve miles in circuit; Prepesinthus; Cythnos; and then, by far the most famous among the Cyclades, and lying in the very middle of them, Delos itself, so famous for its temple of Apollo, and its extensive commerce. This island long floated on the waves, and, as tradition says, was the only one that had never experienced an earthquake, down to the time of M. Varro; Mucianus however has informed us, that it has been twice so visited. Aristotle states that this island received its name from the fact of its having so suddenly made its appearance on emerging from the sea; Aglaosthenes, however, gives it the name of Cynthia, and others of Ortygia, Asteria, Lagia, Chlamydia, Cynthus, and, from the circumstance of fire having been first discovered here, Pyrpile. Its circumference is five miles only; Moint Cynthus here raises his head.

Next to this island is Rhene, which Anticlides calls by the name of Celadussa, and Callidemus, Artemite; Scyros, which the old writers have stated to be twenty miles in circumference, but Mucianus 160; Oliaros; and Paros, with a city of the same name, distant from Delos thirty-eight miles, and famous for its marble; it was first called Platea, and after that, Minois. At a distance of seven miles from this last island is Naxos, with a town of the same name; it is eighteen miles distant from Delos. This island was formerly called Strongyle, then Dia, and then Dionysias, in consequence of the fruitfulness of its vineyards; others again have called it the Lesser Sicily, or Callipolis. It is seventy-five miles in circumference; half as large again as Paros.

THE HELLESPONT — THE LAKE MÆOTIS

The fourth great Gulf of Europe begins at the Hellespont and ends at the entrance of the Mæotish.[1] But in order that the several portions of the Euxine and its coasts may be the better known, we must briefly embrace the form of it in one general view. This vast sea, lying in front of Asia, is shut out from Europe by the projection of the shores of the Chersonesus, and effects an entrance into those countries by a narrow channel only, of the width, as already mentioned, of seven stadia, thus separating Europe from Asia. The entrance of these Straits is called the Hellespont; over it Xerxes, the king of the Persians, constructed a bridge of boats, across which he led his army. A narrow channel extends thence a distance of eighty-six miles, as far as Priapus, a city of Asia, at which Alexander the Great passed over. At this point the sea becomes wider, and after some distance again takes the form of a narrow strait. The wider part is known as the Propontis, the Straits as the Thracian Bosporus, being only half-a-mile in width, at the place where Darius, the father of Xerxes, led his troops across by a bridge. The extremity of this is distant from the Hellespont 239 miles.

We then come to the vast sea called the Euxine (Black Sea), which invades the land as it retreats afar. As the shores bend inwards, this sea with a vast sweep stretches far away, curving on both sides after the manner of a pair of horns, so much so that in shape it bears a distinct resemblance to a Scythian bow. In the middle of the curve it is joined by the mouth of Lake Mæotis, which is called the Cimmerian Bosporus, and is two miles and a half in width. Between the two Bospori, the Thracian and the Cimmerian, there is a distance in a straight line, of 500 miles, as Polybius informs us. We learn from Varro and most of the ancient writers, that the circumference of the Euxine is altogether 2150 miles; but to this number Cornelius Nepos adds 350 more; while Artemidorus makes it 2919 miles, Agrippa 2360, and Mucianus 2425. In a similar manner some writers have fixed the length of the European shores of this sea at 1478 miles, others again at 1172. M. Varro gives the measurement as follows: from the mouth of the Euxine to Apollonia 187 miles, and to Callatis the same distance; thence to the mouth of the Ister 125 miles; to the Borysthenes 250; to Chersonesus, a town of the Heracleotæ, 325; to Panticapæum by some called Bosporus, at the very extremity of the shores of Europe, 212 miles; the whole of which added together, makes 1337 miles. Agrippa makes the distance from Byzantium to the river Ister 560 miles, and from thence to Panticapæum, 635.

---

1 Now generally known as the Palus Mæotis or Sea of Azof.

On leaving Lake Buges, above the Lake Mæotis we come to the Sauromatae and the Essedones. Along the coast, as far as the river Tanais,[2] are the Mæotae, from whom the lake derives its name, and the last of all, in the rear of them, the Arimaspi. We then come to the Riphæan mountains, and the region known by the name of Pterophoros, because of the perpetual fall of snow there, the flakes of which resemble feathers; a part of the world which has been condemned by the decree of nature to lie immersed in thick darkness; suited for nothing but the generation of cold, and to be the asylum of the chilling blasts of the northern winds.

Behind these mountains, and beyond the region of the northern winds, there dwells, if we choose to believe it, a happy race, known as the Hyperboreans,[3] a race that lives to an extreme old age, and which has been the subject of many marvellous stories. At this spot are supposed to be the hinges upon which the world revolves, and the extreme limits of the revolutions of the stars. Here we find light for six months together, given by the sun in one continuous day, who does not, however, as some ignorant persons have asserted, conceal himself from the vernal equinox to autumn. On the contrary, to these people there is but one rising of the sun for the year, and that at the summer solstice, and but one setting, at the winter solstice. This region, warmed by the rays of the sun, is of a most delightful temperature, and exempt from every noxious blast. The abodes of the natives are the woods and groves; the gods receive their worship singly and in groups, while all discord and every kind of sickness are things utterly unknown. Death comes upon them only when satiated with life; after a career of feasting, in an old age sated with every luxury, they leap from a certain rock there into the sea; and this they deem the most desirable mode of ending existence. Some writers have placed these people, not in Europe, but at the very verge of the shores of Asia, because we find there a people called the Attacori, who greatly resemble them and occupy a very similar locality. Other writers again have placed them midway between the two suns, at the spot where it sets to the Antipodes and rises to us; a thing however that cannot possibly be, in consequence of the vast tract of sea which there intervenes. Those writers who place them nowhere but under a day which lasts for six months, state that in the morning they sow, at mid-day they reap, at sunset they gather in the fruits of the trees, and during the night conceal themselves in caves.

GERMANY

The whole of the shores of this sea as far as the Scaldis, a river of Germany, is inhabited by nations, the dimensions of whose respective territories it is quite impossible to state, so immensely do the authors differ who have touched upon this subject. The Greek writers and some of our own countrymen have stated the coast

---

2   Now the Don.
3   Inhabitants of the most northern region of the earth. In early Greek legend the Hyperboreans were a people who lived beyond the north wind, and were not exposed to its blasts, but enjoyed a land of perpetual sunshine and abundant fruits. They were free from disease, violence, and war. Their natural life lasted 1,000 years, and was spent in the worship of Apollo. In later times the Greeks gave the name to the inhabitants of northern countries generally.

Book IV - Europe (II)

of Germany to be 2500 miles in extent, while Agrippa, comprising Rhætia and Noricum in his estimate, makes the length to be 686 miles, and the breadth 148.

There are five German races; the Vandili, parts of whom are the Burgundiones, the Varini, the Carini, and the Gutones; the Ingaevones, forming a second race, a portion of whom are the Cimbri, the Teutoni, and the tribes of the Chauci. The Istaevones, who join up to the Rhine, and to whom the Cimhri belong, are the third race; whUe the Hermiones, formiug a fourth, dwell in the interior, and include the Suevi, the Hermunduri, the Chatti, and the Cherusci; the fifth race is that of the Peucini, who are also the Basternæ, adjoining the Daci previously mentioned. The more famous rivers that flow into the ocean are the Guttalus, the Vistillus or Vistula, the Albis, the Visurgis, the Amisius, the Rhine, and the Mosa. In the interior is the long extent of the Hercynian range, which in grandeur is inferior to none.

BRITANNIA

Opposite to this coast is the island called Britannia, so celebrated in the records of Greece and of our own country. It is situate to the north-west, and, with a large tract of intervening sea, lies opposite to Germany, Gaul, and Spain, by far the greater part of Europe. Its former name was Albion; but at a later period, all the islands, of which we shall just now briefly make mention, were included under the name of "Britanniæ." This island is distant from Gesoriacum, on the coast of the nation of the Morini, at the spot where the passage across is the shortest, fifty miles. Pytheas and Isidorus say that its circumference is 4875 miles. It is barely thirty years since any extensive knowledge of it was gained by the successes of the Roman arms, and even as yet they have not penetrated beyond the vicinity of the Caledonian forest. Agrippa believes its length to be 800 miles, and its breadth 300; he also thinks that the breadth of Hibernia is the same, but that its length is less by 200 miles. This last island is situate beyond Britannia, the passage across being the shortest from the territory of the Silures, a distance of thirty miles. Of the remaining islands none is said to have a greater circumference than 125 miles. Among these there are the Orcades, forty in number, and situate within a short distance of each other, the seven islands called Acmodæ, the Haebudes, thirty in number, and, between Hibernia and Britannia, the islands of Mona, Monapia, Kicina, Vectis, Limnus, and Andros. Below it are the islands called Samnis and Axantos, and opposite, scattered in the German Sea, are those known as the Glaesariæ, but which the Greeks have more recently called the Electrides, from the circumstance of their producing electrum or amber. The most remote of all that we find mentioned is Thule, in which there is no night at the summer solstice, when the sun is passing through the sign of Cancer, while on the other hand at the winter solstice there is no day. Some writers are of opinion that this state of things lasts for six whole months together

GAUL

The whole of Gaul (France) that is comprehended under the one general name of Comata, is divided into three races of people, which are more especially kept distinct from each other by the following rivers. From the Scaldis to the Sequana it is Belgic Gaul; from the Sequana to the Garumna it is Celtic Gaul or Lugdunensis;

and from the Garumna to the promontory of the Pyrensean range it is Aquitanian Gaul, formerly called Aremorica. Agrippa makes the entire length of the coast of Gaul to be 1800 miles, measured from the Rhine to the Pyrenees; and its length, from the ocean to the mountains of Gehenna and Jura, excluding therefrom Gallia Narbonensis, he computes at 420 miles, the breadth being 318.

Book V
Africa and Asia

THE TWO MAURITANIAS

The Greeks have given the name of Libya[1] to Africa, and have called the sea that lies in front of it the Libyan Sea. It has Egypt for its boundary, and no part of the earth is there that has fewer gulfs or inlets, its shores extending in a lengthened line from the west in an oblique direction. The names of its peoples, and its cities in especial, cannot possibly be pronounced with correctness, except by the aid of their own native tongues. Its population, too, for the most part dwells only in fortresses.

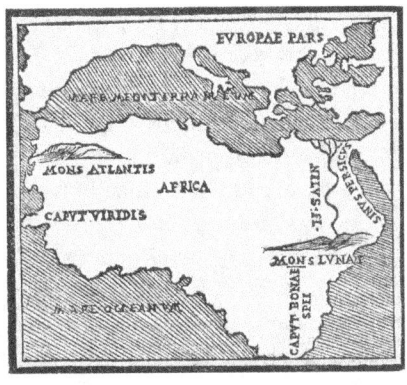

On our entrance into Africa, we find the two Mauritanias, which, until the time of Caius Cæsar, the son of Grermanicus, were kingdoms; but, suffering under his cruelty, they were divided into two provinces.

There were formerly two towns, Lissa and Cotte, beyond the Pillars of Hercules; but, at the present day, we only find that of Tingi, which was formerly founded by Antæus. It is thirty miles distant from Belon, a town of Baetica, where the passage across is the shortest. At a distance of twenty-five miles from Tingi, upon the shores of the ocean, we come to Julia Constantia Zilis, a colony of Augustus. At this place, according to the story, was the palace of Antæus; this was the scene of

---

1 Not reckoning under that appellation the country of Egypt, which was more generally looked upon as forming part of Asia.

his combat with Hercules, and here were the gardens of the Hesperides. An arm of the sea flows into the land here, with a serpentine channel, and, from the nature of the locality, this is interpreted at the present day as having been what was really represented by the story of the dragon keeping guard there. This tract of water surrounds an island, the only spot which is never overflowed by the tides of the sea, although not quite so elevated as the rest of the land in its vicinity. Upon this island, also, there is still in existence the altar of Hercules; but of the grove that bore the golden fruit, there are no traces left, beyond some wild olive-trees.

MOUNT ATLAS

Suetonius Paulinus,[2] whom we have seen Consul in our own time, was the first Roman general who advanced a distance of some miles beyond Mount Atlas. He has given us the same information as we have received from other sources with reference to the extraordinary height of this mountain, and at the same time he has stated that all the lower parts about the foot of it are covered with dense and lofty forests composed of trees of species hitherto unknown. The height of these trees, he says, is remarkable; the trunks are without knots, and of a smooth and glossy surface; the foliage is like that of the cypress, and besides sending forth a powerful odour, they are covered with a flossy down, from which, by the aid of art, a fine cloth might easily be manufactured, similar to the textures made from the produce of the silk-worm. He informs us that the summit of this mountain is covered with snow even in summer, and says that having arrived there after a march of ten days, he proceeded some distance beyond it as far as a river which bears the name of Ger;[3] the road being through deserts covered with a black sand, from which rocks that bore the appearance of having been exposed to the action of fire, projected every here and there; localities rendered quite uninhabitable by the intensity of the heat, as he himself experienced, although it was in the winter season that he visited them. We also learn from the same source that the people who inhabit the adjoining forests, which are full of all kinds of elephants, wild beasts, and serpents, have the name of Canarii; from the circumstance that they partake of their food in common with the canine race, and share with it the entrails of wild beasts.

The province of Tingitana is 170 miles in length. Of the nations in this province, the principal one, was formerly that of the Mauri, who have given to it the name of Mauritania, and have been by many writers called the Maurusii. This nation has been greatly weakened by the disasters of war, and is now dwindled down to a few families only.

NUMIDIA

At the river Ampsaga Numidia begins. By the Greeks this region was called Metagonitis; and the Numidians received the name of "Nomades" from their frequent changes of pasturage; upon which occasions they were accustomed to carry their mapalia, or in other words, their houses, upon wagons.

---

2   The same general who afterwards conquered the Britons under Boadicea or Bonduca.
3   Niger?

BOOK V - AFRICA AND ASIA

AFRICA

Beyond the river Tusca begins the region of Zeugitana, and that part which properly bears the name of Africa.

We here find three promontories; the White Promontory,[4] the Promontory of Apollo,[5] facing Sardinia, and that of Mercury,[6] opposite to Sicily, Projecting into the sea these headlands form two gulfs.

THE SYRTES

A third Gulf is divided into two smaller ones, those of the two Syrtes,[7] which are rendered perilous by the shallows of their quicksands and the ebb and flow of the sea. Polybius states the distance from Carthage to the Lesser Syrtis, the one which is nearest to it, to be 300 miles.

Africa, from the river Ampsaga to this limit, includes 516 peoples, who are subject to the Roman sway, of which six are colonies; among them Uthina and Tuburbi.

CYRENAICA

The region of Cyrenaica, also called Pentapolis, is rendered famous by the oracle of Hammon, which is distant 400 miles from the city of Cyrene; also by the Fountain of the Sun there, and five cities in especial, those of Berenice, Arsinöe, Ptolemais, Apollonia, and Cyrene itself. Berenice is situate upon the outer promontory that hounds the Syrtis; it was formerly called the city of the Hesperides (previously mentioned), according to the fables of the Greeks, which very often change their localities. Not far from the city, and running before it, is the river Lethon, and with it a sacred grove, where the gardens of the Hesperides are said to have formerly stood; this city is distant from Leptis 375 miles.

COUNTRIES ON THE INTERIOR OF AFRICA

If we pass through the interior of Africa in a southerly direction, beyond the Gætuli, after having traversed the intervening deserts, we shall find, first of all the Liby-Egiptians, and then the country where the Leucæthiopians dwell. Beyond these are the Nigritae, nations of Ethiopia, so called from the river Nigris. After passing all these peoples, there are vast deserts towards the east until we come to the Garamantes, the Augylæ, and the Troglodytæ; the opinion of those being exceedingly well founded who place two Æthiopias beyond the deserts of Africa, and more particularly that expressed by Homer, who tells us that the Æthiopians are divided into two nations, those of the east and those of the west. The river Nigris has the same characteristics as the Nile; it produces the calamus, the papyrus, and just the same animals, and it rises at the same seasons of the year. Its source is between the Tarrælian Æthiopians and the Œcalicæ. Magium, the city of the latter people, has been placed by some writers amid the deserts, and, next to them the Atlan-

---

4   Ras-el-Abiad, or Cape Blanco on the Syrian coast.
5   Ras Sidi Ali-al-Mekhi or Cape Farina.
6   Ras-Addar or Cape Bon.
7   The modern Lempta occupies its site.

tes; then the Ægipani, half men, half beasts, the Blemmyæ, the Gamphasantes, the Satyri, and the Hamantopodes.

The Atlantes, if we believe what is said, have lost all characteristics of humanity; for there is no mode of distinguishing each other among them by names, and as they look upon the rising and the setting sun, they give utterance to direful imprecations against it, as being deadly to themselves and their lands; nor are they visited with dreams like the rest of mortals. The Troglodytæ make excavations in the earth, which serve them for dwellings; the flesh of serpents is their food; they have no articulate voice, but only utter a kind of squeaking noise; and thus are they utterly destitute of all means of communication by language. The Garamantes have no institution of marriage among them, and live in promiscuous concubinage with their women. The Augylæ worship no deities but the gods of the infernal regions. The Gamphasantes, who go naked, and are unacquainted with war, hold no intercourse whatever with strangers. The Blemmyæ are said to have no heads, their mouths and eyes being seated in their breasts. The Satyri,[8] beyond their figure, have nothing in common with the manners of the human race, and the form of the Ægipani is such as is commonly represented in paintings. The Himantopodes are a race of people with feet resembling thongs, upon which they move along by nature with a serpentine, crawling kind of gait. The Pharusii, descended from the ancient Persians, are said to have been the companions of Hercules when on his expedition to the Hesperides. Beyond the above, I have met with nothing relative to Africa worthy of mention.

EGYPT AND THEBAIS

Joining on to Africa is Asia, the extent of which, according to Timosthenes, from the Canopic mouth of the Nile to the mouth of the Euxine, is 2089 miles. Prom the mouth of the Euxine to that of Lake Mæotis is, according to Eratosthenes, 1545 miles. The whole distance to the Tanais, including Egypt, is, according to Artemidorus and Isidorus, 6375 miles. The seas of Egypt, which are several in number, have received their names from those who dwell upon their shores, for which reason they will be mentioned together.

Egypt is the country which lies next to Africa; in the interior it runs in a southerly direction, as far as the territory of the Æthiopians, who lie extended at the back of it. The river Nile, dividing itself, forms on the right and left the boundary of its lower part, which it embraces on every side By the Canopic mouth of that river it is separated from Africa, and by the Pelusiæ from Asia, there being a distance between the two of 170 miles. For this reason it is that some persons have reckoned Egypt among the islands, the Nile so dividing itself as to give a triangular form to the land which it encloses; from which circumstance also many persons have named Egypt the Delta,[9] after that of the Greek letter so called.

---

8   So called from their supposed resemblance in form to the Satyrs of the ancient mythology, who were represented as little hairy men with horns, long ears, and tails.

9   By reason of its triangular form Δ.

The upper part of Egypt, which borders on Æthiopia, is known as Thebais. This district is divided into prefectures of towns, which are generally designated as "Nomes."

THE RIVER NILE

The sources of the Nile are unascertained, and, travelling as it does for an immense distance through deserts and burning sands, it is only known to us by common report, having neither experienced the vicissitudes of warfare, nor been visited by those arms which have so effectually explored all other regions. It rises, so far indeed as King Juba was enabled to ascertain, in a mountain of Lower Mauritania, not far from the ocean; immediately after which it forms a lake of standing water, which bears the name of Nilides. In this lake are found the several kinds of fish known by the names of alabeta, coracinus, and silurus; a crocodile also was brought thence as a proof that this really is the Nile, and was consecrated by Juba himself in the temple of Isis at Cæsarea, where it may be seen at the present day. In addition to these facts, it has been observed that the waters of the Nile rise in the same proportion in which the snows and rains of Mauritania increase. Pouring forth from this lake, the river disdains to flow through arid and sandy deserts, and for a distance of several days' journey conceals itself; after which it bursts forth at another lake of greater magnitude in the country of the Massæsyli a people of Mauritania Cæsariensis, and thence casts a glance around, as it were, upon the communities of men in its vicinity, giving proofs of its identity in the same peculiarities of the animals which it produces. It then buries itself once again in the sands of the desert, and remains concealed for a distance of twenty days' journey, till it has reached the confines of Æethiopia. Here, when it has once more become sensible of the presence of man, it again emerges, at the same source, in all probability, to which writers have given the name of Niger, or Black. After this, forming the boundary-line between Africa and Æethiopia, its banks, though not immediately peopled by man, are the resort of numbers of wild beasts and animals of various kinds. Giving birth in its course to dense forests of trees, it travels through the middle of Æthiopia. Proceeding onwards, it divides innumerable islands in its course. It does not obtain the name of "Nile" until its waters have again met and are united in a single stream; and even then, for some miles both above and below the point of confluence, it has the name of Siris. Homer has given to the whole of this river the name of Ægyptus, while other writers again have called it Triton. Every now and then its course is interrupted by islands which intervene, and which only serve as so many incentives to add to the impetuosity of its torrent; and though at last it is hemmed in by mountains on either side, in no part is the tide more rapid and precipitate. Its waters then hastening onwards, it is borne along to the spot in the country of the Æthiopians which is known by the name of "Catadupi";[10] where, at the last Cataract, the complaint is, not that it flows, but that it rushes, with an immense noise between the rocks that lie in its way; after which it becomes more

---

10 Or the "Cataracts," for which it is the Greek name. The most northerly of these cataracts, called the First Cataract, is, and always has been, the southern boundary of Egypt.

smooth, the violence of its waters is broken and subdued, and, wearied out as it were by the length of the distance it has travelled, it discharges itself, though by many mouths, into the Egyptian sea. During certain days of the year, however, the volume of its waters is greatly increased, and as it traverses the whole of Egypt, it inundates the earth, and, by so doing, greatly promotes its fertility.

There have been various reasons suggested for this increase of the river. Of these, however, the most probable are, either that its waters are driven back by the Etesian winds which are blowing at this season of the year from an opposite direction, and that the sea which lies beyond is driven into the mouths of the river; or else that its waters are swollen by the summer rains of Æthiopia, which fall from the clouds conveyed thither by the Etesian winds from other parts of the earth. Timæus the mathematician has alleged a reason of an occult nature; he says that the source of the river is known by the name of Phiala, and that the stream buries itself in channels underground, where it sends forth vapours generated by the heat among the steaming rocks amid which it conceals itself; but that, during the days of the inundation, in consequence of the sun approaching nearer to the earth, the waters are drawn forth by the influence of his heat, and on being thus exposed to the air, overflow; after which, in order that it may not be utterly dried up, the stream hides itself once more. He says that this takes place at the rising of the Dog-Star, when the sun enters the sign of Leo, and stands in a vertical position over the source of the river, at which time at that spot there is no shadow thrown.

The Nile begins to increase at the next new moon after the summer solstice. While it is rising it has been pronounced criminal for kings or prefects even to sail upon its waters. The measure of its increase is ascertained by means of wells. Its most desirable height is sixteen cubits; if the waters do not attain that height, the overflow is not universal; but if they exceed that measure, by their slowness in receding they tend to retard the process of cultivation.

When the waters have reached their greatest height, the people open the embankments and admit them to the lands. As each district is left by the waters, the business of sowing commences. This is the only river in existence that emits no vapours.

THE CITIES OF EGYPT

Egypt, besides its boast of extreme antiquity, asserts that it contained, in the reign of King Amasis, 20,000 inhabited cities; in our day they are still very numerous, though no longer of any particular note. Still however we find the following ones mentioned as of great renown: the city of Apollo; next, that of Leucothea; then Great Diospolis, otherwise Thebes, known to fame for its hundred gates; Coptos, which from its proximity to the Nile, forms its nearest emporium for the merchandise of India and Arabia.

With the greatest justice, however, we may lavish our praises upon Alexandria, built by Alexander the Great on the shores of the Egyptian Sea, upon the soil of Africa, at twelve miles distance from the Canopic Mouth and near Lake Mareotis. The plan of this city was designed by the architect Dinochares, who is memorable for the genius which he displayed in many ways. Building the city upon a wide space of ground fifteen miles in circumference, he formed it in the circular shape of a Macedonian chlamys,[11] uneven at the edge, giving it an angular projection on the right and left; while at the same time he devoted one-fifth part of the site to the royal palace.

THE COASTS OF ARABIA, SITUATE ON THE EGYPTIAN SEA

Beyond the Pelusiac Mouth is Arabia, which extends to the Red Sea, and joins the Arabia known by the surname of Happy, so famous for its perfumes and its wealth. It is remarkable for its sterility, except in the parts where it joins up to Syria, and it has nothing remarkable in it except Mount Casius.

SYRIA

Next to these countries Syria occupies the coast, once the greatest of lands, and distinguished by many names; for the part which joins up to Arabia was formerly called Palæstina, Judæa, Cœle, and Phœnice. The country in the interior was called Damascena, and that further on and more to the south, Babylonia. The part that lies between the Euphrates and the Tigris was called Mesopotamia, that beyond Taurus Sophene, and that on this side of the same chain Comagene. Beyond Armenia was the country of Adiabene, anciently called Assyria, and at the part where it joins up to Cilicia, it was called Antiochia. The whole of the tract of sea that lies in front of these shores is called the Phœnician Sea. The Phœnician people enjoy the glory of having been the inventors of letters, and the first discoverers of the sciences of astronomy, navigation, and the art of war.

JUDÆA

Beyond Idumaea and Samaria, Judæa extends far and wide. That part of it which joins up to Syria is called Galilæa, while that which is nearest to Arabia and Egypt bears the name of Peræa. This last is thickly covered with rugged mountains, and is separated from the rest of Judæa by the river Jordanes.

The river Jordanes rises from the spring of Panias. This is a delightful stream, and, so far as the situation of the localities will allow of, winds along in its course and lingers among the dwellers upon its banks. With the greatest reluctance, as it were, it moves onward towards Asphaltites,[12] a lake of a gloomy and unpropitious nature, by which it is at last swallowed up, and its bepraised waters are lost sight of on being mingled with the pestilential streams of the lake.

Asphaltites produces nothing whatever except bitumen, to which indeed it owes its name. The bodies of animals will not sink in its waters, and even those of bulls and camels float there. In length it exceeds 100 miles being at its greatest breadth twenty-five, and at its smallest six. Arabia of the Nomades faces it on

---

11 The *chlamys* was a scarf or cloak worn over the shoulders, and especially used by military persons of high rank. It did not reach lower than the knees, and was open in front, covering only the neck, back, and shoulders.

12 The Lake of Sodom, or the Dead Sea, in which the Cities of the Plain were swallowed up.

the east, and Machærus on the south, at one time, next to Hierosolyma, the most strongly fortified place in Judæa. On the same side lies Callirrhoë, a warm spring, remarkable for its medicinal qualities, and which, by its name, indicates the celebrity its waters have gained.

Lying on the west of Asphaltites, and sufficiently distant to escape its noxious exhalations, are the Esseni, a people that live apart from the world, and marvellous beyond all others throughout the whole earth, for they have no women among them; to sexual desire they are strangers; money they have none; the palm-trees are their only companions. Day after day, however, their numbers are fully recruited by multitudes of strangers that resort to them, driven thither to adopt their usages by the tempests of fortune, and wearied with the miseries of life. Thus it is, that through thousands of ages, incredible to relate, this people eternally prolongs its existence, without a single birth taking place there; so fruitful a source of population to it is that weariness of life which is felt by others.

THE EUPHRATES

This river rises in Caranitis, a præfecture of Greater Armenia, according to the statement of those who have approached the nearest to its source. It first flows past Derxene, and then Anaitica, shutting out the regions of Armenia from Cappadocia. From this spot it is navigable as far as Sartona, thence to Melitene and to Elegia, when it meets the range of Mount Taurus, but no effectual resistance is offered to its course, although the chain is here twelve miles in width. At its passage between the mountains, the river hears the name of Omma; hut afterwards, when it has passed through, it receives that of Euphrates.

THE ISLANDS WHICH LIE IN FRONT OF ASIA

Of the islands which lie before Asia the first is the one located in the Canopic Mouth of the Nile, and which received its name, it is said, from Canopus, the pilot of Menelaüs. A second, called Pharos, is joined by a bridge to Alexandria, and was made a colony by the Dictator Cæsar. In former times it was one day's sail from the mainland of Egypt; at the present day it directs ships in their course by means of the fires which are lighted at night on the tower there; for in consequence of the insidious nature of the shoals, there are only three channels by which Alexandria can be approached, those of Steganus, Posideum and Taurus.

In the Phoenician Sea, before Joppe there is the island of Paria, the whole of it forming a town. Here, they say, Andromeda was exposed to the monster; the island also of Arados, between which and the continent, as we learn from Mucianus, at a depth of fifty cubits in the sea, fresh water is brought up from a spring at the very bottom by means of leather pipes.

RHODES

But the fairest of them all is the free island of Rhodes, 125, or, if we would rather believe Isidorus, 103 miles in circumference. It contains the inhabited cities of Liudos, Camirus, and Ialysus, now called Rhodos. It is distant from Alexandria in Egypt, according to Isidorus, 583 miles; but, according to Eratosthenes, 469 miles.

Book VI
The Black Sea, India and the Far East

THE EUXINE SEA AND THE MARYANDINI

The Euxine Sea (Black Sea), which in former times had the name of Axenus, from the savage and inhospitable character of the nations living on its borders, by a peculiar whim of nature, which is continually giving way before the greedy inroads of the sea, lies between Europe and Asia. It was not enough

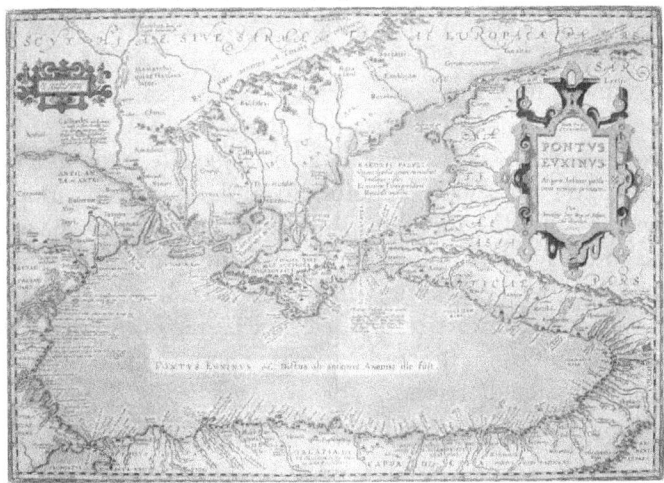

for the ocean to have surrounded the earth, and then deprived us of a considerable portion of it, thus rendering still greater its uninhabitable proportion. That all this has taken place in spite, as it were, of the earth, is manifested by the existence of so many straits and such numbers of narrow passages formed against the will of nature —that of the Hellespont, being only eight hundred and seventy-five paces in width, while at the two Bospori the passage across may be effected by oxen swimming, a fact from which they have both derived their name. And then besides, although they are thus severed, there are certain points on which these coasts stand in the relation of brotherhood towards each other —the singing of birds and the barking of dogs on the one side can be heard on the other, and an intercourse can be maintained between these two worlds by the medium even of the human voice, if the winds should not happen to carry away the sound thereof.

The length of the borders of the Euxine from the Bosporus to the Lake Mæotis has been reckoned by some waiters at fourteen hundred and thirty-eight miles; Eratosthenes, however, says that it is one hundred less.

THE CIMMERIAN BOSPORUS

The length of the peninsula which projects between the Enxine and Lake Mæotis, is not more than sixty-seven miles and a half, and the width across never less than two jugera;[1] it has the name of Eion. The shores of the Bosporus then take a curve both on the side of Europe and of Asia, thus forming the Mæotis.

The towns at the entrance of the Bosporus are, first Hermonassa, next Cepi, founded by the Milesians, and then Stratoclia and Phanagoria, and the almost deserted town of Apaturos, and, at the extremity of the mouth, Cimmerium. After passing Cimmerium, the coast is inhabited by diverse nations and tribes.

THE RIVERS CYRUS AND ARAXES

The river Cyrus takes its rise in the mountains of the Heniochi, by some writers called the Coraxici; the Araxes rises in the same mountains as the river Euphrates, at a distance from it of six miles only and after being increased by the waters of the Usis, falls itself, as many authors have supposed, into the Cyrus, by which it is carried into the Caspian Sea.

The more famous towns in Lesser Armenia are Cassarea, Aza, and Nicopolis in the Greater Arsamosata, which lies near the Euphrates, Carcathiocerta upon the Tigris, Tigranocerta which stands on an elevated site, and, on a plain adjoining the river Araxes, Artaxata.[2] According to Aufidius, the circumference of the whole of Armenia is five thousand miles, while Claudius Cæsar makes the length, from Dascusa to the borders of the Caspian Sea, thirteen hundred miles, and the breadth, from Tigranocerta to Iberia, half that distance. It is a well-known fact, that this country is divided into prefectures, called "Strategies," some of which singly formed a kingdom in former times; they are one hundred and twenty in number, with barbarous and uncouth names.

---

1   The jugerum was 100 Grecian or 104 Roman feet in length.
2   The ancient capital of Armenia. Hannibal, who took refuge at the court of Artaxias when Antiochus was no longer able to afford him protection, superintended the building of it.

Book VI - The Black Sea, India and the Far East

ALBANIA, IBERIA, AND THE ADJOINING NATIONS

The whole plain which extends away from the river Cyrus is inhabited by the nation of the Albani, and, after them, by that of the Iberi, who are separated from them by the river Alazon, which flows into the Cyrus from the Caucasian chain.

THE PASSES OF THE CAUCASUS

After passing the last, we come to the Gates of Caucasus,[3] by many persons most erroneously called the Caspian Passes; a vast work of nature, which has suddenly wrenched asunder in this place a chain of mountains. At this spot are gates barred up with beams shod with iron, while beneath the middle there runs a stream which emits a most fetid odour; on this side of it is a rock, defended by a fortress, the name of which is Cumania, erected for the purpose of preventing the passage of the innumerable tribes that lie beyond. Here, then, we may see the habitable world severed into two parts by a pair of gates.

NATIONS ON THE VICINITY OF THE SCYTHIAN OCEAN

Having now stated all that bears reference to the interior of Asia, let us cross in imagination the Riphæan Mountains, and traverse the shores of the ocean to the right. On three sides does this ocean wash the coasts of Asia, as the Scythian Ocean on the north, the Eastern Ocean on the east, and the Indian Ocean on the south; and it is again divided into various names, derived from the numerous gulfs which it forms, and the nations which dwell upon its shores. A great part of Asia, however, which lies exposed to the north, through the noxious effects of those freezing climates, consists of nothing but vast deserts. From the extreme north north-east to the point where the sun rises in the summer, it is the country of the Scythians. Still further than them, and beyond the point where north north-east begins, some writers have placed the Hyperboreans, who are said, indeed, by the majority to be a people of Europe. After passing this point the first place that is known is Lytarmis, a promontory of Celtica, and next to it the river Carambucis where the chain of the Riphæan Mountains terminates, and with it the extreme rigour of the climate; here, too, we have heard of a certain people being situate, called the Arimphæi, a race not much unlike the Hyperboreans. Their habitations are the groves, and the berries their diet; long hair is held to be disgraceful by the women as well as the men, and they are mild in their manners. Hence it is that they are reported to be a sacred race, and are never molested even by the savage tribes which border upon them, and not only they, but such other persons as well as may have fled to them for refuge. Beyond these we come straight to the Scythians, the Cimmerii, the Cisianthi, the Georgi, and a nation of Amazons. These last extend to the Caspian and Hyrcanian Sea.

THE CASPIAN AND HYRCANIAN SEA

Bursting through, this sea makes a passage from the Scythian Ocean into the back of Asia, receiving various names from the nations which dwell upon its banks,

---

3   There are two chief passes over the chain of the Caucasus, both of which were known to the ancients.

the two most famous of which are the Caspian and the Hyrcanian races. Clitarchus is of opinion that the Caspian Sea is not less in area than the Euxine. Eratosthenes gives the measure of it on the south-east, along the coast of Cadusia and Albania, as five thousand four hundred stadia.

Its waters make their way into this sea by a very narrow mouth, but of considerable length; and where it begins to enlarge, it curves obliquely with horns in the form of a crescent, just as though it would make a descent from its mouth into Lake Mæotis, resembling a sickle in shape. The first of its gulfs is called the Scythian Gulf; it is inhabited on both sides, by the Scythians, who hold communication with each other across the Straits. Then along the coast there are the Albani, the descendants of Jason, it is said; that part of the sea which lies in front of them, bears the name of 'Albanian.' This nation, which lies along the Caucasian chain, comes down as far as the river Cyrus, which forms the boundary of Armenia and Iberia.

MEDIA AND THE CASPIAN GATES

Ecbatana, the capital of Media, was built by king Seleucus, at a distance from Great Seleucia of seven hundred and fifty miles, and twenty miles from the Caspian Gates. The remaining towns of the Medians are Phazaca, Aganzaga, and Apamea, surnamed Rhagiane. The reason of these passes receiving the name of "Gates," is the same that has been stated above. The chain of mountains is suddenly broken by a passage of such extreme narrowness that, for a distance of eight miles, a single chariot can barely find room to move along; the whole of this pass has been formed by artificial means. Both on the right hand and the left are overhanging rocks, which look as though they had been exposed to the action of fire; and there is a tract of country, quite destitute of water.

On the other side of these gates we come to the deserts of Parthia and the mountain chain of Cithenus; and after that, the most pleasant locality of all Parthia, Choara by name. Here were two cities of the Parthians, built in former times for their protection against the people of Media, Calliope, and Issatis, the last of which stood formerly on a rock. Hecatompylos, the capital of Parthia, is distant from the Caspian Gates one hundred and thirty-three miles. In such an effectual manner is the kingdom of Parthia shut out by these passes.

After leaving these gates we find the nation of the Caspii, ex tending as far as the shores of the Caspian, a race which has given its name to these gates as well as to the sea.

THE SERES

After we have passed the Caspian Sea and the Scythian Ocean, our course takes an easterly direction, such being the turn here taken by the lino of the coast. The first portion of these shores, after we pass the Scythian Promontory, is totally uninhabitable, owing to the snow, and the regions adjoining are uncultivated, in consequence of the savage state of the nations which dwell there. Here are the abodes of the Scythian Anthropophagi, who feed on human flesh. Hence it is that all around them consists of vast deserts, inhabited by multitudes of wild beasts, which are continually lying in wait, ready to fall upon human beings just as savage as themselves. After leaving these, we again come to a nation of the Scythians, and then again to desert tracts tenanted by wild beasts, until we reach a chain of mountains which runs up to the sea, and bears the name of Tabis. It is not, however, before we have traversed very nearly one half of the coast that looks towards the north-east, that we find it occupied by inhabitants.

The first people that are known of here are the Seres,[4] so famous for the wool that is found in their forests. After steeping it in water, they comb off a white down that adheres to the leaves; and then to the females of our part of the world they give the twofold task of unravelling their textures, and of weaving the threads afresh. So manifold is the labour, and so distant are the regions which are thus ransacked to supply a dress through which our ladies may in public display their charms. The Seres are of inoffensive manners, but, bearing a strong resemblance therein to all savage nations, they shun all intercourse with the rest of mankind, and await the approach of those who wish to traffic with them.

THE NATIONS OF INDIA

But we come now to nations as to which there is a more general agreement among writers. Where the chain of Emodus[5] rises, the nations of India begin, which borders not only on the Eastern sea, but on the Southern as well, which we have already mentioned as being called the Indian Ocean. That part which faces the east runs in a straight line a distance of eighteen hundred and seventy-five miles until it comes to a bend, at which the Indian Ocean begins. Here it takes a turn to the south, and continues to run in that direction a distance of two thousand four hundred and seventy-five miles, according to Eratosthenes, as far as the river Indus, the boundary of India on the west. Many authors have represented the entire length of the Indian coast as being forty days and nights' sail, and-as being, from north to south, two thousand eight hundred and fifty miles. Agrippa states its length to be three thousand three hundred miles, and its breadth, two thousand three hundred.

In this region, the appearance of the heavens is totally changed, and quite different is the rising of the stars; there are two summers in the year, and two harvests, while the winter intervenes between them during the time that the Etesian winds are blowing; during our winter too, they enjoy light breezes, and their seas are navigable. In this country there are nations and cities which would be found to be quite innumerable, if a person should attempt to enumerate them. The followers of Alexander the Great have stated in their writings, that there were no less than five thousand cities in that portion of India which they vanquished by force of arms, not one of which was smaller than that of Cos; that its nations were eight in number, that India forms one-third of the whole earth, and that its populations are innumerable.

---

4   The people of Serica, which country with Ptolemy corresponds to the north-western part of China, and the adjacent portions of Tibet and Chinese Tartary.

5   Western Himalayan foothills (TN).

THE GANGES

Some writers have stated that this river, like the Nile, takes its rise from unknown sources, and, in a similar manner, waters the neighbouring territory; others, again, say that it rises in the mountains of Scythia. They state also that nineteen rivers discharge their waters into it. The last nation situate on the banks of the Ganges is that of the Gangarides Calingæ; the city where their king dwells has the name of Protalis.

This king has sixty thousand foot-soldiers, one thousand horses, and seven hundred elephants, always caparisoned ready for battle. The people of the more civilized nations of India are divided into several classes. One of these classes tills the earth, another attends to military affairs, others again are occupied in mercantile pursuits, while the wisest and the most wealthy among them have the management of the affairs of state —act as judges, and give counsel to the king. The fifth class, entirely devoting themselves to the pursuit of wisdom, which in these countries is almost held in the same veneration as religion, always end their life by a voluntary death upon the lighted pile. In addition to these, there is a class in a half-savage state, and doomed to endless labour; by means of their exertions, all the classes previously mentioned are supported. It is their duty to hunt the elephant, and to tame him when captured; for it is by the aid of these animals that they plough; by these animals they are conveyed from place to place; these in especial they look upon as constituting their flocks and herds; by their aid they wage their wars, and fight in defence of their territories. Strength, age, and size, are the points usually considered in making choice of these animals.

THE INDUS

The Indus, called Sindis by the natives, rises in that branch of the Caucasian range which bears the name of Paropanisus, and runs in an easterly direction, receiving in its course the waters of nineteen rivers. Of two islands, which it forms in its course, the one, which is known as Prasiane, is of very considerable size; the other, which is smaller, is called Pafale. According to the accounts given by the most moderate writers, this river is navigable for a distance of twelve hundred and fifty miles, and after following the sun's course to the west, in some degree, discharges itself into the ocean.

TAPROBANE

Taprobane (Ceylon), under the name of the "land of the Antichthones," was long looked upon as another world; the age and the arms of Alexander the Great were the first to give satisfactory proof that it is an island. Onesicritus, the commander of his fleet, has informed us that the elephants of this island are larger, and better adapted for warfare than those of India; and from Megasthenes we learn that it is divided by a river, that the inhabitants have the name of Palaeogoni, and that their country is more productive of gold and pearls of great size than even India. Eratosthenes has also given the dimensions of this island, as being seven thousand stadia in length, and five thousand in breadth; he states also that there are no cities, but villages to the number of seven hundred. The sea that lies between the island and the mainland is full of shallows, not more than six paces in depth; but in certain channels it is of such extraordinary depth, that no anchor has ever found a bottom. For this reason it is that the vessels are constructed with prows at either end; so that there may be no necessity for tacking while navigating these channels, which are extremely narrow. In traversing their seas, the people of Taprobane take no observations of the stars, and indeed the Greater Bear is not visible to them; but they carry birds out to sea, which they let go from time to time, and so follow their course as they make for the land.

Thus much we learn from the ancient writers; it has fallen to our lot, however, to obtain a still more accurate knowledge of these people; for during the reign of the Emperor Claudius, an embassy came from even this distant island to Rome. From these persons we learned that in Taprobane there are five hundred towns, and that there is a harbour that lies facing the south, and adjoining the city of Paltesimundus, the most famous city in the isle, the king's place of residence, and containing a population of two hundred thousand.

VOYAGES TO INDIA

But before we enter into any details respecting those countries, it will be as well to mention what Onesicritus has stated, who commanded the fleet of Alexander, and sailed from India into the heart of Persia, and what has been more recently related by Juba; after which I shall speak of the route along these seas which has been discovered in later years, and is followed at the present day. The journal of the voyage of Onesicritus and Nearchus has neither the names of the stations, nor yet the distances set down in it; and, first of all, it is not sufficiently explained where Xylenepolis was, and near what river, a place founded by Alexander, and from which, upon setting out, they took their departure. Still, however, the following places are mentioned by them, which are worthy of our notice. The town of Arbis,; the river Xabrus, navigable for vessels, and opposite to it an island, at a distance of seventy stadia; Alexandria, built by Leonnatus by order of Alexander in the territories of this people; Argenus, with a very convenient harbour; the river Tonberos, a navigable stream, around whose banks are the Pasiræ; then come the Ichthyophagi, who extend over so large a tract of coast that it took thirty days to sail past their territory; and an island known by the names of the "Island of the Sun" and the "Bed of the Nymphs," the earth of which is red, and in which every animal instantly dies; the cause of which, however, has not been ascertained. Next to these is the nation of the Ori, and then the Hyctanis, a river of Carmania, with an excellent harbour at its mouth, and producing gold.

They next came to the Promontory of Carmania.

Nearchus states in his writings that the coast of Carmania extends a distance of twelve hundred and fifty miles, from its frontier to the river Sabis is one hundred miles. This region is known by the name of Armuzia. The cities of Carmania are Zetis and Alexandria.

THE PERSIAN AND THE ARABIAN GULFS

The sea then makes a two-fold indentation in the land upon these coasts, under the name of Eubrum or "Red," given to it by our countrymen; while the Greeks have called it Erythrum, from king Erythras, or, according to some writers, from its red colour, which they think is produced by the reflection of the sun's rays; others again are of opinion that it arises from the sand and the complexion of the soil, others from some peculiarity in the nature of the water. Be this as it may, this body of water is divided into two gulfs. The one which lies to the east is called the Persian Gulf, and is two thousand five hundred miles in circumference, according to Eratosthenes. Opposite to it lies Arabia, the length of which is fifteen hundred miles. On the other side again, Arabia is bounded by the Arabian Gulf. The sea as it enters this gulf is called the Azanian Sea.

In the angle of Carmania are the Chelonophagi, who cover their cabins with the shells of turtles, and live upon their flesh; these people inhabit the next promontory that is seen after leaving the river Arbis with the exception of the head, they are covered all over with long hair, and are clothed in the skins of fishes.

Beyond their district, in the direction of India, is said to be the desert island of Caicandrus, near to which, with a strait flowing between them, is Stoidis, celebrated for its valuable pearls. After passing the promontory are the Armozei, joining up to the Carmani. Here is a place called Portus Macedonum, and the Altars of Alexander, situate on a promontory, besides the rivers Saganos, Baras, and Salsa. Beyond the last river we come to the promontory of Themisteas, and the island of Aphrodisias, which is peopled. Here Persis begins, at the river Oratis, which separates it from Elymais. Persis itself, looking towards the west, has a line of coast live hundred and fifty miles in length; it is a country opulent even to luxury, but has long since changed its name for that of "Parthia." I shall now devote a few words to the Parthian empire.

MESOPOTAMIA

The whole of Mesopotamia formerly belonged to the Assyrians, being covered with nothing but villages, with the exception of Babylonia[6] and Ninus.[7]

Babylon, the capital of the nations of Chaldæa, long enjoyed the greatest celebrity of all cities throughout the whole world; and it is from this place that the remaining parts of Mesopotamia and Assyria received the name of Babylonia. The circuit of its walls, which were two hundred feet in height, was sixty miles. These walls were also fifty feet in breadth, reckoning to every foot three fingers breadth beyond the ordinary measure of our foot. The river Euphrates flowed through the city, with quays of marvellous workmanship erected on either side. The temple

---

6   The great seat of empire of the Babylonio-Chaldæan kingdom. It either occupied the site, it is supposed, or stood in the immediate vicinity of the tower of Babel. In the reign of Labynedus, Nabonnetus, or Belshazzar, it was taken by Cyrus. In the reign of Augustus, a small part only of Babylon was still inhabited, the remainder of the space within the walls being under cultivation.

7   Nineveh.

there of Jupiter Belus is still in existence; he was the first inventor of the science of Astronomy. In all other respects it has been reduced to a desert, having been drained of its population in consequence of its vicinity to Seleucia, founded for that purpose by Nicator, at a distance of ninety miles, on the confluence of the Tigris and the canal that leads from the Euphrates. Seleucia, however, still bears the surname of Babylonia; it is a free and independent city, and retains the features of the Macedonian manners. It is said that the population of this city amounts to six hundred thousand, and that the outline of its walls resembles an eagle with expanded wings; its territory, they say, is the most fertile in all the East.

THE TIGRIS

There is, besides the above, another town in Mesopotamia, on the banks of the Tigris and near its confluence with the Euphrates, the name of which is Digba. But it will be as well now to give some particulars respecting the Tigris itself. This river rises in the region of Greater Armenia, from a very remarkable source, situate on a plain. The name of the spot is Elegosine, and the stream, as soon as it begins to flow, though with a slow current, has the name of Diglito. When its course becomes more rapid, it assumes the name of Tigris, given to it on account of its swiftness, that word signifying an arrow in the Median language. It then flows into Lake Arethusa, the waters of which are able to support all weighty substances thrown into them, and exhale nitrous vapours.

ARABIA

Arabia, inferior to no country throughout the whole world, is of immense extent, running downwards, from Mount Amanus, over against Cilicia and Commagne; many of the Arabian nations having been removed to those countries by Tigranes the Great, while others again have migrated of their own accord to the shores of our sea and the coast of Egypt. As for Arabia itself, it is a peninsula, running out between the Red and the Persian Seas; and it is by a kind of design, apparently on the part of nature, that it is surrounded by the sea in such a manner as to resemble very much the form and size of Italy, there being no difference either in the climate of the two countries, as they lie in the same latitudes. This, too, renders it equally fertile with the countries of Italy.

Ælius Gallus, a member of the Equestrian order, is the sole person who has hitherto carried the Roman arms into these lands. He brought back with him the following discoveries: that the Nomades live upon milk and the flesh of wild beasts, and that the other nations, like the Indians, extract a sort of wine from the palm-tree, and oil from sesame. He says that the most numerous of these tribes are the Homeritæ and the Minæi, that their lands are fruitful in palms and shrubs, and that their chief wealth is centred in their flocks. We also learn from the same source that the Cerbani and the Agraei excel in arms, but more particularly the Chatramotitæ; that the territories of the Carrei are the most extensive and most fertile; but that the Sabæi are the richest of all in the great abundance of their spice-bearing groves, their mines of gold, their streams for irrigation, and their ample produce of honey and wax.

The Arabs either wear the mitra,[8] or else go with their hair unshorn, while the beard is shaved, except upon the upper lip; some tribes, however, leave even the beard unshaved. A singular thing too, one half of these almost innumerable tribes live by the pursuits of commerce, the other half by rapine; take them all in all, they are the richest nations in the world, seeing that such vast wealth flows in upon them from both the Roman and the Parthian Empires; for they sell the produce of the sea or of their forests, while they purchase nothing whatever in return.

THE GULFS OF THE RED SEA

We will now trace the rest of the coast that lies opposite to that of Arabia. Timosthenes has estimated the length of the whole gulf at four days' sail, and the breadth at two, making the Straits to be seven miles and a half in width. Eratosthenes says that the length of the shore from the mouth of the gulf is thirteen hundred miles on each side, while Artemidorus states that the length on the Arabian side is seventeen hundred and fifty miles.

TROGLODYTICE

Troglodytice comes next, by the ancients called Midoë, and by some Michoë; here is Mount Pentedactylos, some islands called Stenæ Deiræ, the Halonnesi, a group of islands not less in number, Cardamine, and Topazos, which last has given its name to the precious stone so called. The gulf is full of islands.

After passing this place we come to the Azanian Sea, a promontory by some writers called Hispalus, Lake Mandalum, and the island of Colocasitis, with many others lying out in the main sea, upon which multitudes of turtles are found. We then come to the town of Suche, the island of Daphnidis, and the town of the Adulitæ, a place founded by Egyptian runaway slaves. This is the principal mart for the Troglodytæ, as also for the people of Æthiopia. To this place they bring ivory in large quantities, horns of the rhinoceros, hides of the hippopotamus, tortoise-shell, sphingiæ,[9] and slaves.

ÆTHIOPIA

The whole of this country has successively had the names of Ætheria, Atlantia, and last of all, Æthiopia, from Æthiops, the son of Vulcan. It is not at all surprising that towards the extremity of this region the men and animals assume a monstrous form, when we consider the changeableness and volubility of fire, the heat of which is the great agent in imparting various forms and shapes to bodies. Indeed, it is reported that in the interior, on the eastern side, there is a people that have no noses, the whole face presenting a plane surface; that others again are destitute of the upper lip, and others are without tongues. Others again, have the mouth grown together, and being destitute of nostrils, breathe through one passage only, imbibing their drink through it by means of the hollow stalk of the oat, which there

---

8 The "mitra," which was a head-dress especially used by the Phrygians, was probably of varied shape, and may have been the early form of the eastern turban.

9 These monkeys were much valued by the Roman ladies for pets, and very high prices were given for them.

grows spontaneously and supplies them with its grain for food. Some of these nations have to employ gestures by nodding the head and moving the limbs, instead of speech. Some writers have also stated that there is a nation of Pygmies, which dwells among the marshes in which the river Nile takes its rise; while on the coast of Æthiopia, where we paused, there is a range of mountains, of a red colour, which have the appearance of being always burning.

Bion makes mention also of some other towns situate on islands, the whole distance being twenty days' journey from Sembobitis to Meroë; a town in an adjoining island, under the queen of the Semberritæ, with another called Asara, and another, in a second island, called Darde. The name of a third island is Medoë, upon which is the town of Asel, and a fourth is called Garodes.

Beyond is the region of Sirbitum, at which the mountains terminate, and which by some writers is said to contain the maritime Æthiopians, the Nisacæthæ, and the Nisyti, a word which signifies "men with three or four eyes" —not that the people really have that conformation, but because they are remarkable for the unerring aim of their arrows. In a more westerly direction are the Nigroæ, whose king has only one eye, and that in the forehead, the Agriophagi, who live principally on the flesh of panthers and lions, the Pamphagi, who will eat anything, the Anthropophagi, who live on human flesh, the Cynamolgi, a people with the heads of dogs, the Artabatitæ, who have four feet, and wander about after the manner of wild beasts; and, after them, the Hesperiæ and the Perorsi. Some tribes, too, of the Æthiopians subsist on nothing but locusts, which are smoke-dried and salted as their provision for the year; these people do not live beyond their fortieth year.

Book VII

Man, his Birth, his Organization, and the Invention of the Arts

Such then is the present state of the world, and of the countries, nations, more remarkable seas, islands, and cities which it contains. The nature of the animated beings which exist upon it, is hardly in any degree less worthy of our contemplation than its other features; if, indeed, the human mind is able to embrace the whole of so diversified a subject. Our first attention is justly due to Man, for whose sake all other things appear to have been produced by Nature; though, on the other hand, with so great and so severe penalties for the enjoyment of her bounteous gifts, that it is far from easy to determine, whether she has proved to him a kind parent, or a merciless step-mother.

We have already given a general description of the human race in our account of the different nations. Nor, indeed, do I now propose to treat of their manners and customs, which are of infinite variety and almost as numerous as the various groups themselves, into which mankind is divided; but yet there are some things, which, I think, ought not to be omitted; and more particularly, in relation to those peoples which dwell at a considerable distance from the sea among which, I have no doubt, that some facts will appear of an astounding nature, and, indeed, incredible to many. Who, for instance, could ever believe in the existence of the Æthiopians, who had not first seen them? Indeed what is there that does not appear marvellous, when it comes to our knowledge for the first time how many things, too, are looked upon as quite impossible, until they have been actually effected But it is the fact, that every moment of our existence we are distrusting the power and the majesty of Nature, if the mind, instead of grasping her in her entirety, considers her only in detail. Not to speak of peacocks, the spotted skins of tigers and panthers, and the rich colours of so many animals, a trifling thing apparently to speak of, but of inestimable importance, when we give it due consideration, is the existence of so many languages among the various nations, so many modes of speech, so great a variety of expressions; that to another, a man who is of a different country, is almost the same as no man at all. And then, too, the human features and countenance, although composed of but some ten parts or little more, are so fashioned, that among so many thousands of men, there are no two in existence who cannot be distinguished from one another, a result which no art could possibly have produced, when confined to so limited a number of combinations.

THE WONDERFUL FORMS OF DIFFERENT NATIONS

I have previously mentioned, a nation remarkable for having but one eye, and that placed in the middle of the forehead. This race is said to carry on a perpetual warfare with the Griffins, a kind of monster, with wings, as they are commonly[1] represented, for the gold which they dig out of the mines, and which these wild beasts retain and keep watch over with a singular degree of cupidity, while the Arimaspi are equally desirous to get possession of it.

The Anthropophagi, whom we have previously mentioned, were in the habit of drinking out of human skulls, and placing the scalps, with the hair attached, upon their breasts, like so many napkins. The same author relates, that there is, in Albania, a certain race of men, whose eyes are of a sea-green colour, and who have white hair from their earliest childhood, and that these people see better in the night than in the day.

Crates of Pergamus relates, that there formerly existed in the vicinity of Parium, in the Hellespont, a race of men whom he calls Ophiogenes, and that by their touch they were able to cure those who had been stung by serpents, extracting the poison by the mere imposition of the hand. Varro tells us, that there are still a few individuals in that district, whose saliva effectually cures the stings of serpents. The same, too, was the case with the tribe of the Psylli, in Africa. In the bodies of these people there was by nature a certain kind of poison, which was fatal to serpents, and the odour of which overpowered them with torpor; with them it was a custom to expose children immediately after their birth to the fiercest serpents, and in this manner to make proof of the fidelity of their wives, the serpents not being repelled by such children as were the offspring of adultery.

Above the Nasamones, and the Machlyæ, who border upon them, are found, as we learn from Calliphanes, the nation of the Androgyni, a people who unite the two sexes in the same individual, and alternately perform the functions of each. Aristotle also states, that their right breast is that of a male, the left that of a female.

There are among the Triballi and the Illyrii, some persons of this description, who also have the power of fascination with the eyes, and can even kill those on

---

1 The figures of the Gryphons, Griffons or Griffins are found not uncommonly on the friezes and walls at Pompeii (See Book X, Fabulous birds). In the East, where there were no safe places of deposit for money, it was the custom to bury it in the earth; hence, for the purpose of scaring depredators, the story was carefully circulated that hidden treasures were guarded by serpents and dragons.

whom they fix their gaze for any length of time, more especially if their look denotes anger; the age of puberty is said to be particularly obnoxious to the malign influence of such persons.

A still more remarkable circumstance is, the fact that these persons have two pupils in each eye. Apollonides says, that there are certain females of this description in Scythia, who are known as Bythiæ, and Phylarchus states that a tribe of the Thibii in Pontus, and many other persons as well, have a double pupil in one eye, and in the other the figure of a horse. He also remarks, that the bodies of these persons will not sink in water, even though weighed down by their garments.

India, and the region of Æthiopia more especially, abounds in wonders. It is a well-known fact, that many of the people here never expectorate, are subject to no pains, either in the head, the teeth, or the eyes, and rarely in any other parts of the body; so well is the heat of the sun calculated to strengthen the constitution. Their philosophers, who are called Gymnosophists, remain in one posture, with their eyes immovably fixed upon the sun, from its rising to its setting, and, during the whole of the day, they are accustomed to stand in the burning sands on one foot, first one and then the other.

There is a tribe of men who have the heads of dogs, and clothe themselves with the skins of wild beasts. Instead of speaking, they bark; and, furnished with claws, they live by hunting and catching birds. According to the story, as given by Ctesias, the number of these people is more than a hundred and twenty thousand; and the same author tells us, that there is a certain race in India, of which the females are pregnant once only in the course of their lives, and that the hair of the children becomes white the instant they are born. He speaks also of another race of men, who are known as Monoeoli, who have only one leg, but are able to leap with surprising agility.

Among the mountainous districts of the eastern parts of India, in what is called the country of the Catharéludi, we find the Satyr, an animal of extraordinary swiftness. These go sometimes on four feet, and sometimes walk erect; they have also the features of a human being. On account of their swiftness, these creatures are never to be caught, except when they are either aged or sickly.

Megasthenes places among the Nomades of India, a people who are called Scyritæ. These have merely holes in their faces instead of nostrils, and flexible feet, like the body of the serpent. At the very extremity of India, on the eastern side, near the source of the river Ganges, there is the nation of the Astomi, a people who have no mouths; their bodies are rough and hairy, and they cover themselves with a down plucked from the leaves of trees. These people subsist only by breathing and by the odours which they inhale through the nostrils. They support themselves upon neither meat nor drink; when they go upon a long journey they only carry with them various odoriferous roots and flowers, and wild apples, that they may not be without something to smell at. But an odour, which is a little more powerful than usual, easily destroys them.

Artemidorus states that in the island of Taprobane (Ceylon), life is prolonged to an extreme length, while, at the same time, the body is exempt from weakness. According to Durisis, some of the Indians have connection with beasts, and from this union a mixture of half man, half beast, is produced. Among the Calingæ, a nation also of India, the women conceive at five years of age, and do not live beyond their eighth year. In other places again, there are men born with long hairy tails, and of remarkable swiftness of foot; while there are others that have ears so large as to cover the whole body.

MARVELLOUS BIRTHS

That three children are sometimes produced at one birth, is a well-known fact; the case, for instance, of the Horatii and the Curiatii. Where a greater number of children than this is produced at one birth, it is looked upon as portentous, except, indeed, in Egypt, where the water of the river Nile, which is used for drink, is a promoter of fecundity. Very recently, towards the close of the reign of the Emperor Augustus, now deified, a certain woman of the lower orders, at Ostia, whose name was Fausta, brought into the world, at one birth, two male children and two females, a presage, no doubt, of the famine which shortly after took place.

Individuals are occasionally born, who belong to both sexes; such persons we call by the name of hermaphrodites; they were formerly called Androgyni, and were looked upon as monsters, but at the present day they are employed for sensual purposes.

The change of females into males is undoubtedly no fable. We find it stated in the Annals, that, in the consulship of P. Licinius Crassus and C. Cassius Longinus, a girl, who was living at Casinum with her parents, was changed into a boy. Licinius Mucianus informs us that he once saw at Argos a person whose name was then Arescon, though he had been formerly called Arescusa; that this person had been married to a man, but that, shortly after, a beard and marks of virility made their appearance, upon which he took to himself a wife. He had also seen a boy at Smyrna, to whom the very same thing had happened. I myself saw in Africa one L. Cossicius, a citizen of Thysdris, who had been changed into a man the very day on which he was married to a husband.

THE GENERATION OF MAN

In other animals the period of gestation and of birth is fixed and definite, While man, on the other hand, is born at all seasons of the year, and without any certain period of gestation for one child is born at the seventh month, another at the eighth, and so on, even to the beginning of the tenth and eleventh.

On the tenth day after conception, pains are felt in the head, vertigo, and dimness of the sight; these signs, together with loathing of food and rising of the stomach, indicate the formation of the future human being. If it is a male that is conceived, the colour of the pregnant woman is more healthy, and the birth less painful; the child moves in the womb upon the fortieth day. In the conception of a child of the other sex, all the symptoms are totally different; the mother experiences an almost insupportable weight, there is a slight swelling of the legs and the groin, and the first movement of the child is not felt until the ninetieth day. But, whatever the sex of the child, the mother is sensible of the greatest languor at the time when the hair of the foetus first begins to grow, and at the full moon; at which latter time it is that children newly born are exposed to the greatest danger. In addition to this, the mode of walking, and indeed everything that can be mentioned, is of consequence in the case of a woman who is pregnant. Thus, for instance, women who have used too much salted meat will bring forth children without nails; parturition, too, is more difficult, if they do not hold their breath. It is fatal, too, to yawn during labour and abortion ensues, if the female should happen to sneeze just after the sexual congress.

STRIKING INSTANCES OF RESEMBLANCE

It is universally known that well-formed parents often produce defective children; and on the other hand, defective parents children who are well formed, or else imperfect in the same part of the body as the parents. It is a well-known fact also, that marks, moles, and even scars, are reproduced in members of the same family in successive generations. The mark which the Daci make on their arms for the purpose of denoting their origin, is known to last even to the fourth generation.

We have heard it stated that three members of the family of the Lepidi have been born, though not in an uninterrupted succession, with one of the eyes covered with a membrane. We observe, too, that some children strongly resemble their grandfather, and that of twins one child is like the father, while the other resembles the mother; and have known cases where a child that was born a year after another, resembled him as exactly as though they had been twins.

These strong features of resemblance proceed, no doubt, from the imagination of the parents, over which we may reasonably believe that many casual circumstances have a very powerful influence; such, for instance, as the action of the eyes, the ears, or the memory, or impressions received at the moment of conception. A thought even, momentarily passing through the mind of either of the parents, may he supposed to produce a resemblance to one of them separately, or else to the two combined. Hence it is that the varieties are much more numerous in the appearance of man than in that of other animals; seeing that, in the former, the rapidity of the ideas, the quickness of the perception, and the varied powers of the intellect, tend to impress upon the features peculiar and diversified marks; while in the case of the other animals, the mind is immovable, and just the same in each and all individuals of the same species.

There exists a kind of peculiar antipathy between the bodies of certain persons, which, though barren with respect to each other, are not so when united to others such, for instance, was the case with Augustus and Livia. Certain individuals, again, both men and women, produce only females, others males; and, still more frequently, children of the two sexes alternately; the mother of the Gracchi, for instance, who had twelve children, and Agrippina, the mother of Germanicus, who had nine. Some women, again, are barren in their youth, while to others it is given to bring forth once only during their lives. Some women never go to their full time, or if, by dint of great care and the aid of medicine, they do give birth to a living child, it is mostly a girl.

Women cease to bear children at their fiftieth year, and, with the greater part of them, the monthly discharge ceases at the age of forty. But with respect to the male sex, it is a well-known fact, that King Masinissa, when he was past his eighty-sixth year, had a son born to him, whom he named Metimanus, and that Cato the Censor, after he had completed his eightieth year, had a son by the daughter of his client, Salonius.

REMARKABLE CIRCUMSTANCES CONNECTED WITH THE MENSTRUAL DISCHARGE

Among the whole range of animated beings, the human female is the only one that has the monthly discharge, and in whose womb are found what we term "moles."[2] These moles consist of a shapeless mass of flesh, devoid of all life, and capable of resisting either the edge or the point of the knife; they are movable in the body, and obstruct the menstrual discharge; sometimes, too, they are productive of fatal consequences to the woman, in the same manner as a real foetus while, at other times, they remain in the body until old age; in some cases, again, they are discharged, in consequence of an increased action of the bowels. Something of a very similar nature is produced in the body of the male, which is called a "schirrus"; this was the case with Oppius Capito, a man of praetorian rank.

It would indeed be a difficult matter to find anything which is productive of more marvellous effects than the menstrual discharge. On the approach of a woman in this state, must will become sour, seeds which are touched by her become sterile, grafts wither away, garden plants are parched up, and the fruit will fall from the tree beneath which she sits. Her very look, even, will dim the brightness of mirrors, blunt the edge of steel, and take away the polish from ivory. A swarm of bees, if looked upon by her, wHl die immediately; brass and iron will instantly become rusty, and emit an offensive odour; while dogs which may have tasted of the matter so discharged are seized with madness, and their bite is venomous and incurable.

SOME ACCOUNT OF THE TEETH, AND SOME FACTS CONCERNING INFANTS

It is a matter beyond doubt, that in young children the front teeth are produced at the seventh month, and, nearly always, those in the upper jaw the first. These are shed in the seventh year, and are then replaced by others. Some infants are even born with teeth; such was the case with Manius Curius, who, from this circumstance, received the name of Dentatus. When this phenomenon happened in the case of a female, it was looked upon in the time of the kings as an omen of some inauspicious event. At the birth of Valeria, under such circumstances as these, it was the answer of the soothsayers, that any city to which she might happen to be carried, would be destroyed; she was sent to Suessa Pometia, at that time a very flourishing place, but the prediction was ultimately verified by its destruc-

---

2   A somewhat shapeless, compact fleshy mass occurring in the uterus, either due to the retention and continued life of the whole or a part of the fetal envelops after the death of the fetus (a maternal or true mole), or being some other body liable to be mistaken for this, as the membrane in membranous dysmenorrhea, or perhaps a polypus (a false mole) (TN).

tion. Some female children are born with the sexual organs closed, a thing of very unfavourable omen; of which Cornelia, the mother of the Gracchi, is an instance.

In addition to this, it is generally supposed that we may form prognostics from the teeth. The number of teeth allotted to all men, with the exception of the nation of the Turduli, is thirty-two; those persons who have a greater number, are thought to be destined to be long-lived. Women have fewer teeth than men. Those females who happen to have two canine teeth on the right side of the upper jaw, have promise of being the favourites of fortune, as was the case with Agrippina, the mother of Domitius Nero; when they are on the left side, it is just the contrary.

We find it stated that Zoroaster was the only human being who ever laughed on the same day on which he was born. We hear, too, that his brain pulsated so strongly that it repelled the hand when laid upon it, a presage of his future wisdom.

EXAMPLES OF UNUSUAL SIZE

It is a well-known fact, that, at the age of three years, the body of each person is half the height that it will ever attain. Taking it all in all, it is observed that in the human race, the stature is almost daily becoming less and less, and that sons are rarely taller than their parents, the fertility of the seed being dried up by the heat of that conflagration to which the world is fast approaching.[3] A mountain of the island of Crete having been burst asunder by the action of an earthquake, a body was found there standing upright, forty-six cubits in height;[4] by some persons it is supposed to have been that of Orion while others again are of opinion that it was that of Otus. It is generally believed, from what is stated in ancient records, that the body of Orestes, which was disinterred by command of an oracle, was seven cubits in height. It is now nearly one thousand years ago, that that divine poet Homer was unceasingly complaining, that men were of less stature in his day than they had formerly been.

INSTANCES OF EXTRAORDINARY STRENGTH, AGILITY, SIGHT AND MEMORY

Varro, speaking of persons remarkable for their strength, gives us an account of Tributanus, a celebrated gladiator, and skilled in the use of the Samnite arms;[5] he was a man of meagre person, but possessed of extraordinary strength. Vinnius Valens, who served as a centurion in the prætorian guard of Augustus, was in the habit of holding up waggons laden with casks, until they were emptied; and of stopping a carriage with one hand, and holding it back, against all the efforts of the horses to drag it forward. Varro, also, gives the following statement: "Fusius, who used to be called the 'bumpkin Hercules,' was in the habit of carrying his

---

3   It was one of the tenets of the Stoics, that the world was to be alternately destroyed by water and by fire. The former element having laid it waste on the occasion of the flood of Deucalion, the next great catastrophe, according to them, is to be produced by fire. Pliny has previously alluded to this opinion.

4   The Roman cubit was 1½ Roman feet, or 17.4 English inches. 46 cubits = 66 feet or 20 m.

5   The gladiators, called Samnites, were armed with the peculiar "scutum," or oblong shield, used by the Samnites, a greave on the left leg, a sponger on the breast, and a helmet with a crest.

own mule; while Salvius was able to mount a ladder, with a weight of two hundred pounds attached to his feet, the same to his hands, and two hundred pounds on each shoulder."

It was considered a very great thing for Philippides to run one thousand one hundred and sixty stadia,[6] the distance between Athens and Lacedaemon, in two days, until Amystis, the Lacedaemonian courier, and Philonides, the courier of Alexander the Great, ran from Sicyon to Elis in one day, a distance of thirteen hundred and five stadia.[7]

Instances of acuteness of sight are to be found stated, which, indeed, exceed all belief. Cicero informs us, that the Iliad of Homer was written on a piece of parchment so small as to be enclosed in a nut-shell. He makes mention also of a man who could distinguish objects at a distance of one hundred and thirty-five miles. Callicrates used to carve ants and other small animals in ivory, so minute in size, that other persons were unable to distinguish their individual parts.

It would be far from easy to pronounce what person has been the most remarkable for the excellence of his memory, that blessing so essential for the enjoyment of life, there having been so many who have been celebrated for it. King Cyrus knew all the soldiers of his army by name. L. Scipio the names of all the Roman people. Cineas, the ambassador of king Pyrrhus, knew by name all the members of the senate and the equestrian order, the day after his arrival at Rome, Mithridates, who was king of twenty-two nations, administered their laws in as many languages, and could harangue each of them, without employing an interpreter. There was in Greece a man named Charmidas, who, when a person asked him for any book in a library, could repeat it by heart, just as though he were reading.

VIGOUR OF MIND

The most remarkable instance, I think, of vigour of mind in any man ever born, was that of Cæsar, the Dictator. I am not at present alluding to his valour and courage, nor yet his exulted genius, which was capable of embracing everything under the face of heaven, but I am speaking of that innate vigour of mind, which was so peculiar to him, and that promptness which seemed to act like a flash of lightning. We find it stated that he was able to write or read, and, at the same time, to dictate and listen. He could dictate to his secretaries four letters at once, and those on the most important business; and, indeed, if he was busy about nothing else, as many as seven.

HEROIC EXPLOITS

But now, as it belongs fully as much to the glorious renown of the Roman Empire, as to the victorious career of a single individual, I shall proceed on this occasion to make mention of all the triumphs and titles of Pompeius Magnus; the splendour of his exploits having equalled not only that of those of Alexander the

---

6   132 miles o 213 km.
7   150 miles or 240 km.

Great, but even of Hercules, and perhaps of Father Liber[8] even. After having recovered Sicily, where he first commenced his career as a partizan of Sylla, but in behalf of the republic, after having conquered the whole of Africa, and reduced it to subjection, and after having received for his share of the spoil the title of "Great," he was decreed the honours of a triumph; although he was only of equestrian rank, a thing that had never occurred before. After having put an end to the civil war, which indeed was the primary cause of all the foreign ones, he, though still of only equestrian rank, again entered Home in the triumphal chariot, having proved himself a general thus often before having been a soldier, After this, he was dispatched to the shores of all the various seas, and then to the East.

The most glorious, however, of all glories, resulting from these exploits, was, as he himself says, in the speech which he made in public relative to his previous career, that Asia, which he received as the boundary of the empire, he left its centre. If any one should wish, on the other hand, in a similar manner, to pass in review the exploits of Cæsar, who has shown himself greater still than Pompeius, why then he must enumerate all the countries in the world, a task, I may say, without an end.

INSTANCES OF EXTREME COURAGE

A minute enquiry by whom the greatest valour has ever been exhibited, would lead to an endless discussion, more especially if all the fables of the poets are to be taken for granted. L. Siccius Dentatus, who was tribune of the people in the consulship of Spurius Tarpeius and A. Aterius, has very numerous testimonies in his favour. This hero fought one hundred and twenty battles, was eight times victorious in single combat, and was graced with forty-five wounds in the front of the body, without one on the back. The same man also carried off thirty-four spoils,[9] was eighteen times presented with the victor's spear,[10] and received twenty-five pendants,[11] eighty-three tores,[12] one hundred and sixty bracelets, twenty-six crowns, (of which fourteen were civic, eight golden, three mural, and one obsidional), a fisc[13] of money, ten prisoners, and twenty oxen altogether.

The military honours of Manlius Capitolinus would have been no less splendid than his, if they had not been all effaced at the close of his life. Before his seven-

---

8   "Father Liber" is one of the names of Bacchus.
9   When a Roman overcame an enemy with whom he had been personally engaged, he took possession of some part of his armour and dress, which might bear testimony to the victory; this was termed the "spolium."
10 "Hasta pura"; these words, according to Hardouin, signify a lance without an iron head. We are told that it was given to him who gained the first victory in a battle; it was also regarded as an emblem of supreme power, and as a mark of the authority which one nation claimed over another.
11 "Phaleris." These were bosses, discs or crescents of metal, sometimes gold. They were mostly used in pairs, and as ornaments for the helmet; but we more commonly read of them as attached to the harness of horses.
12 Golden "armillæ," or bracelets, were worn by the Gauls on the arms and the legs. The Sabines also wore them on the left arm, at the time of the foundation of Rome.
13 The word "fiscus" signifies a wicker basket or pannier, probably of peculiar construction, in which the Romans were accustomed to keep and carry about large sums of money.

teenth year, he had gained two spoils, and was the first of equestrian rank who received a mural crown; he also gained six civic crowns, thirty- seven donations, and had twenty-three scars on the fore-part of his body. He saved the life of P. Servilius, the master of the horse, receiving wounds on the same occasion in the shoulders and the thigh. Besides all this, unaided, he saved the Capitol, when it was attacked by the Gauls, and through that, the state itself; a thing that would have been the most glorious act of all, if he had not so saved it, in order that he might, as its king, become its master. But in all matters of this nature, although valour may effect much, fortune does still more.

MEN OF REMARKABLE GENIUS AND WISDOM

Among so many different pursuits, and so great a variety of works and objects, who can select the palm of glory for transcendent genius? Unless perchance we should agree in opinion that no more brilliant genius ever existed than the Greek poet Homer, whether it is that we regard the happy subject of his work, or the excellence of its execution. For this reason it was that Alexander the Great —and it is only by judges of such high estate that a sentence, just and unbiassed by envy, can be pronounced in the case of such lofty claims— when he found among the spoils of Darius, the king of Persia, a casket for perfumes, enriched with gold, precious stones, and pearls, covered as he was with the dust of battle, deemed it beneath a warrior to make use of unguents, and, when his friends were pointing out to him its various uses, exclaimed, "Nay, but by Hercules! let the casket be used for preserving the poems of Homer".

Apollo impeached by name the assassins of the poet Archilochus at Delphi. While the Lacedemonians were besieguig Athens, Father Liber ordered the funeral rites to be performed for Sophocles, the very prince of the tragic buskin; repeatedly warning their king, Lysander, in his sleep, to allow of the burial of his favourite. Upon this, the king made enquiry who had lately died in Athens; and understanding without any difficulty from the Athenians to whom the god referred, he allowed the funeral rites to be performed without molestation.

MEN WHO HAVE BEEN REMARKABLE FOR WISDOM

Dionysius the tyrant, who otherwise manifested a natural propensity for cruelty and pride, sent a vessel crowned with garlands to meet Plato, that high-priest of wisdom; and on his disembarcation, received him on the shore, in a chariot drawn by four white horses. Isocrates was able to sell a single oration of his for twenty talents. Æschines, the great Athenian orator, after he had read to the Ehodians the speech which he had made on the accusation of Demosthenes, read the defence made by Demosthenes, through which he had been driven into exile among them. When they expressed their admiration of it, "How much more," said he, "would you have admired it, if you had heard him deliver it himself"; a striking testimony, indeed, given in adversity, to the merit of an enemy!

Also the nobles of Rome have given their testimonies in favour of foreigners, even Cn. Pompeius, after having finished the war against Mithridates, when he went to call at the house of Posidonius, the famous teacher of philosophy, forbade

Book VII - Man, his Birth, his Organization...

the lictor to knock at the door, as was the usual custom and he, to whom both the eastern and the western world had yielded submission, ordered the fasces to be lowered before the door of a learned man. Cato the Censor, after he had heard the speech of Cameades, who was one of the embassy sent from Athens, of three men famous for their learning, gave it as his opinion, that the ambassadors ought to be dismissed as soon as possible, because, in consequence of his ingenious method of arguing, it became extremely difficult to distinguish truth from falsehood.

M. Varro[14] is the only person, who, during his lifetime, saw his own statue erected. This was placed in the first public library that was ever built, and which was formed by Asinius Pollio with the spoils of our enemies. The fact of this distinction being conferred upon him by one who was in the first rank, both as an orator and a citizen, and at a time, too, when there was so great a number of men distinguished for their genius, was not less honourable to him, in my opinion, than the naval crown which Pompeius Magnus bestowed upon him in the war against the pirates.

INSTANCES OF THE HIGHEST DEGREE OF AFFECTION

Infinite is the number of examples of affection which have been known in all parts of the world; but one in particular occurred at Rome, to which no other can possibly be compared. A woman of quite the lower class, and whose name has consequently not come down to us, having lately given birth to a child, obtained permission to visit her mother, who was confined in prison; but was always carefully searched by the gaoler before being admitted, to prevent her from introducing any food. At last, however, she was detected nourishing her mother with the milk of her breast; upon which, in consideration of the marvellous affection of the daughter, the mother was pardoned, and they were both maintained for the rest of their days at the public charge; the spot, too, was consecrated to Piety, a temple to that goddess being built on the site of the prison, in the consulship of C. Quintius and M. Acilius, where the theatre of Marcellus now stands.

The father of the Gracchi, on finding (two) serpents in his house, consulted the soothsayers, and received an answer to the effect, that he would survive if the serpent of the other sex was put to death. —"No," said he, "rather kill the serpent of my own sex, for Cornelia is still young, and may yet bear children." Thus did he shew himself ready, at the same moment, to spare his wife and to benefit the state; and shortly after, his wish was accomplished.

TEN VERY FORTUNATE CIRCUMSTANCES WHICH HAVE HAPPENED TO THE SAME PERSON

Q. Metellus, in the funeral oration which he made in praise of his father, L. Metellus, who had been pontiff, twice consul, dictator, master of the horse, one of the quindecemvirs for dividing the lands, and the first who had elephants in his triumphal procession, the same having been taken in the first Punic war, has left it written to the effect that his father had attained the ten greatest and best things, in the search after which wise men have spent all their lives. For, as he states, he was

---

14 M. Varro, the philosopher, sometimes called "the most learned" of the Romans.

anxious to become the first warrior, the best orator, the bravest general, that the most important of all business should be entrusted to his charge, that he should enjoy the very highest honours, that he should possess consummate wisdom, that he should be regarded as the most distinguished senator, that he should by honourable means acquire a large fortune, that he should leave behind him many children, and that he should be the most illustrious person in the state.

The son also, of the same Q. Metellus, who has given the above account of his father, is considered himself to have been one of the rarest instances of human felicity. For, in addition to the very considerable honours which he obtained, and the surname which he acquired from the conquest of Macedonia, he was carried to the funeral pile by his four sons, one of whom had been prætor, three of them consuls, two had obtained triumphs, and one had been censor; each of which honours falls to the lot of a very few only. And yet, in the very full-blown pride of his dignity, as he was returning from the Campus Martius at mid-day when the Forum and the Capitol are deserted, he was seized by the tribune, Caius Atinius Labeo, whom, during his censorship, he had ejected from the senate, and was dragged by him to the Tarpeian rock, for the purpose of being precipitated therefrom. The numerous band, however, who called him by the name of father, flew to his assistance, though tardily, and only just, as it were, at the very last moment, to attend his funeral obsequies, seeing that he could not lawfully offer resistance, or repel force by force in the sacred case of a tribune; and he was just on the very point of perishing, the victim of his virtues and the strictness of his censorship, when he was saved by the intervention of another tribune —only obtained with the greatest difficulty—, and so rescued from the very jaws of death. He afterwards had to subsist on the bounty of others, his property having been consecrated[15] by the very man whom he had degraded; and who, as if that had not satiated his vengeance, still farther wreaked his malice upon him, by throwing a rope around his neck, and twisting it with such extreme violence that the blood flowed from out of his ears.

THE GREATEST LENGTH OF LIFE

Not only the differences of climate, but the multitude of instances named, and the peculiar destiny attached to each of us from the moment of his birth, tend to render one very uncertain in forming any general conclusion respecting the length and duration of human life. Hesiod, who was the first to make mention of this subject, while he states many circumstances about the age of man, which appear to me to be fabulous, gives to the crow nine times the ordinary duration of our life, to the stag four times the length of that of the crow, to the raven three times the length of that of the stag, besides other particulars with reference to the phoenix

---

15   Cicero, in his oration "Pro Lomo sua," sec. 47, refers to the consecration of the property of Metellus, as a case analogous to that of his own house, which had been similarly consecrated by Clodius. It seems to have been the custom, when a person had been capitally condemned, for the tribune of the people to consecrate his property, with certain formalities, to some god or goddess; after which it could not, under ordinary circumstances, be recovered, whether the sentence was revoked or not. Cicero had been capitally condemned through the instrumentality of Clodius, and obliged to fly from Rome.

and the Nymphs of a still more fabulous nature. The poet Anacreon gives one hundred and fifty years to Arganthonius, the king of the Tartessii; ten more to Cinaras, the king of Cyprus, and two hundred to Ægimius. Theopompus gives one hundred and fifty-three years to Epimenides of Cnossus; according to Hellenicus, some of the nation of the Epii, in Ætolia, have completed their two hundredth year; and his account is confirmed by Damastes, who relates that Pictoreus, one of this nation, who was remarkable for his size and strength, lived even to his three hundredth year.

Let us proceed, however, to what is admitted to be true. It is pretty nearly certain, that Arganthonius of Gades reigned eighty years, and he is supposed to have commenced his reign when be was forty. Masinissa, beyond a doubt, reigned sixty years, and Gorgias, the Sicilian, lived one hundred and eight.

Among women also, Livia, the wife of Rutilius, exceeded her ninety-sixth year; during the reign of Claudius, Statilia, a member of a noble family, died at the age of ninety-nine; Terentia, the wife of Cicero, lived one hundred and three years, and Clodia, the wife of Ofilius, one hundred and fifteen; she had fifteen children.

THE VARIETY OF DESTINIES AT THE BIRTH OF MAN

The present conjuncture would appear to demand from me some opinion upon the science of the stars. Epigenes used to maintain that human life could not be possibly prolonged to one hundred and twelve years, and Berosus that it could exceed one hundred and seventeen. The system is still in existence which Petosiris and Necepsos transmitted to us, and called by them "tartemorion," from the division of the signs into four portions; from which it would appear, that life, in the region of Italy, may possibly be extended to one hundred and twenty-four years. They maintain that, reckoning from the commencement of an ascending sign, no life can possibly exceed a period of ninety degrees from that point; which periods they call by the name of "anaphoræ"; they say also, that these anaphoræ may be intercepted by meeting With malign stars or their rays even, or those of the sun. To theirs the school of Æsculapius succeeded, which admits that the allotted duration of life is regulated by the stars, but that it is quite uncertain what is the greatest extent of the period. These say that long life is uncommon, because a very great number of persons are born at critical moments in the hours of the lunar days; for example, in the seventh and the fifteenth hours, both by day and night; these individuals are subject to the malign influence of that ascending scale of the years which is termed the "climacteric," and never hardly, when born under these circumstances, exceed the fifty-fourth year.

DEATH

And now to speak of the premonitory signs of death. Among these are laughter, in madness; in cases of delirium, the patient carefully folding the fringe or the plaits of the bed-clothes; insensibility to the attempts of those who would rouse them from sleep; and involuntary discharges from the body, which it is not necessary here to particularize; but the most unequivocal signs of all, are certain appearances of the eyes and the nose, a lying posture with the face continually upwards, an irregular and feeble motion of the pulse, and the other symptoms, which have been observed by that prince of physicians, Hippocrates. At the same time that there are innumerable signs of death, there are none of health and safety; so much so, that Cato the Censor, when speaking to his son in relation to those who appear to be in good health, declared, as though it had been the enunciation of some oracle, that precocity in youth is a sign of an early death.

PERSONS WHO HAVE COME TO LIFE AGAIN AFTER BEING LAID OUT FOR BURIAL

Aviola, a man of consular rank, came to life again when on the funeral pile; but, reason of the violence of the flames, no assistance could be rendered him, in consequence of which he was burnt alive. The same thing is said to have happened to L. Lamia, a man of praetorian rank. Messala, Rufus, and many other authors, inform us, that C. Ælius Tubero, who had filled the office of praetor, was also rescued from the funeral pile. Such then is the condition of us mortals; to these and the like vicissitudes of fortune are we born; so much so, that we cannot be sure of any thing, no, not even that a person is dead. With reference to the soul of man, we find, among other instances, that the soul of Hermotinus of Clazomenae was in the habit of leaving his body, and wandering into distant countries, whence it brought back numerous accounts of various things, which could not have been obtained by any one but a person who was present. The body, in the meantime, was left apparently lifeless. At last, however, his enemies, the Cantharidae, as they were called, burned the body, so that the soul, on its return, was deprived of its sheath, as it were.

BURIAL

The burning of the body after death, among the Romans, is not a very ancient usage; for formerly, they interred it. After it had been ascertained, however, in the foreign wars, that bodies which had been buried were sometimes disinterred, the custom of burning them was adopted. Many families, however, still observed the ancient rites, as, for example, the Cornelian family, no member of which had his body burnt before Sylla, the Dictator; who directed this to be done, because, having previously disinterred the dead body of Caius Marius, he was afraid that others might retaliate on his own. The term "sepultus" applies to any mode whatever of disposing of the dead body; while, on the other hand, the word "humatus" is applicable solely when it is deposited in the earth.

THE MANES, OR DEPARTED SPIRITS OF THE SOUL

After burial come the different quiddities as to the existence of the Manes.[16] All men, after their last day, return to what they were before the first; and after

---

16 In Roman antiquity, the spirits of the dead were considered as tutelary divinities of their families; the deified shades of the dead, according to the belief that the soul continued to exist and to have relations with earth after the body had perished. Three times a year a pit called the mundus was officially opened in the comitium of the Roman Forum, to permit the manes to come forth. The manes were also honoured at certain festivals, as the Parentalia and Feralia; oblations were made to them, and the flame maintained on the altar of the household was a homage to them (TN.)

death there is no more sensation left in the body or in the soul than there was before birth. But this same vanity of ours extends even to the future, and lyingly fashions to itself an existence even in the very moments which belong to death itself; at one time it has conferred upon us the immortality of the soul; at another transmigration; and at another it has given sensation to the shades below, and paid divine honours to the departed spirit, thus making a kind of deity of him who has but just ceased to be a man. As if, indeed, the mode of breathing with man was in any way different from that of other animals, and as if there were not many other animals to be found whose life is longer than that of man, and yet for whom no one ever presaged anything of a like immortality. For what is the actual substance of the soul, when taken by itself? Of what material does it consist? Where is the seat of its thoughts? How is it to see, or hear, or how to touch? And then, of what use is it, or what can it avail, if it has not these faculties? Where, too, is its residence, and what vast multitudes of these souls and spirits must there be after the lapse of so many ages? But all these are the mere figments of childish ravings, and of that mortality which is so anxious never to cease to exist. It is a similar piece of vanity, too, to preserve the dead bodies of men; just like the promise that he shall come to life again, which was made by Democritus; who, however, never has come to life again himself. Out upon it! What downright madness is it to suppose that life is to recommence after death! or indeed, what repose are we ever to enjoy when we have been once born, if the soul is to retain its consciousness in heaven, and the shades of the dead in the infernal regions? This pleasing delusion, and this credulity, quite cancel that chief good of human nature, death, and, as it were, double the misery of him who is about to die, by anxiety as to what is to happen to him after it. And, indeed, if life really is a good, to whom can it be so to have once lived?

How much more easy, then, and how much more devoid of all doubts, is it for each of us to put his trust in himself, and guided by our knowledge of what our state has been before birth, to assume that after death will be the same.

THE INVENTORS OF VARIOUS THINGS

Before we quit the consideration of the nature of man, it appears only proper to point out those persons who have been the authors of different inventions. Father Liber was the first to establish the practice of buying and selling; he also invented the diadem, the emblem of royalty, and the triumphal procession. Ceres introduced corn, the acorn having been previously used by man for food; it was she, also, who introduced into Attica the art of grinding corn and of making bread, and other similar arts into Sicily; and it was from these circumstances that she came to be regarded as a divinity. She was the first also to establish laws though, according to some, it was Rhadamanthus. I have always been of opinion, that letters were of Assyrian origin, but other writers, Gellius, for instance, suppose that they were invented in Egypt by Mercury; others, again, will have it that they were discovered by the Syrians; and that Cadmus brought from Phœnicia sixteen letters into Greece. To these, Palamedes, it is said, at the time of the Trojan war, added these four, Θ, Ξ,

Φ, and Χ. Simonides, the lyric poet, afterwards added a like number, Ζ, Η, Ψ, and Ω; the sounds denoted by all of which are now received into our alphabet.

Aristotle, on the other hand, is rather of opinion, that there were originally eighteen letters, Α Β Γ Δ Ε Ζ Ι Κ Λ Ν Ο Π Ρ Σ Τ Υ Φ, and that two, Θ namely and Χ, were introduced by Epicharmus, and not by Palamedes. Aristides says, that a certain person of the name of Menos, in Egypt, invented letters fifteen years before the reign of Phoroneus, the most ancient of all the kings of Greece, and this he attempts to prove by the monuments there. On the other hand, Epigenes, a writer of very great authority, informs us that the Babylonians have a series of observations on the stars, for a period of seven hundred and twenty thousand years, inscribed on baked bricks. Berosus and Critodemus, who make the period the shortest, give it as four hundred and ninety thousand years. From this statement, it would appear that letters have been in use from all eternity. The Pelasgi were the first to introduce them into Latium.

The Egyptians were the first who established a monarchical government, and the Athenians, after the time of Theseus, a democracy. Phalaris, of Agrigentum, was the first tyrant that existed; the Lacedæmonians were the introducers of slavery; and the first capital punishment inflicted was ordered by the Areiopagus. The first battles were fought by the Africans against the Egyptians, with clubs, which they are in the habit of calling phalangæ. Prœtus and Acrisius were the first to use shields, in their contests with each other; or, as some say, Chalcus, the son of Athamas. Midias, the Messenian, invented the coat of mail, and the Lacedæmonians the helmet, the sword, and the spear. Greaves and crests were first used by the Carians; Scythes, the son of Jupiter, it is said, invented the bow and arrows, though some say that arrows were invented by Perses, the son of Perseus. Lances were invented by the Ætolians; the javelin, with the thong attached, by Ætolus

The art of divination by means of birds we owe to Car, from whom Caria derives its name; Orpheus extended it to other animals. Delphus taught us the art of divining by the inspection of entrails; Amphiaraüs divination by fire; and Tiresias, the Theban, presages from the entrails of birds. We owe to Amphictyon the interpretation of portents and of dreams, and to Atlas, the son of Libya, the art of astrology, or else, according to other accounts, to the Egyptians or the Assyrians. Anaximander, the Milesian, invented the astronomical sphere; and Æolus, the son of Hellen, gave us the theory of the winds.

We are indebted to the Phœnicians for the first observation of the stars in navigation; the Copæ invented the oar, and the Platæans gave it its broad blade. Icarus was the person who invented sails, and Daedalus the mast and yards; the Samians, or else Pericles, the Athenian, transports for horses, and the Thracians, long covered vessels — before which time they used to fight only from the prow or the stern. Pisæus, the Tyrrhenian, added the beak to ships; Eupalaraus, the anchor; Anacharsis, that with two flukes; Pericles, the Athenian, grappling-irons, and hooks like hands; and Tiphys, the helm and rudder. Minos was the first who waged war by means of ships; Hyperbius, the son of Mars, the first who killed an animal; and Prometheus, the first who slew the ox.

WHEN THE FIRST TIMEPIECES WERE MADE

The third point of universal agreement was the division of time, a subject which afterwards appealed to the reasoning faculties. This art was first invented in Greece; the same was also introduced at Rome, but at a later period. In the Twelve Tables, the rising and setting of the sun are the only things that are mentioned relative to time. Some years afterwards, the hour of midday was added, the summoner of the consuls proclaiming it aloud, as soon as, from the senate-house, he caught sight of the sun between the Rostra and the Græeostasis he also proclaimed the last hour, when the sun had gone down from the Mænian column to the prison. This, however, could only be done in clear weather, but it was continued until the first Punic war. The first sun-dial is said to have been erected among the Romans twelve years before the war with Pyrrhus, by L. Papirius Cursor, at the temple of Quirinus, on which occasion he dedicated it in pursuance of a vow which had been made by his father. This is the account given by Fabius Vestalis; but he makes no mention of either the construction of the dial or the artist, nor does he inform us from what place it was brought, or in whose works he found this statement made.

M. Varro says that the first sun-dial, erected for the use of the public, was fixed upon a column near the Rostra, in the time of the first Punic war, by the consul M. Valerius Messala, and that it was brought from the capture of Catina, in Sicily: this being thirty years after the date assigned to the dial of Papirius, and the year of Rome 491. The lines in this dial did not exactly agree with the hours it served, however, as the regulator of the Roman time ninety-nine years, until Q. Marcius Philippus, who was censor with L. Paulus, placed one near it, which was more carefully arranged; an act which was most gratefully acknowledged, as one of the very best of his censorship. The hours, however, still remained a matter of uncertainty, whenever the weather happened to be cloudy, until the ensuing lustrum;[17] at which time Scipio Nasica, the colleague of Lsenas, by means of a clepsydra, was the first to divide the hours of the day and the night into equal parts; and this time-piece he placed under cover and dedicated, in the year of Rome 595 for so long a period had the Romans remained without any exact division of the day. We will now return to the history of the other animals, and first to that of the terrestrial.

---

17 A lustrum was a term for a five-year period in Ancient Rome (TN).

BOOK VIII
The Nature of the Terrestrial Animals

ELEPHANTS

Let us now pass on to the other animals, and first of all to the land animals. The elephant is the largest of them all, and in intelligence approaches the nearest to man. It understands the language of its country, it obeys commands, and it remembers all the duties which it has been taught. It is sensible alike of the pleasures of love and glory, and, to a degree that is rare among men even, possesses notions of honesty, prudence, and equity; it has a religious respect also for the stars, and a veneration for the sun and the moon. It is said by some authors, that, at the first appearance of the new moon, herds of these animals come down from the forests of Mauritania to a river, the name of which is Amilo; and that they there purify themselves in solemn form by sprinkling their bodies with water; after which, having thus saluted the heavenly body, they return to the woods, carrying before them the young ones which are fatigued. They are supposed to have a notion, too, of the differences of religion and when about to cross the sea, they cannot be prevailed upon to go on board the ship, until their keeper has promised upon oath that they shall return home again. They have been seen, too, when worn out by disease, (for even these vast masses are liable to disease,) lying on their back, and throwing the grass up into the air, as if deputing the earth to intercede for them with its prayers. As a proof of their extreme docility, they pay homage to the king, fall upon their knees, and offer him the crown.

The first harnessed elephants that were seen at Rome, were in the triumph of Pompeius Magnus over Africa, when they drew his chariot. In the exhibition of gladiators which was given by Germanicus, the elephants performed a sort of dance with their uncouth and irregular movements. It was a common thing to see them throw arrows with such strength, that the wind was unable to turn them from their course, to imitate among themselves the combats of the gladiators, and to frolic through the steps of the Pyrrhic dance.

It is a well-known fact, that one of these animals, who was slower than usual in learning what was taught him, and had been frequently chastised with blows, was found conning over his lesson in the night-time. Mutianus, who was three times consul, informs us that one of these animals had been taught to trace the Greek letters, and that he used to write in that language the following words: "I have myself written these words, and have dedicated the Celtic spoils." Mutianus states also, that he himself was witness to the fact, that when some elephants were being landed at Puteoli and were compelled to leave the ship, being terrified at the length of the platform, which extended from the vessel to the shore, they walked backwards, in order to deceive themselves by forming a false estimate of the distance.

THE INSTINCT OF WILD ANIMALS IN PERCEIVING DANGER

It is a wonderful thing, that most animals are aware why it is that they are sought after, and what it is, that, under all circumstances, they have to guard against. When an elephant happens to meet a man in the desert, who is merely wandering about, the animal, it is said, shows himself both merciful and kind, and even points out the way. But the very same animal, if he meets with the traces of a man, before he meets the man himself, trembles in every limb, for fear of an ambush, stops short and scents the wind, looks around him, and snorts aloud with rage; and then, without trampling upon the object, digs it up, and passes it to the next one, who again passes it to the one that follows, and so on from one to the other, till it comes to the very last. The herd then faces about, returns, and ranges itself in order of battle; so strongly does the odour, in all cases, attach itself to the human footstep, even though, as is most frequently the case, the foot itself is not naked. In the same way, too, the tigress, which is the dread of the other wild beasts, and which sees, without alarm, the traces even of the elephant itself, is said at once, upon seeing the footsteps of man, to carry off her whelps.

Elephants always move in herds. The oldest takes the lead, and the next in age brings up the rear. When they are crossing a river, they first send over the smallest, for fear lest the weight of the larger ones may increase the depth of the channel, by working away the bed of the river. We learn from Antipater, that King Antiochus had two elephants, which he employed in his wars, and to which he had given the names of celebrated men; and that they were aware too of this mark of distinction.

These animals are sensible to feelings of modesty; they never couple but in secret the male alter it has attained its fifth year, the female after the age of ten. It is said, that their intercourse takes place only every second year, and for five days only, and no more; on the sixth day they plunge into a river, before doing which they will not rejoin the herd. Adulterous intercourse is unknown to them, and they have none of those deadly combats for the possession of the female, which take place among the other animals.

THE COMBATS OF ELEPHANTS

There is a famous combat mentioned of a Roman with an elephant, when Hannibal compelled our prisoners to fight against each other. The one who had survived all the others he placed before an elephant, and promised him his life if he should slay it; upon which the man advanced alone into the arena, and, to the great regret of the Carthaginians, succeeded in doing so. Hannibal, however, thinking that the news of this victory might cause a feeling of contempt for these animals, sent some horsemen to kill the man on his way home. In our battles with Pyrrhus it was found, on making trial, that it was extremely easy to cut off the trunks of these animals.

In the second consulship of Pompeius, at the dedication of the temple of Venus Victrix, twenty elephants, or, as some say, seventeen, fought in the Circus against a number of Gætulians, who attacked them with javelins. One of these animals fought in a most astonishing manner; being pierced through the feet, it dragged itself on its knees towards the troop, and seizing their bucklers, tossed them aloft into the air: and as they came to the ground they greatly amused the spectators, for they whirled round and round in the air, just as if they had been thrown up with a certain degree of skill, and not by the frantic fury of a wild beast.

The elephant is said to display such a merciful disposition towards animals that are weaker than itself, that, when it finds itself in a flock of sheep, it will remove with its trunk those that are in the way, lest it should unintentionally trample upon them. They will never do any mischief except when provoked, and they are of a disposition so sociable, that they always move about in herds, no animal being less fond of a solitary life. When surrounded by a troop of horsemen, they place in the centre of the herd those that are weak, weary, or wounded, and then take the front rank each in its turn, just as though they acted under command and in accordance with discipline. When taken captive, they are very speedily tamed, by being fed on the juices of barley.

THE WAY IN WHICH ELEPHANTS ARE CAUGHT

In India they are caught by the keeper guiding one of the tame elephants towards a wild one which he has found alone or has separated from the herd; upon which he beats it, and when it is fatigued mounts and manages it just the same way as the other. In Africa they take them in pit-falls; but as soon as an elephant gets into one, the others immediately collect boughs of trees and pile up heaps of earth, so as to form a mound, and then endeavour with all their might to drag it out. It was formerly the practice to tame them by driving the herds with horsemen into a narrow defile, artificially made in such a way as to deceive them by its length; and when thus enclosed by means of steep banks and trenches, they were rendered tame by the effects of hunger; as a proof of which, they would quietly take a branch that was extended to them by one of the men. At the present day, when we take them for the sake of their tusks, we throw darts at their feet, which are in general the most tender part of their body. The Troglodytæ, who inhabit the confines of Æthiopia, and who live entirely on the flesh of elephants procured by the chase, climb the trees which lie near the paths through which these animals usually pass. Here they keep a watch, and look out for the one which comes last in the train; leaping down upon its haunches, they seize its tail with the left hand, and fix their feet firmly upon the left thigh. Hanging down in this manner, the man, with his right hand, hamstrings the animal on one side, with a very sharp hatchet. The elephant's pace being retarded by the wound, he cuts the tendons of the other ham, and then makes his escape; all of which is done with the very greatest celerity.

IN WHAT COUNTRIES THE ELEPHANT IS FOUND; THE ANTIPATHY OF THE ELEPHANT AND THE DRAGON

Africa produces elephants, beyond the deserts of the Syrtes, and in Mauritania; they are found also in the countries of the Æthiopians and the Troglodytæ, as mentioned above. But it is India that produces the largest, as well as the dragon,[1] which is perpetually at war with the elephant, and is itself of so enormous a size, as easily to envelope the elephants with its folds, and encircle them in its coils. The contest is equally fatal to both; the elephant, vanquished, falls to the earth, and by its weight, crushes the dragon which is entwined around it.

The sagacity which every animal exhibits in its own behalf is wonderful, but in these it is remarkably so. The dragon has much difficulty in climbing up to so great a height, and therefore, watching the road, which bears marks of their footsteps when going to feed, it darts down upon them from a lofty tree. The elephant knows that it is quite unable to struggle against the folds of the serpent, and so seeks for trees or rocks against which to rub itself. The dragon is on its guard against this, and tries to prevent it, by first of all confining the legs of the elephant with the folds of its tail; while the elephant, on the other hand, endeavours to disengage itself with its trunk. The dragon, however, thrusts its head into its nostrils, and thus, at the same moment, stops the breath and wounds the most tender parts. When it is met unexpectedly, the dragon raises itself up, faces its opponent, and flies more especially at the eyes; this is the reason why elephants are so often found blind, and worn to a skeleton with hunger and misery.

There is another story, too, told in relation to these combats; the blood of the elephant, it is said, is remarkably cold; for which reason, in the parching heats of summer, it is sought by the dragon with remarkable avidity. It lies, therefore, coiled up and concealed in the rivers, in wait for the elephants, when they come to drink; upon which it darts out, fastens itself around the trunk, and then fixes its teeth behind the ear, that being the only place which the elephant cannot protect with the trunk. The dragons, it is said, are of such vast size, that they can swallow the whole of the blood; consequently, the elephant, being thus drained of its blood, falls to the earth exhausted; while the dragon, intoxicated with the draught, is crushed beneath it, and so shares its fate.

---

1   By the term "dragon," we may suppose that Pliny refers to some of the great serpents which exist in hot climates, and are of such vast size, that they might perhaps be able to perform some of the exploits here ascribed to the dragon.

BOOK VIII - THE NATURE OF THE TERRESTRIAL ANIMALS

DRAGONS/SERPENTS

Æthiopia produces dragons, not so large as those of India, but still, twenty cubits in length. The Æthiopians are known as the Asachæi, among whom they most abound; and we are told, that on those coasts four or five of them are found twisted and interlaced together like so many osiers in a hurdle, and thus setting sail, with their heads erect, they are borne along upon the waves, to find better sources of nourishment in Arabia.

Megasthenes informs us, that in India, serpents grow to such an immense size, as to swallow stags and bulls; while Metrodorus says, that about the river Rhyndacus, in Pontus, they seize and swallow the birds that are flying above them, however high and however rapid their flight. It is a well-known fact, that during the Punic war, at the river Bagrada, a serpent one hundred and twenty feet in length was taken by the Roman army under Regulus, being besieged, like a fortress, by means of balistæ and other engines of war. The serpents which in Italy are known by the name of boa, render these accounts far from incredible, for they grow to such a vast size, that a child was found entire in the stomach of one of them, which was killed on the Vaticanian Hill during the reign of the Emperor Claudius. These are nourished, in the first instance, with the milk of the cow, and from this they take their name.

LIONS

The noble appearance of the lion is more especially to be seen in that species which has the neck and shoulders covered with a mane, which is always acquired at the proper age by those produced from a lion; while, on the other hand, those that are the offspring of the leopard, are always without this distinction. The female also has no mane. The sexual passions of these animals are very violent, and render the male quite furious. This is especially the case in Africa, where, in consequence of the great scarcity of water, the wild beasts assemble in great numbers on the banks of a few rivers. This is also the reason why so many curious varieties of animals are produced there, the males and females of various species coupling promiscuously with each other. Hence arose the saying, which was common in Greece even, that "Africa is always producing something new." The lion recognizes, by the peculiar odour of the leopard, when the lioness has been unfaithful to him, and avenges himself with the greatest fury. Hence it is, that the female, when she has been guilty of a lapse, washes herself, or else follows the lion at a considerable distance.

There are two species of lions; in the one the body is shorter and more compact, and the mane more crisp and curly; these are more timid than those with a longer body and straight hair, which, in fact, have no fear of wounds. They swallow their food whole, without mastication, so far as they are able; and when they have taken more than the stomach can possibly receive, they extract part of it by thrusting their claws into the throat; the same too, if, when full, they have occasion to take to flight. Polybius tells us, that when they become aged they will attack men, as they have no longer sufficient strength for the pursuit of wild beasts. It is then that they lay siege to the cities of Africa; and for this reason it was, that he, as well as

Scipio, had seen some of them hung upon a cross; it being supposed that others, through dread of a similar punishment, might be deterred from committing the like outrages.

COMBATS OF LIONS AT ROME

Q. Scævola, when he was curule ædile, was the first to exhibit at Rome a combat of a number of lions; and L. Sylla, who was afterwards Dictator, during his prætorship, gave the spectacle of a fight of one hundred lions with manes. Alter him, Pompeius Magnus exhibited six hundred lions in the Circus, three hundred and fifteen of which had manes; Cæsar, the Dictator, exhibited four hundred.

WONDERFUL FEATS PERFORMED BY LIONS

It was formerly a very difficult matter to catch the lion, and it was mostly done by means of pit-falls. In the reign, however, of the Emperor Claudius, accident disclosed a method which appears almost disgraceful to the name of such an animal; a Gætulian shepherd stopped a lion, that was rushing furiously upon him, by merely throwing his cloak over the animal; a circumstance which afterwards afforded an exhibition in the arena of the Circus, when the frantic fury of the animal was paralyzed in a manner almost incredible by a light covering being thrown over its head, so much so, that it was put into chains without the least resistance; we must conclude, therefore, that all its strength lies in its eyes.

Anthony subjected lions to the yoke, and was the first at Home to harness them to his chariot and this during the civil war, after the battle on the plains of Pharsalia; not, indeed, without a kind of ominous presage, a prodigy that foretold at the time how that generous spirits were about to be subdued. Mentor, a native of Syracuse, was met in Syria by a lion, who rolled before him in a suppliant manner; though smitten with fear and desirous to escape, the wild beast on every side opposed his flight, and licked his feet with a fawning air. Upon this. Mentor observed on the paw of the lion a swelling and a wound; from which, after extracting a splinter, he relieved the creature's pain. There is a picture at Syracuse, which bears witness to the truth of this transaction.

In the same manner, too, Elpis, a native of Samos, on landing from a vessel on the coast of Africa, observed a lion near the beach, opening his mouth in a threatening manner; upon which he climbed a tree, in the hope of escaping, while, at the same time, he invoked the aid of Father Liber; for it is the appropriate time for invocations when there is no room left for hope. The wild beast did not pursue him as he fled, although he might easily have done so; but, lying down at the foot of the tree, by the open mouth which had caused so much terror, tried to excite his compassion. A bone, while he was devouring his food with too great avidity, had stuck fast between his teeth, and he was perishing with hunger; such being the punishment inflicted upon him by his own weapons, every now and then he would look up and supplicate him, as it were, with mute entreaties. Elpis, not wishing to risk trusting himself to so formidable a beast, remained stationary for some time, more at last from astonishment than from fear. At length, however, he descended from the tree and extracted the bone, the lion in the meanwhile extending his head, and aiding in the operation as far as it was necessary for him to do. The story goes on to say, that as long as the vessel remained off that coast, the lion showed his sense of gratitude by bringing whatever he had chanced to procure in the chase.

TIGERS

The late Emperor Augustus was the first person who exhibited at Rome a tame tiger on the stage. This was in the consulship of Q. Tubero and Fabius Maximus, at the dedication of the theatre of Marcellus, on the fourth day before the nones of May; the late Emperor Claudius exhibited four at one time.

Hyrcania and India produce the tiger, an animal of tremendous swiftness, a quality which is more especially tested when we deprive it of all its whelps, which are always very numerous. They are seized by the hunter, who lies in wait for them, being provided with the fleetest horse he can possibly obtain, and which he frequently changes for a fresh one. As soon as the female finds her lair empty —for the male takes no care whatever of his offspring— headlong she darts forth, and traces them by the smell. Her approach is made known by her cries, upon which the hunter throws down one of the whelps; this she snatches up with her teeth, and more swift, even, under the weight, returns to her lair, and then again sets out in pursuit; and this she continues to do, until the hunter has reached his vessel, while the animal vainly vents her fury upon the shore.

WILD BEASTS THAT KILL WITH ITS EYES

Among the Hesperian Æthiopians is the fountain of Nigris, by many, supposed to be the head of the Nile. Near this fountain, there is found a wild beast, which is called the catoblepas; an animal of moderate size, and in other respects sluggish in the movement of the rest of its limbs; its head is remarkably heavy, and it only

carries it with the greatest difficulty, being always bent down towards the earth. Were it not for this circumstance, it would prove the destruction of the human race; for all who behold its eyes, fall dead upon the spot.

There is the same power also in the serpent called the basilisk. It is produced in the province of Cyrene, being not more than twelve fingers in length. It has a white spot on the head, strongly resembling a sort of a diadem. When it hisses, all the other serpents fly from it; and it does not advance its body, like the others, by a succession of folds, but moves along upright and erect upon the middle. It destroys all shrubs, not only by its contact, but those even that it has breathed upon; it burns up all the grass too, and breaks the stones, so tremendous is its noxious influence. It was formerly a general belief that if a man on horseback killed one of these animals with a spear, the poison would run up the weapon and kill, not only the rider, but the horse as well. To this dreadful monster the effluvium of the weasel is fatal, a thing that has been tried with success, for kings have often desired to see its body when killed; so true is it that it has pleased Nature that there should be nothing without its antidote. The weasel is thrown into the hole of the basilisk, which is easily known from the soil around it being infected. The weasel destroys the basilisk by its odour, but dies itself in this struggle of nature against its own self.

In Italy also it is believed that there is a noxious influence in the eye of the wolf; it is supposed that it will instantly take away the voice of a man, if it is the first to see him.

CAMELS

Camels are found feeding in herds in the East. Of these there are two different kinds, those of Bactria and those of Arabia; the former kind having two humps on the back, and the latter only one; they have also another hump under the breast, by means of which they support themselves when reclining. Both of these species, like the ox, have no teeth in the upper jaw. They are all of them employed as beasts of burthen, in carrying loads on the back, and they answer the purpose of cavalry in battle. Their speed is the same with that of the horse, but their power of holding out in this respect is proportioned in each to its natural strength; it will never go beyond its accustomed distance, nor will it receive more than its usual load. The camel has a natural antipathy to the horse. It can endure thirst for four days even, and when it has the opportunity of obtaining water, it drinks, as it were, both for past and future thirst, having first taken care to trouble the water by trampling in it; without doing which, it would find no pleasure in drinking. They live fifty years, some indeed as much as one hundred. These animals, too, are liable to fits of frenzy. A peculiar mode of castrating them, and the females, even, when required for the purposes of war, has been discovered; it renders them more courageous, by the destruction of all sexual feelings.

THE RHINOCEROS

The rhinoceros has a single horn projecting from the nose. This is another natural-born enemy of the elephant.[2] It prepares itself for the combat by sharpening its horn against the rocks; and in fighting directs it chiefly against the belly of its adversary, which it knows to be the softest part. The two animals are of equal length, but the legs of the rhinoceros are much the shorter; its skin is the colour of box-wood.

WEREWOLF

That men have been turned into wolves, and again restored to their original form, we must confidently look upon as untrue. But, as the belief of it has become

---

2   The other enemy is the dragon, as described before in the present Book.

Book VIII - The Nature of the Terrestrial Animals

so firmly fixed in the minds of the common people, as to have caused the term "Versipellis"[3] to be used as a common form of imprecation, I will here point out its origin. Euanthes, a Grecian author of no mean reputation, informs us that the Arcadians assert that a member of the family of one Anthus is chosen by lot, and then taken to a certain lake in that district, where, after suspending his clothes on an oak, he swims across the water and goes away into the desert, where he is changed into a wolf and associates with other animals of the same species for a space of nine years. If he has kept himself from beholding a man during the whole of that time, he returns to the same lake, and, after swimming across it, resumes his original form, only with the addition of nine years in age to his former appearance.

Agriopas, who wrote an account of the victories gained at the Olympic games, informs us that Demænetus, the Parrhasian, during a sacrifice of human victims, which the Arcadians were offering up to the Lycæan Jupiter, tasted the entrails of a boy who had been slaughtered; upon which he was turned into a wolf, but, ten years afterwards, was restored to his original shape and his calling of an athlete, and returned victorious in the pugilistic contests at the Olympic games.

THE LYNX, THE SPHINX, THE CROCOTTA, AND THE MONKEY

Æthiopia produces the lynx in abundance, and the sphinx, which has brown hair and two mammæ on the breast, as well as many monstrous kinds of a similar nature; horses with wings, and armed with horns, which are called pegasi;[4] the crocotta, an animal which looks as though it had been produced by the union of the wolf and the dog, for it can break any thing with its teeth, and instantly on swallowing it digest it with the stomach; monkeys, too, with black heads, the hair of the ass, and a voice quite unlike that of any other animal. There are oxen, too, like those of India, some with one horn, and others with three; the leucrocotta,[5] a wild beast of extraordinary swiftness, the size of the wild ass, with the legs of a stag, the neck, tail, and breast of a lion, the head of a badger, a cloven hoof, the mouth slit up as far as the ears, and one continuous bone instead of teeth; it is said, too, that this animal can imitate the human voice.

Ctesias informs us, that among these same Æthiopians, there is an animal found, which he calls the mantichora; it has a triple row of teeth, which fit into each other like those of a comb, the face and ears of a man, and azure eyes, is of the colour of blood, has the body of the lion, and a tail ending in a sting, like that of the scorpion. Its voice resembles the union of the

---

3   Shape-changer, who can metamorphose to different shape (TN).

4   The pegasus and the rhinoceros together may have given rise to that fabulous animal, the unicorn.

5   The leucrocotta is a mythic animal who has the ability to imitate the voices of men to lure prey.

sound of the flute and the trumpet; it is of excessive swiftness, and is particularly fond of human flesh.

ABOUT SERPENTS

With reference to serpents, it is generally known, that they assume the colour of the soil in which they conceal themselves. The different species of them are innumerable. The cerastes has little horns, often four in number, projecting from the body, by the movement of which it attracts birds, while the rest of its body lies concealed. The amphisbæna has two heads, that is to say, it has a second one at the tail, as though one mouth were too little for the discharge of all its venom. Some serpents have scales, some a mottled skin, and they are all possessed of a deadly poison. The jaculus darts from the branches of trees; and it is not only to our feet that the serpent is formidable, for these fly through the air even, just as though they were hurled from an engine. The neck of the asp putts out, and there is no remedy whatever against its sting, except the instant excision of the affected part. This reptile, which is thus deadly, is possessed of this one sense, or rather affection; the male and the female are generally found together, and the one cannot live without the other; hence it is that, if one of them happens to be killed, the other takes incredible pains to avenge its death. It follows the slayer of its mate, and will single him out among ever such a large number of people, by a sort of instinctive knowledge; with this object it overcomes all difficulties, travels any distance, and is only to be avoided by the intervention of rivers or an accelerated flight. It is really difficult to decide, whether Nature has altogether been more liberal of good or of evil. First of all, however, she has given to this pest but weak powers of sight, and has placed the eyes, not in the front of the head, so that it may see straight before it, but in the temples, so that it is more frequently put in motion by the approach of the footstep than through the sight.

THE HIPPOPOTAMUS

The Nile produces the hippopotamus, another wild beast, of a still greater size. It has the cloven hoof of the ox; the back, the mane, and the neighing of the horse; and the turned-up snout, the tail, and the hooked teeth of the wild boar, but is not so dangerous. The hide is impenetrable, except when it has been soaked with water; and it is used for making shields and helmets. This animal lays waste the standing corn, and determines beforehand what part it shall ravage on the following day; it is said also, that it enters the field backwards, to prevent any ambush being laid for it on its return.

Book VIII - The Nature of the Terrestrial Animals

PROGNOSTICS OF DANGER DERIVED FROM ANIMALS

The same Nature has also bestowed upon many animals as well, the faculty of observing the heavens, and of presaging the winds, rains, and tempests, each in its own peculiar way. It would be an endless labour to enumerate them all; just as much as it would be to point out the relation of each to man. For, in fact, they warn us of danger, not only by their fibres and their entrails, to which a large portion of mankind attach the greatest faith, but by other kinds of warnings as well. When a building is about to fall down, all the mice desert it before-hand, and the spiders with their webs are the first to drop. Divination from birds has been made a science among the Romans, and the college of its priests is looked upon as peculiarly sacred. In Thrace, when all parts are covered with ice, the foxes are consulted, an animal which, in other respects, is baneful from its craftiness. It has been observed, that this animal applies its ear to the ice, for the purpose of testing its thickness; hence it is, that the inhabitants will never cross frozen rivers and lakes until the foxes have passed over them and returned.

AMPHIBIOUS ANIMALS

The beavers of the Euxine, when they are closely pressed by danger, themselves cut off the same part, as they know that it is for this that they are pursued. This substance is called castoreum by the physicians. In addition to this, the bite of this animal is terrible; with its teeth it can cut down trees on the banks of rivers, just as though with a knife. If they seize a man by any part of his body, they will never loose their hold until his bones are broken and crackle under their teeth. The tail is like that of a fish in the other parts of the body they resemble the otter; they are both of them aquatic animals, and both have hair softer than down.

The seal, too, lives equally in the sea and on land, being possessed of the same degree of intelligence as the beaver. It vomits forth its gall, which is useful for many purposes in medicine; also the rennet, which serves as a remedy in epilepsy; for it is well aware that it is hunted for these substances. Theophrastus informs us, that lizards also cast their skins like the serpent, and instantly devour them, thus depriving us of a powerful remedy for epilepsy; he says, too, that the bite of the lizard is fatal in Greece, but harmless in Italy.

STAGS

Stags, although the most mild of all animals, have still their own feelings of malignancy; when hard pressed by the hounds, of their own accord they fly for refuge to man; and when the females bring forth, they are less anxious to avoid the paths which bear traces of human footsteps, than solitary spots which offer a retreat to wild beasts. They become pregnant after the rising of the constellation Arcturus; they bring forth after a gestation of eight months, and sometimes produce two young ones. They separate after conception, but the males, upon being thus abandoned, become maddened with the fury of their passion; they dig up the earth, and their muzzles become quite black, until they have been washed by the rain.

Stags cross the sea in herds, swimming in a long line, the head of each resting on the haunches of the one that precedes it, each in its turn falling back to the rear.

This has been particularly remarked when they pass over from Cilicia to the island of Cyprus. Though they do not see the land, they still are able to direct themselves by the smell.

THE CHAMELEON

Africa is almost the only country that does not produce the stag, but then it produces the chameleon, although it is much more commonly met with in India. Its figure and size are that of a lizard, only that its legs are straight and longer. Its sides unite under its belly, as in fishes, and its spine projects in a similar manner. Its muzzle is not unlike the snout of a small hog, so far as in so small an animal it can be. Its tail is very long, and becomes smaller towards the end, coiling up in folds like that of the viper. It has hooked claws, and a slow movement like that of the tortoise; its body is rough like that of the crocodile; its eyes are deep sunk in the orbits, placed very near each other, very large, and of the same colour as the body. It never closes them, and when the animal looks round, it does so, not by the motion of the pupil, but of the white of the eye. It always holds the head upright and the mouth open, and is the only animal which receives nourishment neither by meat nor drink, nor anything else, but from the air alone. Towards the end of the dog-days it is fierce, but at other times quite harmless. The nature of its colour, too, is very remarkable, for it is continually changing; its eyes, its tail, and its whole body always assuming the colour of whatever object is nearest, with the exception of white and red. After death, it becomes of a pale colour. It has a little flesh about the head, the jaws, and the root of the tail, but none whatever on the rest of the body. It has no blood whatever, except in the heart and about the eyes, and its entrails are without a spleen. It conceals itself during the winter months, just like the lizard.

BEARS

Bears couple in the beginning of winter, and not after the fashion of other quadrupeds; for both animals lie down and embrace each other. The female then retires by herself to a separate den, and there brings forth on the thirtieth day, mostly five young ones. When first born, they are shapeless masses of white flesh, a little larger than mice their claws alone being prominent. The mother then licks them gradually into proper shape. There is nothing more uncommon than to see a she-bear in the act of parturition. The male remains in his retreat for forty days, the female four months. If they happen to have no den, they construct a retreat with branches and shrubs, which is made impenetrable to the rain and is lined with soft leaves. During the first fourteen days they are overcome by so deep a sleep, that they cannot be aroused by wounds even. They become wonderfully fat, too, while in this lethargic state. This fat is much used in medicine; and it is very useful in preventing the hair from falling off. At the end of these fourteen days they sit up, and find nourishment by sucking their fore-paws.

The head of the bear is extremely weak, whereas, in the lion, it is remarkable for its strength; on which account it is, that when the bear, impelled by any alarm, is about to precipitate itself from a rock, it covers its head with its paws. In the arena of the Circus they are often to be seen killed by a blow on the head with the fist. The people of Spain have a belief, that there is some kind of magical poison in the brain of the bear, and therefore burn the heads of those that have been killed in their public games; for it is averred, that the brain, when mixed with drink, produces in man the rage of the bear.

HEDGEHOGS

Hedgehogs also lay up food for the winter; rolling themselves on apples as they lie on the ground, they pierce one with their quills, and then take up another in the mouth, and so carry them into the hollows of trees. These animals also, when they conceal themselves in their holes, afford a sure sign that the wind is about to change from north-east to south. When they perceive the approach of the hunter, they draw in the head and feet, and all the lower part of the body, which is covered by a thin and defenceless down only, and then roll themselves up into the form of a ball, so that there is no way of taking hold of them but by their quills. When they are reduced to a state of desperation, they discharge a corrosive urine, which injures their skin and quills, as they are aware that it is for the sake of them that they are hunted.

THE DOG

Among the animals, also, that are domesticated with mankind, there are many circumstances that are far from undeserving of being known; among these, there are more particularly that most faithful friend of man, the dog, and the horse. We have an account of a dog that fought against a band of robbers, in defending its master; and although it was pierced with wounds, still it would not leave the body, from which it drove away all birds and beasts. Another dog, again, in Epirus, recognized the murderer of its master, in the midst of an assemblage of people, and, by biting and barking at him, extorted from him a confession of his crime. A king of the Garamantes also was brought back from exile by two hundred dogs, which maintained the combat against all his opponents. The people of Colophon and Castabala kept troops of dogs, for the purposes of war; and these used to fight in the front rank, and never retreat; they were the most faithful of auxiliaries, and yet required no pay. After the defeat of the Cimbri, their dogs defended their moveable houses, which were carried upon wagons. Jason, the Lycian, having been slain, his dog refused to take food, and died of famine. A dog, to which Darius gives the name of Hyrcanus, upon the funeral pile of King Lysimachus being lighted, threw itself into the flames, and the dog of King Hiero did the same. Philistus also gives a similar account of Pyrrhus, the dog of the tyrant Gelon; and it is said, also, that the dog of Nicomedes, king of Bithynia, tore Consingis, the wife of that king, in consequence of her wanton behaviour, when toying with her husband.

Dogs are the only animals that are sure to know their masters; and if they suddenly meet him as a stranger, they will instantly recognize him. They are the only animals that will answer to their names, and recognize the voices of the family. They recollect a road along which they have passed, however long it may be. Next to man, there is no living creature whose memory is so retentive. By sitting down on the ground, we may arrest their most impetuous attack, even when prompted by the most violent rage.

In daily life we have discovered many other valuable qualities in this animal; but its intelligence and sagacity are more especially shown in the chase. It discovers and traces out the tracks of the animal, leading by the leash the sportsman who accompanies it straight up to the prey; and as soon as ever it has perceived it, how silent it is, and how secret but significant is the indication which it gives, first by the tail and afterwards by the nose! Hence it is, that even when worn out with old age, blind, and feeble, they are carried by the huntsman in his arms, being still able to point out the coverts where the game is concealed, by snuffing with their muzzles at the wind. The Indians raise a breed between the dog and the tiger, and for this purpose tie up the females in the forests when in heat. The first two litters they look upon as too savage to be reared, but they bring up the third.

The Gauls do the same with the wolf and the dog and their packs of hounds have, each of them, one of these dogs, which acts as their guide and leader. This dog they follow in the chase, and him they carefully obey; for these animals have even a notion of subordination among themselves. It is asserted that the dogs keep running when they drink at the Nile, for fear of becoming a prey to the voracity of the crocodile. When Alexander the Great was on his Indian expedition, he was presented by the king of Albania with a dog of unusual size; being greatly delighted with its noble appearance, he ordered bears, and after them wild boars, and then deer, to be let loose before it; but the dog lay down, and regarded them with a kind of immoveable contempt. The noble spirit of the general became irritated by the sluggishness thus manifested by an animal of such vast bulk, and he ordered it to be killed. The report of this reached the king, who accordingly sent another dog, and at the same time sent word that its powers were to be tried, not upon small animals, but upon the lion or the elephant; adding, that he had had originally but two, and that if this one were put to death, the race would be extinct. Alexander, without delay, procured a lion, which in his presence was instantly torn to pieces. He then ordered an elephant to be brought, and never was he more delighted with any spectacle; for the dog, bristling up its hair all over the body, began by thundering forth a loud barking, and then attacked the animal, leaping at it first on one side and then on the other, attacking it in the most skilful manner, and then again retreating at the opportune moment, until at last the elephant, being rendered quite giddy by turning round and round, fell to the earth.

THE NATURE OF THE HORSE

King Alexander had also a very remarkable horse it was called Bucephalus, either on account of the fierceness of its aspect, or because it had the figure of a bull's head marked on its shoulder. It is said, that he was struck with its beauty when he was only a boy, and that it was purchased from the stud of Philonicus, the Pharsalian, for thirteen talents. When it was equipped with the royal trappings, it would suffer no one except Alexander to mount it, although at other times it would allow any one to do so. A memorable circumstance connected with it in battle is recorded of this horse; it is said that when it was wounded in the attack upon Thebes, it would not allow Alexander to mount any other horse. Many other circumstances, also, of a similar nature, occurred respecting it; so that when it died, the king duly performed its obsequies, and built around its tomb a city, which he named after it.

It is said, also, that Cæsar, the Dictator, had a horse, which would allow no one to mount but himself, and that its forefeet were like those of a man; indeed it is thus represented in the statue before the temple of Venus Genetrix. The late Emperor Augustus also erected a tomb to his horse; on which occasion Germanicus Cæsar wrote a poem, which still exists.

These animals possess an intelligence which exceeds all description. Those who have to use the javelin are well aware how the horse, by its exertions and the supple movements of its body, aids the rider in any difficulty he may have in throwing his weapon. They will even present to their master the weapons collected on the ground. The horses too, that are yoked to the chariots in the Circus, beyond a doubt, display remarkable proofs how sensible they are to encouragement and to glory. In the Secular games, which were celebrated in the Circus, under the Emperor Claudius, when the charioteer Corax, who belonged to the white party, was thrown from his place at the starting-post, his horses took the lead and kept it, opposing the other chariots, overturning them, and doing every thing against the other competitors that could have been done, had they been guided by the most skilful charioteer; and while we quite blushed to behold the skill of man excelled by that of the horse, they arrived at the goal, after going over the whole of the prescribed course.

THE GENERATION OF THE HORSE

The female of this animal carries her young for eleven months, and brings forth in the twelfth. The connection takes place at the vernal equinox, and generally in both sexes, at the age of two years; but the colt is much stronger when the parents are three years old. The males are capable of covering up to the thirty-third year, and it is not till after the twentieth that they are taken for this purpose from the Circus.

The mare brings forth standing upright, and is attached, beyond all other animals, to her offspring. The horse is born with a poisonous substance on its forehead, known as hippomanes, and used in love philtres; it is the size of a fig, and of a black colour; the mother devours it immediately on the birth of the foal, and until she has done so, she will not suckle it. When this substance can he rescued from the mother, it has the property of rendering the animal quite frantic by the smell. If a foal has lost its mother, the other mares in the herd that have young, will take charge of the orphan. It is said that the young of this animal cannot touch the earth with the mouth for the first three days after its birth.

It is well known that in Lusitania, in the vicinity of the town of Olisipo and the river Tagus, the mares, by turning their faces towards the west wind as it blows, become impregnated by its breezes, and that the foals which are conceived in this way arc remarkable for their extreme fleetness; but they never live beyond three years.

THE OXEN; THEIR GENERATION

We find it stated, that the oxen of India are of the height of camels, and that the extremity of their horns are four feet asunder. In our part of the world the most valuable oxen are those of Epirus, owing, it is said, to the attention paid to their breed by King Pyrrhus. This perfection was acquired by not permitting them to breed until after their fourth year. By these means he brought them to a very large size, and descendants of this breed are still to be seen at the present day. But in our times, we set heifers to breed in their first year, or, at the latest, in their second. Bulls are fit for breeding in their fourth year; one being sufficient, it is said, for ten cows during the whole year. If the bull, after covering, goes to the right side, the produce will be a male; if to the left, a female. Conception takes place after a single union; but if, by any accident, it should not have taken place, the cow seeks the male again, at the end of twenty days. She brings forth in the tenth month; whatever may be produced before that time cannot be reared. Some writers say, that the birth takes place the very day on which the tenth month is completed. This animal but rarely produces twins. The time of covering begins at the rising of the Dolphin, the day before the nones of January, and continues for the space of thirty days. Sometimes it takes place in the autumn; and among those nations which live upon milk, they manage so as to have a supply of it at all times of the year. Bulls never cover more than twice in the same day. The ox is the only' animal that walks backwards while it is feeding; among the Garamantes, they feed in no other manner. The females live fifteen years at the longest, and the males twenty; they arrive at their full vigour in their fifth year.

Bulls are selected as the Very choicest of victims, and are offered up as the most approved sacrifice for appeasing the gods. Of all the animals that have long tails, this is the only one whose tail is not of proportionate length at the moment of birth; and in this animal alone it continues to grow until it reaches its heels. It is on this account, that in making choice of a calf for a victim, due care is taken that its tail reaches to the pastern joint; if it is shorter than this, the sacrifice is not deemed acceptable to the gods.

THE EGYPTIAN APIS

In Egypt an ox is even worshipped as a deity; they call it Apis. It is distinguished by a conspicuous white spot on the right side, in the form of a crescent. There is a knot also under the tongue, which is called "cantharus." This ox is not allowed to live beyond a certain number of years; it is then destroyed by being drowned in the fountain of the priests. They then go, amid general mourning, and seek another ox to replace it; and the mourning is continued, with their heads shaved, until such time as they have found one; it is not long, however, at any time, before they meet with a successor. When one has been found, it is brought by the priests to Memphis. There are two temples appropriated to it, which are called thalami, and to these the people resort to learn the auguries. According as the ox enters the one or the other of these places, the augury is deemed favourable or unfavourable. It gives answers to individuals, by taking food from the hand of those who consult it. It turned away from the hand of Germanicus Cæsar, and not long after he died. In general it lives in secret; but, when it comes forth in public, the multitudes make way for it, and it is attended by a crowd of boys, singing hymns in honour of it; it

Book VIII - The Nature of the Terrestrial Animals

appears to be sensible of the adoration thus paid to it, and to court it. These crowds, too, suddenly become inspired, and predict future events.

SHEEP, AND THEIR PROPAGATION

Many thanks, too, do we owe to the sheep, both for appeasing the gods, and for giving us the use of its fleece. As oxen cultivate the fields which yield food for man, so to sheep are we indebted for the defence of our bodies. The generative power lasts in both sexes from the second to the ninth year, sometimes to the tenth. The lambs produced at the first birth are but small. The season for coupling, in all of them, is from the setting of Arcturus, that is to say, the third day before the ides of May, to the setting of Aquila, the tenth day before the calends of August. The period of gestation is one hundred and fifty days. The lambs that are produced after this time are feeble; the ancients called those that were born after it, cordi.

THE DIFFERENT KINDS OF WOOL

The most esteemed wool of all is that of Apulia, and that which in Italy is called Grecian wool, in other countries Italian. The fleeces of Miletus hold the third rank. The Apulian wool is shorter in the hair, and only owes its high character to the cloaks that are made of it. The sheep are not shorn in all countries; in some places it is still the custom to pull off the wool. There are various colours of wool; so much so, indeed, that we want terms to express them all.

GOATS AND THEIR PROPAGATION

The goat occasionally brings forth as many as four at a birth; but this is rarely the case. It is pregnant five months, like the sheep. Goats become barren when very fat. There is little advantage to be derived from their bringing forth before their third year, or after the fourth, when they begin to grow old. They are capable of generating in the seventh month, and while they are still sucking. In both sexes those that have no horns are considered the most valuable. A single coupling in the day is not sufficient, the second and the following ones are more effectual. They conceive in the month of November, so as to bring forth in the month of March, when the buds are bursting; this is sometimes the case with them when only one year old, and always with those of the second year; but the produce of those which are three years old is the most valuable. They continue to bring forth for a period of eight years. Cold produces abortion. When their eyes are surcharged, the female discharges the blood from the eye by pricking it with the point of a bulrush, and the male with the thorn of a bramble.

It is said also, that they have the power of seeing by night as well as in the day, for which reason those persons who are called Nyctalopes, recover the power of seeing in the evening, by eating the liver of the he-goat. In Cilicia, and in the vicinity of the Syrtes, the inhabitants shear the goat for the purpose of clothing themselves. It is said that the she-goats in the pastures will never look at each other at sun-set, but lie with their backs towards one another, while at other times of the day they lie facing each other and in family groups. They all have long hair hanging down from the chin, which is called by us aruncus. If any one of the flock is taken hold of and dragged by this hair, all the rest gaze on in stupid astonishment; and the same happens when any one of them has eaten of a certain herb Their bite is very destructive to trees, and they make the olive barren by licking it; for which reason they are not sacrificed to Minerva.[6]

THE WILD BOAR

The flesh of the wild boar is also much esteemed. Cato, the Censor, in his orations, strongly declaimed against the use of the brawn of the wild boar. The animal used to be divided into three portions, the middle part of which was laid by, and is called boar's chine.

The wild sow brings forth once only in the year. The males arc very fierce during the rutting time; they fight with each other, having first hardened their sides by rubbing them against the trees, and covered themselves with mud. The females, as is the case with animals of every kind, become more fierce just after they have brought forth. The wild boar is not capable of generating before the first year. The wild boar of India has two curved teeth, projecting from beneath the muzzle, a cubit in length; and the same number projecting from the forehead, like the horns of the young bull. The hair of these animals, in a wild state, is the colour of copper, the others are black. No species whatever of the swine is found in Arabia.

APES

The different kinds of apes, which approach the nearest to the human figure, are distinguished from each other by the tail. Their shrewdness is quite wonderful. It is said that, imitating the hunters, they will besmear themselves with bird-lime, and put their feet into the shoes, which, as so many snares, have been prepared for them. Mucianus says, that they have even played at chess, having, by practice, learned to distinguish the different pieces, which are made of wax. He says that the species which have tails become quite melancholy when the moon is on the wane, and that they leap for joy at the time of the new moon, and adore it.

ANIMALS WHICH ARE TAMED IN PART ONLY

Hares are seldom tamed, and yet they cannot properly be called wild animals; indeed, there are many species of them which are neither tame nor wild, but of a sort of intermediate nature; of the same kind there are among the winged animals, swallows and bees, and among the sea animals, the dolphin.

Many persons have placed that inhabitant of our houses, the mouse, in this class also; an animal which is not to be despised, for the portents which it has afforded, even in relation to public events. By gnawing the silver shields at Lanuvium, mice prognosticated the Marsian war; and the death of our general, Carbo, at Clusium, by gnawing the latchets with which he fastened his shoes. To be visited by white mice is considered as indicative of a fortunate event; but our Annals are full of instances in which the singing of a mouse has interrupted the auspices.

---

6   Since Minerva is the patroness of olive tree.

Book IX
The Natural History of Fishes

We have now given an account of the animals which we call terrestrial, and which live as it were in a sort of society with man.

Among the marine animals there are many to be found that exceed in size any of the terrestrial animals even; the evident cause of which is the superabundance of moisture with which they are supplied. Very different is the lot of the winged animals, whose life is passed soaring aloft in the air. But in the seas, spread out as they are far and wide, forming an element at once so delicate and so vivifying, and receiving the generating principles from the regions of the air, as they are ever produced by Nature, many animals are to be found, and indeed, most of those that are of monstrous form; from the fact, no doubt, that these seeds and first principles of being are so utterly conglomerated and so involved, the one with the other, from being whirled to and fro, now by the action of the winds and now by the waves. Hence it is that the vulgar notion may very possibly be true, that whatever is produced in any other department of Nature, is to be found in the sea as well; while, at the same time, many other productions are there to be found which nowhere else exist. That there are to be found in the sea the forms, not only of terrestrial animals, but of inanimate objects even, is easily to be understood by all who will take the trouble to examine the grape-fish, the sword-fish, the saw-fish, and the cucumber-fish, which last so strongly resembles the real cucumber both in colour and in smell. We shall find the less reason then to be surprised to find that in so small an object as a shell-fish the head of the horse is to be seen protruding from the shell.

THE SEA MONSTERS OF THE OCEANS

But the most numerous and largest of all these animals are those found in the Indian seas; among which there are balænæ,[1] four jugera in extent, and the pristis,[2] two hundred cubits long; here also are found cray-fish four cubits in length, and in the river Ganges there are to be seen eels three hundred feet long. But at sea it is more especially about the time of the solstices that these monsters are to be seen. For then it is that in these regions the whirlwind comes sweeping on, the rains descend, the hurricane comes rushing down, hurled from the mountain heights, while the sea is stirred up from the very bottom, and the monsters are driven from their depths and rolled upwards on the crest of the billow. At other times again, there are such vast multitudes of tunnies met with, that the fleet of Alexander the Great was able to make head against them only by facing them in order of battle, just as it would have done an enemy's fleet. Had the ships not done this, but proceeded in a straggling manner, they could not possibly have made their escape. No noises, no sounds, no blows had any effect on these fish; by nothing short of the clash of battle were they to be terrified, and by nothing less than their utter destruction were they overpowered.

The largest animals found in the Indian Sea are the pristis and the balæna; while of the Gallic Ocean the physeter[3] is the most bulky inhabitant, raising itself aloft like some vast column, and as it towers above the sails of ships, belching forth, as it were, a deluge of water. In the ocean of Gades there is a tree, with outspread branches so vast, that it is supposed that it is for that reason it has never yet entered the Straits. There are fish also found there which are called sea-wheels, in consequence of their singular conformation; they are divided by four spokes, the nave being guarded on every side by a couple of eyes.

TRITONS AND NEREIDS

The Triton

A deputation of persons from Olisipo, that had been sent for the purpose, brought word to the Emperor Tiberius that a triton had been both seen and heard in a certain cavern, blowing a conch-shell, and of the form under which they are usually represented. Nor yet is the figure generally attributed to the nereids at all a fiction; only in

---

1   It is not accurately known what fish was meant by the ancients, under the name of balænæ." According to some writers, it is considered to be the same with what we call the "orca."

2   As Hardouin remarks, we can learn neither from the works of Pliny, nor yet of Lilian, what fish the pristis really was. From Nonius Marcellus, we find that it was a very long fish of large size, but narrow body. Hardouin says that it was a fish of the cetaceous kind, found in the Indian'seas, which, in his time, was known by some as the "vivella," with a long bony muzzle serrated on either side, evidently meaning the saw-fish. Pristis was a favourite name given by the Romans to their ships. In the boat-race described by Virgil in the Æneid, one of the boats is so called.

3   "A blower," probably one sperm whale, so called from its blowing forth the water.

Book IX - The Natural History of Fishes

them, the portion of the body that resembles the human figure is still rough all over with scales. For one of these creatures was seen upon the same shores, and as it died, its plaintive murmurs were heard even by the inhabitants at a distance. The legatus of Gaul, too, wrote word to the late Emperor Augustus that a considerable number of nereids had been found dead upon the sea-shore. I have, too, some distinguished informants of equestrian rank, who state that they themselves once saw in the ocean of Gades a sea-man, which bore in every part of his body a perfect resemblance to a human being, and that during the night he would climb up into ships; upon which the side of the vessel where he seated himself would instantly sink downward, and if he remained there any considerable time, even go under water.

WHETHER FISHES BREATHE AND SLEEP

Balænæ have the mouth in the forehead; and hence it is that, as they swim on the surface of the water, they discharge vast showers of water in the air. It is universally agreed, however, that they respire, as do a very few other animals in the sea, which have lungs among the internal viscera; for without lungs it is generally supposed that no animal can breathe. Those, too, who are of this opinion are of opinion also that no fishes that have gills are so constituted as to inhale and exhale alternately, nor, in fact, many other kinds of animals even, which are entirely destitute of gills. This, I find, was the opinion of Aristotle, who, by his learned researches on the subject, has induced many others to be of the same way of thinking. I shall not, however, conceal the fact, that I for one do not by any means at once subscribe to this opinion, for it is very possible, if such he the will of Nature, that there may he other organs fitted for the purposes of respiration, and acting in the place of lungs; just as in many animals a different liquid altogether takes the place of blood. There are other weighty reasons as well, which induce me to be of opinion that all aquatic animals respire.

DOLPHINS

The swiftest not only of the sea animals, but of all animals whatever, is the dolphin. He is more rapid in his movements than a bird, more instantaneous than the flight of an arrow, and were it not for the fact that his mouth is situate much below his muzzle, almost, indeed, in the middle of the belly, not a fish would be able to escape his pursuit. But Nature, in her prudence, has thrown certain impediments in his way; for unless he turns, and throws himself on his back, he can seize nothing, and it is this circumstance more especially that gives proof of his extraordinary swiftness. For, if pressed by hunger, he will follow a fish, as it flies down, to the very bottom of the water, and then after holding his breath thus long, will dart again to the surface to respire, with the speed of an arrow discharged from a bow; and often, on such occasions, he is known to leap out of the water with such a bound, as to fly right over the sails of a ship.

Dolphins generally go in couples; the females bring forth their young in the tenth month, during the summer season, sometimes two in number. They suckle their young at the teat like the balæna, and even carry them during the weakness of infancy; in addition to which, long after they are grown up, they accompany them, so great is their affection for their progeny.

The dolphin is an animal not only friendly to man, but a lover of music as well; he is charmed by melodious concerts, and more especially by the notes of the water-organ. He does not dread man, as though a stranger to him, but comes to meet ships, leaps and bounds to and fro, vies with them in swiftness, and passes them even when in full sail.

Hegesidemus informed us, that in the city of Iasus there was a boy, Hermias by name, who used to traverse the sea on a dolphin's back, but that on one occasion a tempest suddenly arising, he lost his life, and was brought back dead; upon which, the dolphin, who thus admitted that he had been the cause of his death, would not return to the sea, but lay down upon the dry land, and there expired.

Theophrastus informs us, that the very same thing happened at Naupactus also; nor, in fact, is there any limit to similar instances. The Amphilochians and the Tarentines have similar stories also about children and dolphins; and all these give an air of credibility to the one that is told of Arion, the famous performer on the lyre. The mariners being on the point of throwing him into the sea, for the purpose of taking possession of the money he had earned, he prevailed upon them to allow him one more song, accompanied with the music of his lyre. The melody attracted numbers of dolphins around the ship, and, upon throwing himself into the sea, he was taken up by one of them, and borne in safety to the shore of the Promontory of Tsenarum.

TURTLES AND HOW THEY ARE CAUGHT

The Indian Sea produces turtles of such vast size, that with the shell of a single animal they are able to roof a habitable cottage and among the islands of the Red Sea, the navigation is mostly carried on in boats formed of these shells. They are to be caught in many ways; but they are generally taken when they have come up to the surface of the water just before midday, a season at which they experience great delight in floating on the calm surface, with the back entirely out of the water. Here the delightful sensations which attend a free respiration beguile them to such a degree, and render them so utterly regardless of their safety, that their shell becomes dried up by the heat of the sun, so much so, indeed, that they are unable to descend, and, having to float against their will, become an easy prey to the fishermen. It is said also, that they leave the water at night for the purpose of feeding, and eat with such avidity as to quite glut themselves; upon which, they become weary, and the moment that, on their return in the morning, they reach the sea, they fall asleep on the surface of the water. The noise of their snoring betrays them, upon which the fishermen stealthily swim towards the animals, three to each turtle; two of them, in a moment, throw it on its back, while a third slings a noose around it, as it lies face upwards, and then some more men, who are ready on shore, draw it to land.

Book IX - The Natural History of Fishes

DISTRIBUTION OF AQUATIC ANIMALS INTO VARIOUS SPECIES

The integuments of the aquatic animals are many in number. Some are covered with a hide and hair, as the seal and hippopotamus, for instance; others again, with a hide only, as the dolphin; others again, with a shell, as the turtle; others, with a coat as hard as a stone, like the oyster and other shell-fish; others, with a crust, such as the cray-fish; others, with a crust and spines, like the sea-urchin; others, with scales, as fishes in general; others, with a rough skin, as the squatina, the skin of which is used for polishing wood and ivory; others, with a soft skin, like the murena; and others with none at all, like the octopus.

Those aquatic animals which are covered with hair are viviparous, such, for instance, as the pristis, the balæna, and the seal. This last brings forth its young on land, and, like the sheep, produces an after-birth. In coupling, they adhere after the manner of the canine species; the female sometimes produces even more than two, and rears her young at the breast. She does not take them down to the sea until the twelfth day, and after that time makes them become used to it by degrees.

There are seventy-four species of fishes, exclusive of those that are covered with crusts; the kinds of which are thirty in number. We shall, on another occasion, speak of each individually; but, for the present, we shall treat only of the nature of the more remarkable ones.

FISHES OF THE LARGEST SIZE

Tunnies are among the most remarkable for their size; we have found one weighing as much as fifteen talents, the breadth of its tail being five cubits and a palm. In some of the rivers, also, there are fish of no less size, such, for instance, as the silurus of the Nile, the isox of the Rhenus, and the attilus of the Padus, which, naturally of an inactive nature, sometimes grows so fat as to weigh a thousand pounds, and when taken with a hook, attached to a chain, requires a yoke of oxen to draw it on land. An extremely small fish, which is known as the clupea, attaches itself, with a wonderful tenacity, to a certain vein in the throat of the attilus, and destroys it by its bite. The silurus carries devastation with it wherever it goes, attacks every living creature, and often drags beneath the water horses as they swim.

In the Ganges, a river of India, there is a fish found which they call the platanista; it has the muzzle and the tail of the dolphin, and measures sixteen cubits in length. Statius Sebosus says, a thing that is marvellous in no small degree, that in the same river there are fishes found, called worms; these have two gills, and are sixty cubits in length.

WHY FISHES LEAP ABOVE THE SURFACE OF THE WATER.

There is a little animal, in appearance like a scorpion, and of the size of a spider. This creature, by means of its sting, attaches itself below the fin to the tunny and the fish known as the sword-fish and which often exceeds the dolphin in magnitude, and causes it such excruciating pain, that it will often leap on board of a ship even. Fish will also do the same at other times, when in dread of the violence of other fish, and mullets more especially, which are of such extraordinary swiftness, that they will sometimes leap over a ship, if lying cross-wise.

AUGURIES DERIVED FROM FISHES

Auguries are also derived from this department of Nature, and fishes afford presages of coming events. While Augustus was walking on the sea-shore, during the time of the Sicilian war, a fish leapt out of the sea, and fell at his feet. The diviners, who were consulted, stated that this was a proof that those would fall beneath the feet of Cæsar who at that moment were in possession of the seas —it was just at this time that Sextus Pompeius had adopted Neptune as his father, so elated was he with his successes by sea.

GILLS AND SCALES

Some fishes have numerous gills, others again single ones, others double; it is by means of these that they discharge the water that has entered the mouth. A sign of old age is the hardness of the scales, which are not alike in all. There are two lakes of Italy at the foot of the Alps, called Larius and Verbanus, in which there are to be seen every year, at the rising of the Vergiliæ,[4] fish remarkable for the number of their scales, and the exceeding sharpness of them, strongly resembling hob-nails[5] in appearance; these fish, however, are only to be seen during that month, and no longer.

THE FINS OF FISH, AND THEIR MODE OF SWIMMING

Hence it is that there is a difference, also, in the fins of fish, which have been given them to serve in place of feet, none having more than four, some two only, and others none. It is in Lake Fucinus only that there is a fish found that has eight fins for swimming. Those fishes which are long and slimy, have only two at most, such, for instance, as eels and congers; others, again, have none, such as the murena, which is also without gills. All these fish make their way in the sea by an undulatory motion of the body, just as serpents do on land; on dry land, also, they are able to crawl along, and hence those of this nature are more long-lived than the others. Some of the flat-fish, also, have no fins, the pastinacæ, for instance —for these swim broad-wise— those, also, which are known as the "soft" fish, such as the polypi, for their feet serve them in stead of fins.

EELS

Eels live eight years; they are able to survive out of water as much as six days, when a north-east wind blows; but when the south wind prevails, not so many. In winter, they cannot live if they are in very shallow water, nor yet if the water is troubled. Hence it is that they are taken more especially about the rising of the Vergiliæ, when the rivers are mostly in a turbid state. These animals seek their food at night; they are the only fish the bodies of which, when dead, do not float upon the surface.

---

4   Constellation of the Pleiades.
5   Clavorum caligariuni, "nails for the caliga". This was a strong, heavy sandal, worn by the Roman soldiers. It was worn by the centurions, but not by the superior officers.

THE ECHENEIS, AND ITS USES IN ENCHANTMENTS

There is a very small fish that is in the habit of living among the rocks, and is known as the echeneis.[6] It is believed that when this has attached itself to the keel of a ship its progress is impeded. For this reason, also, it has a disgraceful repute, as being employed in love philtres, and for the purpose of retarding judgments and legal proceedings, evil properties, which are only compensated by a single merit that it possesses, it is good for staying fluxes of the womb in pregnant women, and preserves the fœtus up to birth; it is never used, however, for food. Aristotle is of opinion that this fish has feet, so strong is the resemblance, by reason of the form and position of the fins.

Mucianus speaks of a murex[7] of larger size than the purple, with a head that is neither rough nor round; and the shell of which is single, and falls in folds on either side. He tells us, also, that some of these creatures once attached themselves to a ship freighted with children of noble birth, who were being sent by Periander for the purpose of being castrated, and that they stopped its course in full sail; and he further says, that the shell-fish which did this service are duly honoured in the temple of Venus, at Cnidos. Trebius Niger says that this fish is a foot in length, and that it can retard the course of vessels, five fingers in thickness; besides which, it has another peculiar property —when preserved in salt, and applied, it is able to draw up gold which has fallen into a well, however deep it may happen to be.

FISHES WHICH EMERGE AND FLY ABOVE THE WATER

The sea-swallow, being able to fly, bears a strong resemblance to the bird of that name; the sea-kite too, flies as well.

There is a fish that comes up to the surface of the sea, known, from the following circumstance, as the lantern-fish; thrusting from its mouth a tongue that shines like fire, it emits a most brilliant light on calm nights. Another fish, which, from its horns, has received its name, raises them nearly a foot and a half above the surface of the water. The sea-dragon, if caught and thrown on the sand, works out a hole for itself with its muzzle, with the most wonderful celerity.

THE OCTOPUS

There are numerous kinds of octopus. The land octopus is larger than that of the sea; they all of them use their arms as feet and hands; and in coupling they employ the tail, which is forked and sharp. The octopus has a sort of passage in the back,

---

6   This is the Echeneis remora of Linnæus.

7   Cuvier says, that the shell-fish to which Pliny here ascribes a power similar to that of the remora, is, if we may judge from his description of it, of the genus called Cypræa, and has very little doubt that its peculiar form caused its consecration to Venus, fully as much as its supposed miraculous powers.

by which it lets in and discharges the water, and which it shifts from side to side, sometimes carrying it on the right, and sometimes on the left. It swims obliquely, with the head on one side, which is of surprising hardness while the animal is alive, being puffed out with air. In addition to this, they have cavities dispersed throughout the claws, by means of which, through suction, they can adhere to objects; which they hold, with the head upwards, so tightly, that they cannot be torn away. They cannot attach themselves, however, to the bottom of the sea, and their retentive powers are weaker in the larger ones. These are the only soft fish that come on dry land, and then only where the surface is rugged: a smooth surface they would not come near. They feed upon the flesh of shell-fish, the shells of which they can easily break in the embrace of their arms; hence it is that their retreat may be easily detected by the pieces of shell which lie before it.

I must not omit here the observations which L. Lucullus, the proconsul of Bætica, made with reference to the octopus. He says that it is remarkably fond of shell-fish, and that these, the moment that they feel themselves touched by it, close their valves, and cut off the feelers of the octopus, thus making a meal at the expense of the plunderer. In addition, the same author states, that there is not an animal in existence, that is more dangerous for its powers of destroying a human being when in the water. Embracing his body, it counteracts his struggles, and draws him under with its feelers and its numerous suckers, when, as often is the case, it happens to make an attack upon a shipwrecked mariner or a child. If, however, the animal is turned over, it loses all its power; for when it is thrown upon the back, the arms open of themselves.

THE SAILING NAUPLIUS

Mucianus also relates that he had seen, in the Propontis, another curious resemblance to a ship in full sail. There is a shell-fish, he says, with a keel, just like that of the vessel which we know by the name of acatium, with the poop curving inwards, and a prow with the beak attached. In this shell-fish there lies concealed also an animal known as the nauplius, which bears a strong resemblance to the sæpia, and only adopts the shell-fish as the companion of its pastimes. There are two modes, he says, which it adopts in sailing; when the sea is calm, the voyager hangs down its arms, and strikes the water with a pair of oars as it were; but if, on the other hand, the wind invites, it extends them, employing them by way of a helm, and turning the mouth of the shell to the wind. The pleasure experienced by the shell-fish is that of carrying the other, while the amusement of the nauplius consists in steering; and thus, at the same moment, is an instinctive joy felt by these two creatures, devoid as they are of all sense, unless, indeed, a natural antipathy to man —for it is a well-known fact, that to see them thus sailing along, is a bad omen, and that it is portentous of misfortune to those who witness it.

PEARLS

The first rank then, and the very highest position among all valuables, belongs to the pearl. It is the Indian Ocean that principally sends them to us; and thus have they, amid those monsters so frightful and so huge which we have already

Book IX - The Natural History of Fishes

described, to cross so many seas, and to traverse such lengthened tracts of land, scorched by the ardent rays of a burning sun; and then, too, by the Indians themselves they have to be sought in certain islands, and those but very few in number. The most productive of pearls is the island of Taprobane, and that of Stoïdis; Perimula, also, a promontory of India. But those are most highly valued which are found in the vicinity of Arabia, in the Persian Gulf, which forms a part of the Red Sea.

The origin and production of the shell-fish is not very different from that of the shell of the oyster. When the genial season of the year exercises its influence on the animal, it is said that, yawning, as it were, it opens its shell, and so receives a kind of dew, by means of which it becomes impregnated; and that at length it gives birth, after many struggles, to the burden of its shell, in the shape of pearls, which vary according to the quality of the dew. If this has been in a perfectly pure state when it flowed into the shell, then the pearl produced is white and brilliant, but if it was turbid, then the pearl is of a clouded colour also; if the sky should happen to have been lowering when it was generated, the pearl will be of a pallid colour; from all which it is quite evident that the quality of the pearl depends much more upon a calm state of the heavens than of the sea, and hence it is that it contracts a cloudy hue, or a limpid appearance, according to the degree of serenity of the sky in the morning.

If, again, the fish is satiated in a reasonable time, then the pearl produced increases rapidly in size. Those which are produced in a perfectly healthy state consist of numerous layers, so that they may be looked upon, not inappropriately, as similar in conformation to the callosities on the body of an animal; and they should therefore be cleaned by experienced hands. It is wonderful, however, that they should be influenced thus pleasurably by the state of the heavens, seeing that by the action of the sun the pearls are turned of a red colour, and lose all their whiteness, just like the human body. Hence it is that those which keep their whiteness the best are the pelagiæ, or main-sea pearls, which lie at too great a depth to be reached by the sun's rays; and yet these even turn yellow with age, grow dull and wrinkled, and it is only in their youth that they possess that brilliancy which is so highly esteemed in them. When old, too, the coat grows thick, and they adhere to the shell, from which they can only be separated with the assistance of a file. Those pearls which have one surface flat and the other spherical, opposite to the plane side, are for that reason called tympania, or tambour-pearls. I have seen pearls still adhering to the shell; for which reason the shells were used as boxes for unguents. In addition to these facts, we may remark that the pearl is soft in the water, but that it grows hard the instant it is taken out.

THE MUREX AND THE PURPLE

And yet pearls may be looked upon as pretty nearly a possession of everlasting duration —they descend from a man to his heir, and they are alienated from one to another just like any landed estate. But the colours that are extracted from the murex[8] and the purple fade from hour to hour; and yet luxury, which has similarly acted as a mother to them, has set upon them prices almost equal to those of pearls.

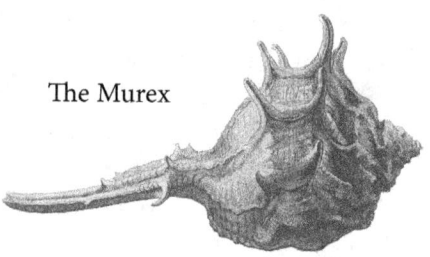

The Murex

Purples live mostly seven years. Like the murex, they keep themselves in concealment for thirty days, about the time of the rising of the Dog-star; in the spring season they unite in large bodies, and by rubbing against each other, produce a viscous spittle, from which a kind of wax is formed. The murex does the same; but the purple has that exquisite juice which is so greatly sought after for the purpose of dyeing cloth, situate in the middle of the throat. This secretion consists of a tiny drop contained in a white vein, from which the precious liquid used for dyeing is distilled, being of the tint of a rose somewhat inclining to black. The rest of the body is entirely destitute of this juice. It is a great point to take the fish alive; for when it dies, it spits out this juice. From the larger ones it is extracted after taking off the shell; but the small fish are crushed alive, together with the shells, upon which they eject this secretion.

THE SENSITIVENESS OF WATER ANIMALS

I am inclined to wonder at the circumstance that some persons have been found who were of opinion that the water animals are devoid of all sense. The torpedo[9] is very well aware of the extent of its own powers, and that, too, although it experiences no benumbing effects from them itself. Lying concealed in the mud, it awaits the approach of the fish, and, at the moment that they are swimming above in supposed security, communicates the shock, and instantly darts upon them; there is no delicate morsel in existence that is preferred to the liver of this fish. And no less wonderful, too, is the shrewdness manifested by the sea-frog,[10] which is known by us as the "fisher." Stirring up the mud, it protrudes from the surface two little horns, which project from beneath the eyes, and so attracts the small fish which are sporting around it, until at last they approach so close that it is able to seize them. In a similar manner, too, the squatina and the rhombus conceal themselves, but extend their fins, which, as they move to and fro, resemble little worms; the ray also does the same. The sting-ray, too, lies lurking in ambush, and pierces the fish as they pass with the sting with which it is armed. Another proof of instinctive shrewdness is the fact, that although the ray is the very slowest of all the fish in its movements, it is found with the mullet in its belly, which is the swiftest of them all.

---

8   Or "conchylium." We find that Pliny generally makes a difference between the colours of the "murex," or "conchylium," and those of the "purpura," or "purple." Cuvier says, that they were the names of different shell-fish which the ancients employed for dyeing in purple of various shades.

9   The "torpedo" is a type of fish that can produce electricity to protect itself.

10   The *Lophius piscatorius* of Linnæus, angler, European angler or common monkfish.

SPONGES

We find three kinds of sponges mentioned; the first are thick, very hard, and rough, and are called "tragi"; the second, are thick, and much softer, and are called "mani"; of the third, being fine and of a closer texture, tents for sores are made; this last is known as "Achillium." All of these sponges grow on rocks, and feed upon shell and other fish, and slime. It would appear that these creatures, too, have some intelligence; for as soon as ever they feel the hand about to tear them off, they contract themselves, and are separated with much greater difficulty; they do the same also when the waves buffet them to and fro. The small shells that are found in them, clearly show that they live upon food; about Torone it is even said that they will survive after they have been detached, and that they grow again from the roots which have been left adhering to the rock. They leave a colour similar to that of blood upon the rock from which they have been detached, and those more especially which are produced in the Syrtes of Africa.

THE DOG-FISH

Vast numbers of dog-fish[11] infest the seas in the vicinity of the sponges, to the great peril of those who dive for them. These persons say that a sort of dense cloud gradually thickens over their heads, bearing the resemblance of some kind of animal like a flat-fish, and that, pressing downward upon them, it prevents them from returning to the surface. It is for this reason that they carry stilettos with them, which are very sharp at the point, and attached to them by strings; for if they did not pierce the object with the help of these, it could not be got rid of. This, however, is entirely the result, in my opinion, of the darkness and their own fears; for no person has ever been able to find, among living creatures, the fish-cloud or the fish-fog, the name which they give to this enemy of theirs.

The divers, however, have terrible combats with the dog-fish, which attack with avidity the groin, the heels, and all the whiter parts of the body. The only means of ensuring safety, is to go boldly to meet them, and so, by taking the initiative, strike them with alarm; for, in fact, this animal is just as frightened at man, as man is at it; and they are on quite an equal footing when beneath the water. But the moment the diver has reached the surface, the danger is much more imminent; for he loses the power of boldly meeting his adversary while he is endeavouring to make his way out of the water, and his only chance of safety is in his companions, who draw him along by a cord that is fastened under his shoulders. While he is engaging with the enemy, he keeps pulling this cord with his left hand, according as there may be any sign of immediate peril, while with the right he wields the stiletto, which he is using in his defence. At first they draw him along at a moderate pace, but as soon as ever they have got him close to the ship, if they do not whip him out in an instant, with the greatest possible celerity, they see him snapped asunder; and many a time, too, the diver, even when already drawn out, is dragged from their hands, through neglecting to aid the efforts of those who are assisting him, by rolling up his body

---

11   It is pretty clear that under the name of "canicula," "dog-fish," "canis marinus," or "seadog," Pliny includes the whole genus of sharks.

in the shape of a ball. The others, it is true, are in the meantime brandishing their pronged fish-spears; but the monster has the craftiness to place himself beneath the ship, and so wage the warfare in safety.

THE GENERATION OF FISHES

The curiosity and wonder which have been excited in mankind by this subject, will not allow me any longer to defer giving an account of the generation of these animals. Fishes couple by rubbing their bellies against one another; an operation, however, that is performed with such extraordinary celerity as to escape the sight. Dolphins also, and other animals of the cetaceous kind, couple in a similar manner, though the time occupied in so doing is somewhat longer. The female fish, at the season for coupling, follows the male, and strikes against its belly with its muzzle; while the male in its turn, when the female is about to spawn, follows it and devours' the eggs. But with them, the simple act of coupling is not sufficient for the purposes of reproduction; it is necessary for the male to pass among the eggs which the female has produced, in order to sprinkle them with its vitalizing fluid. This does not, however, reach all the eggs out of so vast a multitude; indeed, if it did, the seas and lakes would soon be filled, seeing that each female produces these eggs in quantities innumerable.

Frogs leap the one upon the other, the male with its forefeet clasping the armpits of the female, and with its hinder ones the haunches. The female produces tiny pieces of black flesh, which are known by the name of gyrini,[12] and are only to be distinguished by the eyes and tail; very soon, however, the feet are developed, and the tail, becoming bifurcate, forms the hind legs. It is a most singular thing, but, after a life of six months' duration, frogs melt away into slime, though no one ever sees how it is done; after which they come to life again in the water during the spring, just as they were before. This is effected by some occult operation of Nature, and happens regularly every year.

Mussels, also, and scallops are produced in the sand by the spontaneous operations of nature. Those which have a harder shell, such as the murex and the purple, are formed from a viscous fluid like saliva, just as gnats are produced from liquids tinned sour, and the fish called the apua, from the foam of the sea when warm, after the fall of a shower.

Those fish, again, which are covered with a stony coat, such as the oyster, are produced from mud in a putrid state, or else from the foam that has collected around ships which have been lying for a long time in the same position, about posts driven into the earth, and more especially around logs of wood. It has been discovered, of late years, in the oyster-beds, that the animal discharges an impregnating liquid, which has the appearance of milk. Eels, again, rub themselves against rocks, upon which, the particles which they thus scrape from off their bodies come to life, such being their only means of reproduction. The various kinds of fishes do not couple out of their own kind, with the exception of the squatina and the ray.

---

12 Tadpoles.

Book IX - The Natural History of Fishes

The fish that is produced from the union of these two, resembles a ray in the fore part, and bears a name among the Greeks compounded of the two.

LAND FISHES

Besides these, there are still some wonderful kinds of fishes which we find mentioned by Theophrastus; he says, that when the waters subside, which have been admitted for the purposes of irrigation in the vicinity of Babylon, there are certain fish which remain in such holes as may contain water; from these they come forth for the purpose of feeding, moving along with their fins by the aid of a rapid movement of the tail. If pursued, he says, they retreat to their holes, and, when they have reached them, will turn round and make a stand. The head is like that of the sea-frog, while the other parts are similar to those of the gobio, and they have gills like other fish. He says also, that in the vicinity of Heraclea and Cromna, and about the river Lycus, as well as in many parts of the Euxine, there is one kind of fish which frequents the waters near the banks of the rivers, and makes holes for itself, in which it lives, even when the water retires and the bed of the river is dry; for which reason these fishes have to be dug out of the ground, and only show by the movement of the body that they are still alive. He says also, that in the vicinity of the same Heraclea, when the river Lycus ebbs, the eggs are left in the mud, and that the fish, on being produced from these, go forth to seek their food by means of a sort of fluttering motion —their gills being but very small, in consequence of which they are not in need of water; for this reason it is that eels also can live so long out of water; and that their eggs come to maturity on dry land, like those of the sea-tortoise.

THE MICE OF THE NILE

But all these things, singular as they are, still are rendered credible by a marvel which exceeds them all, at the time of the inundation of the Nile; for, the moment that it subsides, little mice are found, the first rudiments of which have been formed by the generative powers of the waters and the earth; in one part of the body they are already alive, while in that which is of later formation, they are still composed of earth.

Book X
The Natural History of Birds

THE OSTRICH

The history of the birds follows next, the very largest of which, and indeed almost approaching to the nature of quadrupeds, is the ostrich of Africa or Æthiopia. This bird exceeds in height a man sitting on horseback, and can surpass him in swiftness, as wings have been given to aid it in running; in other respects ostriches cannot be considered as birds, and do not raise themselves from the earth. They have cloven talons, very similar to the hoof of the stag; with these they fight, and they also employ them in seizing stones for the purpose of throwing at those who pursue them. They have the marvellous property of being able to digest every substance without distinction, but their stupidity is no less remarkable; for although the rest of their body is so large, they imagine, when they have thrust their head and neck into a bush, that the whole of the body is concealed. Their eggs are prized on account of their large size, and are employed as vessels for certain purposes, while the feathers of the wing and tail are used as ornaments for the crest and helmet of the warrior.

THE PŒNIX

Æthiopia and India, more especially, produce birds of diversified plumage, and such as quite surpass all description. In the front rank of these is the phoenix, that famous bird of Arabia; though I am not quite sure that its existence is not all a fable. It is said that there is only one in existence in the whole world, and that one has not been seen very often. We are told that this bird is of the size of an eagle, and has a brilliant golden plumage around the neck, while the rest of the body is of a purple colour; except the tail, which is azure, with long feathers intermingled of a roseate hue; the throat is adorned with a crest, and the head with a tuft of feath-

ers. The first Roman who described this bird, and who has done so with the greatest exactness, was the senator Manilius, so famous for his learning; which he owed, too, to the instructions of no teacher. He tells us that no person has ever seen this bird eat, that in Arabia it is looked upon as sacred to the sun, that it lives five hundred and forty years, that when it becomes old it builds a nest of cassia and sprigs of incense, which it fills with perfumes, and then lays its body down upon them to die; that from its bones and marrow there springs at first a sort of small worm, which in time changes into a little bird; that the first thing that it does is to perform the obsequies of its predecessor, and to carry the nest entire to the city of the Sun near Panchaia, and there deposit it upon the altar of that divinity.

THE EAGLE

Of all the birds with which we are acquainted, the eagle is looked upon as the most noble, and the most remarkable for its strength. There are six different kinds; the one called "melanaetos" by the Greeks, and "valeria" in our language, the least in size of them all, but the most remarkable for its strength, is of a blackish colour. It is the only one among all the eagles that feeds its young; for the others, as we shall mention just now, drive them away; it is the only one too that has neither cry nor murmur; it is an inhabitant of the mountains. The second kind is the pygargus, an inhabitant of the cities and plains, and distinguished by the whiteness of its tail. The third is the morphnos, which Homer also calls the "perenos," while others, again, call it the "plangus" and the "anataria" is the second in size and strength, and dwells in the vicinity of lakes. Phemonoe, who was styled the "daughter of Apollo," has stated that this eagle has teeth, but that it has neither voice nor tongue. This eagle has the instinct to break the shell of the tortoise by letting it fall from aloft, a circumstance which caused the death of the poet Æschylus. An oracle, it is said, had predicted his death on that day by the fall of a house, upon which he took the precaution of trusting himself only under the canopy of the heavens.

The fourth kind of eagle is the "perenopterus," also called the "oripelargus"; it has much the appearance of the vulture, with remarkably small wings, while the rest of the body is larger than the others; but it is of a timid and degenerate nature, so much so, that even a raven can beat it. It is always famishing and ravenous, and has a plaintive murmuring cry. It is the only one among the eagles that will carry off the dead carcase; the others settle on the spot where they have killed their prey. The character of this species causes the fifth one to be known by the distinctive name of "gnesios," as being the genuine eagle, and the only one of untainted lineage; it is of moderate size, of rather reddish colour, and rarely to be met with. The haliætus is the last, and is remarkable for its bright and piercing eye. It poises itself

Book X - The Natural History of Birds

aloft, and the moment it catches sight of a fish in the sea below, pounces headlong upon it, and cleaving the water with its breast, carries off its prey.

Caius Marius, in his second consulship, assigned the eagle exclusively to the Roman legions. Before that period it had only held the first rank, there being four others as well, the wolf, the minotaur, the horse, and the wild boar, each of which preceded a single division. Some few years before his time it had begun to be the custom to carry the eagle only into battle, the other standards being left behind in camp; Marius, however, abolished the rest of them entirely. Since then, it has been remarked that hardly ever has a Roman legion encamped for the winter, without a pair of eagles making their appearance at the spot.

The first and second species of eagle, not only prey upon the whole of the smaller quadrupeds, but will attack deer even. Rolling in the dust, the eagle covers its body all over with it, and then perching on the antlers of the animal, shakes the dust into its eyes, while at the same time it beats it on the head with its wings, until the creature at last precipitates itself down the rocks. Nor, indeed, is this one enemy sufficient for it; it has still more terrible combats with the dragon,[1] and the issue is much more doubtful, although the battle is fought in the air. The dragon seeks the eggs of the eagle with a mischievous avidity; while the eagle, in return, carries it off whenever it happens to see it; upon these occasions, the dragon coils itself about the wings of the bird in multiplied folds, until at last they fall to the earth together.

HAWKS

We find no less than sixteen kinds of hawks mentioned; among these are the ægithus, which is lame of one leg, and is looked upon as the most favourable omen for the augurs on the occasion of a marriage, or in matters connected with property in the shape of cattle; the triorchis also, so called from the number of its testicles, and to which Phemonoë has assigned the first rank in augury. This last is by the Romans known as the "buteo"; indeed there is a family that has taken its surname from it, from the circumstance of this bird having given a favourable omen by settling upon the ship of one of them when he held a command. The Greeks call one kind "epileus"; the only one, indeed, that is seen at all seasons of the year, the others taking their departure in the winter.

The various kinds are distinguished by the avidity with which they seize their prey; for while some will only pounce on a bird while on the ground, others will only seize it while hovering round the trees, others, again, while it is perched aloft, and others while it is flying in mid air. Hence it is that pigeons, on seeing them, are aware of the nature of the danger to which they are exposed, and either settle on the ground or else fly upwards, instinctively protecting themselves by taking due precautions against their natural propensities.

CROWS – BIRDS OF ILL OMEN

Crows, have another kind of food. Nuts being too hard for their beak to break, the crow flies to a great height, and then lets them fall again and again upon the

---

1 By the "dragon" he means some large serpent.

stones or tiles beneath, until at last the shell is cracked, after which the bird is able to open them. This is a bird with a very ill-omened garrulity, though it has been highly praised by some. It is observed, that from the rising of the constellation Arcturus until the arrival of the swallow, it is but rarely to be seen about the sacred groves and temples of Minerva; in some places, indeed, not at all, Athens for instance. In addition to these facts, it is the only one that continues to feed its young for some time after they have begun to fly. The crow is most inauspicious at the time of incubation, or, in other words, just after the summer solstice.

THE WOOD-PECKER

There are some small birds also, which have hooked talons; the wood-pecker, for example, surnamed "of Mars," of considerable importance in the auspices. To this kind belong the birds which make holes in trees, and climb stealthily up them, like cats; mounting with the head upwards, they tap against the bark, and learn by the sound whether or not their food lies beneath; they are the only birds that hatch their young in the hollows of trees. It is a common belief, that if a shepherd drives a wedge into their holes, they apply a certain kind of herb, immediately upon which it falls out. Trebius informs us that if a nail or wedge is driven with ever so much force into a tree in which these birds have made their nest, it will instantly fly out, the tree making a loud cracking noise the moment that the bird has lighted upon the nail or wedge.

These birds have held the first rank in auguries, in Latium, since the time of the king who has given them their name. One of the presages that was given by them, I cannot pass over in silence. A woodpecker came and lighted upon the head of Æelius Tubero, the City prætor, when sitting on his tribunal dispensing justice in the Forum, and showed such tameness as to allow itself to be taken with the hand; upon which the augurs declared that if it was let go, the state was menaced with danger, but if killed, disaster would befall the prætor; in an instant he tore the bird to pieces, and before long the omen was fulfilled.

BIRDS WHICH HAVE HOOKED TALONS

Many birds of this kind feed also on acorns and fruit, but only those which are not carnivorous, with the exception of the kite; though when it feeds on anything but flesh, it is a bird of ill omen.

The birds which have hooked talons are never gregarious; each one seeks its prey by itself. They nearly all of them soar to a great height, with the exception of the birds of the night, and more especially those of larger size. They all have large wings, and a small body; they walk with difficulty, and rarely settle upon stones, being prevented from doing so by the curved shape of their talons.

THE DUNGHILL COCK

Next after the peacock, the animal that acts as our watchman by night, and which Nature has produced for the purpose of arousing mortals to their labours, and dispelling their slumbers, shows itself most actuated by feelings of vanity. The cock knows how to distinguish the stars, and marks the different periods of the day, every three hours, by his note. These animals go to roost with the setting of the sun, and at the fourth watch of the camp recall man to his cares and toils. They do not allow the rising of the sun to creep upon us unawares, but by their note proclaim the coming day, and they prelude their crowing by clapping their sides with their wings. They exercise a rigorous sway over the other birds of their kind, and, in every place where they are kept, hold the supreme command. This, however, is only obtained after repeated battles among themselves, as they are well aware that they have weapons on their legs, produced for that very purpose, as it were, and the contest often ends in the death of both the combatants at the same moment. If, on the other hand, one of them obtains the mastery, he instantly by his note proclaims himself the conqueror, and testifies by his crowing that he has been victorious; while his conquered opponent silently slinks away, and, though with a very bad grace, submits to servitude.

THE GOOSE

The goose also keeps a vigilant guard; a fact which is well attested by the defence of the Capitol, at a moment when, by the silence of the dogs, the commonwealth had been betrayed for which reason it is that the Censors always, the first thing of all, attend to the farming-out of the feeding of the sacred geese.

Our people only esteem the goose for the goodness of its liver. When they are crammed, this grows to a very large size, and on being taken from the animal, is made still larger by being soaked in honeyed milk.

A second income, too, is also to be derived from the feathers of the white goose. In some places, this animal is plucked twice a year, upon which the feathers quickly grow again. Those are the softest which lie nearest to the body, and those that come from Germany are the most esteemed: the geese there are white, but of small size, and are called *gantæ*. The price paid for their feathers is five denarii per pound. It is from this fruitful source that we have repeated charges brought against the commanders of our auxiliaries, who are in the habit of detaching whole cohorts from the posts where they ought to be on guard, in pursuit of these birds: indeed, we have come to such a pitch of effeminacy, that now-a-days, not even the men can think of lying down without the aid of the goose's feathers, by way of pillow.

THE CRANES

By the departure of the cranes, which were in the habit of waging war with them, the nation of the Pygmies now enjoys a respite. The tracts over which they travel must be immense, if we only consider that they come all the way from the Eastern Sea. These birds agree by common consent at what moment they shall set out, fly aloft to look out afar, select a leader for them to follow, and have sentinels duly posted in the rear, which relieve each other by turns, utter loud cries, and with their voice keep the whole flight in proper array. During the night, also, they place sentinels on guard, each of which holds a little stone in its claw; if the bird should happen to fall asleep, the claw becomes relaxed, and the stone falls to the ground, and so convicts it of neglect. The rest sleep in the meanwhile, with the head beneath the wing, standing first on one leg and then on the other; the leader looks out, with neck erect, and gives warning when required. These birds, when tamed, are very frolicsome, and even when alone will describe a sort of circle, as they move along, with their clumsy gait.

THE NIGHTINGALE

The song of the nightingale is to be heard, without intermission, for fifteen days and nights, continuously, when the foliage is thickening, as it bursts from the bud; a bird which deserves our admiration in no slight degree. First of all, what a powerful voice in so small a body! Its note, how long, and how well sustained! And then, too, it is the only bird the notes of which are modulated in accordance with the strict rules of musical science. At one moment, as it sustains its breath, it will prolong its note, and then at another, will vary it with different inflexions; then, again, it will break into distinct chirrups, or pour forth an endless series of roulades. Then it will warble to itself, while taking breath, or else disguise its voice in an instant; while sometimes, again, it will twitter to itself, now with a full note, now with a grave, now again sharp, now with a broken note, and now with a prolonged one. Sometimes, again, when it thinks fit, it will break out into quavers, and will run through, in succession, alto, tenor, and bass; in a word, in so tiny a throat is to be found all the melody that the ingenuity of man has ever discovered through the medium of the invention of the most exquisite flute; so much so, that there can be no doubt it was an infallible presage of his future sweetness as a poet, when one of these creatures perched and sang on the infant lips of the poet Stesichorus.

THE TIMES OF INCUBATION OF BIRDS

The birds that have a note, with the exception of those previously mentioned, do not by any chance produce their young before the vernal or after the autumnal equinox. As to the broods produced before the summer solstice, it is very doubtful if they will survive, but those hatched after it thrive well.

THE HALCYONES

It is for this that the halcyon[2] is more especially remarkable; the seas, and all those who sail upon their surface, well know the days of its incubation. This bird is a little larger than a sparrow, and the greater part of its body is of an azure blue colour, with only an intermixture of white and purple in some of the larger feathers, while the neck is long and slender. There is one kind that is remarkable for its larger size and its note; the smaller ones are heard singing in the reed-beds. It is a thing of very rare occurrence to see a halcyon, and then it is only about the time of the setting of the Vergiliæ, and the summer and winter solstices; when one is sometimes to be seen to hover about a ship, and then immediately disappear. They hatch their young at the time of the winter solstice, from which circumstance those days are known as the "halcyon days"; during this period the sea is calm and navigable, the Sicilian sea in particular. They make their nest during the seven days before the winter solstice, and sit the same number of days after. Their nests are truly wonderful; they are of the shape of a ball slightly elongated, have a very

---

2   The king-fisher, or *Alcedo ispida* of Linnæus.

narrow mouth, and bear a strong resemblance to a large sponge. It is impossible to cut them asunder with iron, and they are only to be broken with a strong blow, upon which they separate, just like foam of the sea when dried up. It has never yet been discovered of what material they are made; some persons think that they are formed of sharp fish-bones, as it is on fish that these birds live. They enter rivers also; their eggs are five in number.

PIGEONS

Chastity is especially observed by it, and promiscuous intercourse is a thing quite unknown. Although inhabiting a domicile in common with others, they will none of them violate the laws of conjugal fidelity; not one will desert its nest, unless it is either widower or widow. Although, too, the males are very imperious, and sometimes even extremely exacting, the females put up with it; for in fact, the males sometimes suspect them of infidelity, though by nature they are incapable of it. On such occasions the throat of the male seems quite choked with indignation, and he inflicts severe blows with the beak; and then afterwards, to make some atonement, he falls to billing, and by way of pressing his amorous solicitations, sidles round and round the female with his feet. They both of them manifest an equal degree of affection for their offspring; indeed, it is not infrequent that this is a ground for correction, in consequence of the female being too slow in going to her young. When the female is sitting, the male renders her every attention that can in any way tend to her solace and comfort. The first thing that they do is to eject from the throat some saltish earth, which they have digested, into the mouths of the young ones, in order to prepare them in due time to receive their nutriment. It is a peculiarity of the pigeon and of the turtle-dove, not to throw back the neck when drinking, but to take in the water at a long draught, just as beasts of burden do.

DIFFERENT MODES OF FLIGHT IN BIRDS

The flight of the pigeon also leads me to consider that of other birds as well. All other animals have one determinate mode of progression, which in every kind is always the same; it is birds alone that have two modes of moving —the one on the ground, the other in the air. Some of them walk, such as the crow, for instance; some hop, as the sparrow and the blackbird; some, again, run, as the partridge and the woodhen; while others throw one foot before the other, the stork and the crane, for instance. Then again, in their flight, some birds expand their wings, and, poising themselves in the air, only move them from time to time; others move them more frequently, but then only at the extremities; while others expand them so as to expose the whole of the side. On the other hand, some fly with the greater part of the wings kept close to the side; and some, after striking the air once, others twice, make their way through it, as though pressing upon it enclosed beneath their wings; other birds dart aloft in a vertical direction, others horizontally, and others come falling straight downwards. You would almost think that some had been hurled upwards with a violent effort, and that others, again, had fallen straight down from aloft; while others are seen to spring forward in their flight. Ducks alone, and the other birds of that kind, in an instant raise themselves aloft, taking a spring from the spot where they stand straight upwards towards the heavens; and this they can do from out of the water even; hence it is that they are the only birds that can make their escape from the pitfalls which we employ for the capture of wild beasts.

The vulture and the heavier wild birds can only fly after taking a run, or else by commencing their flight from an elevated spot. They use the tail by way of rudder. There are some birds that are able to see all around them; others, again, have to turn the neck to do so. Some of them eat what they have seized, holding it in their feet. Many, as they fly, utter some cry; while on the other hand, many, in their flght, are silent. Some fly with the breast half upright, others with it held downwards, others fly obliquely, or else side-ways, and others following the direction of the bill. Some, again, are borne along with the head upwards; indeed the fact is, that if we were to see several kinds at the same moment, we should not suppose that they have to make their way in the same element.

A SEDITION THAT AROSE AMONG THE ROMAN PEOPLE, IN CONSEQUENCE OF A RAVEN SPEAKING

Let us do justice, also, to the raven, whose merits have been attested not only by the sentiments of the Roman people, but by the strong expression, also, of their indignation. In the reign of Tiberius, one of a brood of ravens that had bred on the top of the temple of Castor, happened to. fly into a shoemaker's shop that stood opposite; upon which, from a feeling of religious veneration, it was looked upon as doubly recommended by the owner of the place. The bird, having been taught to speak at an early age, used every morning to fly to the Rostra, which look towards the Forum; here, addressing each by his name, it would salute Tiberius, and then the Cæsars Germanicus and Drusus, after which it would proceed to greet the Roman populace as they passed, and then return to the shop; for several years it was remarkable for the constancy of its attendance. The owner of another shoemaker's shop in the neighbourhood, in a sudden fit of anger killed the bird, enraged, as he would have had it appear, because with its ordure it had soiled some shoes of his. Upon this, there was such rage manifested by the multitude, that he was at once driven from that part of the city, and soon after put to death. The funeral, too, of the bird was celebrated with almost endless obsequies; the body was placed upon a litter carried upon the shoulders of two Æthiopians, preceded by a piper, and borne to the pyre with garlands of every size and description. The pyre was erected on the right-hand side of the Appian Way, at the second milestone from the City, in the field generally known as the "field of Rediculus." Thus did the rare talent of a bird appear a sufficient ground to the Roman people for honouring it with funeral obsequies, as well as for inflicting punishment on a Roman citizen; and that, too, in a city in which no such crowds had ever escorted the funeral of any one out of the whole number of its distinguished men, and where no one had been found to avenge the death of Scipio Æemilianus, the man who had destroyed Carthage and Numantia. This event happened in the consulship of M. Servilius and Gains Cestius, on the fifth day, before the calends of April.

FABULOUS BIRDS

The griffon

I look upon the birds as fabulous which are called "pegasi," and are said to have a horse's head; as also the griffons, with long ears and a hooked beak. The former are said to be natives of Scythia, the latter of Ethiopia. The same is my opinion, also, as to the tragopan many writers, however, assert that it is larger than the eagle, has curved horns on the temples, and a plumage of iron colour, with the exception of the head, which is purple. Nor yet do the sirens obtain any greater credit with me, although Dinon, the father of Clearchus, a celebrated writer, asserts that they exist in India, and that they charm men by their song, and, having first lulled them to sleep, tear them to pieces. The person, however, who may think fit to believe in these tales, may probably not refuse to believe also that dragons licked the ears of Melampodes, and bestowed upon him the power of understanding the language of birds; as also what Democritus says, when he gives the names of certain birds, by the mixture of whose blood a serpent is produced, the person who eats of which will be able to understand the language of birds; as well as the statements which the same writer makes relative to one bird in particular, known as the "galerita," –indeed the science of augury is already too much involved in embarrassing questions, without these fanciful reveries.

THE BAT

Among the winged animals, the only one that is viviparous is the bat; it is the only one, too, that has wings formed of a membrane. This is, also, the only winged creature that feeds its young with milk from the breast. The mother clasps her two young ones as she flies, and so carries them along with her. This animal, too, is said to have but one joint in the haunch, and to be particularly fond of gnats.

Book XI
The Various Kinds of Insects and Organs of Animals

We shall now proceed to a description of the insects, a subject replete with endless difficulties; for, in fact, there are some authors who have maintained that they do not respire, and that they are destitute of blood. The insects are numerous, and form many species, and their mode of life is like that of the terrestrial animals and the birds. Some of them are furnished with wings, bees for instance; others are divided into those kinds which have wings, and those which are without them, such as ants; while others, again, are destitute of both wings and feet. All these animals have been very properly called "insects," from the incisures or divisions which separate the body, sometimes at the neck, and sometimes at the corselet, and so divide it into members or segments, only united to each other by a slender tube. In some insects, however, this division is not complete, as it is surrounded by wrinkled folds; and thus the flexible vertebræ of the creature, whether situate at the abdomen, or whether only at the upper part of the body, are protected by layers, overlapping each other; indeed, in no one of her works has Nature more fully displayed her exhaustless ingenuity.

In large animals, on the other hand, or, at all events, in the very largest among them, she found her task easy and her materials ready and pliable; but in these minute creatures, so nearly akin as they are to non-entity, how surpassing the intelligence, how vast the resources, and how ineffable the perfection which she has displayed. Where is it that she has united so many senses as in the gnat? —not to speak of creatures that might be mentioned of still smaller size. Where, I say, has she found room to place in it the organs of sight? Where has she centred the sense of taste? Where has she inserted the power of smell? And where, too, has she implanted that sharp shrill voice of the creature, so utterly disproportionate to the smallness of its body? With what astonishing subtlety has she united the wings to the trunk, elongated the joints of the legs, framed that long, craving concavity for a belly, and then inflamed the animal with an insatiate thirst for blood, that of man more especially! What ingenuity has she displayed in providing it with a sting, so well adapted for piercing the skin! And then too, just as though she had the most extensive field for the exercise of her skill, although the weapon is so minute that it can hardly be seen, she has formed it with a twofold mechanism, providing it with a point for the purpose of piercing, and at the same moment making it hollow, to adapt it for suction.

What teeth, too, has she inserted in the teredo, to adapt it for piercing oak even with a sound which fully attests their destructive power! While at the same time she has made wood its principal nutriment. We give all our admiration to the shoulders of the elephant as it supports the turret, to the stalwart neck of the bull, and the might with which it hurls aloft whatever comes in its way, to the onslaught of the tiger, or to the mane of the lion; while, at the same time, Nature is nowhere to be seen to greater perfection than in the very smallest of her works. For this reason then, I must beg of my readers, notwithstanding the contempt they feel for many of these objects, not to feel a similar disdain for the information I am about to give relative thereto, seeing that, in the study of Nature, there are none of her works that are unworthy of our consideration.

BEES

But among them all, the first rank, and our especial admiration, ought, in justice, to be accorded to bees, which alone, of all the insects, have been created for the benefit of man. They extract honey and collect it. They form their combs and collect wax, an article that is useful for a thousand purposes of life; they are patient of fatigue, toil at their labours, form themselves into political communities, hold councils together in private, elect chiefs in common, and, a thing that is the most remarkable of all, have their own code of morals.

Bees keep within the hive during the winter —for whence are they to derive the strength requisite to withstand frosts and snows, and the northern blasts? The same, in fact, is done by all insects, but not to so late a period; as those which conceal themselves in the walls of our houses, are much sooner sensible of the returning warmth. They do not come forth to ply their labours until the bean blossoms; and then not a day do they lose in inactivity, while the weather is favourable for their pursuits.

First of all, they set about constructing their combs, and forming the wax, or, in other words, making their dwellings and cells; after this they produce their young, and then make honey and wax from flowers, and extract bee-glue from the tears of those trees which distil glutinous substances, the juices, gums, and resins, namely, of the willow, the elm, and the reed. With these substances, as well as others of a more bitter nature, they first line the whole inside of the hive, as a sort of protection against the greedy propensities of other small insects, as they are well aware that they are about to form that which will prove an object of attraction to them.

HOW BEES WORK

The manner in which bees carry on their work is as follows. In the day time a guard is stationed at the entrance of the hive, like the sentries in a camp. At night they take their rest until the morning, when one of them awakes the rest with a humming noise, repeated twice or thrice, just as though it were sounding a trumpet. They then take their flight in a body, if the day is likely to turn out fine; for they have the gift of foreknowing wind and rain, and in such case will keep close within their dwellings. On the other hand, when the weather is fine the swarm issues forth, and at once applies itself to its work, some loading their legs from the flowers, while others fill their mouths with water, and charge the downy surface of their bodies with drops of liquid. Those among them that are young go forth to their labours, and collect the materials already mentioned, while those that are more aged stay within the hives and work. The bees whose business it is to carry the flowers, with their fore feet load their thighs, which Nature has made rough for the purpose, and with their trunks load their fore feet; bending beneath their load, they then return to the hive, where there are three or four bees ready to receive them and aid in discharging their burdens. For, within the hive as well, they have their allotted duties to perform; some are engaged in building, others in smoothing the combs, while others again are occupied in passing on the materials, and others in preparing food from the provision which has been brought; that there may be no unequal division, either in their labour, their food, or the distribution of their time, they do not even feed separately.

Commencing at the vaulted roof of the hive, they begin the construction of their cells, and, just as we do in the manufacture of a web, they construct their cells from top to bottom, taking care to leave two passages around each compartment, for the entrance of some and the exit of others. The combs, which are fastened to the hive in the upper part, and in a slight degree also at the sides, adhere to each other, and are thus suspended altogether. They do not touch the floor of the hive, and are either angular or round, according to its shape; sometimes, in fact, they are both angular and round at once, when two swarms are living in unison, but have dissimilar modes of operation. They prop up the combs that are likely to fall, by means of arched pillars, at intervals springing from the floor, so as to leave them a passage for the purpose of effecting repairs. The first three ranks of their cells are generally left empty when constructed, that there may be nothing exposed to view which may invite theft; and it is the last ones, more especially, that are filled with honey hence it is that the combs are always taken out at the back of the hive.

The bees that are employed in carrying look out for a favourable breeze, and if a gale should happen to spring up, they poise themselves in the air with little stones, by way of ballast. When the wind is contrary, they fly close to the ground, taking care, however, to keep clear of the brambles. It is wonderful what strict watch is kept upon their work; all instances of idleness are carefully remarked, the offenders are chastised, and on a repetition of the fault, punished with death. Their sense of cleanliness, too, is quite extraordinary; everything is removed that might he in the way, and no filth is allowed to remain in the midst of their work. The ordure even of those that are at work within, that they may not have to retire to any distance, is all collected in one spot, and on stormy days, when they are obliged to cease their ordinary labours, they employ themselves in carrying it out. When it grows towards evening, the buzzing in the hive becomes gradually less and less, until at last one of their number is to be seen flying about the hive with the same loud humming noise with which they were aroused in the morning, thereby giving the signal, as it were, to retire to rest; in this, too, they imitate the usage of the camp. The moment the signal is heard, all is silent.

WASPS AND HORNETS

Wasps build their nests of mud in lofty places, and make wax therein; hornets, on the other hand, build in holes or under ground. With these two kinds the cells are also hexagonal, but, in other respects, though made of the bark of trees, they strongly resemble the substance of a spider's web. Their young also are found at irregular intervals, and are of unshapely appearance; while one is able to fly, another is still a mere pupa, and a third only in the maggot state. It is in the autumn, too, and not in the spring, that all their young are produced; and they grow during the full moon more particularly. The wasp which is known as the ichneumon, a smaller kind than the others, kills one kind of spider in particular, known as the phalangium; after which it carries the body to its nest, covers it over with a sort of gluey substance, and then sits and hatches from it its young. In addition to this, they are all of them carnivorous, while on the other hand bees will touch no animal substance whatever. Wasps more particularly pursue the larger flies, and after catching them cut off the head and carry away the remaining portion of the body.

Wild hornets live in the holes of trees, and in winter, like other insects, keep themselves concealed; their life does not exceed two years in length. It is not infrequent that their sting is productive of an attack of fever, and there are authors who say that thrice nine stings will suffice to kill a man.

THE SILK-WORM

There is another class also of these insects produced in quite a different manner. These last spring from a grub of larger size, with two horns of very peculiar appearance. The larva then becomes a caterpillar, after which it assumes the state in which it is known as bombylis, then that called necydalus, and after that, in six months, it becomes a silk-worm. These insects weave webs similar to those of the spider, the material of which is used for making the more costly and luxurious garments of females, known as "bombycina." Pamphile, a woman of Cos, the daughter of Platea, was the first person who discovered the art of unravelling these webs and spinning a tissue therefrom; indeed, she ought not to be deprived of the glory of having discovered the art of making vestments which, while they cover a woman, at the same moment reveal her naked charms.

SPIDERS

It is by no means an absurdity to append to the silk-worm an account of the spider, a creature which is worthy of our especial admiration. There are numerous kinds of spiders. Those that bear the name of phalangium are of small size, with bodies spotted and running to a point; their bite is venomous, and they leap as they move from place to place. Another kind, again, is black, and the fore-legs are remarkable for their length. They have all of them three joints in the legs. The smaller kind of wolf-spider does not make a web, but the larger ones make their holes in the earth, and spread their nets at the narrow entrance thereof. A third kind, again, is remarkable for the skill which it displays in its operations. These spin a large web, and the abdomen suffices to supply the material for so extensive a work, whether it is that, at stated periods the excrements are largely secreted in the abdomen, as Democritus thinks, or that the creature has in itself a certain faculty of secreting a peculiar sort of woolly substance. With what wondrous art does it conceal the snares that lie in wait for its prey in its checkered nettings! How little, too, would it seem that there is any such trap laid in the compactness of its web and the tenacious texture of the woof, which would appear of itself to be finished and arranged by the exercise of the very highest art! How loose, too, is the body of the web as it yields to the blasts, and how readily does it catch all objects which come in its way!

SCORPIONS

In a similar manner to the spider, the land scorpion also produces maggots similar to eggs, and dies in a similar manner. This animal is a dangerous scourge, and has a venom like that of the serpent; with the exception that its effects are far more painful, as the person who is stung will linger for three days before death ensues. The sting is invariably fatal to virgins, and nearly always so to matrons. It is so to men also, in the morning, when the animal has issued from its hole in a fasting state, and has not yet happened to discharge its poison by any accidental stroke. The tail is always ready to strike, and ceases not for an instant to menace, so that no opportunity may possibly be missed. The animal strikes too with a sidelong blow, or else by turning the tail upwards. For this pest of Africa, the southern winds have provided means of flight as well, for as the breeze bears them along, they extend their arms and ply them like so many oars in their flight; the same Apollodorus, however, asserts that there are some which really have wings. In Scythia, the scorpion is able to kill the swine even with its sting, an animal which, in general, is proof against poisons of this kind in a remarkable degree. When stung, those swine which are black die more speedily than others, and more particularly if they happen to throw themselves into the water. When a person has been stung, it is generally supposed that he may be cured by drinking the ashes of the scorpion mixed with wine.

LOCUSTS

Those insects which have feet, move sideways. Some of them have the hind feet longer than the fore ones, and curving outwards, the locust, for example.

These creatures lay their eggs in large masses, in the autumn, thrusting the end of the tail into holes which they form in the ground. These eggs remain underground throughout the winter, and in the ensuing year, at the close of spring, small locusts issue from them, of a black colour, and crawling along without legs and wings. Hence it is that a wet spring destroys their eggs, while, if it is dry, they multiply in great abundance.

They are looked upon as a plague inflicted by the anger of the gods; for as they fly they appear to be larger than they really are, while they make such a loud noise with their wings, that they might be readily supposed to be winged creatures of quite another species. Their numbers, too, are so vast, that they quite darken the sun. Those from Africa are the ones which chiefly devastate Italy. The Parthians look upon them as a choice food, and the grasshopper as well.

INSECTS THAT ARE PARASITES OF MAN

In dead carrion there are certain animals produced, and in the hair, too, of living men. It was through such vermin as this that the Dictator Sylla, and Aleman, one of the most famous of the Grecian poets, met their deaths. These insects infest birds too, and are apt to kill the pheasant, unless it takes care to bathe itself in the dust. Of the animals that are covered with hair, it is supposed that the ass and the sheep are the only ones that are exempt from these vermin. They are produced, also, in certain kinds of cloth, and more particularly those made of the wool of sheep which have been killed by the wolf. I find it stated, also, by authors, that some kinds of water which we use for bathing are more productive of these parasites than others. Even wax is found to produce mites, which are supposed to be the very smallest of all living creatures. Other insects, again, are engendered from filth, acted upon by the rays of the sun-these fleas are called "petauristæ," from the activity which they display in their hind legs. Others, again, are produced with wings, from the moist dust that is found lying in holes and corners.

THE PYRALLIS OR PYRAUSTA

That fire, which is so destructive to matter, produces certain animals; for in the copper-smelting furnaces of Cyprus, in the very midst of the fire, there is to be seen flying about a four-footed animal with wings, the size of a large fly; this creature is called the "pyrallis," and by some the "pyrausta." So long as it remains in the fire it will live, but if it comes out and flies a little distance from it, it will instantly die.

HERE PLINY STOPS WRITING ABOUT INSECTS AND INSTEAD WRITES ABOUT DIFFERENT ORGANS OF ALL KINDS OF ANIMALS

DIFFERENT KINDS OF HORNS

Horns, too, of various forms have been granted to many animals of the aquatic, marine, and reptile kind, but those which are more properly understood under that name belong to the quadrupeds only; for I look upon the tales of Actæon and of Cippus even, in Latin story, as nothing more nor less than fables. And, indeed, in no department of her works has Nature displayed a greater capriciousness. In providing animals with these weapons, she has made merry at their expense; for some she has spread them out in branches, the stag, for instance; to others she has given them in a more simple form. In others, again, she has flattened them in the shape of a man's hand, with the fingers extended, from which circumstance the animal has received the name of "platyceros." To the roebuck she has given branching horns, but small, and has made them so as not to fall off and be cast each year; while to the ram she has given them of a contorted and spiral form, as though she were providing it with a cæstus for offence. The horns of the bull, again, are upright and threatening. In this last kind, the females, too, are provided with them, while in most it is only the males. The chamois has them, curving backwards; while in the fallow deer they bend forward. The strepsiceros, which in Africa bears the name of addax, has horns erect and spiral, grooved and tapering to a sharp point, so much so, that you would almost take them to be the sides of a lyre. In the oxen of Phrygia, the horns are moveable, like the ears; and among the cattle of the Troglodytæ, they are pointed downwards to the ground, for which reason it is that they are obliged to feed with the head on one side. Other animals, again, have a single horn, and that situate in the middle of the head, or else on the nose, as already stated.

Then, again, in some animals the horns are adapted for butting, and in others for goring; with some they are curved inwards, with others outwards, and with others, again, they are fitted for tossing; all which objects are effected in various ways, the horns either lying backwards, turning from, or else towards each other, and in all cases running to a sharp point. In one kind, also, the horns are used for the purpose of scratching the body, instead of hands.

THE BRAIN

The brain exists in all animals which have blood, and in those sea animals as well, which we have already mentioned as mollusks, although they are destitute of blood, the polypus, for instance. Man, however, has, in proportion to his body, the most voluminous brain of all. This, too, is the most humid, and the coldest of all the viscera, and is enveloped above and below with two membranous integuments, for either of which to be broken is fatal. In addition to these facts, we may remark that the brain is larger in men than in women. In man the brain is destitute of blood and veins, and in other animals it has no fat.

The brain is the most elevated of all the viscera, and the nearest to the roof of the head; it is equally devoid of flesh, blood, and excretions. The senses hold this organ as their citadel; it is in this that are centred all the veins which spring from the heart; it is here that they terminate; this is the very culminating point of all, the regulator of the understanding. With all animals it is advanced to the fore-part of the head, from the fact that the senses have a tendency to the direction in which we look. From the brain proceeds sleep, and its return it is that causes the head to nod. Those creatures, in fact, which have no brain, never sleep.

THE EYES

Below the forehead are the eyes, which form the most precious portion of the human body. Eyes, however, have not been granted to all animals; oysters have none, but, with reference to some of the shell-fish, the question is still doubtful.

Among quadrupeds the mole has no sight, though it has something that bears a resemblance to eyes, if we remove the membrane that is extended in front of them. Among birds also, it is said that a species of heron, which is known as the "leucus," is wanting of one eye; a bird of most excellent augury, when it flies towards the south or north, for it is said that it portends thereby that there is about to be an end of perils and alarms.

The eyes vary in colour in the human race only; in all other animals they are of one uniform colour peculiar to the kind, though there are some horses that have eyes of an azure colour. But in man the varieties and diversities are most numerous; the eyes being either large, of middling size, remarkably small, or remarkably prominent. In addition to this, there are some persons who can see to a very great distance. The vision of many stands in need of the rays of the sun; such persons cannot see on a cloudy day, nor yet after the sun has set. Others, again, have bad sight in the day-time, but a sight superior to that of others by night.

It is only some few beasts of burden that are subject to maladies of the eyes towards the increase of the moon; but it is man alone that is rescued from blindness by the discharge of the humours that have caused it. Many persons have had their sight restored after being blind for twenty years; while others, again, have been denied this blessing from their very birth, without there being any blemish in the eyes

The most learned authors say that there are veins which communicate from the eye to the brain, but I am inclined to think that the communication is with the stomach; for it is quite certain that a person never loses the eye without feeling sickness at the stomach. It is an important and sacred duty, of high sanction among the Romans, to close the eyes of the dead, and then again to open them when the body is laid on the funeral pile, the usage having taken its rise in the notion of its being improper that the eyes of the dead should be beheld by man, while it is an equally great offence to hide them from the view of heaven.

The eyes of animals that see at night in the dark, cats, for instance, are shining and radiant, so much so, that it is impossible to look upon them; those of the she-goat, too, and the wolf are resplendent, and emit a light like fire. The eyes of the seal and the hyena change successively to a thousand colours; and the eyes, when dried, of most of the fishes will give out light in the dark, just in the same way as the trunk of the oak when it has become rotten with extreme old age.

THE TEETH

Teeth are arranged in three different ways, serrated, in one continuous row, or else protruding from the mouth. When serrated they unite together, just like those of a comb, in order that they may not be worn by rubbing against one another, as in serpents, fishes, and dogs, for instance. In some creatures they are set in one continuous row, man and the horse, for instance; while in the wild boar, the elephant, and the hippopotamus, they protrude from the mouth. Among those set in one continuous row, the teeth which divide the food are broad and sharp, while those which grind it are double; the teeth which lie between the incisive and the molar teeth, are those known as the canine or dog-teeth; these are by far the largest in those animals which have serrated teeth. There are many fishes that have teeth upon the tongue and over the whole of the mouth, in order that, by the multitude of the bites which they inflict, they may soften those articles of food which they could not possibly manage by tearing.

The asp also, and other serpents, have similar teeth; but in the upper jaw, on the right and left, they have two of extreme length, which are perforated with a small tube in the interior, just like the sting of the scorpion, and it is through these that they eject their venom. No winged creatures have teeth, with the sole exception of the bat. The camel is the only one among the animals without horns, that has no fore-teeth in the upper jaw.

THE HEART; THE BLOOD; THE VITAL SPIRIT

In all other animals but man the heart is situate in the middle of the breast; in man alone it is placed just below the pap on the left-hand side, the smaller end terminating in a point, and bearing outward. It is among the fish only that this point is turned towards the mouth. It is asserted that the heart is the first among the viscera that is formed in the fœtus, then the brain, and last of all, the eyes; it is said, too, that the eyes are the first organs that die, and the heart the very last of all. The heart also is the principal seat of the heat of the body; it is constantly palpitating, and moves as though it were one animal enclosed within another. It is also enveloped in a membrane equally supple and strong, and is protected by the bulwarks formed by the ribs and the bone of the breast, as being the primary source and origin of life. It contains within itself the primary receptacles for the spirit and the blood, in its sinuous cavity, which in the larger animals is threefold, and in all twofold at least; here it is that the mind has its abode. From this source proceed two large veins, which branch into the fore-part and the back of the body, and which, spreading out in a series of branches, convey the vital blood by other smaller veins over all parts of the body. This is the only one among the viscera that is not affected by maladies, nor is it subject to the ordinary penalties of human life; but when injured, it produces instant death.

THE GALL

In the liver is the gall,[1] which, however, does not exist in every animal. At Chalcis, in Eubœa, none of the cattle have it, while in the cattle of the Isle of Naxos, it is of extraordinary size, and double, so that to a stranger either of these facts would appear as good as a prodigy. The horse, the mule, the ass, the stag, the roe-buck, the wild boar, the camel, and the dolphin have no gall, but some kinds of rats and mice have it. Some few men are without it, and such persons enjoy robust health and a long life. When the gall is black, it is productive of madness in man, and if it is wholly expelled death will ensue. Hence it is, too, that the word "bile" has been employed by us to characterize a harsh, embittered disposition; so powerful are the effects of this secretion, when it extends its influence to the mind. In addition to

---

1 The gall bladder is situated in a fossa between the quadrate and right medial lobes of the liver. It acts as a reservoir for bile (TN).

this, when it is dispersed over the whole of the body, it deprives the eyes, even, of their natural colour; and when ejected, will tarnish copper vessels even, rendering everything black with which it comes in contact; so that no one ought to be surprised that it is the gall which constitutes the venom of serpents.

It is said, that in the small liver of the mouse the number of lobes corresponds to the day of the moon, and that they are found to be just as many in number as she is days old; in addition to which, it is said that it increases at the winter solstice. In the rabbits of Bætica, the liver is always found to have a double lobe. Ants will not touch one lobe of the liver of the bramble-frog, in consequence of its poisonous nature, it is generally thought. The liver is remarkable for its powers of preservation, and sieges have afforded us remarkable instances of its being kept so long as a hundred years.

RESEMBLANCE OF THE APE TO MAN

As to the various kinds of apes, they offer a perfect resemblance to man in the face, the nostrils, the ears, and the eyelids; being the only quadrupeds, in fact, that have eyelashes on the lower eyelid. They have mammæ also on the breast, arms and legs, which bend in opposite directions, and nails upon the hands and fingers, the middle finger being the longest. They differ somewhat from man in the feet; which, like the hands, are of remarkable length, and have a print similar to that of the palm of our hand. They have a thumb also, and articulations similar to those in man. The males differ from man in the sexual parts only, while all the internal viscera exactly resemble those of man.

PARTS OF THE HUMAN BODY TO WHICH RELIGIOUS IDEAS ARE ATTACHED

In accordance with the usages of various nations, certain religious ideas have been attached to the knees. It is the knees that suppliants clasp, and it is to these that they extend their hands; it is the knees that they worship like so many altars, as it were; perhaps, because in them is centred the vital strength. For in the joint of either knee, the right as well as the left, there is on the fore-side of each a certain empty space, which bears a strong resemblance to a mouth, and through which, like the throat, if it is once pierced, the vital powers escape. There are also certain religious ideas attached to other parts of the body, as is testified in raising the back of the right hand to the lips, and extending it as a token of good faith. It was the custom of the ancient Greeks, when in the act of supplication, to touch the chin. The seat of the memory lies in the lower part of the ear, which we touch when we summon a witness to depose upon memory to an arrest. The seat, too, of Nemesis lies behind the right ear, a goddess which has never yet found a Latin name, no, not in the Capitol even. It is to this part that we apply the finger next the little finger, after touching the mouth with it, when we silently ask pardon of the gods for having let slip an indiscreet word.

THE SEXUAL PARTS — HERMAPHRODITES

In some animals, the males have the sexual parts behind. In the wolf, the fox, the weasel, and the ferret, these parts are bony; and it is the genitals of the last-mentioned animal that supply the principal remedies for calculus in the human bladder. It is said also that the genitals of the bear are turned into a horny substance the moment it dies. Among the peoples of the East the very best bow-strings are those which are made of the member of the camel. These parts also, among different nations, are made the object of certain usages and religious observances; and the Galli, the priests of the Mother of the gods, are in the habit of castrating themselves, without any dangerous results. On the other hand, there is in some few women a monstrous resemblance to the male conformation, while hermaphrodites appear to partake of the nature of both. Instances of this last conformation were seen in quadrupeds in Nero's reign, and for the first time, I imagine; for he ostentatiously paraded hermaphrodite horses yoked to his car, which had been found in the territory of the Treviri, in Gaul; as if, indeed, it was so remarkably fine a sight to behold the ruler of the earth seated in a chariot drawn by monstrosities.

In sheep and cattle the testicles hang down to the legs, while in the boar they are knit up close to the body. In the dolphin they are very long, and are concealed in the lower part of the belly. In the elephant, also, they are quite concealed. In oviparous animals they adhere to the interior of the loins; these animals are the most speedy in the venereal congress. Fishes and serpents have no testicles, but in place of them they have two veins, which run from the renal region to the genitals. The bird known as the "buteo," has three testicles. Man is the only creature in which the testicles are ever broken, either accidentally or by some natural malady; those who are thus afflicted form a third class of half men, in addition to hermaphrodites and eunuchs. In all species of animals the male is more courageous than the female, with the exception of the panther and the bear.

SIGNS OF VITALITY AND MORAL DISPOSITION OF MAN, FROM THE LIMBS

I am greatly surprised that Aristotle has not only believed, but has even committed it to writing, that there are in the human body certain prognostics of the duration of life. He has set down the following as indications of a short life: few teeth, very long fingers, a leaden colour, and numerous broken lines in the palm of the hand. On the other hand, he looks upon the following as prognostics of a long life: stooping in the shoulders, one or two long unbroken lines in the hand, a greater number than two-and-thirty teeth, and large ears. He does not, I imagine, require that all these symptoms should unite in one person, but looks upon them as individually significant; in my opinion, however, they are utterly frivolous, all of them, although they obtain currency among the vulgar. Our own writer, Trogus, has in a similar manner set down the physiognomy as indicative of the moral disposition; one of the very gravest of the Roman authors, whose own words I will here subjoin:

"Where the forehead is broad, it is significant of a dull and sluggish understanding beneath; and where it is small, it indicates an unsteady disposition. A rounded forehead denotes an irascible temper, it seeming as though the swelling anger had left its traces there. Where the eyebrows are extended in one straight line, they denote effeminacy in the owner, and when they are bent downwards towards the nose, an austere disposition. On the other hand, when the eyebrows are bent towards the temples, they are indicative of a sarcastic disposition; but when they lie very low, they denote malice and envy. Long eyes are significant of a spiteful, malicious nature and where the corners of the eyes next the nose are fleshy, it is a sign also of a wicked disposition. If the white of the eye is large, it bears tokens of impudence, while those who are incessantly closing the eyelids are inconstant. Largeness of the ears is a sign of loquacity and foolishness."

Book XII
The Natural History of Trees

The trees and forests are regarded as the most valuable benefits conferred by Nature upon mankind. It was from the forest that man drew his first aliment, by the leaves of the trees was his cave rendered more habitable, and by their bark was his clothing supplied; even at this very day, there are nations that live under similar circumstances to these.

The trees formed the first temples of the gods, and even at the present day, the country people, preserving in all their simplicity their ancient rites, consecrate the finest among their trees to some divinity; indeed, we feel ourselves inspired to adoration, not less by the sacred groves and their very stillness, than by the statues of the gods, resplendent as they are with gold and ivory. Each kind of tree remains immutably consecrated to its own peculiar divinity, the beech to Jupiter, the laurel to Apollo, the olive to Minerva, the myrtle to Venus, and the poplar to Hercules; besides which, it is our belief that the Sylvans, the Fauns, and various kinds of goddess Nymphs, have the tutelage of the woods, and we look upon those deities as especially appointed to preside over them by the will of heaven. In more recent times, it was the trees that by their juices, more soothing even than corn, first mollified the natural asperity of man; and it is from these that we now derive the oil of the olive that renders the limbs so supple, the draught of wine that so efficiently recruits the strength, and the numerous delicacies which spring up spontaneously at the various seasons of the year.

But, in addition to this, the trees have a thousand other uses, all of which are indispensable to the full enjoyment of life. It is by the aid of the tree that we plough the deep, and bring near to us far distant lands; it is by the aid of the tree, too, that we construct our edifices. The statues, even, of the deities were formed of the wood of trees, in the days when no value had been set as yet on the dead carcase of a wild beast, and when, luxury not yet deriving its sanction from the gods themselves, we had not to behold, resplendent with the same ivory, the heads of the divinities and the feet of our tables. It is related that the Gauls, separated from us as they were by the Alps, which then formed an almost insurmountable bulwark, had, as their chief motive for invading Italy, its dried figs, its grapes, its oil, and its wine. We may offer some excuse, then, for them, when we know that they came in quest of these various productions, though at the price even of war.

EXOTIC TREES

But who is there that will not, with good reason, be surprised to learn that a tree has been introduced among us from a foreign clime for nothing but its shade? I mean the plane,[1] which was first brought across the Ionian Sea to the Isle of Diomedes, there to be planted at his tomb, and was afterwards imported thence into Sicily, being one of the very first exotic trees that were introduced into Italy.

For we find in Italy some plane-trees, which are known as chamæplatani, in consequence of their stunted growth; for we have discovered the art of causing abortion in trees even, and hence, even in the vegetable world we shall have occasion to make mention of dwarfs, an unprepossessing subject in every case. This result is obtained in trees, by a peculiar method adopted in planting and lopping them.

The cherry and the peach, and all those trees which have either Greek or foreign names, are exotics; those, however, of this number, which have begun to be naturalized among us, will be treated of when I come to speak of the fruit-trees in general. For the present, I shall only make mention of the really exotic trees, beginning with the one that is applied to the most salutary uses. The citron tree, called the Assyrian, and by some the Median apple, is an antidote against poisons. The leaf is similar to that of the arbute, except that it has small prickles running across it. As to the fruit, it is never eaten, but it is remarkable for its extremely powerful smell, which is the case, also, with the leaves; indeed, the odour is so strong, that it will penetrate clothes, when they are once impregnated with it, and hence it is very useful in repelling the attacks of noxious insects. The tree bears fruit at all seasons of the year; while some is falling off, other fruit is ripening, and other, again, just bursting into birth. Various nations have attempted to naturalize this tree among them, for the sake of its medical properties, by planting it in pots of clay, with holes drilled in them, for the purpose of introducing the air to the roots; and I would here remark, once for all, that it is as well to remember that the best plan is to pack all slips of trees that have to be carried to any distance, as close together as they can possibly be placed. It has been found, however, that this tree will grow nowhere except in Media or Persia.

THE TREES OF INDIA

In describing the country of the Seres (Book VI), we have already made mention of the wool-bearing trees which it produces; and we have, likewise, touched

---

1   The Platanus orientalis of Linnæus.

upon the extraordinary magnitude of the trees of India. Virgil has spoken in glowing terms of the ebony-tree, one of those which are peculiar to India, and he further informs us, that it will grow in no other country. Herodotus, however, has preferred to ascribe it to Æthiopia; and states that the people of that country were in the habit of paying to the kings of Persia, every third year, by way of tribute, one hundred billets of ebony-wood, together with a certain quantity of gold and ivory. Nor ought we here to omit the fact, inasmuch as the same author has stated to that effect, that the Æthiopians were also in the habit of paying, by way of tribute, twenty large elephants' teeth. So high was the esteem in which ivory was held in the year from the building of our city.

There is in India, also, a kind of thorn very similar to ebony, though it may be distinguished from it, by the aid of a lantern even; for, on the application of flame, it will instantly run across the tree. We will now proceed to describe those trees which were the admiration of Alexander the Great in his victorious career, when that part of the world was first revealed by his arms.

There is another tree in India, of still larger size, and even more remarkable for the size and sweetness of its fruit, upon which the sages of India live. The leaf of this tree resembles, in shape, the wing of a bird, being three cubits in length, and two in breadth. It puts forth its fruit from the bark, a fruit remarkable for the sweetness of its juice, a single one containing sufficient to satisfy four persons. The name of this tree is "pala," and of the fruit, "ariena." They are found in the greatest abundance in the country of the Sydraci, a territory which forms the extreme limit of the expedition of Alexander.

Macir, too, is a vegetable substance that is brought from India, being a red bark that grows upon a large root, and bears the name of the tree that produces it; what the nature of this tree is, I have not been able to ascertain. A decoction of this bark, mixed with honey, is greatly employed in medicine, as a specific for dysentery.

In the vicinity, too, of India, is Bactriana, in which region we find bdellium[2] that is so highly esteemed. This tree is of a black colour, and about the size of the olive; it has leaves like those of the robur,[3] and bears a fruit similar to that of the wild fig, and in nature resembling a kind of gum. This fruit is by some persons called brochon, by others malacha, and by others, again, maldacon. When of a black colour, and rolled up in cakes, it bears the name of hadrobolon. This substance ought to be transparent and the colour of wax, odoriferous, unctuous when subjected to friction, and bitter to the taste, though without the slightest acidity.

TREES OF PERSIA

Adjoining the countries which we have previously mentioned is Persia, lying along the shores of the Red Sea, the tides of which penetrate far into the land. The trees in these regions are of a marvellous nature; for, corroded by the action of the

---

2   A name given to two aromatic gum-resins, similar to myrrh, but weaker. Indian bdellium is believed to be the product of *Balsamodendron Mukul*. They are used for the same purposes as myrrh, but chiefly as an ingredient in plasters and as a perfume (TN).

3   A very hard-wooded variety of oak (TN).

salt, and bearing a considerable resemblance to vegetable substances that have been thrown up and abandoned by the tide, they are seen to embrace the arid sands of the seashore with their naked roots, just like so many polypi. When the tide rises, buffeted by the waves, there they stand, fixed and immoveable; nay, more, at high water they are completely covered; a fact which proves to conviction, that they derive their nutriment from the salt contained in the water. The size of these trees is quite marvellous; in appearance they strongly resemble the arbute; the fruit, which on the outside is very similar to the almond, has a spiral kernel within.

In the same gulf, there is the island of Tylos, covered with a forest on the side which looks towards the East, where it is washed also by the sea at high tides. Each of the trees is in size as large as the fig; the blossoms are of an indescribable sweetness, and the fruit is similar in shape to a lupine, but so rough and prickly, that it is never touched by any animal. On a more elevated plateau of the same island, we find trees that bear wool, but of a different nature from those of the Seres; as in these trees the leaves produce nothing at all, and, indeed, might very readily be taken for those of the vine, were it not that they are of smaller size. They bear a kind of gourd, about the size of a quince; which, when arrived at maturity, bursts asunder and discloses a ball of down, from which a costly kind of linen cloth is made.

FRANKINCENSE

Next in affinity to cardamomum would have been cinnamomum, and this we should have now proceeded to speak of, were it not more convenient first to make mention of the treasures of Arabia, and the reasons for which that country has received the names of "Happy" and "Blest." The chief productions of Arabia are frankincense and myrrh, which last it bears in common with the country of the Troglodytæ. There is no country in the world that produces frankincense except Arabia, and, indeed, not the whole of that. Almost in the very centre of that region, are the Atramitæ. This district looks towards the north-east, and is rendered inaccessible by rocks on every side, while it is bounded on the right by the sea, from which it is shut out by cliffs of tremendous height. The soil of this territory is said to be of a milky white, a little inclining to red. In this district some lofty hills take their rise, and the trees, which spring up spontaneously, run downwards along the declivities to the plains.

The forest is allotted in certain portions; indeed, there is no one left to watch the trees after the incisions are made, and yet no one is ever known to plunder his neighbour. The incense which has accumulated during the summer is gathered in the autumn; it is the purest of all, and is of a white colour. The second gathering takes place in spring, incisions being made in the bark for that purpose during the winter; this, however, is of a red colour, and not to be compared with the other incense. The first, or superior kind of incense, is known as carfiathum, the latter is called dathiathum. It is thought, also, that the incense which is gathered from the tree while young is the whitest, though the produce of the old trees has the most powerful smell.

The incense, after being collected, is carried on camels' backs to Sabota, at which place a single gate is left open for its admission. To deviate from the high road while conveying it, the laws have made a capital offence. At this place the priests take by measure, and not by weight, a tenth part in honour of their god, whom they call Sabis; indeed, it is not allowable to dispose of it before this has been done; out of this tenth the public expenses are defrayed, for the divinity generously entertains all those strangers who have made a certain number of days' journey in coming thither.

MYRRH

According to some authors, myrrh is the produce of a tree that grows in the same forests as the incense-tree, though most say that they grow in different places; but the fact is that myrrh grows in many parts of Arabia.

Myrrh is grown also by being transplanted, and when thus cultivated is greatly preferred to that which is grown in the forests. The plant is greatly improved by raking and baring the roots; indeed, the cooler the roots are kept, the better it is.

Incisions are made in the myrrh-tree twice a year, and at the same season as in the incense-tree; but in the case of the myrrh-tree they are all made the way up from the root as far as the branches which are able to bear it. The tree spontaneously exudes, before the incision is made, a liquid which bears the name of stacte, and to which there is no myrrh that is superior. Second only in quality to this is the cultivated myrrh; of the wild or forest kind, the best is that which is gathered in summer. They give no tithes of myrrh to the god, because it is the produce of other countries as well; but the growers pay the fourth part of it to the king of the Gebanitæ. Myrrh is bought up indiscriminately by the common people, and then packed into bags; but our perfumers separate it without any difficulty, the principal tests of its goodness being its unctuousness and its aromatic smell.

CINNAMOMUM AND CASSIA

Fabulous antiquity, and Herodotus more particularly, have related that cinnamomum[4] and cassia are found in the nests of certain birds, and principally that of the phœnix, in the districts where Father Liber was brought up; and that these substances either fall from the inaccessible rocks and trees in which the nests are built, in consequence of the weight of the pieces of flesh which the birds carry up, or else are brought down by the aid of arrows loaded with lead. It is said, also, that cassia grows around certain marshes, but is protected by a frightful kind of bat armed with claws, and by winged serpents as well. All these tales, however, have been evidently invented for the purpose of enhancing the prices of these commodities.

The cinnamon shrub is only two cubits in height, at the most, the lowest being no more than a palm in height. It is about four fingers in breadth, and hardly has it risen six fingers from the ground, before it begins to put forth shoots and suckers. It has then all the appearance of being dry and withered, and while it is green

---

4 Cinnamon (TN).

it has no odour at all. The leaf is like that of wild marjoram, and it thrives best in dry localities, being not so prolific in rainy weather; it requires, also, to be kept constantly clipped. Though it grows on level ground, it thrives best among tangled brakes and brambles, and hence it is extremely difficult to be gathered. It is never gathered unless with the permission of the god, by whom some suppose Jupiter to be meant; the Æthiopians, however, call him Assabinus. They offer the entrails of forty-four oxen, goats, and rams, when they implore his permission to do so, but after all, they are not allowed to work at it before sunrise or after sunset. A priest divides the branches with a spear, and sets aside one portion of them for the god; after which, the dealer stores away the rest in lumps. There is another account given, which states that a division is made between the gatherers and the sun, and that it is divided into three portions, after which lots are twice drawn, and the share which falls to the sun is left there, and forthwith ignites spontaneously.

Cassia is a shrub also, which grows not far from the plains where cinnamon is produced, but in the mountainous localities; the branches of it are, however, considerably thicker than those of cinnamon. It is covered with a thin skin rather than a bark, and, contrary to what is the case with cinnamon, it is looked upon as the most valuable when the bark falls off and crumbles into small pieces. The shrub is three cubits in height, and the colours which it assumes are threefold; when it first shoots from the ground, for the length of a foot, it is white; after it has attained that height, it is red for half a foot, and beyond that it is black. This last is the part that is held in the highest esteem, and next to it the portion that comes next, the white part being the least valued of all.

BALSAMUM, OPOBALSAMUM AND XYLOBAL-SAMUM

But to all other odours that of balsamum is considered preferable, a plant that has been only bestowed by Nature upon the land of Judæa. In former times it was cultivated in two gardens only, both of which belonged to the kings of that country; one of them was no more than twenty jugera in extent, and the other somewhat smaller. The emperors Vespasianus and Titus had this shrub exhibited at Rome; indeed, it is worthy of signal remark, that since the time of Pompeius Magnus, we have been in the habit of carrying trees even in our triumphal processions.

There are three different kinds of balsamum. The first has a thin and hair-like foliage, and is known by the name of eutheriston. The second is of a rugged appearance, bending downwards, full of branches, and more odoriferous than the first; the name of this is trachy. The third kind is the eumeces, so called, because it is taller than the others; it has a smooth, even, bark. It is the second in quality, the eutheriston being inferior to the trachy. The seed of this plant has a flavour strongly resembling that of wine; it is of a reddish colour, and not without a certain amount of unctuousness. The branches of the shrub are thicker than those of the myrtle. Incisions are made in it either with glass, or else a sharp stone, or knives made of bone; it being highly injurious to touch the vital parts with iron, for in such case it will immediately wither away and die. On the other hand, it will allow of all the superfluous branches being pruned away with an instrument of iron even. The hand of the person who makes the incision is generally balanced by an artificial guide, in order that he may not accidentally inflict a wound in the wood beyond the bark.

A juice distils from the wound, which is known to us as opobalsamum; it is of extraordinary sweetness, but only exudes in tiny drops, which are then collected in wool, and deposited in small horns. When taken from out of these, the substance is placed in new earthen vessels; it bears a strong resemblance to a thick oil, and is of a white colour when fresh. It soon, however, turns red, and as it hardens loses its transparency. When Alexander the Great waged war in those parts, it was looked upon as a fair summer day's work to fill a single concha[5] with this liquid.

---

5   The concha, or "shell," was a Greek and Roman liquid measure, of which there were two sizes. The smaller was half a cyathus, 0.0412 of an English pint; the larger was about three times the size of the former, and was known also as the oxybaphum.

Book XIII
The Natural History of Exotic Trees, and an Account of Perfumes

Thus far we have been speaking of the trees which are valuable for the scents they produce, and each of which is a subject for our wonder in itself. Luxury, however, has thought fit to mingle all of these, and to make a single scent of the whole; hence it is that perfumes have been invented. Who was the first to make perfumes is a fact not recorded. In the times of the Trojan war they did not exist, nor did they use incense when sacrificing to the gods; indeed, people knew of no other smell, or rather stench, I may say, than that of the cedar and the citrus, shrubs of their own growth, as it arose in volumes of smoke from the sacrifices; still, however, even then, the extract of roses was known, for we find it mentioned as conferring additional value on olive-oil.

We ought, by good rights, to ascribe the first use of perfumes to the Persians, for they quite soak themselves in it, and so, by an adventitious recommendation, counteract the bad odours which are produced by dirt. The first instance of the use of perfumes that I have been able to meet with is that of the chest of perfumes which fell into the hands of Alexander, with the rest of the property of King Darius, at the taking of his camp. Since those times this luxury has been adopted by our own countrymen as well, among the most prized and, indeed, the most elegant of all the enjoyments of life, and has begun even to be admitted in the list of honours paid to the dead; for which reason we shall have to enlarge further on that subject. Those perfumes which are not the produce of shrubs will only be mentioned for the present by name; the nature of them will, however, be stated in their appropriate places.

The names of perfumes are due, some of them, to the original place of their composition, others, again, to the extracts which form their bases, others to the trees from which they are derived, and others to the peculiar circumstance under which they were first made; and it is as well, first of all, to know that in this respect the fashion has often changed, and that the high repute of peculiar kinds has been but transitory. In ancient times, the perfumes the most esteemed of all were those of the island of Delos, and at a later period those of Mendes. This degree of esteem is founded, not only on the mode of mixing them and the relative proportions, but according to the degree of favour or disfavour in which the various places which produce the ingredients are held, and the comparative excellence or degeneracy of the ingredients themselves.

The perfume which is the most readily prepared of all, and indeed, in all probability, the very first that was ever made, is that composed of bryon[1] and oil of balanus. In later times the Mendesian perfume was invented, a more complicated mixture, as resin and myrrh were added to oil of balanus, and at the present day they even add metopion as well, an Egyptian oil extracted from bitter almonds; to which have been added omphacium, cardamum, sweet rush, honey, wine, myrrh, seed of balsamum, galbanum, and resin of terebinth, as so many ingredients.

THE PALM-TREE

In other respects, Egypt is the country that is the best suited of all for the production of perfumes; and next to it, Campania, from its abundance of roses.

Judæa, too, is greatly renowned for its perfumes, and even still more so for its palm-trees, the nature of which I shall take this opportunity of enlarging upon. There are some found in Europe also. They are not uncommon in Italy, but are quite barren there. The palms on the coast of Spain bear fruit, but it is sour. The fruit of those of Africa is sweet, but quickly becomes vapid and loses its flavour; which, however is not the case with the fruit of those that grow in the East. From these trees a wine is made, and bread by some nations, and they afford an aliment for numerous quadrupeds. It will be with very fair reason then, that we shall confine our description to the palm-tree of foreign countries. There are none in Italy that grow spontaneously, nor, in fact, in any other part of the world, with the exception of the warm countries; indeed, it is only in the very hottest climates that this tree will bear fruit.

The palm-tree grows in a light and sandy soil, and for the most part of a nitrous quality. It loves the vicinity of flowing water; and as it is its nature to imbibe the whole of the year, there are some who are of opinion that in a year of drought it will receive injury from being manured even, if the manure is not first mixed with running water; this, at least, is the idea entertained by some of the Assyrians.

The varieties of the palm are numerous. First of all, there are those which do not exceed the size of a shrub; they are mostly barren, though sometimes they are known to produce fruit; the branches are short, and the tree is well covered with leaves all round. In many places this tree is used as a kind of rough-cast, as it

---

1   The name "bryon" seems also to have been extended to the buds of various trees of the Conifera class and of the white poplar. It is probably to the buds of the last tree that Pliny here alludes.

were, to protect the walls of houses against damp. The palms of greater height form whole forests, the trunk of the tree being protected all round by pointed leaves, which are arranged in the form of a comb; these, it must be understood, are wild palms, though sometimes, by some wayward fancy or other, they are known to make their appearance among the cultivated varieties. The other kinds are tall, round, and tapering; and being furnished with dense and projecting knobs or circles in the bark, arranged in regular gradation, they are found easy of ascent by the people in the East; in order to do which, the climber fastens a loop of osier round his body and the trunk, and by this contrivance ascends the tree with astonishing rapidity. All the foliage is at the summit, and the fruit as well; this last being situate, not among the leaves, as is the case with other trees, but hanging in clusters from shoots of its own among the branches, and partaking of the nature both of the grape and the apple. The leaves terminate in a sharp edge, like that of a knife, while the sides are deeply indented, a peculiarity which first gave the idea of a troop of soldiers presenting face on two sides at once; at the present day they are split asunder to form ropes and wythes for fastening, as well as light umbrellas for covering the head.

NINE KINDS OF GUM

It is universally agreed, that the best gum is that produced from the Egyptian thorn; it is of variegated appearance, of azure colour, clean, free from all admixture of bark, and adheres to the teeth; the price at which it sells is three denarii per pound. That produced from the bitter almond-tree and the cherry is of an inferior kind, and that which is gathered from the plum-tree is the worst of all. The vine, too, produces a gum, which is of the greatest utility in healing the sores of children; while that which is sometimes found on the olive-tree is used for the tooth-ache. Gum is also found on the elm upon Mount Corycus in Cilicia, and upon the juniper, but it is good for nothing; indeed, the gum of the elm found there is apt to breed gnats. From the sarcocolla also —such is the name of a certain tree— a gum exudes that is remarkably useful to painters and medical men; it is similar to incense dust in appearance, and for those purposes the white kind is preferable to the red. The price of it is the same as that mentioned above.

PAPYRUS – THE USE OF PAPER

We have not as yet taken any notice of the marsh plants, nor yet of the shrubs that grow upon the banks of rivers; before quitting Egypt, however, we must make some mention of the nature of the papyrus, seeing that all the usages of civilized life depend in such a remarkable degree upon the employment of paper —at all events, the remembrance of past events. M. Varro informs us that paper owes its discovery to the victorious career of Alexander the Great, at the time when Alexandria in Egypt was founded by him; before which period paper had not been used, the leaves of the palm having been employed for writing at an early period, and after that the bark of certain trees. In succeeding ages, public documents were inscribed on sheets of lead, while private memoranda were impressed upon linen cloths, or else engraved on tablets of wax; indeed, we find it stated in Homer, that tablets were employed for this purpose even before the time of the Trojan war. It is generally supposed, too, that the country which that poet speaks of as Egypt, was not the same that is at present understood by that name, for the Sebennytic and the Saitic[2] Nomes, in which all the papyrus is produced, have been added since his time by the alluvion of the Nile; indeed, he himself has stated that the main-land was a day and a night's sail from the island of Pharos, which island at the present day is united by a bridge to the city of Alexandria. In later times, a rivalry having sprung up between King Ptolemy and King Eumenes, in reference to their respective libraries, Ptolemy prohibited the export of papyrus; upon which, as Varro relates, parchment was invented for a similar purpose at Pergamus. After this, the use of that commodity, by which immortality is ensured to man, became universally known.

Papyrus grows either in the marshes of Egypt, or in the sluggish waters of the river Nile, when they have overflowed and are lying stagnant, in pools that do not exceed a couple of cubits in depth. The root lies obliquely, and is about the thickness of one's arm; the section of the stalk is triangular, and it tapers gracefully upwards towards the extremity, being not more than ten cubits at most in height. Very much like a thyrsus[3] in shape, it has a head on the top, which has no seed in it, and, indeed, is of no use whatever, except as a flower employed to crown the statues of the gods. The natives use the roots by way of wood, not only for firing, but for various other domestic purposes as well. From the papyrus itself they construct boats also, and of the outer coat they make sails and mats, as well as cloths, besides coverlets and ropes; they chew it also, both raw and boiled, though they swallow the juice only. The papyrus grows in Syria also, on the borders of the same lake around which grows the sweet-scented calamus.

Paper is made from the papyrus, by splitting it with a needle into very thin leaves, due care being taken that they should be as broad as possible. That of the first quality is taken from the centre of the plant, and so in regular succession, according to the order of division. "Hieratica" was the name that was anciently given to it, from the circumstance that it was entirely reserved for the religious books. The paper of the next quality was called "amphitheatrica." The skilful manufactory that was established by Fannius at Rome, was in the habit of receiving this last kind, and there, by a very careful process of insertion, it was rendered much finer; so much so, that from being a common sort, he made it a paper of first-rate quality, and gave his own name to it. Next to this is the Saitic paper, so called from the city of that name, where it is manufactured in very large quantities, though of cuttings of inferior quality.

---

2   His argument is, that paper made from the papyrus could not be known in the time of Homer, as that plant only grew in certain districts which had been rescued from the sea since the time of the poet.

3   This was a pole represented as being carried by Bacchus and his Bacchanalian train. It was mostly terminated by the fir cone, that tree being dedicated to Bacchus, in consequence of the use of its cones and turpentine in making wine.

All these various kinds of paper are made upon a table, moistened with Nile water; a liquid which, when in a muddy state, has the peculiar qualities of glue. This table being first inclined, the leaves of papyrus are laid upon it lengthwise, as long, indeed, as the papyrus will admit of, the jagged edges being cut off at either end; after which a cross layer is placed over it, the same way, in fact, that hurdles are made. When this is done, the leaves are pressed close together, and then dried in the sun; after which they are united to one another, the best sheets being always taken first, and the inferior ones added afterwards. There are never more than twenty of these sheets to a roll.

THE LOTUS

Africa, too, at least that part of it which looks towards our shores, produces a remarkable tree, the lotus, by some known as the "celtis," which has also been naturalized in Italy, though it has been somewhat modified by the change of soil. The finest quality of lotus is that found in the vicinity of the Syrtes and among the Nasamones. It is the same size as the pear-tree, although Cornelius Nepos states to the effect that it is but short. The leaves have numerous incisions, just as with those of the holm-oak. There are many varieties of the lotus, which are characterized more particularly by the difference in their respective fruits. The fruit is of about the size of a bean, and its colour is that of saffron, though before it is ripe it is continually changing its tints, like the grape. It has branches thickly set with leaves, like the myrtle, and not, as with us in Italy, like the cherry. In the country to which this tree is indigenous, the fruit of it is so remarkably sweet and luscious, that it has even given its name to a whole territory, and to a nation who, by their singular hospitality, have even seduced strangers who have come among them, to lose all remembrance of their native country. It is said also, that those who eat this fruit are subject to no maladies of the stomach.

The fruit which has no stone in the inside is the best; this stone in the other kind seems to be of an osseous nature. A wine is also extracted from this fruit very similar to honied wine; according to Nepos, however, it will not last above ten days; he states also that the berries are chopped up with alica, and then put away in casks for the table. Indeed, we read that armies have been fed upon this food when marching to and fro through the territory of Africa. The wood is of a black colour, and is held in high esteem for making flutes; from the root also they manufacture handles for knives, and various other small articles.

Book XIV
The Natural History of Vines and Viticulture

Those which have been hitherto mentioned, are, nearly all of them, exotic trees, which it is impossible to rear in any other than their native soil, and which are not to be naturalized in strange countries. It is now for us to speak of the more ordinary kinds, of all of which Italy may be looked upon as more particularly the parent. At this fact I cannot sufficiently express my astonishment, that of some trees all memory has utterly perished, and that the very names of some, of which we find various authors making mention, have wholly disappeared. As to ourselves, however, we shall continue our researches into matters now lost in oblivion, nor shall we be deterred from pursuing our task by the trivial nature of some of our details, a consideration which has in no way influenced us in our description of the animal world. And yet we find that Virgil, that most admirable poet, has allowed this to influence him, in his omission to enlarge upon the beauties of the garden; for, happy and graceful poet as he is, he has only culled what we may call the flower of his subject; indeed, we find that he has only named in all some fifteen varieties of the grape, three of the olive, the same number of the pear, and the citron of Assyria, and has passed over the rest in silence altogether.

With what then ought we to begin in preference to the vine, the superiority in which has been so peculiarly conceded to Italy, that in this one blessing we may pronounce her to have surpassed those of all other nations of the earth, with the sole exception of those that bear the various perfumes, and even there, when the vine is in flower, there is not a perfume known which in exquisite sweetness can surpass it. The vine has been justly reckoned by the ancients among the trees, on account of its remarkable size. In the city of Populonium, we see a statue of Jupiter formed of the trunk of a single vine, which has for ages remained proof against all decay; and at Massilia, there is a patera made of the same wood. At Metapontum, the temple of Juno has long stood supported by pillars formed of the like material; and even at the present day we ascend to the roof of the temple of Diana at Ephesus, by stairs constructed, it is said, of the trunk of a single vine, that was brought from Cyprus; the vines of that island often attaining a most remarkable size. There is not a wood in existence of a more lasting nature than this; I am strongly inclined, however, to be of opinion that the material of which these various articles were constructed was the wild vine.

THE NATURE OF THE GRAPE, AND THE CULTIVATION OF THE VINE

The cultivated vine is kept down by pruning every year, and all the strength of the tree is drawn as much as possible into the shoots, or else thrown downwards to the sets;[1] indeed, it is only allowed to expand with the view of ensuring an abundant supply of juice, a result which is obtained in various modes according to the peculiarities of the climate and the nature of the soil. In Campania they attach the vine to the poplar; embracing the tree to which it is thus wedded, the vine grasps the branches with its amorous arms, and as it climbs, holds on with its knotted trunk, till it has reached the very summit; the height being sometimes so stupendous that the vintager when hired is wont to stipulate for his funeral pile and a grave at the owner's expense. The vine keeps continually on the increase, and it is quite impossible to separate the two, or rather, I may say, to tear them asunder. Valerianus Cornelius has regarded it as one of the most remarkable facts that could be transmitted to posterity, that single vines have been known to surround villas and country houses with their shoots and creeping tendrils ever on the stretch. At Rome, in the porticoes of Livia, a single vine, with its leaf-clad trellises, protects with its shade the walks in the open air; the fruit of it yields twelve amphoræ of must.[2]

VARIETIES OF THE VINE

Democritus, who has declared that he was acquainted with every variety of the grape known in Greece, is the only person who has been of opinion that every kind could be enumerated; but, on the other hand, the rest of the authors have stated that they are quite innumerable and of infinite extent, an assertion the truth of which will be more evident, if we only consider the vast number of wines. I shall not attempt, then, to speak of every kind of vine, but only of those that are the most remarkable, seeing that the varieties are very nearly as numberless as the districts in which they grow. It will suffice, then, to point out those which are the most remarkable among the vines, or else are peculiar for some wonderful property.

The very highest rank is given to the Aminean grape, on account of the body and durability of its wine, which improves with old age. The second rank belongs to the vines of Nomentum, the wood of which is red, from which circumstance the vines have received from some the name of "rubellæ." The vine known as the "apiana," has received that name from the bee, an insect which is remarkably fond

---

1 Or "layers," "propagines."
2 "Mustum." Pure, unfermented juice of the grape.

BOOK XIV - THE NATURAL HISTORY OF VINES AND VITICULTURE

of it; there are two varieties of this vine. The small Greek grape is not inferior to the Aminean for the excellence of its quality; the berry is remarkably thin-skinned, and the cluster so extremely small, that it is not worth while cultivating it, except on a soil of remarkable richness.

The wines produced from the vines of which we have hitherto made mention, even though the grapes are black, become, all of them, when old, of a white complexion. The other vines are of no note in particular, though sometimes, thanks to some peculiarity either in the climate or the soil, the wines produced from them attain a mature old age; such, for instance, as the Fecenian vine, and the Biturigian, which blossoms at the same time with it, but has not so many grapes.

THE NATURE OF WINES

It is the property of wine, when drunk, to cause a Feeling of warmth in the interior of the viscera, and, when poured upon the exterior of the body, to be cool and refreshing. It will not be foreign to my purpose on the present occasion to state the advice which Androcydes, a man famous for his wisdom, wrote to Alexander the Great, with the view of putting a check on his intemperance; "When you are about to drink wine, O king!" said he, "remember that you are about to drink the blood of the earth; hemlock is a poison to man, wine a poison to hemlock." And if Alexander had only followed this advice, he certainly would not have had to answer for slaying his friends in his drunken fits. In fact, we may Feel ourselves quite justified in saying that there is nothing more useful than wine for strengthening the body, while, at the same time, there is nothing more pernicious as a luxury, if we are not on our guard against excess.

WINES DRUNK BY THE ANCIENT ROMANS

The wines that were the most esteemed among the ancient Romans were those perfumed with myrrh, as mentioned in the play of Plautus, entitled the "Persian," though we find it there stated that calamus ought to be added to it. Hence it is, that some persons are of opinion that they were particularly fond of aromatites; but Fabius Dossennus quite decides the question, in the following line: "I sent them good wine, myrrh-wine"; and in his play called "Acharistio," we find these words: "Bread and pearled barley, myrrh—wine too." I find, too, that Scævola and L. Ælius, and Ateius Capito, were of the same opinion; and then we read in the play known as the "Pseudolus": "But if it is requisite for him to draw forth what is sweet from the place, has he aught of that?" To which Charinus makes answer, "Do you ask the question? He has myrrh wine, raisin wine, defrutum,[3] and honey"; from which it would appear that myrrh wine was not only reckoned among the wines, but among the sweet wines too.

WINE WITH MIRACULOUS PROPERTIES

There are some miraculous properties, too, in certain wines. It is said that in Arcadia there is a wine grown which is productive of fruitfulness in women, and of madness in men; while in Achaia, and more especially in the vicinity of Carynia,

---

3   Must boiled down to half its original quantity.

there is a wine which causes abortion; an effect which is equally produced if a woman in a state of pregnancy happens only to eat a grape of the vine from which it is grown, although in taste it is in no way different from ordinary grapes; again, it is confidently asserted that those who drink the wine of Trœzen never bear children. Thasos, it is said, produces two varieties of wine with quite opposite properties. By one kind sleep is produced, by the other it is prevented. There is also in the same island a vine known as the "theriaca," the wine and grapes of which are a cure for the bites of serpents. The libanian vine also produces a wine with the smell of frankincense, with which they make libations to the gods, while, on the other hand, the produce of that known as "aspendios," is banished from all the altars; it is said, too, that this last vine is never touched by any bird.

WINE-VESSELS — WINE-CELLARS

The various methods of keeping and storing wines in the cellar are very different. In the vicinity of the Alps, they put their wines in wooden vessels hooped around;[4] during their cold winters, they even keep lighted fires, to protect the wines from the effects of the cold. It is a singular thing to mention, but still it has been occasionally seen, that these vessels have burst asunder, and there has stood the wine in frozen masses; a miracle almost, as it is not ordinarily the nature of wine to freeze, cold having only the effect of benumbing it. In more temperate climates, they place their wines in wine-vats, which they bury in the earth, either covering them entirely or in part, according to the temperature. Sometimes, again, they expose their wines in the open air, while at others they are placed beneath sheds for protection from the atmosphere.

The following are among the rules given for the proper management of wines: One side of the wine-cellar, or, at all events, the windows, ought to face the northeast, or at least due east. All dunghills and roots of trees, and everything of a repulsive smell, ought to be kept at as great a distance as possible, wine being very apt to contract an odour. Fig-trees too, either wild or cultivated, ought not to be planted in the vicinity. Intervals should also be left between the vessels, in order to prevent infection, in case of any of them turning bad, wine being remarkably apt to become tainted. The shape, too, of the vessels is of considerable importance; those that are broad and bellying are not so good. We find it recommended too, to pitch them immediately after the rising of the Dog-star, and then to wash them either with sea or salt water, after which they should be sprinkled with the ashes of tree-shoots or else with potters' earth; they ought then to be cleaned out, and perfumed with myrrh, a thing which ought to be frequently done to the wine-cellars as well. Weak, thin wines should be kept in wine-vats sunk in the ground, while those in which the stronger ones are kept should be more exposed to the air. The vessels ought on no account to be entirely filled, room being left for seasoning, by mixing either raisin wine or else defrutum flavoured with saffron; old pitch and sapa are sometimes used for the same purpose. The lids, too, of the wine-vats ought to be seasoned in a similar manner, with the addition of mastich and Bruttian pitch.

---

4   Casks, in fact, similar to those used in France at the present day.

Book XV
The Olive and Other Fruit-trees

Theophrastus, one of the most famous among the Greek writers, who flourished about the year 440 of the City of Rome, has asserted that the olive does not grow at a distance of more than forty miles from the sea. Fenestella tells us that in the year of Rome 173, being the reign of Tarquinius Priscus, it did not exist in Italy, Spain, or Africa; whereas at the present day it has crossed the Alps even, and has been introduced into the two provinces of Gaul and the middle of Spain.

Hesiod, who looked upon an acquaintance with agriculture as conducive in the very highest degree to the comforts of life, has declared that there was no one who had ever gathered fruit from the olive-tree that had been sown by his own hands, so slow was it in reaching maturity in those times; whereas, now at the present day, it is sown in nurseries even, and if transplanted will bear fruit the following year.

Fabianus maintains that the olive will grow neither in very cold climates, nor yet in very hot ones. Virgil has mentioned three varieties of the olive, the orchites, the radius, and the posia; and says that they require no raking or pruning, nor, in fact, any attention whatever. There is no doubt that in the case of these plants, soil and climate are the things of primary importance; but still, it is usual to prune them at the same time as the vine, and they are improved by lopping between them every here and there. The gathering of the olive follows that of the grape, and there is even a greater degree of skill required in preparing oil than in making wine; for the very same olives will frequently give quite different results. The first oil of all, produced from the raw olive before it has begun to ripen, is considered preferable to all the others in flavour; in this kind, too, the first droppings of the press are the most esteemed, diminishing gradually in goodness and value; and this, whether the wicker-work basket is used in making it, or whether, following the more recent plan, the pulp is put in a stick strainer, with narrow spikes and interstices. The riper the berry, the more unctuous the juice, and the less agreeable the taste. To obtain a result both abundant and of excellent flavour, the best time to gather it is when the berry is just on the point of turning black. In this state it is called "druppa" by us, by the Greeks, "drypetis."

It is not with olive oil as it is with wine, for by age it acquires a bad flavour, and at the end of a year it is already old. This, if rightly understood, is a wise provision on the part of Nature; wine, which is only produced for the drunkard, she has seen no necessity for us to use when new; indeed, by the fine flavour which it acquires with age, she rather invites us to keep it; but, on the other hand, she has not willed that we should be thus sparing of oil, and so has rendered its use common and universal by the very necessity there is of using it while fresh.

THE NATURE OF OLIVE OIL

It is one of the properties of oil to impart warmth to the body, and to protect it against the action of cold; while at the same time it promotes coolness in the head when heated. The Greeks, those parents of all vices, have abused it by making it minister to luxury, and employing it commonly in the gymnasium; indeed, it is a well-known fact that the governors of those establishments have sold the scrapings of the oil used there for a sum of eighty thousand sesterces. The majesty of the Roman sway has conferred high honour upon the olive; crowned with it, the troops of the Equestrian order are wont to defile upon the ides of July; it is used, too, by the victor in the minor triumphs of the ovation. At Athens, also, they are in the habit of crowning the conqueror with olive; and at Olympia, the Greeks employ the wild olive for a similar purpose.

THE CULTURE OF THE OLIVE ACCORDING TO CATO

We will now proceed to mention the precepts given by Cato in relation to this subject. Upon a warm, rich soil, he recommends us to sow the greater radius, the Salentina, the orchites,[1] the posia,[2] the Sergian, the Cominian, and the albicera;[3] but with a remarkable degree of prudence he adds, that those varieties ought to be planted in preference which are considered to thrive best in the neighbouring localities. In a cold and meagre soil he says that the Licinian olive should be planted; and he informs us that a rich or hot soil has the effect, in this last variety, of spoiling the oil, while the tree becomes exhausted by its own fertility, and is liable to be attacked by a sort of red moss. He states it as his opinion that the olive grounds ought to have a western aspect, and, indeed, he approves of no other.

According to him, the best method of preserving olives is to put the orchites and the posia, while green, in a strong brine, or else to bruise them first, and preserve them in mastich oil. The more bitter the olive, he says, the better the oil; but

---

1   Oblong olive (TN).
2   Olive species (TN).
3   Pale yellow, wax-white (TN).

they should be gathered from the ground the very moment they fall, and washed if they are dirty. He says that three days will be quite sufficient for drying them, and that if it is frosty weather, they should be pressed on the fourth, care being taken to sprinkle them with salt. Olives, he informs us, lose oil by being kept in a boarded store-room, and deteriorate in quality; the same being the case, too, if the oil is left with the amurca[4] and the pulp, or, in other words, the flesh of the olive that forms the residue and becomes the dregs. For this reason, he recommends that the oil should be poured off several times in the day, and then put into vessels or cauldrons of lead, for copper vessels will spoil it, he says. All these operations, however, should be carried on with presses heated and tightly closed, and exposed to the air as little as possible —for which reason he recommends that wood should never be cut there, the most convenient fuel for the fires being the stones of the berries. From the cauldron the oil should be poured into vats, in order that the pulp and the amurca may be disengaged in a solidified form; to effect which object the vessels should be changed as often as convenient, while at the same time the osier baskets should be carefully cleaned with a sponge, that the oil may run out in as clean and pure a state as possible. In later times, the plan has been adopted of invariably crushing the olives in boiling water, and at once putting them whole in the press —a method of effectually extracting the amurca— and then, after crushing them in the oil-press, subjecting them to pressure once more. It is recommended, that not more than one hundred modii should be pressed at one time; the name given to this quantity is "factus," while the oil that flows out at the first pressure is called the "flos." Four men, working at two presses day and night, ought to be able to press out three factuses of olives.

OTHER KINDS OF FRUIT-TREES

The other fruits found on trees can hardly be enumerated, from their diversity in shape and figure, without reference to their different flavours and juices, which have again been modified by repeated combinations and graftings.

The largest fruit, and, indeed, the one that hangs at the greatest height, is the pine-nut. It contains within a number of small kernels, enclosed in arched beds, and covered with a coat of their own of rusty iron-colour; Nature thus manifesting a marvellous degree of care in providing its seeds with a soft receptacle. Another variety of this nut is the terentina, the shell of which may be broken with the fingers; and hence it becomes a prey to the birds while still on the tree. A third, again, is known as the "sappinia," being the produce of the cultivated pitch-tree; the kernels are enclosed in a skin more than a shell, which is so remarkably soft that it is eaten together with the fruit. A fourth variety is that known as the "pityis"; it is the produce of the pinaster, and is remarkable as a good specific for coughs. The kernels are sometimes boiled in honey among the Taurini, who then call them "aquiceli." The conquerors at the Isthmian games are crowned with a wreath of pine-leaves.

---

4 Amurca is the bitter-tasting, dark-colored, watery sediment that settles out of unfiltered olive oil over time. It is also known as "olive oil lees" (TN).

Under the head of apples, we include a variety of fruits, although of an entirely different nature, such as the Persian apple, for instance, and the pomegranate, of which, when speaking of the tree, we have already enumerated nine varieties. The pomegranate has a seed within, enclosed in a skin; the peach has a stone inside. Some among the pears, also, known as "libralia," show, by their name, what a remarkable weight they attain.

Next comes a vast number of varieties of the plum, the parti-coloured, the black, the white, the barley plum —so called, because it is ripe at barley-harvest— and another of the same colour as the last, but which ripens later, and is of a larger size, generally known as the "asinina," from the little esteem in which it is held. There are the onychina, too, the cerina —more esteemed, and the purple plum; the Armenian, also an exotic from foreign parts, the only one among the plums that recommends itself by its smell.

THE PEACH

The name of "Persica," or "Persian apple," given to this fruit, fully proves that it is an exotic in both Greece as well as Asia, and that it was first introduced from Persia. As to the wild plum, it is a well-known fact that it will grow anywhere; and I am, therefore, the more surprised that no mention has been made of it by Cato, more particularly as he has pointed out the method of preserving several of the wild fruits as well. As to the peach-tree, it has been only introduced of late years, and with considerable difficulty; so much so, that it is perfectly barren in the Isle of Rhodes, the first resting-place that it found after leaving Egypt.

It is quite untrue that the peach which grows in Persia is poisonous, and produces dreadful tortures, or that the kings of that country, from motives of revenge, had it transplanted in Egypt, where, through the nature of the soil, it lost all its evil properties —for we find that it is of the "persea" that the more careful writers have stated all this, a totally different tree, the fruit of which resembles the red myxa, and, indeed, cannot be successfully cultivated anywhere but in the East. The learned have also maintained that it was not introduced from Persis into Egypt with the view of inflicting punishment, but say that it was planted at Memphis by Perseus; for which reason it was that Alexander gave orders that the victors should be crowned with it in the games which he instituted there in honour of his ancestor; indeed, this tree has always leaves and fruit upon it, growing immediately upon the others. It must be quite evident to every one that all our plums have been introduced since the time of Cato.

VARIOUS METHODS OF GRAFTING TREES

This branch of civilized life has long since been brought to the very highest pitch of perfection, for man has left nothing untried here. Hence it is that we find Virgil speaking of grafting the nut-tree on the arbutus, the apple on the plane, and the cherry on the elm. Indeed, there is nothing further in this department that can possibly be devised, and it is a long time since any new variety of fruit has been discovered. Religious scruples, too, will not allow indiscriminate grafting; thus, for instance, it is not permitted to graft upon the thorn, for it is not easy, by any mode

BOOK XV - THE OLIVE AND OTHER FRUIT-TREES

of expiation, to avoid the disastrous effects of lightning; and we are told that as many as are the kinds of trees that have been engrafted on the thorn, so many are the thunderbolts that will be hurled against that spot in a single flash.

HOW TO KEEP VARIOUS FRUITS AND GRAPES

For the better preserving of fruits it is universally recommended that the store-room should be located in a cool, dry spot, with a well-boarded floor, and windows looking towards the north; which in fine weather ought to be kept open. Care should also be taken to keep out the south wind by window panes, while at the same time it should be borne in mind that a north-east wind will shrivel fruit and make it unsightly. Apples are gathered after the autumnal equinox; but the gathering should never begin before the sixteenth day of the moon, or before the first hour of the day. Windfalls should always be kept separate, and there ought to be a layer of straw, or else mats or chaff, placed beneath. They should, also, be placed apart from each other, in rows, so that the air may circulate freely between them, and they may equally gain the benefit of it. The Amerinian apple is the best keeper, the melimelum the very worst of all.

Quinces ought to be stored in a place kept perfectly closed, so as to exclude all draughts; or else they should be boiled in honey or soaked in it. Pomegranates are made hard and firm by being first put in boiling sea-water, and then left to dry for three days in the sun, care being taken that the dews of the night do not touch them; after which they are hung up, and when wanted for use, washed with fresh water. M. Varro recommends that they should be kept in large vessels filled with sand; if they are not ripe, he says that they should be put in pots with the bottom broken out, and then buried in the earth, all access to the air being carefully shut, and care being first taken to cover the stalk with pitch. By this mode of treatment, he assures us, they will attain a larger size than they would if left to ripen on the tree. As for the other kinds of pomes, he says that they should be wrapped up separately in fig-leaves, the windfalls being carefully excluded, and then stored in baskets of osier, or else covered over with potters' earth.

Pears are kept in earthen vessels pitched inside; when filled, the vessels are reversed and then buried in pits. The Tarentine pear, Varro says, is gathered very late, while the Anician keeps very well in raisin wine. Sorb apples, too, are similarly kept in holes in the ground, the vessel being turned upside down, and a layer of plaster placed on the lid; it should be buried two feet deep, in a sunny spot; sorbs are also hung, like grapes, in the inside of large vessels, together with the branches.

FIGS

Of all the remaining fruits that are included under the name of "pomes," the fig is the largest; some, indeed, equal the pear, even, in size.

Speaking of figs, Cato has the following remarks: "Plant the fig called the 'marisca' on a chalky or open site, but for the African variety, the Herculanean, the Saguntine, the winter fig and the black Telanian with a long stalk, you must select a richer soil, or else a ground well manured." Since his day there have so many names and kinds come up, that even on taking this subject into consideration, it must be apparent to every one how great are the changes which have taken place in civilized life.

There are winter figs, too, in some of the provinces, the Mœsian, for instance; but they are made so by artificial means, such not being in reality their nature. Being a small variety of the fig-tree, they cover it up with manure at the end of autumn, by which means the fruit on it is overtaken by winter while still in a green state; then when the weather, becomes milder the fruit is uncovered along with the tree, and so restored to light. Just as though it had come into birth afresh, the fruit imbibes the heat of the new sun with the greatest avidity —a different sun, in fact, to that which originally gave it life— and so ripens along with the blossom of the coming crop; thus attaining maturity in a year not its own, and this in a country, too, where the greatest cold prevails.

HISTORICAL ANECDOTES CONNECTED WITH THE FIG

The mention by Cato of the variety which bears the name of the African fig, strongly recalls to my mind a remarkable fact connected with it and the country from which it takes its name.

Burning with a mortal hatred to Carthage, anxious, too, for the safety of his posterity, and exclaiming at every sitting of the senate that Carthage must be destroyed, Cato one day brought with him into the Senate-house a ripe fig, the produce of that country. Exhibiting it to the assembled senators, "I ask you," said he, "when, do you suppose, this fruit was plucked from the tree?" All being of opinion that it had been but lately gathered, —"Know then," was his reply, "that this fig was plucked at Carthage but the day before yesterday, so near is the enemy to our walls." It was immediately after this occurrence that the third Punic war commenced, in which Carthage was destroyed, though Cato had breathed his last, the year after this event. In this trait which are we the most to admire? Was it ingenuity and foresight on his part, or was it an accident that was thus aptly turned to advantage? which, too, is the most surprising, the extraordinary quickness of the passage which must have been made, or the bold daring of the man? The thing, however, that is the most astonishing of all is the fact that a city thus mighty, the rival of Rome for the sovereignty of the world during a period of one hundred and twenty years, owed its fall at last to an illustration drawn from a single fig!

In the Forum even, and in the very midst of the Comitium of Rome, a fig-tree is carefully cultivated, in memory of the consecration which took place on the occasion of a thunderbolt which once fell on that spot; and still more, as a memorial of the fig-tree which in former days overshadowed Romulus and Remus, the founders of our empire, in the Lupercal Cave. This tree received the name of "ruminalis," from the circumstance that under it the wolf was found giving the breast to the two infants. A group in bronze was afterwards erected to consecrate the remembrance of this miraculous event, as, through the agency of Attus Navius the augur, the tree itself had passed spontaneously from its original locality to the Comitium in the Forum. And not without some direful presage is it that that tree has withered away, though, thanks to the care of the priesthood, it has been since replaced.

THE SORB

There are four varieties of the sorb; there being some that have all the roundness of the apple, while others are conical like the pear, and a third sort are of an oval shape, like some of the apples; these last, however, are apt to be remarkably acid. The round kind is the best for fragrance and sweetness, the others having a vinous flavour; the finest, however, are those which have the stalk surrounded with tender leaves. A fourth kind is known by the name of "torminalis"; it is only employed, however, for remedial purposes. The tree is a good bearer, but does not resemble the other kinds, the leaf being nearly that of the plane-tree; the fruit, too, is particularly small. Cato speaks of sorbs being preserved in boiled wine.

THE WALNUT

The walnut, which would almost claim precedence of the sorb in size, yields the palm to it in reference to the esteem in which they are respectively held; and this, although it is so favourite an accompaniment of the Fescennine songs at nuptials. This nut, taken as a whole, is very considerably smaller than the pine nut, but the kernel is larger in proportion. Nature, too, has conferred upon it a peculiar honour, in protecting it with a two-fold covering, the first of which forms a hollowed cushion for it to rest upon, and the second is a woody shell. It is for this reason that this fruit has been looked upon as a symbol consecrated to marriage, its offspring being thus protected in such manifold ways; an explanation which bears a much greater air of probability than that which would derive it from the rattling which it makes when it bounds from the floor. The Greek names that have been given to this fruit fully prove that it, like many others, has been originally introduced from Persia; the best kinds being known in that language by the names of "Persicum," and "basilicon; these, in fact, being the names by which they were first known to us. It is generally agreed, too, that one peculiar variety has derived its name of "caryon," from the headache which it is apt to produce by the pungency of its smell.

The green shell of the walnut is used for dyeing wool, and the nuts, while still small and just developing themselves, are employed for giving a red hue to the hair; a discovery owing to the stains which they leave upon the hands. When old, the nut becomes more oleaginous. This is the only fruit that Nature has enclosed in a covering formed of pieces soldered together; the shell, in fact, forming a couple of boats, while the kernel is divided into four separate compartments by the intervention of a ligneous membrane.

THE MYRTLE

The nature of the juices that are found in the myrtle are particularly remarkable, for it is the only one of all the trees, the berries of which produce two kinds of oil as well as of wine, besides myrtidanum. The berry of this was also put to another use in ancient times, for before pepper was known it was employed in place of it as a seasoning; so much so, indeed, that a name has been derived from it for the highly-seasoned dish which to this day is known by the name of "myrtatum." It is by the aid of these berries, too, that the flavour of the flesh of the wild boar is improved, and they generally form one of the ingredients in the flavouring of our sauces.

This tree was seen for the first time in the regions of Europe, which commence on this side of the Ceraunian mountains, growing at Circeii, near the tomb of Elpenor there; it still retains its Greek name,[5] which clearly proves it to be an exotic. There were myrtles growing on the site now occupied by Rome, at the time of its foundation; for a tradition exists to the effect that the Romans and the Sabines, after they had intended fighting, on account of the virgins who had been ravished by the former, purified themselves, first laying down their arms, with sprigs of myrtle, on the very same spot which is now occupied by the statues of Venus Cluacina; for in the ancient language "cluere" means to purify.

This tree is employed, too, for a species of fumigation; being selected for that purpose, because Venus, who presides over all unions, is the tutelary divinity of the tree. I am not quite sure, too, whether this tree was not the very first that was planted in the public places of Rome, the result of some ominous presage by the augurs of wondrous import. For at the Temple of Quirinus, or, in other words, of Romulus himself, one of the most ancient in Rome, there were formerly two myrtle-trees, which grew for a long period just in front of the temple; one of these was called the Patrician tree, the other the Plebeian. The Patrician myrtle was for many years the superior tree, full of sap and vigour; indeed, so long as the Senate maintained its superiority, so did the tree, being of large growth, while the Plebeian tree presented a meagre, shrivelled appearance. In later times, however, the latter tree gained the superiority, and the Patrician myrtle began to fail just at the period of the Marsic War, when the power of the Senate was so greatly weakened; and little by little did this once majestic tree sink into a state of utter exhaustion and sterility. There was an ancient altar also, consecrated' to Venus Myrtea, known at the present day by the name of Murcia.

Cato makes mention of three varieties of the myrtle, the black, white, and the conjugula, perhaps so called from its reference to conjugal unions, and belonging to the same species as that which grew where Cluacina's statues now stand; at the present day the varieties are differently distinguished into the cultivated and the wild myrtle, each of which includes a kind with a large leaf.

The myrtle has played its part, also, in the successes of war. Posthumius Tubertus, who gained a victory over the Sabines in his consulship, was the first person who entered the City enjoying the honour of an ovation, for having achieved this success with ease and without bloodshed; upon which occasion he made his entry crowned with the myrtle of Venus Victrix, and thereby rendered her tree an object of regard to our enemies even. Ever since this occasion, the wreath of those who have enjoyed an ovation has been made of myrtle, with the exception of M. Crassus, who, on his victory over the fugitive slaves and Spartacus, made his entry crowned with laurels.

---

5   μυρσίνη, was its Greek name.

THE LAUREL

The laurel is especially consecrated to triumphs, is remarkably ornamental to houses, and guards the portals of our emperors and our pontiffs; there suspended alone, it graces the palace, and is ever on guard before the threshold. Cato speaks of two varieties of this tree, the Delphic and the Cyprian. Pompeius Lenæus has added another, to which he has given the name of "mustax," from the circumstance of its being used for putting under the cake known by the name of "mustaceum." He says that this variety has a very large leaf, flaccid, and of a whitish hue; that the Delphic laurel is of one uniform colour, greener than the other, with berries of very large size, and of a red tint approaching to green. He says, too, that it is with this laurel that the victors at Delphi are crowned, and warriors who enjoy the honours of a triumph at Rome. The Cyprian laurel, he says, has a short leaf, is of a blackish colour, with an imbricated edge, and crisped.

This tree is emblematical of peace; when a branch of it is extended, it is to denote a truce between enemies in arms. For the Romans more particularly it is the messenger of joyful tidings, and of victory; it accompanies the despatches of the general, and it decorates the lances and javelins of the soldiers and the fasces which precede their chief. It is of this tree that branches are deposited on the lap of Jupiter All-good and All-great, so often as some new victory has imparted universal gladness. This is done, not because it is always green, nor yet because it is an emblem of peace —for in both of those respects the olive would take the precedence of it— but because it is the most beauteous tree on Mount Parnassus, and was pleasing for its gracefulness to Apollo even; a deity to whom the kings of Rome sent offerings at an early period, as we learn from the case of L. Brutus. Perhaps, too, honour is more particularly paid to this tree because it was there that Brutus earned the glory of asserting his country's liberties, when, by the direction of the oracle, he kissed that laurel-bearing soil. Another reason, too, may be the fact, that of all the shrubs that are planted and received in our houses, this is the only one that is never struck by lightning. It is for these reasons, in my opinion, that the post of honour has been awarded to the laurel more particularly in triumphs, and not, as Massurius says, because it was used for the purposes of fumigation and purification from the blood of the enemy.

Book XVI
The Natural History of the Forest Trees

In the East many nations that dwell on the shores of the ocean don't have trees; and I myself have personally witnessed the condition of the Chauci,[1] both the Greater and the Lesser, situate in the regions of the far North. In those climates a vast tract of land, invaded twice each day and night by the overflowing waves of the ocean, opens a question that is eternally proposed to us by Nature, whether these regions are to be looked upon as belonging to the land, or whether as forming a portion of the sea?

Here a wretched race is found, inhabiting either the more elevated spots of land, or else eminences artificially constructed, and of a height to which they know by experience that the highest tides will never reach. Here they pitch their cabins; and when the waves cover the surrounding country far and wide, like so many mariners on board ship are they; when, again, the tide recedes, their condition is that of so many shipwrecked men, and around their cottages they pursue the fishes as they make their escape with the receding tide.

The forests cover all the rest of Germany, and by their shade augment the cold. But the highest of them all are those not far distant from the Chauci already mentioned, and more particularly in the vicinity of the two lakes there. The very shores are lined with oaks, which manifest an extraordinary eagerness to attain their growth; undermined by the waves or uprooted by the blasts, with their entwining roots they carry vast forests along with them, and, thus balanced, stand upright as they float along, while they spread afar their huge branches like the rigging of so

---

1 The Chauci were an ancient Germanic tribe living in the low-lying region between the Rivers Ems and Elbe, on both sides of the Weser and ranging as far inland as the upper Weser (TN).

many ships. Many is the time that these trees have struck our fleets with alarm, when the waves have driven them, almost purposely it would seem, against their prows as they stood at anchor in the night; and the men, destitute of all remedy and resource, have had to engage in a naval combat with a forest of trees!

In the same northern regions, too, is the Hercynian Forest, whose gigantic oaks, uninjured by the lapse of ages, and contemporary with the creation of the world, by their near approach to immortality surpass all other marvels known. Not to speak of other matters that would surpass all belief, it is a well-known fact that their roots, as they meet together, up-heave vast hills; or, if the earth happens not to accumulate with them, rise aloft to the very branches even, and, as they contend for the mastery, form arcades, like so many portals thrown open, and large enough to admit of the passage of a squadron of horse.

All these trees, in general, belong to the glandiferous class,[2] and have ever been held in the highest honour by the Roman people.

It is with the leaves of this class of trees that our civic crown is made, the most glorious reward that can be bestowed on military valour, and, for this long time past, the emblem of the imperial clemency; since the time, in fact, when, after the impiety of civil war, it was first deemed a meritorious action not to shed the blood of a fellow-citizen. Far inferior to this in rank are the mural crown, the vallar, and the golden one, superior though they may be in the value of the material; inferior, too, in merit, is the rostrate crown, though ennobled, in recent times more particularly, by two great names, those of M. Varro, who was presented with it by Pompeius Magnus, for his great achievements in the Piratic War, and of M. Agrippa, on whom it was bestowed by Cæsar, at the end of the Sicilian War, which was also a war against pirates.

In ancient times crowns were presented to none but a divinity, hence it is that Homer awards them only to the gods of heaven and to the entire army; but never to an individual, however great his achievements in battle may have been. It is said, too, that Father Liber was the first of all who placed a crown on his head, and that it was made of ivy. In succeeding times, those engaged in sacrifices in honour of the gods began to wear them, the victims being decked with wreaths as well. More recently, again, they were employed in the sacred games; and at the present day they are bestowed on such occasions, not upon the victor, indeed, but upon his country, which receives, it is proclaimed, this crown at his hands. Hence arose the usage of conferring wreaths upon warriors when about to enjoy a triumph, for them to consecrate in the temples; after which it became the custom to present them at our games.

Romulus presented Hostus Hostilius with a crown of leaves, for being the first to enter Fidense. This crown was made at first of the leaves of the holm oak, but afterwards those of the æsculus were preferred, as being a tree sacred to Jupiter; this, however, was soon employed indifferently with the oak, according as each

---

2   Not only oaks, but a variety of other trees, were included under this name by the ancients; the "glans" embracing not only the acorn, but the mast of the beech, and the hard fruits of other trees.

might happen to present itself, the honourable distinction given to the acorn being the only thing observed.

THE ACORN

It is a well-known fact that acorns at this very day constitute the wealth of many nations, and that, too, even amid these times of peace. Sometimes, also, when there is a scarcity of corn they are dried and ground, the meal being employed for making a kind of bread. Even to this very day, in the provinces of Spain, we find the acorn introduced at table in the second course; it is thought to be sweeter when roasted in the ashes. By the law of the Twelve Tables, there is a provision made that it shall be lawful for a man to gather his acorns when they have fallen upon the land of another.

The acorn of the beech is similar in appearance to a kernel, enclosed in a shell of triangular shape. The leaf is thin and one of the very lightest, is similar in appearance to that of the poplar, and turns yellow with remarkable rapidity. From the middle of the leaf, and upon the upper side of it, there mostly shoots a little green berry, with a pointed top. The beech is particularly agreeable to rats and mice; and hence it is, that where this tree abounds, those creatures are sure to be plentiful also. The leaves are also very fattening for dormice, and good for thrushes too. Almost all trees bear an average crop but once in two years; this is the case with the beech more particularly.

The best acorn, and the very largest, is that which grows upon the oak, and the next to it is the fruit of the aæsculus;[3] that of the robur, again, is diminutive, and the fruit of the cerrus has a meagre, wretched look, being enclosed in a calyx covered with prickles, like the outer coat of the chesnut. With reference to the acorn of the oak, that which grows upon the female tree is sweeter and more tender, while that of the male is more solid and compact. The acorn, however, of the latifolia is the most esteemed, an oak so called from the remarkable broadness of its leaves.

USES FOR THE BARK AND WOOD OF THE TREES

The bark also of the beech, the lime, the fir, and the pitch-tree is extensively used by the peasantry. Panniers and baskets are made of it, as also the large flat hampers which are employed for the carriage of corn and grapes; roofs of cottages, too, are made of this material. When a spy has been sent out he often leaves information for his general, written upon fresh bark, by cutting letters in the parts of it that are the most juicy. The bark of the beech is also employed for religious purposes in certain sacred rites. This tree, however, when deprived of its bark, will not survive.

The best shingles are those made of the wood of the robur; the next best being those furnished by the other glandiferous trees and the beech. Those most easily made are cut from the wood of the resinous trees, but they do not last, with the exception of those made of pine. Cornelius Nepos informs us, that Rome was roofed solely with shingles down to the time of the war with Pyrrhus, a period of

---

3   Variety of oak tree (TN).

four hundred and seventy years. It is well known that it was remarkable for the fine forests in its vicinity. Even at the present day, the name of Jupiter Fagutalus points out in what locality there stood a grove of beeches; the Querquetulan Gate shows where the oak once stood, and the Viminal Hill is the spot where the "vimen" was sought in ancient times.

THE PITCH-TREE

The pitch-tree loves the mountain heights and cold localities. This is a funereal tree, and, as an emblem of death, is placed before the door of the deceased, and is left to grow in the vicinity of the funeral pile. Still, however, it is now some time since it was admitted into our gardens, in consequence of the facility with which it is clipped into various shapes. It gives out considerable quantities of resin, which is intermingled with white granulations like pearls, and so similar in appearance to frankincense, that when mixed, it is impossible to distinguish them; hence the adulterations we find practised in the Seplasia.[4] All this class of trees have a short bristly leaf, thick and hard, like that of the cypress. The branches of the pitch-tree are of moderate size, and extend from almost the very root of the tree, adhering to the sides like so many arms; the same is the case with the fir, the wood of which is held in great esteem for ship-building.

This tree grows upon the summits of lofty mountains, as though, in fact, it had an antipathy to the sea, and it does not at all differ from the pitch-tree in appearance; the wood is also very highly esteemed for the construction of rafters, and many other appliances of life. A flow of resin, which in the pitch-tree constitutes its great merit, is looked upon as a defect in the fir, though it will generally exude in some small quantity on exposure of the wood, to the action of the sun. On the other hand, the wood which in the fir-tree is remarkably fine, in the pitch-tree is only used for making shingles, vats, and a few other articles of joiners' work.

Another kind of resinous tree has the same localities, and is very similar in appearance; it is known as the larch. The wood of this tree is far more valuable, being unimpaired by time, and proof against all decay; it is of a reddish colour, and of an acrid smell. Resin flows from this wood in still greater quantities; it is of the colour of honey, more viscous than the other varieties, and never turns hard.

The wood of all these trees, when set fire to, gives out immoderate volumes of sooty smoke, and sputters every now and then with a sudden crackling noise, while it sends out red-hot charcoal to a considerable distance —with the sole exception of that of the larch, which will neither burn nor char, nor, in fact, suffer any more from the action of fire than a stone. All these trees are evergreens, and are not easily distinguished by the foliage, even by those who are best acquainted with them, so nearly related are they to one another.

---

4   A great street in Capua, which consisted entirely of the shops of sellers of unguents and perfumes.

METHODS OF MAKING TAR AND PITCH

In Europe, tar is extracted from the torch-tree[5] by the agency of fire; it is employed for coating ships and for many other useful purposes. The wood of the tree is chopped into small billets, and then put into a furnace, which is heated by fires lighted on every side. The first steam that exudes flows in the form of water into a reservoir made for its reception; in Syria this substance is known as "cedrium"; and it possesses such remarkable strength, that in Egypt the bodies of the dead, after being steeped in it, are preserved from all corruption.

The liquid that follows is of a thicker consistency, and constitutes pitch, properly so called. This liquid, thrown again into a brazen cauldron, and mixed with vinegar, becomes still thicker, and when left to coagulate, receives the name of "Bruttian" pitch. It is used, however, only for pitching the insides of wine-vats and other vessels, it differing from the other kinds in being more viscous, of a redder colour, and more unctuous than is usually the case. All these varieties of pitch are prepared from the pitch-tree, by putting red-hot stones, with the resinous wood, in troughs made of strong oak; or if these troughs are not attainable, by piling up billets of the wood in the method employed for the manufacture of charcoal. It is this pitch that is used for seasoning wine, being first pounded and reduced to a fine powder; it is of a blacker colour, too, than the other sort. The same resin, if boiled gently with water, and then strained off, becomes viscous, and assumes a red colour; it is then known as "distilled pitch"; for making this, the refuse portions of the resin and the bark of the tree are generally selected.

We must not omit, too, that the Greeks call by the name of zopissa[6] the pitch mixed with wax which has been scraped from off the bottoms of sea-going ships. This composition is found much more efficient for all those purposes in which pitch and resin are employed, in consequence of the superior hardness which has been imparted to it by the sea-salt.

The pitch-tree is opened on the side that faces the sun, not by means of an incision, but of a wound made by the removal of the bark; this opening being generally two feet in width and one cubit from the ground, at the very least. The body of the tree, too, is not spared in this instance, as in others, for even the very chips from off it are considered as having their use; those, however, from the lower part of the tree are looked upon as the best, the wood of the higher parts giving the resin a bitter taste. In a short time all the resinous juices of the entire tree come to a point of confluence in the wound so inflicted; the same process is adopted also with the torch-tree. When the liquid ceases to flow, the tree is opened in a similar manner in some other part, and then, again, elsewhere; after which the whole tree is cut down, and the pith of it is used for burning.

---

5   Numerous varieties of the coniferæ supply us with tar, and Pliny is in error in deriving it solely from the torch-tree, the Pinus mugho of Linnæus.
6   Apparently meaning "boiled pitch."

GERMINATION AND BLOSSOM OF TREES

All trees germinate, however, even those which do not blossom. In this respect there is a very considerable difference in relation to the various localities; for in the same species we find that the tree, when planted in a marshy spot, will germinate earlier than elsewhere; next to that, the trees that grow on the plains, and last of all those that are found in the woods; the wild pear, too, is naturally later in budding than the other pears. At the first breath of the west wind the cornel buds, and close upon it the laurel; then, a little before the equinox, we find the lime and the maple germinating. Among the earlier trees, too, are the poplar, the elm, the willow, the alder, and the nut-trees. The plane buds, too, at an early period.

Others, again, germinate at the beginning of spring, the holly, for instance, the terebinth, the paliurus, the chesnut, and the glandiferous trees. On the other hand, the apple is late in budding, and the cork-tree the very last of all. Some trees germinate twice, whether it is that this arises from some exuberant fertility of the soil, or from the inviting temperature of the atmosphere; this takes place more particularly in the several varieties of the cereals. Excessive germination, however, has a tendency to weaken and exhaust the tree.

Besides the spring budding, some trees have naturally another budding, which depends upon the influence of their own respective constellations. The winter budding takes place at the rising of the Eagle, the summer at that of the Dog-star, and a third budding again at that of Arcturus. Some persons think that these two buddings are common to all trees, but that they are to be remarked more particularly in the fig, the vine, and the pomegranate; seeing that, when this is the case, the crop of figs, in Thessaly and Macedonia more particularly, is remarkably abundant; but it is in Egypt more especially that illustrations of this vast abundance are to be met with. All the trees in general, when they have once begun to germinate, proceed continuously with it; the robur, however, the fir-tree, and the larch germinate intermittently, ceasing thrice, and as many times beginning to bud again, and hence it is that they shed the scales of their bark three several times; a thing that takes place with all trees during the period of germination, the outer coat of the tree bursting while it is budding.

Of the trees which, as we have already stated, bud in winter at the rising of the Eagle, the almond blossoms the first of all, in the month of January namely, while by March the fruit is well developed. Next to it in blossoming is the plum of Armenia, and then the tuber and the early peach, the first two being exotics, and the latter forced by the agency of cultivation. Among the forest trees, the first that blossoms in the course of nature is the elder, which has the most pith of any, and the male cornel, which has none at all. Among the cultivated trees we next have the apple, and immediately after the pear, the cherry, and the plum. Next to these is the laurel, and then the cypress, and after that the pomegranate and the fig; the vine, too, and the olive are budding when these last trees are in flower, the period of their conception being the rising of the Vergiliæ, that being their constellation. As for the vine, it blossoms at the summer solstice, and the olive begins to do so a little later.

Book XVI - The Natural History of the Forest Trees

TREES WHICH BEAR NO FRUIT, LOOKED UPON AS ILL-OMENED

The only ones among all the trees that bear nothing whatever, not so much as any seed even, are the tamarisk, which is used only for making brooms, the poplar, the alder, the Atinian elm, and the alaternus, which has a leaf between that of the holm-oak and the olive. Those trees are regarded as sinister, and are considered inauspicious, which are never propagated from seed, and bear no fruit. Cremutius informs us, that this tree, being the one upon which Phyllis hanged herself, is never green. Those trees which produce a gum open of themselves after germination; the gum never thickens until after the fruit has been removed.

THE TRUNKS AND BRANCHES OF TREES

Some trees are of a simple form, and have but a single trunk rising from the root, together with numerous branches; such as the olive, for instance, the fig, and the vine; others again are of a shrubby nature, such as the paliurus, the myrtle, and the filbert; which last, indeed, is all the better, and the more abundant its fruit, the more numerous its branches. In some trees, again, there is no trunk at all, as is the case with one species of box, and the lotus of the parts beyond sea. Some trees are bifurcated, while there are some that branch out into as many as five parts. Others, again, divide in the trunk but have no branches, as in the case of the elder; while others have no division in the trunk but throw out branches, such as the pitch-tree, for instance.

In some trees the branches are symmetrically arranged, the pitch-tree and the fir, for example; while with others they are dispersed without any order or regularity, as in the robur, the apple, and the pear. In the fir the branches are thrown out from the trunk straight upwards, pointing to the sky, and not drooping downwards from the sides of the trunk. It is a singular thing, but this tree will die if the ends of its branches are cut, though, if taken off altogether, no bad effect is produced. If it is cut, too, below the place where the branches were, the part of the tree which is left will continue to live; but if, on the other hand, the top only of the tree is removed, the whole of it will die.

The branches of the apple-tree have a peculiar conformation; knots are formed which resemble the muzzles of wild beasts, several smaller ones being united to a larger.

Some of the branches are barren, and do not germinate; this takes place either from a natural deficiency of strength, or else some injury received in consequence of having been cut, and the cicatrix impeding the natural functions. The same that the branch is in the trees that spread out, is the eye in the vine, and the joint in the reed. All trees are naturally the thickest in the parts that are nearest the ground. The fir, the larch, the palm, the cypress, and the elm, and, indeed, every tree that has but a single trunk, develop themselves in their remarkable height. Among the branchy trees the cherry is sometimes found to yield a beam forty cubits in length by two in thickness throughout. Some trees divide into branches from the very ground, as in the apple-tree, for example.

THE CYPRESS

The cypress is an exotic, and has been reckoned one of the trees that are naturalized with the greatest difficulty; so much so, indeed, that Cato has expatiated upon it at greater length and more frequently than any of the others. This tree is naturally of a stubborn disposition, bears a fruit that is utterly useless, a berry that causes a wry face when tasted, and a leaf that is bitter; it also gives out a disagreeable pungent smell, and its shade is far from agreeable. The wood that it furnishes is but scanty, so much so indeed, that it may be almost regarded as little more than a shrub. This tree is sacred to Pluto, and hence it is used as a sign of mourning placed at the entrance of a house; the female tree is for a long time barren. The pyramidal appearance that it presents has caused it not to be rejected, but for a long time it was only used for marking the intervals between rows of pines; at the present day, however, it is clipped and trained to form hedge-rows, or else is thinned and lengthened out in the various designs employed in ornamental gardening, and which represent scenes of hunting, fleets, and various other objects; these it covers with a thin small leaf, which is always green.

THE IVY

It is said that the ivy now grows in Asia, though Theophrastus has denied that such is the fact, and asserts that it grows nowhere in India, except upon Mount Meros. He says, too, that Harpalus used every possible exertion to naturalize it in Media, but to no purpose; and that Alexander, in consequence of the rarity of this plant, had himself crowned with it, after the example of Father Liber, when returning victorious with his army from India; and at the present day even, it is used to decorate the thyrsus of that god, and the casques and bucklers employed by the nations of Thrace in their sacred ceremonials. The ivy is injurious to all trees and plants, and makes its way through tombs and walls; it forms a haunt much frequented by serpents, for its refreshing coolness; so that it is a matter for astonishment that there should have been such remarkable veneration for this plant.

The two principal kinds in the ivy, as in other plants, are the male tree and the female. The male is said to have a larger trunk than the female, and a leaf that is harder and more unctuous, with a flower nearly approaching to purple; indeed, the flower of both the male and female tree strongly resembles the wild-rose, were it not destitute of smell. Each of these kinds of ivy is divided into three other varieties; the white ivy, the black, and a third known as the helix.

WATER PLANTS

Among those plants which thrive best in cold localities, it will be only proper to mention the aquatic shrubs. In the first rank, we find the reed, equally indispensable for the emergencies of war and peace, and used among the appliances of luxury even. The northern nations make use of reeds for roofing their houses, and the stout thatch thus formed will last for centuries even; in other countries, too, they make light vaulted ceilings with them. Reeds are employed, too, for writing upon paper, those of Egypt more particularly, which have a close affinity to the papyrus;

the most esteemed, however, are the reeds of Cnidos, and those which grow in Asia, on the margin of the Anaitic Lake there.

The reed of our country is naturally of a more fungous nature, being formed of a spongy cartilage, which is hollow within, and covered by a thin, dry, woody coat without; it easily breaks into splinters, which are remarkably sharp at the edge. In other respects, it is of a thin, graceful shape, articulated with joints, and tapering gradually towards the top, which ends in a thick, hairy tuft. This tuft is not without its uses, as it is employed for filling the beds used in taverns, in place of feathers; or else, when it has assumed a more ligneous consistency, it is pounded, as we see done among the Belgæ, and inserted between the joints of ships, to close the seams, a thing that it does most effectually, being more tenacious than glue, and adhering more firmly than pitch.

It is by the aid of the reed that the nations of the East decide their wars; fixing in it a barbed point, they inflict a wound from which the arrow cannot be withdrawn. By the addition of feathers they accelerate the flight of this instrument of death, and the weapon, if it breaks in the wound, furnishes the combatants with a weapon afresh. With these missiles the warriors darken the very rays of the sun. It is for this reason more particularly that they desire a clear and serene sky, and hold in abhorrence all windy and rainy weather, which has the effect of compelling them, in spite of themselves, to be at peace with one another.

THE JUICES OF TREES

There is a juice in the bark of trees, which must be looked upon as their blood, though it is not of a similar nature in all. In the fig it is of a milky consistency, and has the peculiar property of curdling milk, and so forming cheese. In the cherry-tree this juice is gummy, in the elm clammy, in the apple viscous and fatty, while in the vine and the pear it is watery. The more viscous this humour is, the more long-lived the tree. In a word, we find in the bodies of trees –as with all other beings that are animated– skin, blood, flesh, sinews, veins, bones, and marrow; the bark serving them in place of skin. It is a singular fact connected with the mulberry-tree, that when the medical men wish to extract its juice, if the incision is lightly made, by a blow with a stone, and at the second hour of the day in spring, the juice will flow; but if, on the other hand, a wound is inflicted to any depth, it has all the, appearance of being dried up.

Immediately beneath the bark in most trees there is a fatty substance, which, from its colour, has obtained the name of alburnum; it is soft, and is the very worst part of the wood, and in the robur even will very easily rot, being particularly liable to wood-worm, for which reason it is invariably removed. Beneath this fat lies the flesh of the tree, and then under that, its bones, or, in other words, the choicest part of the wood. Those trees which have a dry wood, the olive, for instance, bear fruit every other year only; this is more the case with them than with those the wood of which is of a fleshy nature, such as the cherry, for instance. It is not all trees, too, that have this fat and flesh in any abundance, the same as we find to be the case among the more active animals. The box, the cornel, and the olive have none at all, nor yet any marrow, and a very small proportion, too, of blood. In the same way, too, the service-tree has no bones, and the elder no flesh, while both of them have marrow in the greatest abundance. Reeds, too, have hardly any flesh.

THE VEINS AND FIBRES OF TREES

In the flesh of some trees we find both fibres and veins; they are easily distinguished. The veins are larger, while the fibres are of whiter material, and are to be found in those woods more particularly which are easily split. Hence it is that if the ear is applied to the extremity of a beam of wood, however long, a tap with a graver even upon the other end may be distinctly heard, the sound penetrating by the passages which run straight through it; by these means it is that we ascertain whether timber runs awry, or is interrupted by knots. The tuberosities which we find on trees resemble the kernels that are formed in flesh; they contain neither veins nor fibres, but only a kind of tough, solid flesh, rolled up in a sort of ball; it is these tuberosities that are the most esteemed parts in the citrus and the maple. As to the other kinds of wood which are employed for making tables, the trees are split into planks lengthwise, and the parts are then selected along which the fibres run, and properly rounded; for the wood would be too brittle to use if it were cut in segments crosswise.

THE FELLING OF TREES

The proper time for felling trees that are wanted for barking, the round, tapering trees, for instance, that are employed in temples and for other purposes, is at the period of germination; for at other times it is quite impossible to detach the bark from the rotten wood that adheres to it, while the wood itself assumes a blackish hue. Squared logs, and wood from which the bark has been lopped, are generally cut in the period that intervenes between the winter solstice and the prevalence of the west winds; or else, if it is necessary to anticipate that period, at the setting of Arcturus and before that of the Lyre, the very earliest period being the summer solstice; the days of these respective constellations will be mentioned in the appropriate place.

In general it is looked upon as quite sufficient to use all due precaution that a tree is not rough-hewn before it has borne its yearly crop. The robur, if cut in spring, is subject to the attacks of wood-worm, but if cut in winter, will neither rot nor warp; otherwise it is very liable to bend and become awry, as well as to crack; the same is the case, too, with the cork-tree, even if cut down at the proper time. The state of the moon, too, is of infinite importance, and it is generally recommended that trees should be cut only between the twentieth and the thirtieth days of the month. It is generally agreed, however, by all, that it is the very best time for felling timber, when the moon is in conjunction with the sun, a day which is called by some persons the interlunium, and by others the moon's silence. At all events, it was under these circumstances that Tiberius Cæsar gave orders for the larches to be cut in Rhætia, that were required for the purpose of rebuilding the bridge of the Naumachia after it had been destroyed by fire.

THE AGE OF TREES

The life of some trees might really be looked upon as of infinite duration, if we only think of the dense wilds and inaccessible forests in some parts of the world. In relation, however, to those, the date of which is still within the memory of man, there are some olive-trees still in existence at Liternum, which were planted by the hand of the first Scipio Africanus, as also a myrtle there of extraordinary size; beneath them there is a grotto, in which, it is said, a dragon keeps watch over that hero's shade. There is a lotus[7] tree in the open space before the Temple of Lucina at Rome, which was built in the year of the City 379. How much older the tree is than the temple, is a matter of doubt; but that it is older is quite certain, for it was from that same grove that the goddess Lucina derived her name; the tree in question is now about four hundred and fifty years old. The lotus tree, which is known as the Capillata, is still older than this, though it is uncertain what is its age; it received that name from the circumstance of the Vestal Virgins suspending locks of their hair from it.

There is another lotus in the Vulcanal, which Romulus erected with the tenth part of the spoil taken from the enemy; according to Massurius, it is generally considered to be as old as the City. The roots of this tree penetrate as far as the Forum of Cæsar, right across the meeting-places of the municipalities. There was a cypress of equal age growing with it till towards the latter part of Nero's reign, when it fell to the ground, and no attempts were made to raise it again.

Still older than the City is the holm-oak that stands on the Vaticanian Hill; there is an inscription in bronze upon it, written in Etruscan characters, which states that even in those days it was an object of religious veneration. The foundation of the town of Tibur, too, dates many years before that of the City of Rome; there are three holm-oaks there, said to be more ancient than Tiburnus even, who was the founder of that place; the tradition is that in their vicinity he was inaugurated. Tradition states also that he was a son of Amphiaraüs, who died before Thebes, one generation before the period of the Trojan war.

MISTLETOE

There are three varieties of the mistletoe. That which grows upon the fir and the larch has the name of stelis in Euboea; and there is the hyphear of Arcadia. It grows also upon the oak, the robur, the holm-oak, the wild plum, and the terebinth, but upon no other tree. It is most plentiful of all upon the oak, and is then known as "adasphear." In all the trees, with the exception of the holmoak and the oak, there is a considerable difference in its smell and pungency, and the leaf of one kind has a disagreeable odour; both varieties, however, are sticky and bitter. The hyphear is the best for fattening cattle with; it begins, however, by purging off all defects, after which it fattens all such animals as have been able to withstand the purging. It is generally said, however, that those animals which have any radical malady in the intestines cannot withstand its drastic effects. This method of treatment is generally adopted in the summer for a period of forty days.

---

7 The *Celtis australis* of Linnæus.

We must not omit to mention the admiration that is lavished upon this plant by the Gauls. The Druids —for that is the name they give to their magicians— held nothing more sacred than the mistletoe and the tree that bears it, supposing always that tree to be the robur. Of itself the robur is selected by them to form whole groves, and they perform none of their religious rites without employing branches of it; so much so, that it is very probable that the priests themselves may have received their name from the Greek name for that tree. In fact, it is the notion with them that everything that grows on it has been sent immediately from heaven, and that the mistletoe upon it is a proof that the tree has been selected by God himself as an object of his especial favour.

The mistletoe, however, is but rarely found upon the robur; and when found, is gathered with rites replete with religious awe. This is done more particularly on the fifth day of the moon, the day which is the beginning of their months and years, as also of their ages, which, with them, are but thirty years. This day they select because the moon, though not yet in the middle of her course, has already considerable power and influence; and they call her by a name which signifies, in their language, the all-healing. Having made all due preparation for the sacrifice and a banquet beneath the trees, they bring thither two white bulls, the horns of which are bound then for the first time. Clad in a white robe the priest ascends the tree, and cuts the mistletoe with a golden sickle, which is received by others in a white cloak. They then immolate the victims, offering up their prayers that God will render this gift of his propitious to those to whom he has so granted it. It is the belief with them that the mistletoe, taken in drink, will impart fecundity to all animals that are barren, and that it is an antidote for all poisons.

Book XVII
The Natural History of the Cultivated Trees

We have described the trees which grow spontaneously on land and in the sea,[1] and it now remains for us to speak of those which owe their formation, properly speaking, rather than birth, to art and the inventive genius of man. Here, however, I cannot but express my surprise, that after the state of penury in which man lived, as already described, in primitive times, holding the trees of the forest in common with the wild beasts, and disputing with them the possession of the fruits that fell, and with the fowls of the air that of the fruits as they hung on the tree, luxury has now attached to them prices so enormous.

THE INFLUENCE OF WEATHER UPON THE TREES

Trees are fond of a site more particularly that faces the north-east; the breezes rendering their foliage more thick and exuberant, and imparting additional solidity to the wood. This is a point, however, upon which most people are very greatly deceived; thus in vineyards, for instance, the props ought not to be placed in such a position as to shelter the stems from the wind in that quarter, it being only against the northern blasts that this precaution should be taken. Nay, even more than this, if the cold weather only comes on in due season, it contributes very materially to the strengthening of the trees, and promotes the process of germination; while, on the other hand, if at that period the southern breezes should caress them, they will grow weak and languid, and more particularly so, if the blossom is just coming on. If rainy weather, too, should happen to follow close upon blossoming, the total destruction of the fruit is the necessary result; indeed, if the weather should be only cloudy, or south winds happen to prevail, it is quite sufficient to ensure the loss

---

1   Pliny alludes to various kinds of fucus or sea-weed.

of the fruit in the almond and the pear. Rains, if prevalent about the rising of the Vergiliæ, are most injurious to the vine and the olive, as it is at that season that germination is commencing with them; indeed, this is a most critical four days for the olive, being the period at which the south wind, as we have already stated, brings on its dark and lowering clouds. The cereals, too, ripen more unfavourably when south winds prevail, though at the same time it proceeds with greater rapidity. All cold, too, is injurious to vegetation, which comes with the northern winds, or out of the proper season. It is most advantageous to all plants for north-east winds to prevail throughout the winter.

In this season, too, showers are very necessary, and the reason is self-evident; the trees, being exhausted by the fruit they have borne, and weakened by the loss of their leaves, are, of course, famished and hungry; and it is the showers that constitute their aliment. Experience has led us to believe that there is nothing more detrimental than a warm winter; for it allows the trees, the moment they have parted with their fruits, to conceive again, or, in other words, to germinate, and then exhaust themselves by blossoming afresh. And what is even worse than this, should there be several years of such weather in succession, even the trees themselves will die; for there can be little doubt that the effort must of necessity be injurious, when they put forth their strength, and are at the same time deprived of their natural sustenance.

Those trees which are the slowest in bringing their fruits to maturity, and require a more prolonged supply of nutriment, receive benefit also from late rains, such as the vine, the olive, and the pomegranate, for instance.

WHAT SOILS ARE TO BE CONSIDERED THE BEST

Next after the influences of the heavens, we have to treat of those of the earth, a task that is in no way more easy than the previous one. It is but rarely that the same soil is found suited to trees as well as corn; indeed, the black earth which prevails in Campania is not everywhere found suited to the vine, nor yet that which emits light exhalations, or the red soil that has been so highly praised by many. The cretaceous earth that is found in the territory of Alba Pompeia, and an argillaceous soil, are preferred to all others for the vine, although, too, they are remarkably rich, a quality that is generally looked upon as not suited to that plant. On the other hand, again, the white sand of the district of Ticinum, the black sand of many other places, and the red sand as well, even though mixed with a rich earth, will prove unproductive.

The very signs, also, from which we form our judgement are often very deceptive; a soil that is adorned with tall and graceful trees is not always a favourable one, except, of course, for those trees. What tree, in fact, is there that is taller than the fir? and yet what other plant could possibly exist in the same spot?

Cato, briefly and in his peculiar manner, characterizes the defects that exist in the various soils. "Take care," he says, "where the earth is rotten not to shake it either with carts or by driving cattle over it." Now what are we to suppose that this term "rotten" means, as applied to a soil, about which he is so vastly apprehensive as to almost forbid our setting foot upon it? Let us only form a comparison by thinking what it is that constitutes rottenness in wood, and we shall find that the faults which are held by him in such aversion are the being arid, full of holes, rough, white, mouldy, worm eaten, in fact, just like pumice-stone; and thus has Cato said more in a single word than we could have possibly found means to express in a description, however long.

METHODS TO ENRICH THE EARTH

There is another method, which has been invented both in Gaul and Britain, of enriching earth by the agency of itself, being known as marl.[2] This soil is looked upon as containing a greater amount of fecundating principles, and acts as a fat in relation to the earth, just as we find glands existing in the body, which are formed by a condensation of the fatty particles into so many kernels. This mode of proceeding, too, has not been overlooked by the Greeks; indeed, what subject is there that they have not touched upon? They call by the name of leucargillon a white argillaceous earth which is used in the territory of Megara, but only where the soil is of a moist, cold nature.

Of the marls that are found to be of an unctuous nature, the best is the white. There are several varieties of it; the most pungent and biting being the one already mentioned. Another kind is the white chalk that is used for cleaning silver; it is taken from a considerable depth in the ground, the pits being sunk, in most instances, as much as one hundred feet. These pits are narrow at the mouth, but the shafts enlarge very considerably in the interior, as is the case in mines; it is in Britain more particularly that this chalk is employed. The good effects of it are found to last full eighty years; and there is no instance known of an agriculturist laying it twice on the same land during his life. A third variety of white marl is known as glisomarga; it consists of fullers' chalk mixed with an unctuous earth, and is better for promoting the growth of hay than grain; so much so, in fact, that between harvest and the ensuing seed-time there is cut a most abundant crop of grass.

ASHES AND MANURE

The agriculturists of the parts of Italy beyond the river Padus, are such admirers of ashes for this purpose, that they even prefer it as a manure to the dung of beasts of burden; indeed, they are in the habit of burning dung for this purpose, on account of its superior lightness. They do not, however, use them indiscriminately upon the same soil, nor do they employ ashes for promoting the growth of shrubs, nor, in fact, of some of the cereals, as we shall have occasion to mention hereafter. There are some persons who are of opinion also that dust imparts nutriment to grapes, and cover them with it while they are growing, taking care to throw it also upon the roots of the vines and other trees.

---

2   A natural mixture of potter's earth and calcareous stones, or subcarbonate of chalk. Fée remarks, that the ancients were not acquainted with the proper method of applying it. Marl only exercises its fertilizing influence after being reduced to dust by the action of the atmosphere, by absorbing the oxygen of the air, and giving to vegetation the carbonic acid that is necessary for their nourishment.

There are various kinds of manure, the use of which is of very ancient date. In the times of Homer even, the aged king is represented as thus enriching the land by the labour of his own hands. Tradition reports that King Augeas was the first in Greece to make use of it, and that Hercules introduced the practice into Italy; which country has, however, immortalized the name of its king, Stercutus, the son of Faunus, as claiming the honour of this invention. M. Varro assigns the first rank for excellence to the dung of thrushes kept in aviaries, and lauds it as being not only good for land, but excellent food for oxen and swine as well; indeed, he goes so far as to assert that there is no food that they will grow fat upon more speedily. We really have some reason to augur well of the manners of the present day, if it is true that in the days of our ancestors there were aviaries of such vast extent as to be able to furnish manure for the fields.

It is recommended, also, that the dung-heap should be kept in the open air, in a spot deep sunk and well adapted to receive the moisture; it should be covered, too, with straw, that it may not dry up with the sun, care being taken to drive a stake of robur into the ground, to prevent serpents from breeding there. It is of the greatest consequence that the manure should be laid upon the land while the west winds prevail, and during a dry moon.

PROPAGATION OF TREES

Having now treated at sufficient length of the requisite conditions of the weather and the soil, we shall proceed to speak of those trees which are the result of the care and inventive skill of man. Indeed, the varieties of them are hardly less numerous than of those which are produced by Nature, so abundantly have we testified our gratitude in return for her numerous bounties. For these trees, we find, are reared either from seed, or else by transplanting, by layers, by slips torn from the stock, by cuttings, by grafting, or by cutting into the trunk of the tree.

It is Nature herself that has taught us most of these methods, and more particularly that of sowing seed, as it was very soon evident how the seed on falling to the ground revived again in germination. Indeed, there are some trees that are capable of being propagated in no other way, the chesnut and the walnut, for instance; with the sole exception, of course, of such as are employed for coppice wood. By this method, too, as well as the others, some trees are propagated, though from a seed of a different nature, such, for instance, as the vine, the apple, and the pear; the seed being in all these cases in the shape of a pip, and not the fruit itself, as in that of the chesnut and the walnut. The medlar, too, can also be propagated by the agency of seed. All trees, however, that are grown by this method are very slow in coming to maturity, degenerate very rapidly, and must often be renewed by grafting; indeed, the chesnut even sometimes requires to be grafted.

On the other hand, there are some trees which have the property of never degenerating, in whatever manner they are reproduced, the cypress, palm, and laurel, for instance; for we find that the laurel is capable of being propagated in several ways. We have already made mention of the various kinds of laurel; those known as the Augustan, the baccalis, and the tinus are all reproduced in a similar manner.

The berries are gathered in the month of January, after they have been dried by the north-east winds which then prevail; they are then kept separate and exposed to the action of the air, being liable to ferment if left in a heap. After this, they are first seasoned with smoke, and then steeped in urine, preparatory to sowing. A trench is then dug, about a palm in depth, and somewhere about twenty of the berries are then put into it, being laid in a heap; this is usually done in the month of March. These kinds of laurel admit of being propagated from layers also; but the triumphal laurel can be reproduced from cuttings only. All the varieties of the myrtle are produced in Campania from the berry only, but at Rome from layers.

With reference to the plants that are propagated from seed, Mago treats at considerable length of the nut-trees; he says that the almond should be sown in a soft argillaceous earth, upon a spot that looks towards the south; that it thrives also in a hard, warm soil, but that in a soil which is either unctuous or moist, it is sure to die, or else to bear no fruit. He recommends also for sowing those more particularly which are of a curved shape like a sickle, and the produce of a young tree, and he says that they should be steeped for three days in diluted manure, or else the day before they are sown in honey and water. He says, also, that they should be put in the ground with the point downwards, and the sharp edge towards the north-east; and that they should be sown in threes and placed triangularly, at the distance of a palm from each other, care being taken to water them for ten days, until such time as they have germinated.

Walnuts when sown are placed lengthwise, lying upon the sides where the shells are joined; and pine nuts are mostly put, in sevens, into perforated pots, or else sown in the same way as the berries are in the laurels which are re-produced by seed.

Nature, too has taught us the art of forming nurseries; when from the roots of many of the trees we see shooting up a dense forest of suckers, an offspring that is destined to be killed by the mother that has borne them. For by the shade of the tree these suckers are indiscriminately stifled, as we often see the case in the laurel, the pomegranate, the plane, the cherry, and the plum. There are some few trees, the elm and the palm for instance, in which the branches spare the suckers; however, they never make their appearance in any of the trees except those in which the roots, from their fondness for the sun and rain, keep close, as they range, to the surface of the ground.

Nature has also discovered another method, which is very similar to the last —for slips torn away from the tree will live. In adopting this plan, care should be taken to pull out the haunch of the slip where it adheres to the stock, and so remove with it a portion of the fibrous body of the parent tree. It is in this way that the pomegranate, the hazel, the apple, the sorb, the medlar, the ash, the fig, and more particularly the vine, are propagated. The quince, however, if planted in this way will degenerate, and it has been consequently found a better plan to cut slips and plant them; a method which was at first adopted for making hedges, with the elder, the quince, and the bramble, but came afterwards to be applied to cultivated trees, such as the poplar, the alder, and the willow, which last will grow if even the slip is planted upside down.

SEED-PLOTS

In laying out a seed-plot it is necessary that a soil of the very highest quality should be selected; for it is very often requisite that a nurse should be provided for the young plants, who is more ready to humour them than their parent soil. The ground should therefore be both dry and nutritious, well turned up with the mattock, replete with hospitality to the stranger plants, and as nearly as possible resembling the soil to which it is intended they should be transplanted. But, a thing that is of primary importance, the stones must be carefully gathered from off the ground, and it should be walled in, to ensure its protection from the depredations of poultry; the soil too, should have as few chinks and crannies as possible, so that the sun may not be enabled to penetrate and burn up the roots. The young trees should be planted at distances of a foot and a-half; for if they happen to touch one another, in addition to other inconveniences, they are apt to breed worms; for which reason it is that they should be hoed as often as possible, and all weeds pulled up, the young plants themselves being carefully pruned, and so accustomed to the knife.

THE HOLES FOR TRANSPLANTING

But it is more particularly necessary in transplanting, that the trees should always be removed to a soil that is similar, or else superior, to the one in which they grew before. If taken from warm or early ripening localities, they ought not to be removed to cold or backward sites, nor yet, on the other hand, from these last to the former. If the thing can possibly be done, the holes for transplanting should be dug sufficiently long before to admit of their being covered throughout with a thick coat of grass. Mago recommends that they should be dug a whole year beforehand, in order that they may absorb the heat of the sun and the moisture of the showers; or, if circumstances do not admit of this, that fires should be made in the middle of them some two months before transplanting, that being only done just after rain has fallen. He says, too, that in an argillaceous or a hard soil, the proper measurement is three cubits every way, and on declivitous spots one palm more, care being taken in every case to make the hole like the chimney of a furnace, narrower at the orifice than at the bottom. Where the earth is black, the depth should be two cubits and a palm, and the hole dug in a quadrangular form.

Some persons recommend that a tree should not be transplanted before it is two years old, nor yet after three, while others, again, are of opinion that if it is one year old it is quite sufficient; Cato thinks that it ought to be more than five fingers in thickness at the time. The same author, too, would not have omitted, if it had been of any importance, to recommend that a mark should be made on the bark for the purpose of pointing out the southern aspect of the tree; so that, when transplanted, it may occupy exactly the same position that it has previously done; from an apprehension that the north side of the tree, on finding itself opposite to a southern sun, might split, and the south side be nipped by the north-eastern blasts.

TREES PROPAGATED FROM LAYERS

Nature; too, has taught us the art of reproduction from layers. The bramble, by reason of its thinness and the excessive length to which it grows, bends downwards, and throws the extremities of its branches into the earth; these immediately take root again, and would fill every place far and wide, were it not that the arts of cultivation put a check to it; so much so, indeed, that it would almost appear that men are born for nothing else but to take care of the earth. Hence it is, that a thing that is in itself most noxious and most baneful, has taught us the art of reproduction by layers and quicksets. The ivy, too, has a similar property.

Cato says, that in addition to the vine, the fig, as well as the olive, the pomegranate, every variety of the apple, the laurel, the plum, the myrtle, the filbert, the nut of Præste, and the plane, are capable of being propagated by layers.

GRAFTING

Nature has also taught us the art of grafting by means of seed. We see a seed swallowed whole by a famished bird; when softened by the natural heat of the crop, it is voided, with the fecundating juices of the dung, upon some soft couch formed by a tree; or else, as is often the case, is carried by the winds to some cleft in the bark of a tree. Hence it is that we see the cherry growing upon the willow, the plane upon the laurel, the laurel upon the cherry, and fruits of various tints and hues all springing from the same tree at once. It is said, too, that the jackdaw, from its concealment of the seeds of plants in holes which serve as its store-houses, gives rise to a similar result.

THE DISEASES OF TREES

Having now treated sufficiently at length of the planting and cultivation of trees, we shall proceed, in order that nothing may be omitted, to describe other details relative to their nature, which are of considerable importance, when taken in connection with all that precedes. Trees, we find, are attacked by maladies; and, indeed, what created thing is there that is exempt from these evils? Still however, the affections of the forest trees, it is said, are not attended with danger to them, and the only damage they receive is from hail-storms while they are budding and blossoming; with the exception, indeed, of being nipped either by heat or cold blasts in unseasonable weather; for frost, when it comes at the proper times, as we have already stated, is serviceable to them. "Well but," it will be said, "is not the vine sometimes killed with cold?" No doubt it is, and this it is through which we detect inherent faults in the soils, for it is only in a cold soil that the vine will die. Just in the same way, too, in winter we approve of cold, so long as it is the cold of the weather, and not of the ground. It is not the weakest trees, too, that are endangered in winter by frost, but the larger ones. When they are thus attacked, it is the summit that dries away the first, from the circumstance that the sap becomes frozen before it is able to arrive there.

Some diseases of trees are common to them all, while others, again, are peculiar to individual kinds, Worms are common to them all, and so, too, is sideration, with pains in the limbs, which are productive of debility in the various parts. Thus do we apply the names of the maladies that prevail among mankind to those with which the plants are afflicted. In the same way, too, we speak of their bodies being mutilated, the eyes of the buds being burnt up, with many other expressions of a similar nature. It is in accordance with the same phraseology that we say that trees are afflicted with hunger or indigestion, both of which result from the comparative amount of sap that they contain; while some, again, are troubled with obesity, as in the case of all the resinous trees, which, when suffering from excessive fatness, are changed into a torch-tree. When the roots, too, begin to wax fat, trees, like animals, are apt to perish from excess of fatness. Sometimes, too, a pestilence will prevail in certain classes of trees, just as among men, we see maladies attack, at one time the slave class, and at another the common people, in cities or in the country, as the case may be.

The disease known as sideration entirely depends upon the heavens; and hence we may class under this head, the ill effects produced by hail-storms, carbunculation,[3] and the damage caused by hoar-frosts. When the approach of spring tempts the still tender shoots to make their appearance, and they venture to burst forth, the malady attacks them, and scorches up the eyes of the buds, filled as they are with their milky juices; this is what upon flowers they call "charcoal" blight. The consequences of hoar-frost to plants are even more dangerous still, for when it has once settled, it remains there in a frozen form, and there is never any wind to remove it, seeing that it never prevails except in weather that is perfectly calm and serene. Sideration, however, properly so called, is a certain heat and dryness that prevails at the rising of the Dog-star, and owing to which grafts and young trees pine away and die, the fig and the vine more particularly. The olive, also, besides the worm, to which it is equally subject with the fig, is attacked by the measles, or as some think fit to call it, the fungus or platter; it is a sort of blast produced by the heat of the sun. Cato says that the red moss is also deleterious to the olive. An excessive fertility, too, is very often injurious to the vine and the olive. Scab is a malady common to all trees. Eruptions, too, and the attacks of a kind of snail that grows on the bark, are diseases peculiar to the fig, but not in all countries; for there are some maladies that are prevalent in certain localities only.

Rain, too, is productive of the caterpillar, a noxious insect that eats away the leaves, and, some of them, the blossoms as well; and this in the olive even, as we find the case at Miletus; giving to the half-eaten tree a most loathsome appearance. This pest is produced by the prevalence of a damp, languid heat; and if the sun should happen to shine after this with a more intense heat and burn them up, this pest only gives place to another just as bad, the aspect only of the evil being changed.

There is still one other affection that is peculiar to the olive and the vine, known as the "cobweb," the fruit being enveloped in a web, as it were, and so stifled. There are certain winds, too, that are particularly blighting to the olive and the vine, as also to other fruits as well; and then besides, the fruits themselves, independently

---

3   The effects produced upon young shoots by frost.

of the tree, are very much worm-eaten in some years, the apple, pear, medlar, and pomegranate for instance. In the olive the presence of the worm may be productive of a twofold result; if it grows beneath the skin, it will destroy the fruit, but if it is in the stone, it will only gnaw it away, making the fruit all the larger.

PRODIGIES CONNECTED WITH TREES

Among the maladies which affect the various trees, we may find room for portentous prodigies also. For we find some trees that have never had a leaf upon them; a vine and a pomegranate bearing fruit adhering to the trunk, and not upon the shoots or branches; a vine, too, that bore grapes but had no leaves; and olives that have lost their leaves while the fruit remained upon the tree. There are some marvels also connected with trees that are owing to accident; an olive that was completely burnt, has been known to revive, and in Bœotia, some fig trees that had been quite eaten away by locusts budded afresh. Trees, too, sometimes change their colour, and turn from black to white; this, however, must not always be looked upon as portentous, and more particularly in the case of those which are grown from seed; the white poplar, too, often becomes black.

Another kind of prodigy, too, is the springing up of a tree in some extraordinary and unusual place, the head of a statue, for instance, or an altar, or upon another tree even. A fig-tree shot forth from a laurel at Cyzicus, just before the siege of that city; and so in like manner, at Tralles, a palm issued from the pedestal of the statue of the Dictator Cæsar, at the period of his civil wars. So, too, at Rome, in the Capitol there, in the time of the wars against Perseus, a palm-tree grew from the head of the statue of Jupiter, a presage of impending victory and triumphs. This palm, however, having been destroyed by a tempest, a fig-tree sprang up in the very same place, at the period of the lustration[4] made by the censors M. Messala and C. Cassius, a time at which, according to Piso, an author of high authority, all sense of shame had been utterly banished. Above all the prodigies, however, that have ever been heard of, we ought to place the one that was seen in our own time, at the period of the fall of the Emperor Nero, in the territory of Marrucinum; a plantation of olives, belonging to Vectius Marcellus, one of the principal members of the Equestrian order, bodily crossed the public highway, while the fields that lay on the opposite side of the road passed over to supply the place which had been thus vacated by the olive-yard.

---

4   Ceremonial purification; especially, a religious act of purgation or cleansing by the use of water or certain sacrifices or ceremonies, or both, performed among the ancients upon persons, armies, cities, localities, animals, etc. The ceremony was practised by the Greeks chiefly to free its subjects from the pollution of crime, but by the Romans as a general means of securing a divine blessing, and in some cases at regular fixed intervals, as of the whole people every five years (TN).

Book XVIII
The Natural History of Agriculture

We now pass on to the Natural History of the various grains, of the garden plants and flowers, and indeed of all the other productions, with the exception of the trees and shrubs, which the Earth, in her bounteousness, affords us, a boundless field for contemplation, if even we regard the herbs alone, when we take into consideration the varieties of them, their numbers, the flowers they produce, their odours, their colours, their juices, and the numerous properties they possess.

Romulus was the first who established the Arval[1] priesthood at Rome. This order consisted of the eleven sons of Accra Placentia, his nurse, together with Romulus himself, who assumed the appellation of the twelfth of the brotherhood. Upon this priesthood he bestowed, as being the most august distinction that he could confer upon it, a wreath of ears of corn, tied together with a white fillet; and this in fact, was the first chaplet that was ever used at Rome. This dignity is only ended with life itself, and whether in exile or in captivity, it always attends its owner. In those early days, two jugera of land were considered enough for a citizen of Rome, and to none was a larger portion than this allotted. And yet, at the present day, men who but lately were the slaves of the Emperor Nero have been hardly content with pleasure-gardens that occupied the same space as this; while they must have fishponds, forsooth, of still greater extent, and in some instances I might add, perhaps, kitchens even as well.

Numa first established the custom of offering corn to the gods, and of propitiating them with the salted cake; he was the first, too, as we learn from Hemina,

---

1   *Arvorum sacerdotes*, the priests of the fields.

to parch spelt,[2] from the fact that, when in this state, it is more wholesome as an aliment. This method, however, he could only establish one way; by making an enactment, to the effect that spelt is not in a pure state for offering, except when parched. He it was, too, who instituted the Fornacalia, festivals appropriated for the parching of corn, and others, observed with equal solemnity, for the erection and preservation of the "termini," or boundaries of the fields; for these termini, in those days, they particularly regarded as gods; while to other divinities they gave the names of Seia, from "sero," "to sow," and of Segesta, from tile "segetes," or "crops of standing corn," the statues of which goddesses we still see erected in the Circus. A third divinity it is forbidden by the rules of our religion to name even beneath a roof. In former days, too, they would not so much as taste the corn when newly cut, nor yet wine when just made, before the priests had made a libation of the first-fruits.

THE JUGERUM OF LAND

That portion of land used to be known as a "jugerum,"[3] which was capable of being ploughed by a single "jugum," or yoke of oxen, in one day; an "actus" being as much as the oxen could plough at a single spell, fairly estimated, without stopping. This last was one hundred and twenty feet in length; and two in length made a jugerum. The most considerable recompense that could be bestowed upon generals and valiant citizens, was the utmost extent of land around which a person could trace a furrow with the plough in a single day. The whole population, too, used to contribute a quarter of a sextarius of spelt, or else half a one, per head.

From agriculture the earliest surnames were derived. Thus, for instance, the name of Pilumnus was given to him who invented the "pilum," or pestle of the bake-house, for pounding corn; that of Piso was derived from "piso," to grind corn; and those of Fabius, Lentulus, and Cicero, from the several varieties of leguminous plants in the cultivation of which respectively these individuals excelled.[4] King Servius was the first who impressed upon our copper coin the figures of sheep and oxen.

The various ranks, too, and distinctions in the state had no other origin than the pursuits of agriculture. The rural tribes held the foremost rank, and were composed of those who possessed lands; while those of the city, a place to which it was looked upon as ignominious to be transferred, had the discredit thrown upon them of being an indolent race. Hence it was that these last were only four in number, and received their names from the several parts of the City which they respectively inhabited; being the Suburran, the Palatine, Colline, and Exquiline tribes.

---

2   A species of grain (*Triticum spelta*) related to wheat, formerly much cultivated in southern Europe and still grown in some districts (TN).

3   The common measure of land, a surface 240 Roman feet long and 120 wide, equal to 0.622 acre, or 0.252 hectare.

4   St Augustin, *De Civ. Dei.*, mentions a goddess, Bubona, the tutelar divinity of oxen. Nothing seems to be known of these games.

Every ninth day the rural tribes used to visit the city for the purpose of marketing, and it was for this reason that it was made illegal to hold the comitia[5] upon the Nundinæ; the object being that the country people might not be called away thereby from the transaction of their business. In those days repose and sleep were enjoyed upon straw. Even to glory itself, in compliment to corn, the name was given of "adorea."

THE PROPER ARRANGEMENTS FOR A FARM-HOUSE

The proper plan to be pursued is this; the farm-house must not be unsuitable for the farm, nor the farm for the house; and we must be on our guard against following the examples of L. Lucullus and Q. Scævola, who, though living in the same age, fell into the two opposite extremes; for whereas the farm-house of Scævola was not large enough for the produce of his farm, the farm of Lucullus was not sufficiently large for the house he built upon it; an error which gave occasion to the reproof of the censors, that on his farm there was less of ground for ploughing than of floor for sweeping. The proper arrangements for a farm-house are not to be made without a certain degree of skill.

It is generally agreed, that a farm-house ought neither to be built near a marsh, nor with a river in front of it; for, as Homer has remarked, with the greatest correctness, unwholesome vapours are always exhaled from rivers before the rising of the sun. In hot localities, a farm-house should have a northern aspect, but where it is cold, it should look towards the south; where, on the other hand, the site is temperate, the house should look due east. "The dwarf-elder," says Cato, "the wild plum, the bramble, the small bulb,[6] trefoil, meadow grass, the oak, and the wild pear and wild apple, are all of them indicative of a corn land. The same is the case, too, where the land is black, or of an ashy colour. All chalky soils are scorching, unless they are very thin; the same, too, with sand, unless it is remarkably fine. These remarks, however, are more applicable to champaign localities than declivities."

MAXIMS OF THE ANCIENTS ON AGRICULTURE

In what way, then, can land be most profitably cultivated? Why, in the words of our agricultural oracles, "by making good out of bad." But here it is only right that we should say a word in justification of our forefathers, who in their precepts on this subject had nothing else in view but the benefit of mankind; for when they use the term "bad" here, they only mean to say that which costs the smallest amount of money.

It was in the same spirit, too, that those oracles of ours have given utterance to these other precepts, to the effect that he is a bad agriculturist who has to buy what his farm might have supplied him with; that the man is a bad manager who does in the day-time what he might have done in the night, except, indeed, when the

---

5   In Roman antiquity, assemblies of the people. They were of three kinds: The most ancient assembly, that of the 30 curiæ, or comitia curiata, in which the old patrician families found representation. Each curia had one vote, and the assembly acted on matters of state and affairs of family and religion (TN).

6   Probably one of the genus *Allium sphserocephalum* of Linnaeus.

state of the weather does not allow it; that he is a worse manager still, who does on a work-day what he might have done on a feast-day;[7] but that he is the very worst of all, who works under cover in fine weather, instead of labouring in the fields.

I cannot refrain from taking the present opportunity of quoting one illustration afforded us by ancient times, from which it will be found that it was the usage in those days to bring before the people even questions connected with the various methods employed in agriculture, and will be seen in what way men were accustomed to speak out in their own defence. C. Furius Chresimus, a freedman, having found himself able, from a very small piece of land, to raise far more abundant harvests than his neighbours could from the largest farms, became the object of very considerable jealousy among them, and was accordingly accused of enticing away the crops of others by the practice of sorcery. Upon this, a day was named by Spurius Calvinus, the curule ædile, for his appearance. Apprehensive of being condemned, when the question came to be put to the vote among the tribes, he had all his implements of husbandry brought into the Forum, together with his farm servants, robust, well-conditioned, and well-clad people, Piso says. The iron tools were of first-rate quality, the mattocks were stout and strong, the plough-shares ponderous and substantial, and the oxen sleek and in prime condition. When all this had been done, "Here, Roman citizens," said he, "are my implements of magic; but it is impossible for me to exhibit to your view, or to bring into this Forum, those midnight toils of mine, those early watchings those sweats, and those fatigues." Upon this, by the unanimous voice of the people, he was immediately acquitted. Agriculture, in fact, depends upon the expenditure of labour and exertion; and hence it is that the ancients were in the habit of saying, that it is the eye of the master that does more towards fertilizing a field than anything else.

We shall give the rest of these precepts in their appropriate places, according as we find them adapted to each variety of cultivation; but in the meantime we must not omit some of a general nature, which here recur to our recollection, and more particularly that maxim of Cato, as profitable as it is humane; "Always act in such away as to secure the love of your neighbours." He then proceeds to state his reasons for giving this advice, but it appears to me that no one surely can entertain the slightest doubt upon the subject. One of the very first recommendations that he gives is to take every care that the farm servants are kept in good condition. It is a maxim universally agreed upon in agriculture, that nothing must be done too late; and again, that everything must be done at its proper season; while there is a third precept, which reminds us that opportunities lost can never be regained.

THE DIFFERENT KINDS OF GRAIN

As the field is now prepared, we shall proceed to speak of the nature of the various kinds of grain; we must premise, however, that there are two principal classes of grain, the cereals, comprising wheat and barley, and the legumina, such as the

---

7   Virgil, *Georg.* I. 268, *et seq.*, speaks of the work that might be done on feast days —making hedges, for instance, irrigating land, catching birds, washing sheep, and burning weeds.

BOOK XVIII - THE NATURAL HISTORY OF AGRICULTURE

bean and the chick-pea, for instance. The difference between these two classes is too well known to require any further description.

SPELT

Of all these grains barley is the lightest, its weight rarely exceeding fifteen pounds to the modius, while that of the bean is twenty-two. Spelt is much heavier than barley, and wheat heavier than spelt. In Egypt they make a meal of olyra,[8] a third variety of corn that grows there. The Gauls have also a kind of spelt peculiar to that country; they give it the name of "brace," while to us it is known as "sandala"; it has a grain of remarkable whiteness. Another difference, again, is the fact that it yields nearly four pounds more of bread to the modius than any other kind of spelt. Verrius states that for three hundred years the Romans made use of no other meal than that of corn.

WHEAT

There are numerous kinds of wheat which have received their names from the countries where they were first produced. For my part, however, I can compare no kind of wheat to that of Italy either for whiteness or weight, qualities for which it is more particularly distinguished; indeed it is only with the produce of the more mountainous parts of Italy that the foreign wheats can be put in comparison. Among these the wheat of Bœotia occupies the first rank, that of Sicily the second, and that of Africa the third.

And it is this whiteness that is still one of the peculiar merits of the Italian wheat; a circumstance which makes me the more surprised to find that none of the Greek writers of a later period have made any reference to it.

BARLEY – RICE

Of all the cereals the first that is sown is barley. In India, there is both a cultivated and a wild barley, from which they make excellent bread. But the most favourite food of all there is rice, from which they prepare a drink[9] similar to that made from barley in other parts of the world. The leaves of rice are fleshy, very like those of the leek, but broader; the stem is a cubit in height, the blossom purple, and the root globular, like a pearl in shape.

POLENTA

Barley is one of the most ancient aliments of man, a fact that is proved by a custom of the Athenians, mentioned by Menander, as also by the name of "hordearii,"[10] that used to be given to gladiators. The Greeks, too, prefer barley to anything else for making polenta. This food is made in various ways; in Greece, the barley is first steeped in water, and then left a night to dry. The next day they parch it, and then grind it in the mill. Some persons parch it more highly, and then sprinkle it again with a little water; after which they dry it for grinding. Others shake the grain

---

8   *Triticum monococcum*, according to some. Fée identifies it with the *Triticum spelta* of Linnæus.
9   Like our rice-milk, probably.
10 Or " barley-fed."

from out of the ear while green, and, after cleaning and soaking it in water, pound it in a mortar. They then wash the paste in baskets, and leave it to dry in the sun; after which they pound it again, clean it, and grind it in the mill. But whatever the mode of preparation adopted, the proportions are always twenty pounds of barley to three pounds of linseed, half a pound of coriander, and fifteen drachmæ of salt; the ingredients are first parched, and then ground in the mill.

Those who want it for keeping, store it in new earthen vessels, with fine flour and bran. In Italy, the barley is parched without being steeped in water, and then ground to a fine meal, with the addition of the ingredients already mentioned, and some millet as well. Barley bread, which was extensively used by the ancients, has now fallen into universal disrepute, and is mostly used as a food for cattle only.

PTISAN

With barley, too, the food called ptisan[11] is made, a most substantial and salutary aliment, and one that is held in very high esteem. Hippocrates, one of the most famous writers on medical science, has devoted a whole volume to the praises of this aliment. The ptisan of the highest quality is that which is made at Utica; that of Egypt is prepared from a kind of barley, the grain of which grows with two points. In Baltic and Africa, the kind of barley from which this food is made is that which Turranius calls the "smooth" barley; the same author expresses an opinion, too, that olyra and rice are the same. The method of preparing ptisan is universally known.

THE NATURE OF BARLEY

Barley-meal, too, is employed for medicinal purposes; and it is a curious fact, that for beasts of burden they make a paste of it, which is first hardened by the action of fire, and then ground. It is then made up into balls, which are introduced with the hand into the paunch, the result of which is, that the vigour and muscular strength of the animal is considerably increased. In some kinds of barley, the ears have two rows of grains, and in others more; in some cases, as many as six. The grain itself, too, presents certain differences, being long and thin, or else short or round, white, black, or, in some instances, of a purple colour. This last kind is employed for making polenta; the white is ill adapted for standing the severity of the weather.

WHEAT

There is no grain that displays a greater avidity than wheat, and none that absorbs a greater quantity of nutriment. With all propriety I may justly call winter wheat the very choicest of all the varieties of wheat. It is white, destitute of all flavour, and not oppressive to the stomach.

Wheat furnishes bread of the very finest quality and the most esteemed delicacies of the bakers. Wheat yields a fine flour of the very highest quality. In African wheat the modius ought to yield half a modius of fine flour and five sextarii of

---

11 Similar to our pearl barley, probably. Pearl-barley, is barley that has been processed to remove its fibrous outer hull and polished to remove some or all of the bran layer.

pollen, that being the name given to fine wheat meal, in the same way that winter wheat is generally known as "flos," or the "flower." This fine meal is extensively used in copper works and paper manufactories. In addition to the above, the modius should yield four sextarii of coarse meal, and the same quantity of bran. The finest wheaten flour will yield one hundred and twenty-two pounds of bread, and the fine meal of winter wheat one hundred and seventeen, to the modius of grain. When the prices of grain are moderate, meal sells at forty asses the modius, bolted wheaten flour at eight asses more, and bolted flour of wheat, at sixteen asses more.

THE MODE OF GRINDING CORN

All the grains are not easily broken. In Etruria they first parch the spelt in the ear, and then pound it with a pestle shod with iron at the end. In this instrument the iron is notched at the bottom, sharp ridges running out like the edge of a knife, and concentrating in the form of a star; so that if care is not taken to hold the pestle perpendicularly while pounding, the grains will only be splintered and the iron teeth broken. Throughout the greater part of Italy, however, they employ a pestle that is only rough at the end, and wheels turned by water, by means of which the corn is gradually ground. I shall here set forth the opinions given by Mago as to the best method of pounding corn. He says that the wheat should be steeped first of all in water, and then cleaned from the husk; after which it should be dried in the sun, and then pounded with the pestle; the same plan, he says, should be adopted in the preparation of barley. In the latter case, however, twenty sextarii of grain require only two sextarii of water. When lentils are used, they should be first parched, and then lightly pounded with, the bran; or else, adopting another method, a piece of unbaked brick and half a modius of sand should be added to every twenty sextarii of lentils.

MILLET – LEAVEN

Campania is particularly prolific in millet, and a fine white porridge is made from it; it makes a bread, too, of remarkable sweetness. The nations of Sarmatia live principally on this porridge, and even the raw meal, with the sole addition of mares' milk, or else blood extracted from the thigh of the horse. The Æthiopians know of no other grain but millet and barley.

Millet is more particularly employed for making leaven; and if kneaded with must,[12] it will keep a whole year. The same is done, too, with the fine wheat-bran of the best quality; it is kneaded with white must three days old, and then dried in the sun, after which it is made into small cakes. When required for making bread, these cakes are first soaked in water, and then boiled with the finest spelt flour, after which the whole is mixed up with the meal; and it is generally thought that this is the best method of making bread. The Greeks have established a rule that for a modius of meal eight ounces of leaven is enough.

WHEN BAKERS WERE FIRST INTRODUCED AT ROME

There were no bakers at Rome until the war with King Perseus, more than five hundred and eighty years after the building of the City. The ancient Romans used

---

12   Or grape-juice. This must have tended to affect the taste of the bread.

to make their own bread, it being an occupation which belonged to the women, as we see the case in many nations even at the present day. We have the fact, too, well ascertained, in the opinion of Ateius Capito, that the cooks in those days were in the habit of making the bread for persons of affluence, while the name of "pistor" was only given to the person who pounded, or "pisebat," the spelt. In those times, they had no cooks in the number of their slaves but used to hire them for the occasion from the market. The Gauls were the first to employ the bolter that is made of horse-hair; while the people of Spain make their sieves and meal-dressers of flax, and the Egyptians of papyrus and rushes.

ALICA

But among the very first things of all, we ought to speak of the method employed in preparing alica,[13] a most delightful and most wholesome food, and which incontestably confers upon Italy the highest rank among the countries that produce the cereals. This delicacy is prepared, no doubt, in Egypt as well, but of a very inferior quality, and not worth our notice. In Italy, however, it is prepared in numerous places, the territories of Verona and Pisæ, for example; but that of Campania is the most highly esteemed. There, at the foot of mountains capped with clouds, runs a plain, not less in all than forty miles in extent. The land here is dusty on the surface, but spongy below, and as porous as pumice. The inconveniences that generally arise from the close vicinity of mountains are here converted into so many advantages; for the soil, acting on it as a sort of filter, absorbs the water of the abundant rains that fall; the consequence of which is, that the water not being left to soak or form mud on the surface, the cultivation is greatly facilitated thereby.

Alica is prepared from the grain called zea, which is known to us as "seed" wheat. The grain is cleansed in a wooden mortar, for fear lest stone, from its hardness, should have the effect of grating it. The motive power for raising the pestle, as is generally known, is supplied by slaves working in chains, the end of it being enclosed in a case of iron. After the husks have been removed by this process, the pure grain is broken to pieces, the same implements being employed.

THE LEGUMINOUS PLANTS – THE BEAN

We now come to the history of the leguminous plants, among which the place of honour must be awarded to the bean;[14] indeed, some attempts have even been made to use it for bread. Bean meal is known as "lomentum"; and, as is the case with the meal of all leguminous plants, it adds considerably, when mixed with flour, to the weight of the bread. Beans are on sale at the present day for numerous purposes, and are employed for feeding cattle, and man more particularly. They are mixed, also, among most nations, with wheat, and panicum[15] more particularly, either whole or lightly broken. In our ancient ceremonials, too, bean pottage occupies its place in the religious services of the gods. Beans are mostly eaten

---

13 Porridge, gruel.
14 The *Faba vullaris* of the modern naturalists. It is supposed to have originally come from Persia.
15 A variety of millet, Italian millet (TN).

together with other food, but it is generally thought that they dull the senses, and cause sleepless nights attended with dreams. Hence it is that the bean has been condemned by Pythagoras; though, according to some, the reason for this denunciation was the belief which he entertained that the souls of the dead are enclosed in the bean; it is for this reason, too, that beans are used in the funereal banquets of the Parentalia. According to Varro, it is for a similar cause that the Flamen[16] abstains from eating beans; in addition to which, on the blossom of the bean, there are certain letters of ill omen to be found.

There are some peculiar religious usages connected with the bean. It is the custom to bring home from the harvest a bean by way of auspice, which, from that circumstance, has the name of "referiva." In sales by public auction, too, it is thought lucky to include a bean in the lot for sale. It is a fact, too, that the bean is the only one among all the grains that fills out at the increase of the moon, however much it may have been eaten away; it can never be thoroughly boiled in sea-water, or indeed any other water that is salt.

The bean is the first leguminous plant that is sown; that being done before the setting of the Vergiliæ, in order that it may pass the winter in the ground. Virgil recommends that it should be sown in spring, according to the usage of the parts of Italy near the Padus; but most people prefer the bean that has been sown early to that of only three months' growth; for, in the former case, the pods as well as the stalk afford a most agreeable fodder for cattle. When in blossom more particularly, the bean requires water; but after the blossom has passed off, it stands in need of but very little. It fertilizes the ground in which it has been sown as well as any manure hence it is that in the neighbourhood of Thessaly and Macedonia, as soon as it begins to blossom, they turn up the ground.

THE LUPINE

The lupine is the next among the leguminous plants that is in extensive use, as it serves for food for man in common with the hoofed quadrupeds. To prevent it from springing out of the pod while being gathered, and so lost, the best plan is to gather it immediately after a shower. Of all the seeds that are sown, there is not one of a more marvellous nature than this, or more favoured by the earth. First of all, it turns every day with the sun, and shows the hour to the husbandman, even though the weather should happen to be cloudy and overcast. It blossoms, too, no less than three times, and so attached is it to the earth, that it does not require to be covered with the soil; indeed, this is the only seed that does not require the earth to be turned up for sowing it. It thrives more particularly on a sandy, dry, and even gravelly soil; and requires no further care to be taken in its cultivation. To such a degree is it attached to the earth, that even though left upon a soil thickly covered

---

16   In Roman antiquity, a priest devoted to the service of one particular deity. Originally there were three priests so called: the flamen Dialis, consecrated to Jupiter; the flamen Martialis, sacred to Mars; and the flamen Quirinalis, who superintended the rites of Quirinus or Romulus (TN).

with brambles, it will throw out a root amid the leaves and brakes, and so contrive to reach the ground.

THE DISEASES OF GRAIN – THE OAT

The foremost feature of disease in wheat is the oat.[17] Barley, too, will degenerate into the oat; so much so, in fact, that the oat has become an equivalent for corn; for the people of Germany are in the habit of sowing it, and make their porridge of nothing else. This degeneracy is owing more particularly to humidity of soil and climate; and a second cause is a weakness in the seed, the result of its being retained too long in the ground before it makes its appearance above it. The same, too, will be the consequence, if the seed is decayed when put in the ground. This may be known, however, the moment it makes its appearance, from which it is quite evident that the defect lies in the root. There is another form of disease, too, which closely resembles the oat, and which supervenes when the grain, already developed to its full size, but not ripe, is struck by a noxious blast, before it has acquired its proper body and strength; in this case, the seed pines away in the ear, by a kind of abortion, as it were, and totally disappears.

The wind is injurious to wheat and barley, at three periods of the year in particular; when they are in blossom, directly the blossom has passed off, and just as the seed is beginning to ripen. In this last case, the grain wastes away, while in the two former ones it is prevented from being developed. Gleams of sunshine, every now and then, from the midst of clouds, are injurious to corn. Maggots, too, breed in the roots, when the rains that follow the seed-time are succeeded by a sudden heat, which encloses the humidity in the ground. Maggots make their appearance, also, in the grain, when the ear ferments through heat succeeding a fall of rain. There is a small beetle, too, known by the name of "cantharis,"[18] which eats away the blade. All these insects die, however, as soon as their nutriment fails them. Oil, pitch, and grease are prejudicial to grain, and care should be taken not to let them come in contact with the seed that is sown. Rain is only beneficial to grain while in the blade; it is injurious to wheat and barley while they are in blossom, but is not detrimental to the leguminous plants, with the exception of the chick-pea. When grain is beginning to ripen, rain is injurious, and to barley in particular. There is a white grass that grows in the fields, very similar to panicum in appearance, but fatal to cattle. As to darnel, the tribulus, the thistle, and the burdock, I can consider them, no more than the bramble, among the maladies that attack the cereals, but rather as so many pests inflicted on the earth. Mildew, a malady resulting from the inclemency of the weather, and equally attacking the vine and corn, is in no degree less injurious. It attacks corn most frequently in localities which are exposed to dews, and in valleys which have not a thorough draught for the wind; windy and

---

17   Plinius borrows this notion of the oat being wheat in a diseased state, from Theophrastus. Singularly enough, it was adopted by the learned Buffon.

18   Some coleopterous insect, probably, now unknown, and not the *Cantharis vesicatoria*, or "Spanish fly," as some have imagined. Dioscorides and Athenæus state to the same effect as Pliny.

elevated spots, on the other hand, are totally exempt from it. Another evil, again, in corn, is over-luxuriance, when it falls to the ground beneath the weight of the grain. One evil, however, to which all crops in common, the chick-pea even, are exposed, is the attacks of the caterpillar, when the rain, by washing away the natural saltness of the vegetation, makes it all the more tempting for its sweetness.

DIFFERENT SYSTEMS OF CULTIVATION EMPLOYED BY VARIOUS NATIONS

As we have now spoken at sufficient length of the several varieties of grain and soil, we shall proceed to treat of the methods adopted in tilling the ground, taking care, in the very first place, to make mention of the peculiar facilities enjoyed by Egypt in this respect. In that country, performing the duties of the husbandman, the Nile begins to overflow, as already stated, immediately after the summer solstice or the new moon, gradually at first, but afterwards with increased impetuosity, as long as the sun remains in the sign of Leo, When the sun has passed into Virgo, the impetuosity of the overflow begins to slacken, and when he has entered Libra the river subsides. Should it not have exceeded twelve cubits in its overflow, famine is the sure result; and this is equally the case if it should chance to exceed sixteen; for the higher it has risen, the more slowly it subsides, and, of course, the seed time is impeded in proportion. It was formerly a very general belief that immediately upon the subsiding of the waters the Egyptians were in the habit of driving herds of swine over the ground, for the purpose of treading the seed into the moist soil. At the present day even, the operation is not attended with much greater labour. It is well known, however, that the seed is first laid upon the slime that has been left by the river on its subsidence, and then ploughed in; this being done at the beginning of November. After this is done, a few persons are employed in stubbing, an operation known there as "botanismos." The rest of the labourers, however, have no occasion to visit the land again till a little before the calends of April, and then it is with the reaping-hook. The harvest is completed in the month of May. The stem is never so much as a cubit in length, as there is a stratum of sand beneath the slime, from which last alone the grain receives its support. The best wheat of all is that of the region of Thebais, Egypt being of a marshy character.

The method adopted at Seleucia in Babylonia is very similar to this, but the fertility there is still greater, owing to the overflow of the Euphrates and Tigris, the degree of irrigation being artificially modified in those parts. In Syria, too, the furrows are made extremely light, while in many parts of Italy, again, it takes as many as eight oxen to pant and blow at a single plough. All the operations of agriculture, but this in particular, should be regulated by the oracular precept: "Remember that every locality has its own tendencies."

ARRANGEMENT OF THE STARS ACCORDING TO THE TERRESTRIAL DAYS AND NIGHTS

In the first place, it is almost an utter impossibility to calculate with a fair degree of accuracy the days of the year and the movements of the sun. To the three hundred and sixty-five days there are still to be added the intercalary days, the result of the additional quarters of a day and night; hence it is, that it is found impossible to ascertain with exactness the proper periods for the appearance of the stars. To this we must add, too, a certain degree of uncertainty connected with these matters, that is universally admitted; thus, for instance, bad and wintry weather will often precede, by several days, the proper period for the advent of that season, a state of things known to the Greeks as προχειμάζειν;[19] while at another time, it will last longer than usual, a state of circumstances known as ἐπιχειμάζειν.[20] The effects, too, of the changes that take place in the seasons will sometimes be felt later, and at other times earlier, upon their reaching the face of the earth; and we not unfrequently hear the remark made, upon the return of fine weather, that the action of such and such a constellation is now completed. And then, again, as all these phenomena depend upon certain stars, arranged and regulated in the vault of heaven, we find intervening, in accordance with the movements of certain stars, hailstorms and showers, themselves productive of no slight results, and apt to interfere with the anticipated regular recurrence of the seasons. Nor are we to suppose that these disappointments fall upon the human race only, for other animated beings, as well as ourselves, are deceived in regard to them, although endowed with even a greater degree of sagacity upon these points than we are, from the fact of their very existence depending so materially upon them. Hence it is, that we sometimes see the summer birds killed by too late or too early cold, and the winter birds by heat coming out of the usual season. It is for this reason, that Virgil has recommended us to study the courses of the planets, and has particularly warned us to watch the passage of the cold star Saturn.

There have been three great schools of astronomy, the Chaldæan, the Ægyptian, and the Grecian. To these has been added a fourth school, which was established by the Dictator Cæsar among ourselves, and to which was entrusted the duty of regulating the year in conformity with the sun's revolution, under the auspices of Sosigenes, an astronomer of considerable learning and skill. His theory, too, upon the discovery of certain errors, has since been corrected, no intercalations having been made for twelve successive years, upon its being found that the year which before had anticipated the constellations, was now beginning to fall behind them.

THE EPOCHS OF THE SEASONS

The year is divided into four periods or seasons, the recurrence of which is indicated by the increase or diminution of the daylight. Immediately after the winter solstice the days begin to increase, and by the time of the vernal equinox, or in other words, in ninety days and three hours, the day is equal in length to the night. After this, for ninety-four days and twelve hours, the days continue to increase, and the nights to diminish in proportion, up to the summer solstice; and from that point the days, though gradually decreasing, are still in excess of the nights for ninety-two days, twelve hours, until the autumnal equinox. At this period the days are of equal length with the nights, and after it they continue to decrease inversely to the nights until the winter solstice, a period of eighty-eight days and three hours.

---

19 "To be an early winter."
20 "To be a long winter."

In all these calculations, it must be remembered, equinoctial hours are spoken of, and not those measured arbitrarily in reference to the length of any one day in particular. All these seasons, too, commence at the eighth degree of the signs of the Zodiac. The winter solstice begins at the eighth degree of Capricorn, the eighth day before the calends of January, in general; the vernal equinox at the eighth degree of Aries; the summer solstice, at the eighth degree of Cancer; and the autumnal equinox at the eighth degree of Libra; and it is rarely that these days do not respectively give some indication of a change in the weather.

These four seasons again, are subdivided, each of them, into two equal parts. Thus, for instance, between the summer solstice and the autumnal equinox, the setting of the Lyre, on the forty-sixth day, indicates the beginning of autumn; between the autumnal equinox and the winter solstice, the morning setting of the Vergiliæ, on the forty-fourth day, denotes the beginning of winter; between the winter solstice and the vernal equinox, the prevalence of the west winds on the forty-fifth day, denotes the commencement of spring; and between the vernal equinox and the summer solstice, the morning rising of the Vergiliæ, on the forty-eighth day, announces the commencement of summer. We shall here make seed-time, or in other words, the morning setting of the Vergiliæ, our starting-point; and shall not interrupt the thread of our explanation by making any mention of the minor constellations, as such a course would only augment the difficulties that already exist. It is much about this period that the stormy constellation of Orion departs, after traversing a large portion of the heavens.

CAUSES OF STERILITY

But we ought always to bear in mind, more particularly, that there are two varieties of evils that are inflicted upon the earth by the heavens. The first of these, known by us under the name of "tempests," comprehends hail-storms, hurricanes and other calamities of a similar nature; when these take place at the full moon, they come upon us with additional intensity. These tempests take their rise in certain noxious constellations, as already stated by us on several occasions, Arcturus, for instance, Orion, and the Kids.

The other evils that are thus inflicted upon us, supervene with a bright, clear sky, and amid the silence of the night, no one being sensible of them until we have perceived their effects. These dispensations are universal and of a totally different character from those previously mentioned, and have various names given to them, sometimes mildew, sometimes blast, and sometimes coal blight; but in all cases sterility is the infallible result. It is of these last that we have now to speak, entering into details which have not hitherto been treated of by any writer; and first of all we will explain the causes of them.

Independently of the moon, there are two principal causes of these calamities, which emanate more particularly from two quarters of the heavens of but limited extent. On the one hand, the Vergiliæ exercise an especial influence on our harvests, as it is with their rising that the summer begins, and with their setting, the winter; thus embracing, in the space of six months, the harvest, the vintage, and the ripening of all the vegetable productions. In addition to this, there is a circular tract in the heavens, quite visible to the human eye even, known as the Milky Way. It is the emanations from this, flowing as it were from the breast, that supply their milky nutriment to all branches of the vegetable world. Two constellations more particularly mark this circular tract, the Eagle in the north, and Canicula in the south. This circle traverses also Sagittarius and Gemini, and passing through the centre of the sun, cuts the equinoctial line below, the constellation of the Eagle making its appearance at the point of intersection on the one side, and Canicula on the other. Hence it is that the influences of both these constellations develop themselves upon all cultivated lands; it being at these points only that the centre of the sun is brought to correspond with that of the earth. If, then, at the moments of the rising and the setting of these constellations, the air, soft and pure, transmits these genial and milky emanations to the earth, the crops will thrive and ripen apace; but if on the other hand, the moon, sheds her chilling dews, the bitterness thereof infuses itself into these milky secretions, and so kills the vegetation in its birth. The measure of the injury so inflicted on the earth depends, in each climate, upon the combination of the one or other of these causes; and hence it is that it is not felt in equal intensity throughout the whole earth, nor even precisely at the same moment of time.

The life led by the ancients was rude and illiterate; still, as will be readily seen, the observations they made were not less remarkable for ingenuity than are the theories of the present day. With them there were three set periods for gathering in the produce of the earth, and it was in honour of these periods that they instituted the festive days, known as the Robigalia, the Floralia, and the Vinalia. The Robigalia were established by Numa in the fortieth year of his reign, and are still celebrated on the seventh day before the calends of May, as it is at this period that mildew mostly makes its first attacks upon the growing corn. Varro fixes this crisis at the moment at which the sun enters the tenth degree of Taurus, in accordance with the notions that prevailed in his day; but the real cause is the fact, that thirty-one days after the vernal equinox, according to the observations of various nations, the Dog-star sets between the seventh and fourth before the calends of May, a constellation baneful in itself, and to appease which a young dog should first be sacrificed. The same people also, in the year of the City 513, instituted the Floralia, a festival held upon the fourth before the calends of May, in accordance with the oracular injunctions of the Sibyl, to secure a favourable season for the blossoms and flowers. Varro fixes this day as the time at which the sun enters the fourteenth degree of Taurus. If there should happen to be a full moon during the four days at this period, injury to the corn and all the plants that are in blossom, will be the necessary result. The First Vinalia, which in ancient times were established on the ninth before the calends of May, for the purpose of tasting the wines, have no signification whatever in reference to the fruits of the earth, any more than the festivals already mentioned have in reference to the vine and the olive; the germination of these last not commencing, in fact, till the rising of the Vergiliæ, on the Sixth day before the ides of May. This, again, is another period of four days, which should never be blemished by dews, as the chilling constellation of Arcturus, which sets on the following day, will be sure to nip the vegetation; still less ought there to be a full moon at this period.

On the fourth before the nones of June, the Eagle rises again in the evening, a critical day for the olives and vines in blossom, if there should happen to be a full moon. For my part, I am of opinion that the eighth before the calends of July, the day of the summer solstice, must be a critical day, for a similar reason; and that the rising of the Dog-star, twenty-three days after the summer solstice, must be so too, in case the moon is then in conjunction; for the excessive heat is productive of injurious effects, and the grape becomes prematurely ripened, shrivelled, and tough. Again, if there is a full noon on the fourth before the nones of July, when Canicula rises to the people of Egypt, or at least on the sixteenth before the calends of August, when it rises in Italy, it is productive of injurious results. The same is the case, too, from the thirteenth day before the calends of August, when the Eagle sets, to the tenth before the calends of that month. The Second Vinalia, which are celebrated on the fourteenth before the calends of September, bear no reference to these influences. Varro fixes them at; the period at which the Lyre begins its morning setting, and says that this indicates the beginning of autumn, the day having been set apart for the purpose of propitiating the weather; at the present day, however, it is observed that the Lyre sets on the sixth before the ides of August.

Within these periods there are exerted the sterilizing influences of the heavens, though I am far from denying that they may be considerably modified by the nature of the locality according as it is cold or hot. Still, however, it is sufficient for me to have demonstrated the theory; the modifications of its results depending, in a great degree, upon attentive observation. It is beyond all question too, that either one of these two causes will be always productive of its own peculiar effects, the full moon, I mean, or else the moon's conjunction.

REMEDIES AGAINST THESE NOXIOUS INFLUENCES

When you have reason to fear these influences, make bonfires in the fields and vineyards of cuttings or heaps of chaff, or else of the weeds that have been rooted up; the smoke will act as a good preservative. The smoke, too, of burning chaff will be an effectual protection against the effects of fogs, when likely to be injurious. Some persons recommend that three crabs should be burnt alive among the trees on which the vines are trained, to prevent these from being attacked by coal blight; while others say that the flesh of the silurus should be burnt in a slow fire, in such a way that the smoke may be dispersed by the wind throughout the vineyard.

Varro informs us, that if at the setting of the Lyre, which is the beginning of autumn, a painted grape is consecrated in the midst of the vineyard, the bad weather will not be productive of such disastrous results as it otherwise would. Archibius has stated, in a letter to Antiochus, king of Syria, that if a bramble-frog is buried in a new earthen vessel, in the middle of a corn-field, there will be no storms to cause injury.

THE HARVEST

The mode of getting in the harvest varies considerably. In the vast domains of the provinces of Gaul a large hollow frame, armed with teeth and supported on two wheels, is driven through the standing corn, the beasts being yoked behind it; the result being, that the ears are torn off and fall within the frame. In other countries the stalks are cut with the sickle in the middle, and the ears are separated by the aid of paddle-forks. In some places, again, the corn is torn up by the roots; and it is asserted by those who adopt this plan, that it is as good as a light turning up for the ground, whereas, in reality, they deprive it of its juices. There are differences in other respects also; in places where they thatch their houses with straw, they keep the longest haulms for that purpose; and where hay is scarce, they employ the straw for litter. The straw of panicum is never used for thatching, and that of millet is mostly burnt; barley-straw, however, is always preserved, as being the most agreeable of all as a food for oxen. In the Gallic provinces panicum and millet are gathered, ear by ear, with the aid of a comb carried in the hand.

In some places the corn is beaten out by machines upon the threshing-floor, in others by the feet of mares, and in others with flails. The later wheat is cut, the more prolific it is; but it is got in early, the grain is finer and stronger. The best rule is to cut it before the grain hardens, and just as it is changing colour; though the oracles on husbandry say that it is better to begin the harvest two days too soon than two days too late. Winter and other wheat must be treated exactly the same way both on the threshing-floor and in the granary. Spelt, as it is difficult to be threshed, should be stored with the chaff on, being only disengaged of the straw and the beard.

THE METHODS OF STORING CORN

Connected with this branch of our subject is the method of storing corn. Some persons recommend that granaries should be built for the purpose at considerable expense, the walls being made of brick, and not less than three feet thick; the corn, they say, should be let in from above, the air being carefully excluded, and no windows allowed. Others, again, say that the granary should have an aspect in no direction but the north-east or north, and that the walls should be built without lime, that substance being extremely injurious to corn. In some places they build their granaries of wood, and upon pillars, thinking it the best plan to leave access for the air on every side, and from below even. Some persons think, however, that the grain diminishes in bulk if laid on a floor above the level of the ground, and that it is liable to ferment beneath a roof of tiles. Many persons say, too, that the grain should never be stirred up to air it, as the weevil is never known to penetrate beyond four fingers in depth; consequently, beyond that depth there is no danger. According to Columella, the west wind is beneficial to grain, a thing that surprises me, as that wind is generally a very parching one. Some persons recommend that, before housing the corn, a bramble-frog should be hung up by one of the hind legs at the threshold of the granary. To me it appears that the most important precaution of all is to house the grain at the proper time; for if it is unripe when cut, and not sufficiently firm, or if it is got in a heated state, it follows of necessity that noxious insects will breed in it.

The chick-pea is the only grain in which no insect will breed while in the granary. Some persons place upon the heaps of the leguminous grains pitchers full of vinegar and coated with pitch, a stratum of ashes being laid beneath; and they fancy that if this is done, no injury will happen.

THE REVOLUTIONS OF THE MOON

I shall now proceed to add some necessary information relative to the moon, the winds, and certain signs and prognostics, in order that I may complete the observations I have to make with reference to the sidereal system. Virgil has even gone so far, in imitation of Democritus, as to assign certain operations to certain days of the moon; but my sole object shall be, as indeed it has been throughout this work, to consult that utility which is based upon a knowledge and appreciation of general principles.

All vegetable productions are cut, gathered, and housed to more advantage while the moon is on the wane than while it is on the increase. Manure must never be touched except when the moon is on the wane; and land must be manured more particularly while the moon is in conjunction, or else at the first quarter. Take care to geld your boars, bulls, rams, and kids, while the moon is on the wane. Put eggs under the hen at a new moon. Make your ditches in the night-time, when the moon is at full. Cover up the roots of trees, while the moon is at full. Where the soil is humid, put in seed at the moon's conjunction, and during the four days about that period. It is generally recommended, too, to give an airing to corn and the leguminous grains, and to garner them, towards the end of the moon; to make seed-plots when the moon is above the horizon; and to tread out the grape, to fell timber, and to do many other things that have been mentioned in their respective places, when the moon is below it.

THE THEORY OF THE WINDS

The theory of the winds[21] is of a somewhat more intricate nature. After observing the quarter in which the sun rises on any given day, at the sixth hour of the day take your position in such a manner as to have the point of the sun's rising on your left; you will then have the south directly facing you, and the north at your back; a line drawn through a field in this direction is called the "cardinal" line. The observer must then turn round, so as to look upon his shadow, for it will be behind him. Having thus changed his position, so as to bring the point of the sun's rising on that day to the right, and that of his setting to the left, it will be the sixth hour of the day, at the moment when the shadow straight before him is the shortest. Through the middle of this shadow, taken lengthwise, a furrow must be traced in the ground with a hoe, or else a line drawn with ashes, some twenty feet in length, say; in the middle of this line, or, in other words, at the tenth foot in it, a small circle must then be described; to this circle we may give the name of the "umbilicus," or

---

21 Many Pliny's statements are drawn from Aristotle's Treatise, *De Mundo*.

"navel." That point in the line which lies on the side of the head of the shadow will be the point from which the north wind blows. You who are engaged in pruning trees, be it your care that the incisions made in the wood do not face this point; nor should the vine-trees or the vines have this aspect, except in the climates of Africa, Cyrenæ, or Egypt. When the wind blows, too, from this point, you must never plough, nor, in fact, attempt any other of the operations of which we shall have to make mention.

That part of the line which lies between the umbilicus and the feet of the shadow will look towards the south, and indicate the point from which the south wind blows, to which, as already mentioned, the Greeks have given the name of Notus. When the wind comes from this quarter, you, husbandman, must never fell wood or touch the vine. In Italy this wind is either humid or else of a burning heat, and in Africa it is accompanied with intense heat and fine clear weather. In Italy the bearing branches should be trained to face this quarter, but the incisions made in the trees or vines when pruned must never face it. Let those be on their guard against this wind upon the four days at the rising of the Vergiliæ, who are engaged in planting the olive, as well as those who are employed in the operations of grafting or inoculating.

It will be as well, too, here to give some advice, in reference to the climate of Italy, as to certain precautions to be observed at certain hours of the day. You, woodman, must never lop the branches in the middle of the day; and you, shepherd, when you see midday approaching in summer, and the shadow gradually decreasing, drive your flocks from out of the sun into some well-shaded spot. When you lead the flocks to pasture in summer, let them face the west before midday, and after that time, the east; if this precaution is not adopted, calamitous results will ensue; the same, too, if the flocks are led in winter or spring to pastures covered with dew. Nor must you let them feed with their faces to the north, as already mentioned; for the wind will either close their eyes or else make them bleared, and they will die of looseness. If you wish to have females, you should let the dams have their faces towards the north while being covered.

WEATHER PROGNOSTICS

Having now explained the theory of the winds, it seems to me the best plan, in order to avoid any repetition, to pass on to the other signs and prognostics that are indicative of a change of weather. I find, too, that this is a kind of knowledge that greatly interested Virgil, for he mentions the fact, that during the harvest even, he has often seen the winds engage in a combat that was absolutely ruinous to the improvident agriculturist.

In the first place, then, we will consider those prognostics of the weather which are derived from the sun. If the sun is bright at its rising, and not burning hot, it is indicative of fine weather, but if pale, it announces wintry weather accompanied with hail. If the sun is bright and clear when it sets, and if it rises with a similar appearance, the more assured of fine weather may we feel ourselves. If it is hidden in clouds at its rising, it is indicative of rain, and of wind, when the clouds are of

Book XVIII - The Natural History of Agriculture

a reddish colour just before sunrise; if black clouds are intermingled with the red ones, they betoken rain as well. When the sun's rays at its rising or setting appear to unite, rainy weather may be looked for.

If, at its rising, the sun is surrounded with a circle, wind may be looked for in the quarter in which the circle breaks; but if it disappears equally throughout, it is indicative of fine weather. If the sun at its rising throws out its rays afar through the clouds, and the middle of its disk is clear, there will be rain; and if its rays are seen before it rises, both rain and wind as well. If a white circle is seen round the sun at its setting, there will be a slight storm in the night; but if there is a mist around it, the storm will be more violent. If the sun is pale at sunset, there will be wind, and if there is a dark circle round it, high winds will arise in the quarter in which the circle breaks.

PROGNOSTICS DERIVED FROM THE MOON

The prognostics derived from the moon, assert their right to occupy our notice in the second place. In Egypt, attention is paid, more particularly, to the fourth day of the moon. If, when the moon rises, she shines with a pure bright light, it is generally supposed that we shall have fine weather; but if she is red, there will be wind, and if of a swarthy hue, rain. If upon the fifth day of the moon her horns are obtuse, they are always indicative of rain, but if sharp and erect, of wind, and this on the fourth day of the moon more particularly. If her northern horn is pointed and erect, it portends wind; and if it is the lower horn that presents this appearance, the wind will be from the south; if both of them are erect, there will be high winds in the night. If upon the fourth day of the moon she is surrounded by a red circle, it is portentous of wind and rain.

In Varro we find it stated to the following effect: "If, at the fourth day of the moon, her horns are erect, there will be great storms at sea, unless, indeed, she has a circlet around her, and that circlet unblemished; for by that sign we are informed that there will be no stormy weather before full moon. If, at the full moon, one half of her disk is clear, it is indicative of fine weather, but if it is red, of wind, and if black, of rain. If a darkness comes over the face of the moon, covered with clouds, in whatever quarter it breaks, from that quarter wind may be expected. If a twofold circle surrounds the moon, the storm will be more violent, and even more so still, if there are three circles, or if they are black, broken, and disjointed. If the new moon at her rising has the upper horn obscured, there will be a prevalence of rainy weather, when she is on the wane; but if it is the lower horn that is obscured, there will be rain before full moon; if, again, the moon is darkened in the middle of her disk, there will be rain when she is at full. If the moon, when full, has a circle round her, it indicates wind from the quarter in the circle which is the brightest; but if at her rising the horns are obtuse, they are portentous of a frightful tempest. If, when the west wind prevails, the moon does not make her appearance before her fourth day, there will be a prevalence of stormy weather throughout the month. If on the sixteenth day the moon has a bright, flaming appearance, it is a presage of violent tempests."

PROGNOSTICS DERIVED FROM THE STARS

In the third rank must be placed the prognostics derived from the stars. These bodies are sometimes to be seen shooting to and fro; when this happens, winds immediately ensue, in that part of the heavens in which the presage has been afforded. When the heavens are equally bright throughout their whole expanse, at the periods previously mentioned, the ensuing autumn will be fine and cool. If the spring and summer have passed not without some rain, the autumn will be fine and settled, and there will be but little wind; when the autumn is fine, it makes a windy winter. When the brightness of the stars is suddenly obscured, though without clouds or fog, violent tempests may be expected. If numerous stars are seen to shoot, leaving a white track behind them, they presage wind from that quarter. If they follow in quick succession from the same quarter, the wind will blow steadily, but if from various quarters of the heavens, the wind will shift in sudden gusts and squalls. If circles are seen to surround any of the planets, there will be rain. In the constellation of Cancer, there are two small stars to be seen, known as the Aselli, the small space that lies between them being occupied by a cloudy appearance, which is known as the Manger; when this cloud is not visible in a clear sky, it is a presage of a violent storm. If a fog conceals from our view the one of these stars which lies to the north-east, there will be high winds from the south; but if it is the star which lies to the south that is so obscured, then the wind will be from the north-east. The rainbow, when double, indicates the approach of rain; but if seen after rain, it gives promise, though by no means a certain one, of fine weather. Circular clouds around some of the stars are indicative of rain.

PROGNOSTICS DERIVED FROM THUNDER

When, in summer, there is more thunder than lightning, wind may be expected from that quarter; but if, on the other hand, there is not so much thunder as lightning, there will be a fall of rain. When it lightens in a clear sky, there will be rain, and if there is thunder as well, stormy weather; but if it lightens from all four quarters of the heavens, there will be a dreadful tempest. When it lightens from the north-east only, it portends rain on the following day; but when from the north, wind may be expected from that quarter. When it lightens on a clear night from the south, the west, or the north-west, there will be wind and rain from those quarters. Thunder in the morning is indicative of wind, and at midday of rain.

PROGNOSTICS DERIVED FROM CLOUDS

When clouds are seen moving in a clear sky, wind may be expected in the quarter from which they proceed; but if they accumulate in one spot, as they approach the sun they will disperse. If the clouds are dispersed by a north-east wind, it is a presage of high winds, but if by a wind from the south, of rain. If at sunset the clouds cover the heavens on either side of the sun, they are indicative of tempest; if they are black and lowering in the east, they threaten rain in the night, but if in the west, on the following day. If the clouds spread in large numbers from the east, like fleeces of wool in appearance, they indicate a continuance of rain for the next three days. When the clouds settle on the summits of the mountains, there will be stormy weather; but if the clouds clear away, it will be fine. When the clouds are white and lowering, a hailstorm, generally known as a "white" tempest, is close at hand. An isolated cloud, however small, though seen in a clear sky, announces wind and storm.

PROGNOSTICS DERIVED FROM AQUATIC ANIMALS AND BIRDS

The animals, too, afford us certain presages; dolphins, for instance, sporting in a calm sea, announce wind in the quarter from which they make their appearance. When they throw up the water in a billowy sea, they announce the approach of a calm. The loligo,[22] springing out of the water, shell-fish adhering to various objects, sea-urchins fastening by their stickles upon the sand, or else burrowing in it, are so many indications of stormy weather; the same, too, when frogs croak more than usual, or coots make a chattering in the morning. Divers, too, and ducks, when they clean their feathers with the bill, announce high winds; which is the case also when the aquatic birds unite in flocks, cranes make for the interior, and divers and sea-mews forsake the sea or the creeks. Cranes when they fly aloft in silence announce fine weather, and so does the owlet, when it screeches during a shower; but it is heard in fine weather, it presages a storm. Ravens, too, when they croak with a sort of gurgling noise and shake their feathers, give warning of the approach of wind, if their note is continuous; but if, on the other hand, it is smothered, and only heard at broken intervals, we may expect rain, accompanied with high winds. Jackdaws, when they return late from feeding, give notice of stormy weather, and the same with the white birds, when they unite in flocks, and the land birds, when they descend with cries to the water and besprinkle themselves, the crow more particularly. The swallow, too, when it skims along the surface of the water, so near as to ripple it every now and then with its wings, and the birds that dwell in the trees, when they hide themselves in their nests, afford similar indications; geese, too, when they set up a continuous gabbling, at an unusual time, and the heron, when it stands moping in the middle of the sands.

---

22 The ink-fish; *Sepia loligo* of Linnæus.

Book XIX
The Nature and Cultivation of Flax, and an Account of Various Garden Plants

We have now imparted a knowledge of the constellations and of the seasons, in a method unattended with difficulty for the most ignorant even, and free from every doubt; indeed, to those who understand these matters rightly, the face of the earth contributes in no less a degree to a due appreciation of the celestial phenomena, than does the science of astronomy to our improvement in the arts of agriculture.

To commence, then, with a production which is of an utility that is universally recognized, and is employed not only upon dry land but upon the seas as well, we will turn our attention to flax, a plant which is reproduced from seed, but which can neither be classed among the cereals nor yet among the garden plants. What department is there to be found of active life in which flax is not employed? and in what production of the earth are there greater marvels revealed to us than in this?

HOW FLAX IS SOWN; ITS VARIETIES

Flax is mostly sown in sandy soils, and after a single ploughing only. There is no plant that grows more rapidly than this; sown in spring, it is pulled up in summer, and is, for this reason as well, productive of considerable injury to the soil.

But it is the province of Nearer Spain that produces a linen of the greatest lustre, an advantage which it owes to the waters of a stream which washes the city of Tarraco[1] there. The fineness, too, of this linen is quite marvellous, and here it is that the first manufactories of cambric[2] were established. From the same province, too, of Spain, the flax of Zoëla has of late years been introduced into Italy, and has

---
1   Now Tarragona.
2   "Carbasus." This was probably the Spanish name originally for fine flax, and hence came to signify the cambrics, or fine linen tissues made of it. It seems, however, to have after-

been found extremely serviceable for the manufacture of hunting-nets. Zoëla is a city of Callæcia, in the vicinity of the Ocean. The flax, too, of Cumæ, in Campania, has its own peculiar merits in the manufacture of nets for fishing and fowling; it is employed, also, for making hunting-nets. For it is from flax, in fact, that we prepare various textures, destined to be no less insidious to the brute creation than they are to ourselves. It is with toils made from the flax of Cumæ that wild boars are taken, the meshes being proof against their bristles, equally with the edge of the knife; before now, too, we have seen some of these toils of a fineness so remarkable as to allow of being passed through a man's ring, running ropes and all, a single individual being able to carry an amount of nets sufficient to environ a whole forest.

The flax of Egypt, though the least strong of all as a tissue, is that from which the greatest profits are derived. There are four varieties of it, the Tanitic, the Pelusiac, the Butic, and the Tentyritic. The upper part of Egypt, in the vicinity of Arabia, produces a shrub, known by some as "gossypium," but by most persons as "xylon"; hence the name of "xylina," given to the tissues that are manufactured from it. The shrub is small, and bears a fruit, similar in appearance to a nut with a beard, and containing in the inside a silky substance, the down of which is spun into threads. There is no tissue known, that is superior to those made from this thread, either for whiteness, softness, or dressing; the most esteemed vestments worn by the priests of Egypt are made of it. There is a fourth kind of tissue, known by the name of "othoninum," which is made from a kind of marshreed, the panicule only being employed for the purpose. In Asia, again, there is a thread made from broom, which is employed in the construction of fishing-nets, being found to be remarkably durable; for the purpose of preparing it, the shrub is steeped in water for ten days. The Æthiopians, also, and the people of India, prepare a kind of thread from a fruit which resembles our apple, from gourds that grow upon trees.

THE MODE OF PREPARING FLAX

In our part of the world the ripeness of flax is usually ascertained by two signs, the swelling of the seed, and its assuming a yellowish tint. It is then pulled up by the roots, made up into small sheaves that will just fill the hand, and hung to dry in the sun. It is suspended with the roots upwards the first day, and then for the five following days the heads of the sheaves are placed, reclining one against the other, in such a way that the seed which drops out may fall into the middle. After the wheat harvest is over, the stalks of flax are plunged in water that has been warmed in the sun, and are then submitted to pressure with a weight; for there is nothing known that is more light and buoyant than this. When the outer coat is loosened, it is a sign that the stalks have been sufficiently steeped; after which they are again turned with the heads downwards, and left to dry as before in the sun; when thoroughly dried, they are beaten with a tow-mallet on a stone.

The part that lies nearest to the outer coat is known by the name of "stuppa"; it is a flax of inferior quality, and is mostly employed for making the wicks of lamps.

---

wards been extended to all kinds of linen tissues, as we find the name given indifferently to linen garments, sail-cloth, and awnings for the theatres.

Book XIX - The Nature and Cultivation of Flax... 219

This, however, requires to be combed out with iron spikes, until the whole of the outer skin is removed. The inner part presents numerous varieties of flax, esteemed respectively in proportion to their whiteness and their softness. Spinning flax is held to be an honourable employment for men even; the husks, or outer coats, are employed for heating furnaces and ovens.

ESPARTO

For the fact is that esparto did not begin to be employed till many ages after the time of Homer; indeed, not before the first war that the Carthaginians waged in Spain. This, too, is a plant that grows spontaneously, and is incapable of being reproduced by sowing, it being a species of rush, peculiar to a dry, arid soil, a morbid production confined to a single country only; for in reality it is a curse to the soil, as there is nothing whatever that can be sown or grown in its vicinity. There is a kind of esparto grown in Africa, of a stunted nature, and quite useless for all practical purposes.

When taken up it is made into sheaves, and laid in heaps for a couple of days, while it retains its life and freshness; on the third day the sheaves are opened out and spread in the sun to dry, after which it is again made up into sheaves, and placed under cover. It is then put to soak in sea-water, this being the best of all for the purpose, though fresh water will do in case sea-water cannot be procured; this done, it is again dried in the sun, and then moistened afresh. If it is wanted for immediate use, it is put in a tub and steeped in warm water, after which it is placed in an upright position to dry; this being universally admitted to be the most expeditious method of preparing it. To make it ready for use, it requires to be beaten out. Articles made of it are proof, more particularly, against the action of fresh or sea-water; but on dry land, ropes of hemp are generally preferred. Indeed, we find that esparto receives nutriment even from being under water, by way of compensation, as it were, for the thirst it has had to endure upon its native soil.

TRUFFLES

As we have here made a beginning of treating of the marvels of Nature, we shall proceed to examine them in detail; and among them the very greatest of all, beyond a doubt, is the fact that any plant should spring up and grow without a root. Such, for instance, is the vegetable production known as the truffle;[3] surrounded on every side by earth, it is connected with it by no fibres, not so much as a single thread even, while the spot in which it grows, presents neither protuberance nor cleft to the view. It is found, in fact, in no way adhering to the earth, but enclosed within an outer coat; so much so, indeed, that though we cannot exactly pronounce it to be composed of earth, we must conclude that it is nothing else but a callous concretion of the earth.

---

3 The truffles are part of the *Tuberaceae* family of fungi. They have a mycorrhizal symbiotic relationship with trees, such as chestnut, walnut and especially those of the Oak genus such as oaks and holm oaks (TN).

Truffles generally grow in dry, sandy soils, and spots that are thickly covered with shrubs; in size they are often larger than a quince, and are found to weigh as much as a pound. There are two kinds of them, the one full of sand, and consequently injurious to the teeth, the other free from sand and all impurities.

When there have been showers in autumn, and frequent thunder-storms, truffles are produced, thunder contributing more particularly to their development; they do not, however, last beyond a year, and are considered the most delicate eating when gathered in spring.

THE PLEASURES OF THE GARDEN

Having made mention of these productions, it now remains for us to return to the cultivation of the garden, a subject recommended by its own intrinsic merits to our notice; for we find that in remote antiquity, even, there was nothing looked upon with a greater degree of admiration than the gardens of the Hesperides, those of the kings Adonis and Alcinoüs, and the Hanging Gardens. The kings of Rome cultivated their gardens with their own hands; indeed, it was from his garden that Tarquinius Superbus sent to his son that cruel and sanguinary message of his. In our laws of the Twelve Tables, we find the word "villa," or "farm," nowhere mentioned; it is the word "hortus" that is always used with that signification, while the term "heredium" we find employed for "garden."

There are certain religious impressions, too, that have been attached to this species of property, and we find that it is in the garden and the Forum only that statues of satyrs are consecrated, as a protection against the evil effects of spells and sorcery; although in Plautus, we find the gardens spoken of as being under the tutelage of Venus. At the present day, under the general name of gardens, we have pleasure-grounds situate in the very heart of the City, as well as extensive fields and villas.

Epicurus, that connoisseur in the enjoyments of a life of ease, was the first to lay out a garden at Athens; up to his time it had never been thought of, to dwell in the country in the middle of the town. At Rome, on the other hand, the garden constituted of itself the poor man's field, and it was from the garden that the lower classes procured their daily food.

In this department even, humble as it is, we are still destined to find certain productions that are denied to the community at large, and the very cabbages pampered to such an enormous extent that the poor man's table is not large enough to hold them.

DIFFERENT KINDS OF PLANTS WHICH GROW IN GARDENS

Of some plants the fruits are in the earth, of others both in the earth and out of it, and of others, again, out of the earth solely. Some of them increase as they lie upon the ground, gourds and cucumbers, for instance; the same products will grow also in a hanging position, but they are much heavier even then than any of the fruits that grow upon trees. The cucumber, however, is composed of cartilage and a fleshy substance, while the gourd consists of rind and cartilage; this last is the only vegetable production the outer coat of which becomes of a ligneous nature, when ripe. Radishes, turnips, and rape are hidden in the earth, and so, too, are elecampane, skirrets, and parsnips, though in a different manner. There are some plants, again, to which we shall give the name of "ferulaceous," anise and mallows.

In the class of ferulaceous plants we must include hemp also. There are some plants, again, to which we must give the appellation of "fleshy"; such as those spongy productions which are found growing in damp meadows. As to the fungus, with a hard, tough flesh, we have already made mention of it when speaking of wood and trees; and of truffles, which form another variety, we have but very recently given a description.

VEGETABLES OF A CARTILAGINOUS NATURE – CUCUMBERS

The cucumber belongs to the cartilaginous class of plants, and grows above the ground. It was a wonderful favourite with the Emperor Tiberius, and, indeed, he was never without it; for he had raised beds made in frames upon wheels, by means of which the cucumbers were moved and exposed to the full heat of the sun; while, in winter, they were withdrawn, and placed under the protection of frames glazed with mirror-stone. We find it stated, also, by the ancient Greek writers, that the cucumber ought to be propagated from seed that has been steeped a couple of days in milk and honey, this method having the effect of rendering them all the sweeter to the taste. The cucumber, while growing, may be trained to take any form that may be wished; in Italy the cucumbers are green and very small, while those grown in some of the provinces are remarkably large, and of a wax colour or black.

GOURDS

Gourds resemble the cucumber in nature, at least in their manner of growing; they manifest an equal aversion to the winter, too, while they require constant watering and manure. Both cucumbers and gourds are sown in holes a foot and a half deep, between the vernal equinox and the summer solstice, at the time of the Parilia more particularly. Some persons, however, think it better to sow gourds after the calends of March, and cucumbers after the nones, and at the time of the Quinquatria. The cucumber and the gourd climb upwards in a precisely similar manner, their shoots creeping along the rough surface of the walls, even to the very roof, so great is their fondness for elevated spots.

The gourd admits of being applied to more numerous uses than the cucumber even; the stem is used as an article of food when young, but at a later period it changes its nature, and its qualities become totally different; of late, gourds have come to be used in baths for jugs and pitchers, but for this long time past they have been employed as casks for keeping wine.

RADISHES

Radishes are composed of an outer coat and a cartilaginous substance, and in many instances the rind is found to be thicker than the bark of some trees. This plant is remarkable for its pungency, which increases in proportion to the thickness of the rind; in some cases, too, the surface of it assumes a ligneous nature. Radishes are flatulent to a remarkable degree, and are productive of eructations; hence it is that they are looked upon as an aliment only fit for low-bred people, and this more particularly if coleworts are eaten directly after them. If, on the other hand, they are eaten with green olives, the eructations produced are not so frequent, and less offensive. In Egypt the radish is held in very high esteem, on account of the abundance of oil that is extracted from the seed. Indeed, the people of that country sow this plant in preference to any other, whenever they can get the opportunity, the profits derived from it being larger than those obtained from the cultivation of corn, and the imposts levied upon it considerably less; there is no grain known that yields a larger quantity of oil.

The radish requires to be sown in a loose, humid soil, has a great aversion to manure, and is content with a dressing solely of chaff; so fond is it of the cold, that in Germany it is known to grow as large as an infant in size. For the spring crop, it is sown immediately after the ides of February; and then again about the time of the Vulcanalia, this last crop being looked upon as the best; many persons, however, sow radishes in March, April, and September.

Medical men recommend raw radishes to be eaten fasting, with salt, for the purpose of collecting the crude humours of the viscera; and in this way they prepare them for the action of emetics. It is said, too, that the juices of this plant are absolutely necessary for the cure of certain diseases of the diaphragm; for it has been found by experiment, in Egypt, that the phthiriasis which attaches itself to the internal parts of the heart, cannot possibly be eradicated by any other remedy, the kings of that country having ordered the bodies of the dead to be opened and examined, for the purpose of enquiring into certain diseases.

PARSNIPS

The other kinds which have been classified by us among the cartilaginous plants, are of a more ligneous nature; and it is a singular thing, that they have, all of them, a strong flavour. Among these, there is one kind of wild parsnip which grows spontaneously; by the Greeks it is known as "staphylinos." Another kind of parsnip is grown either from the root transplanted, or else from seed, at the beginning of spring or in the autumn; Hyginus says that this may be done in February, August, September, and October, the ground being dug to a very considerable depth for the purpose. The parsnip begins to be fit for eating at the end of a year, but it is still better at the end of two; it is reckoned more agreeable eating in autumn, and more particularly if cooked in the saucepan; even then, however, it preserves its strong pungent flavour, which it is found quite impossible to get rid of.

The hibiscum differs from the parsnip in being more slender; it is rejected as a food, but is found useful for its medicinal properties. There is a fourth kind, also, which bears a similar degree of resemblance to the parsnip; by our people it is called the "gallica," while the Greeks, who have distinguished four varieties of it, give it the name of "daucus." We shall have further occasion to mention it among the medicinal plants.

ONION

Garlic and onions are invoked by the Egyptians, when taking an oath, in the number of their deities. The Greeks have many varieties of the onion, the Sardian onion, the Samothracian, the Alsidenian, the setanian, the schistan, and the Ascalonian, so called from Ascalon, a city of Judæa. They have, all of them, a pungent smell, which draws tears from the eyes, those of Cyprus more particularly, and those of Cnidos the least of all. In all of them the body is composed of a cartilage of an unctuous nature. The variety known as the setanian is the smallest of them all, with the exception of the Tusculan onion, but it is sweet to the taste. The schistan and the Ascalonian kinds are used for storing. The schistan onion is left during the winter with the leaves on; in the spring it is stripped of them, upon which offsets make their appearance at the same divisions as the leaves; it is to this circumstance that this variety owes its name. Taking the hint from this fact, it is recommended to strip the other kinds of their leaves, to make them bulb all the better, instead of running to seed.

The Ascalonian onion is of a peculiar nature, being barren in some measure in the root; hence it is that the Greeks have recommended it to be reproduced from seed, and not from roots; the transplanting, too, they say, should be done later in the spring, at the time the plant germinates, the result being that it bulbs with all the greater rapidity, and hastens, as it were, to make up for lost time; great dispatch, however, is requisite in taking it up, for when ripe it rots with the greatest rapidity. If propagated from roots, it throws out a long stalk, runs rapidly to seed, and dies.

In addition to these particulars, it is recommended that the ground intended for sowing onions should be turned up three times, care being taken to remove all roots and weeds; ten pounds of seed is the proper proportion for a jugerum. Savory too, they say, should be mixed with them, the onions being all the finer for it; the ground, too, should be stubbed and hoed four times at least, if not oftener. In Italy, the Ascalonian onion is sown in the month of February. The seed of the onion is gathered when it begins to turn black, and before it becomes dry and shrivelled.

GARLIC

Garlic is generally supposed, in the country more particularly, to be a good specific for numerous maladies. The external coat consists of membranes of remarkable fineness, which are universally discarded when the vegetable is used; the inner part being formed by the union of several cloves, each of which has also a separate coat of its own. The flavour of it is pungent, and the more numerous the cloves the more pungent it is. Like the onion, it imparts an offensive smell to the breath; but this is not the case when it is cooked. The various species of garlic are distinguished by the periods at which they ripen; the early kind becomes fit for use in sixty days. Another distinction, too, is formed by the relative size of the heads.

For the purpose of depriving all these plants of their strong smell, it is recommended to set them when the moon is below the horizon, and to take them up when she is in conjunction. Independently of these precautions, we find Menander, one of the Greek writers, recommending those who have been eating garlic to eat immediately afterwards a root of beet roasted on hot coals; if this is done, he says, the strong smell of the garlic will be effectually neutralized.

If garlic or onions are wanted to keep some time, the heads should be dipped in salt water, made lukewarm; by doing this, they will be all the better for keeping, though quite worthless for reproduction. Some persons content themselves with hanging them over burning coals, and are of opinion that this is quite sufficient to prevent them from sprouting; for it is a well-known fact, that both garlic and onions sprout when out of the ground, and that after throwing out their thin shoots they shrivel away to nothing.

THE NATURE OF THE VARIOUS SEEDS

In most plants the seed is round, in some oblong; it is broad and foliaceous in some, orage for instance, while in others it is narrow and grooved, as in cummin. There are differences, also, in the colour of seeds, which is either black or white; while some seeds are woody and hard, in radishes, mustard, and rape, the seeds are enclosed in pods. In parsley, coriander, anise, fennel, and cummin, the seed has no covering at all, while in blite, beet, orage, and basil, it has an outer coat, and in the lettuce it is covered with a fine down. There is no seed more prolific than that of basil it is generally recommended to sow it with the utterance of curses and imprecations, the result being that it grows all the better for it; the earth, too, is rammed down when it is sown, and prayers offered that the seed may never come up. The seeds which are enveloped in an outer coat, are dried with considerable difficulty, that of basil more particularly; hence it is that all these seeds are dried artificially, their fruitfulness being greatly promoted thereby.

Plants in general come up better when the seed is sown in heaps than when it is scattered broad-cast; leeks, in fact, and parsley are generally grown by sowing the seed in little bags; in the case of parsley, too, a hole is made with the dibble, and a layer of manure inserted.

All garden plants grow either from seed or from slips, and some from both seed and suckers, such as rue, wild marjoram, and basil, for example —this last being usually cut when it is a palm in height. Some kinds, again, are reproduced from both seed and root, as in the case of onions, garlic, and bulbs, and those other plants of which, though annuals themselves, the roots retain their vitality.

THE LETTUCE

The Greeks have distinguished three varieties of the lettuce; the first with a stalk so large, that small garden gates, it is said, have been made of it; the leaf of this lettuce is somewhat larger than that of the herbaceous, or green lettuce, but extremely narrow, the nutriment seeming to be expended on the other parts of the plant. The second kind is that with a rounded stalk; and the third is the low, squat lettuce generally known as the Laconian lettuce.

Some persons have made distinctions in reference to their respective colours, and the times for sowing them; the black lettuce is sown in the month of January, the white in March, and the red in April; and they are fit for transplanting, all of them, at the end of a couple of months.

BEET

Beet is the smoothest of all the garden plants. The Greeks distinguish two kinds of beet, according to the colour, the black and the white. The last, which is the kind generally preferred, has but very little seed, and is generally known as the Sicilian beet; just as it is the white lettuce that is held in the highest degree of esteem. Our people, also, distinguish two varieties of beet, the spring and the autumn kinds, so called from the periods of sowing; although sometimes we find beet sown in June even. This is a plant, too, that is sometimes transplanted; and it thrives all the better, like the lettuce, if the roots are well covered with manure, in a moist soil. Beet is mostly eaten with lentils and beans; it is prepared also in the same way as cabbage, with mustard more particularly, the pungency of which relieves its insipidity. Medical men are of opinion that beet is a more unwholesome vegetable than cabbage; hence it is that I never remember seeing it served at table. Indeed, there are some persons who scruple to taste it even, from a conviction that it is a food suitable only for persons of a robust constitution.

CABBAGES

Cabbage and coleworts, which at the present day are the most highly esteemed of all the garden vegetables, were held in little repute, I find, among the Greeks; but Cato, on the other hand, sings the wondrous praises of the cabbage, the medicinal properties of which we shall duly enlarge upon when we come to treat of that subject. Cato distinguishes three varieties of the cabbage; the first, a plant with leaves wide open, and a large stalk; a second, with crisped leaves, to which he gives the name of "apiaca"; and a third, with a thin stalk, and a smooth, tender leaf, which with him ranks the lowest of all. Cabbages may be sown the whole year through, as we find that they are cut at all periods of the year; the best time, however, for sowing them is at the autumnal equinox, and they are usually transplanted as soon as five leaves are visible. In the ensuing spring after the first cutting, the plant yields sprouts, known to us as "cymæ." These sprouts, in fact, are small shoots thrown out from the main stem, of a more delicate and tender quality than the cabbage itself.

WILD AND CULTIVATED ASPARAGUS

Of all the garden plants, asparagus is the one that requires the most delicate attention in its cultivation. We have already spoken at considerable length of its origin, when treating of the wild plants, and have mentioned that Cato recommends it to be grown in reed-beds. There is another kind, again, of a more uncultivated nature than the garden asparagus, but less pungent than wild sperage; it grows upon the mountains in different countries, and the plains of Upper Germany are quite full of it, so much so, indeed, that it was a not unhappy remark of Tiberius Cæsar, that a weed grows there which bears a remarkably strong resemblance to asparagus. That which grows spontaneously upon the island of Nesis, off the coast of Campania, is looked upon as being by far the best of all.

Garden asparagus is reproduced from roots, the fibres of which are exceedingly numerous, and penetrate to a considerable depth. When it first puts forth its shoots, it is green; these in time lengthen out into stalks, which afterwards throw out streaked branches from the head; asparagus admits, also, of being grown from seed.

THISTLES

Thistles are grown two different ways, from plants set in autumn, and from seed sown before the nones of March; in which latter case they are transplanted before the ides of November, or, where the site is a cold one, about the time that the west winds prevail. They are sometimes manured even, and if such is the will of heaven, grow all the better for it. They are preserved, too, in a mixture of honey and vinegar, with the addition of root of laser and cummin —so that a day may not pass without our having thistles at table.

RUE

Rue, too, is generally sown while the west winds prevail, as well as just after the autumnal equinox. This plant has an extreme aversion to cold, moisture, and dung; it loves dry, sunny localities, and a soil more particularly that is rich in brick clay; it requires to be nourished, too, with ashes, which should be mixed with the seed as well, as a preservative against the attacks of caterpillars. The ancients held rue in peculiar esteem; for I find that honied wine flavoured with rue was distributed to the people, in his consulship, by Cornelius Cethegus, the colleague of Quintus Flamininus, after the closing of the Comitia. This plant has a great liking for the fig-tree, and for that tree only; indeed, it never thrives better than when grown beneath that tree.

PARSLEY

Parsley is sown immediately after the vernal equinox, the seed being lightly beaten, first in a mortar. It is thought that, by doing this, the parsley will be all the more crisped, or else by taking care to beat it down when sown with a roller or the feet. It is a peculiarity of this plant, that it changes colour; it has the honour, in Achaia, of forming the wreath of the victors in the sacred contests of the Nemean Games.

MINT

It is at the same season, too, that mint is transplanted; or, if it has not yet germinated, the matted tufts of the old roots are used for the purpose. This plant, too, is no less fond of a humid soil than parsley; it is green in summer and turns yellow in winter. There is a wild kind of mint, known to us as "mentastrum"; it is reproduced by layers, like the vine, or else by planting the branches upside down. It was the sweetness of its smell that caused this plant to change its name among the Greeks, its former name with them being "mintha," from which the ancient Romans derived their name for it; whereas now, of late, it has been called by them ἡδύοσμον.[4] The mint that is used in the dishes at rustic entertainments pervades the tables far and wide with its agreeable odour. When once planted, it lasts a considerable

---

4 "Sweet-smelling."

length of time; it bears, too, a strong resemblance to pennyroyal, a property of which is, as mentioned by us more than once, to flower when kept in our larders.

POPPY

There are certain plants which are grown in company with others, the poppy, for instance, sown with cabbages and purslain, and rocket with lettuce. Of the cultivated poppy there are three kinds, the first being the white poppy, the seed of which, parched, and mixed with honey, used to be served up in the second course at the tables of the ancients; at the present day, too, the country people sprinkle it on the upper crust of their bread, making it adhere by means of the yolk of eggs, the under crust being seasoned with parsley and gith to heighten the flavour of the flour. The second kind is the black poppy, from which, upon an incision being made in the stalk, a milky juice distils; and the third is that known to the Greeks by the name of "rhœas"; and by us as the wild poppy. This last grows spontaneously, but in fields, more particularly, which have been sown with barley; it bears a strong resemblance to rocket, grows to the height of a cubit, and bears a red flower, which quickly fades; it is to this flower that it is indebted for its Greek name. As to the other kinds of poppies which spring up spontaneously, we shall have occasion to speak of them when treating of the medicinal plants.

THE MALADIES OF GARDEN PLANTS

The garden plants, too, like the rest of the vegetable productions, are subject to certain maladies. Thus, for instance, basil, when old, degenerates into wild thyme, while the seed of an old cabbage produces rape, and vice-versa. Cummin, too, if not kept well hoed, is killed by hæmodorum,[5] a plant with a single stalk, a root similar to a bulb in appearance, and never found except in a thin, meagre soil. Besides this, cummin is liable to a peculiar disease of its own, the scab; basil, too, turns pale at the rising of the Dog-star. All plants, indeed, will turn of a yellow complexion on the approach of a woman who has the menstrual discharge upon her.

There are various kinds of insects, too, that breed upon the garden plants; fleas, for instance, upon turnips, and caterpillars and maggots upon radishes, as well as lettuces and cabbages; besides which, the last two are exposed to the attacks of slugs and snails. The leek, too, is infested with peculiar insects of its own; which may very easily be taken, however, by laying dung upon the plants, the insects being in the habit of burrowing in it. Sabinus Tiro says, in his book entitled "Cepurica," which he dedicated to Mæcenas, that it is not advisable to touch rue, cunila,[6] mint, or basil with any implement of iron.

REMEDIES FOR PLANT MALADIES AND INSECTS THAT ATTACK THEM

The same author recommends as a remedy against ants, which are by no means the slightest plague in a garden that is not kept well watered, to stop up the mouths of their holes with sea-slime or ashes. But the most efficient way of destroying them is with the aid of the plant heliotropium; some persons, too, are of opinion

---

5   Or, according to some readings, "limodorum," a parasitical plant.
6   A species of origanum (TN).

that water in which an unburnt brick has been soaked is injurious to them. The best protection for turnips is to sow a few fitches with them, and for cabbages chickpeas, these having the effect of keeping away caterpillars. If, however, this precaution should have been omitted, and the caterpillars have already made their appearance, the best remedy is to throw upon the vegetables a decoction of wormwood, or else of house-leek, known to some as "aïzoüm." If cabbage-seed, before it is sown, is steeped in the juice of house-leek, the cabbages, it is said, are sure not be attacked by any insect.

Book XX
Remedies Derived from the Garden Plants

We are now about to enter upon an examination of the greatest of all the operations of Nature; we are about to discourse to man upon his aliments, and to compel him to admit that he is ignorant by what means he exists. And let no one, misled by the apparent triviality of the names which we shall have to employ, regard this subject as one that is frivolous or contemptible; for we shall here have to set forth the state of peace or of war which exists between the various departments of Nature, the hatreds or friendships which are maintained by objects dumb and destitute of sense, and all, too, created for the sake of man alone. To these states, known to the Greeks by the respective appellations "sympathia" and "antipathia," we are indebted for the first principles of all things; for hence it is that water has the property of extinguishing fire, that the sun absorbs water, that the moon produces it, and that each of those heavenly bodies is from time to time eclipsed by the other.

Hence it is, too, descending from the contemplation of a loftier sphere, that the loadstone possesses the property of attracting iron, and another stone, again, that of repelling it; and that the diamond, that pride of luxury and opulence, though infrangible by every other object, and presenting a resistance that cannot be overcome, is broken asunder by a he-goat's blood, in addition to numerous other marvels of which we shall have to speak on more appropriate occasions, equal to this or still more wonderful even. My only request is that pardon may be accorded me for beginning with objects of a more humble nature, though still so greatly conducive to our health; I mean the garden plants, of which I shall now proceed to speak.

THE WILD CUCUMBER

We have already stated that there is a wild cucumber, considerably smaller than the cultivated one. From this cucumber the medicament known as "elaterium" is prepared, being the juice extracted from the seed. To obtain this juice the fruit is cut before it is ripe; indeed, if this precaution is not taken at an early period, the seed is apt to spurt out and be productive of danger to the eyes. After it is gathered, the fruit is kept whole for a night, and on the following day an incision is made in it with a reed. The seed, too, is generally sprinkled with ashes, with the view of retaining in it as large a quantity of the juice as possible. When the juice is extracted, it is received in rain water, where it falls to the bottom; after which it is thickened in the sun, and then divided into lozenges, which are of singular utility to mankind for healing dimness of sight, diseases of the eyes, and ulcerations of the eyelids. It is said that if the roots of a vine are touched with this juice, the grapes of it will be sure never to be attacked by birds.

The root, too, of the wild cucumber, boiled in vinegar, is employed in fomentations for the gout, and the juice of it is used as a remedy for tooth-ache. Dried and mixed with resin, the root is a cure for impetigo and the skin diseases known as "psora"[1] and "lichen";[2] it is good, too, for imposthumes of the parotid glands and inflammatory tumours, and restores the natural colour to the skin when a cicatrix has formed. The juice of the leaves, mixed with vinegar, is used as an injection for the ears, in cases of deafness.

THE GOURD

There is found also a wild gourd, called "somphos" by the Greeks, empty within, and long and thick in shape, like the finger; it grows nowhere except upon stony spots. The juice of this gourd, when chewed, is very beneficial to the stomach.

There is another variety of the wild gourd, known as the "colocynthis";[3] this kind is full of seeds, but not so large as the cultivated one. The pale colocynthis is better than those of a grass-green colour. Employed by itself when dried, it acts as a very powerful purgative; used as an injection, it is a remedy for all diseases of the intestines, the kidneys, and the loins, as well as for paralysis. The seed being first removed, it is boiled down in hydromel to one half; after which it is used as an injection, with perfect safety, in doses of four oboli. It is good, too, for the stomach, taken in pills composed of the dried powder and boiled honey. In jaundice seven seeds of it may be taken with beneficial effects, with a draught of hydromel immediately after.

The pulp of this fruit, taken with wormwood and salt, is a remedy for tooth-ache, and the juice of it, warmed with vinegar, has the effect of strengthening loose teeth. Rubbed in with oil, it removes pains of the spine, loins, and hips; in addition to which, really a marvellous thing to speak of! the seeds of it, in even numbers, attached to the body in a linen cloth, will cure, it is said, the fevers to which the

---

1 Itch-scab, probably.
2 A disease of the skin, in which the scab assumes the form almost of a lichen or moss.
3 The *Cucumis colocynthus* of Linnæus, or Coloquintida, so remarkable for its bitterness.

Greeks have given the name of "periodic." The juice, too, of the cultivated gourd[4] shred in pieces, applied warm, is good for ear-ache, and the flesh of the inside, used without the seed, for corns on the feet and the suppurations known to the Greeks as "apostemata." When the pulp and seeds are boiled together, the decoction is good for strengthening loose teeth, and for preventing toothache; wine, too, boiled with this plant, is curative of defluxions of the eyes. The leaves of it, bruised with fresh cypress-leaves, or the leaves alone, boiled in a vessel of potters' clay and beaten up with goose-grease, and then applied to the part affected, are an excellent cure for wounds. Fresh shavings of the rind are used as a cooling application for gout, and burning pains in the head, in infants more particularly; they are good, too, for erysipelas, whether it is the shavings of the rind or the seeds of the plant that are applied to the part affected. The juice of the scrapings, employed as a liniment with rose-oil and vinegar, moderates the burning heats of fevers; and the ashes of the dried fruit applied to burns are efficacious in a most remarkable degree.

RAPE

Rape, too, has its medicinal properties. Warmed, it is used as an application for the cure of chilblains, in addition to which, it has the effect of protecting the feet from cold. A hot decoction of rape is employed for the cure of cold gout; and raw rape, beaten up with salt, is good for all maladies of the feet. Rape-seed, used as a liniment, and taken in drink, with wine, is said to have a salutary effect against the stings of serpents, and various narcotic poisons; and there are many persons who attribute to it the properties of an antidote, when taken with wine and oil.

Wild rape[5] is mostly found growing in the fields; it has a tufted top, with a white seed, twice as large as that of the poppy. This plant is often employed for smoothing the skin of the face and the body generally, meal of fitches, barley, wheat, and lupines, being mixed with it in equal proportions.

THE CULTIVATED RADISH

The cultivated radish purges the stomach, attenuates the phlegm, acts as a diuretic, and detaches the bilious secretions. A decoction of the rind of radishes in wine, taken in the morning in doses of three cyathi, has the effect of breaking and expelling calculi of the bladder. A decoction, too, of this rind in vinegar and water, is employed as a liniment for the stings of serpents. Taken fasting in the morning with honey, radishes are good for a cough. Parched radish-seed, as well as radishes themselves, chewed, is useful for pains in the sides. A decoction of the leaves, taken in drink, or else the juice of the plant taken in doses of two cyathi, is an excellent remedy for phthiriasis. Pounded radishes, too, are employed as a liniment for inflammations under the skin, and the rind, mixed with honey, for bruises of recent date. Lethargic persons are recommended to eat them as hot as possible, and the seed, parched and then pounded with honey, will give relief to asthmatic patients.

---

4 The cultivated cucumber.
5 The *Brassica napus, var. a* of Linnæus.

Radishes, too, are useful as a remedy for poisons, and are employed to counteract the effects of the sting of the cerastes and the scorpion; indeed, after having rubbed the hands with radishes or radish-seed, we may handle those reptiles with impunity. If a radish is placed upon a scorpion, it will cause its death. Radishes are useful, too, in cases of poisoning by fungi or henbane.

Radishes are good, too, for curing ulcerations of the intestines and suppurations of the thoracic organs, if eaten with honey. Taken with vinegar or honey, radishes expel worms from the intestines; and a decoction of them boiled down to one-third, taken in wine, is good for intestinal hernia. Employed in this way, too, they have the effect of drawing off the superfluous blood. Hippocrates recommends females whose hair falls off, to rub the head with radishes, and he says that for pains of the uterus, they should be applied to the navel.

Radishes have the effect, too, of restoring the skin, when scarred, to its proper colour; and the seed, steeped in water, and applied topically, arrests the progress of ulcers known as phagedænic. Democritus regards them, taken with the food, as an aphrodisiac; and it is for this reason, perhaps, that some persons have spoken of them as being injurious to the voice. The leaves, but only those of the long radish, are said to have the effect of improving the eye-sight.

ONIONS

There are no such things in existence as wild onions. The cultivated onion is employed for the cure of dimness of sight, the patient being made to smell at it till tears come into the eyes; it is still better even if the eyes are rubbed with the juice. It is said, too, that onions are soporific, and that they are a cure for ulcerations of the mouth, if chewed with bread. Fresh onions in vinegar, applied topically, or dried onions with wine and honey, are good for the bites of dogs, care being taken not to remove the bandage till the end of a couple of days. Applied, too, in the same way, they are good for healing excoriations. Roasted in hot ashes, many persons have applied them topically, with barley meal, for eye fluxes and ulcerations of the genitals. The juice, too, is employed as an ointment for sores of the eyes. Mixed with honey, it is used as a liniment for the stings of serpents and all kinds of ulcerous sores. In combination with woman's milk, it is employed for affections of the ears; and in cases of singing in the ears and hardness of hearing, it is injected into those organs with goose-grease or honey. In cases where persons have been suddenly struck dumb, it has been administered to them to drink, mixed with water. In cases, too, of toothache, it is sometimes introduced into the mouth as a gargle for the teeth; it is an excellent remedy also for all kinds of wounds made by animals, scorpions more particularly.

In cases of alopecy and itch-scab, bruised onions are rubbed on the parts affected; they are also given boiled to persons afflicted with dysentery or lumbago. Onion peelings, burnt to ashes and mixed with vinegar, are employed topically for stings of serpents and multipedes.

GARLIC

Garlic has very powerful properties, and is of great utility to persons on changes of water or locality. The very smell of it drives away serpents and scorpions, and, according to what some persons say, it is a cure for wounds made by every kind of wild beast, whether taken with the drink or food, or applied topically. Taken in wine, it is a remedy for the sting of the hæmorrhoïs[6] more particularly, acting as an emetic. We shall not be surprised too, that it acts as a powerful remedy for the bite of the shrew-mouse, when we find that it has the property of neutralizing aconite, otherwise known as "pardalianches." It neutralizes henbane, also, and cures the bites of dogs, when applied with honey to the wound. It is taken in drink also for the stings of serpents; and of its leaves, mixed with oil, a most valuable liniment is made for bruises on the body, even when they have swelled and formed blisters.

Hippocrates is of opinion also, that fumigations made with garlic have the effect of bringing away the after-birth; and he used to employ the ashes of garlic, mixed with oil, for the cure of running ulcers of the head. Some persons have prescribed boiled garlic for asthmatic patients; while others, again, have given it raw. The ancients used to give raw garlic in cases of madness, and Diocles administered it boiled for phrenitis. Beaten up, and taken in vinegar and water, it is very useful as a gargle for quinsy. Three heads of garlic, beaten up in vinegar, give relief in toothache; and a similar result is obtained by rinsing the mouth with a decoction of garlic, and inserting pieces of it in the hollow teeth.

Mixed with sulphur and resin, garlic draws out the humours from fistulous sores, and employed with pitch, it will extract an arrow even from the wound. In cases of leprosy, lichen, and eruptions of the skin, it acts as a detergent, and effects a cure, in combination with wild marjoram, or else reduced to ashes, and applied as a liniment with oil and garum.[7]

CABBAGE

It would be too lengthy a task to enumerate all the praises of the cabbage, more particularly as the physician Chrysippus has devoted a whole volume to the subject, in which its virtues are described in reference to each individual part of the human body. Dieuches has done the same, and Pythagoras too, in particular. Cato, too, has not been more sparing in its praises than the others; and it will be only right to examine the opinions which he expresses in relation to it, if for no other purpose than to learn what medicines the Roman people made use of for six hundred years.

Cato esteems the curly cabbage the most highly of all, and next to it, the smooth cabbage with large leaves and a thick stalk. He says that it is a good thing for headache, dimness of the sight, and dazzling of the eyes, the spleen, stomach, and tho-

---

6 This serpent is described by Lucan, in the *Pharsalia*, where a fearful account is given of the effects of its sting. Nicander, in his Theriaca, informs us that those bitten by the hæmorrhoïs die with the blood flowing from the nose and ears, whence its name.

7 A fish-sauce much prized by the Romans, made of small fish preserved in a certain kind of pickle (TN).

racic organs, taken raw in the morning, in doses of two acetabula, with oxymel,[8] coriander, rue, mint, and root of silphium. He says, too, that the virtue of it is so great that the very person even who beats up this mixture feels himself all the stronger for it; for which reason he recommends it to be taken mixed with these condiments, or, at all events, dressed with a sauce compounded of them. For the gout, too, and diseases of the joints, a liniment of it should be used, he says, with a little rue and coriander, a sprinkling of salt, and some barley meal; the very water even in which it has been boiled is wonderfully efficacious, according to him, for the sinews and joints. For wounds, either recent or of long standing, as also for carcinoma, which is incurable by any other mode of treatment, he recommends fomentations to be made with warm water, and, after that, an application of cabbage, beaten up, to the parts affected, twice a-day. He says, also, that fistulas and sprains should be treated in a similar way, as well as all humours which it may be desirable to bring to a head and disperse; and he states that this vegetable, boiled and eaten fasting, in considerable quantities, with oil and salt, has the effect of preventing dreams and wakefulness; also, that if, after one boiling, it is boiled a second time, with the addition of oil, salt, cummin, and polenta, it will relieve gripings in the stomach; and that, if eaten in this way without bread, it is more beneficial still. Among various other particulars, he says, that if taken in drink with black wine, it has the effect of carrying off the bilious secretions; and he recommends the urine of a person who has been living on a cabbage diet to be preserved, as, when warmed, it is a good remedy for diseases of the sinews. I will, however, here give the identical words in which Cato expresses himself upon this point: "If you wash little children with this urine," says he, "they will never be weak and puny."

ASPARAGUS

Asparagus is said to be extremely wholesome as an aliment to the stomach. With the addition of cummin, it dispels flatulency of the stomach and colon; it sharpens the eyesight also, acts as a mild aperient upon the stomach, and, boiled with wine, is good for pains in the chest and spine, and diseases of the intestines. For pains in the loins and kidneys asparagus-seed is administered in doses of three oboli, taken with an equal proportion of cummin-seed. It acts as an aphrodisiac, and is an extremely useful diuretic, except that it has a tendency to ulcerate the bladder.

The root, also, pounded and taken in white wine, is highly extolled by some writers, as having the effect of disengaging calculi, and of soothing pains in the loins and kidneys; there are some persons, too, who administer this root with sweet wine for pains in the uterus. Boiled in vinegar the root is very beneficial in cases of elephantiasis. It is said that if a person is rubbed with asparagus beaten up in oil, he will never be stung by bees.

---

8   A mixture of vinegar or acetic acid and honey (TN).

BOOK XX - REMEDIES DERIVED FROM THE GARDEN PLANTS

PARSLEY

Parsley is held in universal esteem; for we find sprigs of it swimming in the draughts of milk given us to drink in country-places; and we know that as a seasoning for sauces, it is looked upon with peculiar favour. Applied to the eyes with honey, which must also be fomented from time to time with a warm decoction of it, it has a most marvellous efficacy in cases of defluxion of those organs or of other parts of the body; as also when beaten up and applied by itself, or in combination with bread or with polenta. Fish, too, when found to be in an ailing state in the preserves, are greatly refreshed by giving them green parsley. As to the opinions entertained upon it among the learned, there is not a single production dug out of the earth in reference to which a greater diversity exists.

RUE

One of the most active, however, of all the medicinal plants, is rue. The cultivated kind has broader leaves and more numerous branches than the other. Wild rue is more violent in its effects, and more active in every respect. The juice of it is extracted by beating it up, and moistening it moderately with water; after which it is kept for use in boxes of Cyprian copper. Given in large doses, this juice has all the baneful effects of poison, and that of Macedonia more particularly, which grows on the banks of the river Aliacmon. It is a truly wonderful thing, but the juice of hemlock has the property of neutralizing its effects. Thus do we find one thing acting as the poison of another poison, for the juice of hemlock is very beneficial, rubbed upon the hands and face of persons employed in gathering rue.

In other respects, rue is one of the principal ingredients employed in antidotes, that of Galatia more particularly. Every species of rue, employed by itself, has the effect also of an antidote, if the leaves are bruised and taken in wine. It is good more particularly in cases of poisoning by wolf's bane and mistletoe, as well as by fungi, whether administered in the drink or the food. Employed in a similar manner, it is good for the stings of serpents; so much so, in fact, that weasels, when about to attack them, take the precaution first of protecting themselves by eating rue. Rue is good, too, for the injuries by scorpions and spiders, the stings of bees, hornets, and wasps, the noxious effects produced by cantharides and salamanders, and the bites of mad dogs. The juice is taken in doses of one acetabulum, in wine; and the leaves, beaten up or else chewed, are applied topically, with honey and salt, or boiled with vinegar and pitch. It is said that people rubbed with the juice of rue, or even having it on their person, are never attacked by these noxious creatures, and that serpents are driven away by the stench of burning rue. The most efficacious, however, of all, is the root of wild rue, taken with wine; this too, it is said, is more beneficial still, if drunk in the open air.

For cardiac diseases, Diocles prescribes applications of rue, in combination with vinegar, honey, and barley-meal; and for the iliac passion, he says that it should be mixed with meal, boiled in oil, and spread upon the wool of a sheep's fleece. Many persons recommend, for purulent expectorations, two drachmæ of dried rue to one and a half of sulphur; and, for spitting of blood, a decoction of three sprigs in wine. It is given also in dysentery, with cheese, the rue being first beaten up in wine; and it has been prescribed, pounded with bitumen, as a potion for habitual shortness of breath. For persons suffering from violent falls, three ounces of the seed is recommended. A pound of oil, in which rue leaves have been boiled, added to one sextarius of wine, forms a liniment for parts of the body which are frost-bitten.

MINT

The very smell of mint reanimates the spirits, and its flavour gives a remarkable zest to food; hence it is that it is so generally an ingredient in our sauces. It has the effect of preventing milk from turning sour, or curdling and thickening; hence it is that it is so generally put into milk used for drinking, to prevent any danger of persons being choked by it in a curdled state. It is administered also for this purpose in water or honied wine. It is generally thought, too, that it is in consequence of this property that it impedes generation, by preventing the seminal fluids from obtaining the requisite consistency. In males as well as females it arrests bleeding, and it has the property, with the latter, of suspending the menstrual discharge. Taken in water, with amylum, it prevents looseness in cœliac complaints. Syriation employed this plant for the cure of abscesses of the uterus, and, in doses of three oboli, with honied wine, for diseases of the liver; he prescribed it also, in pottage, for spitting of blood. It is an admirable remedy for ulcerations of the head in children, and has the effect equally of drying the trachea when too moist, and of bracing it when too dry. Taken in honied wine and water, it carries off purulent phlegm.

PENNYROYAL

Pennyroyal partakes with mint, in a very considerable degree, the property of restoring consciousness in fainting fits; slips of both plants being kept for the purpose in glass bottles filled with vinegar. It is for this reason that Varro has declared that a wreath of pennyroyal is more worthy to grace our chambers than a chaplet of roses; indeed, it is said that, placed upon the head, it materially alleviates head-ache. It is generally stated, too, that the smell of it alone will protect the head against the injurious effects of cold or heat, and that it acts as a preventive of thirst; also, that persons exposed to the sun, if they carry a couple of sprigs of pennyroyal behind the ears, will never be incommoded by the heat. For various pains, too, it is employed topically, mixed with polenta and vinegar.

POPPY

With reference to the cultivated varieties, the calyx of the white poppy is pounded, and is taken in wine as a soporific; the seed of it is a cure, also, for elephantiasis. The black poppy acts as a soporific, by the juice which exudes from incisions made in the stalk, at the time when the plant is beginning to flower, Diagoras says; but when the blossom has gone off, according to Iollas. This is done at the third hour, in a clear, still, day, or, in other words, when the dew has thoroughly dried upon the poppy. It is recommended to make the incision just beneath the head and calyx of the plant; this being the only kind, in fact, into the head of which the incision is made. This juice, like that of any other plant, is received in wool; or else, if it is in very minute quantities, it is scraped off with the thumb nail just as it is from the lettuce, and so again on the following day, with the portion that has since dried there. If obtained from the poppy in sufficiently large quantities, this juice thickens, after which it is kneaded out into lozenges, and dried in the shade. This juice is possessed not only of certain soporific qualities, but, if taken in too large quantities, is productive of sleep unto death even; the name given to it is "opium."

The principal test of the purity of opium is the smell, which, when genuine, is so penetrating as to be quite insupportable. The next best test is that obtained by lighting it at a lamp; upon which it ought to burn with a clear, brilliant flame, and to give out a strong odour when extinguished; a thing that never happens when opium has been drugged, for, in such case, it lights with the greatest difficulty, and the flame repeatedly goes out. There is another way of testing its genuineness, by water; for, if it is pure, it will float like a thin cloud upon the surface, but, if adulterated, it will unite in the form of blisters on the water. But the most surprising thing of all is the fact, that the sun's heat in summer furnishes a test; for, if the drug is pure, it will sweat and gradually melt, till it has all the appearance of the juice when fresh gathered.

There is one variety of wild poppy known as "ceratitis."[9] It is of a black colour, a cubit in height, and has a thick root covered with bark, with a head resembling a small bud, bent and pointed at the end like a horn. The leaves of this plant are smaller and thinner than those of the other wild poppies, and the seed, which is very diminutive, is ripe at harvest. Taken with honied wine, in doses of half an acetabulum, the seed acts as a purgative. The leaves, beaten up in oil, are a cure for the white specks which form on the eyes of beasts of burden. The root, boiled down to one half, in doses of one acetabulum to two sextarii of water, is prescribed for maladies of the loins and liver, and the leaves, employed with honey, are a cure for carbuncles.

WILD THYME

Wild thyme, it is said, borrows its name, "serpyllum," from the fact that it is a creeping plant, a property peculiar to the wild kind, that which grows in rocky places more particularly. The cultivated thyme is not a creeping plant, but grows upwards, as much a palm in height. That which springs up spontaneously, grows the most luxuriantly, its leaves and branches being whiter than those of the other kinds. Thyme is efficacious as a remedy for the stings of serpents, the cenchris more particularly; also for the sting of the scolopendra, both sea and land, the leaves and branches being boiled for the purpose in wine. Burnt, it puts to flight all venomous creatures by its smell, and it is particularly beneficial as an antidote to the venom of marine animals.

A decoction of it in vinegar is applied for head-ache, with rose oil, to the temples and forehead, as also for phrenitis and lethargy; it is given, too, in doses of four drachmæ, for gripings of the stomach, strangury, quinsy, and fits of vomiting. It is taken in water, also, for liver complaints. The leaves are given in doses of four

---

9   The *Glaucium Corniculatum* of Persoon; the horned poppy, or glaucium.

oboli, in vinegar, for diseases of the spleen. Beaten up in two cyathi of oxymel, it is used for spitting of blood.

THE COMPOSITION OF THERIACA

But as we are now about to leave the garden plants, we will take this opportunity of describing a very famous preparation extracted from them as an antidote against the stings of all kinds of venomous animals; it is inscribed in verse upon a stone in the Temple of Æsculapius at Cos.

Take two denarii of wild thyme, and the same quantity of opopanax and meum respectively; one denarius of trefoil seed; and of aniseed, fennel-seed, ammi, and parsley, six denarii respectively, with twelve denarii of meal of fitches. Beat up these ingredients together, and pass them through a sieve; after which they must be kneaded with the best wine that can be had, and then made into lozenges of one victoriatus each; one of these is to be given to the patient, steeped in three cyathi of wine. King Antiochus the Great, it is said, employed this theriaca against all kinds of venomous animals, the asp excepted.

Book XXI
Flowers – Garlands – Bees – Wild plants

Cato has recommended that flowers for making chaplets should also be cultivated in the garden; varieties remarkable for a delicacy which it is quite impossible to express, inasmuch as no individual can find such facilities for describing them as Nature does for bestowing on them their numerous tints. The other plants she has produced for our use and our nutriment, and to them accordingly she has granted years and even ages of duration; but as for the flowers and their perfumes, she has given them birth for but a day —a mighty lesson to man, we see, to teach him that that which in its career is the most beauteous and the most attractive to the eye, is the very first to fade and die.

Even the limner's art itself possesses no resources for reproducing the colours of the flowers in all their varied tints and combinations, whether we view them in groups alternately blending their hues, or whether arranged in festoons, each variety by itself, now assuming a circular form, now running obliquely, and now disposed in a spiral pattern; or whether, as we see sometimes, one wreath is interwoven within another.

GARLANDS AND CHAPLETS

The ancients used chaplets of diminutive size, called "stroppi"; from which comes our name for a chaplet, "strophiolum." Indeed, it was only by very slow degrees that this last word became generalized, as the chaplets that were used at sacrifices, or were granted as the reward of military valour, asserted their exclusive right to the name of "corona."

For in early times it was the usage to crown the victors in the sacred contests with branches of trees; and it was only at a later period, that they began to vary their tints by the combination of flowers, to heighten the effect in turn by their colour and their smell.

Chaplets of flowers being now the fashion, it was not long before those came into vogue which are known to us as Egyptian chaplets; and then the winter chaplets, made for the time at which Earth refuses her flowers, of thin laminæ of horn stained various colours. By slow degrees, too, the name was introduced at Rome, these garlands being known there at first as "corollæ," a designation given them to express the remarkable delicacy of their texture. In more recent times, again, when the chaplets presented were made of thin plates of copper, gilt or silvered, they assumed the name of "corollaria."

Chaplets, however, were always held in a high degree of estimation, those even which were acquired at the public games. For it was the usage of the citizens to go down in person to take part in the contests of the Circus, and to send their slaves and horses thither as well. Hence it is that we find it thus written in the laws of the Twelve Tables: "If any person has gained a chaplet himself, or by his money, let the same be given to him as the reward of his prowess." There is no doubt that by the words "gained by his money," the laws meant a chaplet which had been gained by his slaves or horses. Well then, what was the honour acquired thereby? It was the right secured by the victor, for himself and for his parents, after death, to be crowned without fail, while the body was laid out in the house, and on its being carried to the tomb.

On other occasions, chaplets were not indiscriminately worn, not even those which had been won in the games.

Indeed the rules upon this point were remarkably severe. L. Fulvius, a banker, having been accused, at the time of the Second Punic War, of looking down from the balcony of his house upon the Forum, with a chaplet of roses upon his head, was imprisoned by order of the Senate, and was not liberated before the war was brought to a close. P. Munatius, having placed upon his head a chaplet of flowers taken from the statue of Marsyas, was condemned by the Triumviri to be put in chains.

In those days, too, chaplets were employed in honour of the gods, the Lares,[1] public as well as domestic, the sepulchres, and the Manes.[2] The highest place, however, in public estimation, was held by the plaited chaplet; such as we find used by the Salii in their sacred rites, and at the solemnization of their yearly banquets. In later times, the rose chaplet has been adopted, and luxury arose at last to such a pitch that a chaplet was held in no esteem at all if it did not consist entirely of leaves sown together with the needle. More recently, again, they have been imported from India, or from nations beyond the countries of India.

---

1   The lares were guardian deities in ancient Roman religion or tutelary gods of home. The statues of domestic Lares were placed at the table during family meals; their presence, cult, and blessing seem to have been required at all important family events (TN).

2   The manes were chthonic deities sometimes thought to represent souls of deceased loved ones. They were associated with the Lares (TN).

THE ROSE

The people of our country were acquainted with but very few garland flowers among the garden plants, and those few hardly any but the violet and the rose.

The rose forms an ingredient in our unguents; it is employed also by itself for certain medicinal purposes, and is used in plasters and eye-salves for its penetrating qualities; it is used, also, to perfume the delicacies of our banquets, and is never attended with any noxious results.

The essential points of difference in the rose are the number of the petals, the comparative number of thorns on the stem, the colour, and the smell. The number of the petals, which is never less than five, goes on increasing in amount, till we find one variety with as many as a hundred, and thence known as the "centifolia"; in Italy, it is to be found in Campania, and in Greece, in the vicinity of Philippi, though this last is not the place of its natural growth.

THE LILY

The lily holds the next highest rank after the rose, and has a certain affinity with it in respect of its unguent and the oil extracted from it, which is known to us as "lirinon." Blended, too, with roses, the lily produces a remarkably fine effect; for it begins to make its appearance, in fact, just as the rose is in the very middle of its season. There is no flower that grows to a greater height than the lily, sometimes, indeed, as much as three cubits; the head of it being always drooping, as though the neck of the flower were unable to support its weight. The whiteness of the lily is quite remarkable, the petals being striated on the exterior; the flower is narrow at the base, and gradually expanding in shape like a tapering cup with the edges curving outwards, the fine pistils of the flower, and the stamens with their antheræ of a saffron colour, standing erect in the middle. Hence the perfume of the lily, as well as its colour, is two-fold, there being one for the petals and another for the stamens. The difference, however, between them is but very small, and when the flower is employed for making lily unguents and oils, the petals are never rejected.

THE VIOLET

Next after the roses and the lilies, the violet is held in the highest esteem; of this there are several varieties, the purple, the yellow, and the white, all of them reproduced from plants, like the cabbage. The purple violet, which springs up spontaneously in sunny spots, with a thin, meagre soil, has larger petals than the others, springing immediately from the root, which is of a fleshy substance. This violet has a name, too, distinct from the other wild kinds, being called "ion," and from it the ianthine cloth takes its name.

THE IRIS

There is still another distinction, which ought not to be omitted, the fact, that many of the odoriferous plants never enter into the composition of garlands, the iris and the saliunca, for example, although, both of them, of a most exquisite odour. In the iris, it is the root only that is held in esteem, it being extensively employed in perfumery and medicine. The iris of the finest quality is that found in Illyricum, and in that country, even, not in the maritime parts of it, but in the forests on the banks of the river Drilon and near Narona. The next best is that of Macedonia, the plant being extremely elongated, white, and thin. The iris of Africa occupies the third rank, being the largest of them all, and of an extremely bitter taste.

SHRUBS

The leaves, also, of smilax and ivy are employed in chaplets; indeed, the clusters of these plants are held in the very highest esteem for this purpose. There are also other kinds of shrubs, which can only be indicated by their Greek names, little attention having been paid by the framers of our language to this branch of nomenclature. Most of them grow in foreign countries, it is true; but still, it is our duty to make some mention of them, as it is of Nature in general that we are speaking, and not of Italy in particular.

TREFOIL

The leaves of trefoil also are employed for making chaplets. There are three varieties; the first being called by the Greeks sometimes "minyanthes," and sometimes "asphaltion"; the leaves of it, which the garland-makers employ, are larger than those of the other kinds.

There are the same number of varieties, also, of origanum employed in making chaplets, one of which is destitute of seed, the other, which is also odoriferous, being known as the Cretan origanum.

THYME

There are also as many varieties of thyme employed, the one white, the other dark; it flowers about the summer solstice, when the bees cull from it. From this plant a sort of augury is derived, as to how the honey is likely to turn out; for the bee-keepers have reason to look for a large crop when the thyme blossoms in considerable abundance. Thyme receives great injury from showers of rain, and is very apt to shed its blossom. The seed of thyme is so minute as to be imperceptible, and yet that of origanum, which is also extremely minute, does not escape the sight.

The honey of Attica is generally looked upon as the best in all the world; for which reason it is that the thyme of that country has been transplanted, being reproduced, as already stated, with the greatest difficulty, from the blossom. But there is also another peculiarity in the nature of the thyme of Attica, which has greatly tended to frustrate these attempts; it will never live except in the vicinity of breezes from the sea. In former times, it was the general belief that this is the case with all kinds of thyme, and that this is the reason why it does not grow in Arcadia; at a period when it was universally supposed, too, that the olive never grows beyond three hundred stadia from the sea. But, at the present day, we know for certain that in the province of Gallia Narbonensis the Stony Plains are quite overgrown with thyme; this being, in fact, the only source of revenue to those parts, thousands of sheep being brought thither from distant countries to browse upon the plant.

THE DURATION OF LIFE OF VARIOUS FLOWERS

At the very utmost, the white violet never lasts longer than three years; should it exceed that period, it is sure to degenerate. The rose-tree will last so long as five years without being pruned or cauterized, methods by which it is made to grow young again. We have already stated that the nature of the soil is of the very greatest importance; for in Egypt, we find, all these plants are perfectly inodorous, and it is only the myrtle that has any particular smell. In some countries, too, the germination of all the plants precedes that in other parts of the world by so long a period as two months even. The rose-beds should be well spaded immediately after the west winds begin to prevail, and, a second time, at the summer solstice; every care, however, should be paid, between these two periods, to keeping the ground well raked and cleaned.

BEES AND BEEHIVES

Bees and beehives, too, are a subject extremely well suited to a description of gardens and garland plants, while, at the same time, where they are successfully managed, they are a source, without any great outlay, of very considerable profit. For bees, then, the following plants should be grown: thyme, apiastrum, the rose, the various violets, the lily, the cytisus, the bean, the fitch, cunila, the poppy, conyza, cassia, the melilote, melissophyllum, and the cerintha. This last is a plant with a white leaf, bent inwards, the stem of it being a cubit in height, with a flower at the top presenting a concavity full of a juice like honey. Bees are remarkably fond of the flowers of these plants, as also the blossoms of mustard, a thing that is somewhat surprising, seeing that it is a well-known fact that they will not so much as touch the blossoms of the olive; for which reason, it will be as well to keep that tree at a distance from them.

There are other trees, again, which should be planted as near the hives as possible, as they attract the swarm when it first wings its flight, and so prevent the bees from wandering to any considerable distance.

The greatest care, too, should be taken to keep the cornel at a distance from the hives; for if the bees once taste the blossoms of it, they will speedily die of flux and looseness. The best remedy in such case is to give them sorb apples beaten up with honey, or else human urine or that of oxen, or pomegranate seeds moistened with Aminean wine. It is a very good plan, too, to plant broom about the hives, the bees being extremely fond of the blossoms.

In relation to the food of bees, I have ascertained a very singular fact, and one that well deserves to be mentioned. There is a village, called Hostilia, on the banks of the river Padus; the inhabitants of it, when food fails the bees in their vicinity, place the hives in boats and convey them some five miles up the river in the night. In the morning the bees go forth to feed, and then return to the boats; their locality being changed from day to day, until at last, as the boats sink deeper and deeper in the water, it is ascertained that the hives are full, upon which they are taken home, and the honey is withdrawn.

POISONED HONEY

Indeed, the food of bees is of the very greatest importance, as it is owing to this that we meet with poisonous honey even. At Heraclia in Pontus, the honey is extremely pernicious in certain years, though it is the same bees that make it at other times. Authors, however, have not informed us from what flowers this honey is extracted; we shall, therefore, take this opportunity of stating what we have ascertained upon the subject.

There is a certain plant which, from the circumstance that it proves fatal to beasts of burden, and to goats in particular, has obtained the name of "ægolcthron,"[3] and the blossoms of which, steeped in the rains of a wet spring, contract most noxious properties, Hence it is that it is not every year that these dangerous results are experienced. The following are the signs of the honey being poisonous; it never thickens, the colour is redder than usual, and it emits a peculiar smell which immediately produces sneezing; while, at the same time, it is more weighty than a similar quantity of good honey. Persons, when they have eaten of it, throw themselves on the ground to cool the body, which is bathed with a profuse perspiration.

MADDENING HONEY

In the country of the Sanni, in the same part of Pontus, there is another kind of honey, which, from the madness it produces, has received the name of "mænomenon." This evil effect is generally attributed to the flowers of the rhododendron, with which the woods there abound; and that people, though it pays a tribute to the Romans in wax, derives no profit whatever from its honey, in consequence of these dangerous properties. In Persis, too, and in Gætulia, a district of Mauritania Cœsariensis, bordering on the country of the Massæsyli, there are poisonous honeycombs found; and some, too, only partly so, one of the most insidious things that possibly could happen, were it not that the livid colour of the honey gives timely notice of its noxious qualities.

BEEHIVES

The hives ought to have an aspect due east, but never looking towards the north-east or the west. The best hives are those made of bark, the next best those of fennel-giant, and the next of osier; many persons, too, have them made of mirror-stone, for the purpose of watching the bees at work within. It is the best plan to anoint the hives all over with cow-dung. The lid of the hive should be made to slide from behind, so as to admit of being shut to within, in case the hive should prove too large or their labours unproductive; for, if this is not done, the bees are apt to become discouraged and abandon their work. The slide may then be gradually withdrawn, the increase of space being imperceptible to the bees as the work progresses. In winter, too, the hives should be covered with straw, and subjected to repeated fumigations, with burnt cow-dung more particularly. As this is of kindred

---

3   "Goats' death." Fée says that this is the *Rhododendron Ponticum* of Linnæus. Desfontaines identifies it with the *Azalea Pontica* of modern botany.

origin with the bees,[4] the smoke produced by it is particularly beneficial in killing all such insects as may happen to breed there, such as spiders, for instance, moths, and wood-worms; while, at the same time, it stimulates the bees themselves to increased activity. In fact, there is little difficulty in getting rid of the spiders, but to destroy the moths, which are a much greater plague, a night must be chosen in spring, just when the mallow is ripening, there being no moon, but a clear sky; torches are then lighted before the hives, upon which the moths precipitate themselves in swarms into the flame.

THE METHOD OF PREPARING WAX

Wax is made from the honeycombs after the honey has been extracted. For this purpose, they are first cleaned with water, and then dried three days in the shade; on the fourth day they are melted on the fire in a new earthen vessel, with sufficient water to cover them, after which the liquor is strained off in a wicker basket. The wax is then boiled again with the same water and in the same pot, and poured into vessels of cold water, the interior of which has been well rubbed with honey. The best wax is that known as Punic wax, the next best being that of a remarkably yellow colour, with the smell of honey. This last comes from Pontus. The next in quality is the Cretan wax.

The Punic wax is prepared in the following manner; yellow wax is first blanched in the open air, after which it is boiled in water from the open sea, with the addition of some nitre. The flower of the wax, or, in other words, the whitest part of it, is then skimmed off with spoons, and poured into a vessel containing a little cold water. After this, it is again boiled in sea-water by itself, which done, the vessel is left to cool. When this operation has been three times repeated, the wax is left in the open air upon a mat of rushes, to dry in the light of the sun and moon; for while the latter adds to its whiteness, the sun helps to dry it. In order, however, that it may not melt, it is the practice to cover it with a linen cloth; if, when it has been thus refined, it is boiled once more, the result is a wax of the greatest possible whiteness.

Punic wax is considered the best for all medicinal preparations. Wax is made black by the addition of ashes of papyrus, and a red colour is given to it by the admixture of alkanet; indeed, by the employment of various pigments, it is made to assume various tints, in which state it is used for making models, and for other purposes without number, among which we may mention varnishing walls and armour, to protect them from the air.

WILD PLANTS

We now come to the plants which grow spontaneously, and which are employed as an aliment by most nations, the people of Egypt in particular, where they abound in such vast quantities, that, extremely prolific as that country is in corn, it is perhaps the only one that could subsist without it; so abundant are its resources in the various kinds of food to be obtained from plants.

---

4   Pliny probably alludes to the notion entertained by the ancients that bees might be reproduced from the putrefied entrails of an ox, as wasps from those of a horse.

In Italy, however, we are acquainted with but very few of them; those few being the strawberry, the tamnus,[5] the butcher's broom, the sea batis, and the garden batis, known by some persons as Gallic asparagus; in addition to which we may mention the meadow parsnip and the hop, which may be rather termed amusements for the botanist than articles of food.

THE COLOCASIA

But the plant of this nature that is the most famous in Egypt is the colocasia,[6] known as the "cyamos" to some. It is gathered in the river Nile, and the stalk of it, boiled, separates into fine filaments when chewed, like those of the spider's web. The head, protruding from among the leaves, is very remarkable; and the leaves, which are extremely large, even when compared with those of trees, are very similar to those of the plant found in our rivers, and known by the name of "personata." So much do the people of that country take advantage of the bounteousness displayed by their river, that they are in the habit of plaiting the leaves of the colocasia with such skill as to make vessels of various shapes, which they are extremely fond of using for drinking vessels. At the present day, however, this plant is cultivated in Italy.

PRICKLY PLANTS

For some plants, in fact, are thorny, while others, again, are destitute of prickles; the species of thorny plants are very numerous. The asparagus and the scorpio[7] are essentially thorny plants, having no leaves at all upon them. Some plants, again, that are prickly have leaves as well, such as the thistle, for instance, the erynge, the glycyrriza, and the nettle; all these plants being provided with leaves that prick or sting. Some plants have thorns at the base of their leaves, the tribulus and the anonis for instance; others, again, have thorns, not on the leaves but on the stem, the pheos for example, known as the stœbe to some. The hippophaës[8] has thorns at the joints; the tribulus presents the peculiarity of bearing a fruit that is thorny.

THE CACTOS

The cactos, too, is a plant that grows only in Sicily, having peculiar characteristics of its own; the root throws out stalks which creep along the ground, the leaves being broad and thorny. The name given to these stalks is "cactos," and they are not disliked as an article of food, even when old. The plant, however, has one stem which grows upright, and is known by the name of "pternix"; it has the same sweet flavour as the other parts, though it will not keep. The seed of it is covered with a kind of down, known as "pappus"; when this is removed, as well as the rind of the fruit, it is tender, and like the pith of the palm; the name given to it is "ascalias."

---

5   Species of wild grape (TN).
6   The *Arum colocasia* of Linnæus.
7   The *Spartium scorpius* of Linnæus: scorpion-grass, or scorpion-wort.
8   Perhaps the *Euphorbia spinosa* of Linnæus.

THE CYPERUS

The cyperus[9] is a rush of angular shape, white near the ground, and black and solid at the top. The lower leaves are more slender than those of the leek, and those at the top are small, with the seed of the plant lying between them. The root resembles a black olive, and when it is of an oblong shape, the plant is known as the "cyperis," being employed in medicine to a great extent. The cyperus most highly esteemed is that of the vicinity of the Temple of Jupiter Hammon, the next best being that of Rhodes, the next that of Thrsæ, and the worst of all that of Egypt, a circumstance which tends greatly to add to the misunderstanding on the subject, as that country produces the cypiros[10] as well; but the cypiros which grows there is extremely hard, and has hardly any smell at all, while all the other varieties of it have an odour strongly resembling that of nard.

The cyperus, employed medicinally, is possessed of certain depilatory properties. It is used in liniments for hang-nails and ulcerous sores of the genitals and of all parts of the body which are of a humid nature, ulcers of the mouth, for instance. The root of it is a very efficacious remedy for the stings of serpents and scorpions. Taken in drink, it removes obstructions of the uterus, but if employed in too large doses, it is liable to cause prolapsus of that organ. It acts also as a diuretic, and expels calculi of the bladder; properties which render it extremely useful in dropsy. It is employed topically, also, for serpiginous ulcers, those of the throat more particularly, being usually applied with wine or vinegar.

MEDICINAL USES OF THE LILY AND THE NARCISSUS

The roots of the lily ennoble that flower in manifold ways by their utility in a medicinal point of view. Taken in wine, they are good for the stings of serpents, and in cases of poisoning by fungi. For corns on the feet, they are applied boiled in wine, not being taken off before the end of three days. A decoction of them with grease or oil, has the effect of making the hair grow again upon burns. Taken with honied wine, they carry off corrupt blood by stool; they are good, also, for the spleen and for hernia, and act as an emmenagogue. Boiled in wine and applied with honey, they are curative of wounds of the sinews. They are good, too, for lichens, leprous sores, and scurf upon the face, and they efface wrinkles of the body.

The petals of the lily are boiled in vinegar, and applied, in combination with polium,[11] to wounds; if it should happen, however, to be a wound of the testicles, it is the best plan to apply the other ingredients with henbane and wheat-meal. Lily-seed is applied in cases of erysipelas, and the flowers and leaves are used as a cataplasm for inveterate ulcers. The juice which is extracted from the flower is called "honey" by some persons, and "syrium" by others; it is employed as an emollient for the uterus, and is also used for the purpose of promoting perspirations, and for bringing suppurations to a head.

---

9 A large genus of plants belonging to the Sedge family, and including the species called galingale, several bulrushes, and the Egyptian papyrus.

10 Several sorts of gladiolus (TN).

11 Perhaps *Teucrium polium*, known popularly as felty germander (TN).

Two varieties of the narcissus are employed in medicine, the one with a purple flower, and the herbaceous narcissus. This last is injurious to the stomach, and hence it is that it acts both as an emetic and as a purgative; it is prejudicial, also, to the sinews, and produces dull, heavy pains in the head; hence it is that it has received its name, from "narce," and not from the youth Narcissus, mentioned in fable. The roots of both kinds of narcissus have a flavour resembling that of wine mixed with honey. This plant is very useful, applied to burns with a little honey, as also to other kinds of wounds, and sprains. Applied topically, too, with honey and oatmeal, it is good for tumours, and it is similarly employed for the extraction of foreign substances from the body.

Beaten up in polenta and oil it effects the cure of contusions and blows inflicted by stones; and, mixed with meal, it effectually cleanses wounds, and speedily removes black morphews from the skin. Of this flower oil of narcissus is made, good for softening indurations of the skin, and for warming parts of the body that have been frost-bitten. It is very beneficial, also, for the ears, but is very apt to produce head-ache.

THE VIOLET

There are both wild and cultivated violets. The purple violet is of a cooling nature; for inflammations they are applied to the stomach in the burning heats, and for pains in the head they are applied to the forehead. Violets, in particular, are used for eye fluxes, prolapsus of the anus and uterus, and suppurations. Worn in chaplets upon the head, or even smelt at, they dispel the fumes of wine and headache; and, taken in water, they are a cure for quinsy. The purple violet, taken in water, is a remedy for epilepsy, in children more particularly; violet seed is good for the stings of scorpions.

On the other hand, the flower of the white violet opens suppurations, and the plant itself disperses them. Both the white and the yellow violet check the menstrual discharge, and act as diuretics. When fresh gathered, they have less virtue, and hence it is that they are mostly used dry, after being kept a year. The yellow violet, taken in doses of half a cyathus to three cyathi of water, promotes menstruation; and the roots of it, applied with vinegar, assuage affections of the spleen, as also the gout. Mixed with myrrh and saffron, they are good for inflammation of the eyes. The leaves, applied with honey, cleanse ulcerous sores of the head, and, combined with cerate,[12] they are good for chaps of the anus and other moist parts of the body. Employed with vinegar, they effect the cure of abscesses.

MEDICINAL USES OF THE IRIS

The red iris is better than the white one. It is very beneficial to attach this plant to the bodies of infants more particularly when they are cutting their teeth, or are suffering from cough; it is equally good, too, to inject a few drops of it when children are suffering from tape-worm. The other properties of it differ but very little

---

12 A thick ointment composed of wax, lard, or oil, with other ingredients, applied externally for various medical purposes. (TN).

from those of honey. It cleanses ulcerous sores of the head, and inveterate abscesses more particularly. Taken in doses of two drachmæ with honey, it relaxes the bowels; and an infusion of it is good for cough, gripings of the stomach, and flatulency; taken with vinegar, too, it cures affections of the spleen. Mixed with oxycrate it is good for the bites of serpents and spiders, and, in doses of two drachmæ with bread or water, it is employed for the cure of the stings of scorpions. It is applied also topically with oil to the bites of dogs, and to parts that are excoriated; employed in a similar manner, too, it is good for pains in the sinews, and in combination with resin it is used as a liniment for lumbago and sciatica. The properties of this plant are of a warming nature. Inhaled at the nostrils, it produces sneezing and cleanses the brain, and in cases of head-ache it is applied topically in combination with the quince or the sparrow-quince. It dispels the fumes of wine also, and difficulties of breathing and taken in doses of two oboli it acts as an emetic; applied as a plaster with honey, it extracts splinters of broken bones. Powdered iris is employed also for whitlows, and, mixed with wine, for corns and warts, in which case it is left for three days on the part affected.

Chewed, it is a corrective of bad breath and offensive exhalations of the armpits, and the juice of it softens all kinds of indurations of the body. This plant acts as a soporific, but it wastes the seminal fluids; it is used also for the treatment of chaps of the anus and condylomata, and it heals all sorts of excrescences on the body.

THYME

Thyme should be gathered while it is in flower, and dried in the shade. There are two kinds of thyme; the white thyme with a ligneous root, which grows upon declivities, and is the most esteemed of the two, and another variety, which is of a darker colour, and bears a swarthy flower. They are, both of them, considered to be extremely beneficial to the sight, whether used as an article of food or as a medicament, and to be good for inveterate coughs. Used as an electuary, with vinegar and salt, they facilitate expectoration, and taken with honey, they prevent the blood from coagulating. Applied externally with mustard, they dispel chronic fluxes of the throat, as well as various affections of the stomach and bowels. Still, however, these plants must be used in moderation, as they are of a heating nature, for which reason it is that they act so astringently upon the bowels. In cases of ulceration of the intestines, the dose should be one denarius of thyme to one sextarius of oxymel; the same proportions, too, should be taken for pains in the sides, between the shoulder-blades, or in the thoracic organs. Taken with oxymel, these plants are used for the cure of intestinal diseases, and a similar draught is administered in cases of alienation of the senses and melancholy.

Thyme is given also for epilepsy, when the fits come on, the smell of it reviving the patient; it is said, too, that epileptic persons should sleep upon soft thyme. It is good, also, for hardness of breathing, and for asthma and obstructions of the menstrual discharge. A decoction of thyme in water, boiled down to one-third, brings away the dead fœtus, and it is given to males with oxymel, as a remedy for flatulency, and in cases of swelling of the abdomen or testicles and of pains in the bladder. Applied with wine, it removes tumours and fluxes, and, in combination with vinegar, callosities and warts. Mixed with wine, it is used as an external application for sciatica; and, beaten up with oil and sprinkled upon wool, it is employed for diseases of the joints, and for sprains. It is applied, also, to burns, mixed with hogs' lard. For maladies of the joints of recent date, thyme is administered in drink, in doses of three oboli to three cyathi of oxymel. For loss of appetite, it is given, beaten up with salt.

Book XXII

The Properties of Plants and Fruits

Nature and the earth might have well filled the measure of our admiration, if we had nothing else to do but to consider the properties enumerated in the preceding Book, and the numerous varieties of plants that we find created for the wants or the enjoyment of mankind. And yet, how much is there still left for us to describe, and how many discoveries of a still more astonishing nature! The greater part, in fact, of the plants there mentioned recommend themselves to us by their taste, their fragrance, or their beauty, and so invite us to make repeated trials of their virtues; but, on the other hand. the properties of those which remain to be described, furnish us with abundant proof that nothing has been created by Nature without some purpose to fulfil, unrevealed to us though it may be.

VEGETABLE DYES

I remark, in the first place, that there are some foreign nations which, in obedience to long-established usage, employ certain plants for the embellishment of the person. That, among some barbarous peoples, the females stain the face by means of various plants, there can be little doubt, and among the Daci and the Sarmatæ we find the men even marking their bodies. There is a plant in Gaul, similar to the plantago in appearance, and known there by the name of "glastum"; with it both matrons and girls among the people of Britain are in tile habit of staining the body all over, when taking part in the performance of certain sacred rites; rivalling hereby the swarthy hue of the Æthiopians, they go in a state of nature.

We know, too, that from plants are extracted admirable colours for dyeing; and, not to mention the berries of Galatia, Africa, and Lusitania, which furnish the coccus, a dye reserved for the military costume of our generals, the people of Gaul beyond the Alps produce the Tyrian colours, the purple tint, and all the other hues, by the agency of plants alone. They have not there to seek the murex at tine bottom of the sea, or to expose themselves to be the prey of the monsters of the deep, while tearing it from their jaws, nor have they to go searching in depths to which no anchor has penetrated. Standing on dry land, the people there gather in their dyes just as we do our crops of corn.

THE GRASS CROWN

Of all the crowns with which, in the days of its majesty, the all-sovereign people, the ruler of the earth, recompensed the valour of its citizens, there was none attended with higher glory than the crown of grass. The crowns bedecked with gems of gold, the vallar, mural, rostrate, civic, and triumphal crowns, were, all of them, inferior to this; great, indeed, was the difference between them, and far in the background were they thrown by it. As to all the rest, a single individual could confer them, a general or commander on his soldiers for instance, or, as on some occasions, on his colleague; the senate, too, exempt from the cares and anxieties of war, and the people in the enjoyment of repose, could award them, together with the honours of a triumph.

But as for the crown of grass, it was never conferred except at a crisis of extreme desperation, never voted except by the acclamation of the whole army, and never to any one but to him who had been its preserver. Other crowns were awarded by the generals to the soldiers, this alone by the soldiers, and to the general. This crown is known also as the "obsidional" crown, from the circumstance of a beleaguered army being delivered, and so preserved from fearful disaster. If we are to regard as a glorious and a hallowed reward the civic crown, presented for preserving the life of a single citizen, and him, perhaps, of the very humblest rank, what, pray, ought to be thought of a whole army being saved, and indebted for its preservation to the valour of a single individual?

The crown thus presented was made of green grass, gathered on the spot where the troops so rescued had been beleaguered. Indeed, in early times, it was the usual token of victory for the vanquished to present to the conqueror a handful of grass; signifying thereby that they surrendered their native soil, the land that had nurtured them, and the very right even there to be interred.

THE TRIBULUS

Of the two[1] kinds of tribulus, the one is a garden plant, the other grows in rivers only. There is a juice extracted from them which is employed for diseases of the eyes, it being of a cool and refreshing nature, and, consequently, useful for inflammations and abscesses. Used with honey, this juice is curative of spontaneous ulcerations, those of the mouth in particular; it is good also for affections of the tonsils. Taken in a potion, it breaks calculi of the bladder.

The Thracians who dwell on the banks of the river Strymon feed their horses on the leaves of the tribulus, and employ the kernels as an article of food, making of them a very agreeable kind of bread, which acts astringently upon the bowels. The root, if gathered by persons in a state of chastity and purity, disperses scrofulous

---

1 Probably the *Fagonia Cretica* and the *Trapa natans* of Linnæus.

sores; and the seed, used as an amulet, allays the pains attendant upon varicose veins; pounded and mixed with water, it destroys fleas.

THE NETTLE

What plant can there possibly be that is more an object of our aversion than the nettle?[2] And yet, in addition to its oil, it abounds in medicinal properties. The seed of it, according to Nicander, is an antidote to the poison of hemlock, of fungi, and of quicksilver. Apollodorus prescribes it, too, taken in the broth of a boiled tortoise, for the bite of the salamander, and as an antidote for the poison of henbane, serpents, and scorpions. The stinging pungency even of the nettle has its uses; for, by its contact, it braces the uvula, and effects the cure of prolapsus of the uterus, and of prolapse of the anus in infants. By touching the legs of persons in a lethargy, and the forehead more particularly, with nettles, they are awakened. Applied with salt, the nettle is used to heal the bites of dogs, and beaten up and applied topically, it arrests bleeding at the nostrils, the root in particular. Mixed with salt, also, it is employed for the cure of cancers and foul ulcers; and, applied in a similar manner, it cures sprains and inflamed tumours, as well as imposthumes of the parotid glands and denudations of the bones. The seed of it, taken with boiled must, dispels hysterical suffocations, and, applied topically, it arrests mucous discharges of the nostrils. Taken with hydromel, after dinner, in doses of two oboli, the seed produces a gentle vomit; and a dose of one obolus, taken in wine, has the effect of dispelling lassitude. The seed is prescribed also, parched, and in doses of one acetabulum, for affections of the uterus; and, taken in boiled must, it is a remedy for flatulency of the stomach. Taken in an electuary, with honey, it gives relief in hardness of breathing, and clears the chest by expectoration; applied with linseed, it is a cure for pains in the side, with the addition of some hyssop and a little pepper. The seed is employed also in the form of a liniment for affections of the spleen, and, parched and taken with the food, it acts as a laxative in constipation of the bowels. Hippocrates says that the seed, taken in drink, acts as a purgative upon the uterus; and that taken, parched, with sweet wine, in doses of one acetabulum, or applied externally with juice of mallows, it alleviates pains in that organ. He states also that, used with hydromel and salt, it expels intestinal worms, and that a liniment made of the seed will restore the hair when falling off. Many persons, too, employ the seed topically, with old oil, for diseases of the joints, and for gout, or else the leaves beaten up with bears'-grease; the root, too, pounded in vinegar, is no less useful for the same purposes, as also for affections of the spleen. Boiled in wine, and applied with stale axle-grease and salt, the root disperses inflamed tumours, and, dried, it is used as a depilatory.

THE ANCHUSA

The root of the anchusa,[3] too, is made use of, a plant a finger in thickness. It is split into leaves like the papyrus, and when touched it stains the hands the colour

---

2   Only two species of the nettle, Fée remarks, were known to the ancients, the *Urtica urens* and the *U. dioica*.

3   The *Anchusa tinctoria* of Linnæus, alkanet, orcanet, or dyers' bugloss.

of blood; it is used for imparting rich colours to wool. Applied with cerate it heals ulcerous sores, those of aged people in particular; it is employed also for the cure of burns. It is insoluble in water, but dissolves in oil, this being, in fact, the test of its genuineness. It is administered also, in doses of one drachma, in wine, for nephretic pains, or else, if there is fever, in a decoction of balanus; it is employed in a similar manner, also, for affections of the liver and spleen, and for enlarged secretions of the bile. Applied with vinegar, it is used for the cure of leprosy and the removal of freckles. The leaves, beaten up with honey and meal, are applied topically for sprains; and taken in honied wine, in doses of two drachmæ, they arrest looseness of the bowels. A decoction of the root in water, it is said, kills fleas.

THE HELIOTROPIUM

We have spoken more than once of the marvels of the heliotropium, which turns with the sun, in cloudy weather even, so great is its sympathy with that luminary. At night, as though in regret, it closes its blue flower.

There are two species of heliotropium, the tricoccum[4] and the helioscopium,[5] the latter being the taller of the two, though they neither of them exceed half a foot in height. The helioscopium throws out branches from the root, and the seed of it, enclosed in follicules, is gathered at harvest-time. It grows nowhere but in a rich soil, a highly-cultivated one more particularly; the tricoccum, on the other hand, is to be found growing everywhere. I find it stated, that the helioscopium, boiled, is considered an agreeable food, and that taken in milk, it is gently laxative to the bowels; while, again, a decoction of it, taken as a potion, acts as a most effectual purgative. The other kind, which we have spoken of as being called the "tricoccum," and which also bears the name of "scorpiuron," has leaves that are not only smaller than those of the other kind, but droop downwards towards the ground; the seed of it resembles a scorpion's tail, to which, in fact, it owes its latter appellation. It is of great efficacy for injuries received from all kinds of venomous insects and the spider known as the "phalangium," but more particularly for the stings of scorpions, if applied topically. Those who carry it about their person are never stung by a scorpion, and it is said that if a circle is traced on the ground around a scorpion with a sprig of this plant, the animal will never move out of it, and that if a scorpion is covered with it, or even sprinkled with tile water in which it has been steeped, it will die that instant.

THE ASPHODEL

The asphodel is one of the most celebrated of all the plants, so much so, indeed, that by some persons it has been called "heroum."[6] Hesiod has mentioned the fact of its growing in rivers, and Dionysius distinguishes it into male and female. It has been observed that the bulbs of it, boiled with a ptisan, are remarkably good for

---

4   Or "three-grained," probably, Fée says, from the three cells in the capsule. He identifies this plant with the *Croton tinctorium* of Linnæus, the turnsole, or sun-flower.

5   Fée identifies it with the *Heliotropium Europæum* of Linnæus, the heliotrope, or verrucaria.

6   "Plant of the heroes."

Book XXII - The Properties of Plants and Fruits 255

consumption and phthisis, and that bread in which they have been kneaded up with the meal, is extremely wholesome. Nicander recommends also, for the stings of serpents and scorpions, either the stalk or else the seed or bulbs, to be taken in wine, in doses of three drachmæ; and he says that these should be strewed beneath the bed, if there is any apprehension of their presence. The asphodel is prescribed also for wounds inflicted by marine animals of a venomous nature, and the bite of the land scolopendra. It is quite wonderful how the snails, in Campania, seek the stalk of this plant, and dry it by extracting the inside. The leaves, too, are applied with wine to wounds made by venomous animals, and the bulbs are beaten up with polenta and similarly used for affections of the sinews and joints. It is also a very good plan to rub lichens with them chopped up and mixed with vinegar, and to apply them in water to putrid sores, as also to inflammations of the breasts and testicles. Boiled in lees of wine, and applied in a linen pledged, they are used for the cure of eye fluxes.

MUSHROOMS

Among those vegetable productions which are eaten with risk, I shall, with good reason, include mushrooms; a very dainty food, it is true, but deservedly held in disesteem since the notorious crime committed by Agrippina, who, through their agency, poisoned her husband, the Emperor Claudius, and at the same moment, in the person of his son Nero, inflicted another poisonous curse upon the whole world, herself[7] in particular.

Some of the poisonous mushrooms are easily known, being of a rank, unwholesome look, light red without and livid within, with the clefts considerably enlarged, and a pale, sickly margin to the head. These characteristics, however, are not presented by others of the poisonous kinds; but being dry to all appearance and strongly resembling the genuine ones, they present white spots upon the head, on the surface of the outer coat. The earth, in fact, first produces the uterus or receptacle for the mushroom, and then the mushroom within, like the yolk in the egg. Nor is this envelope less conducive to the nutrition of the young mushroom (than is the albumen of the egg to that of the chicken). Bursting forth from the envelope at the moment of its first appearance, as it gradually increases it becomes transformed into a substantial stalk; it is but very rarely, too, that we find two growing from a single foot-stalk. The generative principle of the mushroom is in the slime and the fermenting juices of the damp earth, or of the roots of most of the glandiferous trees. It appears at first in the shape of a sort of viscous foam, and then assumes a more substantial but membranous form, after which, as already stated, the young mushroom appears.

In general, these plants are of a pernicious nature, and the use of them should be altogether rejected; for if by chance they should happen to grow near a hob-nail, a piece of rusty iron, or a bit of rotten cloth, they will immediately imbibe all these foreign emanations and flavours, and transform them into poison. Who, in fact, is able to distinguish them, except those who dwell in the country, or the persons

---

7   She having been put to death by him.

that are in the habit of gathering them? There are other circumstances, too, which render them noxious; if they grow near the hole of a serpent, for instance, or if they should happen to have been breathed upon by one when just beginning to open; being all the more disposed to imbibe the venom from their natural affinity to poisonous substances.

It will therefore be as well to be on our guard during the season at which the serpents have not as yet retired to their holes for the winter. The best sign to know this by is a multitude of herbs, of trees, and of shrubs, which remain green from the time that these reptiles leave their holes till their return; indeed, the ash alone will be quite sufficient for the purpose, the leaves of it never coming out after the serpents have made their appearance, or beginning to fall before they have retired to their holes. The entire existence of the mushroom, from its birth to its death, is never more than seven days.

FUNGI

Fungi are of a more humid nature than the last, and are divided into numerous kinds, all of which are derived solely from the pituitous humours of trees. The safest are those, the flesh of which is red, the colour being more pronounced than that of the mushroom. The next best are the white ones, the stems of which have a head very similar to the apex worn by the Flamens; and a third kind are the suilli, very conveniently adapted for poisoning. What great pleasure, then, can there be in partaking of a dish of so doubtful a character as this?

I would here also give some general directions for the cooking of mushrooms, as this is the only article of food that the voluptuaries of the present day are in the habit of dressing with their own hands, and so feeding upon it in anticipation, being provided with amber-handled knives and silver plates and dishes for the purpose. Those fungi may be looked upon as bad which become hard in cooking; while those, on the other hand, are comparatively innoxious, which admit of being thoroughly boiled, with the addition of some nitre. They will be all the safer if they are boiled with some meat or the stalks of pears; it is a very good plan, too, to eat pears directly after them. Vinegar, too, being of a nature diametrically opposed to them, neutralizes their dangerous qualities.

LASER

Laser,[8] a juice which distils from silphium, and reckoned among the most precious gifts presented to us by Nature, is made use of in numerous medicinal preparations. Employed by itself, it warms and revives persons benumbed with cold, and, taken in drink, it alleviates affections of the sinews. It is given to females in wine, and is used with soft wool as a pessary to promote the menstrual discharge. Mixed with wax, it extracts corns on the feet, after they have been first loosened with the knife; a piece of it, the size of a chick-pea, melted in water, acts as a diu-

---

8   A gum-resin obtained from the north of Africa, and greatly esteemed by the ancients as an antispasmodic, deobstruent, and diuretic. It is supposed to have been produced by Thapsia Garganica or one of the varieties of that plant. Also called asadulcis.

retic. Andreas assures us that, taken in considerable doses even, it is never productive of flatulency, and that it greatly promotes the digestion, both in aged people and females; he says, too, that it is better used in winter than in summer, and that even then, it is best suited for those whose beverage is water; but due care must be taken that there is no internal ulceration. Taken with the food, it is very refreshing for patients just recovering from an illness; indeed, if it is used at the proper time, it has all the virtues of a desiccatory, though it is more wholesome for persons who are in the habit of using it than for those who do not ordinarily employ it.

As to external maladies, the undoubted virtues of this medicament are universally acknowledged; taken in drink, it has the effect, also, of neutralizing the venom of serpents and of poisoned weapons, and, applied with water, it is in general use for the cure of wounds

It would be an endless task to enumerate all the uses to which laser is put, in combination with other substances; and the more so, as it is only our object to treat of simple remedies, it being these in which Nature displays her resources.

PROPOLIS

Honey would be held in no less esteem than laser, were it not for the fact that nearly every country produces it. The uses to which honey is put are quite innumerable, if we only consider the vast number of compositions in which it forms an ingredient. First of all, there is the propolis,[9] which we find in the hives. This substance has the property of extracting stings and all foreign bodies from the flesh, dispersing tumours, ripening indurations, allaying pains of the sinews, and cicatrizing ulcers of the most obstinate nature.

As to honey itself, it is of so peculiar a nature, that it prevents putrefaction from supervening, by reason of its sweetness solely, and not any inherent acridity, its natural properties being altogether different from those of salt. It is employed with the greatest success for affections of the throat and tonsils, for quinsy and all ailments of the mouth, as also in fever, when the tongue is parched. Decoctions of it are used also for peripneumony and pleurisy, for wounds inflicted by serpents, and for the poison of fungi. For paralysis, it is prescribed in honied wine, though that liquor also has its own peculiar virtues. Honey is used with rose-oil, as an injection for the ears; it has the effect also of exterminating nits and foul vermin of the head. It is the best plan always to skim it before using it.

HIDROMEL

While speaking of the uses of honey, we ought also to treat of the properties of hydromel. There are two kinds of hydromel, one of which is prepared at the moment, and taken while fresh, the other being kept to ripen. The first, which is made of skimmed honey, is an extremely wholesome beverage for invalids who take nothing but a light diet, such as strained alica for instance; it reinvigorates

---

9   A red, resinous, odorous substance having some resemblance to wax and smelling like storax. It is collected by bees from the viscid buds of various trees, and used to stop the holes and crevices in their hives to prevent the entrance of cold air, to strengthen the cells, etc. Also called bee-glue (TN).

the body, is soothing to the mouth and stomach, and by its refreshing properties allays feverish heats. I find it stated, too, by some authors, that to relax the bowels it should be taken cold, and that it is particularly well-suited for persons of a chilly temperament, or of a weak and pusillanimous constitution, such as the Greeks, for instance, call "micropsychi."

For there is a theory, remarkable for its extreme ingenuity, first established by Plato, according to which the primary atoms of bodies, as they happen to be smooth or rough, angular or round, are more or less adapted to the various temperaments of individuals; and hence it is, that the same substances are not universally sweet or bitter to all. So, when affected with lassitude or thirst, we are more prone to anger than at other times. These asperities, however, of the disposition, or rather I should say of the mind, are capable of being modified by the sweeter beverages; as they tend to lubricate the passages for the respiration, and to mollify the channels, the work of inhalation and exhalation being thereby unimpeded by any rigidities. Every person must be sensible of this experimentally, in his own case; there is no one in whom anger, affection, sadness, and all the emotions of the mind may not, in some degree, be modified by diet. It will therefore be worth our while to observe what aliments they are which exercise a physical effect, not only upon the body, but the disposition as well.

Hydromel is recommended, too, as very good for a cough; taken warm, it promotes vomiting. With the addition of oil it counteracts the poison of white lead; of henbane, also, and of the halicacabum,[10] if taken in milk, asses' milk in particular. It is used as an injection for diseases of the ears, and in cases of fistula of the generative organs. With crumb of bread it is applied as a poultice to the uterus, as also to tumours suddenly formed, sprains, and all affections which require soothing applications.

WAX

To an account of honey, that of wax is naturally appended. Every kind of wax is emollient and warming, and tends to the formation of new flesh; fresh wax is, however, the best. It is given in broth to persons troubled with dysentery, and the combs themselves are sometimes used in a pottage made of parched alica. Wax counteracts the bad effects of milk; and ten pills of wax, the size of a grain of millet, will prevent milk from coagulating in the stomach. For swellings in the groin, it is found beneficial to apply a plaster of white wax to the pubes.

ALICA

Alica[11] is quite a Roman invention, and not a very ancient one; for otherwise the Greeks would never have written in such high terms of the praises of ptisan in preference. I do not think that it was yet in use in the days of Pompeius Magnus, a circumstance which will explain why hardly any mention has been made of it

---

10 *Cardiospermum halicacabum*, known as the lesser balloon vine, balloon plant or love in a puff, is a climbing plant widely distributed across tropical and subtropical areas of Africa, Australia, and North America that is often found as a weed along roads and rivers (TN).

11 Cultivated emmer wheat (*Triticum dicoccum*); grits or gruel made with it (TN).

Book XXII - The Properties of Plants and Fruits

in the works of the school of Asclepiades. That it is a most excellent preparation no one can have a doubt, whether it is used strained in hydromel, or whether it is boiled and taken in the form of broth or thick pottage. To arrest flux of the bowels, it is first parched and then boiled with honeycomb, but it is more particularly useful when there is a tendency to phthisis after a long illness, the proper proportions being three cyathi of it to one sextarius of water. This mixture is boiled till all the water has gone off by evaporation, after which one sextarius of sheep' or goats' milk is added; it is then taken by the patient daily, and after a time some honey is added. By this kind of nutriment a deep decline may be cured.

PTISAN

To ptisan[12] which is a preparation of barley, Hippocrates has devoted a whole treatise; praises, however, which at the present day are all transferred to "alica," being, as it is, a much more wholesome preparation. Hippocrates, however, recommends it as a pottage, for the comparative ease with which, from its lubricous nature, it is swallowed; as also, because it allays thirst, never swells in the stomach, passes easily through the intestines, and is the only food that admits of being given twice a-day in fever, at least to patients who are in the habit of taking two meals. He forbids it to be given, however, without being first strained; for no part, he says, of the ptisan, except the water, should be used. He says, too, that it must never be taken while the feet are cold, and, indeed, that no drink of any kind should be taken then. With wheat a more viscous kind of ptisan is made, which is found to be still more efficacious for ulcerations of the trachea.

BREAD

Bread too, which forms our ordinary nutriment, possesses medicinal properties, almost without, number. Applied with water and oil, or else rose-oil, it softens abscesses; and, with hydromel, it is remarkably soothing for indurations. It is prescribed with wine to produce delitescence, or when a defluxion requires to be checked; or, if additional activity is required, with vinegar. It is employed also for the morbid defluxions of rheum, known to the Greeks as "rheumatismi," and for bruises and sprains. For all these purposes, however, bread made with leaven, and known as "autopyrus," is the best.

---

12 A decoction of barley with other ingredients; a farinaceous drink.

Book XXIII
Medicinal Uses and Properties of the Cultivated Trees

We have now set forth the various properties, medicinal or otherwise, as well of the cereals as of the other productions which lie upon the surface of the earth, for the purpose either of serving us for food, or for the gratification of our senses with their flowers or perfumes. In the trees, however, Pomona[1] has entered the lists with them, and has imparted certain medicinal properties to the fruits as they hang. Not content with protecting and nourishing, under the shadow of the trees, the various plants which we have already described, she would even appear to be indignant, as it were, at the thought that we should derive more succour from those productions which are further removed from the canopy of heaven, and which have only come into use in times comparatively recent. For she bids man bear in mind that it was the fruits of the trees which formed his first nourishment, and that it was these which first led him to look upwards towards the heavens; and not only this, but she reminds him, too, that even still it is quite possible for him to derive his aliment from the trees, without being indebted to grain for his subsistence.

THE VINE

But, by Hercules! It is the vine more particularly to which she has accorded these medicinal properties, as though she were not contented with her generosity in providing it with such delicious flavours, and perfumes, and essences. "It is to me," she says, "that man is indebted for the greater part of his enjoyments, it is I that produce for him the flowing wine and the trickling oil, it is I that ripen the date and other fruits in numbers so varied; and all this, not insisting, like the

---

1 The goddess who fostered fruit-trees and promoted their culture (TN).

earth, on their purchase at the cost of fatigues and labours. No necessity do I create for ploughing with the aid of oxen, for beating out upon the threshing-floor, or for bruising under the millstone, and all in order that man may earn his food at some indefinite time by this vast expenditure of toil. As for me, all my gifts are presented to him ready prepared; for no anxieties or fatigues do they call, but, on the contrary, they offer themselves spontaneously, and even fall to the ground, if man should be too indolent to reach them as they hang." Vying even with herself, Pomona has done still more for our practical advantage than for the mere gratification of our pleasures and caprices.

THE LEAVES AND SHOOTS OF THE VINE

The leaves and shoots of the vine, employed with polenta, allay headache and reduce inflammations; the leaves, too, applied by themselves with cold water, are good for burning pains in the stomach; and, used with barley-meal, are excellent applications for diseases of the joints. The shoots, beaten up and applied, have the property of drying up all kinds of running tumours, and the juice extracted from them is used as an injection for the cure of dysentery. The tears of the vine, which would appear to be a sort of gum, will heal leprous sores, lichens, and itch-scabs, if treated first with nitre; used with oil, and applied frequently to superfluous hairs, they act as a depilatory, those more particularly which exude from the vine when burnt in a green state; this last liquid has the effect, too, of removing warts. An infusion of the shoots in water, taken in drink, is good for persons troubled with spitting of blood, and for the fainting fits which sometimes ensue upon conception.

The bark of the vine and the dried leaves arrest the flowing of blood from wounds, and make the sores cicatrice more rapidly. The juice of the white vine, extracted from it while green, effectually removes cutaneous eruptions. The ashes of the cuttings of vines, and of the husks of the grapes, applied with vinegar, are curative of condylomata and diseases of the anus; as also of sprains, burns, and swellings of the spleen, applied with rose-oil, rue, and vinegar. Used with wine, but without oil, they make a fomentation for erysipelas and parts of the body which are chafed; they act as a depilatory also. For affections of the spleen the ashes of vine-cuttings, moistened with vinegar, are administered in drink, being taken in doses of two cyathi in warm water; after which the patient must take due care to lie upon the side in which the spleen is situate.

The tendrils, too, which the vine throws out as it climbs, beaten up in water and drunk, have the effect of arresting habitual vomiting. The ashes of the vine, used with stale axle-grease,[2] are good for tumours, act as a detergent upon fistulas, and speedily effect a radical cure; the same, too, with pains and contractions of the sinews, occasioned by cold. Applied with oil, they are useful for contusions, and with vinegar and nitre, for fleshy excrescences upon the bones; in combination with oil, they are good, too, for wounds inflicted by scorpions and dogs. The ashes of the bark, employed by themselves, restore the hair to such parts of the body as have suffered from the action of fire.

---

2   Lard, either salted or fresh (TN).

GRAPES

As to grapes when allowed to gain maturity, the black ones have more marked properties than the others; and hence it is, that the wine made from them is not so agreeable. The white grapes, on the other hand, are sweeter, for, being transparent, the air penetrates them with greater facility.

Grapes fresh gathered are productive of flatulency, and disturb the stomach and bowels; hence it is that they are avoided in fevers, in large quantities more particularly. Indeed, they are very apt to produce oppression of the head, and to bring on the malady known as lethargy. Grapes which have been gathered, and left to hang for some time, are much less injurious, the exposure to the air rendering them beneficial even to the stomach, and refreshing to the patient, as they are slightly cooling, and tend to remove nausea and qualmishness.

Grapes which have been preserved in wine or in must are trying to the head. Next to the grapes which have been left to hang in the air, are those which have been kept in chaff; but as to those which have been preserved among grape husks, they are injurious to the head, the bladder, and the stomach, though at the same time they arrest looseness of the bowels, and are extremely good for patients troubled with spitting of blood. When preserved in must, they are worse even in their effects than when kept among husks; boiled must, too, renders them injurious to the stomach. It is the opinion of medical writers, that grapes kept in rain-water are the most wholesome of all, even though they are by no means agreeable eating; for the benefit of them is particularly experienced in burning pains of the stomach, biliousness arising from a disordered liver, vomiting of bile, and attacks of cholera, as also dropsy and burning fevers.

THE WHITE VINE

The white vine[3] is known to the Greeks by the various names of ampeloleuce, staphyle, melothron, psilotrum, archezostis, cedrostis, and madon. The twigs of this tree are jointed, thin, and climbing, with considerable interstices between the knots. The leaves, attached to the numerous shoots, and about the size of an ivy leaf, are jagged at the edges, like that of the vine. The root of it is large and white, and very like a radish at first; from it issue several stems, similar to asparagus in appearance. These stems, eaten boiled, are both purgative and diuretic. The leaves, too, as well as the stems, are possessed of caustic properties; for which reason they are employed topically with salt, for phagedænic sores, gangrenes, and putrid ulcers of the legs. The fruit of the tree is in the form of grapes thinly scattered, the juice of which is red at first, and afterwards of a saffron colour. This fruit is well known to curriers, who are in the habit of using it in preparing leather. It is employed also in the form of a liniment for itch-scabs and leprous spots; and a decoction of it with wheat, taken in drink, increases the milk in women when nursing. The root of this tree, so renowned for the numerous medicinal purposes to which it is applied, is pounded and taken in wine, in doses of two drachmæ, for the cure of stings inflicted by serpents; it has the effect, also, of removing spots upon the

---

3   The *Bryonia alba* of Linnæus; the bryony, white vine, or white jalap.

face, moles and freckles, as well as scars and bruises; a decoction of it in oil is productive of a similar effect. A decoction of it is given to drink for epilepsy, and to persons troubled with a disordered mind or suffering from vertigo, the dose being one drachma daily, for a whole year; taken in larger quantities, it is apt sometimes to disorder the senses. It is possessed, also, of one very remarkable property, applied with water in the same manner as bryonia, of extracting splintered bones, for which reason it is known to some persons by the name of white bryonia; the other kind, however, which is black, is found to answer the purpose better, in combination with honey and frankincense.

OBSERVATIONS RELATIVE TO WINE

Persons whose wish it is to make flesh, or to keep the bowels relaxed, will do well to drink while taking their food. Those, on the other hand, who wish to reduce themselves, or prevent the bowels from being relaxed, should abstain from drinking while taking their meals, and drink but a very little only when they have done eating. To drink wine fasting is a fashion of recent introduction only, and an extremely bad one for persons engaged in matters of importance, and requiring a continued application of the mental faculties. Wine, no doubt, was taken fasting in ancient times, but then it was as a preparative for sleep and repose from worldly cares; and it is for this reason that, in Homer, we find Helen presenting it to the guests before the repast. It is upon this fact, too, that the common proverb is founded, which says that "wisdom is obscured by wine." It is to wine that we men are indebted for being the only animated beings that drink without being thirsty. When drinking wine, it is a very good plan to take a draught of water every now and then; and to take one long draught of it at the last, cold water taken internally having the effect of instantaneously dispelling inebriation.

It is strongly recommended by Hesiod to drink undiluted wine for twenty days before the rising of the Dog-star, and as many after. Pure wine, too, acts as an antidote to hemlock, coriander, henbane, mistletoe, opium, mercury, as also to stings inflicted by bees, wasps, hornets, the phalangium,[4] serpents, and scorpions; all kinds of poison, in fact, which are of a cold nature, the venom of the hæmorrhois[5] and the prester,[6] in particular, and the noxious effects of fungi. Undiluted wine is good, too, in cases of flatulency, gnawing pains in the thoracic organs, excessive vomitings at the stomach, fluxes of the bowels and intestines, dysentery, excessive perspirations after prolonged fits of coughing, and defluxions of various kinds. In the cardiac disease, it is a good plan to apply a sponge soaked in neat wine to the left breast; in all these cases, however, old white wine is the best. A fomentation of hot wine applied to the genitals of beasts of burden is found to be very beneficial; and, introduced into the mouth, with the aid of a horn, it has the effect of removing all sensations of fatigue. It is asserted that in apes, and other quadrupeds with toes, the growth will be impeded if they are accustomed to drink undiluted wine.

---

4   A kind of venomous spider (TN).
5   A kind of venomous serpent (TN).
6   A kind of serpent, whose bite causes a burning thirst (TN).

VINEGAR

Wine, even when it has lost its vinous properties, still retains some medicinal virtues. Vinegar possesses cooling properties in the very highest degree, and is no less efficacious as a resolvent; it has the property, too, of effervescing, when poured upon the ground. We have frequently had occasion, and shall again have occasion, to mention the various medicinal compositions in which it forms an ingredient. Taken by itself it dispels nausea and arrests hiccup, and if smelt at, it will prevent sneezing; retained in the mouth, it prevents a person from being inconvenienced by the heat of the bath. It is used as a beverage also, in combination with water, and employed as a gargle, it is found by many to be very wholesome to the stomach, particularly convalescents and persons suffering from sun-stroke; used as a fomentation, too, this mixture is extremely beneficial to the eyes. Vinegar is used remedially when a leech has been swallowed; and it has the property of healing leprous sores, scorbutic eruptions, running ulcers, wounds inflicted by dogs, scorpions, and scolopendræ, and the bite of the shrew-mouse. It is good, too, as a preventive of the itching sensations produced by the venom of all stinging animals, and as an antidote to the bite or the millepede.

Applied warm in a sponge, in the proportion of three sextarii to two ounces of sulphur or a bunch of hyssop, vinegar is a remedy for maladies of the anus. To arrest the hemorrhage which ensues upon the operation of lithotomy, and, indeed, all other operations of a similar nature, it is usual to apply vinegar in a sponge, and at the same time to administer it internally in doses of two cyathi, the very strongest possible being employed. Vinegar has the effect also of dissolving coagulated blood; for the cure of lichens, it is used both internally and externally. Used as an injection, it arrests looseness of the bowels and fluxes of the intestines; it is similarly employed, too, for prolapse of the rectum and uterus.

THE LEAVES OF THE OLIVE

The next rank, after the vine, clearly belongs to the olive. The leaves of the olive-tree are astringent, detergent, and binding in the highest degree. Chewed and applied to sores, they are of a healing nature; and applied topically with oil, they are good for head-ache. A decoction of them with honey makes a good liniment for such parts of the body as have been subjected to cauterization, as also for inflammations of the gums, whitlows, and foul and putrid ulcers; combined with honey, they arrest discharges of blood from the nervous parts of the body. The juice of olive leaves is efficacious for carbuncular ulcers and pustules about the eyes, and for prolapse of the pupil; hence it is much employed in the composition of eye-salves, having the additional property of healing inveterate runnings of the eyes, and ulcerations of the eyelids.

This juice is extracted by pouring wine and rain-water upon the leaves, and then pounding them; after which the pulp is dried and divided into lozenges. Used with wool, as a pessary, this preparation arrests menstruation when in excess, and is very useful for the treatment of purulent sores, condylomata, erysipelas, spreading ulcers, and epinyctis.

The blossom, of too, of the olive-tree possesses similar properties. The young branches are burnt when just beginning to blossom, and of the ashes a substitute for spodium is made, upon which wine is poured, and it is then burnt afresh. To suppurations and inflamed tumours these ashes are applied, or else the leaves, beaten up with honey; for the eyes, they are used with polenta. The juice which exudes from the wood, when burnt in a green state, heals lichens, scaly eruptions, and running ulcers.

OMPHACIUM

As to olive oil, we have abundantly treated of its nature and elements already. It now remains to speak of the medicinal properties of the various kinds of oil. The most useful of all is omphacium,[7] and next to that, green oil;[8] in addition to which, we may remark that oil ought to be as fresh as possible, except in cases where old oil is absolutely required. For medicinal purposes, too, oil should be extremely fluid, have an agreeable smell, and be free from all taste, just the converse, in fact, of the property which we look for in food. Omphacium is good for the gums, and if kept from time to time in the mouth, there is nothing better as a preservative of the whiteness of the teeth. It checks profuse perspirations.

CASTOR OIL

Castor oil, taken with an equal quantity of warm water, acts as a purgative upon the bowels. It is said, too, that as a purgative this oil acts more particularly upon the regions of the diaphragm. It is very useful for diseases of the joints, all kinds of indurations, affections of the uterus and ears, and for burns; employed with the ashes of the murex, it heals itch-scabs and inflammations of the anus. It improves the complexion also, and by its fertilizing tendencies promotes the growth of the hair. The cicus, or seed from which this oil is made, no animal will touch; and from these grape-like seeds wicks are made, which burn with a peculiar brilliancy; the light, however, that is produced by the oil is very dim, in consequence of its extreme thickness. The leaves are applied topically with vinegar for erysipelas, and fresh-gathered, they are used by themselves for diseases of the breasts and eye-fluxes; a decoction of them in wine, with polenta and saffron, is good for inflammations of various kinds. Boiled by themselves, and applied to the face for three successive days, they improve the complexion.

CYPRUS AND ITS OIL

The oil of cyprus[9] is naturally warming, and relaxes the sinews. The leaves of the tree are used as an application to the stomach, and the juice of them is applied in a pessary for irritations of the uterus. Fresh gathered and chewed, the leaves are applied to running ulcers of the head, ulcerations of the mouth, gatherings, and

---

7 Juice of unripe fruit, either olives or grapes (TN).
8 An inferior kind of omphacium.
9 Cyprus (*Lawsonia alba*) or henna, is but little known in Europe, but it is employed for many purposes in the East. The leaves, which have a powerful smell, are used for the purpose of dyeing and staining various parts of the body.

condylomatous sores. A decoction of the leaves is very useful also for burns and sprains. Beaten up and applied with the juice of the sparrow-quince, they turn the hair red. The blossoms, applied to the head with vinegar, relieve head-ache, and the ashes of them, burnt in a pot of raw earth, are curative of corrosive sores and putrid ulcers, either employed by themselves, or in combination with honey. The odour exhaled by these blossoms induces sleep.

OIL OF BALSAMUM

The oil of balsamum is by far the most valuable of them all, as already stated by us, when treating of the unguents. It is extremely efficacious for the venom of all kinds of serpents, is very beneficial to the eyesight, disperses films upon the eyes, assuages hardness of breathing, and acts emolliently upon all kinds of gatherings and indurations. It has the effect, also, of preventing the blood from coagulating, acts as a detergent upon ulcers, and is remarkably beneficial for diseases of the ears, head-ache, trembling, spasms, and ruptures. Taken in milk, it is an antidote to the poison of aconite, and used as a liniment upon the access of the shivering fits in fevers, it modifies their violence. Still, however, it should be used but sparingly, as it is of a very caustic nature, and, if not employed in moderation, is apt to augment the malady.

THE PALM

Next in rank after the vine and the olive comes the palm. Dates fresh-gathered have an inebriating effect, and are productive of head-ache; when dried, they are not so injurious. It would appear, too, that they are not wholesome to the stomach; they have an irritating effect on coughs, but are very nourishing to the body. The ancients used to give a decoction of them to patients, as a substitute for hydromel, with the view of recruiting the strength and allaying thirst, the Thebaic date being held in preference for the purpose. Dates are very useful, too, for persons troubled with spitting of blood, when taken in the food more particularly. The dates called caryotæ, in combination with quinces, wax, and saffron, are applied topically for affections of the stomach, bladder, abdomen, and intestines; they are good for bruises also. Date-stones, burnt in a new earthen vessel, produce an ash which, when rinsed, is employed as a substitute for spodium,[10] and is used as an ingredient in eye-salves, and, with the addition of nard, in washes for the eye-brows.

PEARS

All kinds of pears, as an aliment, are indigestible, to persons in robust health, even; but to invalids they are forbidden as rigidly as wine. Boiled, however, they are remarkably agreeable and wholesome, those of Crustumium in particular. All kinds of pears, too, boiled with honey, are wholesome to the stomach. Cataplasms of a resolvent nature are made with pears, and a decoction of them is used to disperse indurations. They are efficacious, also, in cases of poisoning by mushrooms and fungi, as much by reason of their heaviness, as by the neutralizing effects of their juice.

---

10 Vegetal ashes (TN).

The wild pear ripens but very slowly. Cut in slices and hung in the air to dry, it arrests looseness of the bowels, an effect which is equally produced by a decoction of it taken in drink; in which case the leaves also are boiled up together with the fruit. The ashes of pear-tree wood are even more efficacious as an antidote to the poison of fungi.

A load of apples or pears, however small, is singularly fatiguing to beasts of burden; the best plan to counteract this, they say, is to give the animals some to eat, or at least to show them the fruit before starting.

FIGS

The milky juice of the fig-tree possesses kindred properties with vinegar; hence it is, that, like rennet, it curdles milk. This juice is collected before the fruit ripens, and dried in the shade; being used with yolk of egg as a liniment, or else in drink, with starch, to bring ulcers to a head and break them, and for the purposes of an emmenagogue. With meal of fenugreek and vinegar, it is applied topically for gout; it acts also as a depilatory, heals eruptions of the eyelids, lichens and itch-scabs, and relaxes the bowels. The milk of the fig-tree is naturally curative of the stings of hornets, wasps, and similar insects, and is remarkably useful for wounds inflicted by scorpions. Mixed with axle-grease it removes warts. With the leaves and figs still green an application is made for scrofulous and other sores of a nature which requires emollients or resolvents. The leaves, too, used by themselves, are productive of a similar effect. In addition to this, they are employed for other purposes, as a friction for lichens, for example, for alopecy, and other diseases which require caustic applications. The young shoots of the branches are used as an application to the skin in cases of bites inflicted by dogs. With honey they are applied to the ulcers known as honeycomb ulcers; mixed with the leaves of wild poppies they extract splinters of bones; and the leaves beaten up in vinegar are a cure for bites inflicted by dogs. The young white shoots of the black fig are applied topically, with wax, to boils, and bites inflicted by the shrew-mouse; and the ashes of their leaves are used for the cure of gangrenes and the reduction of fleshy excrescences.

Ripe figs are diuretic and laxative; they promote the perspiration, and bring out pimples; hence it is that they are unwholesome in autumn, the perspirations which they excite being always attended with shivering. Dried figs are injurious to the stomach, but are beneficial in a marvellous degree to the throat and pharynx. They are of a warming nature, are productive of thirst, and relax the bowels, but are unwholesome in stomachic complaints and fluxes of the bowels. In all cases they are beneficial for the bladder, hardness of breathing, and asthma, as also for diseases of the liver, kidneys, and spleen. Figs are extremely useful for patients recovering from a long illness, and for persons suffering from epilepsy or dropsy. They are applied topically also in all cases where sores require to be brought to a head, or dispersed; and they are still more efficacious when mixed with lime or nitre.

MULBERRIES

In Egypt and in the Isle of Cyprus there are mulberry-trees of a peculiar kind, being of a nature that is truly marvellous; for, if the outer bark is peeled off, they emit a great abundance of juice; but if a deeper incision is made, they are found to be quite dry. This juice is an antidote to the venom of serpents, is good for dysentery, disperses inflamed tumours and all kinds of gatherings, heals wounds, and allays both head-ache and ear-ache; it is taken in drink for affections of the spleen, and is used as a liniment for the same purpose, as also for fits of shivering. This juice, however, very soon breeds worms.

Among ourselves, too, the juice which exudes from the mulberry-tree is employed for an equal number of purposes; taken in wine, it neutralizes the noxious effects of aconite and the venom of spiders, relaxes the bowels, and expels tapeworm and other animals which breed in the intestines; the bark of the tree, pounded, has also a similar effect. The leaves, boiled in rain-water with the bark of the black fig and the vine, are used for dyeing the hair.

The juice of the fruit has a laxative effect immediately upon the bowels, though the fruit itself, for the moment, acts beneficially upon the stomach, being of a refreshing nature, but productive of thirst. If no other food is taken upon them, mulberries are of a swelling tendency. The juice of unripe mulberries acts astringently upon the bowels.

STOMATICE

From the fruit of the mulberry a medicament is prepared, called "panchrestos,"[11] "stomatice," or "arteriace"; the following is the method employed. Three sextarii of the juice are reduced, at a slow heat, to the consistency of honey; two denarii of dried omphacium[12] or one of myrrh, with one denarius of saffron, are then added, the whole being beaten up together and mixed with the decoction. There is no medicament known that is more soothing than this, for affections of the mouth, the trachea, the uvula, and the stomach. There is also another mode of preparing it; two sextarii of mulberry juice and one of Attic honey are boiled down in the manner above stated.

There are some other marvellous properties, also, which are mentioned in reference to this tree. When the tree is in bud, and before the appearance of the leaves, the germs of the fruit must be gathered with the left hand —the Greeks give them the name of "ricini." These germs, worn as an amulet before they have touched the ground, have the effect of arresting hemorrhage, whether proceeding from a wound, from the mouth, from the nostrils, or from haemorrhoids; for which purposes they are, accordingly, put away and kept. Similar virtues are attributed to a branch just beginning to bear, broken off at full moon, provided also it has not touched the ground; this branch, it is said, attached to the arm, is peculiarly efficacious for the suppression of the menstrual discharge when in excess. The same effect is produced, it is said, when the woman herself pulls it off, whatever time it may happen to be, care being taken not to let it touch the ground, and to wear it attached to the body. The leaves of the mulberry-tree beaten up fresh, or a decoction of them dried, are applied topically for stings inflicted by serpents; an infusion

---

11   "All-healing," "mouth-medicine," and "medicine for the trachea."
12   Juice of unripe fruit, either olives or grapes (TN).

of them, taken in drink, is equally efficacious for that purpose. The juice extracted from the bark of the root, taken in wine or oxycrate, counteracts the venom of the scorpion.

PINE CONES

Pine cones, with the resin in them, are slightly bruised, and then boiled down in water to one-half; the proportion of water being one sextarius to each nut. This decoction, taken in doses of two cyathi, is used for the cure of spitting of blood. The bark of the tree, boiled in wine, is given for griping pains in the bowels. The kernels of the pine-nut allay thirst, and assuage acridities and gnawing pains in the stomach; they tend also to neutralize vicious humours in that region, recruit the strength, and are salutary to the kidneys and the bladder. They would seem, however, to exercise an irritating effect upon the throat, and to increase cough. Taken in water, wine, raisin wine, or a decoction of dates, they carry off bile. For gnawing pains in the stomach of extreme violence, they are mixed with cucumber-seed and juice of purslain; they are employed, too, in a similar manner for ulcerations of the bladder and kidneys, having a diuretic effect.

THE LAUREL

All parts of the laurel, both the leaves, bark, and berries, are of a warming nature; and a decoction of them, the leaves in particular, is very useful for affections of the bladder and uterus. The leaves, applied topically, neutralize the poison of wasps, bees, and hornets, as also that of serpents. Boiled in oil, they promote the menstrual discharge; and the more tender of the leaves beaten up with polenta, are used for inflammations of the eyes, with rue for inflammations of the testicles, and with rose-oil, or oil of iris, for head-ache. Three leaves, chewed and swallowed for three days in succession, are a cure for cough, and beaten up with honey, for asthma. The bark of the root is dangerous to pregnant women; the root itself disperses calculi, and taken in doses of three oboli in aromatic wine, it acts beneficially on the liver. The leaves, taken in drink, act as an emetic; and the berries, pounded and applied as a pessary, or else taken in drink, promote menstruation. Two of the berries with the skin removed, taken in wine, are a cure for inveterate cough and hardness of breathing; if, however, this is accompanied with fever, they are given in water, or else in an electuary with raisin wine, or boiled in hydromel. Employed in a similar manner, they are good for phthisis, and for all defluxions of the chest, as they have the effect of detaching the phlegm and bringing it off.

For stings inflicted by scorpions, four laurel-berries are taken in wine. Applied with oil, they are a cure for epinyctis,[13] freckles, running sores, ulcers of the mouth, and scaly eruptions. The juice of the berries is curative of porrigo and phthiriasis; and for pains in the ears, or hardness of hearing, it is injected into those organs with old wine and oil of roses. All venomous creatures fly at the approach of persons who have been anointed with this juice; taken in drink, the juice of the small-leaved laurel in particular, it is good for stings inflicted by them. The berries,

---

13 A pustule, or an eruption, which appears mostly at night (TN).

used with wine, neutralize the venom of serpents, scorpions, and spiders; they are applied also, topically, with oil and vinegar, in diseases of the spleen and liver, and with honey to gangrenous sores. In cases of lassitude and shivering fits, it is a very good plan to rub the body with juice of laurel-berries mixed with nitre. Some persons are of opinion that delivery is accelerated by taking laurel-root to the amount of one acetabulum, in water, and that, used fresh, it is better than dried. It is recommended by some authorities, to take ten of the berries in drink, for the sting of the scorpion; and in cases of relaxation of the uvula, to boil a quarter of a pound of the berries, or leaves, in three sextarii of water, down to one third, the decoction being used warm, as a gargle. For head-ache, also, it is recommended to bruise an uneven number of the berries in oil, the mixture being warmed for use.

MYRTLE

The white[14] cultivated myrtle is employed for fewer medicinal purposes than the black one. The berries of it are good for spitting of blood, and taken in wine, they neutralize the poison of fungi. They impart an agreeable smell to the breath, even when eaten the day before; thus, for instance, in Menander we find the Synaristosæ eating them. They are taken also for dysentery, in doses of one denarius, in wine; and they are employed lukewarm, in wine, for the cure of obstinate ulcers on the extremities. Mixed with polenta, they are employed topically in ophthalmia, and for the cardiac disease they are applied to the left breast. For stings inflicted by scorpions, diseases of the bladder, head-ache, and fistulas of the eye before suppuration, they are similarly employed; and for tumours and pituitous eruptions, the kernels are first removed and the berries are then pounded in old wine. The juice of the berries acts astringently upon the bowels, and is diuretic; mixed with cerate it is applied topically to blisters, pituitous eruptions, and wounds inflicted by the phalangium; it imparts a black tint, also, to the hair.

---

14 A variety with white berries, but which variety it appears impossible to say.

Book XXIV
Medicaments Derived from the Forest Trees

THE ANTIPATHIES AND SYMPATHIES WHICH EXIST AMONG TREES AND PLANTS

Not even are the forests and the spots in which the aspect of Nature is most rugged are destitute of their peculiar medicines; for so universally has that divine parent of all things distributed her succours for the benefit of man, as to implant medicinal virtues in the trees of the desert even, while at every step she presents us with most wonderful illustrations of those antipathies and sympathies which exist in the vegetable world.

Between the oak and the olive there exists a hatred so inveterate, that transplanted, either of them, to a site previously occupied by the other, they will die. Also, if the oak is planted near the walnut, will perish. There is a mortal feud existing also between the cabbage and the vine; and the cabbage itself, so shunned as it is by the vine, will wither immediately if planted in the vicinity of cyclamen or of origanum. We find it asserted even, that aged trees fit to be felled, are cut with all the greater difficulty, and dry all the more rapidly, if touched by the hand of man before the axe is applied: it is a common belief, too, that when their load consists of fruit, beasts of burden are immediately sensible of it, and will instantly begin to sweat, however trifling it may be, unless the fruit is duly shown to them before starting. Fennel-giant, as a fodder, is very agreeable for the ass, and yet to other beasts of burden it is a deadly poison; hence it is that the ass is consecrated to Father Liber, to which deity the fennel is also sacred.

Inanimate objects again, even of the most insignificant character, have their own peculiar antipathies. Cooks disengage meat of the brine, when it has been too highly salted, by the agency of fine meal and the inner bark of the linden-tree. Salt again, tends to neutralize the sickly flavour of food when over-sweet. The taste of water, when nitrous or bitter, is modified by the addition of polenta, so much so indeed, as to be rendered potable in a couple of hours; it is for a similar reason, too, that a layer of polenta is put in our linen wine-strainers. A similar property is possessed also by the chalk of Rhodes, and the potter's earth of our own country.

Equal affinities exist as well; pitch, for instance, is extracted by the agency of oil, both of them being of an unctuous nature oil again, will incorporate only with lime, both of them having a natural antipathy to water. Gum is most easily removed with vinegar, and ink with water; in addition to which, there are numberless other instances of sympathy and antipathy which we shall be careful to mention in their appropriate places.

It is in tendencies of this description that the medical art first took its rise; though it was originally intended, no doubt, by Nature, that our only medicaments should be those which universally exist, are everywhere to be found, and are to he procured at no great outlay, the various substances, in fact, from which we derive our sustenance. But at a later period the fraudulent disposition of mankind, combined with an ingenuity prompted by lucre, invented those quack laboratories, in which each one of us is promised an extension of his life —that is, if he will pay for it. Compositions and mixtures of an inexplicable nature forthwith have their praises sung, and the productions of Arabia and India are held in unbounded admiration in the very midst of us. For some trifling sore or other, a medicament is prescribed from the shores of the Red Sea; while not a day passes but what the real remedies are to be found upon the tables of the very poorest man among us. But if the remedies for diseases were derived from our own gardens, if the plants or shrubs were employed which grow there, it would be no art, forsooth, that would rank lower than that of medicine.

THE LOTUS OF ITALY

The berries of the lotus, which is known among us as the "Grecian bean," act astringently upon the bowels; and the shavings of the wood, boiled in wine, are useful in cases of dysentery, excessive menstruation, vertigo, and epilepsy; they also prevent the hair from falling off. It is a marvellous thing—but there is no substance known that is more bitter than the shavings of this wood, or sweeter than the fruit. The sawdust also of the wood is boiled in myrtle-water, and then kneaded and divided into lozenges, which form a medicament for dysentery of remarkable utility, being taken in doses of one victoriatus, in three cyathi of water.

GALL-NUTS

And no fewer are the varieties of the gall-nut: the full-bodied gall-nut, the perforated one, the white, the black, the large, the small, all of them possessed of similar properties; but, however, the one of Commagene is generally preferred. These substances remove fleshy excrescences on the body, and are serviceable for affections of the gums and uvula, and for ulcerations of the mouth. Burnt, and then quenched in wine, they are applied topically in cases of cœliac affections and dysentery, and with honey, to whitlows, hang-nails, malformed nails, running ulcers, condylomatous swellings, and ulcerations of the nature known as phagedænic. A decoction of them in wine is used as an injection for the ears, and as a liniment for the eyes, and in combination with vinegar they are employed for eruptions and tumours.

The inner part of the gall, chewed, allays tooth-ache, and is good for excoriations between the thighs, and for burns. Taken unripe in vinegar, they reduce the volume of the spleen; and, burnt and then quenched in salt and vinegar, they are used as a fomentation for excessive menstruation and prolapse of the uterus. All varieties of the gall-nut stain the hair black.

THE CYPRESS

The leaves of the cypress are pounded and applied to wounds inflicted by serpents, and with polenta, to the head, in cases of sunstroke. They are used also for hernia, and an infusion of them is taken in drink. They are applied with wax to swellings of the testicles, and mixed with vinegar they stain the hair black. Beaten up with twice the quantity of light bread, and then kneaded with Aminean wine, they are found very soothing for pains in the Feet and sinews.

The excrescences of this tree are taken in drink for the stings of serpents and for discharges of blood from the mouth they are used also as a topical application for gatherings. Fresh-gathered and beaten up with axle-grease and bean-meal, they are good for hernia; and an infusion of them is taken in drink for the same complaint. In combination with meal, they are applied topically to imposthumes of the parotid glands, and to scrofulous sores. From these excrescences, pounded along with the seed, a juice is extracted, which, mixed with oil, disperses films of the eyes. Taken in doses of one victoriatus, in wine, and applied at the same time in a pulpy, dried fig, the seeds of which have been removed, this juice cures maladies of the testicles and disperses tumours: mixed with leaven, it heals scrofulous sores.

The root of the cypress, bruised with the leaves and taken in drink, is curative of diseases of the bladder, strangury, and the sting of the phalangium. The shavings of the wood, taken in drink, act as an emmenagogue, and neutralize the venom of the scorpion.

THE PITCH-TREE AND THE LARCH

The leaves of the pitch-tree and the larch, beaten up and boiled in vinegar, are good for tooth-ache. The ashes of the bark are used for excoriations and burns. Taken in drink this substance arrests diarrhœa, and acts as a diuretic; and used as a fumigation, it reduces the uterus when displaced. The leaves of the pitch-tree are particularly good for the liver, taken in doses of one drachma in hydromel.

It is a well-known fact that forests planted solely with trees from which pitch and resin are extracted, are remarkably beneficial for patients suffering from phthisis, or who are unable to recover their strength after a long illness: indeed it is said, that in such cases to breathe the air of localities thus planted, is more beneficial even than to take a voyage to Egypt or to go on a summer's journey to the mountains to drink the milk there, impregnated with the perfumes of plants.

RESINS

There are two principal kinds of resin, the dry and the liquid. The dry resins are extracted from the pine and the pitch-tree, the liquid from the terebinth, the larch, the lentisk, and the cypress; these last producing it in the province of Asia and in Syria. It is an error to suppose that the resin of the pitch-tree is the same as that of the larch; for the pitch-tree yields an unctuous resin, and of the same consistency as frankincense, while that of the larch is thin, like honey in colour, and of a powerful odour. It is but very rarely that medical men make use of liquid resin, and when they do, it is mostly that produced by the larch, which is administered in an egg for cough and ulcerations of the viscera. The resin of the pine, too, is far from extensively used, and that of the other kinds is always boiled before use; on the various methods of boiling it, we have enlarged at sufficient length already.

As to the produce of the various trees, the resin of the terebinth is held in high esteem, as being the most odoriferous and the lightest, the kinds which come from Cyprus and Syria being looked upon as the best. Both these kinds are the colour of Attic honey; but that of Cyprus has more body, and dries with greater rapidity. In the dry resins the qualities requisite are whiteness, purity, and transparency: but whatever the kind, the produce of mountainous districts is always preferred to that of champaign countries, and that of a north-eastern aspect to that of any other quarter. Resins are dissolved in oil as a liniment and emollient cataplasm for wounds; but when they are used as a potion, bitter almonds are also employed. The curative properties of resins consist in their tendency to close wounds, to act as a detergent upon gatherings and so disperse them, and to cure affections of the chest.

THE LENTISK

The seed, bark, and tear-like juices of the lentisk are diuretics, and act astringently upon the bowels; a decoction of them, used as a fomentation, is curative of serpiginous sores, and is applied topically for humid ulcerations and erysipelas; it is employed also as a collutory for the gums. The teeth are rubbed with the leaves in cases of tooth-ache, and they are rinsed with a decoction of the leaves when loose; this decoction has the effect also of staining the hair. The gum of this tree is useful for diseases of the rectum, and all cases in which desiccatives and calorifics are needed; a decoction too of the gum is good for the stomach, acting as a carminative and diuretic; it is applied also to the head, in cases of headache, with polenta. The more tender of the leaves are used as an application for inflammations of the eyes.

The mastich produced by the lentisk is used as a bandoline[1] for the eye-lashes, in compositions for giving a plumpness to the face, and in cosmetics for smoothing the skin. It is employed for spitting of blood and for inveterate coughs, as well as all those purposes for which gum acacia is in request. It is used also for the cure of excoriations; which are fomented either with the oil extracted from the seed,

---

1 A gummy perfumed substance, originally obtained mainly from quince-seeds, used to impart glossiness to the hair, or to fix it in any particular form (TN).

mixed with wax, or else with a decoction of the leaves in oil. Fomentations too are made of a decoction of it in water for diseases of the male organs.

THE POPLAR

A potion prepared from the bark is good for sciatica and strangury, and the juice of the leaves is taken warm for ear-ache. So long as a person holds a sprig of poplar in his hand, there is no fear of chafing between the thighs.

The black poplar which grows in Crete is looked upon as the most efficacious of them all. The seed of it, taken in vinegar, is good for epilepsy. This tree produces a resin also to a small extent, which is made use of for emollient plasters. The leaves, boiled in vinegar, are applied topically for gout. A moisture that exudes from the clefts of the black poplar removes warts, and pimples caused by friction. Poplars produce also on the leaves a kind of sticky juice, from which bees prepare their propolis; indeed this juice, mixed with water, has the same virtues as propolis.

THE JUNIPER

The juniper is of a warming and resolvent nature beyond all other plants; in other respects, it resembles the cedar. There are two species of this tree, also, one of which is larger than the other; the odour of either, burnt, repels the approach of serpents. The seed is good for pains in the stomach, chest, and sides; it dispels flatulency and sudden chills, soothes cough, and brings indurations to a head. Applied topically, it checks the growth of tumours; and the berries, taken in red wine, act astringently upon the bowels; they are applied also to tumours of the abdomen. The seed is used as an ingredient in antidotes of an aperient nature, and is diuretic in its effects. It is used as a liniment for defluxions of the eyes, and is prescribed for convulsions, ruptures, griping pains in the bowels, affections of the uterus, and sciatica, either in a dose of four berries in white wine, or in the form of a decoction of twenty berries in wine.

THE BROOM

The broom[2] is used for making cords; the flowers of it are greatly sought by bees. I have my doubts whether this is not the same plant that the Greek writers have called "sparton," and of which, in those parts of the world, they are in the habit of making fishing-nets. I doubt also whether Homer has alluded to this plant, when he speaks of the seams of the ships —"the sparta"- coming asunder; for it is certain that in those times the spartum of Spain or Africa was not as yet in use, and that vessels made of materials sown together, were united by the agency, not of spartum, but of flax.

The seed of the plant to which the Greeks now give the name of "sparton," grows in pods like those of the kidneybean. It is as strongly drastic as hellebore, and is usually taken fasting, in doses of one drachma and a half, in four cyathi of hydromel. The branches also, with the foliage, are macerated for several days in vinegar, and are then beaten up, the infusion being recommended for sciatica, in doses of one cyathus. Some persons think it a better plan, however, to make an

---

2   Fée thinks that the kind here alluded to is the Spanish broom.

infusion of them in sea-water, and to inject it as an enema. The juice of them is used also as a friction for sciatica, with the addition of oil. Some medical men, too, make use of the seed for strangury. Broom, bruised with axle-grease, is a cure for diseases of the knees.

THE IVY

The medicinal properties of the many varieties of the ivy all are of a doubtful nature; taken in considerable quantities they disturb the mental faculties and purge the brain. Taken internally they are injurious to the sinews, but applied topically they are beneficial to those parts of the body. Ivy possesses properties similar to those of vinegar. All the varieties of the ivy are of a refrigerative nature, and taken in drink they are diuretic. The softer leaves, applied to the head, allay head-ache, acting more particularly upon the brain and the membrane which envelopes that organ. For this purpose the leaves are bruised with vinegar and oil of roses and then boiled, after which some more rose-oil is added. The leaves too are applied to the forehead, and the mouth is fomented with a decoction of them, with which the head is rubbed as well. They are useful also for the spleen, the leaves being applied topically, or an infusion of them taken in drink. A decoction of them is used for cold shiverings in fevers, and for phlegm outbursts; or else they are beaten up in wine for the purpose. The umbels too, taken in drink or applied externally, are good for affections of the spleen, and an application of them is useful for the liver; employed as a pessary, they act as an emmenagogue. The juice of the ivy, the white cultivated kind more particularly, cures diseases of the nostrils and removes habitually offensive smells. Injected into the nostrils it purges the head, and with the addition of nitre it is still more efficacious for that purpose. In combination with oil, the juice is injected for suppurations or pains in the ears. It is a corrective also of the deformities of scars. The juice of white ivy, heated with the aid of iron, is still more efficacious for affections of the spleen; it will be found sufficient, however, to take six of the berries in two cyathi of wine. Three berries of the white ivy, taken in oxymel, expel tape-worm, and in the treatment of such cases it is a good plan to apply them to the abdomen as well.

THE REED

The root of the reed, pounded and applied to the part affected, extracts the prickles of fern from the body, the root of the fern having a similar effect upon splinters of the reed. The scented reed which is grown in Judæa and Syria as an ingredient in our unguents, boiled with hay-grass or parsley-seed, has a diuretic effect; employed as a pessary, it acts as an emmenagogue. Taken in drink, in doses of two oboli, it is curative of convulsions, diseases of the liver and kidneys, and dropsy. Used as a fumigation, and with resin more particularly, it is good for coughs, and a decoction of it with myrrh is useful for scaly eruptions and running ulcers. A juice, too, is collected from it which has similar properties to those of elaterium.

THE PAPYRUS

Of a kindred nature with the reed is the papyrus of Egypt; a plant that is remarkably useful, in a dried state, for dilating and drying up fistulas, and, by its expansive powers, opening an entrance for the necessary medicaments. The ashes of paper prepared from the papyrus are reckoned among the caustics; those of the plant, taken in wine, have a narcotic effect. The plant, applied topically in water, removes callosities of the skin.

ROSEMARY

There are two kinds of rosemary; one of which is barren, and the other has a stem with a resinous seed, known as "cachrys." The leaves have the odour of frankincense. The root, applied fresh, effects the cure of wounds, prolapsus of the rectum, condylomata, and haemorrhoids. The juice of the plant, as well as of the root, is curative of jaundice, and such diseases as require detergents; it is useful also for the sight. The seed is given in drink for inveterate diseases of the chest, and, with wine and pepper, for affections of the uterus; it acts also as an emmenagogue, and is used with meal of darnel as a liniment for gout. It acts also as a detergent upon freckles, and is used as an application in diseases which require calorifics or sudorifics, and for convulsions. The plant itself, or else the root, taken in wine, increases the milk, and the leaves and stem of the plant are applied with vinegar to scrofulous sores; used with honey, they are very useful for cough.

GUM

We have already spoken of the different kinds of gum; the better sort of each kind will be found the most effective. Gum is bad for the teeth; it tends to make the blood coagulate, and is consequently good for discharges of blood from the mouth. It is useful for burns, but is bad for diseases of the trachea. It exercises a diuretic effect, and tends to neutralize all acridities, being astringent in other respects. The gum of the bitter-almond tree, which has the most astringent properties of them all, is calorific also in its effects. Still, however, the gum of the plum, cherry, and vine is greatly preferred; all which kinds, applied topically, are productive of astringent and desiccative effects, and, used with vinegar, heal lichens upon infants. Taken in must, in doses of four oboli, they are good for inveterate coughs.

THE BRAMBLE

Nor yet has Nature destined the bramble to be only an annoyance to mankind, for she has bestowed upon it mulberries of its own, or, in other words, a nutritive aliment even for mankind. These berries are of a desiccative, astringent, nature, and are extremely useful for maladies of the gums, tonsillary glands, and generative organs. They neutralize also the venom of those most deadly of serpents, the hæmorrhoiss and the prester; and the flowers or fruit will heal wounds inflicted by scorpions, without any danger of abscesses forming. The shoots of the bramble have a diuretic effect; and the more tender ones are pounded, and the juice extracted and then dried in the sun till it has attained the consistency of honey, being considered a most excellent remedy, taken in drink or applied externally, for maladies of the mouth and eyes, discharges of blood from the mouth, quinsy, affections of the uterus, diseases of the rectum, and celiac affections. The leaves, chewed, are good for diseases of the mouth, and a topical application is made of them for running ulcers and other maladies of the head. In the cardiac disease they are similarly applied to the left breast by themselves. They are applied topically also for pains in the stomach and for prolapse of the eyes. The juice of them is used as an injection for the ears, and, in combination with cerate of roses, it heals condylomata.

Among the medicaments known as "styptics," there is none that is more efficacious than a decoction of the root of the bramble in wine, boiled down to one third. Ulcerations of the mouth and rectum are bathed with it, and fomentations of it are used for a similar purpose; indeed, it is so remarkably powerful in its effects, that the very sponges which are used become as hard as a stone.

THE TRIXAGO

We shall now add to these plants, certain vegetable productions to which the Greeks have given names belonging to trees, so that it would be doubtful whether they themselves are not trees as well.

The chamædrys[3] is the same plant that in Latin is called "trixago"; some persons, however, call it "chamædrops," and others "teucria." The leaves of it are the size of those of mint, but in their colour and indentations they resemble those of the oak. According to some, the leaves are serrated, and it was these, they say, that first suggested the idea of the saw; the flower of it borders closely upon purple. This plant is gathered in rough craggy localities, when it is replete with juice; and, whether taken internally or applied topically, it is extremely efficacious for the stings of venomous serpents, diseases of the stomach, inveterate coughs, collections of phlegm in the throat, ruptures, convulsions, and pains in the sides. It diminishes the volume of the spleen, and acts as a diuretic and emmenagogue; for which reasons it is very useful in incipient dropsy, the usual dose being a handful of the sprigs boiled down to one third in three heminæ of water. Lozenges too are made of it for the above-named purposes, by bruising it in water. In combination with honey, it heals abscesses and inveterate or sordid ulcers; a wine too is prepared from it for diseases of the chest. The juice of the leaves, mixed with oil, disperses films on the eyes; it is taken also, in vinegar, for diseases of the spleen; employed as a friction, it is of a warming nature.

THE CHAMÆSYCE

The chamæsyce[4] has leaves similar to those of the lentil, and lying close to the ground; it is found growing in dry, rocky, localities. A decoction of it in wine is remarkably useful as a liniment for improving the sight, and for dispersing cataract, cicatrizations, films, and cloudiness of the eyes. Applied in a pledget of linen, as a pessary, it allays pains in the uterus; and used topically it removes warts and excrescences of all kinds. It is very useful also for hardness of breathing.

---

3 Ground oak.
4 Or "ground fig." The *Euphorbia chamæsyce,* or annual spurge.

THE CLEMATIS ECHITES

The Greeks have other varieties also of the clematis, one of which is known as "echites"[5] or "lagine," and by some as the "little scammony." Its stems are about two feet in height, and covered with leaves; in general appearance it is not unlike scammony, were it not that the leaves are darker and more diminutive; it is found growing in vineyards and cultivated soils. It is eaten as a vegetable, with oil and salt, and acts as a laxative upon the bowels. It is taken also for dysentery, with linseed, in astringent wine. The leaves of this plant are applied with polenta for defluxions of the eyes, the part affected being first covered with a pledget of wet linen. Applied to scrofulous sores, they cause them to suppurate, and if some axle-grease is then applied, a perfect cure will be effected. They are applied also to haemorrhoids, with green oil, and are good for phthisis, in combination with honey. Taken with the food, they increase the milk in nursing women, and, rubbed upon the heads of infants, they promote the rapid growth of the hair. Eaten with vinegar, they act as an aphrodisiac.

THE MILLEFOLLIUM

The myriophyllon, by our people known as the "millefolium" has a tender stem, somewhat similar to fennel-giant ill appearance, with vast numbers of leaves, to which circumstance it is indebted for its name. It grows in marshy localities, and is remarkably useful for the treatment of wounds. It is taken in vinegar for strangury, affections of the bladder, asthma, and falls with violence; it is extremely efficacious also for tooth-ache.

In Etruria, the same name is given to a small meadowplant,[6] provided with leaves at the sides, like hairs, and particularly useful for wounds. The people of that country say that, applied with axle-grease, it will knit together and unite the tendons of oxen, when they have been accidentally severed by the plough-share.

THE APROXIS

Pythagoras makes mention, too, of a plant called aproxis, the root of which takes fire[7] at a distance, like naphtha.[8] He says too, that if the human body happens to be attacked by any disease while the cabbage is in blossom, the person, although he may have been perfectly cured, will be sensible of a recurrence of the symptoms,

---

5   Probably the *Asclepias nigra* of Linnæus, black swallow-wort.

6   Possibly the *Achillea millefolium* of Linnæus, our milfoil or yarrow. It is still said to have the property of healing wounds made by edge-tools, for which reason it is known in France as the "carpenter's plant."

7   Fée says that the only cases known of a phenomena resembling this, are those of the *Dictamnus albus*, white dittany, which attracts flame momentarily when in flower, and of the *Tropæolum majus*, or great Indian cress. He thinks, however, that there are some trees so rich in essential oil, that they might possibly ignite as readily as naphtha.

8   In ancient writers, naphtha referred to a more fluid and volatile variety of asphalt or bitumen. Pliny hesitates about including naphtha with bitumen, on account of its volatility and inflammability (TN).

every time that plant comes into blossom; a peculiarity which he attributes to it in common with wheat, hemlock, and the violet.

A PLANT GROWING ON THE HEAD OF A STATUE

It is asserted also, that a plant growing on the head of a statue, gathered in the lappet of any one of the garments, and then attached with a red string to the neck, is an instantaneous cure for head-ache.

A PLANT GROWING ON THE BANKS OF A RIVER

Any plant that is gathered before sunrise on the banks of a stream or river, due care being taken that no one sees it gathered, attached to the left arm without the patient knowing what it is, will cure a tertian fever, they say.

PLANTS THAT TAKE ROOT IN A SIEVE

Plants that take root in a sieve that has been thrown in a hedge-row, if gathered and worn upon the person by a pregnant woman, will facilitate delivery.

PLANTS GROWING UPON DUNGHILLS

A plant that has been grown upon a dungheap in a field, is a very efficacious remedy, taken in water, for quinsies.

PLANTS THAT HAVE BEEN MOISTENED WITH THE URINE OF A DOG

A plant upon which a dog has watered, torn up by the roots, and not touched with iron, is a very speedy cure for sprains.

GRAMEN

Gramen[9] is of all herbaceous productions the most common. As it creeps along the ground it throws out jointed stems, from the joints of which, as well as from the extremity of the stem, fresh roots are put forth every here and there. In all other parts of the world the leaves of it are tapering, and come to a point; but upon Mount Parnassus they resemble the leaves of the ivy, the, plant throwing out a greater number of stems than elsewhere, and bearing a blossom that is white and odoriferous. There is no vegetable production that is more grateful to beasts of burden than this, whether in a green state or whether dried and made into hay, in which last case it is sprinkled with water when given to them. It is said that on Mount Parnassus a juice is extracted from it, which is very abundant and of a sweet flavour.

In other parts of the world, instead of this juice a decoction of it is employed for closing wounds; an effect equally produced by the plant itself, which is beaten up for the purpose and attached to the part affected, thereby preventing inflammation. To the decoction wine and honey are added, and in some cases, frankincense, pepper, and myrrh, in the proportion of one third of each ingredient; after which it is boiled again in a copper vessel, when required for tooth-ache or eyes-fluxes. A decoction of the roots, in wine, is curative of griping pains in the bowels, strangury, and ulcerations of the bladder, and it disperses calculi. The seed is still more

---

9   "Grass." The *Triticum repens*, or *Paspalum dactylon* of Linnæus, our couch-grass.

Book XXIV - Medicaments Derived from the Forest Trees

powerful as a diuretic, arrests looseness and vomiting, and is particularly useful for wounds inflicted by dragons.[10] There are some authorities which give the following prescription for the cure of scrofulous sores and inflamed tumours: From one, two, or three stems, as many as nine joints must be removed, which must then be wrapped in black wool with the grease in it. The party who gathers them must do so fasting, and must then go, in the same state, to the patient's house while he is from home. When the patient comes in, the other must say to him three times, "I come fasting to bring a remedy to a fasting man"; and must then attach the amulet to his person, repeating the same ceremony three consecutive days. The variety of this plant which has seven joints is considered a most excellent amulet for the cure of head-ache. For excruciating pains in the bladder, some recommend a decoction of gramen, boiled down in wine to one half, to be taken immediately after the bath.

---

10 "Draconum." A peculiar kind of serpent.

Book XXV
Medicinal Use of Plants (I)

The more highly esteemed plants of which I am now about to speak, and which are produced by the earth for medicinal purposes solely, inspire me with admiration of the industry and laborious research displayed by the ancients. Indeed there is nothing that they have not tested by experiment or left untried; no discovery of theirs which they have not disclosed, or which they have not been desirous to leave for the benefit of posterity.

This subject has not been treated of by the writers in our own language so extensively as it deserves, eager as they have proved themselves to make enquiry into everything that is either meritorious or profitable. M. Cato, that great master in all useful knowledge, was the first, and, for a long time, the only author who treated of this branch of learning; and briefly as he has touched upon it, he has not omitted to make some mention of the remedial treatment of cattle. After him, another illustrious personage, C. Valgius, a man distinguished for his erudition, commenced a treatise upon the same subject, which he dedicated to the late Emperor Augustus, but left unfinished.

MITHRIDATES

The only person among us, at least so far as I have been able to ascertain, who had treated of this subject before the time of Valgius, was Pompeius Lenæus, the freedman of Pompeius Magnus; and it was in his day, I find, that this branch of knowledge first began to be cultivated among us.

It was to Mithridates that Asclepiades, that celebrated physician, dedicated his works, still extant, and sent them, as a substitute for his own personal attendance, when requested by that monarch to leave Rome and reside at his court. Among the other gifts of extraordinary genius with which he was endowed, Mithridates displayed a peculiar fondness for enquiries into the medical arts; and gathering items of information from all his subjects, extended, as they were, over a large proportion of the world, it was his habit to make copies of their communications, and to take notes of the results which upon experiment had been produced. These memoranda, which he kept in his private cabinet, fell into the hands of Pompeius, when he took possession of the royal treasures; who at once commissioned his freedman, Lenæus the grammarian, to translate them into the Latin language; the result of which was, that his victory was equally conducive to the benefit of the republic and of mankind at large.

GREEK WRITERS

In addition to these, there are some Greek writers who have treated of this subject, and who have been already mentioned on the appropriate occasions. Hence it is that other writers have confined themselves to a verbal description of the plants, indeed some of them have not so much as described them even, but have contented themselves for the most part with a bare recital of their names, considering it sufficient if they pointed out their virtues and properties to such as might Feel inclined to make further enquiries into the subject.

There was nothing more highly admired than an intimate knowledge of plants, in ancient times. It is long since the means were discovered of calculating beforehand, not only the day or the night, but the very hour even at which an eclipse of the sun or moon is to take place; and yet the greater part of the lower classes still remain firmly persuaded that these phenomena are brought about by compulsion, through the agency of herbs and enchantments, and that the knowledge of this art is confined almost exclusively to females. What country, in fact, is not filled with the fabulous stories about Medea of Colchis and other sorceresses, the Italian Circe in particular, who has been elevated to the rank of a divinity even? It is with reference to her, I am of opinion, that Æschylus, one of the most ancient of the poets, asserts that Italy is covered with plants endowed with potent effects, and that many writers say the same of Circeii, the place of her abode. Another great proof too that such is the case, is the fact, that the nation of the Marsi, descendants of a son of Circe, are well known still to possess the art of taming serpents.

Homer, that great parent of the learning and traditions of antiquity, while extolling the fame of Circe in many other respects, assigns to Egypt the glory of having first discovered the properties of plants, and that; too at a time when the portion of that country which is now watered by the river Nilus was not in existence, having been formed at a more recent period by the alluvions of that river. At all events, he states that numerous Egyptian plants were sent to the Helena of his story, by the wife of the king of that country, together with the celebrated nepenthes, which ensured oblivion of all sorrows and forgetfulness of the past, a potion which Helena was to administer to all mortals. The first person, however, of whom the remembrance has come down to us, as having treated with any degree of exactness on the subject of plants, is Orpheus; and next to him Musæus and Hesiod. Orpheus and Hesiod too we find speaking in high terms of the efficacy of fumigations.

In later times again, Pythagoras, that celebrated philosopher, was the first to write a treatise on the properties of plants, a work in which he attributes the origin and discovery of them to Apollo, Æsculapius, and the immortal gods in general. Democritus too, composed a similar work. Both of these philosophers had visited the magicians of Persia, Arabia, Æthiopia, and Egypt, and so astounded were the ancients at their recitals, as to learn to make assertions which transcend all belief. Xanthus, the author of some historical works, tells us, in the first of them, that a young dragon[1] was restored to life by its parent through the agency of a plant to which he gives the name of "ballis," and that one Tylon, who had been killed by a dragon, was restored to life and health by similar means. Juba too assures us that in Arabia a man was resuscitated by the agency of a certain plant. Democritus has asserted that there is a certain herb in existence, which, upon being carried thither by a bird, the name of which we have already given, has the effect, by the contact solely, of instantaneously drawing a wedge from a tree, when driven home by the shepherds into the wood.

These marvels, incredible as they are, excite our admiration nevertheless, and extort from us the admission that, making all due allowance, there is much in them that is based on truth. Hence it is too that I find it the opinion of most writers, that there is nothing which cannot be effected by the agency of plants, but that the properties of by far the greater part of them remain as yet unknown. In the number of these was Herophilus, a celebrated physician, a saying of whose is reported, to the effect that some plants may possibly exercise a beneficial influence, if only trodden under foot. Be this as it may, it has been remarked more than once, that wounds and maladies are sometimes inflamed upon the sudden approach of persons who have been journeying on foot.

MEDICINAL HERBS IN MODERN TIMES

Such was the state of medical knowledge in ancient times, wholly concealed as it was in the language of the Greeks. But the main reason why the medicinal properties of most plants remain still unknown, is the fact that they have been tested solely by rustics and illiterate people, such being the only class of persons that live in the midst of them; in addition to which, so vast is the multitude of medical men always at hand, that the public are careless of making any enquiries about them. Indeed, many of those plants, the medicinal properties of which have been discovered, are still destitute of names.

But the most disgraceful cause of all, why so few simples are known, is the fact that those even who are acquainted with them are unwilling to impart their knowledge; as though, forsooth, they should lose for ever anything that they might think fit to communicate to others! Added to all this, there is no well-ascertained method to guide us to the acquisition of this kind of knowledge; for, as to the discoveries that have been made already, they have been due, some of them, to mere accident, and others again, to say the truth, to the interposition of the Deity.

---

1   Or serpent.

Down to our own times, the bite of the mad dog, the symptoms of which are a dread of water and an aversion to every kind of beverage, was incurable; and it was only recently that the mother of a soldier who was serving in the prætorian guard, received a warning in a dream, to send her son the root of the wild rose, known as the cynorrhodos, a plant the beauty of which had attracted her attention in a shrubbery the day before, and to request him to drink the extract of it. The army was then serving in Lacetania, the part of Spain which lies nearest to Italy; and it so happened that the soldier, having been bitten by a dog, was just beginning to manifest a horror of water when his mother's letter reached him, in which she entreated him to obey the words of this divine warning. He accordingly complied with Her request, and, against all hope or expectation, his life was saved; a result which has been experienced by all who have since availed themselves of the same resource. Before this, the cynorrhodos had been only recommended by writers for one medicinal purpose; the spongy excrescences, they say, which grow in the midst of its thorns, reduced to ashes and mixed with honey, will make the hair grow again when it has been lost by alopecy. I know too, for a fact, that in the same province there was lately discovered in the land belonging to a person with whom I was staying, a stalked plant, the name given to which was dracunculus.[2] This plant, about an inch in thickness, and spotted with various colours, like a viper's skin, was generally reported to be an effectual preservative against the sting of all kinds of serpents. There is also another marvellous property belonging to it; in spring, when the serpents begin to cast their slough, it shoots up from the ground to the height of about a couple of feet, and again, when they retire for the winter it conceals itself within the earth, nor is there a serpent to be seen so long as it remains out of sight. Even if this plant did nothing else but warn us of impending danger, and tell us when to be on our guard, it could not be looked upon otherwise than as a beneficent provision made by Nature in our behalves.

It is not, however, the animals only that are endowed with certain baneful and noxious properties, but, sometimes, waters even, and localities as well. Upon one occasion, in his German campaign, Germanicus Cæsar had pitched his camp beyond the river Rhenus; the only fresh water to be obtained being that of a single spring in the vicinity of the sea-shore. It was found, however, that within two years the habitual use of this water was productive of loss of the teeth and a total relaxation of the joints of the knees; the names given to these maladies, by medical men, were "stomacace"[3] and "sceloturbe." A remedy for them was discovered, however, in the plant known as the "britannica," which is good, not only for diseases of the sinews and mouth, but for quinsy also, and injuries inflicted by serpents. This plant has dark oblong leaves and a swarthy root; the name given to the flower of it is "vibones," and if it is gathered and eaten before thunder has been heard, it will ensure

---

2   Or "little dragon." The *Arum dracunculus* of Linnæus.

3   Fée says that this disease was an "intense gastritis, productive of a fetid breath." It would seem, however, to be neither more nor less than the malady now known as "scurvy of the gums." Galen describes the "sceloturbe," as a kind of paralysis. "Stomacace" means "disease of the mouth"; "sceloturbe" "disease of the legs."

safety in every respect. The Frisii, a nation then on terms of friendship with us, and within whose territories the Roman army was encamped, pointed out this plant to our soldiers; the name given to it, however, rather surprises me, though possibly it may have been so called because the shores of Britannia are in the vicinity, and only separated by the ocean. At all events, it was not called by this name from the fact of its growing there in any great abundance, that is quite certain, for at the time I am speaking of, Britannia was still independent.

MOLY

According to Homer, the most celebrated of all plants is that, which, according to him, is known as moly[4] among the gods. The discovery of it he attributes to Mercury, who was also the first to point out its uses as neutralizing the most potent spells of sorcery. At the present day, it is said, it grows in the vicinity of Lake Pheneus, and in Cyllene, a district of Arcadia. It answers the description given of it by Homer, having a round black root, about as large as an onion, and a leaf like that of the squill; there is no difficulty experienced in taking it up. The Greek writers have delineated it as having a yellow flower, while Homer, on the other hand, has spoken of it as white.

PÆONIA

The plant known as "pæonia"[5] is the most ancient of them all. It still retains the name of him who was the first to discover it, being known also as the "pentorobus" by some, and the "glycyside" by others; indeed, this is one of the great difficulties attendant on forming an accurate knowledge of plants, that the same object has different names in different districts. It grows in umbrageous mountain localities, and puts forth a stem amid the leaves, some four fingers in height, at the summit of which are four or five heads resembling Greek nuts in appearance; enclosed in which, there is a considerable quantity of seed of a red or black colour. This plant is a preservative against the illusions practised by the Fauni in sleep. It is generally recommended to take it up at night; for if the wood-pecker of Mars[6] should perceive a person doing so, it will immediately attack his eyes in defence of the plant.

PANACES ASCLEPION

The panaces, by its very name,[7] gives assurance of a remedy for all diseases; there are numerous kinds of it, and the discovery of its properties has been attributed to

---

4   Fée devotes a couple of pages to the *vexata quæstio* of the identification of this plant, and comes to the conclusion that the Moly of Homer, mentioned on the present occasion, and of Theophrastus, Ovid, and the poets in general is only an imaginary plant; that the white-flowered Moly of Dioscorides and Galen is identical with the *Allium Dioscoridis* of Sibthorpe; and that the yellow-flowered Moly of the author of the Priapeia is not improbably the *Allium Moly* or magicum of Linnæus. Sprengel derives the name "Moly" from the Arabic, and identifies it with the *Allium nigrunm* of Linnæus.
5   The *Pæonia officinalis* of Linnæus, our Peony.
6   The black woodpecker (*Dryocopus martius*), a large woodpecker, called by Linnæus *Picus martius* (TN).
7   The Greek for "all-healing."

the gods. One of these kinds is known by the additional name of "asclepion,"[8] in commemoration of the circumstance that Æsculapius gave the name of Panacia to his daughter. The juice of it, coagulates like that of fennel-giant; the root is covered with a thick rind of a salt flavour.

After this plant has been taken up, it is a point religiously observed to fill the hole with various kinds of grain, a sort of expiation, as it were, to the earth. The juice that is imported from Macedonia is known as "bucolicon," from the fact that the herdsmen there are in the habit of collecting it as it spontaneously exudes; it evaporates, however, with the greatest rapidity. As to the other kinds, that more particularly is held in disesteem which is black and soft, such being a proof, in fact, that it has been adulterated with wax.

HYOSCYAMOS

To Hercules also is attributed the discovery of the plant known as the "apollinaris," and, among the Arabians, as the "altercum" or "altercangenum"; by the Greeks it is called "hyoscyamos."[9] There are several varieties of it; one of them, with a black seed, flowers bordering on purple, and a prickly stem, growing in Galatia. The common kind[10] again, is whiter, more shrub-like, and taller than the poppy. The seed of a third variety is similar to that of irio[11] in appearance; but they have, all of them, the effect of producing vertigo and insanity. A fourth kind again is soft, lanuginous, and more unctuous than the others; the seed of it is white, and it grows in maritime localities. It is this kind that medical men employ, as also that with a red seed. Sometimes, however, the white seed turns of a reddish colour, if not sufficiently ripe when gathered; in which case it is rejected as unfit for use; indeed, none of these plants are gathered until they are perfectly dry. Hyoscyamos, like wine, has the property of flying to the head, and consequently of acting injuriously upon the mental faculties.

LINOZOSTIS, PARTHENION, HERMUPOA, OR MERCURIALIS

Linozostis[12] or parthenion is a discovery attributed to Mercury; hence it is that among the Greeks it is known as "hermupoa" by many, while among us it is universally known as "mercurialis." There are two varieties of this plant, the male and the female, the last possessing more decided properties than the other, and having a stem a cubit in height, and sometimes branchy at the summit, with leaves somewhat narrower than those of ocimum. The joints of the stem lie close together, and the axils are numerous; the seed hangs downwards, having the joints for its basis. In the female plant the seed is very abundant, but in the male it is less so, lies closer to the joints, and is short and wreathed. In the female plant the seed hangs more loosely, and is of a white colour. The leaves of the male plant are swarthy, while

---

8 Probably the *Laserpitium hirsutum* of Lamarck. The *Echinophora tennlifolia* of Linnæus, the thin-leaved prickly parsnip, has also been named.
9 "Swine's bean" —our henbane.
10 The *Hyoscyamus niger* of Linnæus, black henbane.
11 A siliquose plant, called by the Greeks sisymbrium, winter-cresses (TN).
12 The *Mercuralis annua* of Linnæus, male and female; the herb mercury.

those of the female are whiter; the root, which is made no use of, is very diminutive.

Both of these plants grow in cultivated champaign localities. A marvellous property is mentioned as belonging to them; the male plant, they say, ensures the conception of male children, the female plant of females; a result which is ensured by drinking the juice in raisin wine, the moment after conception, or by eating the leaves, boiled with oil and salt, or raw with vinegar. Some persons, again, boil the plant in a new earthen vessel with heliotropium and two or three ears of corn, till it is thoroughly done; and say that the decoction should be taken in drink by the female, and the plant eaten for three days successively, the regimen being commenced the second day of menstruation. This done, on the fourth day she must take a bath, immediately after which the sexual congress must take place.

ACHILLEOS

Achilles too, the pupil of Chiron, discovered a plant which heals wounds, and which, as being his discovery, is known as the "achilleos." It was by the aid of this plant, they say, that he cured Telephus. Other authorities, however, assert that he was the first to discover that verdigris is an extremely useful ingredient in plasters; and hence it is that he is sometimes represented in pictures as scraping with his sword the rust from off a spear into the wound of Telephus. Some again, are of opinion that he made use of both remedies.

MELAMPODIUM, HELLEBORE OR VERATRUM

The repute of Melampus, as being highly skilled in the arts of divination, is universally known. This personage has given a name to one species of hellebore, known as the "Melampodion." Some persons, however, attribute the discovery of this plant to a shepherd of that name, who remarked that his she-goats were violently purged after browsing upon it, and afterwards cured the daughters of Prœtus of madness, by, giving them the milk of these goats. It will be the best plan, therefore, to take this opportunity of treating of the several varieties of hellebore. The two principal kinds are the white[13] and the black;[14] though, according to most authorities, this difference exists in the root only. There are some authors, however, who assure us that the leaves of the black hellebore are similar to those of the plane-tree, only darker, more diminutive, and more jagged at the edges; and who say, that the white hellebore has leaves like those of beet when first shooting, though at the same time of a more swarthy colour, with reddish veins on the under side. The stem, in both kinds, is ferulaceous, a palm in height, and covered with coats like those of the bulbs, the root, too, being fibrous like that of the onion.

The black hellebore kills horses, oxen, and swine; hence it is that those animals avoid it, while they eat the white kind. The proper time, thay say, for gathering this last, is harvest. It grows upon Mount Œta in great abundance; and the best of

---

13 Identified by Fée with the V*eratrum album* and *Veratrum nigrum* of Linnæus, species between which there is little difference.

14 Identified by Tournefort with the *Helleborus niger* of Lamarck. Littré mentions the *Helleborus orientalis* of Linnæus.

all is that found upon one spot on that mountain, in the vicinity of Pyra. Of these kinds it is the black hellebore that is known as the "melampodium"; it is used in fumigations, and for the purpose of purifying houses; cattle, too, are sprinkled with it, a certain form of prayer being repeated. This last plant, too, is gathered with more numerous ceremonies than the other; a circle is first traced around it with a sword, after which, the person about to cut it turns towards the East, and offers up a prayer, entreating permission of the gods to do so. At the same time he observes whether an eagle is in sight —for mostly while the plant is being gathered that bird is near at hand— and if one should chance to fly close at hand, it is looked upon as a presage that he will die within the year. The white hellebore, too, is gathered not without difficulty, as it is very oppressive to the head; more particularly if the precaution has not been used of eating garlic first, and of drinking wine every now and then, care being taken to dig up the plant as speedily as possible.

The best white hellebore is that which acts most speedily as a sternutatory; but it would seem to be a much more formidable plant than the black kind; more particularly if we read in the ancient authors the precautions used by those about to take it, against cold shiverings, suffocation, unnatural drowsiness, continuous hiccup or sneezing, derangements of the stomach, and vomitings, either retarded or prolonged, too sparing or in excess.

In order to secure a beneficial result, due precautions must be taken not to administer hellebore in cloudy weather; for if given at such a time, it is sure to be productive of excruciating agonies. Indeed there is no doubt that summer is a better time for giving it than winter; the body too, by an abstinence from wine, must be prepared for it seven days previously, emetics being taken on the fourth and third days before, and the patient going without his evening meal the previous day. White hellebore, too, is administered in a sweet medium, though lentils or pottage are found to be the best for the purpose. There has been a plan also, lately discovered, of splitting a radish, and inserting the hellebore in it, after which the sections are pressed together; the object being that the strength of the hellebore may be incorporated with the radish, and modified thereby.

CENTAURION OR CHIRONION

Centaury,[15] it is said, effected a cure for Chiron, on the occasion when, while handling the arms of Hercules, his guest, he let one of the arrows fall upon his foot; hence it is that by some it is called "chironion." The leaves of it are large and oblong, serrated at the edge, and growing in thick tufts from the root upwards. The stems, some three cubits in height and jointed, bear heads resembling those of the poppy. The root is large and spreading, of a reddish colour, tender and brittle, a couple of cubits in length, and full of a bitter juice, somewhat inclining to sweet.

This plant grows in rich soils upon declivities; the best in quality being that of Arcadia, Elis, Messenia, Mount Pholoë, and Mount Lycæus; it grows also upon the Alps, and in numerous other localities, and in Lycia they prepare a lycium from

---

15 Fée considers this to be the same with the *Panaces centaurion*, the greater Centaury. Littré also names the *Centaurea centaureum* of Linnæus.

it. So remarkable are its properties for closing wounds, that pieces of meat even, it is said, are soldered together, when boiled with it. The root is the only part in use, being administered in doses of two drachmæ in the several cases hereafter mentioned. If, however, the patient is suffering from fever, it should be bruised and taken in water, wine being used in other cases. A decoction of the root is equally useful for all the same purposes.

ARTEMISIA

Women too have even affected an ambition to give their name to plants; thus, for instance, Artemisia, the wife of King Mausolus, adopted the plant, which before was known by the name of "parthenis." There are some persons, however, who are of opinion that it received this surname from the goddess Artemis Ilithyia,[16] from the fact of its being used for the cure of female complaints more particularly. It is a plant with numerous branches, like those of wormwood, but the leaves of it are larger and substantial.

There are two varieties of it; one has broader[17] leaves than the other,[18] which last is of a slender form, with a more diminutive leaf, and grows nowhere but in maritime districts.

NYMPHÆA OR HERACLEON

The plant called "nymphæa," owes its name, they say, to a Nymph who died of jealousy conceived on account of Hercules, for which reason it is also known as "heracleon" by some. By other persons, again, it is called "rhopalon," from the resemblance of its root to a club. It is taken in drink by persons troubled with lascivious dreams and hence it is that those who take it in drink become impotent for some twelve days, and incapacitated for procreation. That of the first quality is found in Orchomenia and at Marathon; the people of Bœotia call it "madon," and use the seed for food. It grows in spots covered with water; the leaves[19] of it are large, and float upon the surface, while others are to be seen springing from the roots below. The flower is very similar to a lily in appearance, and after the plant has shed its blossom, the place of the flower is occupied by a head like that of the poppy. The stem is slender, and the plant is usually cut in autumn. The root, of a swarthy hue, is dried in the sun; garlic manifests a peculiar antipathy to it.

THE IBERIS

It is but very lately, too, that Servilius Democrates, one of our most eminent physicians, first called attention to a plant to which he gave the name of iberis,[20] a fanciful appellation only, bestowed by him upon this discovery of his in the verses

---

16 Artemis or Diana, the guardian of pregnant women.
17 Probably the *Artemisia chamæmelifolia*, Camomile-leaved mugwort.
18 The *A. arborescens*, the Tree-wormwood is named by Littré.
19 Identified with the *Nymphæa alba* of Linnæus, the White-flowered nymphæa.
20 Fée identifies it with the *Lepidium graminifolium* of Linnæus, Grassleaved pepperwort; Desfontaines with the *L. Iberis* of Linnæus, Bushy pepperwort. Littré gives as its synonym the *Iberis amara* of Linnæus, the White candy-tuft.

by him devoted to it. This plant is found mostly growing in the vicinity of ancient monuments, old walls, and overgrown footpaths; it is an evergreen, and its leaves are like those of nasturtium, with a stem a cubit in height, and a seed so diminutive as to be hardly perceptible; the root, too, has just the smell of nasturtium. Its properties are more strongly developed in summer, and it is only used fresh gathered; there is considerable difficulty in pounding it.

Mixed with a small proportion of axle-grease, it is extremely useful for sciatica and all diseases of the joints; the application being kept on some four hours at the utmost, when used by the male sex, and about half that time in the case of females. Immediately after its removal, the patient must take a warm bath, and then anoint the body all over with oil and wine the same operation being repeated every twenty days, so long as there are any symptoms of pain remaining. A similar method is adopted for the cure of all internal defluxions; it is never applied, however, so long as the inflammation is at its height, but only when it has somewhat abated.

PLANTS DISCOVERED BY ANIMALS

The brute animals also have been the discoverers of certain plants; among them, we will name chelidonia first of all. It is by the aid of this plant that the swallow restores the sight of the young birds in the nest, and even, as some persons will have it, when the eyes have been plucked out. There are two varieties of this plant; the larger[21] kind has a branchy stem, and a leaf somewhat similar to that of the wild parsnip, but larger. The plant itself is some two cubits in height, and of a whitish colour, that of the flower being yellow. The smaller[22] kind has leaves like those of ivy, only rounder and not so white. The juice of it is pungent, and resembles saffron in colour, and the seed is similar to that of the poppy.

These plants blossom, both of them, at the arrival of the swallow, and wither at the time of its departure. The juice is extracted while they are in flower, and is boiled gently in a copper vessel on hot ashes, with Attic honey, being esteemed a sovereign remedy for films upon the eyes. This juice is employed also, unmixed with any other substance, for the eye-salves, which from it take their name of "chelidonia."

THE ARISTOLOCHIA

In the number of the most celebrated plants is the aristolochia, which would appear to have derived its name from females in a state of pregnancy, as being ἀρίστη λοχούσαιχ.[23] Among us, however, it is known as the "malum terræ," or apple of the earth, four different varieties of it being distinguished. One of these has a root covered with tubercles of a rounded shape, and leaves of a mixed appearance, between those of the mallow and the ivy, only softer and more swarthy. The second kind is the male plant, with an elongated root some four fingers in length, and the thickness of a walking-stick. A third variety is extremely thin and long, similar to

---

21   The *Chelidonium majus* of Linnæus, the Greater celandine or swallow-wort.
22   Identified with the *Ranunculus ficaria* of Linnæus, the Pilewort, or Lesser celandine.
23   "Most excellent for pregnancy."

a young vine in appearance; it has the most strongly-marked properties of them all, and is known by the additional names of "clematitis," and "cretica." All these plants are the colour of boxwood, have a slender stem, and bear a purple flower and small berries like those of the caper; the root is the only part that is possessed of any virtues.

The aristolochia that is the most esteemed, however, is that which comes from Pontus; but whatever the soil may happen to be, the more weighty it is, the better adapted it is for medicinal purposes. The aristolochia with a round root is recommended for the stings of serpents. But in this is centred its principal reputation; applied to the uterus with raw beef, as a pessary, immediately after conception, it will ensure the birth of male issue, they say. The fishermen on the coasts of Campania give the round root the name of "poison of the earth"; and I myself have seen them pound it with lime, and throw it into the sea; immediately on which the fish flew towards it with surprising avidity, and being struck dead in an instant, floated upon the surface.

HIERABOTANE OR VERBENACA

But among the Romans there is no plant that enjoys a more extended renown than hierabotane,[24] known to some persons as "peristereon,"[25] and among us more generally as "verbenaca."[26] It is this plant that we have already mentioned as being borne in the hands of envoys when treating with the enemy, with this that the table of Jupiter is cleansed,[27] with this that houses are purified and due expiation made. There are two varieties of it; the one that is thickly covered with leaves[28] is thought to be the female plant; that with fewer leaves,[29] the male. Both kinds have numerous thin branches, a cubit in length, and of an angular form. The leaves are smaller than those of the oak, and narrower, with larger indentations. The flower is of a grey colour, and the root is long and thin. This plant is to be found growing everywhere, in level humid localities. Some persons make no distinction between these two varieties, and look upon them as identical, from the circumstance of their being productive of precisely similar effects.

The people in the Gallic provinces make use of them both for soothsaying purposes, and for the prediction of future events; but it is the magicians more particularly that give utterance to such ridiculous follies in reference to this plant. Persons, they tell us, if they rub themselves with it will be sure to gain the object of their desires; and they assure us that it keeps away fevers, conciliates friendship, and is a cure for every possible disease; they say, too, that it must be gathered about the rising of the Dog-star —but so as not to be shone upon by sun or moon— and that honey-combs and honey must be first presented to the earth by way of expiation.

---

24 "Holy plant."
25 "Pigeon plant."
26 Our "vervain." It was much used in philtres, and was as highly esteemed as the mistletoe by the people of Gaul.
27 On the occasion of the Feasts of Jupiter in the Capitol, prepared by the Septemviri.
28 The *Verbena supina* of Linnæus, Recumbent vervain.
29 The *Verbena officinalis* of Linnæus, Vervain or holy plant.

They tell us also that a circle must first be traced around it with iron; after which it must be taken up with the left hand, and raised aloft, care being taken to dry the leaves, stem, and root, separately in the shade. To these statements they add, that if the banqueting couch is sprinkled with water in which it has been steeped, merriment and hilarity will be greatly promoted thereby.

As a remedy for the stings of serpents, this plant is bruised in wine.

THE THELYPHONON OR SCORPIO

The thelyphonon is a plant known as the "scorpio" to some, from the peculiar form of its roots, the very touch of which kills the scorpion; hence it is that it is taken in drink for stings inflicted by those reptiles. If a dead scorpion is rubbed with white hellebore, it will come to life, they say. The thelyphonon is fatal to all quadrupeds, on the application of the root to the genitals. The leaf too, which bears a resemblance to that of cyclaminos, is productive of a similar effect, in the course of the same day. It is a jointed plant, and is found growing in unbrageous localities. Juice of betony or of plantago is a preservative against the venom of the scorpion.

THE XIPHION OR PHASGANION

The xiphion or phasganion, on the other hand, is found growing in humid localities. On first leaving the ground it has the appearance of a sword; the stem of it is two cubits in length, and the root is fringed like a hazel nut.

This root should always be taken up before harvest, and dried in the shade. The upper part of it, pounded with frankincense, and mixed with an equal quantity of wine, extracts fractured bones of the cranium, purulent matter in all parts of the body, and bones of serpents, when accidentally trodden upon; it is very efficacious, too, for poisons. In cases of head-ache, the head should be rubbed with hellebore, boiled and beaten up in olive oil, or oil of roses, or else with peucedanum steeped in olive oil or rose oil, and vinegar. This last plant, made lukewarm, is very good also for giddiness. It being of a heating nature, the body is rubbed with the root as a sudorific.

MEDICAMENTS FOR DISEASES OF THE EYES

It is generally thought that the greater centaury strengthens the sight, if the eyes are fomented with it steeped in water; and that by employing the juice of the smaller kind, in combination with honey, films and cloudiness may be dispersed, marks obliterated, and small flies removed which have got into the eve. It is thought also that sideritis is curative of albugo in beasts of burden. As to chelidonia, it is marvellously good for all the affections above mentioned. Root of panaces is applied, with polenta, to defluxions of the eyes; and for the purpose of keeping them down, henbane-seed is taken, in doses of one obolus, with an equal proportion of opium, in wine. Juice, too, of gentian is used as a liniment, and it sometimes forms an ingredient in the more active eye-salves, as a substitute for meconium. Euphorbia, applied in the form of a liniment, improves the eyesight, and for ophthalmia juice of plantago is injected into the eyes.

Aristolochia disperses films upon the eyes; and iberis, attached to the head with cinquefoil, is curative of defluxions and other diseases of the eyes. Verbascum is applied topically to eye-fluxes, and vervain is used for a similar purpose, with rose oil and vinegar. For the treatment of cataract and dimness of sight, cyclaminos is reduced to a pulp and divided into lozenges. Juice, too, of peucedanum, as already mentioned, mixed with meconium and oil of roses, is good for the sight, and disperses films upon the eyes. Psyllion, applied to the forehead, arrests eye-fluxes.

HEMLOCK

Hemlock,[30] too, is a poisonous plant, rendered odious by the use made of it by the Athenian people, as an instrument of capital punishment; still, however, as it is employed for many useful purposes, it must not be omitted. It is the seed that is noxious, the stalk being eaten by many people, either green, or cooked in the saucepan. This stem is smooth, jointed like a reed, of a swarthy hue, often as much as two cubits in height, and branchy at the top. The leaves are like those of coriander, only softer, and possessed of a powerful odour. The seed is more substantial than that of anise, and the root is hollow and never used. The seed and leaves are possessed of refrigerating properties; indeed, it is owing to these properties that it is so fatal, the cold chills with which it is attended commencing at the extremities. The great remedy for it, provided it has not reached the vitals, is wine, which is naturally of a warming tendency; but if it is taken in wine. it is irremediably fatal.

A juice is extracted from the leaves and flowers; for it is at the time of its blossoming that it is in its full vigour. The seed is crushed, and the juice extracted from it is left to thicken in the sun, and then divided into lozenges. This preparation proves fatal by coagulating the blood —another deadly property which belongs to it; and hence it is that the bodies of those who have been poisoned by it are covered with spots. It is sometimes used in combination with water as a medium for diluting certain medicaments. An emollient poultice is also prepared from this juice, for the purpose of cooling the stomach; but the principal use made of it is as a topical application, to check eye-fluxes in summer, and to allay pains in those organs. It is employed also as an ingredient in eye-salves, and is used for arresting fluxes in other parts of the body; the leaves, too, have a soothing effect upon all kinds of pains and tumours, and upon eye-fluxes.

Anaxilaüs makes a statement to the effect, that if the mamillæ are rubbed with hemlock (luring virginity, they will always be hard and firm; but a better-ascertained fact is, that applied to the breasts, it dries up the milk in women who recently delivered; as also that, applied to the testicles at the age of puberty, it acts most effectually as an anti-aphrodisiac. As to those cases in which it is recommended to take it internally as a remedy, I shall, for my own part, decline to mention them. The most powerful hemlock is that grown at Susa, in Parthia, the next best being

---

30 "Cicuta." Identified with the *Conium maculatum* of Linnæus. It grows in the vicinity of Athens, and probably formed the basis of the poisons with which that volatile people "recompensed," as Fée remarks, the virtues and exploits of their philosophers and generals. Socrates, Potion, and Philopœmen, are said to have been poisoned with hemlock.

the produce of Laconia, Crete, and Asia. In Greece, the hemlock of the finest quality is that of Megara, and next to it, that of Attica.

PREPARATIONS FOR TREATING OFFENSIVE BREATH

We shall also here make mention of certain preparations for the cure of offensive breath —a most noisome inconvenience. For this purpose, leaves of myrtle and lentisk are taken in equal proportions, with one half the quantity of Syrian nut-galls; they are then pounded together and sprinkled with old wine, and the composition is chewed in the morning. In similar cases, also, ivy berries are used, in combination with cassia and myrrh; these ingredients being mixed, in equal proportions, with wine.

For offensive odours of the nostrils, even though attended with carcinoma, the most effectual remedy is seed of dracontium beaten up with honey. An application of hyssop has the effect of making bruises disappear. Brand marks in the face are healed by rubbing them with mandragora.

Book XXVI
Medicinal Use of Plants (II)

NEW SKIN DISEASES

The face of man has recently been sensible of new forms of disease, unknown in ancient times, not only to Italy, but to almost the whole of Europe. Still, however, they have not as yet extended to the whole of Italy, nor have they made any very great inroads in Illyricum, Gaul, or Spain, or indeed any other parts, to so great an extent as in Rome and its environs. Though unattended with pain, and not dangerous to life, these diseases are of so loathsome a nature, that any form of death would be preferable to them.

THE NATURE OF LICHEN

The most insupportable of all these diseases is the one which, after its Greek appellation, is known to us as "lichen."[1] In consequence, however, of its generally making its first appearance at the chin, the Latin's, by way of joke, originally —so prone are mankind to make a jest of the misfortunes of others— gave it the name of "mentagra";[2] an appellation which has since become established in general use. In many cases, however, this disease spreads over the interior of the mouth, and takes possession of the whole face, with the sole exception of the eyes; after which, it passes downwards to the neck, breast, and hands, covering them with foul furfuraceous eruptions.

This curse was unknown to the ancients, and in the times of our fathers even, having first entered Italy in the middle of the reign of the Emperor Tiberius

---

1   Probably as Littré suggests, a peculiar form of elephantiasis, the leprosy of the middle ages.
2   The "chin disease"; from "mentum," the "chin."

Claudius Cæsar; where it was introduced from Asia, in which country it had lately made its appearance, by a member of the equestrian order at Rome, a native of Perusiun, secretary to the quæstor. The disease, however, did not attack either females or slaves, nor yet the lower orders, or, indeed, the middle classes, but only the nobles, being communicated even by the momentary contact requisite for the act of salutation. Many of those who persevered in undergoing a course of remedial treatment, though cured of the disease, retained scars upon the body more hideous even than the malady itself; it being treated with cauteries, as it was certain to break out afresh, unless means were adopted for burning it out of the body by cauterizing to the very bone.

As to the treatment of lichen, so noisome a disease as it is, we shall here give a number of additional remedies for it, gathered from all quarters, although those already described are by no means few in number. For the cure of lichen plantago is used, pounded, cinquefoil also, root of albucus in combination with vinegar, the young shoots of the fig-tree boiled in vinegar, or roots of marsh-mallow boiled down to one-fourth with glue and vinegar. The sores are rubbed also with pumice, and then fomented with root of rumex bruised in vinegar, or with scum of viscus kneaded up with lime. A decoction, too, of tithymalos with resin is highly esteemed for the same purpose.

But to all these remedies the plant known as "lichen," from its efficacy as a cure, is held in preference. It is found growing among rocks, and has a single broad leaf[3] near the root. and a single long stem, with small leaves hanging from it. This plant has the property also of effacing brand marks, being beaten up with honey for that purpose. There is another kind of lichen also, which adheres entirely to rocks, like moss, and which is equally used as a topical application. The juice of it, dropped into wounds, or applied to abscesses, has the property of arresting haemorrhage; mixed with honey, it is curative of jaundice, the face and tongue being rubbed with it. Under this mode of treatment, the patient is recommended to wash in salt water, to anoint himself with oil of almonds, and to abstain from garden vegetables. For the cure of lichen, root of thapsia is also used, bruised in honey.

ELEPHANTIASIS

Elephantiasis was unknown in Italy before the time of Pompeius Magnus. This malady, too, like those already mentioned, mostly makes its first appearance in the face. In its primary form it bears a considerable resemblance to a small lentil upon the nose; the skin gradually dries up all over the body, is marked with spots of various colours, and presents an unequal surface, being thick in one place, thin in another, indurated every here and there, and covered with a sort of rough scab. At a later period, the skin assumes a black hue, and compresses the flesh upon the bones, the fingers and toes becoming swollen.

This disease was originally peculiar to Egypt. Whenever it attacked the kings of that country, it was attended with peculiarly fatal effects to the people, it being

---

3   Identified by Fée with the *Marchantia polymorpha* of Linnæus, Common Marchantia, or Fountain liverwort, the male plant.

the practice to temper their sitting-baths with human blood, for the treatment of the disease.

THE OLD SYSTEM OF MEDICINE

The remedies which I am here describing, are those which were universally employed in ancient times, Nature herself, so to say, making up the medicines; indeed, for a long time these were the only medicines employed.

Hippocrates, it is well known, was the first to compile a code of medical precepts, a thing which he did with the greatest perspicuity, as his treatises, we find, are replete with information upon the various plants. No less is the information which we gain from the works of Diocles of Carystus, second only in reputation, as well as date, to Hippocrates. The same, too, with reference to the works of Praxagoras, Chrysippus, and, at a later period, Erasistratus of Cos. Herophilus too, though himself the founder of a more refined system of medicine, was extremely profuse of his commendations of the use of simples. At a later period, however, experience, our most efficient instructor in all things, medicine in particular, gradually began to be lost sight of in mere words and verbiage; it being found, in fact, much more agreeable to sit in schools, and to listen to the talk of a professor, than to go a simpling in the deserts, and to be searching for this plant or that at all the various seasons of the year.

THE NEW SYSTEM OF MEDICINE – ASCLEPIADES

Still, however, the ancient theories remained unshaken, based as they were upon the still existing grounds of universally acknowledged experience; until, in the time of Pompeius Magnus, Asclepiades, a professor of rhetoric, who considered himself not sufficiently repaid by that pursuit, and whose readiness and sagacity rendered him better adapted for any other than forensic practice, suddenly turned his attention to the medical art. Having never practised medicine, and being totally unacquainted with the nature of remedies —a knowledge only to be acquired by personal examination and actual experience— as a matter of course, he was obliged to renounce all previously-established theories, and to trust rather to his flowing periods and his well-studied discourses, for gaining an influence upon the minds of his audience.

Reducing the whole art of medicine to an estimation solely of primary causes, he made it nothing but a merely conjectural art, and established it as his creed, that there are five great principles of treatment for all diseases in common: diet, use or non-use of wine, frictions, exercise on foot, and exercise in a carriage or on horseback. As every one perceived that each of these methods of treatment lay quite within his own reach, all, of course, with the greatest readiness gave their assent, willing as they were to believe that to be true which was so easy of acquisition; and hence it was that he attracted nearly all the world about him, as though he had been sent among mankind on a special mission from heaven.

In addition to this, he had a wonderful tact in gaining the full confidence of his patients; sometimes he would make then a promise of wine, and then seize the opportune moment for administering it, while on other occasions, again, he would prescribe cold water; indeed, as Herophilus, among the ancients, had been the first to enquire into the primary causes of disease, and Cleophantus had brought into notice the treatment of diseases by wine, so did Asclepiades, as we learn from M. Varro, prefer to be indebted for his surname and repute to the extensive use made by him of cold water as a remedy. He employed also various other soothing remedies for his patients; thus, for instance, it was he that introduced swinging beds, the motion of which might either lull the malady, or induce sleep, as deemed desirable. It was he, too, that brought baths into such general use —a method of treatment that was adopted with the greatest avidity— in addition to numerous other modes of treatment of a pleasant and soothing nature. By these means he acquired a great professional reputation, and a no less extended fame.

There is, however, one thing, and one thing only, at which we have any ground for indignation, the fact, that a single individual, and he belonging to the most frivolous nation[4] in the world, a man born in utter indigence, should all on a sudden, and that, too, for the sole purpose of increasing his income, give a new code of medical laws to mankind; laws, however, be it remembered, which have been annulled by numerous authorities since his day. The success of Asclepiades was considerably promoted by many of the usages of ancient medicine, repulsive in their nature, and attended with far too much anxiety; thus, for instance, it was the practice to cover up the patient with vast numbers of clothes, and to adopt every possible method of promoting the perspiration; to order the body to be roasted before a fire; or else to be continually sending the patient on a search for sunshine, a thing hardly to be found in a showery climate like that of this city of ours; or rather, so to say, of the whole of Italy, so prolific as it is of fogs and rain. It was to remedy these inconveniences, that he introduced the use of hanging baths, an invention that was found grateful to invalids in the very highest degree.

In addition to this, he modified the tortures which had hitherto attended the treatment of certain maladies; as in quinsy for instance, the cure of which before his time had been usually effected by the introduction of an instrument into the throat. He condemned, and with good reason, the indiscriminate use of emetics, which till then had been resorted to in; most extraordinary degree. He disapproved also of the practice of administering internally potions that are naturally injurious to the stomach, a thing that may truthfully be pronounced of the greater part of them. Indeed it will be as well to take an early opportunity of stating what are the medicaments which act beneficially upon the stomach.

REMARKS AGAINST SUPERSTITIONS

But above all things, it was the follies of magic more particularly that contributed so essentially to his success —follies which had been carried to such a pitch as to destroy all confidence in the remedial virtues of plants. Thus, for instance, it was stoutly maintained that by the agency of the plant aethiopis rivers and standing waters could be dried up, and that by the its very touch all bars and doors might be opened; that if the plant achænis were thrown into the ranks of the enemy it

---

4   Asia Minor. Asclepiades was a native of Prusa in Bithynia.

COUGH

Of all diseases of the chest, cough is the one that is the most oppressive. For the cure of this malady, root of panaces in sweet wine is used, and in cases where it is attended with spitting of blood, juice of henbane. Henbane, too, used as a fumigation, is good for cough; and the same with scordotis,[6] mixed with nasturtium and dry resin, beaten up with honey; employed by itself also, scordotis facilitates expectoration, a property which is equally possessed by the greater centaury, even where the patient is troubled with spitting of blood; for which last juice of plantago is very beneficial. Betony, taken in doses of three oboli in water, is useful for purulent or bloody expectorations; root also of persolata, in doses of one drachma, taken with eleven pine-nuts; and juice of peucedanum.

CHALCETUM

Chalcetum[7] also is the name of a plant, which is pounded with grape husks and applied topically, for the cure of liver complaints. Root of betony acts as a gentle emetic, taken in the same way as hellebore, in doses of four drachmæ in raisin wine or honied wine. Hyssop, too, is beaten up with honey for similar purposes; but it is more efficacious if nasturtium or irio is taken first.

MEDICAMENTS FOR DISEASES OF THE BELLY

But it is the belly, for the gratification of which the greater part of mankind exist, that causes the most suffering to man. Thus, for instance, at one time it will not allow the aliments to pass, while at another it is unable to retain them. Sometimes, again, it either cannot receive the food, or, if it can, cannot digest it; indeed, such are the excesses practised at the present day, that it is through his aliment, more than anything else, that man hastens his end. This receptacle, more troublesome to us than any other part of the body, is ever craving, like some importunate creditor, and makes its calls repeatedly in the day. It is for its sake, more particularly, that avarice is so insatiate, for its sake that luxury is so refined, for its sake that men voyage to the shores even of the Phasis, for its sake that the very depths of the ocean are ransacked. And yet, with all this, no one ever gives a thought how abject is the condition of this part of our body, how disgusting the results of its action upon what it has received! No wonder then, that the belly should have to be indebted to the aid of medicine in the very highest degree

Scordotis, fresh-gathered and beaten up, in doses of one drachma, with wine, arrests flux of the bowels; an effect equally produced by a decoction of it taken

---

5   A magic herb (TN).
6   Teucrium scordium (TN).
7   C. Bauhin identifies it with the *Valeriana locusta* of Linnæus, Corn valerian, Corn-salad, or Lamb's lettuce. Fée considers its identity as still unknown.

in drink. Polemonia, too, is given in wine for dysentery, or two fingers' length of root of verbascum, in water; seed of nymlphæa heraclia, in wine; the upper root of xiphion, in doses of one drachma, in vinegar; seed of plantago, beaten up in wine; plantago itself boiled in vinegar, or else a pottage of alica mixed with the juice of the plant; plantago boiled with lentils; plantago dried and powdered, and sprinkled in drink, with parched poppies pounded; juice of plantago, used as an injection, or taken in drink; or betony taken in wine heated with a red-hot iron.

SCAMMONY

Scammony,[8] also, is productive of derangement of the stomach. It carries off bile, and acts strongly as a purgative upon the bowels; unless, indeed, aloes are added, in the proportion of two drachmæ of aloes to two oboli of scammony. The drug thus called is the juice of a plant that is branchy from the root, and has unctuous, white, triangular, leaves, with a solid, moist root, of a nauseous flavour; it grows in rich white soils. About the period of the rising of the Dog-star, an excavation is made about the root, to let the juice collect; which done, it is dried in the sun and divided into tablets. The root itself, too, or the outer coat of it, is sometimes dried. The scammony most esteemed is that of Colophon, Mysia, and Priene. In appearance it ought to he smooth and shiny, and as much like bull glue as possible; it should present a fungous surface also, covered with minute holes; should melt with the greatest rapidity, have a powerful smell, and be sticky like gum. When touched with the tongue, it should give out a white milky liquid; it ought also to be extremely light, and to turn white when melted.

This last feature is recognized in the spurious scammony also, a compound of meal of fitches and juice of marine tithymalos, which is mostly imported from Judea, and is very apt to choke those who use it. The difference may be easily detected, however, by the taste, as tithymalos imparts a burning sensation to the tongue. To be fully efficacious, scammony should be two years old; before or after that age it is useless. It has been prescribed to be taken by itself also, in doses of four oboli, with hydromel and salt; but the most advantageous mode of using it is in combination with aloes, care being taken to drink honied wine the moment it begins to operate. The root, too, is boiled down in vinegar to the consistency of honey, and the decoction used as a liniment for leprosy. The head is also rubbed with this decoction, mixed with oil, for head-ache.

TITHYMALOS CHARACIAS

The tithymalos is called by our people the "milk plant," and by some persons the "goat lettuce." They say, that if characters are traced upon the body with the milky juice of this plant, and powdered with ashes, when dry, the letters will be perfectly visible; an expedient which has been adopted before now by intriguers, for the purpose of communicating with their mistresses, in preference to a cor-

---

8   The produce of the *Convolvulus scammonia* of Linnæus, the Scammony bind-weed. The scammony of Aleppo is held in the highest esteem, and is very Valuable. That of Smyrna also is largely imported.

respondence by letter. There are numerous varieties of this plant.⁹ The first kind has the additional name of "characias," and is generally looked upon as the male plant. Its branches are about a finger in thickness, red and full of juice, five or six in number, and a cubit in length. The leaves near the root are almost exactly those of the olive, and the extremity of the stem is surmounted with a tuft like that of the bulrush; it is found growing in rugged localities near the sea-shore. The seed is gathered in autumn, together with the tufts, and after being dried in the sun, is beaten out and put by for keeping. As to the juice, the moment the down begins to appear upon the fruit, the branches are broken off and the juice of them is received upon either meal of fitches or else figs, and left to dry therewith. Five drops are as much as each fig ought to receive; and the story is, that if a dropsically patient eats one of these figs he will have as many motions as the fig has received drops. While the juice is being collected, due care must be taken not to let it touch the eyes. From the leaves, pounded, a juice is also extracted, but not of so useful a nature as the other kind; a decoction, too, is made from the branches.

The seed also is used, being boiled with honey and made up into purgative pills. These seeds are sometimes inserted in hollow teeth with wax; the teeth are rinsed too, with a decoction of the root in wine or oil. The juice is used externally for lichens, and is taken internally both as an emetic and to promote alpine evacuation; in other respects, it is prejudicial to the stomach. Taken in drink, with the addition of salt, it carries off pituitous humours; and in combination with saltpeter, removes bile. In cases where it is desirable that it should purge by stool, it is taken with oxycrate, but where it is wanted to act as an emetic, with raisin wine or hydromel; three oboli being a middling dose. The best method, however, of using it, is to eat the prepared figs above-mentioned, just after taking food. In taste, it is slightly burning to the throat; indeed it is of so heating a nature, that, applied externally by itself, it raises blisters on the flesh, like those caused by the action of fire.

REMEDIES FOR GRIPING PAINS IN THE BOWELS

Every kind of panaces¹⁰ is curative of gripings in the bowels; as also betony, except in those cases where they arise from indigestion. Juice of peucedanum is good for flatulency, acting powerfully as a carminative; the same is the case, also, with root of acoron and with daucus, eaten like lettuce as a salad. Ladanum of Cyprus, taken in drink, is curative of intestinal affections; and a similar effect is produced by powdered gentian, taken in warm water, in quantities about as large as a bean. For the same purpose, plantago is taken in the morning, in doses of two spoonfuls, with one spoonful of poppy in four cyathi of wine, due care being taken that it is not old wine. It is given, too, at the last moment before going to sleep, and with the addition of nitre or polenta, if a considerable time has elapsed since the last meal. For colic, an injection of the juice is used, one hemina at a time, even in cases where fever has supervened.

---

9   Known to us by the general name of Euphorbia of Spurge.
10   A plant supposed to cure all diseases; panacea, heal-all. It is a species of Opoponax.

SILAUS

Silaus[11] is a plant which grows in running streams with a gravelly bed. It bears some resemblance to parsley, and is a cubit in height. It is cooked in the same manner as the acid vegetables, and is of great utility for affections of the bladder. In cases where that organ is affected with eruptions, it is used in combination with root of panaces, a plant which is otherwise bad for the bladder.

SCORDION

Scordion reduces swellings of the testicles. Henbane is curative of diseases of the generative organs. Strangury is cured by juice of peucedanum, taken with honey; as also by the seed of that plant. Agaric is also used for the same purpose, taken in doses of three oboli in one cyathus of old wine; root of trefoil, in doses of two drachmæ in wine; and root or seed of daucus, in doses of one drachma. For the cure of sciatica, the seed and leaves of erythrodanum are used, pounded; panaces, taken in drink; polemonia, employed as a friction; and leaves of aristolochia, in the form of a decoction. Agaric, taken in doses of three oboli in one cyathus of old wine, is curative of affections of the tendon known as "platys" and of pains in the shoulders. Cinquefoil is either taken in drink or applied topically for the cure of sciatica; a decoction of scammony is used also, with barley meal; and the seed of either kind of hypericon is taken in wine.

For diseases of the anus and for excoriations plantago is remarkably efficacious; for condylomata, cinquefoil; and for prolaps of the rectum, root of cyclaminos, applied in vinegar. The blue anagallis reduces prolapse of the rectum, while, on the contrary, that with a red flower has a tendency to bear it down. Cotyledons is a marvellous cure for condylomatous affections and haemorrhoids; and root of acoron, boiled in wine and beaten up, is a good application for swelling of the testicles. According to what Cato says, those who carry about them Pontic wormwood, will never experience chafing between the thighs.

APHRODISIACS AND ANTI-APHRODISIACS

Nymphæa heraclia acts most powerfully as an anti-aphrodisiac; the same too if taken once every forty days in drink. Taken in drink fasting, or eaten with the food, it effectually prevents the recurrence of libidinous dreams. The root too, used in the form of a liniment and applied to the generative organs, not only represses all prurient desires, but arrests the seminal secretions as well; for which reason, it is said to have a tendency to make flesh and to improve the voice.

The upper part of the root of xiphion, taken in wine, acts as an aphrodisiac. The same is the case too with the wild crethmos, or agrios as it is called, and with holmium, beaten up with polenta.

---

11   Hardouin thinks that it is the *Apium graveolens* of Linnæus, Smallage; but at the present day it is generally identified with the *Peucedanum silaus* of Linnæus, the Meadow sulphurwort, or saxifrage.

THE ORCHIDS OR SERAPIAS

But there are few plants of so marvellous a nature as the orchids[12] or serapias, a vegetable production with leaves like those of the leek, a stem a palm in height, a purple flower, and a twofold root, formed of tuberosities which resemble the testicles in appearance. The larger of these tuberosities, or, as some say, the harder of the two. Taken in water, is provocative of lust; while the smaller, or, in other words, the softer one, taken in goat's milk, acts as an anti-aphrodisiac. Some persons describe this plant as having a leaf like that of the squill, only smoother and softer, and a prickly stem. The roots heal ulcerations of the mouth, and are curative of pituitous discharges from the chest; taken in wine they act astringently upon the bowels.

Satyrion is also a powerful stimulant. There are two kinds of it; the first[13] has leaves like those of the olive, but longer, a stem four fingers in length, a purple flower, and a double root, resembling the human testicles in shape. This root swells and increases in volume one year, and resumes its original size the next. The other kind is known as the "satyrios orchis," and is supposed to be the female plant. It is distinguished from the former one by the distance between its joints, and its more branchy and shrub-like form. The root is employed in philtres; it is mostly found growing near the sea. Beaten up and applied with polenta, or by itself, it heals tumours and various other affections of the generative organs. The root of the first kind, administered in the milk of a farm-yard sheep, causes erections; taken in water it produces a contrary effect.

SATYRION

The Greeks give the name of "satyrion"[14] to a plant with red leaves like those of the lily, but smaller, not more than three of them making their appearance above ground. The stem, they say, is smooth and bare and a cubit in length, and the root double; the lower part, which is also the larger, promoting the conception of male issue, the upper or smaller part, that of female.

They distinguish also another kind of satyrion, by the name of "erythraïcon"[15] it has seed like that of the vitex,[16] only larger, smooth, and hard; the root, they say, is covered with a red rind, and is white within and of a sweetish taste; it is mostly found in mountainous districts. The root, we are told, if only held in the hand, acts as a powerful aphrodisiac, and even more so, if it is taken in rough, astringent wine. It is administered in drink, they say, to rams and he-goats when inactive and sluggish; and the people of Sarmatia are in the habit of giving it to their stallions when

---

12 Identified by Littré with the *Orchids undulatifolia*, and by Fée with the *Orchis morio* of Linnæus, the Female orchis, or Female fool-stones.

13 Identified by Desfontaines with the *Orchis pyramidalis*. and by Fée with the *O. papilionacea* of Linnæus.

14 Littré identifies it with the *Aceras anthropophora* of Linnæus; Desfontaines with the *Orchis bifolia*, the Butterfly orchis. The *Iris florentina* of Linnæus has also been named; but, though with some doubt, Fée is inclined to prefer the *Tulipa Clusiana*, or some other kind of tulip.

15 Mostly identified with the *Erythronium dens canis* of Linnæus.

16 The chaste-tree, Abraham's balm: *Vitex agnus castus* of Linnæus (TN).

fatigued with covering, a defect to which they give the name of "prosedamum." The effects of this plant are neutralized by the use of hydromel or lettuces.

MALADIES WHICH ATTACK THE WHOLE OF THE BODY

Having now finished the detail of the diseases which are perceptible in individual parts of the body, we shall proceed to speak of those which attack the whole of the body. The following I find mentioned as general remedies; in preference to anything else, an infusion of dodecatheos,[17] should be taken in drink, and then the roots of the several kinds of panaces, in maladies of long standing more particularly; seed, too, of panaces should be used for intestinal complaints. For all painful affections of the body we find juice of scordium recommended, as also that of betony; this last, taken in a potion, is particularly excellent for removing a wan and leaden hue of the skin, and for improving its general appearance.

ONOTHERAS OR ONEAR

Among the various evils by which the whole of the body in common is afflicted, that of wakefulness is the most common. Among the remedies for it we find panaces mentioned, clymenus, and aristolochia, the odour of the plant being inhaled and the head rubbed with it. Aizoüm, or houseleek, is beneficial, wrapped in black cloth and placed beneath the pillow, without the patient being aware of it. The onotheras[18] too, or onear, taken in wine, has certain exhilarating properties; it has leaves like those of the almond tree, a rose-coloured flower, numerous branches, and a long root, with a vinous smell when dried; an infusion of this root has a soothing effect upon wild beasts even.

MEDICAMENTS FOR JAUNDICE

It is upon the eyes in particular that jaundice is productive of so remarkable an effect; the bile penetrating between the membranes, so extremely delicate as they are and so closely united. Hippocrates tells us that the appearance of jaundice on or after the seventh day in fevers is a fatal symptom; but I am acquainted with some instances in which the patients survived after having been reduced to this apparently hopeless state. We may remark also, that jaundice sometimes comes on without fever supervening. It is combated by taking the greater centaury in drink; agaric, in doses of three oboli in old wine; or leaves of vervain, in doses of three oboli, taken for four consecutive days in one hemina of mulled wine. But the most speedy cure of all is effected by using juice of cinquefoil, in doses of three cyathi, with salt and honey. Root of cyclaminos is also taken in drink in doses of three drachmæ, the patient sitting in a warm room free from all cold and draughts, the infusion expelling the bile by its action as a sudorific.

Leaves of tussilago are also used in water for this purpose; the seed of either kind of linozostis, sprinkled in the drink, or made into a decoction with chickpease or wormwood; hyssop berries taken in water; the plant lichen, all other veg-

---

17 An herb, so called after the twelve greater gods; perhaps *Primula vulgaris*, Linneo (TN).

18 Identified with the *Epilobium roseum* of Linnæus. Rose-coloured willow-herb.

etables being carefully abstained from while it is being used; polythrix, taken in wine; and struthion, in honied wine.

REMEDIES FOR ABSCESSES AND INFLAMMATIONS

Abscesses and inflammations are cured by an application of leaves of argemonia. For indurations and gatherings of all descriptions a decoction of vervain or cinquefoil in vinegar is used; leaves or root of verbascum; a liniment made of wine and hyssop; root of acoron, a decoction of it being used as a fomentation; or else aizoüm. Contusions also, hard tumours, and fistulous abscesses are treated with illecebra.[19]

All kinds of foreign substances which have pierced the flesh are extracted by using leaves of tussilago, daucus, or seed of leontopodium pounded in water with polenta. To suppurations, leaves of pycnocomon are applied, beaten up with polenta, or else the seed of that plant, or orchis. An application of root of satyrion is said to be a most efficacious remedy for deep-seated diseases of the bones. Corrosive ulcers and all kinds of gatherings are treated with sea-weed, used before it has dried. Root, too, of alcima disperses gatherings.

MEDICAMENTS FOR HAEMORRHAGE

The red seed of the plant called "pæmonia"[20] arrests haemorrhage; the root also is possessed of similar properties. But it is clymenus that should be employed, when there are discharges of blood at the mouth or nostrils, from the bowels, or from the uterus. In such cases, lysimachia also is taken in drink, applied topically, or introduced into the nostrils; or else seed of plantago, or cinquefoil, is taken in drink, or employed in the form of a liniment. Hemlock seed is introduced into the nostrils, for discharges of blood there, or else it is pounded and applied in water; aizoüm also, and root of astragalus. Ischæmon and achillea likewise arrest haemorrhage.

MEDICAMENTS FOR RUPTURES AND SPRAINS

For ruptures, sprains, and falls with violence, the greater centaury is used; root of gentian pounded or boiled; juice of betony —this last being employed also for ruptures produced by straining the vocal organs or sides— panaces; scordium; or aristolochia taken in drink. For contusions and falls, agaric is taken, in doses of two oboli, in three cyathi of honied wine, or if there are symptoms of fever, hydromel; the verbascum, also, with a golden flower; root of acoron the several varieties of Aizoüm, the juice of the larger kind being particularly efficacious; juice of symphytum, or a decoction of the root of that plant; daucus, unboiled; erysithales, a plant with a yellow flower and a leaf like that of acanthus, taken in wine; chamærops; irio, taken in pottage.

---

19 Sedum acre, commonly known as the goldmoss stonecrop, mossy stonecrop, goldmoss sedum, biting stonecrop and wallpepper (TN).
20 Our peony.

MEDICAMENTS FOR WARTS AND APPLICATIONS FOR THE REMOVAL OF SCARS

Argemonia with vinegar, or root of batrachion, removes warts; this last having the effect also of bringing off malformed nails. The juice or the leaves, applied topically, of either kind of linozostis, remove warts. All the varieties of tithymalos are efficacious for the removal of every kind of wart, as also of hangnails and wens. Ladanum imparts a fresh colour and seemly appearance to scars.

The traveller who carries artemisia attached to his person, or elelisphacus,[21] will never be sensible of lassitude, it is said.

REMEDIES FOR FEMALE DISEASES

One great remedy for all female diseases in common, is the black seed of the herbaceous plant pæonia, taken in hydromel; the root also is an effectual emmenagogue. Seed of panaces, mixed with wormwood, acts as an emmenagogue and as a sudorific; the same, too, with scordotis, taken internally or applied topically. Betony, in doses of one drachma to three cyathi of wine, is taken for various affections of the uterus, as also directly after child-birth. Excessive menstruation is arrested by a pessary of achillea, or else a sitting-bath composed of a decoction of that plant. Seed of henbane in wine is used as a liniment for diseases of the breasts, and the root is employed in the form of a plaster for uterine affections; chelidonia, too, is applied to the breasts.

Roots of panaces, applied as a pessary, bring away the after-birth and the dead fœtus, and the plant itself, taken in wine, or used as a pessary with honey, acts as a detergent upon the uterus. Polemonia, taken in wine, brings away the after-birth; used as a fumigation, it is good for suffocations of the uterus. Juice of the smaller centaury, taken in drink, or employed as a fomentation, acts as an emmenagogue. The root also of the larger centaury, similarly used, is good for pains in the uterus; scraped and used as a pessary, it expels the dead fœtus. For pains of the uterus, plantago is applied as a pessary, in wool, and for hysterical suffocations, it is taken in drink. But it is dittany that is of the greatest efficacy in cases of this description; it acts as an emmenagogue, and is an expellent of the fœtus when dead or lying transversely in the uterus. In these cases the leaves of it are taken, in doses of one obolus, in water; indeed so active is it in its effects that ordinarily it is forbidden to be introduced into the chamber of a woman lying-in. Not only is it thus efficacious when taken in drink, but even when applied topically or used as a fumigation. Bastard-dittany possesses pretty nearly the same virtues, but it acts as an emmenagogue also, boiled in doses of one denarius in unmixed wine. Aristolochia, however, is employed for a greater number of purposes; in combination with myrrh and pepper, either taken in drink or used as a pessary, it acts as a powerful emmenagogue, and brings away the dead fœtus and the after-birth. This plant, the smaller kind in particular, used either as a fomentation, fumigation, or pessary, acts as a preventive of prolapse of the uterus.

Hysterical suffocations and irregularities of the menstrual discharge are treated with agaric, taken in doses of three oboli, in one cyathus of old wine; vervain is

---

21 A kind of sage (TN).

used also in similar cases, as a pessary, with fresh hog's lard; or else antirrhinum,[22] with rose oil and honey. Root of Thessalian nymphæa, used as a pessary, is curative of pains in the uterus; taken in red wine, it arrests uterine discharges. Root of cyclaminos, on the other hand, taken in drink and employed as a pessary, acts as an emmenagogue; a decoction of it, used as a sitting-bath, cures affections of the bladder. Cissanthemos,[23] taken in drink, brings away the after-birth, and is curative of diseases of the uterus. The upper part of the root of xiphion, taken in doses of one drachma, in vinegar, promotes menstruation. A fumigation of burnt peucedanum has a soothing effect in cases of hysterical suffocation. Psyllion, taken in the proportion of one drachma to three cyathi of hydromel, is particularly good for promoting the lochial discharge. Seed of mandragora, taken in drink, acts as a detergent upon the uterus; the juice, employed in a pessary, promotes menstruation and expels the dead fetus. The seed of this plant, used with live sulphur, arrests menstruation when in excess; while batrachion, on the other hand, acts as an emmenagogue. This last plant is either used as an article of food, or is taken in drink; in a raw state, as already stated, it has a burning flavour; but when cooked, the taste of it is greatly improved by the addition of salt, oil, and cummin. Daucus, taken in drink, promotes the menstrual discharge, and is an expellent of the after-birth in a very high degree. Ladanum, used as a fumigation, acts as a corrective upon the uterus, and is employed topically for pains and ulcerations of that organ.

22　*Antirrhinum orontium*, weasel's snout (TN).
23　A kind of ivy (TN).

Book XXVII
Medicinal Use of Plants (III)

The further I proceed in this work, the more I am impressed with admiration of the ancients; and the greater the number of plants that remain to be described, the more I am induced to venerate the zeal displayed by the men of former times in their researches, and the kindly spirit manifested by them in transmitting to us the results thereof. Indeed their bounteousness in this respect would almost seem to have surpassed the munificent disposition even of Nature herself, if our knowledge of plants had depended solely upon man's spirit of discovery; but as it is, it is evident beyond all doubt that this knowledge has emanated from the gods themselves, or, at all events, has been the result of divine inspiration, even in those cases where man has been instrumental in communicating it to us. In other words, if we must confess the truth —a marvel surpassed by nothing in our daily experience— Nature herself, that common parent of all things, has at once produced them, and has discovered to us their properties.

But who, I say, can sufficiently venerate the zeal and spirit of research displayed by the ancients? It is they who have shown us that aconite is the most prompt of all poisons in its effects —so much so indeed, that female animals, if the sexual parts are but touched with it, will not survive a single day. According to the fables of mythology, this plant was originally produced from the foam of the dog Cerberus, when dragged by Hercules from the Infernal Regions; for which reason, it is said, it is still so remarkably abundant in the vicinity of Heraclea in Pontus, a spot where the entrance is still pointed out to the shades below.

And yet, noxious as it is, the ancients have shown us how to employ aconite for the benefit of mankind, and have taught us as the result of their experience, that, taken in mulled wine, it neutralizes the venom of the scorpion; indeed such is the nature of this deadly plant, that it kills man, unless it can find in man something else to kill. When such is the case, as though it had discovered in the body a fit rival to contend with, that substance is the sole object of its attack; finding another poison in the viscera, to it alone it confines its onslaught; and thus, a truly marvellous thing! Two poisons, each of them of a deadly nature, destroy one another within the body, and the man survives. Even more than this, the ancients have handed down to us remedies employed by the animals themselves, and have shown how that venomous creatures even effect their own cure. By the contact of aconite the scorpion is struck with torpor, is quite benumbed, assumes a pallid hue, and so confesses itself vanquished. When this is the case, white hellebore is its great auxiliary; the very touch of it dispels its torpor, and the aconite is forced to yield before two foes, its own enemy and the common enemy of all.

ACONITE

The ancients, openly professing their belief that there is no evil without some admixture of good, have asserted that aconite is a remarkably useful ingredient in compositions for the eyes. It may therefore be permitted me, though I have hitherto omitted a description of the poisonous plants, to point out the characteristics of aconite, if only that it may be the more easily detected. Aconite[1] has leaves like those of cyclaminos or of the cucumber, never more than four in number, slightly hairy, and rising from near the root. This root, which is of moderate size, resembles the sea-fish known as the "cammarus,"[2] a circumstance owing to which the plant has received the name of "cammaron" from some. The root is slightly curved, like a scorpion's tail, for which reason some persons have given it the name of "scorpio."

This plant is found growing upon the naked rocks known as "aeonæ"; and hence it is, according to some authorities, that it is called "aconitum," there being not so much as dust even about it to conduce to its nutriment. Such is the reason given for its name by some; but according to others, it receives this appellation from the fact that it fatally exercises the same effects upon the body that the whetstone does upon the edge of iron, being no sooner employed than its effects are felt.

ALOE

The aloe[3] bears a resemblance to the squill, except that it is larger, and has more substantial leaves, with streaks running obliquely. The stem is tender, red in the middle, and not unlike that of the anthericus.[4] It has a single root, which runs straight downwards, like a stake driven into the ground; its smell is powerful, and

---

1 The ancients no doubt knew several plants under the common name of Aconitum. The one here described, is identified by Fée with the *Doronicum pardalianches* of Linnæus, Leopard's bane.

2 A kind of crab.

3 The ancients probably included under this name several distinct species of the aloe. They were well acquainted, Fée says, with the Indian aloe, but probably not with that of Africa. As described by Pliny, he identifies it with the *Aloe perfoliata* of Linnæus; Desfontaines gives the *Aloe umbellata*.

4 Flowering stem of the asphodel (TN).

it has a bitter taste. The most esteemed aloes are those imported from India, but it grows in the Asiatic provinces as well. This last kind, however, is never used, except that the leaves are applied fresh to wounds; indeed, these leaves, as well as the juice, are glutinous to a marvellous degree, and it is for this property that it is grown in vessels of a conical form, in the same way as the greater Aizoüm. Some persons make incisions in the stem to obtain the juice, before the seed is ripe, while others, again, make them in the leaves as well. Tear like drops are also found adhering to it, which exude spontaneously; hence it is that some recommend that the place should be paved where it is grown, to prevent this juice from being absorbed.

Some authors have stated, that there is found in Judæa, beyond Hierosolyma, a mineral[5] aloe, but that it is inferior to the other kinds, being of a darker colour and more humid than any of the rest. Aloes of the finest quality should be unctuous and shining, of a red colour, brittle, compact, like the substance of liver, and easily liquefied. That which is hard and black should be rejected; the same, too, when it is mixed with sand or adulterated with gum and acacia, a fraud which may be easily detected by the taste.

This plant is of an astringent nature, binding, and slightly calorific. It is employed for numerous purposes, but principally as a purgative, it being almost the only one of all the medicaments which produce that effect, that is at the same time a good stomachic, and does not exercise the slightest noxious influence upon the stomach. It is taken in doses of one drachma, and, in cases of derangement of the stomach, it is administered two or three times a day, in the proportion of one spoonful to two cyathi of warm or cold water, at intervals, according to the nature of the emergency. As a purgative it is mostly taken in doses of three drachmæ; and it operates still more efficaciously, if food is eaten directly afterwards. Used with astringent wine, it prevents the hair from falling off, the head being rubbed with it the contrary way of the hair, in the sun. Applied to the temples and forehead with rose oil and vinegar, or used as an infusion, in a more diluted form, it allays headache. It is generally agreed that it is remedial for all diseases of the eyes, but more particularly for prurigo and scaly eruptions of the eye-lids; as also for marks and bruises, applied in combination with honey, Pontic honey in particular.

ALSINE

Alsine,[6] a plant known as "myosoton"[7] to some, grows in the woods, to which fact it is indebted for its name of "alsine."[8] It begins to make its appearance at midwinter, and withers in the middle of summer. When it first puts forth, the leaves bear a strong resemblance to the ears of mice. It grows in gardens, and upon walls more particularly; when rubbed, it emits a smell like that of cucumber. It is used for

---

5   Pliny alludes to the bitumen of Judæa, much used by the Egyptians for the purposes of embalmment.

6   Identified by Sprengel with the *Cerastium aquaticum*, and by other authorities with the *Alsine media* of Linnæus, the Common chickweed.

7   "Mouse-ear."

8   From the Greek ἄλσος, a "grove."

abscesses, inflammations, and all those purposes for which helxine[9] is employed; its properties, however, are not so active. It is applied topically, also, to eye-fluxes, and to sores upon the generative organs, and ulcerations, with barley meal. The juice is used as an injection for the ears.

APARINE

Aparine,[10] otherwise called "omphalocarpos"[11] or "philanthropos," is a ramose, hairy, plant, with five or six leaves at regular intervals, arranged circularly around the branches. The seed is round, hard, concave, and of a sweetish taste. It grows in cornfields, gardens, and meadows, and, by the aid of its prickly points, adheres to the clothes. The seed is employed to neutralize the venom of serpents, being taken in doses of one drachma, in wine; it is useful also for the bite of the phalangium.[12] The leaves, applied topically, arrest haemorrhage from wounds. The juice is used as an injection for the ears.

ALCIBIUM

I have not found it stated by authors what kind of plant alcibium[13] is; but the root, I find, and the leaves, are pounded and employed, both externally and internally, for injuries inflicted by serpents. When the leaves are used, a handful of them is bruised in three cyathi of undiluted wine; the root is employed in the proportion of three drachmæ to the same quantity of wine.

ABSINTHIUM OR WORMWOOD

There are numerous kinds of absinthium; the Santonic,[14] for instance, so called from a city in Gaul, and the Pontic,[15] which comes from Pontus, where the cattle are fattened upon it, a diet which causes them to be destitute of gall. The Pontic wormwood, we may remark, is of the finest quality, superior to that of Italy, and much more bitter; the pith, however, of the Pontic wormwood is sweet. As to its general utility, a plant so commonly found and applied to such numerous uses, people are universally agreed; but with the Romans more particularly it has been always held in the highest esteem, from the fact of its being employed in their religious ceremonials. Thus, for instance, upon the Latin Festival, it is the custom to have a race of four-horsed chariots in the Capital, and for the conqueror to be presented with a draught of wormwood; from the circumstance, no doubt, that our forefathers were of opinion that good health was the most valuable reward they could bestow upon his skill.

This plant is very strengthening to the stomach, and hence it is that wines are flavoured with it. A decoction of it in water is also taken, the following being the

---

9   The *Parietaria officinalis*.
10 It is identified with the *Galiun Aparine* of Linnæus, Ladies' bedstraw, Cleavers, goosegrass, hariff, or catchweed.
11 "Navel-fruit."
12 A venomous spider.
13 Desfontaines identifies the Alcibium with the *Echium rubrum* of Linnæus.
14 The *Artemisia Santonica* of Linnæus, Tartarian southernwood.
15 The *Artemisia Pontica* of Linnæus, Little wormwood, or Roman wormwood.

method employed in preparing it. Six drachmæ of the leaves are boiled, with the branches, in three sextarii of rain water, and the preparation is then left to cool in the open air a day and a night. Salt, too, should be added to it. When old, it is utterly useless. A dilution of wormwood steeped in water is also used. This dilution is made by leaving the vessel covered up for three days, any kind of water being used. Pounded wormwood is but rarely employed, and the same with the extracted juice of the seed. In cases, however, where it is extracted, the seed is subjected to pressure as soon as it begins to swell, after which it is soaked for three days in water, if used fresh, and seven, if dry. It is then boiled in a copper vessel, in the proportion of ten heminæ to forty-five sextarii of water, after which it is strained off and boiled gently to the consistency of honey, in the same way as the juice is extracted from the smaller centaury. The juice, however, of wormwood, thus extracted, is bad for the head and stomach; whereas the decoction, on the other hand, is wholesome in the highest degree, as it acts astringently upon the stomach, carries off bile, is a powerful diuretic, has a soothing effect upon the bowels, and assuages pains in the intestines. With the addition of sile,[16] Gallic nard, and a little vinegar, it dispels nausea and flatulency, and expels intestinal worms. It removes qualmishness, promotes the digestion, and, with the addition of rue, pepper, and salt, disperses crudities of the stomach.

The ancients were in the habit of giving wormwood as a purgative, the dose being six drachmæ of the seed with three of salt and one cyathus of honey, in one sextarius of sea water kept for some time. This preparation, however, is rendered more efficacious by doubling the proportion of salt; the seed, too, must be bruised with the greatest care, as there is considerable difficulty in pounding it. Some authorities have prescribed the dose above mentioned to he given in polenta, with the addition of pennyroyal; while others recommend the leaves to be given to children in a dried fig, to disguise their bitterness. Taken with iris, wormwood acts as a detergent upon the thoracic organs; for jaundice it is used raw, with parsley or adiantum. In cases of flatulency, it is sipped every now and then, warmed in water; for liver complaints it is taken with Gallic nard, and for diseases of the spleen, with vinegar, pap, or figs. Taken in vinegar it neutralizes the bad effects of fungi and of viscus; in wine it is an antidote to the poison of hemlock, and to the bite of the shrew-mouse, and is curative of wounds inflicted by the sea-dragon and the scorpion. It contributes also very greatly to the improvement of the sight, and is used as an external application, with raisin wine, for defluxions of the eyes, and with honey, for bruises.

TWO VARIETIES OF FERN

Of fern there are two varieties, equally destitute of blossom and of seed.[17] The Greeks give the name of "pteris," and sometimes "blachnon," to the kind[18] in which

---

16   The *Seseli tortuosum* of Linnæus.

17   From this remark, Fée is of opinion that Pliny had in view more particularly the *Pteris aquilina* and the *Blechnum spicatum* of Linnæus, plants in which the seed is not easily detected.

18   Identified by Fée with the *Polypodium filix mas* of Linnæus, the Male fern.

numerous shoots take their rise from a single root, exceeding two cubits even in length, and with a not unpleasant smell; this plant is thought to be the male fern.

The other kind is known to the Greeks as "thelypteris,"[19] and sometimes, "nymphæa pteris"; it has a single stem only, with comparatively few branches, is shorter, softer, and more tufted than the other, and has channelled leaves growing near the root. Swine are fattened upon the roots of either kind. The leaves of both kinds are arranged on either side in the form of wings, whence the Greek name "pteris." The roots are long, run obliquely, and are of a swarthy colour, more particularly when dried; when wanted for use, they should be dried in the sun. These plants are found growing everywhere, but in cold soils more particularly; they should be taken up, too, at the setting of the Vergiliæ. The root is only used at the end of three years, neither before that period nor after. They act as an expellent of intestinal worms; for tapeworm honey is taken with them, but in other cases sweet wine, for three days.

They are, both of them, extremely detrimental to the stomach, but are laxative to the bowels, carrying off first the bile and then the aqueous humours of the body. When used for tapeworm, it is the best plan to take scammony with them, in equal proportions. For rheumatic defluxions, the root is taken in doses of two oboli, in water, after a day's abstinence from food, a little honey being taken first. Neither kind must ever be given to females; for in pregnancy they are productive of abortion, and in other cases entail sterility. Powdered fern is sprinkled upon sordid ulcers, as also upon the necks of beasts of burden, when chafed. Fern-leaves kill bugs, and serpents will never harbour among them; hence it is a good plan to strew them in places where the presence of those reptiles is suspected. The very smell, too, of burnt fern will put serpents to flight. Medical men have made this distinction as to ferns; that of Macedonia, they say, is the best, and that of Cassiope the next.

THE LITHOSPERMUM

Among all the plants, however, there is none of a more marvellous nature than the lithospermum,[20] sometimes called "exonychon," "diospyron," or "heracleos." It is about five inches in height, with leaves twice the size of those of rue, and small ligneous branches, about the thickness of a rush. It bears close to the leaves a sort of fine beard or spike, standing by itself, on the extremity of which there are small white stones, as round as a pearl, about the size of a chick-pea, and as hard as a pebble. These stones, at the part where they adhere to the stalk, have a small cavity, and contain a seed within.

This plant is found in Italy, no doubt, but that of Crete is the most esteemed. Among all the plants, there is none that I ever contemplated with greater admiration than this; so beauteous is the conformation, that it might be fancied that the hand of an artist had arranged a row of lustrous pearls alternately among the

---

19 "Female fern." Identified by Fée with the *Polypodium filix fœmina* of Linnæus, Female fern or *Pteris aquilina*.

20 Identified by Fée and Desfontaines with the *Lithospermum officinale* of Linnæus, Gremil, gromwell, or stone-crop. Littré mentions the *Lithospermum tenuifiorum* of Linnæus.

leaves; so exquisite too the nicety in thus making a stone to grow upon a plant! The authorities say that this is a creeping plant, and that it lies upon the ground; but for my own part, I have only seen it when plucked, and not while growing. It is well known that these small stones, taken in doses of one drachma, in white wine, break and expel urinary calculi, and are curative of strangury. Indeed, there is no plant that so instantaneously proclaims, at the mere sight of it, the medicinal purposes for which it was originally intended; the appearance of it, too, is such, that it can be immediately recognized, without the necessity of having recourse to any botanical authority.

LAPIDIS MUSCUS OR STONE MOSS

There grows near running streams, a dry, white moss,[21] upon ordinary stones. One of these stones, with the addition of human saliva, is rubbed against another; after which the first stone is used for touching impetigo, the party so doing uttering these words:

φεύγετε χανθαρίδες, λύχος ἄγριος αἷμα διώχει.

"Cantharides begone, a wild wolf seeks your blood."

THE NATRIX

"Natrix"[22] is the name of a plant, the root of which, when taken out of the ground, has just the rank smell of the he-goat. It is used in Picenum for the purpose of keeping away from females what with a singular credulity they call by the name of "Fatui."[23] For my own part, however, I should think that persons requiring to be treated with such medicaments as these, must be labouring under a sort of mental hallucination.

THE PEPLIS

The peplis,[24] known by the various names of "syce,"[25] "meconion," and "mecon aphrodes," is a shrub-like plant, springing from a single, diminutive, root. The leaves of it resemble those of rue, but are a little larger; the seed, which lies beneath the leaves, is round, and smaller than that of the white poppy. It is ordinarily gathered in vineyards, at harvest-time, and is dried with the seed on, receivers being placed beneath to catch it as it falls. This seed, taken in drink, purges the bowels, and carries off bile and pituitous secretions; one acetabulum, taken in three heminæ of hydromel, is a middling dose. It is sprinkled also upon meat and other articles of food, as a laxative medicine.

---

21 Some kind of lichen, probably, but what in particular it is impossible to say.

22 Possibly a fabulous plant; though it is generally identified with the *Ononis natrix* of Linnæus. Poinsinet de Sivry derives its name from the Celto-Germanic words, nat, "night," and ris, "wand"; a name given to it, according to him, for its efficacy in dispelling the illusions of the night.

23 Or "Fauni," the same as our nightmare.

24 Probably the *Euphorbia peplis* of Linnæus.

25 "Fig-plant," "poppy-juice," and "poppy-froth." In reference, no doubt, to its milky juice.

POTERION

Poterion, or, as some call it, "phrynion" or "neuras,"[26] throws out numerous branches, is shrivelled and prickly, and covered with a thick down. The leaves of it are small and round; the branches long, soft, thin, and flexible; and the blossom elongated, and of a grass-green colour. The seed is never used, but it has a pungent flavour and a powerful smell; the plant is found growing upon moist, watery, elevations. The roots are two or three in number, some two cubits in length, sinewy, white, and firm. It is dug up in autumn, and the stem yields a juice like gum, when cut. The root is said to be of wonderful efficacy as an application for the cure of wounds, more particularly of the sinews, even when severed. A decoction of it is also taken, with honey, for relaxations of the sinews, and for weakness or wounds of those parts.

RHACOMA

Rhacoma[27] is imported from the regions situate beyond Pontus. The root of it is similar to black costus, but smaller and somewhat redder, inodorous, and of a hot, astringent flavour; when pounded, it yields a colour like that of wine, but inclining to saffron. Applied topically, it reduces abscesses and inflammations, and heals wounds; used with raisin wine, it allays eye-fluxes; with honey, ecchymosis; and with vinegar, livid marks upon the skin. Reduced to powder, it is sprinkled upon malignant ulcers, and is given internally for spitting of blood, in doses of one drachma, in water. For dysentery and cœliac affections, if unattended with fever, it is administered in wine; but if there is fever, in water. It is pounded more easily when it has been steeped in water the night before. A decoction of it is given, in doses of two drachmæ, for ruptures, convulsions, contusions, and falls with violence.

In cases of pains in the chest, a little pepper and myrrh is added. When the stomach is deranged, it is taken in cold water; and the same in cases of chronic cough, purulent expectorations, liver complaint, affections of the spleen, sciatica, diseases of the kidneys, asthma, and hardness of breathing. Pounded and taken in doses of three oboli, in raisin wine, or used in the form of a decoction, it cures irritations of the trachea; applied with vinegar, it acts as a detergent upon lichens. It is taken in drink, also, for flatulency, cold shiverings, chilly fevers, hiccup, gripings of the bowels, herpetic ulcerations, oppressions of the head, vertigo attended with melancholy, lassitude accompanied with pain, and convulsions.

THE AGES OF PLANTS

Such, then, is all that I have hitherto been enabled to learn or discover, worthy of mention, relative to plants. At the close of this subject, it seems to me that it will not be out of place to remind the reader, that the properties of plants vary according to their age. It is elaterium that preserves its properties the longest of all. The

---

26 The "sinew" plant.
27 It is generally supposed to be the *Rheum Rhaponticum* of Linnæus, Pontic rhubarb.

black chamæleon[28] retains its virtues forty years, centaury not more than twelve, peucedanum and aristolochia six, and the wild vine one year —that is to say, if they are kept in the shade. I would remark, also, that beyond those animals which breed within the plants, there are none that attack the roots of any of those which have been mentioned by me; with the exception, indeed, of the sphondyle, a kind of creeping insect, which infests them all.

HOW THE GREATEST EFFICACY IN PLANTS MAY BE ENSURED

It is also an undoubted truth, that the virtues and properties of all roots are more feebly developed, when the fruit has been allowed to ripen; and that it is the same with the seed, when incisions have been previously made in the root, for the extraction of the juice. The efficacy, too, of all plants is impaired by making habitual use of them; and these substances, if employed daily, lose equally their good or bad properties, when required to be effectual. All plants, too, have more powerful properties, when grown in soils that are cold and exposed to the north-eastern blasts, or in dry localities.

MALADIES PECULIAR TO VARIOUS NATIONS

There are certain differences, also, by no means inconsiderable, in the predispositions of the various nations of the earth. I have been informed, for instance, that the people of Egypt, Arabia, Syria, and Cilicia, are subject to tapeworm and mawworm, while those of Thracia and Phrygia, on the other hand, are totally exempt from them. This, however, is less surprising than the fact that, although Attica and Bœotia are adjoining territories, the Thebans are troubled with these inflictions, while among the people of Athens they are unknown.

Considerations of this description lead me now to turn my attention to the nature of the animated beings themselves, and the medicinal properties which are inborn in them, the most assured remedies, perhaps, for all diseases.

For Nature, in fact, that parent of all things, has produced no animated being for the purpose solely of eating; she has willed that it should be born to satisfy the wants of others, and in its very vitals has implanted medicaments conducive to health. While she has implanted them in mute and inanimate objects even, she has equally willed that these, the most invaluable aids of life, should be also derived from the life of another; a subject for contemplation, marvellous in the highest degree!

---

28 Desfontaines identifies it with the *Centaurea crocodileum* of Linnaeus, and Littre with the *Carduus pycnocephalus* of Linnaeus. Ruellius considers it to be the same plant as the Leucacantha of Dioscorides, which Sprengel identifies with the *Cnicus casabonse*. Fee expresses himself at a loss as to its identity.

Book XXVIII
Medicaments Derived From Living Creatures (I) – Magic and Charms

We should have now concluded our description of the various things[1] that are produced between the heavens and the earth, and it would have only remained for us to speak of the substances that are dug out of the ground itself; did not our exposition of the remedies derived from plants and shrubs necessarily lead us into a digression upon the medicinal properties which have been discovered, to a still greater extent, in those living creatures themselves which are thus indebted for the cure of their respective maladies. For ought we, after describing the plants, the forms of the various flowers, and so many objects rare and difficult to be found, ought we to pass in silence the resources which exist in man himself for the benefit of man, and the other remedies to be derived from the creatures that live among us.

My researches will extend to the usages of foreign countries, and to the customs of barbarous nations, subjects upon which I shall have to appeal to the good faith of other authors; though at the same time I have made it my object to select no facts but such as are established by pretty nearly uniform testimony, and to pay more attention to scrupulous exactness than to copiousness of diction.

It is highly necessary, however, to advertise the reader, that whereas I have already described the natures of the various animals, and the discoveries due to them respectively, it is my present intention to confine myself to the remedial properties which are found in the animal world, a subject which has not been altogether lost sight of in the former portion of this work. These additional details therefore, though of a different nature, must still be read in connexion with those which precede.

---

1 The trees and plants.

MEDICAMENTS DERIVED FROM MAN

We will begin then with man, and our first enquires will be into the resources which he provides for himself; a subject replete with boundless difficulties at the very outset.

Epileptic patients are in the habit of drinking the blood even of gladiators, draughts teeming with life, as it were; a thing that, when we see it done by the wild beasts even, upon the same arena, inspires us with horror at the spectacle! And yet these persons, forsooth, consider it a most effectual cure for their disease, to quaff the warm, breathing, blood from man himself, and, as they apply their mouth to the wound, to draw forth his very life; and this, though it is regarded as an act of impiety to apply the human lips to the wound even of a wild beast! Others there are, again, who make the marrow of the leg-bones, and the brains of infants, the objects of their research!

Among the Greek writers, too, there are not a few who have enlarged upon the distinctive flavours of each one of the viscera and members of the human body, pursuing their researches to the very parings of the nails! as though, forsooth, it could possibly be accounted the pursuit of health for man to make himself a wild beast, and so deserve to contract disease from the very remedies he adopts for avoiding it. To examine human entrails is deemed an act of impiety; what then must it be to devour them?

We read, for instance, in the memoirs of Democritus, still extant, that for some diseases, the skull of a malefactor is most efficacious, while for the treatment of others, that of one who has been a friend or guest is required. Apollonius, again, informs us in his writings, that the most effectual remedy for tooth-ache is to scarify the gums with the tooth of a man who has died a violent death; and, according to Miletus, human gall is a cure for cataract. For epilepsy, Artemon has prescribed water drawn from a spring in the night, and drunk from the skull of a man who has been slain, and whose body remains unburnt. From the skull, too, of a man who had been hanged, Antæus made pills that were to be an antidote to the bite of a mad dog.

Far from us, far too from our writings, be such prescriptions as these! It will be for us to describe remedies only, and not abominations; cases, for instance, in which the milk of a nursing woman may have a curative effect, cases where the human spittle may be useful, or the contact[2] of the human body, and other instances of a similar nature. We do not look upon life as so essentially desirable that it must be prolonged at any cost, be it what it may.

WHETHER WORDS ARE POSSESSED OF ANY HEALING EFFICACY

In reference to the remedies derived from man, there arises first of all one question, of the greatest importance and always attended with the same uncertainty, whether words, charms, and incantations, are of any efficacy or not? For if such is the case, it will be only proper to ascribe this efficacy to man himself; though the wisest of our fellow-men, I should remark, taken individually, refuse to place

---

2   We may here discover the first rudiments of the doctrine of Animal Magnetism.

the slightest faith in these opinions. And yet, in our every-day life, we practically show, each passing hour, that we do entertain this belief, though at the moment we are not sensible of it. Thus, for instance, it is a general belief that without a certain form of prayer it would be useless to immolate a victim, and that, with such an informality, the gods would be consulted to little purpose. And then besides, there are different forms of address to the deities, one form for entreating, another form for averting their ire, and another for commendation.

We see too, how that our supreme magistrates use certain formulæ for their prayers; that not a single word may be omitted or pronounced out of its place, it is the duty of one person to precede the dignitary by reading the formula before him from a written ritual, of another, to keep watch upon every word, and of a third to see that silence is not ominously broken; while a musician, in the meantime, is performing on the flute to prevent any other words being heard. Indeed, there are memorable instances recorded in our Annals, of cases where either the sacrifice has been interrupted, and so blemished, by imprecations, or a mistake has been made in the utterance of the prayer; the result being that the lobe of the liver or the heart has disappeared in a moment, or has been doubled, while the victim stood before the altar.

At the present day, too, it is a general belief, that our Vestal virgins have the power, by uttering a certain prayer, to arrest the flight of runaway slaves, and to rivet them to the spot, provided they have not gone beyond the precincts of the City. If then these opinions be once received as truth, and if it be admitted that the gods do listen to certain prayers, or are influenced by set forms of words, we are bound to conclude in the affirmative upon the whole question. Our ancestors, no doubt, always entertained such a belief, and have even assured us, a thing by far the most difficult of all, that it is possible by such means to bring down lightning from heaven.

PRODIGIES AND PORTENTS

Lucius Piso informs us, in the first Book of his Annals, that King Tullus Hostilius, while attempting, in accordance with the books of Numa, to summon Jupiter from heaven by means of a sacrifice similar to that employed by him, was struck by lightning in consequence of his omission to follow certain forms with due exactness. Many other authors, too, have attested, that by the power of words a change has been effected in destinies and portents of the greatest importance.

And then besides, in the laws themselves of the Twelve Tables, do we not read the following words: "Whosoever shall have enchanted the harvest," and in another place, "Whosoever shall have used pernicious incantations"? Verrius Flaccus cites authors whom he deems worthy of credit, to show that on the occasion of a siege, it was the usage, the first thing of all, for the Roman priests to summon forth the tutelary divinity of that particular town, and to promise him the same rites, or even a more extended worship, at Rome; and at the present day even, this ritual still forms part of the discipline of our pontiffs. Hence it is, no doubt, that the name of the tutelary deity of Rome has been so strictly kept concealed, lest any of our enemies should act in a similar manner. There is no one, too, who does not dread being spell-bound by means of evil imprecations; and hence the practice, after eating eggs or snails, of immediately breaking[3] the shells, or piercing them with the spoon. Hence, too, those love-sick imitations of enchantments which we find described by Theocritus among the Greeks, and by Catullus, and more recently, Virgil, among our own writers. Many persons are fully persuaded that articles of pottery may be broken by a similar agency; and not a few are of opinion even that serpents can counteract incantations, and that this is the only kind of intelligence they possess; so much so, in fact, that by the agency of the magic spells of the Marsi, they may be attracted to one spot, even when asleep in the middle of the night. Some people go so far, too, as to write certain words on the walls of houses, deprecatory of accident by fire.

PEOPLE WITH MAGIC POWERS

We have already, when speaking of the singular peculiarities of various nations, made mention of certain men of a monstrous nature, whose gaze is endowed with powers of fascination; and we have also described properties belonging to numerous animals, which it would be superfluous here to repeat. In some men, the whole of the body is endowed with remarkable properties, as in those families, for instance, which are a terror to serpents; it being in their power to cure persons when stung, either by the touch or by a slight suction of the wound. To this class belong the Psylli, the Marsi, and the people called "Ophiogenes," in the Isle of Cyprus. One Euagon, a member of this family, while attending upon a deputation at Rome, was thrown by way of experiment, by order of the consuls, into a large vessel filled with serpents; upon which, to the astonishment of all, they licked his body all over with their tongues. One peculiarity of this family is the strong offensive smell which proceeds from their body in the spring; their sweat, too, no less than their spittle, was possessed of remedial virtues.

It is said, that if a person takes a stone or other missile which has slain three living creatures, a man, a boar, and a bear, at three blows, and throws it over the roof of a house in which there is a pregnant woman, her delivery, however difficult, will be instantly accelerated thereby. In such a case, too, a successful result will be rendered all the more probable, it a light infantry lance is used, which has been drawn from a man's body without touching the earth; indeed, if it is brought into the house it will be productive of a similar result. In the same way, too, we find it stated in the writings of Orpheus and Archelaiis, that arrows, drawn from a human body without being allowed to touch the ground, and placed beneath the bed, will have all the effect of a philtre; and, what is even more than this, that it is a cure for

---

3   It is a superstition still practised to pierce the shell of an egg after eating it, "lest the witches should come." Holland gives the following Note: "Because afterwards no witches might pricke them with a needle in the name and behalfe of those whom they would hurt and mischeefe, according to the practice of pricking the images of any person in wax; used in the witchcraft of these daies."

epilepsy if the patient eats the flesh of it wild beast killed with an iron weapon with which a human being has been slain.

PROPERTIES OF THE HUMAN SPITTLE

But it is the fasting spittle of a human being, the sovereign preservative against the poison of serpents; while, at the same time, our daily experience may recognize its efficacy and utility, in many other respects. We are in the habit of spitting, for instance, as a preservative from epilepsy, or in other words, we repel contagion thereby; in a similar manner, too, we repel fascinations, and the evil presages attendant upon meeting a person who is lame in the right leg. We ask pardon of the gods, by spitting in the lap, for entertaining some too presumptuous hope or expectation. On the same principle, it is the practice in all cases where medicine is employed, to spit three times on the ground, and to conjure the malady as often; the object being, to aid the operation of the remedy employed. It is usual, too, to mark a boil, when it first makes its appearance, three times with fasting spittle. What we are going to say is marvellous, but it may easily be tested by experiment; if a person repents of a blow given to another, either by hand or with a missile, he has nothing to do but to spit at once into the palm of the hand which has inflicted the blow, and all feelings of resentment will be instantly alleviated in the person struck. This, too, is often verified in the case of a beast of burden, when brought on its haunches with blows; for upon this remedy being adopted, the animal will immediately step out and mend its pace. Some persons, however, before making an effort, spit into the hand in manner above stated, in order to make the blow more heavy.

We may well believe, then, that lichens and leprous spots may be removed by a constant application of fasting spittle; that ophthalmia may be cured by anointing, as it were, the eyes every morning with fasting spittle; that carcinomata may be effectually treated, by kneading the root of the plant known as "apple of the earth," with human spittle; that crick in the neck may be got rid of by carrying fasting spittle to the right knee with the right hand, and to the left knee with the left; and that when an insect has got into the ear, it is quite sufficient to spit into that organ, to make it come out. Among the counter-charms too, are reckoned, the practice of spitting into the urine the moment it is voided, of spitting into the shoe of the right foot before putting it on, and of spitting while a person is passing a place in which he has incurred any kind of peril.

MEDICAMENTS DERIVED FROM THE HUMAN BLOOD

The blood of the human body, come from what part it may, is most efficacious, according to Orpheus and Archelaüs, as an application for quinsy; they say, too, that if it is applied to the mouth of a person who has fallen down in a fit of epilepsy, he will come to himself immediately. Some say that, for epilepsy, the great toes should be pricked, and the drops of blood that exude therefrom applied to the face; or else, that a virgin should touch the patient with her right thumb —a circumstance that has led to the belief that persons suffering from epilepsy should eat the flesh of animals in a virgin state. Æschines of Athens used to cure quinsy, carcinoma, and affections of the tonsillary glands and uvula, with the ashes of burnt excrements, a medicament to which he gave the name of "botryon." There are many kinds of diseases which disappear entirely after the first sexual congress, or, in the case of females, at the first appearance of menstruation; indeed, if such is not the case, they are apt to become chronic, epilepsy in particular. Even more than this, a man, it is said, who has been stung by a serpent or scorpion, experiences relief from the sexual congress; but the woman, on the other hand, is sensible of detriment. We are assured, too, that if persons, when washing their feet, touch the eyes three times with the water, they will never be subject to ophthalmia or other diseases of the eyes.

MEDICAMENTS DERIVED FROM THE DEAD

Scrofula, imposthumes of the parotid glands, and throat diseases, they say, may be cured by the contact of the hand of a person who has been carried off by an early death; indeed there are some who assert that any dead body will produce the same effect, provided it is of the same sex as the patient, and that the part affected is touched with the back of the left hand. To bite off a piece from wood that has been struck by lightning, the hands being held behind the back, and then to apply it to the tooth, is a sure remedy, they say, for toothache. Some persons recommend the tooth to be fumigated with the smoke of a burnt tooth, which has belonged to another person of the same sex; or else to attach to the person a dogtooth, as it is called, which has been extracted from a body before burial. Earth, they say, taken from out of a human skull, acts as a depilatory to the eyelashes; it is asserted, also, that any plant which may happen to have grown there, if chewed, will cause the teeth to come out; and that if a circle is traced round an ulcer with a human bone, it will be effectually prevented from spreading.

MISCELLANEOUS MEDICAMENTS

To sit by a pregnant woman, or by a person to whom any remedy is being administered, with the fingers of one hand inserted between those of the other, acts as a magic spell. If the fingers are thus joined, clasping one or both knees, or if the ham of one leg is first put upon the knee of the other, and then changed about, the omen is of still worse signification. Hence it is, that in councils held by generals and persons in authority, our ancestors forbade these postures, as being an impediment to all business. They have given a similar prohibition also with reference to sacrifices and the offering of public vows; but as to the usage of uncovering the head in presence of the magistrates, that has been enjoined, Varro says, not as a mark of respect, but with a view to health, the head being strengthened by the practice of keeping it uncovered.

To thrust an iron nail into the spot where a person's head lay at the moment he was seized with a fit of epilepsy, is said to have the effect of curing him of that disease. For pains in the kidneys, loins, or bladder, it is considered highly soothing to void the urine lying on the face at full length in a reclining bath. It is quite surprising how much more speedily wounds will heal if they are bound up and tied with a

Book XXVIII - Medicaments Derived From Living Creatures (I)...

Hercules' knot;[4] indeed, it is said, that if the girdle which we wear every day is tied with a knot of this description, it will be productive of certain beneficial effects, Hercules having been the first to discover the fact.

Demetrius, in the treatise which he has compiled upon the number Four, alleges certain reasons why drink should never be taken in proportions of four cyathi or sextarii. As a preventive of ophthalmia, it is a good plan to rub the parts behind the ears, and, as a cure for watery eyes, to rub the forehead. As to the presages which are derived from man himself, there is one to the effect that so long as a person is able to see himself reflected in the pupil of the patient's eye, there need be no apprehension of a fatal termination to the malady.

MEDICAMENTS DERIVED FROM THE URINE

The urine, too, has been the subject not only of numerous theories with authors, but of various religious observances as well, its properties being classified under several distinctive heads; thus, for instance, the urine of eunuchs, they say, is highly beneficial as a promoter of fruitfulness in females. But to turn to those remedies which we may be allowed to name without impropriety; the urine of children who have not arrived at puberty is a sovereign remedy for the poisonous secretions of the asp known as the "ptyas," from the fact that it spits its venom into the eyes of human beings. It is good, too, for the cure of albugo, films and marks upon the eyes, white specks upon the pupils, and maladies of the eyelids. In combination with meal of fitches, it is used for the cure of burns, and, with a head of bulbed leek, it is boiled down to one half, in a new earthen vessel, for the treatment of suppurations of the ears, or the extermination of worms breeding in those organs; the vapour, too, of this decoction acts as an emmenagogue. Salpe recommends that the eyes should be fomented with it, as a means of strengthening the sight; and that it should be used as a liniment for sun scorches, in combination with white of egg, that of the ostrich being the most effectual, the application being kept on for a couple of hours.

Urine is also used for taking out ink spots. Male urine cures gout, witness the fullers for instance, who, for this reason, it is said, are never troubled with that disease. With stale urine some mix ashes of calcined oyster-shells, for the cure of eruptions on the bodies of infants, and all kinds of running ulcers; it is used, too, as a liniment for corrosive sores, burns, diseases of the rectum, chaps upon the body, and stings inflicted by scorpions.

MEDICAMENTS DERIVED FROM THE FEMALE SEX

The remedies said to be derived from the bodies of females closely approach the marvellous nature of prodigies; to say nothing of still-born infants cut up limb by limb for the most abominable practices, expiations made with the menstrual discharge, and other devices which have been mentioned, not only by midwives but by harlots even as well! The smell of a woman's hair, burnt, will drive away serpents, and hysterical suffocations, it is said, may be dispelled thereby. The ashes

---

4 A knot tied very hard, and in which no ends were to be seen.

of a woman's hair, burnt in an earthen vessel, or used in combination with litharge, will cure eruptions and prurigo of the eyes; used in combination with honey they will remove warts and ulcers upon infants; with the addition of honey and frankincense, they will heal wounds upon the head, and fill up all concavities left by corrosive ulcers; used with hogs' lard, they will cure inflammatory tumours and gout; and applied topically to the part affected, they will arrest erysipelas and haemorrhage, and remove itching pimples on the body which resemble the stings of ants.

MEDICAMENTS DERIVED FROM WOMAN'S MILK

As to the uses to which woman's milk has been applied, it is generally agreed that it is the sweetest and the most delicate of all, and that it is the best of remedies for chronic fevers and cœliac affections, when the woman has just weaned her infant more particularly. In cases, too, of sickness at stomach, fevers, and gnawing sensations, it has been found by experience to be highly beneficial; as also, in combination with frankincense, for abscesses of the breasts. When the eyes are bloodshot from the effects of a blow, or affected with pain or defluxion, it is a very good plan to inject woman's milk into them, more particularly in combination with honey and juice of daffodil, or else powdered frankincense. In all cases, however, the milk of a woman who has been delivered of a male child is the most efficacious, and still more so if she has had male twins; provided always she abstains from wine and food of an acrid nature. Mixed with the white of an egg in a liquid state, and applied to the forehead in wool, it arrests defluxions of the eyes. If a frog has spirted its secretions into the eye, woman's milk is a most excellent remedy; and for the bite of that reptile it is used both internally and externally.

It is asserted that if a person is rubbed at the same moment with the milk of both mother and daughter, he will be proof for the rest of his life against all affections of the eyes. Mixed with a small quantity of oil, woman's milk is a cure for diseases of the ears; and if they are in pain from the effects of a blow, it is applied warm with goose-grease. If the ears emit an offensive smell, a thing that is mostly the case in diseases of long standing, wool is introduced into those organs, steeped in woman's milk and honey.

FACTS CONNECTED WITH THE MENSTRUAL DISCHARGE

Over and above these particulars, there is no limit to the marvellous powers attributed to females. For, in the first place, hailstorms, they say, whirlwinds, and lightning even, will be scared away by a woman uncovering her body while her monthly courses are upon her. The same, too, with all other kinds of tempestuous weather; and out at sea, a storm may be lulled by a woman uncovering her body merely, even though not menstruating at the time. As to the menstrual discharge itself, a thing that in other respects, as already stated on a more appropriate occasion, is productive of the most monstrous effects, there are some ravings about it of a most dreadful and unutterable nature. Of these particulars, however, I do not feel so much shocked at mentioning the following. If the menstrual discharge coincides with an eclipse of the moon or sun, the evils resulting from it are irremediable; and no less so, when it happens while the moon is in conjunction with the sun; the congress with a woman at such a period being noxious, and attended with fatal effects to the man. At this period also, the lustre of purple is tarnished by the touch of a woman; so much more baneful is her influence at this time than at any other. At any other time, also, if a woman strips herself naked while she is menstruating, and walks round a field of wheat, the caterpillars, worms, beetles, and other vermin, will fall from off the ears of corn. Metrodorus of Scepsos tells us that this discovery was first made in Cappadocia; and that, in consequence of such multitudes of cantharides being found to breed there, it is the practice for women to walk through the middle of the fields with their garments tucked up above the thighs. In other places, again, it is the usage for women to go barefoot, with the hair dishevelled and the girdle loose; due precaution must be taken, however, that this is not done at sun-rise, for if so, the crop will wither and dry up. Young vines, too, it is said, are injured irremediably by the touch of a woman in this state; and both rue and ivy, plants possessed of highly medicinal virtues, will die instantly upon being touched by her.

Icetidas the physician pledges his word that quartan fever may be cured by sexual intercourse, provided the woman is just beginning to menstruate. It is universally agreed, too, that when a person has been bitten by a dog and manifests a dread of water and of all kinds of drink, it will be quite sufficient to put under his cup a strip of cloth that has been dipped in this fluid; the result being that the hydrophobia will immediately disappear.

MEDICAMENTS DERIVED FROM FOREIGN ANIMALS: ELEPHANT, LION, CAMEL, HYÆNA

The blood of the elephant, the male in particular, arrests all those defluxions known by the name of "rheumatismi." Ivory shavings, it is said, in combination with Attic honey, are good for the removal of spots upon the face; with the sawdust, too, of ivory, hangnails are removed. By the touch of an elephant's trunk head-ache is alleviated, if the animal happens to sneeze at the time more particularly. The right side of the trunk, attached to the body with red earth of Lemnos, acts powerfully as an aphrodisiac. Elephant's blood is good for consumption, and the liver for epilepsy.

Lion's fat, mixed with oil of roses, protects the skin of the face from all kinds of spots, and preserves the whiteness of the complexion; it is remedial also for such parts of the body as have been frozen by snow, and for swellings in the joints. The gall, used as an ointment in combination with water, improves the eyesight, and, employed with the fat of the same animal, is a cure for epilepsy; but a slight taste only must be taken of it, and the patient must run immediately after swallowing it, in order to digest it. A lion's heart, used as food, is curative of quartan fevers, and the fat, taken with oil of roses, of quotidian fevers. Wild beasts will fly from persons anointed with lion's fat, and it is thought to be a preservative even against treacherous practices.

A camel's brains, dried and taken in vinegar, are a cure, they say, for epilepsy; the same, too, with the gall, taken with honey; which is a remedy also for quinsy.

A camel's tail dried, it is said, is productive of diarrhœa, and ashes of burnt camel's dung, mixed with oil, make the hair curl. These ashes, applied topically, are very useful for dysentery, as also taken in drink, the proper dose being a pinch in three fingers at a time; they are curative also of epilepsy. Camel's urine it is said, is very useful to fullers, and is good for the cure of running sores. Barbarous nations, we are told, are in the habit of keeping it till it is five years old, and then taking it as a purgative, in doses of one semisextarius. The hairs of the tail, it is said, plaited and attached to the left arm, are a cure for quartan fevers.

But of all animals, it is the hyæna that has been held in the highest admiration by the magicians, who have gone so far as to attribute to it certain magical virtues even, and the power of alluring human beings and depriving them of their senses.

The hyæna, it is said, is particularly terrible to panthers; so much so, indeed, that they will not attempt to make the slightest resistance to it, and will never attack a man who has any portion of a hyæna's skin about him. A thing truly marvellous to tell of, if the hides of these two animals are hung up facing one another, the hair will fall from off the panther's skin! When the hyæna flies before the hunter, it turns off on the right, and letting the man get before it, follows in his track; should it succeed in doing which, the man is sure to lose his senses and fall from his horse even. But if, on the other hand, it turns off to the left, it is a sign that the animal is losing strength, and that it will soon be taken.

We learn also, from the same sources, that the teeth of the hyæna are useful for the cure of tooth-ache, the diseased tooth being either touched with them, or the animal's teeth being arranged in their regular order, and attached to the patient; that the shoulders of this animal are good for the cure of pains in the arms and shoulders; that the teeth, extracted from the left side of the jaw, and wrapped in the skin of a sheep or he-goat, are an effectual cure for pains in the stomach; that the lights of the animal, taken with the food, are good for cœliac affections; that the lights, reduced to ashes and applied with oil, are also soothing to the stomach.

Persons afflicted with night-mare and dread of spectres, will experience relief, they say, by attaching one of the large teeth of a hyæna to the body, with a linen thread. In fits of delirium too, it is recommended to fumigate the patient with the smoke of one of these teeth, and to attach one in front of his chest, with the fat of the kidneys, or else the liver or skin. They assert also that a pregnant woman will never miscarry, if she wears suspended from her neck, the white flesh from a hyena's breast, with seven hairs and the genitals of a stag, the whole tied up in the skin of a gazelle. The genitals, they say, eaten with honey, act as a stimulant upon a person, according to the sex, and this even though it should be the case of a man who has manifested an aversion to all intercourse with females.

REMEDIES DERIVED FROM THE CROCODILE

The teeth of the right jaw of the crocodile, attached to the right arm as an amulet, acts as an aphrodisiac, that is, if we choose to believe it. The eye-teeth of the animal, filled with frankincense —for they are hollow— are a cure for periodical fevers, care being taken to let the patient remain five days without seeing the person who has attached them to his body. A similar virtue is attributed to the small stones which are found in the belly of this animal, as being a check to the cold shiverings in fevers, when about to come on; and with the same object the Ægyptians are in the habit of anointing their sick with the fat of the crocodile.

The ashes of the skin of the crocodile, applied with vinegar to such parts of the body as are about to undergo an incision, or indeed the very smell of the skin when burning, will render the patient insensible to the knife. The blood of the crocodile, applied to the eyes, effaces marks upon those organs and improves the sight. The body, with the exception of the head and feet, is eaten, boiled, for the cure of sciatica, and is found very useful for chronic coughs, in children more particularly; it is equally good, too, for the cure of lumbago. These animals have a certain fat also, which, applied to the hair, makes it fall off; persons anointed with this fat are effectually protected against crocodiles, and it is the practice to drop it into wounds inflicted by them. A crocodile's heart, attached to the body in the wool of a black sheep without a speck of any other colour, due care too being taken that the sheep was the first lamb yeaned by its dam, will effectually cure a quartan fever, it is said.

MEDICAMENTS DERIVED FROM THE HIPPOPOTAMUS

Between the crocodile, too, and the hippopotamus there is a certain affinity, frequenting as they do the same river, and being both of them of an amphibious nature. Its hide, reduced to ashes and applied with water, is curative of inflamed tumours, and the fat, as well as the dung, used as a fumigation, is employed for the cure of cold agues. With the teeth of the left side of the jaw, the gums are scarified for the cure of tooth-ache. The skin of the left side of the forehead, attached to the groin, acts as an anti-aphrodisiac; and an application of the ashes of the same part will cause the hair to grow when lost through alopecy. The testicles are taken in water, in doses of one drachma, for the cure of injuries inflicted by serpents. The blood is made use of by painters.

MEDICINAL USES OF MILK

We will now return to our own part of the world, speaking, first of all, of certain remedies common to animals in general, but excellent in their nature; such as the use of milk, for example. The most beneficial milk to every creature is the mother's milk. It is highly dangerous for nursing women to conceive; children that are suckled by them are known among us as "colostrati," their milk being thick, like cheese in appearance —the name "colostra," it should be remembered, is given to the first milk secreted after delivery, which assumes a spongy, coagulated form. The most nutritive milk, in all cases, is woman's milk, and next to that goats' milk, to which is owing, probably, the fabulous story that Jupiter was suckled by a goat. The sweetest, next to woman's milk, is camels' milk; but the most efficacious, medicinally speaking, is asses' milk. It is in animals of the largest size and individuals of the greatest bulk, that the milk is secreted with the greatest facility. Goats' milk agrees the best with the stomach, that animal browsing more than grazing. Cows' milk is considered more medicinal, while ewes' milk is sweeter and more nutritive, but not so well adapted to the stomach, it being more oleaginous than any other.

Milk is employed as an injection where excoriations have been caused by the use of strong purgatives; in cases also where dysentery is productive of chafing, it is similarly employed, boiled with sea pebbles or a ptisan of barley. Where, however, the intestines are excoriated, cows' milk or ewes' milk is the best. New milk is used as an injection for dysentery; and in an unboiled state, it is employed for affections of the colon and uterus, and for injuries inflicted by serpents. It is also taken internally as an antidote to the venom of cantharides, the pine-caterpillar, the buprestis,[5] and the salamander. Cows' milk is particularly recommended for persons who have taken colchicum, hemlock, dorycnium,[6] or the flesh of the sea-hare; and asses' milk, in cases where gypsum, white-lead, sulphur, or quick-silver, have been taken internally.

THE VARIOUS USES OF FAT

Among the remedies common to living creatures, fat is the substance held in the next highest esteem, that of swine in particular, which was employed by the ancients for certain religious purposes even; at all events, it is still the usage for the newly-wedded bride, when entering her husband's house, to touch the doorposts with it. There are two methods of keeping hogs' lard, either salted or fresh; indeed, the older it is, the better. The Greek writers have now given it the name of "axungia," or axle-grease, in their works. Nor, in fact, is it any secret, why swine's fat should be possessed of such marked properties, seeing that the animal feeds to such a great extent upon the roots of plants; owing too, to which, its dung is applied to such a vast number of purposes. It will be as well, therefore, to premise, that I shall here speak only of the hog that feeds in the open field, and no other; of which kind it is the female that is much the most useful-if she has never farrowed, more particularly. But it is the fat of the wild boar that is held in by far the highest esteem of all.

The distinguishing properties, then, of swine's-grease, are emollient, calorific, resolvent, and detergent. Some physicians recommend it as an ointment for the gout, mixed with goose grease, bull-suet, and wool-grease; in cases, however, where the pain is persistent, it should be used in combination with wax, myrtle, resin, and pitch. Hogs' lard is used fresh for the cure of burns, and of blains, too, caused by snow; with ashes of burnt barley and nutgalls, in equal proportions, it is employed for the cure of chilblains. It is good also for excoriations of the limbs, and for dispelling weariness and lassitude arising from long journeys.

GALL

But among the substances which are furnished in common by the various animals, it is the gall, we may say, that is the most efficacious of all. The properties of this substance are of a calorific, pungent, resolvent, extractive, and dispersive nature. The gall of the smaller animals is looked upon as the most penetrating; for which reason it is that it is generally considered the most efficacious for the com-

---

5   A venomous beetle, whose sting caused a swelling in cattle (TN).
6   A poisonous plant (TN).

Book XXVIII - Medicaments Derived From Living Creatures (I)...

position of eye-salves. Bull's gall is possessed of a remarkable degree of potency, having the effect of imparting a golden tint to the surface of copper even and to vessels made of other metals. Gall in every case is prepared in the following manner; it is taken fresh, and the orifice of the vesicle in which it is contained being tied fast with a strong linen thread, it is left to steep for half an hour in boiling water; after which it is dried in the shade, and then put away for keeping, in honey.

BLOOD

The blood, also, of the horse is possessed of certain corrosive properties; and so, too, is mare's blood-except, indeed, where the animal has not been covered-it having the effect of cauterizing the margins of ulcers, and so enlarging them. Bull's blood too, taken fresh, is reckoned among the poisons; except, indeed, at Ægira, at which place the priestess of the Earth, when about to foretell coming events, takes a draught of bull's blood before she descends into the cavern; so powerful, in fact, is the agency of that sympathy so generally spoken of, that it may occasionally originate, we find, in feelings of religious awe, or in the peculiar nature of the locality.

PECULIAR REMEDIES DERIVED FROM VARIOUS ANIMALS

We will therefore classify the various remedies, according to the maladies for which they are respectively used; and, first of all, those to which man has recourse for injuries inflicted by serpents. That deer are destructive to those reptiles no one is ignorant; as also of the fact that they drag them from their holes when they find them, and so devour them. And it is not only while alive and breathing that deer are thus fatal to serpents, but even when dead and separated limb from limb. The fumes of their horns, while burning, will drive away serpents, but the bones, it is said, of the upper part of a stag's throat, if burnt upon a fire, will bring those reptiles together. Persons may sleep upon a deer's skin in perfect safety, and without any apprehension of attacks by serpents; its rennet too, taken with vinegar, is an effectual antidote to the stings of those reptiles; indeed, if it has been only touched by a person, he will be for that day effectually protected from them. The testicles, dried, or the genitals of the male animal, are considered to be very wholesome, taken in wine.

As a preservative against the attacks of serpents, the brains and blood of the wild boar are held in high esteem; the liver also, dried and taken in wine with rue; and the fat, used with honey and resin. Similar properties are attributed to the liver of the domesticated boar and the outer filaments, and those only, of the gall, these last being taken in doses of four denarii; the brains also, taken in wine, are equally effectual. The fumes of the burning horns or hair of a she-goat will repel serpents, they say; the ashes, too, of the horns, used either internally or externally, are thought to be an antidote to their poison. A similar effect is attributed to goats' milk, taken with Taminian grapes; to the urine of those animals, taken with squill vinegar; to goats' milk cheese, applied with origanum; and to goat suet, used with wax.

REMEDIES AGAINST ENCHANTMENTS

The dried muzzle of a wolf, they say, is an effectual preservative against the malpractices of magic; and it is for this reason that it is so commonly to be seen fastened to the doors of farm-houses. A similar degree of efficacy, it is thought, belongs to the skin of the neck, when taken whole from the animal. Indeed, so powerful is the influence of this animal, that if a horse only treads in its track, it will be struck with torpor in consequence.

MEDICAMENTS FOR AFFECTIONS OF THE EYES

For eye fluxes, beef suet, boiled with oil, is applied to the parts affected; and for eruptions of those organs, ashes of burnt deer's horns are similarly employed, the tips of the horns being considered the most effectual for the purpose. For the cure of cataract, it is reckoned a good plan to apply a wolf's excrements; the same substance, too, reduced to ashes, is used for the dispersion of films, in combination with Attic honey. Bear's gall, too, is similarly employed; and for the cure of epinyctis,[7] wild boar's lard, mixed with oil of roses, is thought to be very useful. An ass's hoof, reduced to ashes and applied with asses' milk, is used for the removal of marks in the eyes and indurations of the crystalline humours. Beef marrow, from the right fore leg, beaten up with soot, is employed for affections of the eyebrows, and for diseases of the eyelids and corners of the eyes.

She-goats, they say, are never affected with ophthalmia, from the circumstance that they browse upon certain kinds of herbs; the same, too, with the gazelle. Hence it is that we find it recommended, at the time of new moon, to swallow the dung of these animals, coated with wax. As they are able to see, too, by night, it is a general belief that the blood of a hegoat is a cure for those persons affected with dimness of sight to whom the Greeks have given the name of "nyctalopes."

MEDICAMENTS FOR TOOTH-ACHE

The ashes of deer's horns strengthen loose teeth and allay tooth-ache, used either as a friction or as a gargle. Some persons, however, are of opinion that the horn, unburnt and reduced to powder, is still more efficacious for all these purposes. Dentifrices are made both from the powder and the ashes. Another excellent remedy is a wolf's head, reduced to ashes; it is a well-known fact, too, that there are bones generally found in the excrements of that animal; these bones, attached to the body as an amulet, are productive of advantageous effects. For the cure of tooth-ache, hare's rennet is injected into the ear; the head also of that animal, reduced to ashes, is used in the form of a dentifrice, and, with the addition of nard, is a corrective of bad breath. Some persons, however, think it a better plan to mix the ashes of a mouse's head with the dentifrice. In the side of the hare there is a bone found, similar to a needle in appearance; for the cure of tooth-ache it is recommended to scarify the gums with this bone. The pastern-bone of an ox, ignited and applied to loose teeth which ache, has the effect of strengthening them in the sockets; the same bone, reduced to ashes, and mixed with myrrh, is also used as a

---

7   Night-blains, pustules that arise in the night (TN).

dentifrice. The ashes of burnt pig's feet are productive of a similar effect, as also the calcined bones of the cotyloïd cavities in which the hip-bones move. It is a well-known fact, that, introduced into the throat of beasts of burden, these bones are a cure for worms, and that, in a calcined state, they are good for strengthening the teeth.

MEDICAMENTS FOR COUGH AND FOR SPITTING OF BLOOD

A wolf's liver, administered in mulled wine, is a cure for cough; a bear's gall also, mixed with honey; the ashes of the tips of a cow's horn; or else the saliva of a horse, taken in the drink for three consecutive days—in which last case the horse will be sure to die, they say. A deer's lights are useful for the same purpose, dried with the gullet of the animal in the smoke, and then beaten up with honey, and taken daily as an electuary; the spitter deer, be it remarked, is the kind that is the most efficacious for the purpose.

Spitting of blood is cured by taking ashes of burnt deer's horns, or else a hare's rennet in drink, in doses of one-third of a denarius, with Samian earth and myrtle-wine. The dung of this last animal, reduced to ashes and taken in the evening, with wine, is good for coughs that are recurrent at night.

MEDICAMENTS FOR BOWEL COMPLAINTS

To arrest looseness of the bowels, deer's blood is used; the ashes also of deer's horns; the liver of a wild boar, taken fresh and without salt, in wine; a swine's liver roasted, or that of a he-goat, boiled in five semisextarii of wine; a hare's rennet boiled, in quantities the size of a chick-pea, in wine, or, if there are symptoms of fever, in water. To this last some persons add nut-galls, while others, again, content themselves with hare's blood boiled by itself in milk. Ashes; too, of burnt horse-dung are taken in water for this purpose; or else ashes of the part of an old bull's horn which lies nearest the root, sprinkled in water; the blood, too, of a he-goat boiled upon charcoal; or a decoction made from a goat's hide boiled with the hair on.

Cœliac affections and dysentery are cured by taking cow's liver; ashes of deer's horns, a pinch in three fingers swallowed in water; hare's rennet, kneaded up in bread, or, if there is any discharge of blood, taken with polenta; or else boar's dung, swine's dung, or hare's dung, reduced to ashes and mixed with mulled wine.

MEDICAMENTS FOR GOUT AND FOR DISEASES OF THE FEET

For the cure of gout, bears' grease is employed, mixed in equal proportions with bull-suet and wax; some persons add to the composition, hypocisthis[8] and nut-galls. Others, again, prefer he-goat suet, mixed with the dung of a she-goat and saffron, or else with mustard, or sprigs of ivy pounded and used with perdicium, or with flowers of wild cucumber. Cow dung is also used, with lees of vinegar. Some persons speak highly in praise of the dung of a calf which has not begun to graze, or else a bull's blood, without any other addition; a fox, also, boiled alive till only the bones are left; a wolf boiled alive in oil to the consistency of a cerate; he-

---

8   A parasitic plant that grows on the cisthus, Asarum hypocistis, Linn. (TN).

goat suet, with an equal proportion of pellitory, and one-third part of mustard; or ashes of goats' dung, mixed with axle-grease. They say, too, that for sciatica, it is an excellent plan to apply this dung boiling hot beneath the great toes; and that, for diseases of the joints, it is highly efficacious to attach bears' gall or hares' feet to the part affected. Gout, they say, may be allayed by the patient always carrying about with him a hare's foot, cut off from the animal alive.

Bears' grease is a cure for chilblains and all kinds of chaps upon the feet; with the addition of alum, it is still more efficacious. The same results are produced by using goat-suet; a horse's teeth powdered; the gall of a wild boar or hog; or else the lights of those animals, applied with their grease; and this, too, where the soles are blistered, or the feet have been crushed by a substance striking against them. In cases where the feet have been frozen, ashes of burnt hare's fur are used; and for contusions of the feet, the lights of that animal are applied, sliced or reduced to ashes.

MEDICAMENTS FOR FEVERS

Deer's flesh is a febrifuge. Periodical and recurrent fevers are cured, if we are to believe what the magicians tell us, by wearing the right eye of a wolf, salted, and attached as an amulet. For quartan fever, the magicians recommend cats' dung to be attached to the body, with the toe of a horned owl, and, that the fever may not be recurrent, not to be removed until the seventh paroxysm is past. Who, pray, could have ever made such a discovery as this? And what, too, can be the meaning of this combination? Why, of all things in the world, was the toe of a horned owl made choice of?

Other adepts in this art, who are more moderate in their suggestions, recommend for quartan fever, the salted liver of a cat that has been killed while the moon was on the wane, to be taken in wine just before the paroxysms come on. The magicians recommend, too, that the toes of the patient should be rubbed with the ashes of burnt cow-dung, diluted with a boy's urine, and that a hare's heart should be attached to the hands; they prescribe, also, hare's rennet, to be taken in drink just before the paroxysms come on. New goats' milk cheese is also given with honey, the whey being carefully extracted first.

MEDICAMENTS FOR SPRAINS, INDURATIONS AND BOILS

For the cure of sprains the following applications are used; wild boars' dung or swine's dung; calves' dung; wild boars' foam, used fresh with vinegar; goats' dung, applied with honey; and raw beef, used as a plaster. For swellings, swine's dung is used, warmed in an earthen pot, and beaten up with oil. The best emollient for all kinds of indurations upon the body is wolf's fat, applied topically. In the case of sores which are wanted to break, the most effectual plan is to apply cow-dung warmed in hot ashes, or else goats' dung boiled in vinegar or wine. For the cure of boils, beef-suet is applied with salt; but if they are attended with pain, it is melted with oil, and no salt is used. Goat-suet is employed in a similar manner.

MEDICAMENTS FOR THE ITCH

The itch in man is cured very effectually by using the marrow of an ass, or the urine of that animal, applied with the mud it has formed upon the ground. Butter, too, is very good; as also in the case of beasts of burden, if applied with warmed resin; bull glue is also used, melted in vinegar, and incorporated with lime; or goat's gall, mixed with calcined alum. The eruption called "boa," is treated with cow-dung, a fact to which it is indebted for its name. The itch in dogs is cured by an application of fresh cows' blood, which, when quite dry, is renewed a second time, and is rubbed off the next day with strong lye-ashes.

MEDICAMENTS FOR FEMALE DISEASES

Menstruation is promoted by using bull's gall, in unwashed wool, as a pessary; Olympias of Thebe adds hyssop and nitre. Ashes, too, of deer's horns are taken in drink for the same purpose, and for derangements of the uterus they are applied topically, as also bull's gall, used as a pessary with opium, in the proportion of two oboli. It is a good plan, too, to use fumigations for the uterus, made with deer's hair, burnt. Hinds, they say, when they find themselves pregnant, are in the habit of swallowing a small stone. This stone, when found in their excrements, or in the uterus, attached to the body as an amulet, is a preventive of abortion. There are also certain small stones, found in the heart and uterus of these animals, which are very useful for women during pregnancy and in travail.

Where the foetus is felt to be dead in the uterus, the lichens or excrescences from a horse's legs, taken in fresh water, will act as an expellent; an effect produced also by a fumigation made with the hoofs or dry dung of that animal. Procidence of the uterus is arrested by using butter, in the form of an injection; and indurations of that organ are removed by similarly employing ox-gall, with oil of roses, turpentine being applied externally in wool. They say, too, that a fumigation, made from ox-dung, acts as a corrective upon prolapse of the uterus, and facilitates parturition; and that conception is promoted by the use of cows' milk. It is a well-known fact that sterility is often entailed by suffering in child-birth; an evil which may be averted, Olympias of Thebes assures us, by rubbing the parts, before sexual intercourse, with bull's gall, serpents' fat, verdigris, and honey. In cases, too, where menstruation is too abundant, the external parts should be sprinkled with a solution of calf's gall, the moment before the sexual congress; a method which acts emolliently also upon indurations of the abdomen.

STIMULANTS FOR THE SEXUAL PASSIONS

Among the aphrodisiacs, we find mentioned, a wild boar's gall, applied externally; swine's marrow, taken inwardly; asses' fat, mixed with the grease of a gander and applied as a liniment; the virulent substance described by Virgil as distilling from mares when covered; and the dried testicles of a horse, pulverized and mixed with the drink. The right testicle, also, of an ass, is taken in a proportionate quantity of wine, or worn attached to the arm in a bracelet; or else the froth discharged by that animal after covering, collected in a piece of red cloth and enclosed in silver, as Osthanes informs us. Salpe recommends the genitals of this animal to be plunged seven times in boiling oil, and the corresponding parts to be well rubbed therewith. Balcon says that these genitals should be reduced to ashes and taken in drink; or else the urine; that has been voided by a bull immediately after covering; he recommends, also, that the groin should be well rubbed with earth moistened with this urine.

Mouse-dung, on the other hand, applied in the form of a liniment, acts as an anti-aphrodisiac. The lights of a wild boar or swine, roasted, are an effectual preservative against drunkenness; they must, however, be eaten fasting, and upon the same day. The lights of a kid, too, are productive of the same effect.

BOOK XXIX

History of Medicine and Medicaments Derived From Living Creatures (II)

THE ORIGIN OF THE MEDICAL ART

The nature and multiplicity of the various remedies already described or which still remain to be enlarged upon, compel me to enter upon some further details with reference to the art of medicine itself. Commencing by ranking its inventors in the number of the gods, and consecrating for them a place in heaven, the art of medicine, at the present day even, teaches us in numerous instances to have recourse to the oracles for aid.

Its succeeding history, a fact that is truly marvellous, remains enveloped in the densest night, down to the time of the Peloponnesian War; at which period it was restored to light by the agency of Hippocrates, a native of Cos, an island flourishing and powerful in the highest degree, and consecrated to Æsculapius. It being the practice for persons who had recovered from a disease to describe in the temple of that god the remedies to which they had owed their restoration to health, that others might derive benefit therefrom in a similar emergency; Hippocrates, it is said, copied out these prescriptions, and, as our fellow-countryman Varro will have it, after burning the temple to the ground,[1] instituted that branch of medical practice which is known as "Clinics."

In the rules laid down by these professors, changes were effected by Chrysippus with a vast parade of words, and, after Chrysippus, by Erasistratus, son of the daughter of Aristotle. For the cure of King Antiochus –to give our first illustration of the profits realized by the medical art– Erasistratus received from his son, King Ptolemæus, the sum of one hundred talents.

---

1 In order to destroy the medical books and prescriptions there.

Another sect again, known as that of the Empirics —be cause it based its rules upon the results of experiment— took its rise in Sicily, having for its founder Acron of Agrigentum, a man recommended by the high authority of Empedocles the physician.

These several schools of medicine, long at variance among themselves, were all of them condemned by Herophilus, who regulated the arterial pulsation according to the musical scale, correspondingly with the age of the patient. In succeeding years again, the theories of this sect were abandoned, it being found that to belong to it necessitated an acquaintance with literature. Changes, too, were effected in the school, of which, Asclepiades had become the founder. His disciple, Themison, who at first in his writings implicitly followed him, soon afterwards, in compliance with the growing degeneracy of the age, went so far as to modify his own methods of treatment; which, in their turn, were entirely displaced, with the authorization of the late Emperor Augustus, by Antonius Musa, a physician who had rescued that prince from a most dangerous malady, by following a mode of treatment diametrically opposite.

During the reign of the Emperor Nero, that the destinies of the medical art passed into the hands of Thessalus, a man who swept away all the precepts of his predecessors, and declaimed with a sort of frenzy against the physicians of every age; but he was at last eclipsed in credit by Crinas, a native of Massilia, who, to wear an appearance of greater discreetness and more devoutness, united in himself the pursuit of two sciences, and prescribed diets to his patients in accordance with the movements of the heavenly bodies, as indicated by the almanacs of the mathematicians, taking observations himself of the various times and seasons.

It was while these men were ruling our destinies, that all at once, Charmis, a native also of Massilia, took the City by surprise. Not content with condemning the practice or preceding physicians, he proscribed the use of warm baths as well, and persuaded people, in the very depth of winter even, to immerse themselves in cold water. His patients he used to plunge into large vessels filled with cold water, and it was a common thing to see aged men of consular rank make it a matter of parade to freeze themselves; a method of treatment, in favour of which Annæus Seneca gives his personal testimony, in writings still extant.

There can be no doubt whatever, that all these men, in the pursuit of celebrity by the introduction of some novelty or other, made purchase of it at the downright expense of human life. Hence those woeful discussions, those consultations at the bedside of the patient, where no one thinks fit to be of the same opinion as another, lest he may have the appearance of being subordinate to another; hence, too, that ominous inscription to be read upon a tomb, "It was the multitude of physicians that killed me."

The medical art, so often modified and renewed as it has been, is still on the change from day to day, and still are we impelled onwards by the puffs which emanate from the ingenuity of the Greeks. It is quite evident too, that every one among them that finds himself skilled in the art of speech, may forthwith create himself the arbiter of our life and death; as though, forsooth, there were not thousands of nations who live without any physicians at all, though not, for all that, without the aid of medicine. Such, for instance, was the Roman people, for a period of more than six hundred years; a people, too, which has never shown itself slow to adopt all useful arts, and which even welcomed the medical art with avidity, until, after a fair experience of it, there was found good reason to condemn it.

THE OPINIONS ENTERTAINED BY THE ROMANS ON THE ANCIENT PHYSICIANS

"Concerning those Greeks, son Marcus, I will speak to you more at length on the befitting occasion. I will show you the results of my own experience at Athens, and that, while it is a good plan to dip into their literature, it is not worth while to make a thorough acquaintance with it. They are a most iniquitous and intractable race, and you may take my word as the word of a prophet, when I tell you, that whenever that nation shall bestow its literature upon Rome it will mar everything; and that all the sooner, if it sends its physicians among us. They have conspired among themselves to murder all barbarians with their medicine; a profession which they exercise for lucre, in order that they may win our confidence, and dispatch us all the more easily. They are in the common habit, too, of calling us barbarians, and stigmatize us beyond all other nations, by giving us the abominable appellation of Opici.[2] I forbid you to have anything to do with physicians."

REMEDIES DERIVED FROM WOOL AND EGGS

I shall begin then with some remedies that are well known, those namely, which are derived from wool and from the eggs of birds, thus giving due honour to those substances which hold the principal place in the estimation of mankind; though at the same time I shall be necessitated to speak of some others out of their proper place, according as occasion may offer.

The ancient Romans attributed to wool a degree of religious importance even, and it was in this spirit that they enjoined that the bride should touch the doorposts of her husband's house with wool. In addition to dress and protection from the cold, wool, in an unwashed state, used in combination with oil, and wine or vinegar, supplies us with numerous remedies, according as we stand in need of an emollient or an excitant, an astringent or a laxative. Wetted from time to time with these liquids, greasy wool is applied to sprained limbs, and to sinews that are suffering from pain. In the case of sprains, some persons are in the habit of adding salt, while others, again, apply pounded rue and grease, in wool; the same, too, in the case of contusions or tumours. Wool will improve the breath, it is said, if the teeth and gums are rubbed with it, mixed with honey; it is very good, too, for phrenitis, used as a fumigation. To arrest bleeding at the nose, wool is introduced into the nostrils with oil of roses; or it is used in another manner, the ears being well plugged with it. In the case of inveterate ulcers it is applied topically with honey;

---

2 The Opici or Osci were an ancient tribe of Italy, settled in Campania, Latium, and Samnium. From their uncivilized habits the name was long used as a reproachful epithet, equivalent to our words "bumpkin," "clodhopper," or "chawbacon."

soaked in wine or vinegar, or in cold water and oil, and then squeezed out, it is used for the cure of wounds.

Rams' wool, washed in cold water, and steeped in oil, is used for female complaints, and to allay inflammations of the uterus. Prolapsus of the uterus is reduced by using this wool in the form of a fumigation. Greasy wool, used as a plaster and as a pessary, brings away the dead fœtus, and arrests uterine discharges. Bites inflicted by a mad dog are plugged with unwashed wool, the application being removed at the end of seven days. Applied with cold water, it is a cure for agnails; steeped in a mixture of boiling nitre, sulphur, oil, vinegar, and tar, and applied twice a day, as warm as possible, it allays pains in the loins. By making ligatures with unwashed rams' wool about the extremities of the limbs, bleeding is effectually stopped.

REMEDIES DERIVED FROM EGGS

There is a considerable affinity also between wool and eggs, which are applied together as a frontal to the forehead by way of cure for eye fluxes. Wool, however, is not required for this purpose to have been dressed with radicula, the only thing requisite to be combined with it being the white of an egg and powdered frankincense. The white of an egg, also applied by itself, arrests eye fluxes, and has a cooling effect upon inflammations of those organs; some, however, prefer mixing saffron with it, and employ it as an ingredient in eye-salves, in place of water. For ophthalmia in infants there is hardly any remedy to be found, except white of egg mixed with fresh butter. Eggs beaten up with oil, are very soothing for erysipelas, beet leaves being laid on the liniment.

For cœliac fluxes, it is recommended to take the yolks of eggs, with like proportions of pulpy raisins and pomegranate rind, in equal quantities, for three consecutive days; or else to follow another method, and take the yolks of three eggs, with three ounces of old bacon and honey, and three cyathi of old wine; the whole being beaten up to the consistency of honey, and taken in water, when needed, in pieces the size of a hazel nut.

In what various ways eggs are used as food is well known to all, passing downwards, however swollen the throat may be, and warming the parts as they pass. Eggs, too, are the only diet which, while it affords nutriment in sickness, does not load the stomach, possessing at the same moment all the advantages both of food and drink. The shell of an egg becomes soft when steeped in vinegar; it is by the aid of eggs thus prepared, and kneaded up with meal into bread, that patients suffering from the cœliac flux are often restored to strength.

REMEDIES DERIVED FROM THE DOG

In reference to the dog, the usages of our forefathers compel us to enter into some further details. They considered the flesh of sucking whelps to be so pure a meat, that they were in the habit of using them as victims even in their expiatory sacrifices. A young whelp, too, is sacrificed to Genita Mana;[3] and, at the repasts celebrated in honour of the gods, it is still the usage to set whelps' flesh on table; at

---

3   An ancient divinity, who is supposed to have presided over childbirth.

Book XXIX - History of Medicine and Medicaments Derived... 345

the inaugural feasts, too, of the pontiffs, this dish was in common use, as we learn from the Comedies of Plautus. It is generally thought that for narcotic poisons there is nothing better than dogs' blood; and it would appear that it was this animal that first taught man the use of emetics. Other medicinal uses of the dog which are marvellously commended, I shall have occasion to refer to on the appropriate occasions.

REMEDIES DERIVED FROM BUGS

There are some things, of a most revolting nature, but which are recommended by authors with such a degree of assurance, that it would be improper to omit them, the more particularly as it is to the sympathy or antipathy of objects that remedies owe their existence. Thus the bug, for instance, a most filthy insect, and one the very name of which inspires us with loathing, is said to be a neutralizer of the venom of serpents, asps in particular, and to be a preservative against all kinds of poisons. As a proof of this, they tell us that the sting of an asp is never fatal to poultry, if they have eaten bugs that day; and that, if such is the case, their flesh is remarkably beneficial to persons who have been stung by serpents. Of the various recipes given in reference to these insects, the least revolting are the application of them externally to the wound, with the blood of a tortoise; the employment of them as a fumigation to make leeches loose their hold; and the administering of them to animals in drink when a leech has been accidentally swallowed. Some persons, however, go so far as to crush bugs with salt and woman's milk, and anoint the eyes with the mixture; in combination, too, with honey and oil of roses, they use them as an injection for the ears. Field-bugs, again, and those found upon the mallow, are burnt, and the ashes mixed with oil of roses as an injection for the ears.

As to the other remedial virtues attributed to bugs, for the cure of vomiting, quartan fevers, and other diseases, although we find recommendations given to swallow them in an egg, some wax, or in a bean, I look upon them as utterly unfounded, and not worthy of further notice. They are employed, however, for the treatment of lethargy, and with some fair reason, as they successfully neutralize the narcotic effects of the poison of the asp; for this purpose seven of them are administered in a cyathus of water, but in the case of children only four. In cases, too, of strangury, they have been injected into the urinary channel; so true it is that Nature, that universal parent, has engendered nothing without some powerful reason or other. In addition to these particulars, a couple of bugs, it is said, attached to the left arm in some wool that has been stolen from the shepherds, will effectually cure nocturnal fevers; while those recurrent in the daytime may be treated with equal success by enclosing the bugs in a piece of russet-coloured cloth. The scolopendra, on the other hand, is a great enemy to these insects; used in the form of a fumigation, it kills them.

REMEDIES DERIVED FROM THE SALAMANDER

But of all venomous animals it is the salamander that is by far the most dangerous; for while other reptiles attack individuals only, and never kill many persons at a time, the salamander is able to destroy whole nations at once, unless they take the proper precautions against it. For if this reptile happens to crawl up a tree, it infects all the fruit with its poison, and kills those who eat thereof by the chilling properties of its venom, which in its effects is in no way different from aconite. Nay, even more than this, if it only touches with its foot the wood upon which bread is baked, or if it happens to fall into a well, the same fatal effects will be sure to ensue. The saliva, too, of this reptile, if it comes in contact with any part of the body, the sole of the foot even, will cause the hair to fall off from the whole of the body. And yet the salamander, highly venomous as it is, is eaten by certain animals, swine for example; owing, no doubt, to that antipathy which prevails in the natural world.

From what we find stated, it is most probable, that, next to the animals which eat it, the best neutralizers of the poison of this reptile, are, cantharides taken in drink, or a lizard eaten with the food; other antidotes we have already mentioned, or shall notice in the appropriate place. As to what the magicians[4] say, that it is proof against fire, being, as they tell us, the only animal that has the property of extinguishing fire, if it had been true, it would have been made trial of at Rome long before this. Sextius says that the salamander, preserved in honey and taken with the food, after removing the intestines, head, and feet, acts as an aphrodisiac; he denies also that it has the property of extinguishing fire.

REMEDIES FOR THE BITE OF THE MAD DOG

When a person has been bitten by a mad dog, he may be preserved from hydrophobia by applying the ashes of a dog's head to the wound. All ashes of this description, we may here remark once for all, are prepared in the same method; the substance being placed in a new earthen vessel well covered with potter's clay, and put into a furnace. These ashes, too, are very good, taken in drink, and hence some recommend the head itself to be eaten in such cases. Others, again, attach to the body of the patient a maggot, taken from the carcase of a dead dog; or else place the menstruous blood of a bitch, in a linen cloth, beneath his cup, or insert in the wound ashes of hairs from the tail of the dog that inflicted the bite. Dogs will fly from any one who has a dog's heart about him, and they will never bark at a person who carries a dog's tongue in his shoe, beneath the great toe, or the tail of a weasel which has been set at liberty after being deprived of it. There is beneath the tongue of a mad dog a certain slimy spittle, which, taken in drink, is a preventive of hydrophobia; but much the most useful plan is, to take the liver of the dog that has inflicted the injury, and eat it raw, if possible; should that not be the case, it must be cooked in some way or other, or else a broth must be taken, prepared from the flesh.

There is a small worm[5] in a dog's tongue, known as "lytta" to the Greeks; if this is removed from the animal while a pup, it will never become mad or lose its appetite. This worm, after being carried thrice round a fire, is given to persons

---

4   He probably alludes to the Magi of Persia here, as most of the stories about the salamander appear to bear the aspect of an Eastern origin.

5   This is still the vulgar notion; but in reality there is no worm, but certain white pustules beneath the tongue, which break spontaneously at the end of twelve days after birth. Puppies

Book XXIX - History of Medicine and Medicaments Derived... 347

who have been bitten by a mad dog, to prevent them from becoming mad. This madness, too, is prevented by eating a cock's brains; but the virtue of these brains lasts for one year only, and no more. They say, too, that a cock's comb, pounded, is highly efficacious as an application to the wound; as also, goose-grease, mixed with honey. The flesh also of a mad dog is sometimes salted, and taken with the food, as a remedy for this disease.

REMEDIES FOR HEAD-ACHE AND FOR WOUNDS ON THE HEAD

A good remedy for head-ache are the heads taken from the snails which are found without[6] shells, and in an imperfect state. In these heads there is found a hard stony substance, about as large as a common pebble; on being extracted from the snail, it is attached to the patient, the smaller snails being pounded and applied to the forehead. Wool-grease, too, is used for a similar purpose; the bones of a vulture's head, worn as an amulet; or the brains of that bird, mixed with oil and cedar resin, and applied to the head and introduced into the nostrils. The brains of a crow or owlet, are boiled and taken with the food; or a cock is put into a coop, and kept without food a day and a night, the patient submitting to a similar abstinence, and attaching to his head some feathers plucked from the neck or the comb of the fowl. The ashes, too, of a weasel are applied in the form of a liniment; a twig is taken from a kite's nest, and laid beneath the patient's pillow; or a mouse's skin is burnt, and the ashes applied with vinegar; sometimes, also, the small bone is extracted from the head of a snail that has been found between two cart ruts, and after being passed through a gold ring, with a piece of ivory, is attached to the patient in a piece of dog's skin; a remedy well known to most persons, and always used with success.

REMEDIES FOR DISEASES OF THE EYES

According to what the magicians say, glaucoma may be cured by using the brains of a puppy seven days old; the probe being inserted in the right side (of the eye), if it is the right eye that is being operated on, and in the left side, if it is the left. The fresh gall, too, of the asio, a kind of owl, with feathers standing erect like ears. Apollonius of Pitanæ used to prefer dog's gall, in combination with honey, to that of the hyæna, for the cure of cataract, as also of albugo. The heads and tails of mice, reduced to ashes and applied to the eyes, improve the sight, it is said; a result which is ensured with even greater certainty by using the ashes of a dormouse or wild mouse, or else the brains or gall of an eagle. The ashes and fat of a field-mouse, beaten up with Attic honey and antimony, are remarkably useful for watery eyes.

For the cure of cataract, the ashes of a weasel are used, as also the brains of a lizard or swallow. Weasels, boiled and pounded, and so applied to the forehead, allay eye fluxes, either used alone, or else with fine flour or with frankincense. Employed in a similar manner, they are very good for sun-stroke, or in other words, for injuries inflicted by the sun. It is a remarkably good plan, too, to burn these

---

are still "wormed," as it is called, as a preventive of hydrophobia, it is said, and of a propensity to gnaw objects which come in their way. The "worming"consists in the breaking of these pustules.

6   He means slugs probably.

animals alive, and to use their ashes, with Cretan honey, as a liniment for films upon the eyes.

The cobweb of the common fly-spider, that which lines its hole more particularly, applied to the forehead across the temples, in a compress of some kind or other, is said to be marvellously useful for the cure of eye fluxes; the web must be taken, however, and applied by the hands of a boy who has not arrived at the years of puberty; the boy, too, must not show himself to the patient for three days, and during those three days neither of them must touch the ground with his feet uncovered. The white spider with very elongated, thin, legs, beaten up in old oil, forms an ointment which is used for the cure of albugo. The spider, too, whose web, of remarkable thickness, is generally found adhering to the rafters of houses, applied in a piece of cloth, is said to be curative of eye-fluxes. The green scarabæus has the property of rendering the sight more piercing of those who gaze upon it; hence it is that the engravers of precious stones use these insects to steady their sight.

REMEDIES FOR PAINS AND DISEASES OF THE EARS

A sheep's gall, mixed with honey, is a good detergent of the ears. Pains in those organs are allayed by injecting a bitch's milk; and hardness of hearing is removed by using dogs' fat, with wormwood and old oil, or else goose-grease. Some persons add juice of onions and of garlic, in equal proportions. The eggs, too, of ants are used, by themselves, for this purpose; these insects being possessed, in fact, of certain medicinal properties, and bears, it is well known, curing themselves when sick, by eating them as food. Goose-grease, and indeed that of all birds, is prepared by removing all the veins and leaving the fat, in a new, shallow, earthen vessel, well covered, to melt in the sun, some boiling water being placed beneath it; which done, it is passed through linen strainers, and is then put by in a cool spot, in a new earthen vessel, for keeping; with the addition of honey it is less liable to turn rancid.

Millepedes, known also as "centipedes" or "multipedes," are insects belonging to the earth-worm genus, hairy, with numerous feet, forming curves as they crawl, and contracting themselves when touched; the Greeks give to this insect the name of "oniscos," others, again, that of "tylos." Boiled with leek-juice in a pomegranate rind, it is highly efficacious, they say, for pains in the ears; oil of roses being added to the preparation, and the mixture injected into the ear opposite to the one affected.

Book XXX
The Magic Art. Medicaments Derived From Living Creatures (III)

In former parts of this work, I have had occasion, more than once, when the subject demanded it, to refute the impostures of the magic art, and it is now my intention to continue still further my exposure thereof. Indeed, there are few subjects on which more might be profitably said, were it only that, being, as it is, the most deceptive of all known arts, it has exercised the greatest influence in every country and in nearly every age. And no one can be surprised at the extent of its influence and authority, when he reflects that by its own energies it has embraced, and thoroughly amalgamated with itself, the three other sciences[1] which hold the greatest sway upon the mind of man.

That it first originated in medicine, no one entertains a doubt; or that, under the plausible guise of promoting health, it insinuated itself among mankind, as a higher and more holy branch of the medical art. Then, in the next place, to promises the most seductive and the most flattering, it has added all the resources of religion, a subject upon which, at the present day, man is still entirely in the dark. Last of all, to complete its universal sway, it has incorporated with itself the astrological art; there being no man who is not desirous to know his future destiny, or who is not ready to believe that this knowledge may with the greatest certainty be obtained, by observing the face of the heavens. The senses of men being thus enthralled by a three-fold bond, the art of magic has attained an influence so mighty, that at the present day even, it holds sway throughout a great part of the world, and rules the kings of kings in the East.

There is no doubt that this art originated in Persia, under Zoroaster, this being a point upon which authors are generally agreed; but whether there was only one

---

1   "Artes." Medicine, religion, and the art of divination.

Zoroaster, or whether in later times there was a second person of that name, is a matter which still remains undecided. Eudoxus informs us that this Zoroaster existed six thousand years before the death of Plato, an assertion in which he is supported by Aristotle. Hermippus, again, an author who has written with the greatest exactness on all particulars connected with this art, and has commented upon the two millions of verses left by Zoroaster, besides completing indexes to his several works, has left a statement, that Agonaces was the name of the master from whom Zoroaster derived his doctrines, and that he lived five thousand years before the time of the Trojan War. The first thing, however, that must strike us with surprise, is the fact that this art, and the traditions connected with it, should have survived for so many ages, all written commentaries thereon having perished in the meanwhile; and this, too, when there was no continuous succession of adepts, no professors of note, to ensure their transmission.

The first person, so far as I can ascertain, who wrote upon magic, and whose works are still in existence, was Osthanes, who accompanied Xerxes, the Persian king, in his expedition against Greece. It was he who first disseminated, as it were, the germs of this monstrous art, and tainted therewith all parts of the world through which the Persians passed. Authors who have made diligent enquiries into this subject, make mention of a second Zoroaster, a native of Proconnesus, as living a little before the time of Osthanes. That it was this same Osthanes, more particularly, that inspired the Greeks, not with a fondness only, but a rage, for the art of magic, is a fact beyond all doubt; though at the same time I would remark, that in the most ancient times, and indeed almost invariably, it was in this branch of science, that was sought the highest point of celebrity and of literary renown. At all events, Pythagoras, we find, Empedocles, Democritus, and Plato, crossed the seas, in order to attain a knowledge thereof, submitting, to speak the truth, more to the evils of exile than to the mere inconveniences of travel. Returning home, it was upon the praises of this art that they expatiated —it was this that they held as one of their grandest mysteries.

There is also a marvellous coincidence, in the fact that the two arts —medicine, I mean, and magic— were developed simultaneously; medicine by the writings of Hippocrates, and magic by the works of Democritus, about the period of tile Peloponnesian War, which was waged in Greece in the year of the City of Rome 300.

The Gallic provinces were pervaded by the magic art, and that even down to a period within memory; for it was the Emperor Tiberius that put down their Druids, and all that tribe of wizards and physicians. At the present day, struck with fascination, Britannia still cultivates this art, and that, with ceremonials so august, that she might almost seem to have been the first to communicate them to the people of Persia. To such a degree are nations throughout the whole world, totally different as they are and quite unknown to one another, in accord upon this one point!

Such being the fact, then, we cannot too highly appreciate the obligation that is due to the Roman people, for having put an end to those monstrous rites, in accordance with which, to murder a man was to do an act of the greatest devoutness, and to eat his flesh was to secure the highest blessings of health.

THE VARIOUS BRANCHES OF MAGIC

According to what Osthanes tells us, there are numerous sorts of magic. It is practised[2] with water, for instance, with balls, by the aid of the air, of the stars, of lamps, basins, hatchets, and numerous other appliances; means by which it engages to grant a foreknowledge of things to come, as well as converse with ghosts and spirits of the dead. All these practices, however, have been proved by the Emperor Nero, in our own day, to be so many false and chimerical illusions; entertaining as he did a passion for the magic art, unsurpassed even by his enthusiastic love for the music of the lyre, and for the songs of tragedy; so strangely did his elevation to the highest point of human fortune act upon the deep-seated vices of his mind! It was his leading desire to command the gods of heaven, and no aspiration could he conceive more noble than this. Never did person lavish more favours upon any one of the arts; and for the attainment of this, his favourite object, nothing was wanting to him, neither riches, nor power, nor aptitude at learning, and what not besides, at the expense of a suffering world.

MEDICAMENTS DERIVED FROM LIVING CREATURES – TOOTH-ACHE

But to proceed with the remedies for tooth-ache, the magicians tell us, that it may be cured by using the ashes of the head of a dog that has died in a state of madness. The head, however, must be burnt without the flesh, and the ashes injected with oil of cyprus[3] into the ear on the side affected. For the same purpose also, the left eye-tooth of a dog is used. the gum of the affected tooth being lanced with it; one of the vertebræ also of a dragon or of an enhydris, which is a male white serpent. The eye-tooth, too, of this last, is used for scarifying the gums; and when the pain affects the teeth of the upper jaw, they attach to the patient two of the upper teeth of the serpent, and, similarly, two of the lower ones for tooth-ache in the lower jaw. Persons who go in pursuit of the crocodile, anoint themselves with the fat of this animal. The gums are also scarified with the frontal bones of a lizard, taken from it at full moon, and not allowed to touch the ground; or else the mouth is rinsed with a decoction of dogs' teeth in wine, boiled down to one half.

Ashes of dogs' teeth, mixed with honey, are useful for difficult dentition in children, and a dentifrice is similarly prepared from them. Hollow teeth are plugged with ashes of burnt mouse-dung, or with a lizard's liver, dried. To eat a snake's heart, or to wear it, attached to the body, is considered highly efficacious. There are some among the magicians, who recommend a mouse to be eaten twice a month, as a preventive of tooth-ache.

---

2   These kinds of divination, rather than magic, were called hydromancy, sphæromancy, aëromancy, astromancy, lychnomancy, lecanomancy, and axinomancy.

3   A tree growing in Cyprus and Egypt; the flower of which yielded the cyprinum, the *Lawsonia alba* of Linnæus (TN).

REMEDIES FOR QUINSY AND SCROFULA

For quinsy we have very expeditious remedies in goose-gall, mixed with elaterium and honey, an owlet's brains, or the ashes of a burnt swallow, taken in warm water; which last remedy we owe to the poet Ovid. But of all the remedies spoken of as furnished by the swallow, one of the most efficacious is that derived from the young of the wild swallow, a bird which may be easily recognized by the peculiar conformation of its nest. By far the most effectual, however, of them all, are the young of the bank-swallow, that being the name given to the kind which builds its nest in holes on the banks of rivers. Many persons recommend the young of any kind of swallow as a food, assuring us that the person who takes it need be in no apprehension of quinsy for the whole of the ensuing year. The young of this bird are sometimes stifled and then burnt in a vessel with the blood, the ashes being administered to the patient with bread or in the drink; some, however, mix with them the ashes of a burnt weasel, in equal proportion. The same remedies are recommended also for scrofula, and they are administered for epilepsy, once a day, in drink. Swallows preserved in salt are taken for quinsy, in doses of one drachma, in drink; the nest, too, of the bird, taken internally, is said to be a cure for the same disease.

Millepedes, it is thought, used in the form of a liniment, are peculiarly efficacious for quinsy; some persons, also, administer eleven of them, bruised in one semi-sextarius of hydromel, through a reed, they being of no use whatever if once touched by the teeth.

For ulcerated scrofula, a weasel's blood is employed, or the animal itself, boiled in wine; but not in cases where the tumours have been opened with the knife. It is said, too, that a weasel, eaten with the food, is productive of a similar effect; sometimes, also, it is burnt upon twigs, and the ashes are applied with axle-grease. In some instances, a green lizard is attached to the body of the patient, a fresh one being substituted at the end of thirty days. Some persons preserve the heart of this animal in a small silver vessel, as a cure for scrofula in females.

REMEDIES FOR PAINS IN THE STOMACH

One of the very best remedies for affections of the stomach, is to use a snail diet. They must first be left to simmer in water for some time, without touching the contents of the shell, after which, without any other addition, they must be grilled upon hot coals, and eaten with wine and garum; the snails of Africa being the best of all for the purpose. The efficacy of this remedy has been proved in numerous instances of late. Another point, too, to be observed, is to take an uneven number of them. Snails, however, have a juice, it should be remembered, which imparts to the breath an offensive smell. For patients troubled with spitting of blood, they are remarkably good, the shell being first removed, and the contents bruised and administered in water.

River snails, and those with a white shell, have a strong, rank, juice, and forest snails are by no means good for the stomach, having a laxative effect upon the bowels; the same, too, with all kinds of small snails. Sea-snails, on the other hand, are more beneficial to the stomach; but it is for pains in that region that they are found the most efficacious; the best plan, it is said, is to eat them alive, of whatever kind they may happen to be, with vinegar.

REMEDIES FOR DYSENTERY

Dysentery is cured by taking the broth of a leg of mutton, boiled with linseed in water; by eating old ewe-milk cheese; or by taking mutton suet boiled in astringent wine. This last is good, too, for the iliac passion, and for inveterate coughs. Dysentery is removed also, by taking a spotted lizard from beyond seas, boiled down till the skin only is left, the head, feet, and intestines, being first removed. A couple of snails also, and an egg, are beaten up, shells and all, in both cases, and made lukewarm in a new vessel, with some salt, three cyathi of water, and two cyathi of raisin-wine or date-juice, the decoction being taken in drink. Ashes, too, of burnt snails, are very serviceable, taken in wine with a modicum of resin.

The snails without shells, as mostly found in Africa, are remarkably useful for dysentery, five of them being burnt with half a denarius of gum acacia, and taken, in doses of two spoonfuls, in myrtle wine or any other kind of astringent wine, with an equal quantity of warm water. Some persons employ all kinds of African snails indiscriminately in this manner; while others, again, make use of a similar number of African snails or broad-shelled snails, as an injection, in preference; in cases, too, where the flux is considerable, they add a piece of gum acacia, about the size of a bean. For dysentery and tenesmus, the cast-off slough of a snake is boiled in a pewter vessel with oil of roses; if prepared in any other kind of vessel, it is applied with an instrument made of pewter. Chicken-broth is also used as a remedy for these affections; but the broth of an old cock, strongly salted, acts more powerfully as a purgative upon the bowels. A pullet's craw, grilled and administered with salt and oil, has a soothing effect upon cœliac affections; but it is absolutely necessary that neither fowl nor patient should have eaten corn for some time before. Pigeons' dung, also, is grilled and taken in drink. The flesh of a ring-dove, boiled in vinegar, is curative of dysentery and cœliac affections; and for the cure of the former, a thrush is recommended, roasted with myrtleberries; a blackbird, also; or honey, boiled, in which the bees have died.

REMEDIES FOR URINARY CALCULI AND AFFECTIONS OF THE BLADDER

For the cure of urinary calculi, it is a good plan to rub the abdomen with mouse-dung. The flesh of a hedge-hog is agreeable eating, they say, if killed with a single blow upon the head, before it has had time to discharge its urine upon its body (persons who eat this flesh, it is said, will never by any possibility suffer from strangury). The flesh of a hedgehog thus killed, is a cure for urinary obstructions of the bladder; and the same, too, with fumigations made therewith. If, on the other hand, the animal has discharged its urine upon its body, those who eat the flesh will be sure to be attacked by strangury, it is said.

It is very beneficial also for urinary affections to eat thrushes with myrtleberries, or grasshoppers grilled on a shallow-pan; or else to take the millepedes, known as "onisci," in drink. For pains in the bladder, a decoction of lambs' feet is used. Chicken-broth relaxes the bowels and mollifies acridities; swallows' dung, too, with honey, employed as a suppository, acts as a purgative.

REMEDIES FOR COLD SHIVERINGS

A remedy for cold shiverings, according to Nicander, is a dead amphisbæna, or its skin only, attached to the body; in addition to which, he informs us that if one of these reptiles is attached to a tree that is being felled, the persons hewing it will never feel cold, and will fell it all the more easily. For so it is, that this is the only one among all the serpents that faces the cold, making its appearance the first of all, and even before the cuckoo's note is heard. There is another marvellous fact also mentioned, with reference to the cuckoo; if, upon the spot where a person hears this bird for the first time, he traces round the space occupied by his right foot and then digs up the earth, it will effectually prevent fleas from breeding, wherever it is thrown.

REMEDIES FOR JAUNDICE

Jaundice is combated by administering ear-wax to the patient, or else the filth that adheres to the udders of sheep, in doses of one denarius, with a modicum of myrrh, in two cyathi of wine; the ashes, also, of a dog's head, mixed with honied wine; a millepede, in one semi-sextarius of wine; earth-worms, in hydromel with myrrh; wine in which a hen's feet have been washed, after being first cleansed with water —the hen must be one with yellow feet— the brains of a partridge or of an eagle, in three cyathi of wine; the ashes of a ring-dove's feathers or intestines, in honied wine, in doses of three spoonfuls; or ashes of sparrows burnt upon twigs, in doses of two spoonfuls, in hydromel.

REMEDIES FOR FEVERS

In the treatment of quartan fevers, clinical medicine is, so to say, pretty nearly powerless; for which reason we shall insert a considerable number of remedies recommended by professors of the magic art, and, first of all, those prescribed to be worn as amulets; the dust, for instance, in which a hawk has bathed itself, tied up in a linen cloth, with a red string, and attached to the body; the longest tooth of a black dog; or the wasp known by the name of "pseudosphex,"[4] which is always to be seen flying alone, caught with the left hand and attached beneath the patient's chin. Some use for this purpose the first wasp that a person sees in the current year. Other amulets are, a viper's head, severed from the body and wrapped in a linen cloth; a viper's heart, removed from the reptile while still alive; the muzzle of a mouse and the tips of its ears, wrapped in red cloth, the animal being set at liberty after they are removed; the right eye plucked from a living lizard, and enclosed with the head, separated from the body, in goat's skin; the scarabænus also that forms pellets and rolls them along.

It is on account of this kind of scarabæus that the people of a great part of Egypt worship those insects as divinities; an usage for which Apion gives a curious rea-

---

4 "Bastard-wasp."

Book XXX - The Magic Art. Medicaments Derived From Living...

son, asserting, as he does, by way of justifying the rites of his nation, that the, insect in its operations pictures the revolution of the sun.

REMEDIES FOR CARBUNCLES

Carbuncles are removed by an application of pigeons' dung, either alone or in combination with linseed and oxymel; or of bees that have died in the honey. A sprinkling of polenta upon the sores is also used. For carbuncles and other sores of the generative organs, wool-grease is used as a remedy, with refuse of lead; and for incipient carbuncles, sheep's dung is employed. Tumours and all other affections that stand in need of emollients are treated most effectually with goose-grease; that of cranes, too, is equally efficacious.

REMEDIES FOR BURNS

For burns, the ashes of a dog's head are used; ashes of burnt dormice, with oil; sheep's dung, with wax; ashes also of burnt snails, an application so effectual, as not to leave a scar even. Viper's fat, too, is used, and ashes of burnt pigeons' dung, applied with oil.

METHODS FOR ARRESTING HAEMORRHAGE

Bleeding at the nostrils is arrested by mutton suet taken from the caul, introduced into the nostrils; by draing up rennet, lamb's rennet in particular, mixed with water, into the nostrils, or by using it as an injection, a remedy which succeeds even where other remedies; have failed; by making up goose grease into a bolus with an equal quantity of butter, and plugging the nostrils with it; or by using the earth that adheres to snails, or else the snails themselves, extracted from the shell. Excessive discharges from the nostrils are arrested also by applying crushed snails, or cobwebs, to the forehead. For issues of blood from the brain, the blood or brains of poultry are used, as also pigeons' dung, thickened and kept for the purpose. In cases where there is and immoderate flow of blood from a wound, an application of horse-dung, burnt with egg-shells, is marvellously good for stopping it.

REMEDIES FOR BROKEN BONES

For fractures of the joints, ashes of sheep's thigh-bones are particularly useful, applied in combination with wax; and the remedy is all the more efficacious, if a sheep's jaw-bones are burnt with the other ingredients, together with a deer's antler, and some wax dissolved in oil of roses. For broken bones, a dog's brains are used, spread upon a linen cloth, with wool laid upon the surface and moistened every now and then. The fractured bone will mostly unite in the course of fourteen days; and a cure equally expeditious may be effected by using the ashes of burnt field-mice, with honey, or of burnt earthworms; a substance which is extremely useful for the extraction of splintered bones.

REMEDIES FOR FEMALE COMPLAINTS

For diseases incident to females, a ewe's placenta is very useful; sheep's dung, too, is equally good. A fumigation of burnt locusts, applied to the lower parts, affords relief to strangury, in females more particularly. If immediately after conception, a woman eats a cock's testicles every now and then, the child of which she is pregnant will become a male, it is said. The ashes of a burnt porcupine, taken in drink, are a preventive of abortion; bitches' milk facilitates delivery; and the afterbirth of a bitch, provided it has not touched the ground, will act as an expellent of the fœtus. Milk, taken as a drink, strengthens the loins of women when in travail. Mouse-dung, diluted with rain water, reduces the breasts of females, when swollen after delivery. The ashes of a burnt hedge-hog, applied with oil, act as a preventive of abortion. Delivery is facilitated, in cases where the patient has taken, either goose-dung in two cyathi of water, or the liquid that escapes from the uterus of a weasel by its genitals.

Earth-worms, applied topically, effectually prevent pains in the sinews of the neck and shoulders; taken in raisin wine, they expel the after-birth, when retarded. Applied by themselves, earthworms ripen abscesses of the breasts, open them, draw the humours, and make them cicatrice; taken in honied wine, they promote the secretion of the milk. In hay-grass there are small worms found, which, attached to the neck, act as a preventive of premature delivery; they are removed, however, at the moment of childbirth, as otherwise they would have the effect of impeding delivery; care must be taken, also, not to put them on the ground.

VARIOUS KINDS OF DEPILATORIES

Bats' blood has all the virtues of a depilatory; but if applied to the cheeks of youths, it will not be found sufficiently efficacious, unless it is immediately followed up by an application of copper rust or hemlock seed; this method having the effect of entirely removing the hair, or at least reducing it to the state of a fine down. It is generally thought, too, that bats' brains are productive of a similar effect; there being two kinds of these brains, the red and the white. Some persons mix with the brains the blood and liver of the same animal; others, again, boil down a viper in three semisextarii of oil, and, after boning it, use it as a depilatory, first pulling out the hairs that are wanted not to grow. The gall of a hedgehog is a depilatory, more particularly if mixed with bats' brains and goats' milk; the ashes, too, of a burnt hedgehog are used for a similar purpose. If, after plucking out the hairs that are wanted not to grow, or if, before they make their appearance, the parts are well rubbed with the milk of a bitch with her first litter, no hairs will grow there. The same result is ensured, it is said, by using the blood of a tick taken from off a dog, or else the blood or gall of a swallow.

Ants' eggs, they say, beaten up with flies, impart a black colour to the eyebrows. If it is considered desirable that the colour of the infant's eyes should be black, the pregnant woman must eat a rat. Ashes of burnt earth-worms, applied with oil, prevent the hair from turning white.

APHRODISIACS AND ANTI-APHRODISIACS

A lizard drowned in a man's urine has the effect of an anti-aphrodisiac upon the person whose urine it is; for this animal is to be reckoned among the philtres, the magicians say. The same property is attributed to the excrements of snails, and to pigeons' dung, taken with oil and wine. The right lobe of a vulture's lungs, attached to the body in the skin of a crane, acts powerfully as a stimulant upon males; an effect equally produced by taking the yolks of five pigeons' eggs, in honey, mixed with one denarius of hog's lard; sparrows, or eggs of sparrows, with the food; or by wearing the right testicle of a cock, attached to the body in a ram's skin. The ashes of a burnt ibis, it is said, employed as a friction with goose-grease and oil of iris, will prevent abortion when a female has once, conceived; while the testicles of a game-cock, on the other hand, rubbed with goose-grease and attached to the body in a ram's skin, have all the effect of an anti-aphrodisiac; the same, too, with the testicles of any kind of dunghill cock, placed, together with the blood of a cock, beneath the bed. Hairs taken from the tail of a she-mule while being covered by the stallion, will make a woman conceive, against her will even, if knotted together at the moment of the sexual congress. If a man makes water upon a dog's urine, he will become disinclined to copulation, they say.

A singular thing, too, is what is told about the ashes of a spotted lizard to the effect that, wrapped in linen and held in the left hand, they act as an aphrodisiac, while, on the contrary, if they are transferred to the right, they will take effect as an anti-aphrodisiac. A bat's blood, too, they say, received on a flock of wool and placed beneath a woman's head, will promote sexual desire; the same being the case also with a goose's tongue, taken with the food or drink.

OTHER MARVELLOUS FACTS CONNECTED WITH ANIMALS

There are still some other marvellous facts related, with reference to the animals which we have mentioned. A dog will not bark at a person who has any part of the secundines of a bitch about him, or a hare's dung or fur. The kind of gnats called "muliones," do not live more than a single day. Persons when taking honey from the hives, will never be touched by the bees if they carry the beak of a woodpecker about them. Swine will be sure to follow the person who has given them a raven's brains, made up into a bolus. The dust in which a she-mule has wallowed, sprinkled upon the body, will allay the flames of desire. Rats may be put to flight by castrating a male rat, and setting it at liberty. If a snake's slough is beaten up with some spelt, salt, and wild thyme, and introduced into the throat of oxen, with wine, at the time that grapes are ripening, they will be in perfect health for a whole year to come; the same, too, if three young swallows are given to them, made up into three boluses. The dust gathered from the track of a snake, sprinkled among bees, will make them return to the hive. If the right testicle of a ram is tied up, he will generate females only. Persons who have about them the sinews taken from the wings or legs of a crane, will never be fatigued with any kind of laborious exertion. Mules will never kick when they have drunk wine.

Of all known substances, it is a mule's hoofs only that are not corroded by the poisonous waters of the fountain Styx; a memorable discovery made by Aristotle, to his great infamy, on the occasion when Antipater sent some of this water to Alexander the Great, for the purpose of poisoning him.

We will now pass on to the aquatic productions.

Book XXXI
Water and Medicaments Derived from Aquatic Animals (I)

We have now to speak of the benefits derived, in a medicinal point of view, from the aquatic animals; for not here even has all-bounteous Nature reposed from her work. Amid waves and billows, and tides of rivers for ever on the ebb and flow, she still unceasingly exerts her powers; and nowhere, if we must confess the truth, does she display herself in greater might, for it is this among the elements that holds sway over all the rest. It is water that swallows up dry land, that extinguishes flame, that ascends aloft, and challenges possession of the very heavens; it is water that, spreading clouds as it does, far and wide, intercepts the vital air we breathe; and, through their collision, gives rise to thunders and lightnings, as the elements of the universe meet in conflict.

What can there be more marvellous than waters suspended aloft in the heavens? And yet, as though it were not enough to reach so high an elevation as this, they sweep along with them whole shoals of fishes, and often stones as well, thus lading themselves with ponderous masses which belong to other elements, and bearing them on high. Falling upon the earth, these waters become the prime cause of all that is there produced; a truly wondrous provision of Nature, if we only consider, that in order to give birth to grain and life to trees and to shrubs, water must first leave the earth for the heavens, and thence bring down to vegetation the breath of life! The admission must be surely extorted from us, that for all our resources the earth is indebted to the bounteousness of water. It will be only proper, therefore, in the first place to set forth some instances of the powerful properties displayed by this element; for as to the whole of them, what living mortal could describe them?

THE DIFFERENT PROPERTIES OF WATER

On all sides, and in a thousand countries, there are waters bounteously springing forth from the earth, some of them cold, some hot, and some possessed of these properties united; those in the territory of the Tarbelli,[1] for instance, a people of Aquitania, and those among the Pyrencæan Mountains, where hot and cold springs are separated by only the very smallest distance. Then, again, there are others that are tepid only, or lukewarm, announcing thereby the resources they afford for the treatment of diseases, and bursting forth, for the benefit of man alone, out of so many animated beings.

Under various names, too, they augment the number of the divinities,[2] and give birth to cities. But nowhere do they abound in greater number, or offer a greater variety of medicinal properties than in the Gulf of Baiæ; some being impregnated with sulphur, some with alum, some with salt, some with nitre, and some with bitumen, while others are of a mixed quality, partly acid and partly salt. In other cases, again, it is by their vapours that waters are so beneficial to man, being so intensely hot as to heat our baths even, and to make cold water boil in our sitting-baths; such, for instance, as the springs at Baiæ; waters which are so hot as to cook articles of food even. There are others, too, those, for example, formerly the property of Licinius Crassus, which send forth their vapours in the sea even, thus providing resources for the health of man in the very midst of the waves!

REMEDIES DERIVED FROM WATER

According to their respective kinds, these waters are beneficial for diseases of the sinews, feet, or hips, for sprains or for fractures; they act, also, as purgatives upon the bowels, heal wounds, and are singularly useful for affections of the head and ears; indeed, the waters of Cicero are good for the eyes.

In Campania, too, are the waters of Sinuessa, remedial, it is said, for sterility in females, and curative of insanity in men.

The tepid waters of Albula, near Rome, have a healing effect upon wounds. Those of Cutilia, again, in the Sabine territory, are intensely cold, and by a kind of suction penetrate the body to such a degree as to have the effect of a mordent almost. They are remarkably beneficial for affections of the stomach, sinews, and all parts of the body, in fact.

The waters of Thespiæ ensure conception to females; the same, too, with those of the river Elatus in Arcadia. The spring Linus, also in Arcadia, acts as a preservative of the fœtus, and effectually prevents abortion. The waters of the river Aphrodisius, on the other hand, in the territory of Pyrrhsæa, are productive of sterility.

The waters of Lake Alphius remove white morphew. The waters of the river Cydnus, in Cilicia, are curative of gout. At Trœzen, on the contrary, all the inhabitants are subject to diseases of the feet, owing to the bad quality of the water there.

---

1   Pliny alludes to the mineral waters of Acqs or Dax on the Adour, in the French department of the Ariège. They are still highly esteemed.

2   Pliny alludes to Neptune, Amphitrite, the Oceanides, Nereides, Tritons, Crenides, Limnades, Potamides, and numerous other minor divinities.

The state of the Tungri, in Gaul, has a spring of great renown, which sparkles as it bursts forth with bubbles innumerable, and has a certain ferruginous taste, only to be perceived after it has been drunk. This water is strongly purgative, is curative of tertian fevers, and disperses urinary calculi; upon the application of fire it assumes a turbid appearance, and finally turns red.

At the Temple of the god Trophonius, in Bœotia, near the river Hercynnus, there are two fountains, one of which aids the memory, while the other is productive of forgetfulness; hence the names which they respectively bear.

DEADLY WATERS – POISONOUS FISHES

There are other marvels again, connected with water, but of a more fatal nature. Ctesias states in his writings, that there is a spring in Armenia, the fishes in which are black, and, if used as food, productive of instantaneous death. I have heard the same, too, with reference to the waters near the sources of the river Danuvius,[3] until a spring is reached which is near its main channel, and beyond which this poisonous kind of fish is not to be found. Hence it is that this spot is generally looked upon as the source of the river. The same, too, is reported of the Lake of the Nymphs, in Lydia. Near the river Pheneus, in Achaia, there flows from the rocks a spring known as the Styx, the waters of which are instantly fatal. And not only this, but there are also small fish in it, Theophrastus says, which are as deadly as the water, a thing that is not the case with the fish of any other poisonous springs. Theopompus says, that at the town of Cychri, in Thrace, the waters are deadly; and Lycus states, that at Leontium there is a spring, the waters of which are fatal at the end of a couple of days to those who drink thereof. Varro speaks also of a spring upon Mount Soracte, some four feet in breadth, the waters of which bubble forth at sunrise, as though they were boiling; birds, he says, which only taste thereof, fall dead close by.

THE WHOLESOMENESS OF WATERS

It is a subject of enquiry among medical men, which kind of water is the most beneficial. They condemn, and with justice, all stagnant, sluggish, waters, and are of opinion that running water is the best, being rendered lighter and more salubrious by its current and its continuous agitation. Hence it is that I am much surprised that persons should be found to set so high a value as they do, upon cistern water. These last give as their reason, however, that rain-water must be the lightest water of all, seeing that it has been able to rise aloft and remain suspended in the air. Hence it is, too, that they prefer snow-water to rain-water, and ice, again, to snow, as being water subtilized to the highest possible degree; on the ground that snow-water and ice-water must be lighter thin ordinary water, and ice, of necessity, considerably lighter. It is for the general interest, however, of mankind, that these notions should be refuted. For, in the first place, this comparative lightness which they speak of, could hardly be ascertained in any other way than by the sensation, there being pretty nearly no difference at all in weight between the kinds of water.

---

3 The Danube.

Nor yet, in the case of rain-water, is it any proof of its lightness that it has made its way upwards into the air, seeing that stones, it is quite evident, do the same; and then, besides, this water, while falling, must of necessity become tainted with the vapours which rise from the earth; a circumstance owing to which it is, that such numerous impurities are to be detected in rain-water, and that it ferments with such extreme rapidity.

What water, then, out of all these various kinds, are we to look upon as best adapted for the human constitution? Different kinds in different localities, is my answer. The kings of Parthia drink no water but that of the Choaspes or of the Eulæus, and, however long their journies, they always have this water carried in their suite. And yet it is very evident that it is not merely because this water is river-water that it is thus pleasing to them, seeing that they decline to drink the water of the Tigris, Euphrates, and so many other streams.

THE IMPURITIES OF WATER

Slime is one great impurity of water; still, however, if a river of this description is full of eels, it is generally looked upon as a proof of the salubrity of its water; just as it is regarded as a sign of its freshness when long worms breed in the water of a spring. But it is bitter water, more particularly, that is held in disesteem, as also the water which swells the stomach the moment it is drunk, a property which belongs to the water at Trœzen. As to the nitrous and salty-acid waters which are found in the deserts, persons travelling across towards the Red Sea render them potable in a couple of hours by the addition of polenta, which they use also as food. Those springs are more particularly condemned which secrete mud, or which give a bad complexion to persons who drink thereof. It is a good plan, too, to observe if water leaves stains upon copper vessels; if leguminous vegetables boil with difficulty in it; if, when gently decanted, it leaves an earthy deposit; or if, when boiled, it covers the vessel with a thick crust.

It is a fault also in water but to have any flavour not only to have a bad smell, at all, even though it be a flavour pleasant and agreeable in itself, or closely approaching, as we often find the case, the taste of milk. Water, to be truly wholesome, ought to resemble air as much as possible. There is only one spring of water in the whole universe, it is said, that has an agreeable smell, that of Chabura, namely, in Mesopotamia; the people give a fabulous reason for it, and say that it is because Juno bathed there. Speaking in general terms, water, to be wholesome, should have neither taste nor smell.

PROSPECTING FOR WATER

It will not be out of place to append here an account of the method employed in prospecting for water. Water is mostly to be found in valleys, whether formed by the intersection of declivities or lying at the lower part of mountains. Many persons have been of opinion that all places with a northern aspect are naturally provided with water; a point upon which it will not be amiss to explain the diversities presented to us by Nature. On the south side of the mountains of Hyrcania it never rains; and hence it is that it is only on the northeast side that they are wooded.

As for Olympus, Ossa, Parnassus, the Apennines, and the Alps, they are covered with wood on every side, and abundantly watered with streams. Some mountains, again, are wooded on the south side, the White Mountains in Crete, for example. On this point, therefore, we may come to the conclusion that there is no rule which in all cases holds good.

The following are indications of the presence of water: rushes, reeds or frogs sitting squatted on a spot for a long time together. As to the wild willow, alder, vitex, reed, and ivy, all of which grow spontaneously on low grounds in which there is a settling of rain water from higher localities, considered as indications of the presence of water, they are all of them of a deceptive nature. A sign much more to be depended upon, is a certain misty exhalation, visible from a distance before sunrise. The better to observe this, some persons ascend an eminence, and lie flat at full length upon the ground, with the chin touching the earth. There is also another peculiar method of judging upon this point, known only to men of experience in these matters; in the very middle of the heats of summer they select the hottest hours of the day, and observe how the sun's rays are reflected in each spot; and if, notwithstanding the general dryness of the earth, a locality is observed to present a moist appearance, they make no doubt of finding water there.

But so intense is the stress upon the eyes in doing this, that it is very apt to make them ache; to avoid which inconvenience, they have recourse to other modes of testing. They dig a hole, for instance, some five feet in depth, and cover it with vessels of unbaked pottery, or with a copper basin well-oiled; they then place a burning lamp on the spot, with an arch-work over it of leaves, and covered with earth on the top. If, after a time, they find the pots wet or broken, the copper covered with moisture, or the lamp extinguished, but not from want of oil, or if a lock of wool that has been left there is found to be moist, it is a sign of the presence of water, beyond all doubt. With some persons it is the practice to light a fire on the spot before they dig the hole, a method which renders the experiment with the vessels still more conclusive.

THE QUALITIES OF WATER AT THE DIFFERENT SEASONS OF THE YEAR

Every kind of water is freshest in winter, not so fresh in summer, still less so in autumn, and least of all in times of drought. River-water, too, is by no means always the same in taste, the state of the bed over which it runs making a considerable difference. For the quality of water, in fact, depends upon the nature of the soil through which it flows, and the juices of the vegetation watered by it; hence it is that the water of the same river is found in some spots to be comparatively unwholesome. The confluents, too, of rivers, are apt to change the flavour of the water, impregnating the stream in which they are lost and absorbed; as in the case of the Borysthenes, for example. In some instances, again, the taste of river-water is changed by the fall of heavy rains. It has happened three times in the Bosporus that there has been a fall of salt rain, a phenomena which proved fatal to the crops. On three occasions, also, the rains have imparted a bitterness to the overflowing streams of the Nilus, which was productive of great pestilence throughout Egypt.

WATERS WHICH HAVE SUDDENLY MADE THEIR APPEARANCE OR CEASED

It frequently happens that in spots where forests have been felled, springs of water make their appearance, the supply of which was previously expended in the nutriment of the trees. This was the case upon Mount Hæmus for example, when, during the siege by Cassander, the Gauls cut down a forest for the purpose of making a rampart. Very often too, after removing the wood which has covered an elevated spot and so served to attract and consume the rains, devastating torrents are formed by the concentration of the waters. It is very important also, for the maintenance of a constant supply of water, to till the ground and keep it constantly in motion, taking care to break and loosen the callosities of the surface crust; at all events, we find it stated, that upon a city of Crete, Arcadia by name, being razed to the ground, the springs and water-courses, which before were very numerous in that locality, all at once dried up; but that, six years after, when the city was rebuilt, the water again made its appearance, just as each spot was again brought into cultivation.

Earthquakes also are apt to discover or swallow up springs of water; a thing that has happened, it is well known, on five different occasions in the vicinity of Pheneus, a town of Arcadia. So too, upon Mount Corycus, a river burst forth; after which, the soil was subjected to cultivation.

Waters, too, sometimes change their colour; as at Babylon, for example, where the water of a certain lake for eleven days in summer is red. In the summer season, too, the current of the Borysthenes is blue, it is said, and this, although its waters are the most rarefied in existence, and hence float upon the surface of those of the Hypanis; though at the same time there is this marvellous fact, that when south winds prevail, the waters of the Hypanis assume the upper place.

THE METHOD OF CONVEYING WATER

The most convenient method of making a watercourse from the spring is by employing earthen pipes, two fingers in thickness, inserted in one another at the points of junction —the one that has the higher inclination fitting into the lower one— and coated with quick-lime macerated in oil. The inclination, to ensure the free flow of the water, ought to be at least one-fourth of an inch to every hundred feet; and if the water is conveyed through a subterraneous passage, there should be air-holes let in at intervals of every two actus. Where the water is wanted to ascend aloft, it should be conveyed in pipes of lead; water, it should be remembered, always rises to the level of its source. If, again, it is conveyed from a considerable distance, it should be made to rise and fall every now and then, so as not to lose its motive power. The proper length for each leaden pipe is ten feet; and if the pipe is five fingers in circumference its weight should be sixty pounds; if eight feet, one hundred; if ten, one hundred and twenty; and so on in the same proportion.

A pipe is called "a ten-finger" pipe when the sheet of metal is ten fingers in breadth before it is rolled up; a sheet one half that breadth giving a pipe "of five fingers." In all sudden changes of inclination in elevated localities, pipes of five fingers should be employed, in order to break the impetuosity of the fall; reservoirs, too, for branches should be made as circumstances may demand.

HOW MINERAL WATERS SHOULD BE USED

I am surprised that Homer has made no mention of hot springs, when, on the other hand, he has so frequently introduced the mention of warm baths; a circumstance from which we may safely conclude that recourse was not had in his time to mineral waters for their medicinal properties, a thing so universally the case at the present day. Waters impregnated with sulphur are good for the sinews, and aluminous waters are useful for paralysis and similar relaxations of the system. Those, again, which are impregnated with bitumen or nitre, the waters of Cutilia, for example, are drunk as a purgative.

Many persons quite pride themselves on enduring the heat of mineral waters for many hours together; a most pernicious practice, however, as they should be used but very little longer than the ordinary bath, after which the bather should be shampooed with cold water, and not leave the bath without being rubbed with oil. This last operation, however, is commonly regarded as altogether foreign to the use of mineral baths; and hence it is, that there is no situation in which men's bodies are more exposed to the chances of disease, the head becoming saturated with the intensity of the odours exhaled, and left exposed, perspiring as it is, to the coldness of the atmosphere, while all the rest of the body is immersed in the water.

THE USES OF SEA-WATER – THE ADVANTAGES OF A SEA-VOYAGE

Sea-water also is employed in a similar manner for the cure of diseases. It is used, made hot, for the cure of pains in the sinews, for reuniting fractured bones, and for its desiccative action upon the body; for which last purpose, it is also used cold. There are numerous other medicinal resources derived from the sea; the benefit of a sea-voyage, more particularly, in cases of phthisis, as already mentioned, and where patients are suffering from hæmoptosis,[4] as lately experienced, in our own memory, for it is not for the purpose of visiting the country, that people so often travel to Egypt, but in order to secure the beneficial results arising from a long sea-voyage. Indeed, the very sea-sickness that is caused by the rocking of the vessel to and fro, is good for many affections of the head, eyes, and chest, all those cases, in fact, in which the patient is recommended to drink an infusion of hellebore. Medical men consider sea-water, employed by itself, highly efficacious for the dispersion of tumours, and, boiled with barley-meal, for the successful treatment of imposthumes of the parotid glands; it is used also as an ingredient in plasters, white plasters more particularly, and for emollient poultices. Sea-water is very good, too, employed as a shower-bath; and it is taken internally, though not without injury to the stomach, both as a purgative and as an expellent, by vomit and by alvine evacuation, of black bile or coagulated blood, as the case may be.

---

4   The coughing up of blood or blood-stained mucus from the bronchi, larynx, trachea, or lungs (TN).

THE VARIOUS KINDS OF SALT

All salt is either native or artificial; both kinds being formed in various ways, but produced from one of these two causes, the condensation or the desiccation, of a liquid. The Lake of Tarentum is dried up by the heat of the summer sun, and the whole of its waters, which are at no time very deep, not higher than the knee in fact, are changed into once mass of salt. The same, too, with a lake in Sicily, Cocanicus by name, and another in the vicinity of Gela. But in the case of these two last, it is only the sides that are thus dried up; whereas in Phrygia, in Cappadocia, and at Aspendus, where the same phenomena are observable, the water is dried up to a much larger extent, to the very middle of the lake, in fact.

Sea-water, again, spontaneously produces another kind of salt, from the foam which it leaves on shore at high-water mark, or adhering to rocks; this being, in all cases, condensed by the action of the sun, and that salt being the most pungent of the two which is found upon the rocks.

There are also three different kinds of native salt. In Bactriana there are two vast lakes; one of them situate on the side of Scythia, the other on that of Ariana, both of which throw up vast quantities of salt. So, too, at Citium, in Cyprus; and, in the vicinity of Memphis, they extract salt from the lake and dry it in the sun. The surface-waters of some rivers, also, condense in the form of salt, the rest of the stream flowing beneath, as though under a crust of ice; such as the running waters near the Caspian Gates for instance, which are known as the "Rivers of Salt." The same is the case, too, in the vicinity of the Mardi and of the people of Armenia. In Bactriana, also, the rivers Ochus and Oxus carry down from the mountains on their banks, fragments of salt. There are also in Africa some lakes, the waters of which are turbid, that are productive of salt. Some hot springs, too, produce salt- those at Pagasæ for example. Such, then, are the various kinds of salt produced spontaneously by water.

Of artificial salt there are several kinds; the common salt, and the most abundant, being made from sea-water drained into salt-pans, and accompanied with streams of fresh water; but it is rain more particularly, and, above all things, the sun, that aids in its formation; indeed without this last it would never dry. In the neighbourhood of Utica, in Africa, they build up masses of salt, like hills in appearance; and when these have been hardened by the action of the sun and moon, no moisture will ever melt them, and iron can hardly divide them. In Crete, however, salt is made without the aid of fresh water, and merely by introducing sea-water into the salt-pans.

FLOWER OF SALT

That which mainly distinguishes the produce of salt-works, in respect of its purity, is a sort of efflorescence, which forms the lightest and whitest part of salt. The name "flower of salt" is given, also, to a substance of an entirely different character, more humid by nature, and of a red or saffron colour; a kind of "rust of salt," as it were, with an unpleasant smell like that of garum, and differing therein not only from froth of salt, but from salt itself. This substance is found in Egypt, and, as it would appear, is conveyed thither by the waters of the Nilus; though it is to be found floating upon the surface of certain springs as well. The best kind is that which yields a certain fatty substance, like oil; for salt even, a thing that is quite marvellous to think of, is not without a degree of unctuousness.

This substance is sophisticated, and coloured with red earth, or, in most instances, with powdered potsherds; an adulteration to be detected by the agency of water, which washes off the fictitious colour, the natural colour being only removable by the agency of oil. Indeed, it is for its colour that perfumers more particularly make such extensive use of this drug. When seen in the vessels, the surface of it is white, but that which lies in the middle is moister, as already stated. It is of an acrid nature, calorific, and bad for the stomach. It acts also as a sudorific, and, taken with wine and water, has a purgative effect upon the bowels. It is very useful, also, as an ingredient in acopa and in detersive compositions, and is remarkably efficacious for the removal of hairs from the eyelids. It is the practice to shake up the sediment, in order to renovate the saffron colour of the drug.

THE NATURE OF SALT

Salt, regarded by itself, is naturally igneous, and yet it manifests an antipathy to fire, and flies[5] from it. It consumers everything, and yet upon living bodies it has an astringent, desiccative, and binding effect, while the dead it preserves from putrefaction, and makes them last for ages even. In respect, however, of its medicinal properties, it is of a mordent, burning, detergent, attenuating, and resolvent nature; it is, however, injurious to the stomach, except that it acts as a stimulant to the appetite, For the cure of injuries inflicted by serpents, it is used with origanum, honey, and hyssop; and for the sting of the cerastes, with origanum, cedar-resin, pitch, or honey. Taken internally with vinegar, it is good for injuries caused by the scolopendra; and, applied topically, with an equal proportion of linseed, in oil or vinegar, for stings inflicted by scorpions. For stings of hornets, wasps, and insects of a similar description, it is applied with vinegar; and, for the cure of hemicrania, ulcers on the head, blisters, pimples, and incipient warts, with veal-suet. It is used also among the remedies for the eyes, and for the removal of fleshy excrescences upon those organs, as also of hangnails upon the fingers or toes. For webs that form upon the eyes it is peculiarly useful, and hence it is that it is so commonly employed as an ingredient in eye-salves, as well as plasters. For all these last mentioned purposes, the salt of Tatta or of Caunus is more particularly in request.

In cases where there is ecchymosis of the eyes, or a bruise from the effects of a blow, salt is applied, with an equal quantity of myrrh and honey, or with hyssop in warm water, the eyes being also fomented with salsugo.

Every kind of salt is useful for the cure of quinsy; but, in addition to this, it is necessary to make external applications simultaneously with oil, vinegar, and tar. Mixed with wine, it is a gentle aperient to the bowels, and, taken in a similar manner, it acts as an expellent of all kinds of intestinal worms. Salt is useful for the removal of corns upon the feet, and of chilblains; for the cure of burns also,

---

5   Pliny alludes to its decrepitation in flame.

it is applied with oil, or else chewed. It acts as a check also upon blisters, and, in cases of erysipelas and serpiginous ulcers, it is applied topically with vinegar or with hyssop. For the cure of carcinoma it is employed in combination with Taminian grapes; and for phagedænic ulcers it is used parched with barley-meal, a linen pledget steeped in wine being laid upon it. In cases of jaundice, it is employed as a friction before the fire, with oil and vinegar, till the patient is made to perspire, for the purpose of preventing the itching sensations attendant upon that disease. When persons are exhausted with fatigue, it is usual to rub them with salt and oil. Many have treated dropsy with salt, have used external applications of salt and oil for the burning heats of fever, and have cured chronic coughs by laying salt upon the patient's tongue. Salt has been used, also, as an injection for sciatica, and has been applied to ulcers of a fungous or putrid nature.

THE VARIOUS KINDS OF NITRUM

And here we must no longer defer giving an account of nitrum;[6] which in its properties does not greatly differ from salt, and deserves all the more to be attentively considered, from the evident fact that the medical men who have written upon it were ignorant of its nature; of all which authors Theophrastus is the one that has given the greatest attention to the point. It is found in small quantities in Media, in certain valleys there that are white with heat and drought; the name given to it being "halmyrax." In Thracia, too, near Philipli, it is found, but in smaller quantities, and deteriorated with earthy substances, being known there as "agrion." As to that prepared from the burnt wood of the oak, it never was made to any very great extent, and the manufacture of it has been long since totally abandoned. Nitrous waters are also found in numerous places, but not sufficiently impregnated to admit of condensation.

The best and most abundant supply is found at Litæ, in Macedonia, where it is known as "Chalastricum"; it is white and pure, and closely resembles salt. In the middle of a certain nitrous lake there, a spring of fresh water issues forth. In this lake the nitrum forms for nine days, about the rising of the Dog-star, and then ceases for the same period, after which it again floats upon the surface, and then again ceases; facts which abundantly prove that it is the peculiar nature of the soil which generates the nitrum, it being very evident that, when the formation is there interrupted, neither the heat of the sun nor the fall of rain is productive of the slightest effect.

In Egypt, again, it is made artificially, and in much greater abundance, but of inferior quality, being tawny and full of stones. It is prepared in pretty nearly the same manner as salt, except that in the salt-pans it is sea-water that is introduced, whereas in the nitre-beds it is the water of the river Nilus; a water which, upon the subsidence of the river, is impregnated with nitrum for forty days together, and not, as in Macedonia, at intermittent periods only.

---

6   Beckmann considers it not to be our "nitre" or "saltpetre," but a general name for impure alkaline salts. Ajasson, without hesitation, pronounces it to be nitrate of potash, neither more or less than our saltpetre.

BOOK XXXI - WATER AND MEDICAMENTS DERIVED FROM AQ. ANIMALS (I)

Viewed medicinally, nitrum is calorific, attenuant, mordent, astringent, desiccative, and ulcerating; it is good, too, in all cases where certain humours require to be drawn out or dispersed, or where gentle mordents or attenuants are required, as in the case of pustules and pimples, for example. Some persons ignite it for this purpose, and, after quenching it in astringent wine, bruise and use it, without oil, at the bath. Applied with dried iris powdered, and green olive oil, it checks immoderate perspiration. Applied topically with a fig, or boiled down to one half in raisin wine, it removes marks upon the eyes and granulations of the eyelids. It is used, also, for the removal of argema,[7] boiled in a pomegranate rind with raisin wine. Used as an ointment, in combination with honey, it improves the eye-sight. It is very useful, also, for tooth-ache, taken as a collutory with wine and pepper, or boiled with a leek. Burnt, and employed as a dentifrice, it restores teeth to their original colour that have turned black; and an application of it, with Samian earth and oil, kills nits and other vermin of the head. Dissolved in wine, it is used as an injection for suppurations of the ears, and, applied with vinegar, it consumes filth that has accumulated there. Introduced dry into the ears, it disperses singings and tinglings in those organs.

SPONGES

Some authorities make the following distinctions; they regard as males those sponges which are pierced with more diminutive holes, are more compact in form and more ready to imbibe, and are stained, to satisfy luxurious tastes, in various colours, sometimes purple even; those, on the other hand, which have holes, larger and running into one another, they consider to be females. Among the male sponges, too, there is one kind, harder than the others, the name given to which is "tragi," and the holes of which are extremely small and numerous. Sponges are made white artificially; the softest being chosen for the purpose, and after they have been steeped the whole summer through with the foam of the sea. They are then exposed to the action of the moon and hoar-frosts, being turned upside down, or, in other words, with that part upwards by which they formerly adhered to the rocks, the object being that they may become white throughout.

That sponges are animated beings, we have already stated; and not only this, but they have a coat of blood even, adhering to them. Some say that they regulate their movements by the sense of hearing, and that at the slightest noise they contract themselves, and emit an abundant moisture; when such is the case, it is said, it is impossible to tear them away from the rocks, and consequently they must be cut, an operation during which they emit a purulent secretion. Those sponges, too, are preferred to all others, which are grown on spots with a north-east aspect, the physicians assuring us that these retain the breath of life the longest of all; a circumstance which renders them additionally useful to the human body, from the union which is thereby effected of their vital principle with our own. It is for this reason, too, that they are preferred as fresh as possible, and in a moist state rather than dry. They are not so useful, however, if applied with hot water, and still less so

---

7   A small ulcer in the eye (TN).

if they are oiled, or applied to the body when just anointed. The compact sponges, it is thought, have less adhesive power than the others.

In the treatment of wounds, sponges are sometimes used as a substitute for greasy wool, either with wine and oil, or with salt and water; the only difference being, that wool acts emolliently upon sores, whereas sponge has an astringent action, and absorbs the vitiated humours. To dropsical patients, bandages of sponge are applied, either dry or steeped in warm water or oxycrate, according as there is a necessity for soothing the skin, or for covering it up and drying it. Sponges are applied, also, in all those diseases where warmth is required, being first soaked in boiling water and then squeezed out between a couple of boards.

Book XXXII
Medicaments Derived from Aquatic Animals (II)

Following the proper order of things, we have now arrived at the culminating point of the wonders manifested to us by the operations of Nature. And even at the very outset, we find spontaneously presented to us an incomparable illustration of her mysterious powers; so much so, in fact, that beyond it we feel ourselves bound to forbear extending our enquiries, there being nothing to be found either equal or analogous to an element in which Nature quite triumphs over herself. For what is there more unruly than the sea, with its winds, its tornadoes, and its tempests? And yet in what department of her works has Nature been more seconded by the ingenuity of man, than in this, by his inventions of sails and of oars? In addition to this, we are struck with the ineffable might displayed by the Ocean's tides, as they constantly ebb and flow, and so regulate the currents of the sea as though they were the waters of one vast river.

THE ECHENEÏS

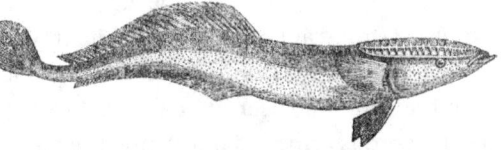

And yet all these forces, though acting in unison, and impelling in the same direction, a single fish, and that of a very diminutive size — the fish known as the "echeneïs"[1] — possesses the power of counteracting them. Winds may blow and storms may rage, and yet the echeneïs controls their fury, restrains their mighty force, and bids ships

---

1   The remora, sometimes called suckerfish, is any of a family (*Echeneidae*) of ray-finned fish in the order *Carangiformes*. Depending on species, they grow to 12-43 in long.

stand still in their career; a result which no cables, no anchors, from their ponderousness quite incapable of being weighed, could ever have produced! A fish bridles the impetuous violence of the deep, and subdues the frantic rage of the universe; and all this by no effort of its own, no act of resistance on its part, no act at all, in fact, but that of adhering to the bark! Trifling as this object would appear, it suffices to counteract all these forces combined, and to forbid the ship to pass onward in its way! Fleets, armed for war, pile up towers and bulwarks on their decks, in order that, upon the deep even, men may fight from behind ramparts as it were. But alas for human vanity! — When their prows, beaked as they are with brass and with iron, and armed for the onset, can thus be arrested and riveted to the spot by a little fish, no more than some half foot in length!

At the battle of Actium, it is said, a fish of this kind stopped the prætorian ship of Antonius in its course. In our own time, too, one of these fish arrested the ship of the Emperor Caius in its course, when he was returning from Astura to Antium; and thus, as the result proved, did an insignificant fish give presage of great events; for no sooner had the emperor returned to Rome than he was pierced by the weapons of his own soldiers.

According to the persons who examined it on that occasion, and who have seen it since, the echeneïs bears a strong resemblance to a large slug. It is a singular thing, but among the Greeks we find writers who state that, worn as an amulet, the echeneïs has the property, as already mentioned, of preventing miscarriage, and of reducing prolapse of the uterus, and so permitting the fœtus to reach maturity; while others, again, assert that, if it is preserved in salt and worn as an amulet, it will facilitate parturition; a fact to which it is indebted for another name which it bears, "odinolytes." Be all this as it may, considering this most remarkable fact of a ship being thus stopped in its course, who can entertain a doubt as to the possibility of any manifestation of her power by Nature, or as to the effectual operation of the remedies which she has centred in her spontaneous productions?

THE TORPEDO

And then, besides, even if we had not this illustration by the agency of the echeneïs, would it not have been quite sufficient only to cite the instance of the torpedo (sting-ray), another inhabitant also of the sea, as a manifestation of the mighty powers of Nature? From a considerable distance even, and if only touched with the end of a spear or staff, this fish has the property of benumbing even the most vigorous arm, and of riveting the feet of the runner, however swift he may be in the race. If, upon considering this fresh illustration, we find ourselves compelled to admit that there is in existence a certain power which, by the very exhalations and, as it were, emanations therefrom, is enabled to affect the members of the human body, what are we not to hope for from the remedial influences which Nature has centred in all animated beings?

THE INSTINCTS OF FISHES

The statements which Ovid has made as to the instincts of fish, in the work of his known as the "Halieuticon,"[2] appear to me truly marvellous. The scarus,[3] for instance, when enclosed in the lobster pot, makes no effort to escape with its head, nor does it attempt to thrust its muzzle between the oziers; but turning its tail towards them, it enlarges the orifices with repeated blows therefrom, and so makes its escape backwards. Should, too, another scarus, from without, chance to see it thus struggling within the kype, it will take the tail of the other in its mouth, and so aid it in its efforts to escape. The lupus,[4] again, when surrounded with the net, furrows the sand with its tail, and so conceals itself, until the net has passed over it. The murena, trusting in the slippery smoothness of its rounded back, boldly faces the meshes of the net, and by repeatedly wriggling its body, makes its escape. The octupus makes for the hooks, and, without swallowing the bait, clasps it with its feelers; nor does it quit its hold until it has eaten off the bait, or perceives itself being drawn out of the water by the rod.

The mullet, too, is aware that within the bait there is a hook concealed, and is on its guard against the ambush; still however, so great is its voracity, that it beats the hook with its tail, and strikes away from it the bait. The bass again, shows less foresight and address, but repentance at its imprudence arms it with mighty strength; for, when caught by the hook, it flounders from side to side, and so widens the wound, till at last the insidious hook falls from its mouth. The murena not only swallows the hook, but catches at the line with its teeth, and so gnaws it asunder. The anthias,[5] Ovid says, the moment it finds itself caught by the hook, turns its body with its back downwards, upon which there is a sharp knife-like fin, and so cuts the line asunder.

According to Licinius Macer, the murena is of the female sex only, and is impregnated by serpents; and hence it is that the fishermen, to entice it from its retreat, and catch it, make a hissing noise in imitation of the hissing of a serpent. He states, also, that by frequently beating the water it is made to grow fat, that a blow with a stout stick will not kill it, but that a touch with a stalk of fennel-giant is instantly fatal. That in the case of this animal, the life is centred in the tail, there can be no doubt, as also that it dies immediately on that part of the body being struck; while, on the other hand, there is considerable difficulty in killing it with a blow upon the head. Persons who have come in contact with the razor-fish[6] smell

---

2   Or "Treatise on Fishes."
3   A genus of acanthopterygian fishes, of which the scarus of the ancient Greeks and Romans is the oldest known species, giving name to the Scaridæ or Scarinæ, and having varying limits; the parrot-wrasses or parrot-fishes.
4   The wolf fish. The *Perca labrax* of Linnæus.
5   A genus of brilliantly coloured fishes found in warm seas, the species longest known being the barbier, *A. anthias*, of the Mediterranean.
6   *Novacula piscis*. There are numerous varieties of it, among which the best known are the *Coryphæna novacula* of Linnæus, the Rason of the Mediterranean, highly esteemed as an article of food, and the *Coryphæna pentedactyle* of Bloch.

of iron. The hardest of all fishes, beyond a doubt, is that known as the "orbis";[7] it is spherical, destitute of scales, and all head.

CORAL

In the same degree that people in our part of the world set a value upon the pearls of India, do the people of India prize coral; it being the prevailing taste in each nation respectively that constitutes the value of things. Coral is produced in the Red Sea also, but of a more swarthy hue than ours. It is to be found also in the Persian Gulf, where it is known by the name of "iace." But the most highly-esteemed of all, is that produced in the vicinity of the islands called Stœchades, in the Gallic Gulf, and near the Æolian Islands and the town of Drepana in the Sea of Sicily. Coral is to be found growing, too, at Graviscæ, and off the coast of Neapolis in Campania; as also at Erythræ, where it is intensely red, but soft, and consequently little valued.

Its form is that of a shrub, and its colour green; its berries are white and soft while under water, but the moment they are removed from it, they become hard and red, resembling the berries of cultivated cornel in size and appearance. They say that, while alive, if it is only touched by a person, it will immediately become as hard as stone; and hence it is that the greatest pains are taken to prevent this, by tearing it up from the bottom with nets, or else cutting it short with a sharp-edged instrument of iron. The reddest coral and the most branchy is held in the highest esteem; but, at the same time, it must not be rough or hard like stone; nor yet, on the other hand, should it be full of holes or hollow.

The berries of coral are no less esteemed by the men in India than are the pearls of that country by the females among us; their soothsayers, too, and diviners look upon coral as an amulet endowed with sacred properties, and a sure preservative against all dangers; hence it is that they equally value it as an ornament and as an object of devotion. Before it was known in what estimation coral was held by the people of India, the Gauls were in the habit of adorning their swords, shields, and helmets with it; but at the present day, owing to the value set upon it as an article of exportation, it has become so extremely rare, that it is seldom to be seen even in the regions that produce it. Branches of coral, hung at the neck of infants, are thought to act as a preservative against danger. Calcined, pulverized, and taken in water, coral gives relief to patients suffering from griping pains in the bowels, affections of the bladder, and urinary calculi. Similarly taken in wine, or, if there are symptoms of fever, in water, it acts as a soporific. It resists the action of fire a considerable time before it is calcined.

AMPHIBIOUS ANIMALS. THE BEAVER

The might of Nature, too, is equally conspicuous in the animals which live upon dry land as well water; the beaver, for instance, more generally known as "castor," and the testicles of which are called in medicine "castorea." Sextius informs us, also, that there are small, tightly knit, and attached to the back-bone, and that it

---

7   Or "globe-fish." The Mola, *Orbis marinus*, or sun-fish of modern Natural History.

is impossible to remove them without taking the animal's life. We learn from him that there is a mode of adulterating them by substituting the kidneys of the beaver, which are of considerable size, whereas the genuine testicles are found to be extremely diminutive; in addition to which, he says that they must not be taken to be bladders, as they are two in number, a provision not to be found in any animal. Within these pouches, he says, there is a liquid found, which is preserved by being put in salt; the genuine castoreum being easily known from the false, by the fact of its being contained in two pouches, attached by a single ligament.

Mixed with oil of roses and peucedanum, and applied to the head, castoreaum is productive of narcotic effects —a result which is equally produced by taking it in water-, for which reason it is employed in the treatment of phrenitis. Used as a fumigation, it acts as an excitant upon patients suffering from lethargy; and similarly employed, or used in the form of a suppository, it dispels hysterical suffocations. It acts also as an emmenagogue and as an expellent of the afterbirth, being taken by the patient, in doses of two drachmæ, with pennyroyal, in water. It is employed also for the cure of vertigo, opisthotonos, fits of trembling, spasms, affections of the sinews, sciatica, stomachic complaints, and paralysis, the patient either being rubbed with it all over, or else taking it as an electuary, bruised and incorporated with seed of vitex, vinegar, and oil of roses, to the consistency of honey. In the last form, too, it is taken for the cure of epilepsy, and in a potion, for the purpose of dispelling flatulency and gripings in the bowels, and for counteracting the effects of poison.

The urine, too, of the beaver, is a neutralizer of poisons, and for this reason is used as an ingredient in antidotes. The best way of keeping it, some think, is in the bladder of the animal.

THE TORTOISE

The tortoise, too, is an animal that is equally amphibious as the beaver, and possessed of medicinal properties as strongly developed; in addition to which, it claims an equal degree of notice for the high price which luxury sets upon its shell, and the singularity of its conformation. Of tortoises, there are various kinds, land tortoises, sea tortoises, tortoises which live in muddy waters, and tortoises which live in fresh waters; these last being known to some Greek authors by the name of "emydes." The flesh of the land-tortoise is employed for fumigations more particularly, and we find it asserted that it is highly salutary for repelling the malpractices of magic, and for neutralizing poisons. These tortoises are found in the greatest numbers in Africa; where the head and feet being first cut off, it is said, they are given to persons by way of antidote. Eaten, too, in a broth made from them, they are thought to disperse scrofula, diminish the volume of the spleen, and effect the cure of epilepsy. The blood of the land-tortoise improves the eyesight, and removes cataracts; it is kept also, made up with meal into pills, which are given with wine when necessary, to neutralize the poison of all kinds of serpents, frogs, spiders, and similar venomous animals. It is found a useful plan, too, in cases of glaucoma, to anoint the eyes with gall of tortoises, mixed with Attic honey, and, for the cure of injuries inflicted by scorpions, to drop the gall into the wound.

Ashes of tortoiseshell, kneaded up with wine and oil, are used for the cure of chaps upon the feet, and of ulcerations. The shavings of the surface of the shell, administered in drink, act as an anti-aphrodisiac; a thing that is the more surprising, from the fact that a powder prepared from the whole of the shell has the reputation of being a strong aphrodisiac. The flesh of the sea-tortoise, mixed with that of frogs, is an excellent remedy for injuries caused by the salamander; indeed there is nothing that is a better neutralizer of the secretions of the salamander than the sea-tortoise. The blood of this animal reproduces the hair when lost through alopecy, and is curative of porrigo and all kinds of ulcerations of the head; the proper method of using it being to let it dry, and then gently wash it off. The gall of the tortoise improves the eye-sight, effaces scars, and cures affections of the tonsillary glands, quinsy, and all kinds of diseases of the mouth, cancers of that part more particularly, as well as cancer of the testicles. Applied to the nostrils it dispels epilepsy, and sets the patient on his feet; incorporated in vinegar with the slough of a snake, it is a sovereign remedy for purulent discharges from the ears.

VARIOUS FROGS

The broth prepared from sea-frogs,[8] boiled in wine and vinegar, is taken internally as a neutralizer of poisons and of the venom of the bramble-toad as also for injuries inflicted by the salamander. For the cure of injuries caused by the seahare and the various serpents above mentioned, it is a good plan to eat the flesh of river-frogs, or to drink the liquor in which they have been boiled; as a neutralizer, too, of the venom of the scorpion, river-frogs are taken in wine. Democritus assures us that if the tongue is extracted from a live frog, with no other part of the body adhering to it, and is then applied —the frog being first replaced in the water— to a woman while asleep, just at the spot where the heart is felt to palpitate, she will be sure to give a truthful answer to any question that may be put to her.

To this the Magi add some other particulars, which, if there is any truth in them, would lead us to believe that frogs ought to be considered much more useful to society than laws. They say, for instance, that if a man takes a frog and transfixes it with a reed, entering the body at the sexual parts and coming out at the mouth, and then dips the reed in the menstrual discharge of his wife, she will be sure to conceive an aversion for all paramours. That the flesh of frogs, attached to the kype or hook, as the case may be, makes a most excellent bait, for purples[9] more particularly, is a well-known fact. Frogs, they say, have a double liver; and of this liver, when exposed to the attacks of ants, the part that is most eaten away is thought to be an effectual antidote to every kind of poison.

There are some frogs, again, which live only among brakes and thickets, for which reason they have received the name of "rubetæ," or "bramble-frogs." They are the largest in size of all the frogs, have two protuberances like horns, and are full of poison. Authors quite vie with one another in relating marvellous stories about them; such, for instance, as that if they are brought into the midst of a con-

---

8   Angler-fish (TN).
9   A gastropod yielding a purple fluid for dyeing, as a murex (TN).

course of people, silence will instantly prevail; as also that by throwing into boiling water a small bone that is found in their right side, the vessel will immediately cool, and the water refuse to boil again until it has been removed. This bone, they say, may be found by exposing a dead bramble-frog to ants, and letting them eat away the flesh; after which the bones must be put into the vessel, one by one.

On the other hand, again, in the left side of this reptile there is another bone, they say, which, thrown into water, has all the appearance of making it boil, and the name given to which is "apocynon." This bone, it is said, has the property of assuaging the fury of dogs, and, if put into the drink, of conciliating love and ending discord and strife. Worn, too, as an amulet, it acts as an aphrodisiac, we are told. The bone, on the contrary, which is taken from the right side, acts powerfully as a refrigerative upon boiling liquids, it is said; attached to the patient in a piece of fresh lamb's-skin, it has the repute of assuaging quartan and other fevers, and of checking amorous propensities. The spleen of these frogs is used as an antidote to the various poisons that are prepared from them; and for all these purposes the liver is considered still more efficacious.

OYSTERS

Oysters, too, neutralize the venom of the sea-hare. Oysters love fresh water and spots where numerous rivers discharge themselves into the sea; hence it is that the pelagia[10] are of such small size and so few in number. Still, however, we do find them breeding among rocks and in places far remote from the contact of fresh water. Generally speaking, they increase in size with the increase of the moon; but it is at the beginning of summer, more particularly, and when the rays of the sun penetrate the shallow waters, that they are swollen with an abundance of milk.[11] This, too, would appear to be the reason why they are so small when found out at sea; the opacity of the water tending to arrest their growth, and the moping consequent thereon producing a comparative indisposition for food.

Oysters are of various colours; in Spain they are red, in Illyricum of a tawny hue, and at Circeii black, both in meat and shell. But in every country, those oysters are the most highly esteemed that are compact without being slimy from their secretions, and are remarkable more for their thickness than their breadth. They should never be taken in either muddy or sandy spots, but from a firm, hard bottom; the meat should be compressed, and not of a fleshy consistence; and the oyster should be free from fringed edges, and lying wholly in the cavity of the shell. Persons of experience in these matters add another characteristic; a fine purple thread, they say, should run round the margins of the beard, this being looked upon as a sign of superior quality, and obtaining for them their name of "calliblephara."

Oysters are slightly laxative to the bowels; and boiled in honied wine, they relieve tenesmus, in cases where it is unattended with ulceration. They act detergently also upon ulcerations of the bladder. Boiled in their shells, unopened just as

---

10 "Deep-sea" oysters.
11 It is at the spawning season that this milky liquid is found in the oyster; a period at which the meat of the fish is considered unwholesome as food.

they come to hand, oysters are marvellously efficacious for rheumatic defluxions. Calcined oyster-shells, mixed with honey, allay affections of the uvula and of the tonsillary glands; they are similarly used for imposthumes of the parotid glands, inflamed tumours, and indurations of the breasts. Applied with water, these ashes are good for ulcerations of the head, and impart a plumpness to the skin in females. They are sprinkled, too, upon burns, and are highly esteemed as a dentifrice. Applied with vinegar, they are good for the removal of prurigo and of pituitous eruptions. Beaten up in a raw state, they are curative of scrofula and of chilblains upon the feet.

SEA-WEED

According to Nicander, sea-weed is also a theriac.[12] There are numerous varieties of it; one, for instance, with an elongated leaf, another red, another again with a broader leaf, and another crisped. The most esteemed kind of all is that which grows off the shores of Crete, upon the rocks there, close to the ground; it being used also for dyeing wool, as it has the property of so fixing the colours as never to allow of their being washed out. Nicander recommends it to be taken with wine.

REMEDIES FOR DISEASES OF THE EYES

The fat of all kinds of fish, both fresh-water as well as sea fish, melted in the sun and incorporated with honey, is an excellent improver of the eye-sight; the same, too, with castoreum, in combination with honey. The gall of the callionymus[13] heals marks upon the eyes and cauterizes fleshy excrescences about those organs; indeed, there is no fish with a larger quantity of gall than this. This fish is known also as the "uranoscopos," from the eyes being situate in the upper part of the head.

The gall of the red sea-scorpion, used with stale oil or Attic honey, disperses incipient cataract; for which purpose, the application should be made three times, on alternate days. A similar method is also employed for removing indurations of the membrane of the eyes. The surmullet, used as a diet, weakens the eyesight, it is said. The sea-hare is poisonous itself, but the ashes of it are useful as an application for preventing superfluous hairs on the eyelids from growing again, when they have been once pulled out by the roots. For this purpose, however, the smaller the fish is, the better. Small scallops, too, are salted and beaten up with cedar resin for a similar purpose, or else the frogs known as "diopetes"[14] and "calamitæ," are used; the blood of them being applied with vine gum to the eyelids, after the hairs have been removed.

REMEDIES FOR TOOTH-ACHE

Tooth-ache is alleviated by scarifying the gums with bones of the sea-dragon, or by rubbing the teeth once a year with the brains of a dog-fish boiled in oil, and kept for the purpose. It is a very good plan too, for the cure of tooth-ache, to lance

---

12 Or antidote.
13 Identified by Ajasson with the white Rascasse of the Mediterranean.
14 Meaning, literally, "Fallen from Jupiter," in reference to their supposed descent from heaven in showers of rain.

the gums with the sting of the sting-ray in some cases. This sting, too, is pounded, and applied to the teeth with white hellebore, having the effect of extracting them without the slightest difficulty. Another of these remedies is, ashes of salted fish calcined in an earthen vessel, mixed with powdered marble. Salted fish rinsed in a new earthen vessel, and then pounded, is very useful for the cure of tooth-ache. Equally good, it is said, are the back-bones of all kinds of salt fish, pounded and applied in a liniment. A decoction is made of a single frog boiled in one hemina of vinegar, and the teeth are rinsed with it, the decoction being retained in the mouth. In cases where a repugnance existed to making use of this remedy, Sallustius Dionysius used to suspend frogs over boiling vinegar by the hind legs, so as to make them discharge their humours into the vinegar by the mouth, using considerable numbers of frogs for the purpose; to those, however, who had a stronger stomach, he prescribed the frogs themselves, eaten with their broth. It is generally thought, too, that this recipe applies more particularly to the double teeth, and that the vinegar prepared as above-mentioned, is remarkably useful for strengthening them when loose.

REMEDIES FOR SCROFULA

Ulcerations of the mouth are cured by an application of brine in which mænæ[15] have been pickled, in combination with calcined heads of the fish, and honey. For the cure of scrofula, it is a good plan to prick the sores with the small bone that is found in the tail of the fish known as the sea-frog; care being taken to avoid making a wound, and to repeat the operation daily, until a perfect cure is effected. The same property, too, belongs to the sting of the sting-ray, and to the sea-hare, applied topically to the sores; but in both cases due care must be taken to remove them in an instant. Shells of sea-urchins are bruised, also, and applied with vinegar; shells also of sea-scolopendræ, applied with honey; and river-crabs pounded or calcined, and applied with honey. Bones, too, of the sæpia, triturated and applied with stale axle-grease, are marvellously useful for this purpose.

REMEDIES FOR PAINS IN THE LIVER AND SIDE

For pains in the liver, a sea-scorpion is killed in wine, and the liquid is taken. The meat, too, of the long mussel is taken with honied wine and water, in equal quantities, or, if there are symptoms of fever, with hydromel. Pains in the side are assuaged by taking the flesh of the hippocampus, grilled, or else the tethea, very similar to the oyster, with the ordinary food. For sciatica, the pickle of the silurus is injected, by way of enema. The flesh of mussels, too, is prescribed, for fifteen days, in doses of three oboli soaked in two sextarii of wine.

REMEDIES FOR INTESTINAL HERNIA, AND FOR DISEASES OF THE RECTUM

For the cure of intestinal hernia the sea-hare is applied, bruised with honey. The liver of the water-snake, and that of the hydrus,[16] bruised and taken in drink, are remedial for urinary calculi. Sciatica is cured by using the pickle of the silurus as an

---

15 Small sea-fish (TN).
16 A genus of venomous sea-snakes, type of a family Hydridæ.

enema, the bowels being first thoroughly purged. For chafing of the fundament, an application is made of heads of mullets and surmullets, reduced to ashes; for which purpose they are calcined in an earthen vessel, and must be applied in combination with honey. Calcined heads, too, of the fish known as mænæ are useful for the cure of chaps and condylomata; as also heads of salted pelamides,[17] reduced to ashes, or calcined tunny, applied with honey.

The torpedo, applied topically, reduces prolapse of the rectum. River-crabs, reduced to ashes, and applied with oil and wax, are curative of chaps of the anus; sea-crabs, too, are equally useful for the purpose.

REMEDIES FOR GOUT, AND FOR PAINS IN THE FEET

For the cure of gout and of diseases of the joints, oil is useful in which the intestines of frogs have been boiled. Ashes, too, of burnt bramble-frogs are similarly employed, with stale grease; in addition to which, some persons use calcined barley, the three ingredients being mixed in equal proportions. It is recommended too, in cases of gout, to rub the parts affected with a sea-hare, fresh caught, and to wear shoes made of beaver's skin, Pontic beaver more particularly, or else of a seal's skin, an animal the fat of which is very useful for the purpose; the same being the case also with bryon, similar to the lettuce in appearance, but with more wrinkled leaves, and destitute of stem. This plant is of a styptic nature, and, applied topically, it tends to modify the paroxysms of gout. The same, too, with sea-weed, of which we have also spoken already; due precaution being taken not to apply it dry.

REMEDIES FOR FEVERS

Recurrent fevers are effectually checked by making the patient taste the liver of a dolphin, just before the paroxysm comes on. Hippocampus are stifled in oil of roses, and the patients are rubbed therewith in cold agues, the fish, also, being worn as an amulet by the patient. In the same way, too, the small stones that are found at full moon in the head of the fish called "asellus" are worn, attached in a piece of linen cloth to the patient's body. A similar virtue is attributed to the longest tooth of the river-fish called phagrus, attached to the patient with a hair, provided he does not see the person who attaches it to him for five days. Frogs are boiled in oil in a spot where three roads meet, and, the flesh being first thrown away, the patients are rubbed with the decoction, by way of cure for quartan fever. Some persons, again, suffocate frogs in oil, and, after attaching them to the patient without his knowing it, anoint him with the oil. The heart of a frog, worn as an amulet, modifies the cold chills in fevers; the same, too, with oil in which the intestines of frogs have been boiled. But the best remedy for quartan fevers, is to wear attached to the body either frogs from which the claws have been removed, or else the liver or heart of a bramble-frog, attached in a piece of russet-coloured cloth.

REMEDIES FOR ULCERS, CARCINOMAS, AND CARBUNCLES

Ulcers of a serpiginous nature, as also the fleshy excrescences which make their appearance in them, are kept in check by applying ashes of calcined heads

---

17   A young tunnyfish, before it is a year old (TN).

of mænæ, or else ashes of the silurus. Carcinomas, too, are treated with heads of salted perch, their efficacy being considerably increased by using some salt along with the ashes, and kneading them up with heads of cunila and olive-oil. Ashes of sea-crabs, calcined with lead, arrest the progress of carcinomatous sores; a purpose for which ashes of river-crabs, in combination with honey and fine lint, are equally useful; though there are some authorities which prefer mixing alum and barley with the ashes. Phagedænic ulcers are cured by an application of dried silurus pounded with sandarach; malignant cancers, corrosive ulcers, and putrid sores, by the agency of stale tunny.

REMEDIES FOR FEMALE DISEASES

The milk is increased in females by eating the glauciscus[18] in its own liquor, or else smarides[19] with a ptisan, or boiled with fennel. Ashes of calcined shells of the murex or purple, applied with honey, are an effectual cure for affections of the breasts; river-crabs, too, and sea-crabs, applied topically, are equally good. The meat of the murex, applied to the breasts, removes hairs growing upon those parts. The squatina, applied topically, prevents the breasts from becoming too distended. Lint greased with dolphin's fat, and then ignited, produces a smoke which acts as an excitant upon females suffering from hysterical suffocations; the same, too, with strombi, left to putrefy in vinegar. Heads of perch or of mænæ, calcined and mixed with salt, oil, and cunila, are curative of diseases of the uterus; used as a fumigation, they bring away the afterbirth. Fat, too, of the seal, melted by the agency of fire, is introduced into the nostrils of females when swooning from hysterical suffocations; and for a similar purpose, the rennet of that animal is applied as a pessary, in wool.

The pulmo marinus,[20] attached to the body as an amulet, is an excellent promoter of menstruation; an effect which is equally produced by pounding live sea-urchins, and taking them in sweet wine. River-crabs, bruised in wine, and taken internally, arrest menstruation. The silurus, that of Africa more particularly, used as a fumigation, facilitates parturition, it is said. Crabs, taken in water, arrest menstruation; but used with hyssop, they act as an emmenagogue, we are told. In cases, too, where the infant is in danger of suffocation at the moment of delivery, a similar drink, administered to the mother, is highly efficacious. Crabs, too, either fresh or dried, are taken in drink, for the purpose of preventing abortion. Hippocrates prescribes them as a promoter of menstruation, and as an expellent of the dead fœtus, beaten up with five roots of lapathum and rue and some soot, and administered in honied wine. Crabs, boiled and taken in their liquor, with lapathum and parsley, promote the menstrual discharge, and increase the milk. In cases of fever, attended

---

18 A bluish-coloured fish, otherwise unknown (TN).

19 Ajasson remarks that many writers have identified the Smaris with the Sardine or the Anchovy. In his opinion, however, it is neither; but he thinks that under this head were included seven or eight varieties of the Pickerel, the principal of which are, the *Sparus smaris* of Linnæus and Lacépède, the *Sparus mana* of Linnæus, or *Sparus mendola* of Lacépède, and the *Sparus haffara* of Lacépède and Linnæus.

20 Or sea-lungs.

with pains in the head and throbbing of the eyes, crabs are said to be highly beneficial to females, given in astringent wine.

OTHER WATER CREATURES

Among the aquatic creatures ought also to be mentioned calamochnos, in Latin known as "adarea," a substance which collects about small reeds, from a mixture of the foam of fresh and of sea water. It possesses certain caustic properties, and hence it is that it is so useful as an ingredient in "acopa"[21] and as a remedy for cold shiverings; it is used too, for removing freckles upon the face of females. The ink of the sæpia is possessed of such remarkable potency, that if it is put into a lamp, Anaxilaüs tells us, the light will become entirely changed, and all present will look as black as Æthiopians. The bramble-frog, boiled in water, and given to swine with their drink, is curative of the maladies with which they are affected; an effect equally produced by the ashes of any other kind of frog. If wood is rubbed with the pulmo marinus, it will have all the appearance of being on fire; so much so, indeed, that a walking-stick, thus treated, will light the way like a torch.

---

21 "Remedies for lassitude."

Book XXXIII

The Natural History of Metals (I)

We are now about to speak of metals, of actual wealth,[1] the standard of comparative value, objects for which we diligently search, within the earth, in numerous ways. In one place, for instance, we undermine it for the purpose of obtaining riches, to supply the exigencies of life, searching for either gold or silver, electrum[2] or copper. In another place, to satisfy the requirements of luxury, our researches extend to gems and pigments, with which to adorn our fingers and the walls of our houses; while in a third place, we gratify our rash propensities by a search for iron, which, amid wars and carnage, is deemed more acceptable even than gold. We trace out all the veins of the earth, and yet, living upon it, undermined as it is beneath our feet, are astonished that it should occasionally cleave asunder or tremble; as though, forsooth, these signs could be any other than expressions of the indignation felt by our sacred parent! We penetrate into her entrails, and seek for treasures in the abodes even of the Manes, as though each spot we tread upon were not sufficiently bounteous and fertile for us!

GOLD

Gold is dug out of the earth, and, in close proximity to it, chrysocolla,[3] a substance which, that it may appear all the more precious, still retains the name[4] which it has borrowed from gold, was not enough for us to have discovered one bane for the human race, but we must set a value too upon the very corrupt matter dis-

---

1   *Ipsæ opes*. The metals were looked upon by the ancients as the only true riches.
2   Electrum is gold mixed with a certain quantity of silver. The word "electrum" is also used to signify amber.
3   A silicate of the protoxid of copper, it may have included borax (TN).
4   Meaning "gold glue," or "gold solder."

charged by gold. While avarice, too, was on the search for silver, it congratulated itself upon the discovery of minium,[5] and devised a use to be made of this red earth.

HOW MUCH GOLD POSSESSED THE ANCIENTS

At Rome, for a long period of time, the quantity of gold was but very small. At all events, after the capture of the City by the Gauls, when peace was about to be purchased, not more than one thousand pounds' weight of gold could be collected. I am by no means unaware of the fact that in the third consulship of Pompeius there was lost from the throne of Jupiter Capitolinus two thousand pounds' weight of gold, originally placed there by Camillus; a circumstance which has led most persons to suppose, that two thousand pounds' weight was the quantity then collected. But in reality, this excess of one thousand pounds was contributed from the spoil taken from the Gauls, amplified as it was by the gold of which they had stripped the temples, in that part of the City which they had captured.

The story of Torquatus,[6] too, is a proof that the Gauls were in the habit of wearing ornaments of gold when engaged in combat; from which it would appear that the sum taken from the Gauls themselves, and the amount of which they had pillaged the temples, were only equal to the amount of gold collected for the ransom, and no more. It appears, therefore, that in the year of the City 364, when Rome was captured by the Gauls, there was but two thousand pounds' weight of gold, at the very most; and this, too, at a period when, according to the returns of the census, there were already one hundred and fifty-two thousand five hundred and seventy-three free citizens in it. In this same city, too, three hundred and seven years later, the gold which C. Marius the younger conveyed to Præneste from the Temple of the Capitol when in flames, and all the other shrines, amounted to thirteen thousand pounds' weight, such being the sum that figured in the inscriptions at the triumph of Sylla; on which occasion it was displayed in the procession, as well as six thousand pounds' weight of silver. The same Sylla had, the day before, displayed in his triumph fifteen thousand pounds' weight of gold, and one hundred and fifteen thousand pounds' weight of silver, the fruit of all his other victories.

THE RIGHT OF WEARING GOLD RINGS

It does not appear that rings were in common use before the time of Cneius Flavius, the son of Annius. This Flavius obtained such high favour with the people, that he was created curule ædile; the additional honour was also conferred on Flavius, of making him tribune of the people at the same time, a thing which occasioned such a degree of indignation, that, as we find stated in the more ancient Annals, "the rings were laid aside!"

Most persons, however, are mistaken in the supposition that on this occasion the members of the equestrian order did the same; for it is in consequence of these additional words, "the phaleræ,[7] too, were laid aside as well," that the name of the

---

5 Red oxid of lead.
6 Who took the golden tore (torques) from the Gaul whom he slew; whence his name.
7 The "phaleræ" were bosses of metal, often gold, attached to the harness of the horse.

equestrian order was added. These rings, too, as the Annals tell us, were laid aside by the nobility, and not[8] by the whole body of the senate.

A second occasion, however, that of the Second Punic War, shows that rings must have been at that period in very general use; for if such had not been the case, it would have been impossible for Hannibal to send the three modii of rings, which we find so much spoken of, to Carthage. It was through a dispute, too, at an auction about the possession of a ring, that the feud first commenced between Cæpio and Drusus, a dispute which gave rise to the Social War, and the public disasters which thence ensued. Not even in those days, however, did all the senators possess gold rings, seeing that, in the memory of our grandsires, many personages who had even filled the prætorship, wore rings of iron to the end of their lives.

In this, as in every other case, luxury has introduced various fashions, either by adding to rings gems of exquisite brilliancy, and so loading the fingers with whole revenues, or else by engraving them with various devices; so that it is in one instance the workmanship, in another the material, that constitutes the real value of the ring. It was the custom at first to wear rings on a single finger only, the one, namely, that is next to the little finger; and this we see the case in the statues of Numa and Servius Tullius In later times, it became the practice to put rings on the finger next to the thumb, even in the case of the statues of the gods; and more recently, again, it has been the fashion to wear them upon the little finger as well. Among the peoples of Gallia and Britannia, the middle finger, it is said, is used for this purpose. At the present day, however, among us, this is the only finger that is excepted, all the others being loaded with rings, smaller rings even being separately adapted for the smaller joints of the fingers.

THE DECURIES OF THE JUDGES

Rings, as soon as they began to be commonly worn, distinguished the second order from the plebeians, in the same manner as the use of the tunic distinguished the senate from those who only were the ring. Still, however, this last distinction was introduced at a later period only, and we find it stated by writers that the public heralds even were formerly in the habit of wearing the tunic with the purple laticlave.[9] But the use of rings, no doubt, was the distinguishing mark of a third and intermediate order, between the plebeians and the senators; and the title of "eques," originally derived from the possession of a war-horse, is given at the present day as an indication of a certain amount of income. This, however, is of comparatively recent introduction; for when the late Emperor Augustus made his regulations for the decuries,[10] the greater part of the members thereof were persons who wore iron rings, and these bore the name, not of "equites," but of "judices," the former name

---

8   Pliny would probably imply hereby that, as he states subsequently, at this period gold rings were not as yet worn by all the members of the senate.

9   One of two broad stripes of purple woven in the stuff of the tunic worn by Roman senators and persons of senatorial rank, extending vertically from the neck down the front, and serving as a badge of their dignity (TN).

10 The "Decuriæ" of "judices," or "judges," were so called, probably, from ten (decem) having been originally chosen from each tribe.

being reserved solely for the members of the squadrons furnished with war-horses at the public charge.

Of these judices, too, there were at first but four decuries only, and in each of these decuries there was hardly one thousand men to be found, the provinces not having been hitherto admitted to the office; an observance which is still in force at the present day, no one newly admitted to the rights of citizenship being allowed to perform the duties of judex as a member of the decuries.

THE EQUESTRIAN ORDER

At length, however, in the ninth year of the reign of the Emperor Tiberius, the equestrian order was united in a single body; and a decree was passed, establishing to whom belonged the right of wearing the ring, in the consulship of C. Asinius Pollio and C. Antistius Vetus, the year from the foundation of the City, 775. It is a matter for surprise, how almost futile, we may say, was the cause which led to this change. C. Sulpicius Galba, desirous in his youth to establish his credit with the Emperor by hunting out grounds for prosecuting the keepers of victualling-houses, made complaint in the senate that the proprietors of those places were in the habit of protecting themselves from the consequences of their guilt by their plea of wearing the golden ring. For this reason, an ordinance was made that no person whatsoever should have this right of wearing the ring, unless, freeborn himself as regarded his father and paternal grandfather, he should be assessed by the censors at four hundred thousand sesterces, and entitled, under the Julian Law, to sit in the fourteen tiers of seats at the theatre. In later times, however, people began to apply in whole crowds for this mark of rank; and in consequence of the diversities of opinion which were occasioned thereby, the Emperor Caius added a fifth decury to the number. Indeed to such a pitch has conceit now arisen, that whereas, under the late Emperor Augustus, the decuries could not be completed, at the present day they will not suffice to receive all the members of the equestrian order, and we see in every quarter persons even who have been but just liberated from slavery, making a leap all at once to the distinction of the golden ring; a thing that never used to happen in former days, as it was by the ring of iron that the equites and the judices were then to be recognized.

COINS OF GOLD AND OTHER METALS

The next[11] crime committed against the welfare of mankind was on the part of who was the first to coin a denarius of gold, a crime the author of which is equally unknown. The Roman people made no use of stamped silver even before the period of the defeat of King Pyrrhus. The "as" of copper weighed exactly one libra. King Servius was the first to make an stamp upon copper. Before his time, according to Timæus, at Rome only the raw metal was used. The form of a sheep was the first figure stamped upon money, and to this fact it owes its name, "pecunia."[12] The highest figure at which one man's property was assessed in the reign of that king

---

11 The first crime having been committed by who introduced the use of gold rings.
12 From "pecus," a sheep.

was one hundred and twenty thousand asses, and consequently that amount of property was considered the standard of the first class.

Silver was not stamped with a mark until the year of the City 485, the year of the consulship of Q. Ogulnius and C. Fabius, five years before the First Punic War; at which time it was ordained that the value of the denarius should be ten libræ of copper, that of the quinarius five libræ, and that of the sestertius two libræ and a half. The weight, however, of the libra of copper was diminished during the First Punic War, the republic not having means to meet its expenditure; in consequence of which, an ordinance was made that the as should in future be struck of two ounces weight. By this contrivance a saving of five-sixths was effected, and the public debt was liquidated. The stamp upon these copper coins was a two-faced Janus on one side, and the beak of a ship of war on the other; the triens,[13] however, and the quadrans,[14] bore the impression of a ship.

The first golden coin was struck sixty-two years after that of silver, the scruple of gold being valued at twenty sesterces; a computation which gave, according to the value of the sesterce then in use, nine hundred sesterces to each libra of gold. In later times, again, an ordinance was made, that denarii of gold should be struck, at the rate of forty denarii to each libra of gold; after which period, the emperors gradually curtailed the weight of the golden denarius, until at last, in the reign of Nero, it was coined at the rate of forty-five to the libra.

CONSIDERATIONS ON MAN'S CUPIDITY FOR GOLD

But the invention of money opened a new field to human avarice, by giving rise to usury and the practice of lending money at interest, while the owner passes a life of idleness; and it was with no slow advances that, not mere avarice only, but a perfect hunger for gold became inflamed with a sort of rage for acquiring; to such a degree, in fact, that Septimuleius, the familiar friend of Caius Gracchus, not only cut off his head, upon which a price had been set of its weight in gold, but, before bringing it to Opimius, poured molten lead into the mouth, and so not only was guilty of the crime of parricide, but added to his criminality by cheating the state. Nor was it now any individual citizen, but the universal Roman name, that had been rendered infamous by avarice, when King Mithridates caused molten gold to be poured into the mouth of Aquilius the Roman general, whom he had taken prisoner; such were the results of cupidity.

SILVER UPON THE ARENA AND THE STAGE

We, too, have done things that posterity may probably look upon as fabulous. Cæsar, who was afterwards dictator, but at that time ædile,[15] was the first person, on the occasion of the funeral games in honour of his father, to employ all the apparatus of the arena in silver; and it was on the same occasion that for the first time

---

13 The third of an "as."
14 The fourth of an "as."
15 In Rome, a magistrate who had the superintendence of public buildings, spectacles, police and other municipal functions. (TN).

criminals encountered wild beasts with implements of silver, a practice imitated at the present day in our municipal towns even.

At the games celebrated by C. Antonius the stage was made of silver; and the same was the case at those celebrated by L. Muræna. The Emperor Caius had a scaffold introduced into the Circus, upon which there were one hundred and twenty-four thousand pounds' weight of silver. His successor Claudius, on the occasion of his triumph over Britain, announced by the inscriptions that among the coronets of gold, there was one weighing seven thousand pounds' weight, contributed by Nearer Spain, and another of nine thousand pounds, presented by Gallia Comata. Nero, who succeeded him, covered the Theatre of Pompeius with gold for one day, the occasion on which he displayed it to Tiridates, king of Armenia.

FOR WHAT REASONS THE HIGHEST VALUE IS SET UPON GOLD

The highest rank has been accorded to this substance, not, in my opinion, for its colour, (which in silver is clearer and more like the light of day, for which reason silver is preferred for our military ensigns, its brightness being seen at a greater distance). Nor yet is it for its weight or malleability that gold has been preferred to other metals, it being inferior in both these respects to lead —but it is because gold is the only substance in nature that suffers no loss from the action of fire, and passes unscathed through conflagrations and the flames of the funeral pile. Nay, even more than this, the oftener gold is subjected to the action of fire, the more refined in quality it becomes; indeed, fire is one test of its goodness, as, when submitted to intense heat, gold ought to assume a similar colour, and turn red and igneous in appearance; a mode of testing which is known as "obrussa."[16]

The first great proof, however, of the goodness of gold, is its melting with the greatest difficulty; in addition to which, it is a fact truly marvellous, that though proof against the most intense fire, if made with wood charcoal, it will melt with the greatest readiness upon a fire made with chaff; and that, for the purpose of purifying it, it is fused with lead.

A thing that is not the case with any other metal, gold is found pure in masses or in the form of dust; and whereas all other metals, when found in the ore, require to be brought to perfection by the aid of fire, this gold that I am speaking of is gold the moment it is found, and has all its component parts already in a state of perfection. And then, more than anything else, gold is subject to no rust, no verdigris, no emanation whatever from it, either to alter its quality or to lessen its weight. In addition to this, gold steadily resists the corrosive action of salt and vinegar, things which obtain the mastery over all other substances.

HOW GOLD IS FOUND

Gold is found in our own part of the world; not to mention the gold extracted from the earth in India by the ants, and in Scythia by the Griffins.[17] Among us it is

---

16 The gold thus tested was called "obrussum," "obryzum," or "obrizum," from the Greek ὄβρυζον, meaning "pure gold."

17 In mythology, an imaginary animal supposed to be generated between the lion and the eagle, and to combine the head, front, and wings of an eagle with the body and hind quarters

procured in three different ways; the first of which is, in the shape of dust, found in running streams, the in Spain, for instance, the Padus in Italy, the Hebrus in Thracia, the Pactolus in Asia, and the Ganges in India; indeed, there is no gold found in a more perfect state than this, thoroughly polished as it is by the continual attrition of the current.

A second mode of obtaining gold is by sinking shafts or seeking it among the debris of mountains. The persons in search of gold in the first place remove the "segutilum," such being the name of the earth which gives indication of the presence of gold. This done, a bed is made, the sand of which is washed, and, according to the residue found after washing, a conjecture is formed as to the richness of the vein.

The third method of obtaining gold surpasses the labours of the Giants[18] even; by the aid of galleries driven to a long distance, mountains are excavated by the light of torches, the duration of which forms the set times for work, the workmen never seeing the light of day for many months together. These mines are known as "arrugiæ"; and not unfrequently clefts are formed on a sudden, the earth sinks in, and the workmen are crushed beneath; so that it would really appear less rash to go in search of pearls and purples at the bottom of the sea, so much more dangerous to ourselves have we made the earth than the water!

ELECTRUM

In all gold ore there is some silver, in varying proportions; a tenth part in some instances, an eighth in others. Whenever the proportion of silver is one-fifth, the ore is known also by the name of "electrum";[19] grains, too, of this metal are often found in the gold known as "canaliense." An artificial electrum, too, is made, by mixing silver with gold. If the proportion of silver exceeds one-fifth, the metal offers no resistance on the anvil.

Electrum, too, was highly esteemed in ancient times, as we learn from the testimony of Homer, who represents the palace of Menelaüs as refulgent with gold and electrum, silver and ivory. At Lindos, in the island of Rhodes, there is a temple dedicated to Minerva, in which there is a goblet of electrum, consecrated by Helena; history states also that it was moulded after the proportions of her bosom. One peculiar advantage of electrum is, its superior brilliancy to silver by lamp-light. Native electrum has also the property of detecting poisons; for in such case, semicircles, resembling the rainbow in appearance, will form upon the surface of the goblet, and emit a crackling noise, like that of flame, thus giving a twofold indication of the presence of poison.

---

of a lion. This animal was supposed to watch over mines of gold and hidden treasures, and was consecrated to the sun. The figure of the griffin is seen on ancient coins, and is borne in coat-armor. It is also a frequent motive in architectural decoration (TN).

18   Who were said to have heaped one mountain on another in their war with the gods.

19   A name also given by the ancients to amber. Artificial "electrum," or gold alloyed with silver, was known in the most ancient times.

EIGHT REMEDIES DERIVED FROM GOLD

Gold is efficacious as a remedy in many ways, being applied to wounded persons and to infants, to render any malpractices of sorcery comparatively innocuous that may be directed against them. Gold, however, itself is mischievous in its effects if carried over the head, in the case of chickens and lambs more particularly. The proper remedy in such case is to wash the gold, and to sprinkle the water upon the objects which it is wished to preserve. Gold, too, is melted with twice its weight of salt, and three times its weight of misy;[20] after which it is again melted with two parts of salt and one of the stone called "schistos." Employed in this manner, it withdraws the natural acridity from the substances torrefied with it in the crucible, while at the same time it remains pure and incorrupt; the residue forming an ash which is preserved in an earthen vessel, and is applied with water for the cure of lichens on the face; the best method of washing it off is with bean-meal. These ashes have the property also of curing fistulas and the discharges known as "hæmorrhoides"; with the addition, too, of powdered pumice, they are a cure for putrid ulcers and sores which emit an offensive smell.

SILVER

After stating these facts, we come to speak of silver ore, the next folly of mankind. Silver is never found but in shafts sunk deep in the ground, there being no indications to raise hopes of its existence, no shining sparkles, as in the case of gold. The earth in which it is found is sometimes red, sometimes of an ashy hue. It is impossible, too, to melt it, except in combination with lead or with galena, this last being the name given to the vein of lead that is mostly found running near the veins of the silver ore. When submitted, too, to the action of fire, part of the ore precipitates itself in the form of lead, while the silver is left floating on the surface, like oil on water.

The vein of silver that is found nearest the surface is known by the name of "crudaria." In ancient times, the excavations used to be abandoned the moment alum[21] was met with, and no further search was made. Of late, however, the discovery of a vein of copper beneath alum, has withdrawn any such limits to man's hopes. The exhalations from silver-mines are dangerous to all animals, but to dogs more particularly. The softer they are, the more beautiful gold and silver are considered.

QUICKSILVER

There is a mineral also found in these veins of silver, which yields a humour that is always liquid, and is known as "quicksilver." It acts as a poison upon everything, and pierces vessels even, making its way through them by the agency of its malignant properties. All substances float upon the surface of quicksilver, with the excep-

---

20 A sulphur-yellow mineral occurring in loose aggregations of small crystalline scales it consists of hydrous sulphate of iron, and is derived from the decomposition of pyrite. Also called yellow copperas and copiapite (TN).

21 Alumen.

tion of gold, this being the only substance that it attracts to itself. Hence it is, that it is such an excellent refiner of gold; for, on being briskly shaken in an earthen vessel with gold, it rejects all the impurities that are mixed with it. When once it has thus expelled these superfluities, there is nothing to do but to separate it from the gold; to effect which, it is poured out upon skins that have been well tawed, and so, exuding through them like a sort of perspiration, it leaves the gold in a state of purity behind.

MINIUM

It is also in silver-mines that minium[22] is found, a pigment held at the present day in very high estimation; and by the Romans in former times not only held in the highest estimation, but used for sacred purposes as well. Verrius enumerates certain authors, upon whose testimony we find it satisfactorily established that it was the custom upon festivals to colour the face of the statue of Jupiter even with minium, as well as the bodies of triumphant generals; and that it was in this guise that Camillus celebrated his triumph. We find, too, that it is through the same religious motives that it is employed at the present day for colouring the unguents used at triumphal banquets, and that it is the first duty of the censors to make a contract for painting the statue of Jupiter with this colour.

THE DIFFERENT KINDS OF SILVER, AND THE MODES OF TESTING IT

There are two kinds of silver. On placing a piece of it upon an iron fire-shovel at a white heat, if the metal remains perfectly white, it is of the best quality; if again it turns of a reddish colour, it is inferior; but if it becomes black, it is worthless. Fraud, however, has devised means of stultifying this test even; for by keeping the shovel immersed in men's urine, the piece of silver absorbs it as it burns, and so displays a fictitious whiteness. There is also a kind of test with reference to polished silver; when the human breath comes in contact with it, it should immediately be covered with steam, the cloudiness disappearing at once.

MIRRORS

It is generally supposed among us that it is only the very finest silver that admits of being laminated, and so converted into mirrors. Pure silver was formerly used for the purpose, but, at the present day, this too has been corrupted by the devices of fraud. But, really, it is a very marvellous property that this metal has, of reflecting objects; a property which, it is generally agreed, results from the repercussion of the air, thrown back as it is from the metal upon the eyes. The same too is the action that takes place when we use a mirror. If, again, a thick plate of this metal is highly polished, and is rendered slightly concave, the image or object is enlarged to an immense extent; so vast is the difference between a surface receiving, and throwing back the air. Even more than this-drinking-cups are now made in such a manner, as to be filled inside with numerous concave facets, like so many mirrors; so that if but one person looks into the interior, he sees reflected a whole multitude of persons.

---

22   Minium is our Cinnabar, a bisulphurate of mercury. This ore is the great source of the mercury of commerce, from which it is obtained by sublimation. When pure, it is the same as the manufactured vermilion of commerce.

Mirrors, too, have been invented to reflect monstrous forms; those, for instance, which have been consecrated in the Temple at Smyrna. This, however, all results from the configuration given to the metal; and it makes all the difference whether the surface has a concave form like the section of a drinking cup, or whether it is convex; whether it is depressed in the middle or elevated; whether the surface has a direction transversely or obliquely; or whether it runs horizontally or vertically; the peculiar configuration of the surface which receives the shadows, causing them to undergo corresponding distortions; for, in fact, the image is nothing else but the shadow of the object collected upon the bright surface of the metal.

However, to finish our description of mirrors on the present occasion; the best, in the times of our ancestors, were those of Brundisium, composed of a mixture of stannum[23] and copper; at a later period, however, those made of silver were preferred, Pasiteles being the first who made them, in the time of Pompeius Magnus. More recently, a notion has arisen that the object is reflected with greater distinctness, by the application to the back of the mirror of a layer of gold.

CÆRULEUM

Cæruleum[24] is a kind of sand. In former times there were three kinds of it; the Egyptian, which was the most esteemed of all; the Scythian, which is easily dissolved, and which produces four colours when pounded, one of a lighter blue and one of a darker blue, one of a thicker consistency and one comparatively thin; and the Cyprian, which is now preferred as a colour to the preceding. Since then, the kinds imported from Puteoli and Spain have been added to the list, this sand having of late been prepared there. Every kind, however, is submitted to a dyeing process, it being boiled with a plant used particularly for this purpose, and imbibing its juices. In other respects, the mode of preparing it is similar to that of chrysocolla. From cæruleum, too, is prepared the substance known as "lomentum," it being washed and ground for the purpose. Lomentum is of a paler tint than cæruleum; the price of it is ten denarii per pound, and that of cæruleum but eight. Cæruleum is used upon a surface of clay, for upon lime it will not hold. A more recent invention is the Vestorian cæruleum, so called from the person who first manufactured it; it is prepared from the finer parts of Egyptian cæruleum, and the price of it is eleven denarii per pound. That of Puteoli is used in a similar manner, as also for windows; it is known as "cylon."

Cæruleum has the medicinal property of acting as a detergent upon ulcers. Hence it is, that it is used as an ingredient in plasters, as also in cauteries. As to sil,[25] it is pounded with the greatest difficulty; viewed as a medicament, it is slightly mordent and astringent, and fills up the cavities left by ulcers. To make it the more serviceable, it is burnt in earthen vessels.

---

23   An alloy of silver and lead (TN).
24   "It is possible that the 'cæruleum' of the ancients may in some cases have been real ultramarine, but properly and in general, it was only copper ochre." Beckmann's *Hist. Inv.* Vol. I.
25   A kind of yellowish earth used as a pigment by ancient painters; yellow ocher (TN).

Book XXXIV
The Natural History of Metals (II)

THE ORES OF BRASS

We must, in the next place, give an account of the ores of brass,[1] a metal which, in respect of utility, is next in value; indeed the Corinthian brass comes before silver, not to say almost before gold itself. It is also the standard of monetary value; hence the terms "æra militum," "tribuni ærarii," "ærarium," "obærati," and "ære diruti."[2] I have already mentioned for what length of time the Roman people employed no coin except brass; and there is another ancient fact which proves that the esteem in which it was held was of equal antiquity with that of the City itself, the circumstance that the third associated body[3] which Numa established, was that of the braziers.

THE DIFFERENT KINDS OF COPPER

The ore is extracted and is then purified by fusion. The metal is also obtained from a coppery stone called "cadmia." The most highly esteemed copper is procured from beyond seas; it was formerly obtained in Campania also, and at present

---

    1   "Æris Metalla." The word "Æs" does not entirely correspond to our word "brass"; the brass of the moderns being a compound of copper and zinc, while the "Æs" of the ancients was mostly composed of copper and tin, and therefore, would be more correctly designated by the word "bronze."

    2   These terms must have come into use when brass, "æs," was the ordinary medium of circulation.. Their meaning is, "soldiers' pay," "tribunes of the treasury," the "public treasury," "made bondmen for debt," and "mulcted of their pay."

    3   "Collegium." The colleges of the priests and of the augurs being the first two associated bodies.

is found in the country of the Bergomates, at the extremity of Italy. It is said to have been lately discovered also in the province of Germany.

CORINTHIAN BRASS

Formerly a mixture was made of copper fused with gold and silver, and the workmanship in this metal was considered even more valuable than the material itself; but, at the present day, it is difficult to say whether the workmanship in it, or the material, is the worst. Indeed, it is wonderful, that while the value of these works has so infinitely increased, the reputation of the art itself is nearly extinct.

BRASS CANDELABRA AND THE STORY OF GEGANIA

Ægina was particularly famous for the manufacture of sockets only for brass candelabra, as Tarentum was for that of the stems; the most complete articles were, therefore, produced by the union of the two. There are persons, too, who are not ashamed to give for one a sum equal to the salary of a military tribune, although, as its name indicates, its only use is to hold a lighted candle. On the sale of one of these brass candelabra, Theon the public crier announced, that the purchaser must also take, as part of the lot, one Clesippus, a fuller, who was hump-backed, and in other respects, of a hideous aspect. The purchase was made by a female named Gegania, for fifty thousand sesterces. Upon her exhibiting these purchases at an entertainment which she gave, the slave, for the amusement of her guests, was brought in naked. Conceiving an infamous passion for him, she first admitted him to her bed, and finally left him all her estate. Having thus become excessively rich, he adored the brass candelabra as much as any divinity, and the story became a sort of pendant to the celebrity of the Corinthian brass candelabra. Still, however, good morals were vindicated in the end, for he erected a splendid monument to her memory, and so kept alive the eternal remembrance of the misconduct of Gegania.

THE FIRST STATUE OF A GOD MADE OF BRASS AT ROME

But after some time the artists everywhere applied themselves to representations of the gods. I find that the first brass image, which was made at Rome, was that of Ceres; and that the expenses were defrayed out of the property that belonged to Spurius Cassius, who was put to death by his own father, for aspiring to the regal office. The practice, however, soon passed from the gods to the statues and representations of men, and this in various forms. The ancients stained their statues with bitumen, which makes it the more remarkable that they were afterwards fond of covering them with gold. I do not know whether this was a Roman invention; but it certainly has the repute of being an ancient practice at Rome.

DIFFERENT KINDS AND FORMS OF STATUES

In former times the statues that were thus dedicated were clad in the toga. Naked statues also, brandishing a spear, after the manner of the youths at their gymnastic exercises, were much admired; these were called "Achillean." The Greek practice is, not to cover any part of the body; while, on the contrary, the Roman and the military statues have the addition of a cuirass.[4] Cæsar, the Dictator, permitted a statue with a cuirass to be erected in honour of him in his Forum. As to the statues which are made in the garb of the Luperci,[5] they are of no older date than those which have been lately erected, covered with a cloak. Mancinus gave directions, that he should be represented in the dress which he wore when he was surrendered to the enemy. It has been remarked by some authors, that L. Attius, the poet, had a statue of himself erected in the Temple of the Muses, which was extremely large, although he himself was very short.

Equestrian statues are also held in esteem in Rome; but they are of Greek origin, no doubt. Among the Greeks, those persons only were honoured with equestrian statues who were victors on horseback in the sacred games; though afterwards the same distinction was bestowed on those who were successful in the races with chariots with two or four horses; hence the use of chariots with us in the statues of those who have triumphed. But this did not take place until a late period; and it was not until the time of the late Emperor Augustus, that we had chariots represented with six horses, as also with elephants.

THE MOST CELEBRATED COLOSSAL STATUES

As to boldness of design, the examples are innumerable; for we see designed, statues of enormous bulk, known as colossal statues and equal to towers in size. Such, for instance, is the Apollo in the Capitol, which was brought by M. Lucullus from Apollonia, a city of Pontus, thirty cubits in height, and which cost five hundred talents; such, too, is the statue of Jupiter, in the Campus Martius, dedicated by the late Emperor Claudius, but which appears small in comparison from its vicinity to the Theatre of Pompeius; and such is that at Tarentum, forty cubits in height, and the work of Lysippus.

But that which is by far the most worthy of our admiration, is the colossal statue of the Sun, which stood formerly at Rhodes, and was the work of Chares the Lindian, a pupil of the above-named Lysippus; no less than seventy cubits in height. This statue fifty-six years after it was erected, was thrown down by an earthquake; but even as it lies, it excites our wonder and admiration.

Colossal statues used also to be made in Italy. At all events, we see the Tuscan Apollo, in the library of the Temple of Augustus, fifty feet in height from the toe; and it is a question whether it is more remarkable for the quality of the metal, or for the beauty of the workmanship. But all these gigantic statues of this kind have been surpassed in our own age by that of Mercury, made by Zenodotus for the city of the Arverni in Gaul, which was ten years in being completed, and the making of which cost four hundred thousand sesterces. Having given sufficient proof there of his artistic skill, he was sent for by Nero to Rome, where he made a colossal

---

4   A piece of defensive armor covering the body from the neck to the girdle, and combining a breastplate and a backpiece.

5   The Luperci were the priests of Pan, who, at the celebration of their games, called Lupercalia, were in the habit of running about the streets of Rome, with no other covering than a goat's skin tied about the loins.

statue intended to represent that prince, one hundred and ten feet in height. In consequence, however, of the public detestation of Nero's crimes, this statue was consecrated to the Sun.

THE DIFFERENT KINDS OF COPPER

We will now return to the different kinds of copper, and its several combinations. In Cyprian copper we have the kind known as "coronarium," and that called "regulare," both of them ductile. The former is made into thin leaves, and, after being coloured with ox-gall, is used for what has all the appearance of gilding on the coronets worn upon the stage. The same substance, if mixed with gold, in the proportion of six scruples of gold to the ounce, and reduced into thin plates, acquires a fiery red colour, and is termed "pyropus." In other mines again, they prepare the kind known as "regulare," as also that which is called "caldarium." These differ from each other in this respect, that, in the latter, the metal is only fused, and breaks when struck with the hammer, whereas the "regulare" is malleable, or ductile, as some call it, a property which belongs naturally to all the copper of Cyprus. In the case, however, of all the other mines, this difference between bar copper and cast brass is produced by artificial means. All the ores, in fact, will produce bar or malleable copper when sufficiently melted and purified by heat. Among the other kinds of copper, the palm of excellence is awarded to that of Campania, which is the most esteemed for vessels and utensils. This last is prepared several ways. At Capua it is melted upon fires made with wood, and not coals, after which it is sprinkled with cold water and cleansed through a sieve made of oak. After being thus smelted a number of times, Spanish silver-lead is added to it, in the proportion of ten pounds of lead to one hundred pounds of copper; a method by which it is rendered pliable, and made to assume that agreeable colour which is imparted to other kinds of copper by the application of oil and the action of the sun. Many parts, however, of Italy, and the provinces, produce a similar kind of metal; but there they add only eight pounds of lead, and, in consequence of the scarcity of wood, melt it several times over upon coals. It is in Gaul more particularly, where the ore is melted between red-hot stones, that the difference is to be seen that is produced by these variations in the method of smelting. Indeed, this last method scorches the metal, and renders it black and friable. Besides, they only melt it twice; whereas, the oftener this operation is repeated, the better in quality it becomes.

CADMIA

The ores of copper furnish a number of resources that are employed in medicine; indeed, all kinds of ulcers are healed thereby with great rapidity. Of these, however, the most useful is cadmia. This substance is formed artificially, beyond a doubt, in the furnaces, also, where they smelt silver, but it is whiter and not so heavy, and by no means to be compared with that from copper. There are several kinds of it. For, as the mineral itself, from which it is prepared artificially, so neces-

Book XXXIV - The Natural History of Metals (II)

sary in fusing copper ore, and so useful in medicine, has the name of "cadmia,"[6] so also is it found in the smelting-furnaces, where it receives other names, according to the way in which it is formed.

Cadmia acts as a desiccative, heals wounds, arrests discharges, acts detergently upon webs and foul incrustations of the eyes, removes eruptions, and produces, in fact, all the good effects which we shall have occasion to mention when speaking of lead. Copper too, itself, when calcined, is employed for all these purposes; in addition to which it is used for white spots and cicatrizations upon the eyes. Mixed with milk, it is curative also of ulcers upon the eyes; for which purpose, the people in Egypt make a kind of eye-salve by grinding it upon whet stones. Taken with honey, it acts as an emetic.

VERDIGRIS

Verdigris[7] is also applied to many purposes, and is prepared in numerous ways. Sometimes it is detached already formed, from the mineral from which copper is smelted; and sometimes it is made by piercing holes in white copper, and suspending it over strong vinegar in casks, which are closed with covers; it being much superior if scales of copper are used for the purpose. Some persons plunge vessels themselves, made of white copper, into earthen pots filled with vinegar, and scrape them at the end of ten days. Others, again, cover the vessels with husks of grapes, and scrape them in the same way, at the end of ten days. Others sprinkle vinegar upon copper filings, and stir them frequently with a spatula in the course of the day, until they are completely dissolved. Others prefer triturating these filings with vinegar in a brazen mortar; but the most expeditious method of all is to add to the vinegar shavings of coronet copper.

It affords a most useful ingredient for eye-salves, and from its mordent action is highly beneficial for watery humours of the eyes. It is necessary, however, to wash the part with warm water, applied with a fine sponge, until its mordency is no longer felt.

IRON ORES

Next to copper we must give an account of the metal known as iron, at the same time the most useful and the most fatal instrument in the hand of mankind. For by the aid of iron we lay open the ground, we plant trees, we prepare our vineyard-trees, and we force our vines each year to resume their youthful state, by cutting away their decayed branches. It is by the aid of iron that we construct houses, cleave rocks, and perform so many other useful offices of life. But it is with iron also that wars, murders, and robberies are effected, and this, not only hand to hand, but from a distance even, by the aid of missiles and winged weapons, now launched from engines, now hurled by the human arm, and now furnished with feathery wings. This last I regard as the most criminal artifice that has been devised

---

6   The "cadmia" of this Chapter is a furnace-calamine, a product of the fusion of the ore of copper, or zinc.

7   "Ærugo." The researches of modern chemists have ascertained the composition of verdigris to be a diacetete of copper.

by the human mind; for, as if to bring death upon man with still greater rapidity, we have given wings to iron and taught it to fly. Let us therefore acquit Nature of a charge that here belongs to man himself.

Iron ores are to be found almost everywhere; for they exist even in the Italian island of Ilva, being easily distinguished by the ferruginous colour of the earth. The method of working the ore is the same as that employed in the case of copper. In Cappadocia, however, it is peculiarly questionable whether this metal is a present due to the water or to the earth; because, when the latter has been saturated with the water of a certain river, it yields, and then only, an iron that may be obtained by smelting.

There are numerous varieties of iron ore; the chief causes of which arise from differences in the soil and in the climate. Some earths produce a metal that is soft, and nearly akin to lead; others an iron that is brittle and coppery, the use of which must be particularly avoided in making wheels or nails, the former kind being better for these purposes. There is another kind, again, which is only esteemed when cut into short lengths, and is used for making hobnails; and another which is more particularly liable to rust. All these varieties are known by the name of "strictura," an appellation which is not used with reference to the other metals, and is derived from the steel that is used for giving an edge. There is a great difference, too, in the smelting; some kinds producing knurrs of metal, which are especially adapted for hardening into steel, or else, prepared in another manner, for making thick anvils or heads of hammers. But the main difference results from the quality of the water into which the red-hot metal is plunged from time to time. The water, which is in some places better for this purpose than in others, has quite ennobled some localities for the excellence of their iron

SEVEN REMEDIES DERIVED FROM IRON

Iron is employed in medicine for other purposes besides that of making incisions. For if a circle is traced with iron, or a pointed weapon is carried three times round them, it will preserve both infant and adult from all noxious influences; if nails, too, that have been extracted from a tomb, are driven into the threshold of a door, they will prevent nightmare. A slight puncture with the point of a weapon, with which a man has been wounded, will relieve sudden pains, attended with stitches in the sides or chest. Some affections are cured by cauterization with red-hot iron, the bite of the mad dog more particularly; for even if the malady has been fully developed, and hydrophobia has made its appearance, the patient is instantly relieved on the wound being cauterized. Water in which iron has been plunged at a white heat, is useful, as a potion, in many diseases, dysentery more particularly.

THE ORES OF LEAD

The nature of lead next comes to be considered. There are two kinds of it, the black and the white.[8] The white is the most valuable; it was called by the Greeks

---

8   It is most probable that the "black lead" of Pliny was our lead, and the "white lead" our tin.

"cassiteros," and there is a fabulous story told of their going in quest of it to the islands of the Atlantic, and of its being brought in barks made of osiers, covered with hides. It is now known that it is a production of Lusitania and Gallæcia. It is a sand found on the surface of the earth, and of a black colour, and is only to be detected by its weight. It is mingled with small pebbles, particularly in the dried beds of rivers. The miners wash this sand, and calcine the deposit in the furnace. It is also found in the gold mines that are known as "alutiæ," the stream of water which is passed through them detaching certain black pebbles, mottled with small white spots and of the same weight as gold. Hence it is that they remain with the gold in the baskets in which it is collected; and being separated in the furnace, are then melted, and become converted into white lead.

Black lead is not procured in Gallæcia, although it is so greatly abundant in the neighbouring province of Cantabria; nor is silver procured from white lead, although it is from black. Pieces of black lead cannot be soldered without the intervention of white lead, nor can this be done without employing oil; white lead, on the other hand, cannot be united without the aid of black lead. White lead was held in estimation in the days even of the Trojan War, a fact that is attested by Homer, who calls it "cassiteros." There are two different sources of black lead; it being procured either from its own native ore, where it is produced without the intermixture of any other substance, or else from an ore which contains it in common with silver, the two metals being fused together. The metal which first becomes liquid in the furnace, is called "stannum"; the next that melts is silver; and the metal that remains behind is galena, the third constituent part of the mineral. On this last being again submitted to fusion black lead is produced, with a deduction of two-ninths.

When copper vessels are coated with stannum, they produce a less disagreeable flavour, and the formation of verdigris is prevented; it is also remarkable, that the weight of the vessel is not increased. As already mentioned, the finest mirrors were formerly prepared from it at Brundisium, until everybody, our maid-servants even, began to use silver ones. At the present day a counterfeit stannum is made, by adding one-third of white copper to two-thirds of white lead.

BLACK LEAD

Black lead is used in the form of pipes and sheets; it is extracted with great labour in Spain, and throughout all the Gallic provinces; but in Britannia it is found in the upper stratum of the earth, in such abundance, that a law has been spontaneously made, prohibiting any one from working more than a certain quantity of it. It is a marvellous fact, that these mines, and these only, when they have been abandoned for some time, become replenished, and are more prolific than before. This would appear to be effected by the air, infusing itself at liberty through the open orifices, just as some women become more prolific after abortion.

REMEDIES DERIVED FROM LEAD

Lead is used in medicine, without any addition, for the removal of scars; if it is applied, too, in plates, to the region of the loins and kidneys, in consequence of its cold nature it will restrain the venereal passions, and put an end to libidinous dreams at night, attended with spontaneous emissions, and assuming all the form of a disease. The orator Calvus, it is said, effected a cure for himself by means of these plates, and so preserved his bodily energies for labour and study. The Emperor Nero could never sing to the full pitch of his voice, unless he had a plate of lead upon his chest; thus showing us one method of preserving the voice. For medicinal purposes the lead is melted in earthen vessels; a layer of finely powdered sulphur being placed beneath, very thin plates of lead are laid upon it, and are then covered with a mixture of sulphur and iron. While it is being melted, all the apertures in the vessel should be closed, otherwise a noxious vapour is discharged from the furnace, of a deadly nature, to dogs in particular. Indeed, the vapours from all metals destroy flies and gnats; and hence it is that in mines there are none of those annoyances.

Book XXXV
An Account of Paintings, Colours, Plastic Art and Earths

I have now given at considerable length an account of the nature of metals, which constitute our wealth, and of the substances that are derived from them; so connecting my various subjects, as, at the same time, to describe an immense number of medicinal compositions which they furnish, the mysteries thrown upon them by the druggists, and the tedious minutiæ of the arts of carving, statuary, and of dyeing. It remains for me to describe the various kinds of earths and stones; a still more extensive series of subjects, each of which has been treated of, by the Greeks more particularly, in a great number of volumes. For my own part, I propose to employ a due degree of brevity, at the same time omitting nothing that is necessary or that is a product of Nature.

I shall begin then with what still remains to be said with reference to painting, an art which was formerly illustrious, when it was held in esteem both by kings and peoples, and ennobling those whom it deigned to transmit to posterity. But at the present day, it is completely banished in favour of marble, and even gold.

PORTRAITS

Correct portraits of individuals were formerly transmitted to future ages by painting; but this has now completely fallen out of fashion. Brazen shields are now set up, and silver faces, with only some obscure traces of the countenance; the very heads, too, of statues are changed, a thing that has given rise before now to many a current sarcastic line; so true it is that people prefer showing off the valuable material, to having a faithful likeness. And yet, at the same time, we tapestry the walls of our galleries with old pictures, and we prize the portraits of strangers; while as to those made in honour of ourselves, we esteem them only for the value of the material, for some heir to break up and melt, and so forestall the noose and slip-knot of the thief. Thus it is that we possess the portraits of no living individuals, and leave behind us the pictures of our wealth, not of our persons.

But on the contrary, in the days of our ancestors, it was these that were to be seen in their halls, and not statues made by foreign artists, or works in bronze or marble; portraits modelled in wax were arranged, each in its separate niche, to be always in readiness to accompany the funeral processions of the family; occasions on which every member of the family that had ever existed was always present. The pedigree, too, of the individual was traced in lines upon each of these coloured portraits. Their archive-rooms, too, were filled with archives and memoirs, stating what each had done when holding the magistracy. On the outside, again, of their houses, and around the thresholds of their doors, were placed other statues of those mighty spirits, in the spoils of the enemy there affixed, memorials which a purchaser even was not allowed to displace; so that the very house continued to triumph even after it had changed its master. A powerful stimulus to emulation this, when the walls each day reproached an unwarlike owner for having thus intruded upon the triumphs of another!

THE HISTORY OF PAINTING

We have no certain knowledge as to the commencement of the art of painting, nor does this enquiry fall under our consideration. The Egyptians assert that it was invented among themselves, six thousand years before it passed into Greece; a vain boast, it is very evident. As to the Greeks, some say that it was invented at Sicyon, others at Corinth; but they all agree that it originated in tracing lines round the human shadow. The first stage of the art, they say, was this, the second stage being the employment of single colours; a process known as "monochromaton," after it had become more complicated, and which is still in use at the present day.

But already, in fact, the art of painting had been perfectly developed in Italy.[1] At all events, there are extant in the temples at Ardea, at this day, paintings of greater antiquity than Rome itself; in which, in my opinion, nothing is more marvellous, than that they should have remained so long unprotected by a roof, and yet preserving their freshness. At Lanuvium, too, it is the same, where we see an Atalanta and a Helena, without drapery, close together, and painted by the same artist. They are both of the greatest beauty, the former being evidently the figure of a virgin, and they still remain uninjured, though the temple is in ruins.

ROMAN PAINTERS

Among the Romans, too, this art very soon rose into esteem, for it was from it that the Fabii, a most illustrious family, derived their surname of "Pictor"; indeed the first of the family who bore it, himself painted the Temple of Salus, in the year of the City 450; a work which lasted to our own times, but was destroyed when the temple was burnt, in the reign of Claudius. Next in celebrity were the paintings of the poet Pacuvius, in the Temple of Hercules, situate in the Cattle Market; he was

---

1 Ajasson remarks, that a great number of paintings have been lately discovered in the Etruscan tombs, in a very perfect state, and probably of very high antiquity.

a son of the sister of Ennius, and the fame of the art was enhanced at Rome by the success of the artist on the stage. After this period, the art was no longer practised by men of rank; unless, indeed, we would make reference to Turpilius, in our own times, a native of Venetia, and of equestrian rank, several of whose beautiful works are still in existence at Verona. He painted, too, with his left hand, a thing never known to have been done by any one before.

WHEN PAINTING WAS FIRST HELD IN HIGH ESTEEM AT ROME

But it was the Dictator Cæsar that first brought the public exhibition of pictures into such high estimation, by consecrating an Ajax and a Medea before the Temple of Venus Genetrix. After him there was M. Agrippa, a man who was naturally more attached to rustic simplicity than to refinement. Still, however, we have a magnificent oration of his, and one well worthy of the greatest of our citizens, on the advantage of exhibiting in public all pictures and statues; a practice which would have been far preferable to sending them into banishment at our country-houses. Severe as he was in his tastes, he paid the people of Cyzicus twelve hundred thousand sesterces for two paintings, an Ajax and a Venus. He also ordered small paintings to be set in marble in the very hottest part of his Warm Baths; where they remained until they were removed a short time since, when the building was repaired.

THE ART OF PAINTING – COLOURS

The art of painting at last became developed, in the invention of light and shade, the alternating contrast of the colours serving to heighten the effect of each. At a later period, again, lustre was added, a thing altogether different from light. The gradation between lustre and light on the one hand and shade on the other, was called "tonos"; while the blending of the various tints, and their passing into one another, was known as "harmoge."

Colours are either sombre or florid, these qualities arising either from the nature of the substances or their mode of combination. The florid colours are those which the employer supplies to the painter at his own expense; minium, namely, armenium, cinnabaris, chrysocolla, indicum, and purpurissum. The others are the sombre colours. Taking both kinds together, some are native colours, and others are artificial. Sinopis, rubrica, parætonium, melinum, cretria and orpiment, are native colours. The others are artificial, more particularly those described by us when speaking of metals; in addition to which there are, among the more common colours, ochra, usta or burnt ceruse, sandarach, sandyx, syricum, and atramentum.

COLOURS USED BY THE ANCIENTS

It was with four colours only, that Apelles, Echion, Melanthius, and Nicomachus, those most illustrous painters, executed their immortal works; melinum for the white, Attic sil for the yellow, Pontic sinopis for the red, and atramentum for the black; and yet a single picture of theirs has sold before now for the treasures of whole cities. But at the present day, when purple is employed for colouring walls even, and when India sends to us the slime of her rivers, and the corrupt blood of her dragons and her elephants, there is no such thing as a picture of high quality produced. Everything, in fact, was superior at a time when the resources of art were so much fewer than they now are. Yes, so it is; and the reason is, as we have already stated, that it is the material, and not the efforts of genius, that is now the object of research.

ENCAUSTIC PAINTING

In ancient times there were but two methods of encaustic[2] painting, in wax and on ivory, with the cestrum or pointed graver. When, however, this art came to be applied to the painting of ships of war, a third method was adopted, that of melting the wax colours and laying them on with a brush, while hot. Painting of this nature, applied to vessels, will never spoil from the action of the sun, winds, or salt water.

THE COLOURING OF TISSUES

In Egypt, too, they employ a very remarkable process for the colouring of tissues. After pressing the material, which is white at first, they saturate it, not with colours, but with mordents that are calculated to absorb colour. This done, the tissues, still unchanged in appearance, are plunged into a cauldron of boiling dye, and are removed the next moment fully coloured. It is a singular fact, too, that although the dye in the pan is of one uniform colour, the material when taken out of it is of various colours, according to the nature of the mordents that have been respectively applied to it; these colours, too, will never wash out. Thus the dye-pan, which under ordinary circumstances, no doubt, would have made but one colour of several, if coloured tissues had been put into it, is here made to yield several colours from a single dye. At the same moment that it dyes the tissues, it boils in the colour; and it is the fact, that material which has been thus submitted to the action of fire becomes stouter and more serviceable for wear, than it would have been if it had not been subjected to the process

PLASTIC ART

On painting we have now said enough, and more than enough; but it will be only proper to append some accounts of the plastic art. Butades, a potter of Sicyon, was the first who invented, at Corinth, the art of modelling portraits in the earth which he used in his trade. It was through his daughter that he made the discovery; who, being deeply in love with a young man about to depart on a long journey, traced the profile of his face, as thrown upon the wall by the light of the lamp. Upon seeing this, her father filled in the outline, by compressing clay upon the surface, and so made a face in relief, which he then hardened by fire along with other articles of pottery. This model, it is said, was preserved in the Nymphæum at Corinth, until the destruction of that city by Mummius. Others, again, assert that the first inventors of the plastic art were Rhœcus and Theodorus, at Samos, a considerable period before the expulsion of the Bacchiadæ from Corinth; and that Damaratus, on taking to flight from that place and settling in Etruria, where he became father of Tarquinius, who was ultimately king of the Roman people, was accompanied

---

2   Pertaining to the art of painting with pigments in which wax enters as a vehicle, or to a painting so executed (TN).

thither by the modellers Euchir, Diopus, and Eugrammus, by whose agency the art was first introduced into Italy.

Butades first invented the method of colouring plastic compositions, by adding red earth to the material, or else modelling them in red chalk; he, too, was the first to make masks on the outer edges of gutter-tiles upon the roofs of buildings; in low relief, and known as "prostypa" at first, but afterwards in high relief, or "ectypa." It was in these designs, too, that the ornaments on the pediments of temples originated; and from this invention modellers first had their name of "plastæ."

WORKS IN POTTERY

Statues of this nature are still in existence at various places. At Rome, in fact, and in our municipal towns, we still see many such pediments of temples; wonderful too, for their workmanship, and, from their artistic merit and long duration, more deserving of our respect than gold, and certainly far less baneful. At the present day even, in the midst of such wealth as we possess, we make our first libation at the sacrifice, not from murrhine vases or vessels of crystal, but from ladles made of earthenware.

Bounteous beyond expression is the earth, if we only consider in detail her various gifts. To omit all mention of the cereals, wine, fruits, herbs, shrubs, medicaments, and metals, bounties which she has lavished upon us, and which have already passed under our notice, her productions in the shape of pottery alone, would more than suffice, in their variety, to satisfy our domestic wants; what with gutter-tiles of earthenware, vats for receiving wine, pipes for conveying water, conduits for supplying baths, baked tiles for roofs, bricks for foundations, the productions, too, of the potter's wheel; results, all of them, of an art, which induced King Numa when established, as a seventh company, that of the makers of earthenware.

Even more than this, many persons have chosen to be buried in coffins made of earthenware. For the service of the table, the Samian pottery is even yet held in high esteem; that, too, of Arretium in Italy, still maintains its high character; while for their cups, and for those only, the manufactories of Surrentum, Asta, Pollentia, Saguntum in Spain, and Pergamus in Asia, are greatly esteemed.

VARIOUS KINDS OF EARTH

But there are other resources also, which are derived immediately from the earth. Who, indeed, cannot but be surprised at finding the most inferior constituent parts of it, known as "dust" only, on the hills about Puteoli, forming a barrier against the waves of the sea, becoming changed into stone the moment of its immersion, and increasing in hardness from day to day; more particularly when mixed with the cement of Cumæ? There is an earth too, of a similar nature found in the districts about Cyzicus; but there, it is not a dust, but a solid earth, which is cut away in blocks of all sizes, and which, after being immersed in the sea, is taken out transformed into stone. The same thing may be seen also, it is said, in the vicinity of Cassandrea; and at Cnidos, there is a spring of fresh water which has the property of causing earth to petrify within the space of eight months. Between Oropus and

Aulis, every portion of the land upon which the sea encroaches becomes transformed into solid rock.

The finer portion of the sand of the river Nilus is not very different in its properties from the dust of Puteoli; not, indeed, that it is used for breaking the force of the sea and withstanding the waves, but only for the purpose, forsooth, of subduing the body for the exercises of the palestra!

FRAMED WALLS

And then, besides, have we not in Africa and in Spain walls of earth, known as framed walls? from the fact that they are moulded, rather than built, by enclosing earth within a frame of boards, constructed on either side. These walls will last for centuries, are proof against rain, wind, and fire, and are superior in solidity to any cement. Even at this day, Spain still beholds watch-towers that were erected by Hannibal, and turrets of earth placed on the very summits of her mountains. It is from the same source, too, that we derive the substantial materials so well adapted for forming the earth-works of our camps and embankments against the impetuous violence of rivers. What person, too, is unacquainted with the fact, that partitions are made of hurdles coated with clay, and that walls are constructed of unbaked bricks?

BRICKS

Earth for making bricks should never be extracted from a sandy or gravelly soil, and still less from one that is stony; but from a stratum that is white and cretaceous, or else impregnated with red earth. If a sandy soil must be employed for the purpose, it should at least be male sand, and no other. The spring is the best season for making bricks, as at midsummer they are very apt to crack. For building, bricks two years old are the only ones that are approved of; and the wrought material of them should be well macerated before they are made.

There are three different kinds of bricks; the Lydian, which is in use with us, a foot-and-a-half in length by a foot in breadth; the tetradoron; and the pentadoron; the word "doron" being used by the ancient Greeks to signify the palm —hence, too, their word "doron" meaning a gift, because it is the hand that gives. These last two kinds, therefore, are named respectively from their being four and five palms in length, the breadth being the same. The smaller kind is used in Greece for private buildings, the larger for the construction of public edifices. At Pitane, in Asia, and in the cities of Maxilua and Calentum in Farther Spain, there are bricks made, which float in water, when dry; the material being a sort of pumice-earth, extremely good for the purpose when it can be made to unite. The Greeks have always preferred walls of brick, except in those cases where they could find silicious stone for the purposes of building; for walls of this nature will last for ever, if they are only built on the perpendicular. Hence it is, that the Greeks have built their public edifices and the palaces of their kings of brick; the wall at Athens, for example, which faces Mount Hymettus; the Temples of Jupiter and Hercules at Patræ, although the columns and architraves in the interior are of stone; the palace of King Attalus at Tralles; the palace of Crœsus at Sardes, now converted into an asylum for aged persons; and that of King Mausolus at Halicarnassus; edifices, all of them, still in existence.

SULPHUR

Let thus much be deemed sufficient on the subject of bricks. Among the other kinds of earth, the one of the most singular nature, perhaps, is sulphur, an agent of great power upon other substances. Sulphur is found in the Æolian Islands, between Sicily and Italy, which are volcanic. But the finest sulphur of all, is that which comes from the Isle of Melos. It is obtained also in Italy, upon the range of hills in the territories of Neapolis and Campania, known as the Leucogæi; when extracted from the mines there, it is purified by the agency of fire.

There are four kinds of sulphur; the first of which is "live" sulphur, known as "apyron" by the Greeks, and found in solid masses, or in other words, in blocks. This, too, is the only sulphur that is extracted in its native state, the others being found in a state of liquescence, and requiring to be purified by being boiled in oil. This kind is green and transparent, and is the only sulphur that is used for medicinal purposes. A second kind is known as the "glebaceous" sulphur, and is solely employed in the workshops of the fullers. The third kind, also, is only used for a single purpose, that of fumigating wool, a process which contributes very greatly to making the wool white and soft; "egula" is the name given to it. The fourth kind is used in the preparation of matches more particularly.

In addition to these several uses, sulphur is of such remarkable virtue, that if it is thrown upon the fire it will at once detect, by the smell, whether or not a person is subject to epilepsy. Anaxilaüs used to employ this substance by way of pastime; putting sulphur in a cup of wine, with some hot coals beneath, he would hand it round to the guests, the light given by it, while burning, throwing a ghastly paleness like that of death upon the face of each. Its properties are calorific and maturative, in addition to which, it disperses abscesses on the body; hence it is that it is used as an ingredient in plasters and emollient poultices. Applied to the loins and kidneys, with grease, when there are pains in those parts, it is marvellously effectual as a remedy. In combination with turpentine, it removes lichens on the face, and leprosy, the preparation being known as "harpax," from the celerity with which it acts upon the skin; for which reason it ought to be removed every now and then. Employed as an electuary, it is good for asthma, purulent expectorations, and stings inflicted by scorpions. Live sulphur, mixed with nitre, and then bruised with vinegar and applied, causes morphew to disappear, and destroys nits in the hair; in combination, too, with sandarach[3] and vinegar, it is good for diseases of the eyelids.

BITUMEN

Nearly approaching to the nature of sulphur is that of bitumen, which in some places assumes the form of a slime, and in others that of an earth; a slime, thrown up by a certain lake in Judæa, and an earth, found in the vicinity of Sidon, a mari-

---

3 A red coloring matter (TN).

time town of Syria. In both these states, it admits of being thickened and condensed. There is also a liquid bitumen, that of Zacynthus, for example, and the bitumen that is imported from Babylon; which last kind is also white; the bitumen, too, of Apollonia is liquid. All these kinds, in Greek, have the one general name of "pissasphaltos," from their strong resemblance to a compound of pitch and bitumen. There is also found an unctuous liquid bitumen, resembling oil, in a spring at Agrigentum, in Sicily, the waters of which are tainted by it. The inhabitants of the spot collect it on the panicles of reeds, to which it very readily adheres, and make use of it for burning in lamps, as a substitute for oil, as also for the cure of itch-scab in beasts of burden.

Its medicinal properties are similar to those of sulphur, it being naturally astringent, dispersive, contractive, and agglutinating; ignited, it drives away serpents by the smell. Babylonian bitumen is very efficacious, it is said, for the cure of cataract and albugo, as also of leprosy, lichens, and pruriginous affections. Bitumen is employed, too, in the form of a liniment, for gout; and every variety of it is useful for making bandolines for eyelashes that are refractory and impede the sight. Applied topically with nitre, it is curative of tooth-ache, and, taken internally, with wine, it alleviates chronic coughs and difficulty of respiration. It is administered in a similar manner for dysentery, and is very good for arresting looseness of the bowels.

ALUMEN

Not less important, or indeed very dissimilar, are the uses that are made of alumen; by which name is understood a sort of brine which exudes from the earth. Of this, too, there are several kinds. In Cyprus there is a white alumen, and another kind of a darker colour. The difference, however, in their colour is but trifling in reality, though the uses made of them are very dissimilar; the white liquid alumen being employed for dyeing wool of bright colours, and the black, on the other hand, for giving wool a tawny or a sombre tint. Gold, too, is purified by the agency of black alumen. Every kind of alumen is a compound of slime and water, or in other words, is a liquid product exuding from the earth; the concretion of it commencing in winter, and being completed by the action of the summer sun. That portion of it which is the first matured, is the whitest in appearance.

Liquid alumen is naturally astringent, indurative, and corrosive; used in combination with honey, it heals ulcerations of the mouth, pimples, and pruriginous eruptions. There is one kind of solid alumen, known to the Greeks as "schiston," which splits into filaments of a whitish colour; for which reason some have preferred giving it the name of "trichitis." It is produced from the mineral ore known to us as "chalcitis," from which copper is also produced, it being a sort of exudation from that mineral, coagulated into the form of scum. This kind of alumen is less desiccative than the others, and is not so useful as a check upon bad humours of the body. Used, however, either in the form of a liniment or of an injection, it is highly beneficial to the ears; as also for ulcerations of the mouth, and for toothache, if retained with the saliva in the mouth.

Book XXXVI

The Natural History of Stones

It now remains for us to speak of stones, for everything of which we have previously treated, down to the present Book, may, by some possibility or other, have the appearance of having been created for the sake of man; but as to the mountains, Nature has made those for herself, as a kind of bulwark for keeping together the bowels of the earth; as also for the purpose of curbing the violence of the rivers, of breaking the waves of the sea, and so, by opposing to them the very hardest of her materials, putting a check upon those elements which are never at rest. And yet we must hew down these mountains, forsooth, and carry them off; and this, for no other reason than to gratify our luxurious inclinations; heights which in former days it was reckoned a miracle even to have crossed!

Our forefathers regarded as a prodigy the passage of the Alps, first by Hannibal, and, more recently, by the Cimbri; but at the present day, these very mountains are cut asunder to yield us a thousand different marbles, promontories are thrown open to the sea, and the face of Nature is being everywhere reduced to a level. We now carry away the barriers that were destined for the separation of one nation from another; we construct ships for the transport of our marbles; and, amid the waves, the most boisterous element of Nature, we convey the summits of the mountains to and fro; a thing, however, that is even less unpardonable than to go on the search amid the regions of the clouds for vessels[1] with which to cool our draughts, and to excavate rocks, towering to the very heavens, in order that we may have the satisfaction of drinking from ice! Let each reflect, when he hears of the high prices set upon these things, when he sees these ponderous masses carted

---

1   Pliny alludes to vessels made of crystal, which, as Dalechamps remarks, was long supposed to be nothing but ice in a concrete form.

and carried away, how many there are whose life is passed far more happily without them. For what utility or for what so-called pleasure do mortals make themselves the agents, or, more truly speaking, the victims of such undertakings, except in order that others may take their repose in the midst of variegated stones? Just as though too, the shades of night, which occupy one half of each man's existence, would forbear to curtail these imaginary delights.

MARBLE AND ITS SCULPTORS

The first artists who distinguished themselves in the sculpture of marble, were Dipœnus and Scyllis, natives of the Isle of Crete. At this period the Medians were still in power, and Cyrus had not begun to reign in Persia; their date being about the fiftieth Olympiad. They afterwards repaired to Sicyon, a state which for a length of time was the adopted country of all such pursuits as these. The people of Sicyon had made a contract with them for the execution of certain statues of the gods; but, before completing the work, the artists complained of some injustice being done them, and retired to Ætolia. Immediately upon this, the state was afflicted with sterility and famine, and dreadful consternation was the result. Upon enquiry being made as to a remedy for these evils, the Pythian Apollo made answer, that Dipœnus and Scyllis must complete the statues of the gods; an object which was attained at the cost of great concessions and considerable sums of money. The statues were those of Apollo, Diana, Hercules, and Minerva; the last of which was afterwards struck by lightning.

Before these artists were in existence, there had already appeared Melas, a sculptor of the Isle of Chios; and, in succession to him, his son Micciades, and his grandson Archermus; whose sons, Bupalus and Athenis, afterwards attained the highest eminence in the art. These last were contemporaries of the poet Hipponax, who, it is well known, lived in the sixtieth Olympiad. Now, if a person only reckons, going upwards from their time to that of their great-grandfather, he will find that the art of sculpture must have necessarily originated about the commencement of the era of the Olympiads.

All these artists, however, used nothing but the white marble of the Isle of Paros, a stone which was known as "lychnites" at first, because, according to Varro, it was cut in the quarries by lamplight. Since their time, many other whiter marbles have been discovered, and very recently that of the quarries of Luna.[2] With reference to the marble of Paros, there is one very marvellous circumstance related; in a single block that was split with wedges, a figure of Silenus made its appearance.

PHIDIAS

We must not omit to remark, that the art of sculpture is of much more ancient date than those of painting and of statuary in bronze; both of which commenced with Phidias, in the eighty-third Olympiad, or in other words, about three hundred and thirty-two years later. Indeed, it is said, that Phidias himself worked in marble, and that there is a Venus of his at Rome, a work of extraordinary beauty, in the

---

2   Carrara marble (TN).

buildings of Octavia. Among all nations which the fame of the Olympian Jupiter has reached, Phidias is looked upon, beyond all doubt, as the most famous of artists; but to let those who have never even seen his works, know how deservedly he is esteemed, we will take this opportunity of adducing a few slight proofs of the genius which he displayed. In doing this, we shall not appeal to the beauty of his Olympian Jupiter, nor yet to the vast proportions of his Athenian Minerva, six and twenty cubits in height, and composed of ivory and gold; but it is to the shield of this last statue that we shall draw attention; upon the convex face of which he has chased a combat of the Amazons, while, upon the concave side of it, he has represented the battle between the Gods and the Giants. Upon the sandals again, we see the wars of the Lapithæ and Centaurs, so careful has he been to fill every smallest portion of his work with some proof or other of his artistic skill. To the story chased upon the pedestal of the statue, the name of the "Birth of Pandora" has been given; and the figures of new-born gods to be seen upon it are no less than twenty in number. The figure of Victory, in particular, is most admirable, and connoisseurs are greatly struck with the serpent and the sphinx in bronze lying beneath the point of the spear. Let thus much be said incidentally in reference to an artist who can never be sufficiently praised; if only to let it be understood that the richness of his genius was always equal to itself, even in the very smallest details.

PRAXITELES

Praxiteles, an artist, who, in the glory which he acquired by his works in marble, surpassed even himself when he executed his Cnidian Venus; for the inspection of which, many persons before now have purposely undertaken a voyage to Cnidos. The artist made two statues of the goddess, and offered them both for sale; one of them was represented with drapery, and for this reason was preferred by the people of Cos, who had the choice; the second was offered them at the same price, but, on the grounds of propriety and modesty, they thought fit to choose the other. Upon this, the Cnidians purchased the rejected statue, and immensely superior has it always been held in general estimation. At a later period, King Nicomedes wished to purchase this statue of the Cnidians, and made them an offer to pay off the whole of their public debt, which was very large. They preferred, however, to submit to any extremity rather than part with it; and with good reason, for by this statue Praxiteles has perpetuated the glory of Cnidos. The little temple in which it, is placed is open on all sides, so that the beauties of the statue admit of being seen from every point of view; an arrangement

Cnidian Venus
Roman marble copy.

which was favoured by the goddess herself, it is generally believed. Indeed, from whatever point it is viewed, its execution is equally worthy of admiration. A certain individual, it is said, became enamoured of this statue, and, concealing himself in the temple during the night, gratified his lustful passion upon it, traces of which are to be seen in a stain left upon the marble.

There are also at Cnidos some other statues in marble, the productions of illustrious artists; a Father Liber by Bryaxis, another by Scopas, and a Minerva by the same hand; indeed, there is no greater proof of the supreme excellence of the Venus of Praxiteles than the fact that, amid such productions as these, it is the only one that we generally find noticed. By Praxiteles, too, there is a Cupid, a statue which occasioned one of the charges brought by Cicero against Verres, and for the sake of seeing which persons used to visit Thespiæ; at the present day, it is to be seen in the Schools of Octavia. By the same artist there is also another Cupid, without drapery, at Parium, a colony of the Propontis; equal to the Cnidian Venus in the fineness of its execution, and said to have been the object of a similar outrage. For one Alcetas, a Rhodian, becoming deeply enamoured of it, left upon the marble similar traces of the violence of his passion.

Cephisodotus, the son of Praxiteles, inherited his father's talent. There is, by him, at Pergamus, a splendid Group of Wrestlers, a work that has been highly praised, and in which the fingers have all the appearance of being impressed upon real flesh rather than upon marble. At Rome there are by him, a Latona, in the Temple of the Palatium; a Venus, in the buildings that are memorials of Asinius Pollio; and an Æsculapius, and a Diana, in the Temple of Juno situate within the Porticos of Octavia.

SCOPAS

Scopas rivals these artists in fame; there are by him, a Venus and a Pothos, statues which are venerated at Samothrace with the most august ceremonials. He was also the sculptor of the Palatine Apollo; a Vesta seated, in the Gardens of Servilius, a work that has been highly praised; to be seen upon the buildings of Asinius Pollio; and some figures of Canephori in the same place. But the most highly esteemed of all his works, are those in the Temple erected by Cneius Domitius, in the Flaminian Circus; a figure of Neptune himself, a Thetis and Achilles, Nereids seated upon dolphins, cetaceous fishes, and sea-horses, Tritons, the train of Phorcus, whales, and numerous other sea-monsters, all by the same hand; an admirable piece of workmanship, even if it had taken a whole life to complete it. In addition to the works by him already mentioned, and others of the existence of which we are ignorant, there is still to be seen a colossal Mars of his, seated, in the Temple erected by Brutus Callæcus, also in the Flaminian Circus; as also, a naked Venus, of anterior date to that by Praxiteles, and a production that would be quite sufficient to establish the renown of any other place.

Scopas had for rivals and contemporaries, Bryaxis, Timotheus, and Leochares, artists whom we are bound to mention together, from the fact that they worked together at the Mausoleum; such being the name of the tomb that was erected by his wife Artemisia in honour of Mausolus, a petty king of Caria, who died in the second year of the hundred and seventh Olympiad. It was through the exertions of these artists more particularly, that this work came to be reckoned one of the Seven Wonders of the World.

WHEN MARBLE WAS FIRST USED IN BUILDINGS

This must suffice for the sculptors in marble, and the works that have gained the highest repute; with reference to which subject it occurs to me to remark, that spotted marbles were not then in fashion. In making their statues, these artists used the marble of Thasos also, one of the Cyclades, and of Lesbos, this last being rather more livid than the other. The poet Menander, in fact, who was a very careful enquirer into all matters of luxury, is the first who has spoken, and that but rarely, of variegated marbles, and, indeed, of the employment of marble in general. Columns of this material were at first employed in temples, not on grounds of superior elegance, (for that was not thought of, as yet), but because no material could be found of a more substantial nature. It was under these circumstances, that the Temple of the Olympian Jupiter was commenced at Athens, the columns of which were brought by Sylla to Rome, for the buildings in the Capitol.

Still, however, there had been a distinction drawn between ordinary stone and marble, in the days of Homer even. The poet speaks in one passage of a person being struck down with a huge mass of marble; but that is all; and when he describes the abodes of royalty adorned with every elegance, besides brass, gold, electrum, and silver, he only mentions ivory.

THE METHOD OF CUTTING MARBLE INTO SLABS

But whoever it was that first invented the art of thus cutting marble, and so multiplying the appliances of luxury, he displayed considerable ingenuity, though to little purpose. This division, though apparently effected by the aid of iron, is in reality effected by sand; the saw acting only by pressing upon the sand within a very fine cleft in the stone, as it is moved to and fro.

The sand of Æthiopia is the most highly esteemed for this purpose; for, to add to the trouble that is entailed, we have to send to Æthiopia for the purpose of preparing our marble —aye, and as far as India even; whereas in former times, the severity of the Roman manners thought it beneath them to repair thither in search of such costly things even as pearls! This Indian sand is held in the next highest degree of estimation, the Æthiopian being of a softer nature, and better adapted for dividing the stone without leaving any roughness on the surface; whereas the sand from India does not leave so smooth a face upon it. Still, however, for polishing marble, we find it recommended to rub it with Indian sand calcined. The sand of Naxos has the same defect; as also that from Coptos, generally known as "Egyptian" sand.

VARIETIES OF MARBLES

The marbles are too well known to make it necessary for me to enumerate their several colours and varieties; and, indeed, so numerous are they, that it would be no easy task to do so. For what place is there, in fact, that has not a marble of its own? In addition to which, in our description of the earth and its various peoples, we have already made it our care to mention the more celebrated kinds of marble. Still, however, they are not all of them produced from quarries, but in many instances lie scattered just beneath the surface of the earth; some of them the most precious even, the green Lace-dæmonian marble, for example, more brilliant in colour than any other; the Augustan also; and, more recently, the Tiberian; which were first discovered, in the reigns respectively of Augustus and Tiberius, in Egypt. These two marbles differ from ophites[3] in the circumstance that the latter is marked with streaks which resemble serpents in appearance, whence its name. There is also this difference between the two marbles themselves, in the arrangement of their spots; the Augustan marble has them undulated and curling to a point; whereas in the Tiberian the streaks are white, not involved, but lying wide asunder.

Of ophites, there are only some very small pillars known to have been made. There are two varieties of it, one white and soft, the other inclining to black, and hard. Both kinds, it is said, worn as an amulet, are a cure for head-ache, and for wounds inflicted by serpents.

Porphyrites, which is another production of Egypt, is of a red colour; the kind that is mottled with white blotches is known as "leptospsephos." The quarries there are able to furnish blocks of any dimensions, however large. Vitrasius Pollio, who was steward in Egypt for the Emperor Claudius, brought to Rome from Egypt some statues made of this stone; a novelty which was not very highly approved of, as no one has since followed his example.

ONYX AND ALABASTRITES

Our forefathers imagined that onyx was only to be found in the mountains of Arabia, and nowhere else; but Sudines was aware that it is also found in Carmania. Drinking-vessels were made of it at first, and then the feet of beds and chairs. Cornelius Nepos relates that great was the astonishment, when P. Lentulus Spinther exhibited amphoræ made of this material, as large as Chian wine-vessels in size; "and yet, five years after," says he, "I saw columns of this material, no less than two-and-thirty feet in height." This stone is called "alabastrites" by some, and is hollowed out into vessels for holding unguents, it having the reputation of preserving them from corruption better than anything else.

VARIOUS STONES

Little inferior to it for the preservation of unguents, in the opinion of many, is the stone, called "lygdinus," that is found in Paros, and never of a larger size than to admit of a dish or goblet being made of it. In former times, it was only imported from Arabia, being remarkable for its extreme whiteness.

Great value is placed also upon two other kinds of stone, of quite a contrary nature; corallitic stone, found in Asia, in blocks not more than two cubits in thickness, and of a white some-what approaching that of ivory, and in some degree

---

3 A kind of marble spotted like a snake (TN).

resembling it; and Alabandic stone, which, on the other hand, is black, and is so called from the district which produces it; though it is also to be found at Miletus, where, however, it verges somewhat more upon the purple. It admits of being melted by the action of fire, and is fused for the preparation of glass.

Thebaic stone, which is sprinkled all over with spots like gold, is found in Africa, on the side of it which lies adjacent to Egypt; the small hones which it supplies being peculiarly adapted, from their natural properties, for grinding the ingredients used in preparations for the eyes. In the neighbourhood of Syene, too, in Thebais, there is a stone found that is now known as "syenites," but was formerly called "pyrrhopœcilon."

OBELISKS

Monarchs, too, have entered into a sort of rivalry with one another in forming elongated blocks of stone, known as "obelisks," and consecrated to the divinity of the Sun.

Mesphres, who reigned in the City of the Sun, was the first who erected one of these obelisks, being warned to do so in a dream; indeed, there is an inscription upon the obelisk to this effect; for the sculptures and figures which we still see engraved thereon are no other than Egyptian letters. At a later period other kings had these obelisks hewn. Sesosthes erected four of them in the above-named city, forty-eight cubits in height. Rhamsesis, too, who was reigning at the time of the capture of Troy, erected one, a hundred and forty cubits high.

There are two other obelisks, which were in Cæsar's Temple at Alexandria, near the harbour there, forty-two cubits in height, and originally hewn by order of King Mesphres. But the most difficult enterprise of all, was the carriage of these obelisks by sea to Rome, in vessels which excited the greatest admiration. Indeed, the late Emperor Augustus consecrated the one which brought over the first obelisk, as a lasting memorial of this marvellous undertaking, in the docks at Puteoli; but it was destroyed by fire.

The one that has been erected in the Campus Martius has been applied to a singular purpose by the late Emperor Augustus; that of marking the shadows projected by the sun, and so measuring the length of the days and nights. With this object, a stone pavement was laid, the extreme length of which corresponded exactly with the length of the shadow thrown by the obelisk at the sixth hour on the day of the winter solstice. After this period, the shadow would go on, day by day, gradually decreasing, and then again would as gradually increase, correspondingly with certain lines of brass that were inserted in the stone; a device well deserving to be known, and due to the ingenuity of Facundus Novus, the mathematician. Upon the apex of the obelisk he placed a gilded ball in order that the shadow of the summit might be condensed and agglomerated, and so prevent the shadow of the apex itself from running to a fine point of enormous extent; the plan being first suggested to him, it is said, by the shadow that is projected by the human head. For nearly the last thirty years, however, the observations derived from this dial have been found not to agree; whether it is that the sun itself has changed its course in consequence of some derangement of the heavenly system; or whether that the whole earth has been in some degree displaced from its centre, a thing that, I have heard say, has been. remarked in other places as well; or whether that some earthquake, confined to this city only, has wrenched the dial from its original position; or whether it is that in consequence of the inundations of the Tiber, the foundations of the mass have subsided, in spite of the general assertion that they are sunk as deep into the earth as the obelisk erected upon them is high.

THE PYRAMIDS

We must make some mention, too, however cursorily, of the Pyramids of Egypt, so many idle and frivolous pieces of ostentation of their resources, on the part of the monarchs of that country. Indeed, it is asserted by most persons, that the only motive for constructing them, was either a determination not to leave their treasures to their successors or to rivals that might be plotting to supplant them, or to prevent the lower classes from remaining unoccupied. There was great vanity displayed by these men in constructions of this description, and there are still the remains of many of them in an unfinished state. There is one to be seen in the Nome of Arsinoïtes; two in that of Memphites, not far from the Labyrinth, of which we shall shortly have to speak; and two in the place where Lake Mœris was excavated, an immense artificial piece of water, cited by the Egyptians among their wondrous and memorable works; the summits of the pyramids, it is said, are to be seen above the water.

The other three pyramids, the renown of which has filled the whole earth, and which are conspicuous from every quarter to persons navigating the river, are situate on the African side of it, upon a rocky sterile elevation. They lie between the city of Memphis and what we have mentioned as the Delta, within four miles of the river, and seven miles and a-half from Memphis, near a village known as Busiris, the people of which are in the habit of ascending them.

THE SPHINX

In front of these pyramids is the Sphinx, a still more wondrous object of art, but one upon which silence has been observed, as it is looked upon as a divinity by the people of the neighbourhood.

It is their belief that King Harmaïs was buried in it, and they will have it that it was brought there from a distance. The truth is, however, that it was hewn from the solid rock; and, from a feeling of veneration, the face of the monster is coloured red. The circumference of the head, measured round the forehead, is one hundred and two feet, the length of the feet being one hundred and forty-three, and the height, from the belly to the summit of the asp on the head, sixty-two.

The largest Pyramid is built of stone quarried in Arabia; three hundred and sixty thousand men, it is said, were employed upon it twenty years, and the three were completed in seventy-eight years and four months. They are described by the following writers; Herodotus, Euhemerus, Duris of Samos, Aristagoras, Dionysius, Artemidorus, Alexander Polyhistor, Butoridas, Antisthenes, Demetrius, Demoteles, and Apion.

The most difficult problem is, to know how the materials for construction could possibly be carried to so vast a height. According to some authorities, as the building gradually advanced, they heaped up against it vast mounds of nitre and salt; which were melted after its completion, by introducing beneath them the waters of the river. Others, again, maintain, that bridges were constructed, of bricks of clay, and that, when the pyramid was completed, these bricks were distributed for erecting the houses of private individuals.

Such are the marvellous Pyramids; but the crowning marvel of all is, that the smallest, but most admired of them was built by Rhodopis, a courtesan! This woman was once the fellow-slave of Æsopus the philosopher and fabulist, and the sharer of his bed; but what is much more surprising is, that a courtesan should have been enabled, by her vocation, to amass such enormous wealth.

LABYRINTHS

We must speak also of the Labyrinths, the most stupendous works, perhaps, on which mankind has expended its labours; and not for chimerical purposes, merely, as might possibly be supposed.

There is still in Egypt, in the Nome of Heracleopolites, a labyrinth, which was the first constructed, three thousand six hundred years ago, they say, by King Petesuchis or Tithöes; although, according to Herodotus, the entire work was the production of no less than twelve kings, the last of whom was Psammetichus. As to the purpose for which it was built, there are various opinions; Demoteles says that it was the palace of King Moteris, and Lyceas that it was the tomb of Mœris, while many others assert that it was a building consecrated to the Sun, an opinion which mostly prevails.

That Dædalus took this for the model of the Labyrinth which he constructed in Crete, there can be no doubt; though he only reproduced the hundredth part of it, that portion, namely, which encloses circuitous passages, windings, and inextricable galleries which lead to and fro. We must not, comparing this last to what we see delineated on our mosaic pavements, or to the mazes formed in the fields for the amusement of children, suppose it to be a narrow promenade along which we may walk for many miles together; but we must picture to ourselves a building filled with numerous doors, and galleries which continually mislead the visitor, bringing him back, after all his wanderings, to the spot from which he first set out. This Labyrinth is the second, that of Egypt being the first. There is a third in the Isle of Lemnos, and a fourth in Italy.

HANGING GARDENS – A HANGING CITY

We read, too, of hanging gardens,[4] and what is even more than this, a hanging city, Thebes in Egypt; it being the practice for the kings to lead forth their armies from beneath, while the inhabitants were totally unconscious of it. This, too, is even less surprising than the fact that a river flows through the middle of the city. If, however, all this had really been the case, there is no doubt that Homer would have mentioned it, he who has celebrated the hundred gates of Thebes.

TEMPLE OF DIANA AT EPHESUS

The most wonderful monument of Græcian magnificence, and one that merits our genuine admiration, is the Temple of Diana at Ephesus, which took one hundred and twenty years in building, a work in which all Asia joined. A marshy soil was selected for its site, in order that it might not suffer from earthquakes, or the chasms which they produce. On the other hand, again, that the foundations of so vast a pile might not have to rest upon a loose and shifting bed, layers of trodden charcoal were placed beneath, with fleeces covered with wool upon the top of them. The entire length of the temple is four hundred and twenty-five feet, and the breadth two hundred and twenty-five. The columns are one hundred and twenty-seven in number, and sixty feet in height, each of them presented by a different king.

REMARKABLE STONES – THE MAGNET

Upon quitting the marbles to pass on to the other more remarkable stones, who can for a moment doubt that the magnet will be the first to suggest itself? For what, in fact, is there endowed with more marvellous properties than this? Or in which of her departments has Nature displayed a greater degree of waywardness? She had given a voice to rocks and had enabled them to answer man, or rather, I should say, to throw back his own words in his teeth. What is there in existence more inert than a piece of rigid stone? And yet, behold! Nature has here endowed stone with both sense and hands. What is there more stubborn than hard iron? Nature has, in this instance, bestowed upon it both feet and intelligence. It allows itself, in fact, to be attracted by the magnet, and, itself a metal which subdues all other elements, it precipitates itself towards the source of an influence at once mysterious and unseen. The moment the metal comes near it, it springs towards the magnet, and, as it clasps it, is held fast in the magnet's embraces. Hence it is that this stone is sometimes known by the name of "sideritis";[5] another name given to it being "heraclion." It received its name "magnes," Nicander informs us, from the person who was the first to discover it, upon Ida. It is found, too, in various other countries, as in Spain, for example. Magnes, it is said, made this discovery, when,

---

4 Probably of Babylon, which were built on terraces raised on arches.
5 "Iron earth"; from σίδηρος, "iron." The magnet, or loadstone itself, is an oxide of iron, known as Oxidulated iron, or Ferroso-ferric oxide; sometimes in combination with quartz or alumine.

upon taking his herds to pasture, he found that the nails of his shoes and the iron ferrel of his staff adhered to the ground.

Sotacus describes five different kinds of magnet; the Æthiopian magnet; that of Magnesia, a country which borders on Macedonia, and lies to the right of the road which leads from the town of Bœbe to Iolcos; a third, from Hyettus in Bœotia; a fourth, from Alexandria in Troas; and a fifth, from Magnesia in Asia. The leading distinction in magnets is the sex, male and female, and the next great difference in them is the colour. Those of Magnesia, bordering on Macedonia, are of a reddish black; those of Bœotia are more red than black; and the kind that is found in Troas is black, of the female sex, and consequently destitute of attractive power. The most inferior, however, of all, are those of Magnesia in Asia; they are white, have no attractive influence on iron, and resemble pumice in appearance. It has been found by experience, that the more nearly the magnet approaches to an azure colour, the better it is in quality. The Æthiopian magnet is looked upon as the best of all, and is purchased at its weight in silver; Zmiris in Æthiopia is the place where it is found, such being the name of a region there, covered with sand.

All these minerals are useful as ingredients in ophthalmic preparations, in certain proportions according to the nature of each; they are particularly good, too, for arresting eye fluxes. Triturated in a calcined state, they have a healing effect upon burns.

In Æthiopia, too, not far from Zmiris, there is a mountain in which the stone called "theamedes" is found, a mineral which repels and rejects all kinds of iron.

THE SARCOPHAGUS STONE

At Assos in Troas, there is found a stone of a laminated texture, called "sarcophagus." It is a well-known fact, that dead bodies, when buried in this stone, are consumed in the course of forty days, with the sole exception of the teeth. According to Mucianus, too, mirrors, body-scrapers, garments, and shoes, that have been buried with the dead, become transformed into stone. In Lycia, and in the East, there are certain stones of a similar nature, which, when attached to the bodies of the living even, corrode the flesh.

CHERNITES

Less active in its properties is chernites, a stone which preserves bodies without consuming them, and strongly resembles ivory in appearance; the body of King Darius, they say, was buried in it. The stone that is known as "porus," is similar to Parian marble in hardness and whiteness, but is not so heavy. Theophrastus mentions also a transparent stone that is found in Egypt, and is similar to stone of Chios in appearance; it is by no means improbable that it may have existed in his time, for stones, we know, disappear, and new kinds are discovered. The stone of Assos, which is saltish to the taste, modifies the attacks of gout, the feet being placed in a vessel made of it for the purpose; in addition to which, in the quarries of this stone, all maladies of the legs disappear, whereas, in mines in general, the legs become affected with disease. "Flower of stone of Assos" is the name given to a soft stone which crumbles into dust, and is found very efficacious in some cases; it resembles red pumice in appearance. In combination with Cyprian wax, this stone is curative of affections of the breasts; and, employed with pitch or resin, it disperses scrofulous sores and inflammatory tumours. Used in the form of an electuary, it is good for phthisis, and, with honey, it causes old sores to cicatrize, and consumes proud flesh. It is used, also, for the cure of wounds of an obstinate nature inflicted by animals, and acts as a desiccative upon suppurations. Plaisters, too, are made of it for gout, bean-meal being incorporated with it for the purpose.

PUMICE

And here, too, I must not omit to give some account of pumice. This name is very generally given, it is true, to those porous pieces of stone, which we see suspended in the erections known as "musæa,"[6] with the view of artificially giving them all the appearance of caverns. But the genuine pumice-stones, that are in use for imparting smoothness to the skin of females, and not females only, but men as well, and, as Catullus says, for polishing books, are found of the finest quality in the islands of Melos and Nisyros and in the Æolian Isles. To be good, they should be white, as light as possible, porous and dry in the extreme, friable, and free from sand when rubbed.

Considered medicinally, pumice is of a resolvent and desiccative nature; for which purpose it is submitted to calcination, no less than three times, on a fire of pure charcoal, it being quenched as often in white wine. It is then washed, like cadmia, and, after being dried, is put by for keeping, in a place as free from damp as possible. In a powdered state, pumice is used in ophthalmic preparations more particularly, and acts as a lenitive detergent upon ulcerations of the eyes. It also makes new flesh upon cicatrizations of those organs, and removes all traces of the marks. Some prefer, after the third calcination, leaving the pumice to cool, and then triturating it in wine. It is employed also as an ingredient in emollient poultices, being extremely useful for ulcerations on the head and generative organs; dentifrices, too, are prepared from it.

SPECULAR STONES

As to the specular[7] stone, it admits of being divided with still greater facility, and can be split into leaves as thin as may be desired. The province of Nearer Spain used formerly to be the only one that furnished it, but at the present day, Cyprus, Cappadocia, and Sicily, supply us with it; and, still more recently, it has been discovered in Africa; they are all, however, looked upon as inferior to the stone which comes from Spain. The sheets from Cappadocia are the largest in size; but then they are clouded. This stone is to be found also in the territory of Bononia, in Italy; but in small pieces only, covered with spots and encrusted in a bed of silex, there being a considerable affinity, it would appear, in their nature.

In Spain, the specular-stone is extracted from shafts sunk in the earth to a very considerable depth; though it is occasionally to be found just beneath the surface,

---

6   Or "temples of the Muses"; evidently grottos in the present instance.
7   Or "Mirror-stone." Transparent Selenite or gypsum; a sulphate of lime.

enclosed in the solid rock, and extracted without difficulty, or else cut away from its bed. In most cases, however, it admits of being dug up, being of an isolated nature, and lying in pieces, like ragstone, but never known as yet to exceed five feet in length. It would appear that this substance is originally a liquid, which, by an animating power in the earth, becomes congealed like crystal; and it is very evident that it is the result of petrifaction, from the fact that, when animals have fallen into the shafts from which it is extracted, the marrow of their bones becomes transformed into stone of a similar nature, by the end of a single winter.

QUICK-LIME

Cato the Censor disapproves of lime prepared from stones of various colours; that made of white stone is the best. Lime prepared from hard stone is the best for building purposes, and that from porous stone for coats of plaster. For both these purposes, lime made from silex is equally rejected. Stone that has been extracted from quarries furnishes a better lime than that collected from the beds of rivers; but the best of all is the lime that is obtained from the molar-stone, that being of a more unctuous nature than the others. It is something truly marvellous, that quick-lime, after the stone has been subjected to fire, should ignite on the application of water!

Lime is also employed very extensively in medicine. For this purpose, fresh lime is selected, which has not been slaked with water. Its properties are caustic, resolvent, and attractive; and it prevents serpiginous ulcers from spreading, being incorporated with vinegar and oil of roses, for the purpose. When this has been effected, it is tempered with wax and oil of roses, and applied to promote cicatrization. In combination with honey, and liquid resin, or hogs' lard, lime is curative of sprains and scrofulous sores.

VARIOUS KINDS OF SAND

There are three kinds of sand; fossil sand, to which one-fourth part of lime should be added; river sand; and sea sand; to both of which last, one third of lime should be added. If, too, one third of mortar is composed of bruised earthenware, it will be all the better. Fossil sand is found in the districts that lie between the Apennines and the Padus, but not in the parts beyond sea.

STUCCO

The great cause of the fall of so many buildings in our City, is, that through a fraudulent abstraction of the lime, the rough work is laid without anything to hold it together. The older, too, the mortar is, the better it is in quality. In the ancient laws for the regulation of building, no contractor was to use mortar less than three months old; hence it is, that no cracks have disfigured the plaster coatings of their walls. These stuccos will never present a sufficiently bright surface, unless there have been three layers of sanded mortar, and two of marbled mortar upon that. In damp localities and places subject to exhalations from the sea, it is the best plan to substitute ground earthenware mortar for sanded mortar. In Greece, it is the practice, first to pound the lime and sand used for plastering, with wooden pestles in a large trough. The test by which it is known that marbled mortar has been properly blended, is its not adhering to the trowel; whereas, if it is only wanted for whitewashing, the lime, after being well slaked with water, should stick like glue. For this last purpose, however, the lime should only be slaked in lumps.

MALTHA

Maltha is a cement prepared from fresh lime; lumps of which are quenched in wine, and then pounded with hogs' lard and figs, both of them, mollifying substances. It is the most tenacious of all cements, and surpasses stone in hardness. Before applying maltha, the substance upon which it is used must be well rubbed with oil.

GYPSUM

Gypsum[8] has a close affinity with limestone, and there are numerous varieties of it. One kind is prepared from a calcined stone, as in Syria, and at Thurii, for example. In Cyprus and at Perrhæbia, gypsum is dug out of the earth, and at Tymphæ it is found just below the level of the soil. The stone that is calcined for this purpose, ought to be very similar to alabastrites, or else of a grain like that of marble. In Syria, they select the hardest stones for the purpose, and calcine them with cow-dung, to accelerate the process. Experience has proved, however, that the best plaster of all is that prepared from specular-stone, or any other stone that is similarly laminated. Gypsum, when moistened, must be used immediately, as it hardens with the greatest rapidity; it admits, however, of being triturated over again, and so reduced to powder. It is very useful for pargetting, and has a pleasing effect when used for ornamental figures and wreaths in buildings.

PAVED FLOORS

Pavements are an invention of the Greeks, who also practised the art of painting them, till they were superseded by mosaics. In this last branch of art, the highest excellence has been attained by Sosus, who laid, at Pergamus, the mosaic pavement known as the "Asarotos œcos"; from the fact that he there represented, in small squares of different colours, the remnants of a banquet lying upon the pavement, and other things which are usually swept away with the broom, they having all the appearance of being left there by accident. There is a dove also, greatly admired, in the act of drinking, and throwing the shadow of its head upon the water; while other birds are to be seen sunning and pluming themselves, on the margin of a drinking-bowl.

TERRACE-ROOF PAVEMENTS

The Greeks have also invented terrace-roof pavements, and have covered their houses with them; a thing that may easily be done in the hotter climates, but a great mistake in countries where the rain is apt to become congealed. In making these pavements, the proper plan is to begin with two layers of boards, running

---

8   The name now given to Sulphate of lime, including the varieties of Alabaster and Selenite. Plaster of Paris is prepared from it.

different ways, and nailed at the extremities, to prevent them from warping. Upon this planking a rough-work must be laid, one-fourth of which consists of pounded pottery; and upon this, another bed of rough-work, two-fifths composed of lime, a foot in thickness, and well beaten down with the rammer. The nucleus is then laid down, a bed six fingers in depth; and upon that, large square stones, not less than a couple of fingers in thickness; an inclination being carefully observed, of an inch and a half to every ten feet. This done, the surface is well rubbed down with a polishing stone. The general opinion is, that oak should never be used for the planking, it being so very liable to warp; and it is considered a good plan to cover the boards with a layer of fern or chaff, that they may be the better able to resist the action of the lime. It is necessary, too, before putting down the planking, to underset it with a bed of round pebbles. Wheat-ear tesselated pavements are laid down in a similar manner.

GLASS

In Syria there is a region known as Phœnice, adjoining to Judæa, and enclosing, between the lower ridges of Mount Carmelus, a marshy district known by the name of Cendebia. In this district, it is supposed, rises the river Belus, which, after a course of five miles, empties itself into the sea near the colony of Ptolemaïs. The tide of this river is sluggish, and the water unwholesome to drink, but held sacred for the observance of certain religious ceremonials. Full of slimy deposits, and very deep, it is only at the reflux of the tide that the river discloses its sands; which, agitated by the waves, separate themselves from their impurities, and so become cleansed. It is generally thought that it is the acridity of the sea-water that has this purgative effect upon the sand, and that without this action no use could be made of it. The shore upon which this sand is gathered is not more than half a mile in extent; and yet, for many ages, this was the only spot that afforded the material for making glass.

The story is, that a ship, laden with nitre, being moored upon this spot, the merchants, while preparing their repast upon the sea-shore, finding no stones at hand for supporting their cauldrons, employed for the purpose some lumps of nitre which they had taken from the vessel. Upon its being subjected to the action of the fire, in combination with the sand of the sea-shore, they beheld transparent streams flowing forth of a liquid hitherto unknown; this, it is said, was the origin of glass.

In process of time, as human industry is ingenious in discovering, it was not content with the combination of nitre, but magnet-stone began to be added as well; from the impression that it attracts liquefied glass as well as iron. In a similar manner, too, brilliant stones of various descriptions came to be added in the melting, and, at last, shells and fossil sand. Some authors tell us, that the glass of India is made of broken crystal, and that, in consequence, there is none that can be compared to it.

In fusing it, light and dry wood is used for fuel, Cyprian copper and nitre being added to the melting, nitre of Ophir more particularly. It is melted, like copper, in contiguous furnaces, and a swarthy mass of an unctuous appearance is the result. Of such a penetrating nature is the molten glass, that it will cut to the very bone any part of the body which it may come near, and that, too, before it is even felt. This mass is again subjected to fusion in the furnace, for the purpose of colouring it; after which, the glass is either blown into various forms, turned in a lathe, or engraved like silver. Sidon was formerly famous for its glass-houses, for it was this place that first invented mirrors.

Such was the ancient method of making glass; but, at the present day, there is found a very white sand for the purpose, at the mouth of the river Volturnus, in Italy. It spreads over an extent of six miles, upon the sea-shore that lies between Cumæ and Liternum, and is prepared for use by pounding it with a pestle and mortar; which done, it is mixed with three parts of nitre, either by weight or measure, and, when fused, is transferred to another furnace. Here it forms a mass of what is called "hammonitrum"; which is again submitted to fusion, and becomes a mass of pure, white, glass.

MARVELLOUS FACTS CONNECTED WITH FIRE

Having now described all the creations of human ingenuity, reproductions, in fact, of Nature by the agency of art, it cannot but recur to us, with a feeling of admiration, that there is hardly any process which is not perfected through the intervention of fire. Submit to its action some sandy soil, and in one place it will yield glass, in another silver, in another minium, and in others, again, lead and its several varieties, pigments, and numerous medicaments. It is through the agency of fire that stones are melted into copper; by fire that iron is produced, and subdued to our purposes; by fire that gold is purified; by fire, too, that the stone is calcined, which is to hold together the walls of our houses.

Some materials, again, are all the better for being repeatedly submitted to the action of fire; and the same substance will yield one product at the first fusion, another at the second, and another at the third. Charcoal, when it has passed through fire and has been quenched, only begins to assume its active properties; and, when it might be supposed to have been reduced to annihilation, it is then that it has its greatest energies. An element this, of immense, of boundless power, and, as to which, it is a matter of doubt whether it does not create even more than it destroys!

Fire even has certain medicinal virtues of its own. When pestilences prevail, in consequence of the obscuration[9] of the sun, it is a well-known fact, that if fires are lighted, they are productive of beneficial results in numerous ways. Empedocles and Hippocrates have proved this in several passages.

"For convulsions or contusions of the viscera," says M. Varro "let the hearth be your medicine-box; for lye of ashes, taken from thence, mixed with your drink, will effect a cure. Witness the gladiators, for example, who, when disabled at the Games, refresh themselves with this drink." Carbuncle too, admits of being successfully treated with oak-charcoal, triturated with honey. So true is it that things

---

9   Pliny probably alludes to eclipses of the sun.

which are despised even, and looked upon as so utterly destitute of all virtues, have still their own remedial properties, charcoal and ashes for example.

I must not omit too, one portentous fact connected with the hearth, and famous in Roman history. In the reign of Tarquinius Priscus, it is said, there appeared upon his hearth a resemblance of the male generative organ in the midst of the ashes. The captive Ocrisia, a servant of Queen Tanaquil, who happened to be sitting there, arose from her seat in a state of pregnancy, and became the mother of Servius Tullius, who eventually succeeded to the throne. It is stated, too, that while the child was sleeping in the palace, a flame was seen playing round his head; the consequence of which was, that it was believed that the Lar of the household was his progenitor.

Book XXXVII

The Natural History of Precious Stones

That nothing may be wanting to the work which I have undertaken, it still remains for me to speak of precious stones; a subject in which the majestic might of Nature presents itself to us, contracted within a very limited space, though, in the opinion of many, nowhere displayed in a more admirable form. According to fabulous lore, the first use of them was suggested by the rocks of Caucasus, in consequence of an unhappy interpretation which was given to the story of the chains of Prometheus; for we are told by tradition, that he enclosed a fragment of this stone in iron, and wore it upon his finger;[1] such being the first ring and the first jewel known.

FAMOUS RINGS AND JEWELS OF LEGEND

With a beginning such as this, the value set upon precious stones increased to such a boundless extent, that Polycrates, the tyrant of Samos, who ruled over the islands and the adjacent shores, when he admitted that his good fortune had been too great, deemed it a sufficient expiation for all this enjoyment of happiness, to make a voluntary sacrifice of a single precious stone; thinking thereby to balance accounts with the inconstancy of fortune, and, by this single cause for regret, abundantly to buy off every ill-will she might entertain. Weary, therefore, of his continued prosperity, he embarked on board a ship, and, putting out to sea, threw the ring which he wore into the waves. It so happened, however, that a fish of remarkable size, one destined for the table of a king, swallowed the jewel, as it would

---

1   This being imposed as a punishment on him, in remembrance of his sacrilegious crimes, when released by Jupiter from the rock. Prometheus and Vulcan, as Ajasson remarks, are personifications of fire, employed for artistic purposes.

have done a bait; and then, to complete the portentous omen, restored it again to the owner in the royal kitchen, by the ruling hand of a treacherous fortune.

The stone in this ring, it is generally agreed, was a sardonyx, and they still show one at Rome, which, if we believe the story, was this identical stone. It is enclosed in a horn of gold, and was deposited, by the Emperor Augustus, in the Temple of Concord, where it holds pretty nearly the lowest rank among a multitude of other jewels that are preferable to it.

Next in note after this ring, is the jewel that belonged to another king, Pyrrhus, who was so long at war with the Romans. It is said that there was in his possession an agate, upon which were to be seen the Nine Muses and Apollo holding a lyre; not a work of art, but the spontaneous produce of Nature, the veins in it being so arranged that each of the Muses had her own peculiar attribute.

PEARLS AND PRECIOUS STONES

It was Pompeius Magnus that first introduced so general a taste for pearls and precious stones; just as the victories, gained by L. Scipio and Cneius Manlius, had first turned the public attention to chased silver, Attalic tissues, and banqueting-couches decorated with bronze; and the conquests of L. Mummius had brought Corinthian bronzes and pictures into notice.

On the occasion of his third triumph, over the Pirates and over the Kings and nations of Asia and Pontus, the anniversary of his birth, he displayed in public, with its pieces, a chess-board, made of two precious stones, three feet in width by two in length, three banqueting-couches; vessels for nine waiters, in gold and precious stones; three golden statues of Minerva, Mars, and Apollo; thirty-three crowns adorned with pearls; a square mountain of gold, with stags upon it, lions, and all kinds of fruit, and surrounded with a vine of gold; as also a musæum,[2] adorned with pearls, with an horologe upon the top of it.

It was the same conquest, too, that first introduced murrhine[3] vessels at Rome; Pompeius being the first to dedicate, at the conclusion of this triumph, vases and cups, made of this material, in the Temple of Jupiter Capitolinus; a circumstance which soon brought them into private use, waiters, even, and eating-utensils made of murrhine being in great request.

ROCK CRYSTAL

Crystal,[4] a substance which assumes a concrete form from excessive congelation, is only to be found in places where the winter snow freezes with the greatest intensity. The East, too, sends us crystal, there being none preferred to the produce of India. It is to be found, also, in Asia, that of the vicinity of Alabanda, Orthosia, and the neighbouring mountains, being held in a very low degree of esteem. In Cyprus, also, there is crystal, but that found upon the Alpine heights in Europe is, in

---

2   Probably meaning a shrine dedicated to the Muses.

3   Modern writers differ as to the material of which these vessels were composed. Some think that they were of variegated glass, and others of onyx; but the more general opinion is, that they were Chinese porcelain.

4   Colourless crystals, quartz, or rock crystal; called "white stone" in jewellery.

general, more highly valued. According to Juba, there is crystal in a certain island of the Red Sea, opposite the coast of Arabia, called "Necron"; as, also, in another neighbouring island which produces the precious stone known as the "topazus"; where a block of crystal was extracted, he says, by Pythagoras, the præfect of King Ptolemæus, no less than a cubit in length.

Cornelius Bocchus informs us that in Lusitania, there have been blocks of crystal found, of extraordinary weight, in sinking shafts in the Ammiensian mountains there, to a water-level for the supply of wells. It is a marvellous fact, stated by Xenocrates of Ephesus, that in Asia and in the Isle of Cyprus, crystal is turned up by the plough; it having been the general belief that it is never to be found in terreous soils, and only in rocky localities.

MARVELLOUS HISTORIES ABOUT AMBER

Next in rank among the objects of luxury, we have amber;[5] an article which, for the present, however, is in request among women only. All these three last-mentioned substances hold the same rank, no doubt, as precious stones; the two former for certain fair reasons; crystal, because it is adapted for taking cool drinks, and murrhine vessels, for taking drinks that are either hot or cold. But as for amber, luxury has not been able, as yet, to devise any justification for the use of it.

After Phaëthon had been struck by lightning, his sisters, they tell us, became changed into poplars, which every year shed their tears upon the banks of the Eridanus, a river known to us as the "Padus." To these tears was given the name of "electrum,"[6] from the circumstance that the Sun was usually called "elector." Such is the story, at all events, that is told by many of the poets, the first of whom were, in my opinion, Æschylus, Philoxenus, Euripides, Satyrus, and Nicander; and the falsity of which is abundantly proved upon the testimony of Italy itself. Those among the Greeks who have devoted more attention to the subject, have spoken of certain islands in the Adriatic Sea, known as the "Electrides," and to which the Padus, they say, carries down electrum.

Other writers, again, who are more guarded in their assertions, have told us, though with an equal degree of untruthfulness, that, at the extremity of the Adriatic Gulf, upon certain inaccessible rocks in that place, there are certain trees which shed their gum at the rising of the Dog-Star. Theophrastus has stated that amber is extracted from the earth in Liguria; Chares, that Phaëthon died in the territory of Hammon, in Æthiopia, where there is a temple of his and an oracle, and where amber is produced; Philemon, that it is a fossil substance, and that it is found in two different localities in Scythia, in one of which it is of a white and waxen colour, and is known as "electrum"; while in the other it is red, and is called "sualiternicum." Sudines says, that it is a tree in reality, that produces amber, and that, in Etruria, this tree is known by the name of "lynx"; an opinion which is also adopted

---

5 "Succinum." It is of vegetable origin, and, according to Göppert, was originally the viscous resin of a tree named by him *Pinites succinifer*.

6 In this case electrum appears to be a synonym for amber, but Pliny also uses the same name to refer to an alloy of silver and gold in other parts of his work.

by Metrodorus. Sotacus expresses a belief that amber exudes from certain stones in Britannia, to which he gives the name of "electrides." Pytheas says that the Gutones, a people of Germany, inhabit the shores of an æstuary of the Ocean called Mentonomon, their territory extending a distance of six thousand stadia; that, at one day's sail from this territory, is the Isle of Abalus, upon the shores of which, amber is thrown up by the waves in spring, it being an excretion of the sea in a concrete form; as, also, that the inhabitants use this amber by way of fuel, and sell it to their neighbours, the Teutones. Timæus, too, is of the same belief, but he has given to the island the name of Basilia.

SEVERAL KINDS OF AMBER

There are several kinds[7] of amber. The white is the one that has the finest odour; but neither this nor the wax-coloured amber is held in very high esteem. The red amber is more highly valued; and still more so, when it is transparent, without presenting too brilliant and igneous an appearance. For amber, to be of high quality, should present a brightness like that of fire, but not flakes resembling those of flame. The most highly esteemed amber is that known as the "Falernian," from its resemblance to the colour of Falernian wine; it is perfectly transparent, and has a softened, transparent, brightness. Other kinds, again, are valued for their mellowed tints, like the colour of boiled honey in appearance.

So highly valued is this as an object of luxury, that a very diminutive human effigy, made of amber, has been known to sell at a higher price than living men even, in stout and vigorous health. Amber, however, is not without its utility in a medicinal point of view; though it is not for this reason that the women are so pleased with it. It is beneficial for infants also, attached to the body in the form of an amulet; and, according to Callistratus, it is good for any age, as a preventive of delirium and as a cure for strangury, either taken in drink or attached as an amulet to the body. This last author, too, has invented a new variety of amber; giving the name of "chryselectrum" to an amber of a golden colour, and which presents the most beautiful tints in the morning. This last kind attracts flame, too, with the greatest rapidity, and, the moment it approaches the fire, it ignites. Worn upon the neck, he says, it is a cure for fevers and other diseases, and, triturated with honey and oil of roses, it is good for maladies of the ears. Beaten up with Attic honey, it is good for dimness of sight; and the powder of it, either taken by itself or with gum mastich in water, is remedial for diseases of the stomach.

PRECIOUS STONES

We will now proceed to speak of the various kinds of precious stones, the existence of which is generally admitted, beginning with those which are the most highly esteemed. Nor shall we content ourselves with doing this only; but, with the view of consulting the general welfare of mankind, we shall also refute the infamous lies that have been promulgated by the magicians; for it is with reference to precious stones, more particularly, that they have circulated most of their fabulous

---

7   These so-called kinds or varieties are mostly accidental variations only in appearance.

ADAMAS

The substance that possesses the greatest value, not only among the precious stones, but of all human possessions, is adamas;[8] a mineral which, for a long time, was known to kings only, and to very few of them. Such was the name given to a nodosity of gold,[9] sometimes, though but rarely, found in the mines, in close proximity with gold, and only there to be found, it was thought. The ancients supposed that adamas was only to be discovered in the mines of Æthiopia, between the Temple of Mercury and the island of Meroë; and they have informed us that it was never larger than a cucumber-seed, or differing at all from it in colour.

At the present day, for the first time, there are no less than six different varieties of it recognized. The Indian adamas is found, not in a stratum of gold, but in a substance of a kindred nature to crystal; which it closely resembles in its transparency and its highly polished hexangular and hexahedral form. In shape it is turbinated, running to a point at either extremity, and closely resembling, marvellous to think of, two cones united at the base. In size, too, it is as large even as a hazel-nut. Resembling that of India, is the adamas of Arabia, which is found in a similar bed, but not so large in size. Other varieties have a pallid hue like that of silver, and are only to be found in the midst of gold of the very finest quality. These stones are tested upon the anvil, and will resist the blow to such an extent, as to make the iron rebound and the very anvil split asunder. Indeed its hardness is beyond all expression, while at the same time it quite sets fire at defiance and is incapable of being heated.

When, by good fortune, this stone does happen to be broken, it divides into fragments so minute as to be almost imperceptible. These particles are held in great request by engravers, who enclose them in iron, and are enabled thereby, with the greatest facility, to cut the very hardest substances known. So great is the antipathy borne by this stone to the magnet, that when placed near, it will not allow of its attracting iron; or if the magnet has already attracted the iron, it will seize the metal and drag it away from the other. Adamas, too, overcomes and neutralizes poisons, dispels delirium, and banishes groundless perturbations of the mind; hence it is

---

8   The word "adamas" is supposed to be derived from the Greek ἀ, privative, and δαμάω, "to subdue," it being supposed to be invincible by fire. The diamond is pure carbon crystallized, and is thought to have been of vegetable origin. Dana has the following remarks upon the word adamas: "This name was applied by the ancients to several minerals differing much in their physical properties. A few of these are quartz, specular iron ore, emery, and other substances of rather high degrees of hardness, which cannot now be identified. It is doubtful whether Pliny had any acquaintance with the real diamond."— (System of Mineralogy, Art. Diamond). We may also add, from the same authority, that the method of polishing diamonds was first discovered in 1456, by Louis Berquen, a citizen of Bruges, previous to which time the diamond was only known in its native uncut state.

9   This statement cannot apply to the "diamond" as known to us, though occasionally grains of gold have been found in the vicinity of the diamond.

that some have given it the name of "ananchites." Metrodorus of Scepsis is the only author, that I know of, who says that this stone is found also in Germany, and in the island of Basilia, where amber is found.

EMERALDS

Next in esteem with us are the pearls of India and Arabia. The third rank, for many reasons, has been given to the smaragdus (Emerald). Indeed there is no stone, the colour of which is more delightful to the eye; for whereas the sight fixes itself with avidity upon the green grass and the foliage of the trees, we have all the more pleasure in looking upon the smaragdus, there being no green in existence of a more intense colour than this. And then, besides, of all the precious stones, this is the only one that feeds the sight without satiating it. Even when the vision has been fatigued with intently viewing other objects, it is refreshed by being turned upon this stone; and lapidaries know of nothing that is more gratefully soothing to the eyes, its soft green tints being wonderfully adapted for assuaging lassitude, when felt in those organs.

And then, besides, when viewed from a distance, these stones appear all the larger to the sight, reflecting as they do, their green hues upon the circumambient air. Neither sunshine, shade, nor artificial light effects any change in their appearance; they have always a softened and graduated brilliancy; and transmitting the light with facility, they allow the vision to penetrate their interior; a property which is so pleasing, also, with reference to water. In form they are mostly concave, so as to reunite the rays of light and the powers of vision; and hence it is, that it is so universally agreed upon among mankind to respect these stones, and to forbid their surface to be engraved. In the case, however, of the stones of Scythia and Egypt, their hardness is such, that it would be quite impossible to penetrate them. When the surface of the smaragdus is flat, it reflects the image of objects in the same manner as a mirror. The Emperor Nero used to view the combats of the gladiators upon a smaragdus.

BERYLS

Beryls, it is thought, are of the same[10] nature as the smaragdus, or at least closely analogous. India produces them, and they are rarely to be found elsewhere. The lapidaries cut all beryls of an hexagonal form; because the colour, which is deadened by a dull uniformity of surface, is heightened by the reflection resulting from the angles. If they are cut in any other way, these stones have no brilliancy whatever. The most esteemed beryls are those which in colour resemble the pure green of the sea; the chrysoberyl being next in value, a stone of a somewhat paler colour, but approaching a golden tint. Closely allied to this last in its brilliancy, but of a more pallid colour, and thought by some to constitute a separate genus, is chrysoprasus. In the fourth rank are reckoned the hyacinthine beryls; and in the fifth, those known as "aëroides." Next, we have the wax-coloured beryls, and, after them,

---

10   The Beryl and the Emerald are only varieties of the same species, the latter owing its colour to oxide of chrome, the former to oxide of iron.

the oleaginous beryls, so called from the resemblance of their colour to that of oil. Last of all, there are the stones which closely resemble crystal in appearance; mostly disfigured by spots and filaments, and of a poor, faint, colour as well; all of them so many imperfections in the stone.

The people of India are marvellously fond of beryls of an elongated form, and say that these are the only precious stones they prefer wearing without the addition of gold; hence it is that, after piercing them, they string them upon the bristles of the elephant. It is generally agreed, however, that those stones should not be perforated which are of the finest quality; and in this case they only enclose the extremities of them in studs of gold.

OPALS

Opals[11] are at once very similar to, and very different from, beryls, and only yield to the smaragdus in value. India, too, is the sole parent of these precious stones, thus completing her glory as being the great producer of the most costly gems. Of all precious stones, it is opal that presents the greatest difficulties of description, it displaying at once the piercing fire of carbunculus, the purple brilliancy of amethystos, and the sea-green of smaragdus, the whole blended together and refulgent with a brightness that is quite incredible. Some authors have compared the effect of its refulgence to that of the colour known as Armenian pigment, while others speak of it as resembling the flame of burning sulphur, or of flame fed with oil.

ONYX

We must give some account also of onyx.[12] This name, though in some places given to a marble, is here used to signify a precious stone. Sudines says, that in this stone there is a white portion which resembles the white of the human-finger nail, in addition to the colours of chrysolithos, sarda, and iaspis. According to Zenothemis, there are numerous varieties of the Indian onyx, the fiery-coloured, the black, and the cornel, with white veins encircling them, like an eye as it were, and in some cases running across them obliquely. Sotacus mentions an Arabian onyx, which differs from the rest; that of India, according to him, presenting small flames, each surrounded by one or more white zones; in a manner altogether different from the Indian sardonyx, which presents a series of white specks, while in this case it is one continuous circle. The Arabian onyx, on the other hand, is black, he says, with a white zone encircling it.

TOPAZOS

Topazos[13] is a stone that is still held in very high estimation for its green tints; indeed, when it was first discovered, it was preferred to every other kind of pre-

---

11 Opals are hydrated silica, the amount of water varying.

12 So called from ὄνυξ, a "finger-nail." It is a variety of the Chalcedony, resembling Agate, but the colours are arranged in flat horizontal planes.

13 Under this name Pliny evidently speaks of the stone known to us as Chrysolite, and possibly of green agate as well. Our Topaz cannot be easily recognized in this Chapter, at all events.

cious stone. It so happened that some Troglodytic pirates, suffering from tempest and hunger, having landed upon an island off the coast of Arabia known as Cytis, when digging there for roots and grass, discovered this precious stone; such, at least, is the opinion expressed by Archelaüs. Juba says that there is an island in the Red Sea called "Topazos," at a distance of three hundred stadia from the main land; that it is surrounded by fogs, and is often sought by navigators in consequence; and that, owing to this, it received its present name, the word "topazin" meaning "to seek," in the language of the Troglodytæ. He states also, that Philon, the king's præfect, was the first to bring these stones from this island; that, on his presenting them to Queen Berenice, the mother of the second Ptolemæus, she was wonderfully pleased with them; and that, at a later period, a statue, four cubits in height, was made of this stone, in honour of Arsinoë, the wife of Ptolemæus Philadelphus, it being consecrated in the temple known as the "Golden Temple."

IASPIS

Iaspis,[14] too, is green, and often transparent; a stone which, if surpassed by many others, still retains the renown which it acquired in former times. Many countries produce this stone; that of India is like smaragdus in colour; that of Cyprus is hard, and of a full sea-green; and that of Persia is sky-blue. Similar to this last is the Caspian iaspis. On the banks of the river Thermodon the iaspis is of an azure colour; in Phrygia, it is purple; and in Cappadocia of an azure purple, sombre, and not refulgent. Amisos sends us an iaspis like that of India in colour, and Chalcedon, a stone of a turbid hue.

But it is of less consequence to distinguish the several localities that furnish it, than it is to remark upon the degrees of excellence which they present. The best kind is that which has a shade of purple, the next best being the rose-coloured, and the next the stone with the green colour of the smaragdus; to each of which the Greeks have given names according to their respective tints. A fourth kind, which is called by them "boria," resembles in colour the sky of a morning in autumn; this, too, will be the same that is known as "aërizusa." There is an iaspis also which resembles sarda in appearance, and another with a violet tint.

Throughout all the East, it is the custom, it is said, to wear iaspis by way of amulet. The variety of this stone which resembles smaragdus in colour is often found with a white line running transversely through the middle; in which case it is known as "monogrammos"; when it is streaked with several lines, it is called "polygrammos." Here, too, I may take the opportunity of exposing the falsehoods of the magicians, who pretend that this stone is beneficial for persons when speaking in public.

AMETHYSTS

We will now commence with another class of precious stones, those of a purple colour, or whose tints are derived from purple. To the first rank belongs the

---

14 Meadow-green jasper.

amethysts[15] of India; a stone which is also found in the part of Arabia that adjoins Syria and is known as Petra, as also in Lesser Armenia, Egypt, and Galatia; the very worst of all, and the least valued, being those of Thasos and Cyprus. The name which these stones bear, originates, it is said, in the peculiar tint of their brilliancy, which, after closely approaching the colour of wine, passes off into a violet without being fully pronounced; or else, according to some authorities, in the fact that in their purple there is something that falls short of a fiery colour, the tints fading off and inclining to the colour of wine.

All these stones are transparent and of an agreeable violet colour, and are easy to engrave. Some prefer giving these stones the name of "pæderos" or of "anteros," while to many they are known as "Venus' eyelid," a name which would seem to be particularly appropriate to the colour and general appearance of the gem. The falsehoods of the magicians would persuade us that these stones are preventive of inebriety, and that it is from this that they have derived their name. They tell us also, that if we inscribe the names of the sun and moon upon this stone, and then wear it suspended from the neck, with some hair of the cynocephalus and feathers of the swallow, it will act as a preservative against all noxious spells. It is said too, that worn in any manner, this stone will ensure access to the presence of kings; and that it will avert hail and the attacks of locusts, if a certain prayer is also repeated which they mention. They make similar promises, too, in reference to the smaragdus, if graven with the figure of an eagle or of a scarabæus; statements which, in my opinion, they cannot have committed to writing without a feeling of contempt and derision for the rest of mankind.

CERAUNIA

Among the white stones also, there is one known as "ceraunia,"[16] which absorbs the brilliancy of the stars. It is of a crystalline formation, of a lustrous azure colour, and is a native of Carmania. Zenothemis admits that it is white, but asserts that it has the figure of a blazing star within. Some of them, he says, are dull, in which case it is the custom to steep them for some days in a mixture of nitre and vinegar; at the end of which period the star makes its appearance, but gradually dies away by the end of as many months.

Sotacus mentions also two other varieties of ceraunia, one black and the other red; and he says that they resemble axes in shape. Those which are black and round, he says, are looked upon as sacred, and by their assistance cities and fleets are attacked and taken; the name given to them is "bætyli," those of an elongated form being known as "ceraunia." They make out also that there is another kind, rarely to

---

15 So called, according to some authorities, from ἀ, "not," μεθύω, "to intoxicate," on account of its being a supposed preservative against inebriety. Ajasson is of opinion that Pliny does not here speaks of the Quartz Amethyst of modern mineralogy, but only the Oriental Amethyst, violet Sapphire, or violet Corundum. It is not improbable, however, that he includes them all, as well as violet Fluor spar, and some other purple stones; inclusive, possibly, of the Garnet.

16 "Thunder-stone". Parisot thinks that these must have been Aërolites or Meteorites.

be met with, and much in request for the practices of magic, it never being found in any place but one that has been struck by lightning.

GALAXIAS

Galaxias,[17] by some called "galactitis," is a stone that closely resembles those next mentioned, but is interspersed with veins of blood-red or white. Galactitis is of the uniform colour of milk, and, when pounded in water, both in taste and colour it marvellously resembles milk. This stone promotes the secretion of the milk in nursing women, it is said; in addition to which, attached to the neck of infants, it produces saliva, and it dissolves when put into the mouth. They say, too, that it deprives persons of their memory; it is in the rivers Nilus and Acheloüs that it is produced. Some persons give the name of "galactitis" to a smaragdus surrounded with veins of white. Gallaica is a stone like argyrodamas, but of a somewhat more soiled appearance; these stones are found in twos and threes clustered together.

HELIOTROPE

Heliotrope[18] is found in Æthiopia, Africa, and Cyprus; it is of a leek-green colour, streaked with blood-red veins. It has been thus named, from the circumstance that, if placed in a vessel of water and exposed to the full light of the sun, it changes to a reflected colour like that of blood; this being the case with the stone of Æthiopia more particularly. Out of the water, too, it reflects the figure of the sun like a mirror, and it discovers eclipses of that luminary by showing the moon passing over its disk. In the use of this stone, also, we have a most glaring illustration of the impudent effrontery of the adepts in magic, for they say that, if it is combined with the plant heliotropium, and certain incantations are then repeated over it, it will render the person invisible who carries it about him.

THE METHODS OF TESTING PRECIOUS STONES

In addition to the particulars which we have already given, when treating of each individual kind of precious stone, it is generally agreed that transparent stones should be tested by a morning light, or even, if necessary, so late as the fourth[19] hour, but never after that hour. The modes of testing stones are numerous; first, by their weight, the genuine stone being the heavier of the two; next, by their comparative coolness, the genuine stone being cooler than the other to the mouth; and, next to that, by their substance; there being blisters perceptible in the body of the fictitious stone, as well as a certain roughness on the surface; filaments, too, an unequal brilliancy, and a brightness that falls short before it reaches the eye. The best mode of testing is to strike off a fragment with an iron saw; but this is a thing not allowed by the dealers, who equally refuse to let their gems be tested by the file. Dust of Obsian stone will not leave a mark upon the surface of a genuine stone; but where the gem is artificial, every mark that is made will leave a white scratch upon

---

17   "Galaxy stone." Ajasson thinks that this may possibly have been an Opal, or a dead white Topaz, traversed by lines of other colours.
18   Also named bloodstone, or blood jasper. It is of a deep-green colour, with red spots.
19   Ten in the morning.

it. In addition to this, there is such a vast diversity in their degrees of hardness, that some stones do not admit of being engraved with iron, and others can only be cut with a graver blunted at the edge. In all cases, however, precious stones may be cut and polished by the aid of adamas; an operation which may be considerably expedited by heating the graver.

Index

A

absinthium 316
achilleos 291
aconite 314
acorn 175
adamas 431
adivination
   auguries from fishes 114
Africa 53
alcibium 316
alica 202
aloe 314
alsine 315
alumen 408
amber 429
amethysts 434
amphibious animals 101
amphisbæna 100
anchusa 253
anti-aphrodisiacs 306
aparine 316
ape 108
aphrodisiacs 306
aproxis 281

aquatic animals
   prognostics derived from 215
Arabia 69
Arabian gulf 68
aristolochia 294
artemisia 293
Asclepiades 301
ashes 187
asparagus 225, 234
asphodel 254
Atlas, mount 54

B

balsamum 150, 267
bark
   use of 175
barley 199, 200
basilisk 97
bat 131
bean 202
bear 102
beaver 374
beehives 243, 244
bees 134

beet 225
beryls 432
birds
  fabulous 131
  prognostics derived from 215
bitumen 407
Black Sea 61
bladder
  remedies for 353
blood 335
boar, wild 108
boils
  medicaments for 338
bowel complaints
  medicaments for 337
bramble 279
brass
  candelabra 394
  Corinthian 394
  ores of 393
bread 259
bricks 406
Britannia 51
broken bones
  remedies for 355
broom 277
bugs
  remedies derived from 345
burns
  remedies for 355

C

cabbage 225, 233
cactos 246
cadmia 396
cæruleum 392
camel 98
  medicaments derived from 331
candelabra 394
carbuncles
  remedies for 355, 380
carcinomas
  remedies for 380
Caspian Gates 64
cassia 149
castor oil 266
catoblepas 97
Caucasus, passes 63
centaurion 292
cerastes 100
ceraunia 435
Ceylon 66
chalcetum 303
chamæsyce 280
chameleon 102
chaplets 239
chernites 419
chironion 292
Cimmerian Bosporus 62
cinnamomum (cinnamon) 149
clematis echites 281
clouds
  prognostics derived from 214
cold shiverings
  remedies for 354
colocasia 246
comets 31
copper 393
  different kinds 396
coral 374
corn
  mode of grinding 201
  storing 210
cough 303
  medicaments for 337
crane 127
crocodile
  medicaments derived from 332
crocotta 99
crow 125
cucumber 221
cucumber, wild 230
cultivation
  systems of 205
cyperus 247
cypress 180, 275
Cyprus
  oil of 266

INDEX 441

D

dead
  medicaments derived from 328
depilatories 356
Diana
  temple of 418
divination
  by animals 101
dog 103
  remedies derived from 344
dog-fish (sharks) 119
dolphin 111
dunghill cock 126
dyes
  vegetable 251
dysentery
  remedies for 353

E

eagle 124
ears
  remedies for 348
earth
  dimensions of 40
  form 36
  nature of 35
earthquakes 38
echeneïs (remora) 371
eclipses 23
eggs
  remedies derived from 343
Egypt 56
Egyptian Apis 106
electrum 389
elephant 91
  and dragon 94
  combats of 93
  how they are caught 93
  medicaments derived from 331
elephantiasis 300
emeralds 432
enchantments
  remedies against 336

equestrian order 386
esparto 219
Ethiopia 70
Europe 43
eyes 139
  beasts that kill with its eyes 97
  medicaments for 336
  remedies for 347

F

farm-house
  proper arrangement 197
feet
  medicaments for 337
female complaints
  remedies for 355
female diseases
  medicaments for 339
  remedies for 381
female sex
  medicaments derived from 329
fern 317
fevers
  medicaments for 338, 354, 380
figs 167, 268
flax 217
frankincense 148
frogs 376
fungi 256

G

gall 334
galaxias 436
gall 141
gall-nuts 274
Ganges 66
garlands 239
garlic 223
Gaul 51
Germany 50
glass 423
goat 107
God 17

gold 383
  coins of 386
  how is found 388
  remedies derived from 390
  rings 384
goose 127
gourd 221, 230
gout
  medicaments for 337
  remedies for 380
grafting 166
gramen 282
grapes 160, 263
Greece 47
  Attica 48
griffon 131
gum 155, 279
gypsum 422

H

haemorrhage
  remedies for 355
halcyon (king-fisher) 128
harvest 210
hawk 125
head-ache
  remedies for 347
heart 141
hedgehog 103
heliotrope 436
heliotropium 254
hellebore 291
Hellespont 49
hemlock 297
heracleon 293
hermaphrodites 142
hidromel 257
hippopotamus 100
  medicaments derived from 333
honey
  maddening 244
  poisoned 244
hornets 136
horns 138

horse 104
hyæna
  medicaments derived from 332
hyoscyamos 290

I

iaspis 434
iberis 293
India 65
Indus 66
intestinal hernia
  remedies for 379
iris 241, 248
iron
  ores of 397
  remedies derived from 398
Italy 44
itch
  medicaments for 339
ivy 180, 278

J

jaundice
  remedies for 354
Judæa 59
jugerum of land 196
juniper 277

L

labyrinths 417
land fishes 121
larch 275
laser 256
laurel 171, 270
lead
  black 399
  ores of 398
  remedies derived from 399
lentisk 276
lettuce 224
leucrocotta 99
lily 241, 247
lion 95

combat of 96
medicaments derived from 331
lithospermum 318
locusts 137
lotus 157, 274
lupine 203
lynx 99

M

magic
  various branches of 351
  powers 326
magnet 418
maltha 422
man
  body size 79
  burial 86
  death 85
  extreme courage 81
  fortunate circumstances 83
  generation of 76
  heroic exploits 80
  length of life 84
  medicaments derived from 324
  remarkable wisdom 82
  spittle 327
  variety of destinies 85
manes 86
mantichora 99
manure 187
marble 410
  varieties of 413
Marvellous Births 76
Media 64
melampodium 291
menstrual discharge 78, 330
mercurialis 290
Mesopotamia 68
mice of the Nile 121
milk
  medicinal uses from 333
millefolium 281
millet 201
minium 391

mint 226, 236
mirrors 391
mistletoe 183
Mithridates 285
moly 289
Moon
  motion 24
  prognostics derived from 213
  revolutions of 211
murex 117
mushrooms 255
myrrh 149
myrtle 169, 271

N

narcissus 247
natrix 319
nauplius 116
nereid 110
nettle 253
nightingale 128
Nile river 57
nitrum
  various kinds 368
Numidia 54
nymphæa 293

O

oat 204
obelisks 415
octopus 115
olive 163
  culture of 164
  leaves of 265
  oil 164
omphacium 266
onion 222, 232
onotheras 308
onyx 433
opals 433
opobalsamum 150
orchids 307
ostrich 123

oxen 105
oysters 377

P

pæonia (peony) 289
painting
　encaustic 404
palm 267
palm-tree 154
panaces 289
papyrus 155, 279
parsley 226, 235
parsnip 222
peach 166
pearls 116, 428
pears 267
pegasi (pegaso) 131
pennyroyal 236
peplis 319
Persian gulf 68
Phidias 410
pigeon 129
pine
　cones 270
pitch 177
pitch-tree 176, 275
planets 16
　motion 19
plastic art 404
pœnix 123
polenta 199
poplar 277
poppy 227, 236
portraits 401
poterion 320
pottery 405
Praxiteles 411
prodigies and portents 325
propolis 257
ptisan 200, 259
pumice 420
purple 117
pyrallis or pyrausta 138
pyramids 416

Q

quick-lime 421
quinsy
　remedies for 352

R

radish, cultivated 231
radishes 221
rainbow 35
rape 231
reed 278
remedies from garden plants 229
resin 276
rhacoma 320
rhinoceros 98
rice 199
rock crystal 428
Roman painters 402
Rome 45
rose 241
rosemary 279
rue 226, 235

S

salamander
　remedies derived from 345
salt
　flower of 366
　nature of 367
　various kinds 366
sand 421
sarcophagus stone 419
satyrion 307
scammony 304
Scopas 412
scordion 306
scorpio 296
scorpion 137
scrofula
　remedies for 379
seasons 33, 206
sea-swallow 115
sea-weed 378

INDEX 445

seed-plots 190
serapias 307
Seres 64
serpent 100
sexual passions
  stimulants 339
sheep 107
shrubs 242
silaus 306
silk-worm 136
silver 387, 390
sorb 169
Spain 44
spelt 199
sphinx 99, 416
spiders 136
sponges 119, 369
sprains
  medicaments for 338
stag 101
stars 19
  colours 28
  distances 29
  harmony 30
  motions 27
  prognostics derived from 214
statues 394
  colossal 395
sterility
  causes of 207
stomach
  remedies for 352
stomatice 269
stone moss 319
stones
  precious 430
  showers of 32
  specular 420
stucco 421
suicksilver 390
sulphur 407
superstitions 302
Syria 59

T

Taprobane (Ceylon) 66
tar 177
teeth 140
thelyphonon 296
theriaca 238
thistles 226
thunder 29, 34
  invocation of 35
  prognostics derived from 214
thyme 242, 249
  wild 237
tiger 97
Tigris river 69
tithymalos 304
tooth-ache
  medicaments for 336
  remedies for 351, 378
topazos 433
torpedo (sting-ray) 372
tortoise 375
tragopan 131
trees 145
  diseases of 191
  exotic 146
  grafting 191
  of India 146
  of Persia 147
  prodigies connected with 193
  propagation of 188
trefoil 242
tribulus 252
triton 110
trixago 280
Troglodytice 70
truffles 219
turtle
  how they are caught 112

U

ulcers
  remedies for 380

urinary calculi
  remedies for 353
urine
  medicaments derived from 329

V

veratrum 291
verbenaca 295
verdigris 397
vine 261
  white 263
vinegar 265
vines 159
violet 241, 248
viticulture 159

W

walnut 169
wasps 136
water
  conveying 364
  deadly 361
  different properties of 360
  impurities of 362
  prospecting for 362
  qualities in different seasons 363
  remedies derived from 360
wax 258
  method of preparing 245
weather 212
werewolf 98
wheat 199
winds
  origin of 34
  theory of 211
wine 161
  vessels and cellars 162
  with miraculous properties 161
woman's milk
  medicaments derived from 330
wood
  use of 175
wood-pecker 126
wool 107
  remedies derived from 343
world
  dimensions 30
world, form and nature 16
wormwood 316

Measurement Units

Greek (G) and Roman (R) money, weights, and measures mentioned by Pliny

Acetabulum. R	1/8 of a Sextarius, 0.128 pint.
Actus. R	120 Pedes or Roman Feet.
Amphora. R.	48 Sextarii, 5 gall. 7.577 pints.
As. R	2 1/8 farthings. Copper.
As (plural asses). R (weight)	See "Libra"
Concha, Smaller, G and R	0.0412 pint.
Concha, Larger, G and R	0.1238 pint.
Congius. R	5.9471 pints.
Cubitus. G	1 foot 6.2016 inches.
Cubitus. R	1 foot 5.4744 inches.
Culeus. R	20 Amphorae, 118 gall. 7.546 pints.
Cyathus. G and R	1/12 of a Sextarius, 0.0825 pint.
Denarius. R	16 Asses, 8½ pence. Silver.
Denarius. R. (weight)	52.5 to 60 grains.
Digitus, or Finger. R	1/16 of a Pes, 0.7281 inch.
Drachma. G	63 grains.
Hemina. R	See "Semisextarius"
Jugerum. R	240 x 120 Pedes or Roman feet.

Libra, or Pound. R	11 ¾ ounces 60.45 grains, avoird.
Modius. R (dry measure)	1/3 of an Amphora, 1 gall. 7.876 pints.
Obolus, oboli G	1½ 5 pence. Silver
Obolus, oboli G. (weight)	10.5 grains.
Palmus, or Handbreadth. R	2.9214 inches.
Pes, or Foot. R	12 Unciae, 11.6496 inches.
Pollex, or Thumb R	See "Unciae" (lineal measure).
Quadrans. R	53,125 farthing. Copper.
Quadrans. R (weight)	3 Unciae, 2¾ ounces 97.21 grs.
Quadrantal. R	See "Amphora"
Quartarius. R	¼ of a Sextarius, 0.2477 pint.
Quinarius. R	½ of a Denarius.
Scripulum, or Scruple. R	1/24 of an Unciae, 18.06 grains.
Semisextarius. R	½ of a Sextarius
Sestertius. R	¼ of a Denarius. Brass or Silver.
Sestertium. R	1000 Sestertii, £7 16s 3d.
Sextarius. R	1/6 of a Congius, 0.9911 pint.
Spithama, or Span. G	9.1008 inches.
Stadium. G and R	1/8 or a Roman mile, 606 feet 9 in.
Teruncius. R	See "Quadrans" (weight & money).
Ulna, or Ell. R	6 feet, 81 inch.
Unciae or Inch. R.	1/12 of a Pes, 0.9708 inch.
Unciae, or Ounce. R	1/12 of a Libra. 233.666 grs.
Urna. R	½ of an Amphora.
Victoriatus. R	See "Quinarius"